THE ROUTLEDGE COMPANION TO DIGITAL CONSUMPTION

The first generation that has grown up in a digital world is now in our university classrooms. They, their teachers and their parents have been fundamentally affected by the digitization of text, images, sound, objects and signals. They interact socially, play games, shop, read, write, work, listen to music, collaborate, produce and co-produce, search and browse very differently than in the pre-digital age.

Adopting emerging technologies easily, spending a large proportion of time online and multitasking are signs of the increasingly digital nature of our everyday lives. Yet consumer research is just beginning to emerge on how this affects basic human and consumer behaviors such as attention, learning, communications, relationships, entertainment and knowledge.

The Routledge Companion to Digital Consumption offers an introduction to the perspectives needed to rethink consumer behavior in a digital age that we are coming to take for granted and which therefore often escapes careful research and reflective critical appraisal.

Russell W. Belk is Kraft Foods Canada Chair in Marketing at the Schulich School of Business, York University, Canada. He is past President of the International Association of Marketing and Development and is a Fellow, past President and Film Festival co-founder of the Association for Consumer Research. He also co-initiated the Consumer Behavior Odyssey and the Consumer Culture Theory Conference. He has received the Paul D. Converse Award and the Sheth Foundation/*Journal of Consumer Research* Award for Long-Term Contribution to Consumer Research. His research involves the meanings of possessions, collecting, gift-giving, materialism, sharing and global consumer culture.

Rosa Llamas is Associate Professor of Marketing at the School of Business, University of León, Spain. Her research interests include the meaning of luxury, materialism, transformative consumer research and global consumer culture. Her work is often cultural, visual, qualitative and interpretive and has been conducted in varied cultural settings.

Routledge Companions in Business, Management and Accounting

Routledge Companions in Business, Management and Accounting are similar to what some publishers call 'handbooks', i.e. prestige reference works providing an overview of a whole subject area or sub-discipline, and which survey the state of the discipline including emerging and cutting-edge areas. These books provide a comprehensive, up to date, definitive work of reference which can be cited as an authoritative source on the subject.

One of the key aspects of the Routledge Companions in Business, Management and Accounting series is their international scope and relevance. Edited by an array of well-regarded scholars, these volumes also benefit from teams of contributors which reflect an international range of perspectives.

Individually, Routledge Companions in Business, Management and Accounting provide an impactful one-stop-shop resource for each theme covered, while collectively they represent a comprehensive learning and research resource for researchers and postgraduates and practitioners.

Published titles in this series include:

THE ROUTLEDGE COMPANION TO DIGITAL CONSUMPTION

Edited by
Russell W. Belk and Rosa Llamas

LONDON AND NEW YORK

First published 2013
by Routledge
2 Park Square, Milton Park, Abingdon, Oxon OX14 4RN

Simultaneously published in the USA and Canada
by Routledge
711 Third Avenue, New York, NY 10017

Routledge is an imprint of the Taylor & Francis Group, an informa business

British Library Cataloguing in Publication Data
A catalogue record for this book is available from the British Library

Library of Congress Cataloging in Publication Data
The Routledge companion to digital consumption / edited by Russell W. Belk and Rosa Llamas.
    p. cm. – (Routledge companions in business, management and accounting)
    Includes bibliographical references and index.
    1. Information technology–Social aspects. 2. Consumer behavior. 3. Consumers–Research.
    I. Belk, Russell W. II. Llamas, Rosa.
    HM851.R6793 2013
    658.8'342–dc23
                2012017247

ISBN: 978-0-415-67992-3 (hbk)
ISBN: 978-0-203-10530-6 (ebk)

Typeset in Bembo
by Taylor & Francis Books

Printed and bound by CPI Group (UK) Ltd, Croydon, CR0 4YY

CONTENTS

LIST OF FIGURES

LIST OF TABLES

NOTES ON CONTRIBUTORS

Pia A. Albinsson is Assistant Professor of Marketing at Appalachian State University, USA. Her work has been published in the *Journal of Consumer Behaviour*, the *European Journal of Marketing* and the *Journal of Public Policy and Marketing*.

Yun Mi Antorini is Assistant Professor in the Department of Language and Business Communications at Aarhus University, Denmark. She has a Master's degree and a PhD from Copenhagen Business School, Denmark. Prior to the PhD she worked as a Strategic Planner in the advertising industry and as a Senior Director of Global Brand Strategies at the LEGO Group. Her research and teaching focus on consumer behaviour such as user innovation and brand community.

Zeynep Arsel is Assistant Professor of Marketing at John Molson School of Business at Concordia University, Canada.

Russell W. Belk is Kraft Foods Canada Chair in Marketing, Schulich School of Business, York University, Canada. He is past President of the International Association of Marketing and Development and is a Fellow, past President and Film Festival co-founder of the Association for Consumer Research. He also co-initiated the Consumer Behavior Odyssey and the Consumer Culture Theory Conference. He has received the Paul D. Converse Award and the Sheth Foundation/*Journal of Consumer Research* Award for Long-Term Contribution to Consumer Research. His research involves the meanings of possessions, collecting, gift-giving, materialism, sharing and global consumer culture.

Ray Benedicktus is Assistant Professor of Marketing at California State University, USA. His research engages topics related to services strategy, multi-channel retailing and consumer attitudes. His research has been published in the *Journal of Retailing*, the *Journal of Business Research*, and the *Journal of Interactive Advertising*.

Tom Boellstorff is Professor of Anthropology at the University of California, Irvine, USA. From 2007–12, he was Editor-in-Chief of *American Anthropologist*. His books include *The Gay Archipelago: Sexuality and Nation in Indonesia* (2005), *A Coincidence of Desires: Anthropology, Queer*

Studies, Indonesia (2007), *Coming of Age in Second Life: An Anthropologist Explores the Virtually Human* (2008), and with Bonnie Nardi, Celia Pearce, and T.L. Taylor, *Ethnography and Virtual Worlds: A Handbook of Method* (2012).

Sammy K. Bonsu is Associate Professor of Marketing at the Schulich School of Business, York University, Canada. He is a student of consumption and identities, with a focused interest on Africa and Diasporan experiences that inform theoretical developments in contemporary consumer cultures and markets. He was a management consultant for several years. These days, when he is not partying with his two older children who have left the nest, he spends the bulk of his time playing with the remaining two not-so-young ones who still live at home – a good excuse for staying away from conferences! Nobody reads his research that has been published in the *Journal of Consumer Research*, the *Journal of Consumer Culture*, the *Journal of Macromarketing*, the *Journal of Contemporary Ethnography* and *Consumption, Markets and Culture*, among others … really, who cares?

Michael Brady is the Carl DeSantis Professor and Chair of the Department of Marketing at Florida State University, USA. His research interests are in managing consumer perceptions of frontline service transactions and the strategic ramifications of branding for service firms.

Norah Campbell is Assistant Professor of Marketing at Trinity College, Dublin, Ireland. She is interested in the philosophy of technology, critiques of services marketing and images of the future in consumer culture.

Sydney Chinchanachokchai is a PhD student at the College of Business, University of Illinois at Urbana-Champaign, USA. Her research interests include consumer multitasking behavior, memory and judgment and cognitive thinking style.

Elanor Colleoni is a Research Fellow at Copenhagen Business School, Denmark. With a background in computer science and sociology, she is currently working on virality and emotions in social media. She is also working on new forms of value in informational capitalism (Arvidsson and Colleoni, 2012).

June Cotte is PhD Program Director, Faculty Scholar, George and Mary Turnbull Fellow and Associate Professor of Marketing at the Ivey Business School, Canada. Her research interests include the consumption of gambling. Her research has appeared in the *Journal of Consumer Research*, the *Journal of Consumer Psychology*, the *MIT/Sloan Management Review*, as well as in the *Wall Street Journal*, and other journals and books.

Marlon Dalmoro is a PhD Candidate in Marketing at the Universidade Federal do Rio Grande do Sul, Brazil. He was also a visiting scholar at the EDHEC Business School, France. His research interests are consumers and market culture.

Peter Darke is Associate Professor of Marketing at the Schulich School of Business at York University, Canada. His research is concerned with consumer judgment and information processing, with a particular interest in the role of trust and suspicion.

Janice Denegri-Knott is a Senior Lecturer at Bournemouth University, UK. She currently teaches consumer culture and behaviour and is a member of the Emerging Consumer Cultures

Group (ECCG). Her research includes digital virtual consumption and its practices, the emergence of new media technology, the socio-historic patterning of consumption and more generally the subject of power in consumer and marketing research.

Kristine de Valck is Associate Professor of Marketing at HEC Paris, France. Her research focuses on online consumer networks, consumer tribes, and the role of Web 2.0 and social media in co-creation, marketing and market research. Her work has been published in the *British Journal of Management, Decision Support Systems, Finanza Marketing e Produzione*, and the *Journal of Marketing*. She has also contributed to various edited books.

Nikhilesh Dholakia is Professor of Marketing and International Business at the University of Rhode Island, USA. His research stream includes issues at the intersection of technology, globalization and consumer culture.

João Pedro dos Santos Fleck is a PhD Candidate in Marketing at the Universidade Federal do Rio Grande do Sul, Brazil. He was also a visiting PhD student at the Schulich Business School, Canada. His research interests are film festivals, fans, gamers and highly involved consumers. He has also been a gamer for most of his life.

Brittany R. L. Duff is Assistant Professor of Advertising at the Charles H. Sandage Department of Advertising at the University of Illinois, USA. Her research focuses on how attention and emotion influence perceptions of advertising.

Debora Dunkle is Director of Research at the Center for Digital Transformation (CDT), University of California, Irvine, USA. Her research focuses on the social and economic impacts of technology, and she has extensive experience in the design and implementation of surveys. She was a research specialist at CRITO for over 20 years, responsible for database management and analysis. She received her PhD from the State University of New York at Buffalo.

Eileen Fischer is a Professor of Marketing and the Anne and Max Tanenbaum Chair of Entrepreneurship and Family Enterprise at Schulich School of Business, York University, Canada. She writes in the fields of both entrepreneurship and consumer research, looking at how markets affect and are affected by consumers and entrepreneurs.

Aubrey R. Fowler III is Assistant Professor of Marketing at Valdosta State University, USA. He is an ardent fan of *Buffy the Vampire Slayer*, Heavy Metal music and the *Star Wars* saga. He has published in the *Journal of Macromarketing* and the *International Journal of Housing Markets and Analysis*.

Mary C. Gilly is Professor of Marketing at the Paul Merage School of Business, University of California, USA. Her research focuses on consumer behavior and the indirect and often unintended consequences of marketing actions. Current projects include a study of household decision-making at a distance via new technologies and an examination of consumer-generated advertising. She has earned National Science Foundation grants focusing on older Americans' use of the Internet. Her research has appeared in the *Journal of Marketing*, the *Journal of Consumer Research*, the *California Management Review* and the *Journal of Retailing*. She recently authored "Why Consumers Shop Online, Who They Are, and What They Want" for *The Internet Encyclopaedia*.

Ian Grant is Honorary Research Fellow in the Department of Marketing at the University of Strathclyde Business School, UK, but is based in Pasadena, USA. His research interests focus on diverse aspects of marketing communications, including the consumption of new forms of media among adolescents, communications account planning, issues of online privacy and mobile marketing.

Jay M. Handelman is Associate Professor of Marketing at Queen's University School of Business, Canada. Some of his work has been published in the *Journal of Marketing*, *Journal of Consumer Research*, the *Journal of Retailing* and the *Journal of the Academy of Marketing Science*, among others.

Andrea Hemetsberger is Professor of Branding at Innsbruck University School of Management, Austria, and Visiting Professor at the Université Paris-Dauphine, France. Her research interests revolve around brands as action nets, the meaning of luxury, philosophical notions of uniqueness, authentication practices of open-source brands, co-creation and the democratization of markets, and the open-source movement in general. Her work has been published in the Journal of Macromarketing, the Journal of Business Research, and Organization Studies amongst others.

Donna L. Hoffman is Albert O. Steffey Professor of Marketing and Co-Director of the Sloan Center for Internet Retailing at the University of California, Riverside, USA. She publishes widely in the areas of online consumer experience and Internet strategy and has been awarded many of the field's most prestigious research awards. She is an Academic Trustee of the Marketing Science Institute and a member of the Procter & Gamble Digital Advisory Board. Her PhD is from the L.L. Thurstone Psychometric Laboratory at the University of North Carolina at Chapel Hill.

Margaret K. Hogg is Fulgoni Professor of Consumer Research and Marketing at Lancaster University, UK. Before joining LUMS in 2004, she was a Reader in Consumer Behaviour at Manchester School of Management, UMIST. She read Politics and Modern History at Edinburgh University, followed by postgraduate studies in history at the Vrije Universiteit, Amsterdam, and then by an MA in Business Analysis at Lancaster University. She spent six years working in Marketing with K Shoes, Kendal. She completed her part-time PhD at Manchester Business School in Consumer Behaviour and Retailing, while lecturing at University College Salford. Her research interests are around the issues of identity, self and consumption. Her work has appeared in refereed journals including the *Journal of Advertising*, the *Journal of Business Research*, the *Journal of Marketing Management* and the *European Journal of Marketing*. She has presented papers at a number of international conferences including the European Marketing Academy (EMAC) and US and European meetings of the Association for Consumer Research (ACR); and AMA Marketing and Public Policy. She is a co-author of the fourth edition of *Consumer Behaviour: A European Perspective* (Pearson 2010).

Robert V. Kozinets is Professor of Marketing and Chair of Marketing Department at Schulich School of Business, York University, Canada. He is a globally recognized expert on social media, marketing research, innovation, and marketing strategy. He has extensive professional consulting and public speaking experience and has published three books and over 100 chapters, proceedings, white papers, cases, and articles in some of the world's top-tier marketing journals.

Gachoucha Kretz is Associate Professor of Marketing at ISC PARIS School of Management, France. She holds a PhD from HEC Paris in the realm of social media marketing and branding, specifically applied to fashion and luxury. Her research focuses on online social networks, luxury and fashion consumers, and luxury and fashion branding. She heads an international Master's course specializing in Luxury Business.

Clinton D. Lanier, Jr. is Assistant Professor of Marketing at the University of St. Thomas, USA. He is a devoted fan of *Harry Potter, Star Trek* and *The Beatles*. He has published in the *Academy of Marketing Science Review, Memorable Customer Experiences* and *Research in Consumer Behavior: Consumer Culture Theory*.

Helene M. Lawson is Professor and Program Director of Sociology and Coordinator of the Gender Studies Program at the University of Pittsburgh at Bradford, USA. She is the author of *Ladies on the Lot* and co-editor of *The Cultural Study of Work*.

Kira Leck is Associate Professor of Psychology at the University of Pittsburgh at Bradford, USA. Her research interests include personality and social psychology, prejudice and discrimination, close relationships and the psychology of music.

Ming Lim is Lecturer in Critical Marketing at the University of Leicester's School of Management, UK, where her research is focused on global branding, international marketing, ethics, digital consumption and technology marketing. She is currently engaged in projects on the ethical and performative aspects of consumer behaviour in healthcare contexts, funded by the Arts and Humanities Research and other leading UK research councils.

Rosa Llamas is Associate Professor of Marketing at the School of Business, University of León, Spain. Her research interests include the meaning of luxury, materialism, transformative consumer research and global consumer culture. Her work is often cultural, visual, qualitative and interpretive and has been conducted in varied cultural settings.

David Lyon is Director of the Surveillance Studies Centre and Professor of Sociology at Queen's University in Kingston, Canada. His webpage at the university is: www.sscqueens.org/davidlyon/.

Mike Molesworth is Senior Lecturer at Bournemouth University, UK. He has a PhD in consumer culture and currently teaches consumer culture and online marketing and is a member of the Emerging Consumer Cultures Group (ECCG). He has published in the areas of consumer culture, especially the consumption of digital technologies, the imagination in consumption and the marketization of higher education and the student as a consumer.

Albert M. Muñiz, Jr. is Associate Professor of Marketing at DePaul University, USA. His research interests are in the sociological aspects of consumer behaviour and branding, including consumer-generated content and online communities. His teaching interests include consumer behaviour, consumer culture and brand management. He received his BS, MS and PhD from the University of Illinois, Urbana-Champaign.

Thomas P. Novak is Albert O. Steffey Professor of Marketing and Co-Director of the Sloan Center for Internet Retailing at the University of California, Riverside, USA, where his current research focuses on social media and online consumer behavior. He has published widely in the area of Internet marketing for the past two decades. He received his PhD from the L.L. Thurstone Psychometric Laboratory at the University of North Carolina at Chapel Hill.

Marie-Agnès Parmentier is Assistant Professor of Marketing at HEC Montréal, Canada. She is an active scholar in the field of consumer culture theory. Her research interests include the pursuit of marketplace identity projects, person-branding and participatory culture in virtual communities of consumption.

Anthony Patterson is Professor of Marketing at the University of Liverpool Management School, UK. Before joining Liverpool, he taught on faculties at the University of Sheffield and the University of Ulster. He holds a PhD in consumer behaviour from the latter institution. Much of his research focuses on providing a snapshot of current cultural practices such as social networking and text messaging and exploring how these phenomena impact on consumer behaviour. His other research interests include city branding, nation branding and book marketing. He is the recipient of the University of Liverpool's Sir Alistair Pilkington Award for Teaching Excellence and his work has appeared in the *Journal of Business Research*, *Psychology & Marketing* and the *Journal of Marketing Management*, among others.

Elfriede Penz is Associate Professor at WU Vienna University of Economics and Business, Austria. Her research focuses on international marketing and consumer behaviour; in particular, it includes studies on new technologies, counterfeits and the influence of the social context. She has published in refereed international journals such as the *Journal of Economic Psychology*, *Psychology & Marketing*, the *International Marketing Review*, the *European Journal of Marketing* and the *Management International Review*. She has presented papers at international conferences including the European Marketing Academy (EMAC), the Association for Consumer Research (ACR), the American Marketing Association (AMA) and the Academy of International Business (AIB, AIB-UK-Ireland). She has received several best paper awards and has been engaged in international teaching and research collaborations.

B. Yasanthi Perera is a Management PhD candidate at New Mexico State University, USA. Her research interests include social entrepreneurship and individual and corporate social responsibility. Her research has been published in the *Journal of Consumer Behaviour* and the *International Journal of Innovation and Learning*.

Jason Pridmore is Senior Researcher on the DigIDeas project that examines the social and ethical implications of digital identification. His research focuses on consumer surveillance practices and the use of new media in marketing practice, specifically marketing techniques such as the use of loyalty cards and social media integration as forms of collaborative surveillance. He is the author of numerous texts on consumer surveillance, including the entry on consumer surveillance in the *Routledge Handbook of Surveillance Studies* (2012) and the expert report on the surveillance of consumers and consumption, part of the report on the surveillance society commissioned by the British Information Commissioner in 2006. Prior to joining the DigIDeas team, Jason was a Post-Doctoral fellow with The New Transparency Project, under the auspices of The Surveillance Project. He received his PhD from the Department of Sociology at Queen's University, Canada, in 2008.

Hope Jensen Schau is Associate Professor and Gary M. Munsinger Chair in Entrepreneurship and Innovation at the University of Arizona, USA. Her research focuses on the impact of technology on marketplace relationships, branding, identity-salient consumption practices and collaborative consumption. She has published in the *Journal of Consumer Research*, the *Journal of Marketing*, *Journal of Retailing*, the *Journal of Advertising*, the *Journal of Macromarketing* and *Business Horizons*.

Jonathan Schroeder is the William A. Kern Professor at Rochester Institute of Technology, USA. His current research involves four intersecting areas: aesthetic leadership, branding, ethics of representation and visual communication-photography, in particular. He is editor-in-chief of *Consumption Markets & Culture*.

Anton Siebert is a PhD Candidate at Witten/Herdecke University, Germany. His research focuses on market system dynamics beyond the Western hemisphere. He is currently working with Markus Giesler and Eva Illouz on a study exploring the relationship among romantic love, the marketplace, and globalization.

Sachil Singh is a PhD candidate in the Department of Sociology at Queen's University in Kingston, Canada. He is currently examining the role of consumer surveillance in South Africa in engineering new social forms of apartheid.

Randy Stein is Post-Doctoral Scholar at the Sloan Center for Internet Retailing at the University of California, Riverside, USA. His research topics include the social cognitive processes involved in social media usage, the ways in which people are automatically influenced by others and the causes of and potential solutions to unwanted decision biases. He received his PhD in Social Psychology from Yale University in 2011.

Vebjørg Tingstad is Professor and Director at the Norwegian Centre for Child Research at the Norwegian University of Science and Technology in Trondheim, Norway. Her current research interest involves childhood, media, consumption and food. Recent publications are *Childhood and Consumer Culture* (with David Buckingham), and a number of journal articles on childhood, commercial television, consumption and methodology. She is also the chief editor of the Nordic journal, *Barn*.

Birgitte Tufte is Professor in the Department of Marketing, Copenhagen Business School, Denmark. Her research focuses on children, media and consumption. Her work has been published in various academic journals and she has authored books and articles such as *Children, Media and Consumption: On the Front Edge* (with Karin M.Ekström) (Nordicom, 2007), and "Children and the Internet," (with Jeanette Rasmussen) in *Understanding Children as Consumers* (Sage, 2010).

Carlos Alberto Vargas Rossi is Associate Professor of Marketing at UFRGS (Universidade Federal do Rio Grande do Sul), Brazil. He has published in the *Journal of Services Research*, the *Journal of the Academy of Marketing Science*, the *Journal of Consumer Marketing*, the *International Journal of Consumer Studies*, the *Journal of Services Marketing*, the *Brazilian Administrative Review* and others.

Ekant Veer is Senior Lecturer of Marketing at the University of Canterbury, New Zealand, and is currently the editor of the *Journal of Research for Consumers*. His research focuses on understanding how consumers who feel stigmatised perceive themselves and how this perception of marginalisation affects their future behaviour, especially on the Internet. His work also looks at using contemporary marketing technologies to drive consumer welfare and societal betterment.

Alladi Venkatesh is Professor of Management and Associate Director, CRITO, University of California, Irvine, USA. His research areas are technology diffusion, aesthetics and consumer culture. He has published in various journals including the *Journal of Marketing*, the *Journal of Consumer Research* (Best Paper award), *Management Science*, *CACM*, the *European Journal of Marketing* and several others. He co-edited *ICT for the Next Billion* (Springer, 2007). He is the past co-editor of *Consumption, Markets & Culture*.

Handan Vicdan is Assistant Professor of Marketing at EMLYON Business School, France. Her research stream includes studies of social, cultural, and technological transformations in how consumers (re)organize their lives; specifically issues of consumer freedom, body, power, resistance, the impact of social media on consumer–marketer collaboration, and the implications of social networking in healthcare.

Kathryn Waite is Lecturer of Marketing in the School of Management and Languages at Heriot Watt University, Edinburgh, UK. She is interested in issues relating to information use and consumer empowerment. Her work currently focuses on online information search behaviour, digital identity, and the marketing of credence services.

Henri Weijo is a PhD student at the Aalto University School of Business in Helsinki, Finland. His research focuses on consumption communities and their role in shaping marketplace cultures.

T. E. Dominic Yeo is Research Assistant Professor at the Department of Communication Studies, Hong Kong Baptist University, where he teaches new media and consumer perspectives in advertising and public relations. His research applies consumer culture perspectives to our understanding of viral propagation, social media and advertising.

Xin Zhao PhD. is Assistant Professor of Marketing at the University of Nebraska-Lincoln. He studies Chinese consumer culture and market development in China. His work has been published in the journal of Consumer Research, Journal of Advertising, and Journal of Advertising Research.

Detlev Zwick is Associate Professor of Marketing at the Schulich School of Business, York University, Canada. His research critically investigates the cultural politics of consumption, marketing and management practice. His work has been published widely in marketing, communications, media culture and sociology journals, as well as in several edited collections. He is the editor (with Julien Cayla) of *Inside Marketing: Practices, Ideologies, Devices* (Oxford, 2011).

PART I

What's digital?

1

LIVING IN A DIGITAL WORLD

Rosa Llamas and Russell Belk

> Men are suddenly nomadic gathers of knowledge, nomadic as never before, free from fragmentally specialism as never before – but also involved in the total social process as never before; since with electricity we extend our central nervous system globally, instantly interrelating every human experience.
>
> (Marshall McLuhan 1964)

> Our technology forces us to live mythically.
>
> (Marshall McLuhan 1967)

Keywords

digital age, digital consumption, *homo connectus*, technoscape

Digital consumption

In January 2012, there was a major winter snow storm in Toronto on the first day of Winter Semester classes at York University. Traffic accidents clogged roads, public transportation was snarled, and sidewalks were buried under a foot of blowing snow. Russ taught a 7:30 a.m. MBA class and students straggled in late and exhausted. When a reasonable number had arrived he asked how many had been on Facebook that morning and about three-fourths of the class raised their hands. He then asked how many had been on Facebook before they got out of bed and nearly a third raised their hands. Clearly there is something compelling about the digital world in which we live. Spending a large proportion of our time online, adopting emerging technologies easily, and multitasking fluidly are all signs of the increasingly digital nature of our everyday lives. New media have been integrated into our daily routines and agendas, shaping, shifting, and transforming the way we interact, play, shop, read, write, work, listen, create, communicate, collaborate, produce, co-produce, search, and browse. Each of these actions is now very different from the way we did these things in the pre-digital age.

New media have altered our daily lives. Even the most mundane routines in the early morning have been replaced by switching on technological devices. Logging on is now first thing in the morning for many, even before getting up. We may text our children to wake them up. Sharing breakfast with the family with a newspaper as our only source of distraction is an increasingly old-fashioned memory as we now substitute computers, mobile phones, and other technological devices for what was once family time (Stone 2009). We then check the traffic online if we cannot work from home and must head to the office. Once there, we are apt to work in a collaborative way using new media. During the day we may browse the net to find restaurants, to book movies and entertainment, to listen to music, watch television and movies, and to keep track of our daily exercise, using specialized apps for each. Technology permeates every aspect of our everyday lives and gives rise to dependence on new media to such an extent that we may feel panic if our Internet connection is down for even a short time.

In the transition from analog to digital representation over the past half century, technically speaking, something has been lost; zeroes and ones substitute discrete approximations for continuous sensory phenomena like colors, sounds, and shapes. But for the consumer far more has been gained than lost. We have gained speed, miniaturization, and a cornucopia of new creations. Digital technologies of the microchip make possible not only a host of new devices and applications, but also new ways to present and fashion our identities through what Foucault (1998) called technologies of the self. The contributions in this volume outline some of these possibilities and the revolutionary changes, both good and bad, that digital devices and applications are bringing to our lives as consumers. Many earlier technologies from fire and language to electricity and photography have also radically changed our lives and spawned explosions of creative opportunities. In the future digital technologies, too, may be eclipsed by nanotechnologies, the "Internet of things" (see Chapter 4 by Campbell in this volume), or some other game-changing ways of interacting with our environment and each other. For the moment, however, we are caught up in the swirl of digital possibilities.

The excitement and anticipation characteristic of the current era of digital consumption are illustrated by the yearly Consumer Electronics Show to which the media swarm in order to report on the next new thing. Apple's new product announcements draw equally rapt media and consumer attention. Numerous websites, blogs, magazines, television shows, and news reports help to sustain the excitement and feed the desires of digital aficionados seeking the magic that each new device and application seems to offer. By the time of his death in 2011, Steve Jobs had been virtually deified (Belk and Tumbat 2005; Deutschman 2000; Isaacson 2011; Kahney 2004), not so much as Prometheus bringing us digital fire as Vulcan forging wondrous new things from digital magma.

Some impacts of digital consumption

Disruptive changes are brought by major new technologies, even if like the automobile, they may be better appreciated after the fact. In a loose play on Foucault's technologies of the self, Abbas and Dervin (2009) suggest that we are now enjoying digital technologies of the self with the power to transform us. And even if they do not fully transform our identities, they have very likely changed our lives. The new economy is one of post-humanization, Feenberg and Barney (2004) state, proclaiming the "symbiosis of humans with machines." Turkle (2011) points out that, metaphorically speaking, some time ago a computer could be considered "a second self, a mirror of mind." Nowadays, such a metaphor is not enough to represent the situation in which "new devices provide space for the emergence of a new state of the self, itself, split between the screen and the physical real, wired into existence through technology" (ibid., p. 16). Particularly for teenagers, "technology has become like a phantom limb, it is so much part of them" (ibid., p. 17). The distinction between the real and the virtual is no longer entirely clear. The line between the two is blurred as the two worlds intertwine in an almost Gibsonesque way – our flesh and blood are now mixed with circuits and devices. We have become wired and wireless selves, *homo connectus*, always logged on (Rainie 2007).

Homo connectus is always on, seeking to know what's going on and what's in, ever catching up on the latest news and updates. They are versatile, chameleonic, tech-savvy, information junkies, juggling several tasks at the same time, so their attention is fragmented. There is a blurred line separating the professional and personal life, so fuzzy that instead of making a distinction between work and leisure time, their days are hybrid, and free time, as understood in the pre-digital age, has vanished. They have adopted non-linear approaches to learning, thinking, playing, and expressing self. They are digital nomads, wired to the world but becoming more and more wireless. App-addiction permeates all spheres of their lives in order to manage a wide range of everyday issues, tracking everything from health status, to caloric intake, to miles run, or sleep patterns, retouching and sharing pictures, learning other languages, exchanging money online, or writing shopping lists.

Homo connectus lives in a digital ecosystem, in a media bubble, in an instant era, a "Nescafe" age. Communication becomes vivid and disinhibited via instant messaging, SMS, and microblogging, which are replacing once-popular e-mail and voice mail. It is fast, alive, fresh, and only semi-intrusive, since it does not impose on the receiver when to respond. Nevertheless netiquette has evolved demanding instant responses. Mobile phones are nowadays more used for data than for calls (Wortham 2010). Instant messaging is becoming more popular while phone calls are becoming obsolete and landlines are rapidly losing ground. This immediacy not only impregnates communications but also other actions available online, actions and proce-dures that in a pre-digital era would have required going to an office, queuing up, and waiting. Digital identity and signatures have replaced physical and ink-based expressions of personality (Hawkins 2011). Mobiles phones are not only a tool for communication but they have acquired a wide variety of uses, "replacing wallets, watches and doorbells" (Watson 2010).

Homo connectus is gregarious and hypersocial, in constant communication (albeit not often face to face) with the digital others on the other side of a screen or keyboard. Hypersociability is enabled by "screen culture." Friendship is also instantaneous in the digital era. The saying "you can count your true friends on the fingers of one hand" is so analog! Friends sprout in the fertile field of the social media, even though the concept of friendship is redefined in the connected world. Inviting hundreds of friends to a party or any other event just takes a few seconds on Facebook and they will accept or decline the invitation immediately. Even previously formal and important announcements like births, engagements, and weddings have migrated from the paper and face-to-face worlds to the digital world, adopting the form of SMS, videos, and other highly creative digital formats. Our language has also muted into a cyberlanguage with a "gr8" deal of new expressions. Sharing status updates with friends as well as personal information, whereabouts, and pictures, engaging in public conversations and communities, and checking-in at various online and offline places are all part of the *homo connectus*'s self-representation today. Socialholics (Polo and Polo 2012) share their knowledge, collaborate with other peers, and engage with social causes. Calling people to take action through social media has been a key ingredient in activist movements like the Arab Spring and Occupy Wall Street. *Homo connectus* gets involved in social and civic activism, supporting and taking part in movements which are shaping the political and economic arena. *Homo connectus* belongs to *The Empathic Civilization* (Rifkin 2010) which has connection, collaboration, and caring engraved in its DNA (Finkelstein and Gavin 2011). In this technoscape there is no room for hierarchies, and seemingly the whole world is brought closer by subscribing to their updates on Facebook or becoming a follower on Twitter.

Homo connectus needs to be connected as much as to breathe; e-mails, messages, and notifications are the foods that feed him/her. But they may get caught in a spiral, checking and rechecking, looking for their daily dose of notifications. An overdose of connection may be stress-inducing, while a lack of connection may cause their anxiety levels to skyrocket. According to one study, the obsessive use of the digital devices leads to high levels of stress in some users who even feel imaginary vibrations from mobile phones that are not buzzing (Schwarze 2012). Not being able to sign off and getting trapped in the net is one of the typical illnesses in the digital age. Practicing digital detachment has proved to be a harsh cure for this illness of the postmodern digerati. Disconnect to reconnect, digital detox, or what Powers (2010) has termed an *Internet Sabbath*, brings several benefits. According to Powers, "Your mind slows down, it really goes to a different place when you've been off the internet for a day or two" (NPR 2010). Finding a "high-tech, high touch" balance is a challenge nowadays. This concept was introduced by Naisbitt in his visionary book, *Megatrends* (1982). He admonishes that we must increase "high touch" in parallel with the rise of "high tech" in our lives for a more emotionally satisfying existence (Naisbitt 2001).

In this constantly "on" world, *homo connectus* no longer enjoys those sacred analog moments, typical of earlier times. Digital devices have intruded on what was once considered "down times," like dinner with the family, the golden moments devoted to reading a newspaper over a cup of coffee, and even the sleep time. They have conquered the most precious moments, and violated the most sacred spaces. One of the recent conquests starring an iPhone was at a concert by the New York Philharmonic Orchestra. The strict protocol of virginal silence was breached by the profane "Marimba" ring tone of someone's iPhone during a particularly emotional part of the symphony. Gilbert Alan, the orchestra's music director, said: "It was so shocking what happened. You're in this very far away spiritual place in the piece. It's like being rudely awakened. All of us were stunned on the stage" (Wakin 2012). Even the lamas in Tibet, one of the most isolated, untouched, and spiritual places on Earth, use mobile phones. The combination of their traditional robes and the new technologies shocks the Western eye which sees with disillusionment how these devices have even conquered the Himalayas.

Homo connectus is always learning and sharing. For this *übersocial* individual, learning is also a social activity. Learning is nowadays multi-linear, visual, and ubiquitous, using both online sources as well as peers to get knowledge and share it with the digital others. In a pre-digital age learning was an individual process based on internalizing knowledge, while in the digital era, it is a social activity of externalizing knowledge (Veen 2007). The *Global Brain* is the term coined in 1982 by Peter Russell to refer to collective intelligence in a networked world. The openness to sharing knowledge has resulted in the so-called *crowd-accelerated innovation*. The term was been coined by Chris Anderson, the curator of TED Talks, and it characterizes the collaborative boost in learning fostered by the Internet. Finkelstein and Gavin (2011) refer to the *Participation Age* to describe how digital media have changed the way information is created, published, managed, and consumed. Other labels include co-creation, infotopia, and we-think.

New technologies have become part of the basic infrastructure of the modern world, reshaping every sphere of our lives. In order to adapt to this new scenario, Nicholas Carr (2011) more critically asserts that "What we're experiencing is, in a metaphorical sense, a reversal of the early trajectory of civilization: we are evolving from cultivators of personal knowledge into hunters and gatherers in the electronic data forest" (p. 138). In the process, Carr contends, we seem fated to sacrifice much of what makes our minds so interesting.

Realms of digital consumption

In the chapters that follow, a vast range of digital consumption topics are addressed. As Venkatesh and Dunkle document in Chapter 2, communication, entertainment, information, shopping, banking, health care, and socializing are among the consumption arenas in which digital technologies have thus far had the greatest impact in transforming our lives. While they emphasize the digitization of aspects of our lives such as bill paying, photo making, storage, display, and television viewing, all of which previously used analog technologies within the home, other chapters add to this list of digital substitutions: blogging (Chapter 5, Arsel and Zhao; Chapter 6, Kretz and de Valck), Internet-based sharing (Chapter 13, Siebert; Chapter 18, Vicdan and Dholakia), gazing (Chapter 14, Veer), dating (Chapter 17, Lawson and Leck), stock trading (Chapter 19, Zwick and Schroeder), gambling (Chapter 23, Cotte), worshiping (Chapter 25, Lanier and Fowler; Chapter 27, Muñiz, Antorini, and Schau), gaming (Chapter 26, Fleck, Dalmoro, and Rossi), protesting (Chapter 34, Handelman), and mourning (Chapter 35, Lim).

In order to more fully consider the impact that such digitally facilitated actions may have in transforming us, other chapters focus on personal and interpersonal processes involved in consuming digital technologies. The influence of new technologies on our social capital and the way they affect our relationships were examined in a study by the Pew Internet and American Life Project (Boase *et al.* 2006). They found out that while some people see the Internet as amplifying relationships both socially and geographically, others see it as creating alienated forms of life that are far from being "authentic" and "real." Technologies are also reshaping the nature of the relationships, so in this digital era a re-examination of concepts such friendship is important.

As Hoffman, Novak, and Stein detail in Chapter 3, motivations for engaging with social media are far from homogeneous. They also join a number of other chapter authors in discussing user roles in not only consuming, but also producing social media content, e.g., Parmentier and Fischer (Chapter 16), Bonsu (Chapter 22), Schau and Gilly (Chapter 7), Hemetsberger (Chapter 15), Lanier and Fowler (Chapter 25), Molesworth and Denegri-Knott (Chapter 20). Although user-generated content may provide an outlet for creativity and enhance the reputation of those producing it, another impact is to influence other users' subsequent consumption of music, movies, fashion, and food, e.g. Arsel and Zhao (Chapter 5), Kretz and de Valck (Chapter 6), and Parmentier and Fischer (Chapter 16). One of the reasons that word of mouth from fellow consumers is trusted is the assumption that those providing their opinions and evaluations are not trying to sell us anything (see Chapter 21, Penz and Hogg). In a broader sense what these consumers are "selling" is themselves. The expanded possibilities for self-presentation through digital media mean that we can say and show aspects of the self that are inappropriate or difficult to display in face-to-face encounters with others. We can display our favorite brands, list our favorite music and movies, make evident who our friends are, show photos, provide updates on our activities, and much more.

However, as Schau and Gilly show in Chapter 7, as our self-representations have migrated from free-form web pages to the templates of social media sites and blog consolidations, creativity has been constrained and we are encouraged to provide the same types of information about ourselves as others do. Our specific content differs, but we are following the equivalent of what Rick Wilk (1995) calls global structures of common difference. That is, the general structure of self-differentiation is similar even though our local articulation within this structure shows some uniqueness. Arsel and Zhao as well as Kretz and de Valck provide rich accounts of why people blog. In addition to expressing actual and ideal self by creating a self-narrative, displaying taste, and revealing brand and style affinities, blogging can also be cathartic, a form of connection providing feelings of community, a way to create a sense of individual power in influencing others' opinions, a way of seeking celebrity, and sometimes a way of earning money, receiving free goods, and acquiring entry to special events. The latter benefits are more likely for those fashion bloggers who acquire significant followings. The rise of influential bloggers is one instance of a more general shift of power within the digitized marketplace from marketers to consumers.

However, the monetized connections between marketers and some bloggers mean that, like product placements, what may appear as spontaneous, innocent, consumer-driven commentary can also be a hidden form of paid promotion. Laws differ from country to country on requirements for disclosing freebies or compensation a blogger has received.

Being influenced in digital consumption

In other cases the presence of the market in digital media is more explicit. Darke, Benedicktus, and Brady examine in Chapter 36 the role of trust in patronage of Internet sellers and why consumers are often willing to pay a premium price to buy directly from a prominent retailer whom they trust. They consider various theoretical models of why online retailing is not the level playing field it was expected to be. In Chapter 23, Cotte reviews another case of seemingly irrational digital consumption: online gambling. In accounting for the more extreme behaviors of gamblers online versus in brick and mortar casinos, she points to the use of more ephemeral electronic money, the anonymity of the player, the lack of the verbal and non-verbal cues present in dealing with embodied others, and the familiarity and safety of gambling online from within the player's home. In turning to her own research with young online gamblers, Cotte finds that contrary to Darke *et al.*, there is a great deal of unwarranted trust in the, usually foreign, online casinos that they patronize. She concludes that the assumption of digital expertise among these "digital natives" is not always warranted.

In Chapter 24, Yeo highlights another case of digital influence in the viral spread of both marketer-generated and consumer-generated digital content. He points out that some of this rapid propagation of content is also seen in pre-digital urban legends, rumors, and word of mouth behaviors. Among the processes involved when video clips and other narratives "go viral" are the fan dynamics addressed by Lanier and Fowler in Chapter 25 as well as the sharing addressed by Siebert in Chapter 13. As with passing along interesting, amazing, or titillating rumors, video spoofs, and word of mouth, passing along digital content that fascinates and entertains those in our social networks can similarly enhance our image as being knowledgeable, fun, and well-connected. However, as Siebert finds in the context of dating couples sharing cellular phones in Indonesia, there can also be intense jealousy when a partner suspects that his/her loved one has been sharing messages with rival love interests. Although, as Lanier and Fowler emphasize, digital fandom can be consumer-driven and oppositional, it can also be producer-driven through transmedia storytelling. But in both cases, as with consumption-related blogging, consumers are engaging with marketers to co-construct the meaning and even co-create the content of the object of their fandom (e.g., with fan fiction authored by consumer-fans using the characters and settings of *Harry Potter* or *Star Trek*).

Such co-construction and consumer participation in production are also evident in many of the practices of crowdsourcing that Hemetsberger analyzes in Chapter 15. In her broad view, crowdsourcing includes not only open source software like Linux, collaborative online projects like Wikipedia, and crowd voting participation in shows like *American Idol* (see Parmentier and Fischer in Chapter 16), but also uploading photos and videos to sites like Flickr and YouTube, submitting profile material to dating sites like eHarmony and Yahoo Personals (see Lawson and Leck in Chapter 17), writing reviews and recommendations on sites like Amazon and Apple's App Store (see Penz and Hogg in Chapter 21), constructing and participating in virtual worlds and games like Second Life and World of Warcraft (see Fleck, Dalmoro, and Rossi in Chapter 26), and participating in social media sites like Facebook and Twitter. In Chapter 22, Bonsu warns that such activity not only can be part of the co-creation of value for both users and the usually commercial entities behind them, but can also be a form of unpaid labor and exploitation of consumers by those who seek to profit from them. This is not to say that consumers may not also benefit in social reputation, enjoyment, connections, celebrity, respect, and even job opportunities based on co-production, but the few originators who benefit from the labor of the many consumers providing content certainly enjoy the vast majority of economic benefits that such collaborations produce.

Benefits and problems of digital consumption

The digitalization of life creates and reinforces changes, from micro routines like the alterations in family life mentioned above to changes at a macro or societal level. On one hand, technology is separating family members even as it enables communication among people around the world. On the other hand, information technology is fostering inequalities among countries giving rise to the "digital divide" regarding possession, creation, and dissemination of knowledge. There is also a "generation divide" segregating the "adaptive immigrants" from the "digital natives" and particularly from the "M-Agers" – youngsters born since 1997 who have always had Internet and mobile devices as a part of their lives and who do not draw a line between the real and the virtual world (Hudson 2011).

The case of co-construction and co-creation in digital environments is another aspect of a broader assessment of the costs and benefits of digital consumption. Much can be said of the new and empowering possibilities that have emerged and will continue to emerge online. These include sharing medical information (Chapter 18, Vicdan and Dholakia), trading stocks (Chapter 19, Zwick and Schroeder), enjoying better communication (Chapter 3, Hoffman, Novak, and Stein; Chapter 8, Patterson; Chapter 2, Venkatesh and Dunkle), fashioning and presenting the self (Chapter 5, Arsel and Zhao; Chapter 7, Schau and Gilly; Chapter 6, Kretz and de Valck), creating new and enhanced or transformed selves (Chapter 4, Campbell; Chapter 20, Molesworth and Denegri-Knott), shopping online (Chapter 21, Penz and Hogg); interactive gaming (Chapter 26, Fleck, Dalmoro, and Rossi; Chapter 20, Molesworth and Denegri-Knott), finding or forming community (Chapter 25, Lanier and Fowler; Chapter 27, Muñiz, Antorini, and Schao; Veer), finding partners (Chapter 17, Lawson and Leck), joining and participating in consumer activist movements (Chapter 31, Albinsson and Perera; Chapter 34, Handelman), and even paying final respects and memorializing the dead (Chapter 35, Lim).

At the same time there are a number of danger areas for consumer well-being that are identified in these chapters. They include threats to privacy (Chapter 29, Grant and Waite; Chapter 28, Singh and Lyon; Chapter 30, Weijo; Chapter 10, Pridmore and Zwick), threats to the young, to women, and to sexual minorities (Chapter 11, Tingstad; Chapter 33, Tufte); threats to our attention span and ability to concentrate (Chapter 32, Chinchanachokchai and Duff), and threats to self-control and "reasonable" spending (Chapter 23, Cotte; Chapter 36, Darke, Benedicktus, and Brady; Chapter 20, Molesworth and Denegri-Knott; Chapter 19, Zwick and Schroeder).

Any attempt to tally or compare the benefits and problems created by digital consumption would be overly simplistic. Furthermore, the impact of digital consumption is largely positive for some and largely negative for others. New media evangelists coexist with digital detractors. And for the many others in the world who are not directly involved in digital consumption, the effects are distant, although in this case too they are two-sided. By not being involved in the digital revolution, they are missing opportunities that are afforded to others; they are being left farther behind in advances in economic, health, communication, entertainment, and the other realms that digital consumption has aided or created. But they are also shielded from spam, digital scams, digital distractions, digital addictions, and the other ills that have accompanied the digital revolution.

Future research

Digital consumption has attracted the attention of a broad array of social sciences, physical sciences, medical sciences, humanities, arts, commerce, politics, athletics, travel, entertainment, communications, and a number of other disciplines. It is difficult to imagine an area of inquiry that is unaffected. With such a broad array of perspectives and the ongoing revolution in digital technologies, there is no single research method that is applicable across these fields. Furthermore, the same ongoing changes in digital technologies that are challenging old methods of research are also providing and necessitating new methods. There are a few exemplary methodological treatments like Boellstorff's (2008) discussion of adapting ethnographic methods to researching Second Life consumption, Kozinet's (2010) development of netnography for researching online groups and forums, and the discussions in Belk, Fischer, and Kozinets (forthcoming). The chapters in this volume by Colleoni (Chapter 12), Kozinets (Chapter 9), Patterson (Chapter 8), Tingstad (Chapter 11), and Pridmore and Zwick (Chapter 10) provide discussions of other techniques for academic and business research on digital consumption.

Theoretically, we are at or near the beginning of trying to understand how digital technologies are shaping human relationships, sense of community, global understanding, personal, group, and national identity, business, leisure, work, governance, religion, culture, creativity, generosity, and other significant spheres of life. The key issue is not about how technology is going to evolve in the future but how we, consumers, are going to evolve through incorporating these technologies as integral parts of our everyday lives. In *What Technology Wants*, Kelly (2010) asserts that technology has been part of our lives forever, but what it is new to our times is the way we interact. According to Kelly, ten thousand years ago, humanity reached a turning point where our ability to modify the biosphere exceeded the planet's ability to modify us. This threshold was the beginning of the *Technium*. We are now at a second inflection point, where the situation has reversed and the ability of the *Technium* to modify us exceeds our capacity to alter it (ibid., p. 197). In this vein, future research should address the new digital consumer instead of merely the consumer of technology.

Future research agendas may also focus on the intersection between the digital age and transformative consumer research, finding new approaches to how technology can help to improve our individual and collective well-being. Collective and creative thinking through digital media can help in seeking solutions to challenges such as sustainability, materialism, and excess in consumption. Through social media, consumers are becoming more powerful and societies are becoming more democratic. Communities and social movements benefit from the viral effects provided by the net. The pro-social agenda of transformative consumer research may be able to leverage these same developments.

The chapters in this volume suggest some of the pressing research needs at the present time. In the short history of digitization we are already long past the point where researchers could ignore these trends and assume that we are merely using new media in the same ways we have used old media. We are also moving past the initial swell of utopian and dystopian takes on digitization as being the salvation or curse of humankind. Technodystopias focused on the extinction of the human being as we know it, and the rise of cyborgs. This dystopian view has been with us at least since the writings of André Leroi-Gourhan in the 1960s (Lenoir 2003). Just as earlier technologies (e.g., the telegraph, the phonograph, photography, film, mechanization) were regarded in extreme ways initially and began to have their most profound effects when they were accepted as a part of everyday life, so it is with digital technologies. Even such advances as written language provoked a twofold reaction among the ancient Greeks. While some were enthusiastic about this "new technology," others like Socrates viewed it as a way to destroy our minds and advised us to "stay away from the alphabet" (Carr 2011; Manguel 1996; Powers 2010). We have moved from an era when the computer was seen as an impersonal device to be loathed and feared for its use in controlling our lives and dehumanizing us, to the present era when computing is ubiquitous and largely embraced as something very personal, useful, and fascinating.

But as Cotte finds, just because we now have a generation of digital natives who have grown up with digital devices (e.g., Palfrey and Gasser 2008; Tapscott 2009), does not necessarily mean that they are all sophisticated, wise, or appropriately cautious users of these devices and applications. Furthermore, just because young people were in the vanguard of adopting and embracing digital technologies, should not restrict us to focusing on issues like identity that may be especially compelling to this age group. Attention is already being paid to events of later life stages such as digital mourning (see Chapter 35, Lim) and disposition of our "digital estate" (Carroll and Romano 2011).

It is our hope that the chapters that follow will stimulate the reader to think about the nature and effects of digital consumption. We also hope that they raise new issues for future research and make us more alert to the implications of new digital developments in the future. More generally, the great attention that digital consumption is beginning to attract should sensitize us to considering the effects of past and future technologies as well.

References

Abbas, Yasmine and Dervin, Fred (2009) *Digital Technologies of the Self*, Newcastle upon Tyne: Cambridge Scholars Publishing.

Belk, Russell, Fischer, Eileen and Kozinets, Robert (forthcoming) *Qualitative Research Methods for Consumer and Market Research*, London: Sage.

Belk, Russell and Tumbat, Gülnur (2005) "The Cult of Macintosh," *Consumption, Markets and Culture*, 8 (September): 205–18.

Boase, Jeffrey, Horrigan, John, Wellman, Barry and Rainie, Lee (2006) *The Strength of Internet Ties*, Washington, DC: Pew Internet & American Life Project, available at: www.pewinternet.org/~/media/Files/Reports/2006/PIP_Internet_ties.pdf.pdf (accessed December 31, 2011).

Boellstorff, Tom (2008) *Coming of Age in Second Life: An Anthropologist Explores the Virtually Human*, Princeton, NJ: Princeton University Press.

Carr, Nicholas (2011) *The Shallows: What the Internet Is Doing to Our Brains*, New York: W.W. Norton & Company.

Carroll, Evan and Romano, John (2011) *Your Digital Afterlife: When Facebook, Flickr, and Twitter Are Your Estate, What's Your Legacy?* Berkeley, CA: New Riders.

Deutschman, Alan (2000) *The Second Coming of Steve Jobs*, New York: Random House.

Feenberg, Andrew and Barney, Darin (2004) *Community in the Digital Age: Philosophy and Practice*, Lanham, MD: Rowman & Littlefield.

Finkelstein, Jim and Gavin, Mary (2011) *Fuse: Making Sense of the New Cogenerational Workplace*, Austin, TX: Greenleaf Book Group.

Foucault, Michel (1998) *Technologies of the Self: A Seminar with Michel Foucault*, ed. Luther Martin, Huck Gutman, and Patrick Hutton, Amherst, MA: University of Massachusetts Press.

Hawkins, Chris (2011) *A History of Signatures: From Cave Paintings to Robo-Signings*, Charleston, NC: CreateSpace.

Hudson, Paul (2011) "The Dawning of the Digital Age," Future Thinkers Update, available at: www.intersperience.com/article_more.asp?art_id=46 (accessed December 31, 2011).

Isaacson, Walter (2011) *Steve Jobs*, New York: Simon & Schuster.

Kahney, Leander (2004) *The Cult of Mac*, San Francisco: No Starch Press.

Kelly, Kevin (2010) *What Technology Wants*, New York: Penguin Group.

Kozinets, Robert V. (2010) *Netnography: Doing Ethnographic Research Online*, London: Sage.

Lenoir, Timothy 2003 "Makeover: Writing the Body into the Posthuman Technoscape Part One: Embracing the Posthuman," in Timothy Lenoir (ed.), *Makeover: Writing the Body into the Posthuman*

Technoscape, two-part special issue of *Configurations*, Baltimore, MD: Johns Hopkins University Press, 2003–4, Part I, *Configurations*, 10(Spring): 203–20.

McLuhan, Marshall (1964) *Understanding Media*, Cambridge, MA: MIT Press.

——(1967) *The Medium Is the Message*, Harmondsworth: Penguin.

Manguel, Alberto (1996) *A History of Reading*, Toronto: Random House Canada.

Naisbitt, John (1982) *Megatrends: Ten New Directions Transforming Our Lives*, New York: Warner Books.

——(2001) *High Tech/High Touch: Technology and Our Accelerated Search for Meaning*, London: Nicholas Brealey Publishing.

NPR (2010) "'Hamlet's BlackBerry': To Surf Or Not To Surf?", National Public Radio, available at: www.npr.org/templates/story/story.php?storyId=128364111 (accessed January 30, 2012).

Palfrey, John and Gasser, Urs (2008) *Born Digital: Understanding the First Generation of Digital Natives*, New York: Basic Books.

Polo, Fernando and Polo, J. Luis (2012) *Socialholic: Todo lo que Necesitas Saber sobre Marketing en Medios Sociales*, Barcelona: Gestión 2000.

Powers, William (2010) *Hamlet's BlackBerry: A Practical Philosophy for Building a Good Life in the Digital Age*, New York: HarperCollins.

Rainie, Lee (2007) *Homo Connectus: The Impact of Technology on People's Everyday Lives*, Washington, DC: Pew Internet & American Life Project, available at: www.pewinternet.org/Presentations/2007/The-impact-of-technology-on-peoples-everyday-lives.aspx (accessed April 5, 2012).

Rifkin, Jeremy (2010) *The Empathic Civilization: The Race to Global Consciousness in a World in Crisis*, Harmondsworth: Penguin Books.

Schwarze, Kelly (2012) "The Stresses of Smartphones," Sugargeek, available at: www.geeksugar.com/Smartphones-Causing-Stress-21316052 (accessed January 26, 2012).

Stone, Brad (2009) "Breakfast Can Wait: The Day's First Stop is Online," *The New York Times*, August 10, p. A1.

Tapscott, Don (2009) *Grown Up Digital*, New York: McGraw-Hill.

Turkle, Sherry (2011) *Alone Together: Why We Expect More from Technology and Less from Each Other*, New York: Basic Books.

Veen, Wim (2007) "Homo Zappiens and the Need for New Education Systems," in *Proceedings of the OECD Conference, "The New Millennium Learner,"* Firenze.

Wakin, Daniel J. (2012) "New York Philharmonic Interrupted by Chimes Mahler Never Intended," Artbeats, *New York Times*, available at: http://artsbeat.blogs.nytimes.com/2012/01/11/new-york-philharmonic-interrupted-by-chimes-mahler-never-intended/ (accessed January 26, 2011).

Watson, Richard (2010) *Future Minds: How the Digital Age Is Changing our Minds, Why This Matters and What We Can Do about It*, London: Nicholas Brealey.

Wilk, Richard (1995) "Learning to Be Local in Belize: Global Systems of Common Difference," in Daniel Miller (ed.), *Worlds Apart: Modernity through the Prism of the Local*, London: Routledge, pp. 110–33.

Wortham, Jenna (2010) "Cellphones Now Used More for Data Than for Calls," *The New York Times*, May 13. Available at: www.nytimes.com/2010/05/14/technology/personaltech/14talk.html (accessed January 26, 2011).

2

DIGITIZING PHYSICAL OBJECTS IN THE HOME

Alladi Venkatesh and Debora Dunkle

Key words

digital culture, digital family, digital objects, digital transformation, networked home

Introduction

Recent research has shown that the Internet has become a major transformational force (Joy *et al.* 2009) and is indispensable to consumers and households in the context of their everyday life (Hoffman *et al.* 2004; Venkatesh *et al.* 2011). For many people, the home computer is as essential as other appliances commonly found in the home. That the personal computer has become an integral part of households is apparent. And, as computers have become integrated into the household and their use has spread across family members, this technology is expected to make and, in a number of households, has already made fundamental changes in home life and in the performance of household tasks. Current trends on the home front indicate that we are witnessing the emergence of the networked home (Venkatesh *et al.* 2003) and a digital culture associated with various daily activities in families. The focus of this research is to empirically examine digitization in the home, particularly as it relates to the impact on family life and activities. Specifically, the main research question posed here is, what is the nature of digital transformation in the home and what key activities of family life are digitized and to what extent?

The emergence of digital culture

When PCs first came into the home in the early 1980s, there was much anticipation and excitement about what the future was going to hold (Rogers 1986). By today's standards, the early home computer was a primitive machine and had limited performance potential. For many, the computer was introduced into the home to do job-related work either for a home-based business or for work outside of the home and to do word processing (Vitalari *et al.* 1985). Families with children also touted the home computer as useful for educational purposes, but this type of use tended to take a back seat to the more business-oriented uses. Since the home computer of the 1980s was in many households a stand-alone unit, the full potential of its use was not realized until after the arrival of the Internet in the mid-1990s. With the introduction of the Internet, some 15 years ago, and accompanied later on by various technological advancements such as Google, broadband connectivity, and more recently, social media, home computing has assumed a more central role in household activities. That is to say, recent technological developments have heralded some rapid changes that point to the emergence of a digital world filled with transformational possibilities.

To put the current trends in a historical perspective, digital technologies are following a technological trajectory that we have witnessed in other areas of our social and cultural life. For example, more than a century ago, we witnessed the emergence of the telephone which was a major technological innovation resulting in changes in communication patterns (Fischer 1994). Similarly, in the world of entertainment, the introduction of the cinema initiated an artistic revolution and heralded a new form of audience engagement (Stanley 1978). This prompted Walter Benjamin ([1936] 1972) to write his famous commentary, "The Work of Art in the Age of Mechanical Reproduction." In the same fashion, social life has undergone radical change with the introduction of the automobile (Flink 1970). In addition, as part of the technological culture, radio (Hilmes and Laviglio 2002) and television (Fiske 1987), similar to the telephone and the movies, have brought about fundamental changes in the areas of mass communication and entertainment. All these developments have one fundamental characteristic. They introduced new forms of behaviors that did not exist before and at the same time displaced some older forms. In a similar fashion currently, the areas of communication and entertainment are converging now into a new digital medium made possible by the Internet and various digital technologies. Henry Jenkins (2006) describes the contemporary digital culture as "convergence culture," while Vaidyanathan (2011) refers to it as the *Googlization* of our social and personal lives.

Thanks to the digital technologies, not only do we find that social and physical distances are shrinking and transactions are becoming instantaneous, but new methods of social interaction are beginning to emerge. As a result, we live in a qualitatively different, digitally constituted world. Terms such as interactivity, connectivity, virtual spaces, digital divide, crowdsourcing, cloud computing, web cultures, social networking and many more are proliferating and are now part of the new digital vocabulary. In the world of communication, face-to-face contacts are being supplanted or reinforced by electronic contacts (RoAne 2008), resulting in the redefining of social distance in the global communication context. In the field of marketing, Hoffman and Novak (1996), Kozinets *et al.* (2010) and others have drawn our attention to new forms of consumer behaviors and practices. Along the same lines, mobile communication technologies (e.g. smartphones) are dramatically altering communication patterns locally and globally (Shankar *et al.* 2010). Newspaper readership is gradually being supplanted by electronic news (Paterson and Domingo 2008) altering the information landscape. The rise of social media and online networks is a major development that is changing the digital landscape quite dramatically (Kozinets *et al.* 2010).

Digital players and lifestyles

In terms of digital demographic segments, children and youth are acknowledged as advanced users of emerging technology in their daily lives (Ito *et al.* 2009; Venkatesh and Behairy 2012). In addition, gender and ethnic differences are disappearing along with other distinctions associated with the digital culture. The general conclusion seems to be that what seems to matter is not so much competence in using the technology but individual life interests and other social needs. Thus, children are most interested in games and similar forms of entertainment. Young females more than males use mobile technologies for communication and texting.

In general, it looks as though people's use of these technologies is based on their lifestyle characteristics and needs. The question that is often asked is, does technology follow life patterns or do life patterns change according to technology? We believe that there is an element of truth in both statements and, more importantly, it is the interaction between the users and technology that gives rise to new lifestyle patterns. It is against this background that we examine the nature of digitization in the context of home life. In the next section we present some theoretical perspectives on the role of technology as an agent of change. This will be followed by an empirical analysis focusing on digitization trends in family life based on survey data.

The role of technology in the home: digital transformation issues

The basic dynamic with respect to home-based technologies is that technologies do play a key role in relation to home life. This can be identified in terms of three possibilities: (1) the enabling role of technology; (2) its mediating role; and (3) its transformative role (Venkatesh 2008; Venkatesh *et al.* 2011). In the simplest of the three, the enabling role suggests that technologies introduce practical efficiencies and show some qualitative and quantitative improvements in existing practices. The focus here is on looking at technology as a tool. For example, if a family buys a bigger car, or a vehicle which goes faster or saves more gas, one might say that the new car performs existing functions by facilitating time and monetary savings and added comfort and the like. Such functional advances are not considered radical changes but we grant that they add efficiency and convenience to the routine activities in the home. This is an example of the enabling role of technology.

In its mediating role, technology assumes a more complex functionality by intervening between the user and their social space. For example, when the cable TV was introduced into the home, it opened up several channels for family viewing and acted as a go-between between the user and the entertainment world. As a mediating technology, the cable (or satellite) TV connects the family with the outside world of entertainment, over which they have no control. The mediating role of technology is a bit more complex than its enabling role because it adds a higher-order dimension to the application of technology for users' benefit not present in its simpler version.

A transformative role is one which alters family life and activities in some fundamental ways. Of course, when the automobile was introduced into the market, it was indeed a transformational technology because over the years, it has changed many aspects of people's living patterns. When the PC entered the home environment, it made it possible for individuals to bring work home, thus altering their work life. And it did not stop here. In the ensuing years, or, as we now call it, in the age of the Internet, families have begun to perform a lot of activities using the computer: for shopping, email and other forms of communication, online banking, information search, home-based learning, telemedicine, home-based business, and so on. When we consider the impact of the Internet on family life, one can easily recognize its transformative role. If we now add digital or smart appliances, the possibilities increase dramatically.

Of course, the same technology can perform different roles under different conditions. Thus, for a user who has never owned a TV set, a new TV can fundamentally alter their viewing habits and transform their life. However, in a family that already has a TV set, a new replacement TV will have a minimal impact. In other words, the role a technology plays is partially dependent on the user and their existing use patterns. The important point is that the various technologies that are now ready to be launched seem to have the potential to change the home life in some major ways. As a large part of this transformation involves the actions of the consumer/user and the overall user environment, one must take them into account seriously.

We would argue that digitization in the home leads to the transformation of domestic technological activity and the emergence of a digital culture.

The digital family and the networked home

It is in this context of a rapidly evolving digital culture that we examine digitization resulting from the family's use of computers. In our earlier and also ongoing work, we have highlighted various possibilities in this regard. First, we presented a conceptual model of the household adoption of computers (Venkatesh 1996), and this was followed by some other studies including an analysis of the post-adoption processes (Shih and Venkatesh 2004), the emergence of the networked home, and the children and family use of computers (Venkatesh *et al.* 2011), and a few others. To put these developments in a time frame, we divide the past 15+ years after the arrival of the Internet into three periods: the early Internet (1995–2000); the Internet growth (2001–06); and Internet maturity (2006–present). During these periods the Internet has contributed to many changes in people's daily activities. These three periods also represent some forms of digital transformation.

Conceptually, we identify the household in terms of eight major activity centers (see Figure 2.1). These activity centers are communication, information, shopping, home management, education/learning, job/work/employment, entertainment/hobbies and social.

Figure 2.1 Household activity centers

Technology in the home has brought about a number of changes in the way things are being done within the activity centers. Particularly interesting is the question of how these activity centers are being digitally transformed. For example, if we consider the home activity of shopping, changes in technology have made it possible now that rather than hopping in the car and driving to the mall for a table lamp, the consumer can now simply 'computer mall shop' without leaving the home. Similarly, the inside of a bank is most likely foreign to many people not just because of ATMs, but also because of the sophisticated online banking sites where accounts can be tracked, bills can be paid and loans can be processed. There are several other examples of this type for other activity centers. In the next section we examine empirically some of these changes by considering the extent to which some physical objects in the home are being digitally replaced.

Empirical analysis

To obtain some idea of how widespread digital replacement is, we conducted a national survey of 1,200 US households,[1] and looked at five household objects that we considered standard for a number of years: the telephone, the newspaper, the file cabinet with family records, the TV, and finally, the photo album. In addition, we also identified households under three categories of telephone ownership: households with both landline and mobile phones, landline only and mobile phones only. The national sample of households was queried regarding the extent to which there has been digital replacement in the home. They were given the following question in relation to each of the five physical objects in question: "For some people the computer has provided a way of replacing a physical device or object with a digitized version. On a scale of 1 to 5 where 1 is 'not at all' and 5 is 'completely' please tell us the extent to which each of the following has happened in your household." In addition to the digital substitution across the entire sample in aggregate, we also analyzed the extent to which the changes observed may be a function of household demographic characteristics including age, education level and household income. We also asked our respondents to indicate the level of transformation in the household resulting from computer use. The results for the study are presented in Figures 2.2a–2.2f and Tables 2.1–2.7.

Results

Information center: replaced a physical newspaper with online news

The physical newspaper appears to be on its way out, being replaced by information and news services available on the Internet. Our results (Figure 2.2a) show that 60 percent of our sample families have replaced newspapers with online news in various degrees. That is, 25 percent report replacement completely and 35 percent partially. The rest of the sample (40 percent) reported that they have not replaced the physical newspaper at all. This seems to be a significant trend in the news category.

In Table 2.1, we present the overall distribution and breakdown by age, education and household income. While there is still a sizeable percentage subscribing or buying a newspaper, it is important to note that age is a significant factor. Younger adults, in contrast to older adults, are more likely to report having switched to accessing online news sites. About one-third of those aged 18–29 reported that they have completely replaced the physical newspaper and a substantial 44 percent of those aged 30–39 reported replacing the physical newspaper with access to online news. Similarly, education is a factor, with college graduates significantly more likely to have made the change than those with a high school education or even only some

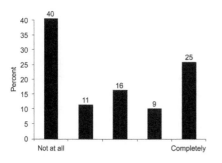

(a) Replaced physical newspaper with online news

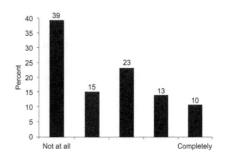

(b) Replaced paper records with digital versions

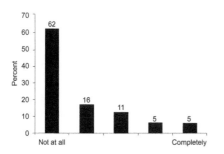

(c) Replaced watching programs on TV to computer/hand-held device

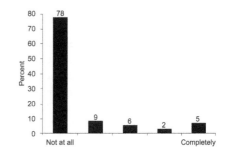

(d) Replaced landline with computer to make calls

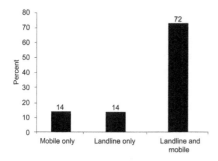

(e) Replaced landline phone with mobile phone

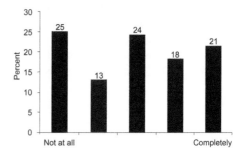

(f) Replaced printing photos with viewing online

Figure 2.2 Distributions of digitized replacement of household objects

college education. Income is much less linear with lower incomes (under $30,000) and higher incomes (over $100,000) more likely to have switched in contrast to mid-level incomes.

Home management center: replaced paper records such as bills, insurance claims, maintenance contracts, warranties with digital versions

As for paper records in the family, 61 percent have replaced them in varying degrees and 39 percent not at all (Figure 2.2b). However, only 10 percent report replacement of paper records completely. Paper records include check writing, medical records, bill payment, insurance

Table 2.1 Replaced a physical newspaper with online news

	Mean score[a]	Not at all								Completely		Total	
		%	(N)	%	(N)	%	(N)	%	(N)	%	(N)	%	(N)
Total	2.69	39.7	(474)	10.5	(126)	15.5	(186)	9.3	(112)	24.8	(297)	100.0	(1195)
Age													
18–29	3.30	22.2	(36)	11.1	(18)	16.7	(27)	14.2	(23)	35.8	(58)	100.0	(162)
30–39	3.44	26.2	(45)	4.7	(8)	12.8	(22)	12.2	(21)	44.2	(76)	100.0	(172)
40–49	2.74	41.9	(98)	7.3	(17)	14.1	(33)	8.1	(19)	28.6	(67)	100.0	(234)
50–59	2.55	41.7	(113)	12.9	(35)	14.8	(40)	9.6	(26)	21.0	(57)	100.0	(271)
60–69	2.22	47.0	(85)	12.2	(22)	23.8	(43)	6.1	(11)	11.0	(20)	100.0	(181)
70 and over	1.80	60.6	(72)	16.0	(19)	11.8	(14)	6.7	(8)	5.0	(6)	100.0	(119)
Household income													
$15,000 and under	2.84	36.5	(23)	11.1	(7)	12.7	(8)	11.1	(7)	28.6	(18)	100.0	(63)
$15,000–$30,000	2.72	43.3	(52)	5.8	(7)	14.2	(17)	9.2	(11)	27.5	(33)	100.0	(120)
$30,000–$50,000	2.42	49.0	(103)	8.6	(18)	12.4	(26)	11.4	(24)	18.6	(39)	100.0	(210)
$50,000–$75,000	2.74	37.6	(80)	10.8	(23)	16.9	(36)	9.4	(20)	25.4	(54)	100.0	(213)
$75,000–$100,000	2.70	39.4	(61)	11.6	(18)	13.5	(21)	11.0	(17)	24.5	(38)	100.0	(155)
More than $100,000	2.94	31.2	(77)	12.1	(30)	19.0	(47)	7.3	(18)	30.4	(75)	100.0	(247)
Education													
High school or less	2.60	43.3	(197)	10.1	(25)	14.2	(35)	8.5	(21)	23.9	(59)	100.0	(247)
Some college	2.47	42.9	(141)	12.5	(41)	18.2	(60)	7.6	(25)	18.8	(62)	100.0	(329)
College graduate	2.85	36.7	(223)	9.4	(57)	15.0	(91)	10.7	(65)	28.3	(172)	100.0	(293)

[a] Scale item scores range from 1 (not at all) to 5 (completely).

records, tax documents, rental/lease agreements, and so on. While the future of physical newspapers seems clear, the paperless home is still a part of the future with over half of households continuing with paper records over digital versions. About one-tenth of the households report being paperless in terms of records of bills, insurance claims, contracts and warranties, etc. In this context we also note that our survey results show that 75 percent of the families use their computer for virtual shopping which can be considered as an activity under home management.

There is a less clear demarcation of what types of households are more paperless than others (Table 2.2). Income variations are not very clear-cut although higher incomes are slightly more likely to store digital versions of records. Age again shows a decline in digitization of household records with those 60 and over significantly less likely to have given up paper records. Similarly, those households with higher levels of education are more likely to have made the transition to digital versions than those with lower levels of education. Nonetheless, no group is truly committed to being paperless. By income level, the percentage range for reported paperless record keeping was as low as 7 percent (households with income between $30,000 and $50,000) to a high of 16 percent (households with income between $75,000 and $100,000). For age groups, the range was from 4 percent (age 70 and over) to a high of 18 percent (ages 30–39).

Entertainment center: replaced watching programs and movies on a TV to watching them on a computer or hand-held device

Utilizing the media substitution theory, Jaye and Johnson (2003), examined the status of traditional media in the online world. We were similarly interested in finding out how families are

Table 2.2 Replaced paper records such as bills, insurance claims, maintenance contracts, warranties with digital versions

	Mean score[a]	Not at all								Completely		Total	
		%	(N)	%	(N)	%	(N)	%	(N)	%	(N)	%	(N)
Total	2.41	38.9	(464)	15.1	(180)	22.6	(270)	13.3	(159)	10.1	(121)	100.0	(1194)
Age													
18–29	2.64	31.7	(51)	16.8	(27)	21.7	(35)	15.5	(25)	14.3	(23)	100.0	(161)
30–39	2.81	26.3	(45)	17.5	(30)	22.2	(38)	16.4	(28)	17.5	(30)	100.0	(171)
40–49	2.47	38.4	(89)	9.9	(23)	26.3	(61)	17.2	(40)	8.2	(19)	100.0	(232)
50–59	2.38	37.0	(101)	16.8	(46)	25.6	(70)	12.1	(33)	8.4	(23)	100.0	(273)
60–69	2.15	48.1	(87)	16.6	(30)	16.6	(30)	9.9	(18)	8.8	(16)	100.0	(181)
70 and over	2.04	52.1	(62)	10.1	(12)	23.5	(28)	10.1	(12)	4.2	(5)	100.0	(119)
Household income													
$15,000 and under	1.98	54.8	(34)	16.1	(10)	12.9	(8)	8.1	(5)	8.1	(5)	100.0	(62)
$15,000–$30,000	2.35	45.8	(55)	9.2	(11)	19.2	(23)	15.8	(19)	10.0	(12)	100.0	(120)
$30,000–$50,000	2.29	40.4	(84)	15.9	(33)	25.5	(53)	11.1	(23)	7.2	(15)	100.0	(208)
$50,000–$75,000	2.37	38.0	(82)	18.5	(40)	20.4	(44)	14.4	(31)	8.8	(19)	100.0	(216)
$75,000–$100,000	2.63	33.8	(52)	14.3	(22)	22.7	(35)	13.6	(21)	15.6	(24)	100.0	(154)
More than $100,000	2.62	31.2	(77)	14.2	(35)	27.5	(68)	15.4	(38)	11.7	(29)	100.0	(247)
Education													
High school or less	2.27	49.6	(122)	9.8	(24)	17.5	(43)	10.2	(25)	13.0	(32)	100.0	(246)
Some college	2.19	45.9	(151)	15.2	(50)	20.1	(66)	11.2	(37)	7.6	(25)	100.0	(329)
College graduate	2.59	30.4	(185)	17.1	(104)	26.3	(160)	15.8	(96)	10.4	(63)	100.0	(608)

[a] Scale item scores range from 1 (not at all) to 5 (completely).

using computers to watch TV programs (Figure 2.2c). We found that 38 percent use the computer or a hand-held device (e.g. iPad) at various degrees and within that range only 5 percent report replacing it completely. It is important to note here that our question is not directed towards what is the percentage of families using computers for hobbies and entertainment. Indeed, about four-fifths of the households report using the home computer for hobbies and entertainment (data not shown). Rather, our interest here is the extent to which one form of entertainment (watching TV programs and movies on the TV) is being replaced by watching these programs and movies on the computer.

The TV set is not going away too soon. While there have been new websites that have TV programs and movie rental companies such as NETFLIX are now offering downloadable movies for viewing, roughly three-fifths (62 percent) of households report that they have not replaced the TV with a computer or hand-held device for viewing programs and movies (see Table 2.3). Only about 5 percent reported that they have made the change to TV on the computer. A further development is that TV sets are now coming equipped with Internet access. At the time of the survey in 2010, approximately 22 percent of the respondents reported that they owned TV sets that could connect to the Internet. Similar to other digital replacements, age is clearly a factor in that as age increases the likelihood of using a computer as a TV decreases. There is a higher proportion of experimentation with the use of the computer as TV in the younger age groups. Level of education is not a factor. But to some extent household income does appear to be a factor with a higher likelihood in the lower-income categories, which may simply be an artefact of age.

Table 2.3 Replaced watching programs and movies on a TV to watching them on a computer or hand-held device

	Mean score^a	Not at all								Completely		Total	
		%	(N)	%	(N)	%	(N)	%	(N)	%	(N)	%	(N)
Total	1.75	61.9	(742)	16.4	(196)	11.4	(137)	5.0	(60)	5.3	(63)	100.0	(1198)
Age													
18–29	2.40	38.3	(62)	19.1	(31)	19.1	(31)	11.1	(18)	12.3	(20)	100.0	(162)
30–39	2.02	50.0	(86)	22.1	(38)	12.2	(21)	7.0	(12)	8.7	(15)	100.0	(172)
40–49	1.73	61.5	(144)	17.5	(41)	12.0	(28)	4.7	(11)	4.3	(10)	100.0	(234)
50–59	1.63	65.9	(180)	15.4	(42)	12.1	(33)	2.9	(8)	3.7	(10)	100.0	(273)
60–69	1.40	76.2	(138)	13.8	(25)	5.0	(9)	3.9	(7)	1.1	(2)	100.0	(181)
70 and over	1.45	74.8	(89)	11.8	(14)	10.1	(12)	0.8	(1)	2.5	(3)	100.0	(119)
Household income													
$15,000 and under	1.94	63.5	(40)	7.9	(5)	11.1	(7)	6.3	(4)	11.1	(7)	100.0	(63)
$15,000–$30,000	1.91	61.7	(74)	9.2	(11)	15.0	(18)	5.0	(6)	9.2	(11)	100.0	(120)
$30,000–$50,000	1.71	63.6	(133)	16.7	(35)	10.0	(21)	4.3	(9)	5.3	(11)	100.0	(209)
$50,000–$75,000	1.59	65.7	(142)	18.5	(40)	9.3	(20)	3.7	(8)	2.8	(6)	100.0	(216)
$75,000–$100,000	1.75	60.0	(93)	16.1	(25)	15.5	(24)	5.2	(8)	3.2	(5)	100.0	(155)
More than $100,000	1.75	58.3	(144)	22.3	(55)	10.1	(25)	4.9	(12)	4.5	(11)	100.0	(247)
Education													
High school or less	1.85	64.0	(158)	11.3	(28)	9.3	(23)	6.9	(17)	8.5	(21)	100.0	(247)
Some college	1.63	65.8	(217)	15.2	(50)	12.4	(41)	3.3	(11)	3.3	(11)	100.0	(330)
College graduate	1.78	59.0	(360)	19.2	(117)	11.8	(72)	5.1	(31)	4.9	(30)	100.0	(610)

^a Scale item scores range from 1 (not at all) to 5 (completely).

Communication center: replaced the landline telephone with the computer to make calls using, for example, Skype or Vonage

In terms of communication, we make a distinction between written communication (e.g. emails displacing hard copies of letter writing, and voice communication). The question of communication replacement (physical vs. virtual) is complex because we are already witnessing a dramatic increase in the use of mobile phones which are replacing the landlines as the principal mode of communication activity for a sizeable segment of the population. It is already well established that as far as written communication is concerned, computers have overtaken handwritten letters by a large proportion and this appears to be less of an issue now as compared to, say ten or 15 years ago. Our own research shows that the highest use of computers is for email with 98 percent of the sample reporting this use. So the question remaining is, to what extent are the computers being used for voice communication and more specifically, are telephones being replaced with computer-assisted voice communication?

WiFi and access to the Internet on the mobile phone pretty much reduce the need for the computer as a telephone. There is very little acceptance of the replacement of the telephone with the computer (Table 2.4); indeed, nearly 78 percent of the households reported "not at all" for this replacement (Figure 2.2d). In addition, age, education and income do not make much of a difference in the replacement value of the computer for the telephone.

The widespread use of mobile phones, particularly the smartphones, has made a considerable dent in the use of landline phones as well as the use of the computer for making cheap to free long-distance phone calls. So we are faced with a voice communication triangle involving

Table 2.4 Replaced the landline telephone with the computer to make calls using, for example, Skype or Vonage

	Mean score[a]	Not at all								Completely		Total	
		%	(N)	%	(N)	%	(N)	%	(N)	%	(N)	%	(N)
Total	1.47	77.7	(928)	9.3	(111)	6.4	(76)	2.1	(25)	4.6	(55)	100.0	(1195)
Age													
18–29	1.57	72.8	(118)	10.5	(17)	8.6	(14)	2.5	(4)	5.6	(9)	100.0	(162)
30–39	1.60	72.7	(125)	8.7	(15)	10.5	(18)	1.7	(3)	6.4	(11)	100.0	(172)
40–49	1.53	78.1	(182)	6.4	(15)	5.6	(13)	3.9	(9)	6.0	(14)	100.0	(233)
50–59	1.43	78.7	(214)	10.7	(29)	3.7	(10)	2.6	(7)	4.4	(12)	100.0	(272)
60–69	1.35	81.2	(147)	9.9	(18)	5.0	(9)	0.0	(0)	3.9	(7)	100.0	(181)
70 and over	1.35	78.0	(92)	11.0	(13)	9.3	(11)	1.7	(2)	0.0	(0)	100.0	(118)
Household income													
$15,000 and under	1.46	77.8	(49)	7.9	(5)	7.9	(5)	3.2	(2)	3.2	(2)	100.0	(63)
$15,000–$30,000	1.55	78.3	(94)	4.2	(5)	8.3	(10)	2.5	(3)	6.7	(8)	100.0	(120)
$30,000–$50,000	1.53	74.0	(154)	11.1	(23)	7.7	(16)	1.9	(4)	5.3	(11)	100.0	(208)
$50,000–$75,000	1.35	83.3	(180)	6.0	(13)	6.0	(13)	1.4	(3)	3.2	(7)	100.0	(216)
$75,000–$100,000	1.54	76.0	(117)	9.7	(15)	5.2	(8)	2.6	(4)	6.5	(10)	100.0	(154)
More than $100,000	1.44	77.9	(191)	11.3	(28)	5.7	(14)	1.2	(3)	4.5	(11)	100.0	(247)
Education													
High school or less	1.51	79.6	(195)	5.7	(14)	6.1	(15)	1.6	(4)	6.9	(17)	100.0	(245)
Some college	1.38	81.5	(268)	8.2	(27)	4.6	(15)	2.7	(9)	3.0	(10)	100.0	(329)
College graduate	1.50	74.8	(456)	11.3	(69)	7.4	(45)	2.0	(12)	4.6	(28)	100.0	(610)

[a] Scale item scores range from 1 (not at all) to 5 (completely).

landlines, computers and mobile phones. As shown in Figure 2.2e, we found that 14 percent of the households have mobile phone only, 14 percent have landline only and 72 percent have both landline and mobile phone. As a further refinement to our analysis, we are able to examine the extent to which age, education and household income level are associated with mobile phone communication (see Table 2.5). Age is a contributing factor as the proportion of mobile phone only households are highest for the younger age groups and steadily declines with age. The age distribution for landline only and landline and mobile phone is fairly similar across age groups with a decided upswing in the landline proportion for those aged 70 and over and a decrease in landline and mobile phone. Mobile phone only decreases by income with a steady increase in the income levels for landline and mobile phone. The proportion of mobile phone only versus landline and mobile phone households is relatively stable across the educational levels.

Social center: replaced printing photos with using a digital picture frame or viewing pictures online

Digital picture frames and online viewing are becoming more and more popular. Nearly one-quarter of the households reported that they have completely replaced photo printing with viewing pictures online or with a digital picture frame (Figure 2.2f). On the other hand, about one-quarter have not joined the digital photo revolution. Age is associated although the differences are not very substantial (Table 2.6): While 25 percent of those aged 18–29 report that

Table 2.5 Landline vs. cell phone households

	Cell phone only		Landline only		Landline and cell phone		Total	
Total	14.2	(170)	13.8	(165)	72.1	(865)	100.0	(1200)
Age								
18–29	45.7	(74)	6.2	(10)	48.1	(78)	100.0	(162)
30–39	22.5	(39)	13.3	(23)	64.2	(111)	100.0	(173)
40–49	9.0	(21)	14.5	(34)	76.5	(179)	100.0	(234)
50–59	8.4	(23)	13.2	(36)	78.4	(214)	100.0	(273)
60–69	4.4	(8)	13.8	(25)	81.8	(148)	100.0	(181)
70 and over	3.4	(4)	23.5	(28)	73.1	(87)	100.0	(119)
Household income								
$15,000 and under	22.2	(14)	20.6	(13)	57.1	(36)	100.0	(63)
$15,000–$30,000	21.5	(26)	19.0	(23)	59.5	(72)	100.0	(121)
$30,000–$50,000	17.1	(36)	10.5	(22)	72.3	(152)	100.0	(210)
$50,000–$75,000	16.2	(35)	9.7	(21)	74.1	(160)	100.0	(216)
$75,000–$100,000	13.5	(21)	10.3	(16)	76.1	(118)	100.0	(155)
More than $100,000	7.7	(19)	8.1	(20)	84.2	(208)	100.0	(247)
Education								
High school or less	19.8	(49)	13.8	(34)	66.4	(164)	100.0	(247)
Some college	16.1	(53)	12.7	(42)	71.2	(235)	100.0	(330)
College graduate	11.1	(68)	14.1	(86)	74.8	(457)	100.0	(611)

Table 2.6 Replaced printing photos with using a digital picture frame or viewing pictures online

	Mean score[a]	Not at all								Completely		Total	
		%	(N)	%	(N)	%	(N)	%	(N)	%	(N)	%	(N)
Total	2.96	25.1	(300)	12.5	(149)	24.3	(290)	17.6	(210)	20.6	(246)	100.0	(1195)
Age													
18–29	3.22	18.5	(30)	11.7	(19)	23.5	(38)	21.6	(35)	24.7	(40)	100.0	(162)
30–39	3.09	22.1	(38)	8.7	(15)	25.6	(44)	25.0	(43)	18.6	(32)	100.0	(172)
40–49	3.00	23.7	(55)	10.8	(25)	27.6	(64)	17.2	(40)	20.7	(48)	100.0	(232)
50–59	3.03	24.9	(68)	13.2	(36)	19.0	(52)	20.1	(55)	22.7	(62)	100.0	(273)
60–69	2.85	26.5	(48)	14.4	(26)	26.5	(48)	12.7	(23)	19.9	(36)	100.0	(181)
70 and over	2.67	33.1	(39)	14.4	(17)	24.6	(29)	8.5	(10)	19.5	(23)	100.0	(118)
Household income													
$15,000 and under	2.63	40.3	(25)	12.9	(8)	11.3	(7)	14.5	(9)	21.0	(13)	100.0	(62)
$15,000–$30,000	3.02	30.8	(37)	6.7	(8)	23.3	(28)	7.5	(9)	31.7	(38)	100.0	(120)
$30,000–$50,000	2.95	25.8	(54)	12.9	(27)	22.5	(47)	17.7	(37)	21.1	(44)	100.0	(209)
$50,000–$75,000	2.97	24.5	(53)	12.0	(26)	25.0	(54)	18.5	(40)	19.9	(43)	100.0	(216)
$75,000–$100,000	3.03	22.7	(35)	9.7	(15)	26.6	(41)	23.4	(36)	17.5	(27)	100.0	(154)
More than $100,000	3.16	16.3	(40)	15.9	(39)	25.2	(62)	21.1	(52)	21.5	(53)	100.0	(246)
Education													
High school or less	2.87	30.4	(75)	10.9	(27)	22.3	(55)	14.2	(35)	22.3	(55)	100.0	(247)
Some college	2.92	27.4	(90)	11.0	(36)	25.3	(83)	14.9	(49)	21.3	(70)	100.0	(328)
College graduate	3.03	21.5	(131)	13.8	(84)	24.5	(149)	20.5	(125)	19.7	(120)	100.0	(609)

[a] Scale item scores range from 1 (not at all) to 5 (completely).

Table 2.7 EMT Model (Enabling-Mediating-Transforming) of computer use

	Percent agreeing 1999	Percent agreeing 2003	Percent agreeing 2008	Percent agreeing 2010	Role of technology
The computer has saved us time at home	48	51	51	55	Enabling
Computers are difficult to use	16	11	13	–	Enabling
Computers have made it easier to organize family/social events	–	34	33	43	Enabling
Households with a computer are run more efficiently than those without a computer	15	22	–	–	Enabling
Computers in the home take away from family interactions	23	27	30	–	Enabling/ Disabling
The computer has increased the amount of job related work I do at home	43	37	33	–	Mediating
Computers are more useful than in the home	40	39	37	–	Mediating
I have more contact with friends and relatives now that I have email	50	54	48	55	Mediating
It would be difficult to imagine life without a computer at home	44	50	58	61	Transforming
The computer has changed the way we do things at home	40	45	–	52	Transforming
The computer is as essential as any other household appliance	38	51	59	63	Transforming
Having the Internet makes me much better informed about the world	47	56	61	66	Transforming
Computers give status to their owners	13	11	–	–	Transforming
Those that are not knowledgeable about computers are falling behind	68	68	68	70	Transforming
Watch less TV as a result of the Internet	29	25	23	–	Transforming
The computer has become part of daily routine at home	52	62	63	72	Transforming
The Internet helps me look for product information that was not possible before	58	72	72	71	Transforming
The computer has replaced the telephone as major communication device	10	16	15	–	Transforming
Reduced our need of daily newspapers	–	–	40	–	Transforming
I do most of my communication with friends using social networking sites	–	–	–	21	Transforming
More productive because we have a computer	–	–	49	48	Transforming
Computer has enabled me to meet new people	–	–	–	22	Transforming

they have completely made the replacement, a full 20 percent of those aged 60–69 and those over 70 years old have also replaced printing with digital. Household income levels do not differentiate nor does educational level. It appears that the digital camera has significantly reduced the need for photo developing services; photo printing is now on the chopping block.

Enabling-Mediating-Transforming (EMT): the model of technology's role

To capture the impact of technology resulting from its Enabling-Mediating-Transforming (EMT) role, we asked our respondents to indicate how computers have affected their lives. The computer has been an instrument of change as seen from the information gathered from our samples of respondents over the ten-year period (Table 2.7) (Venkatesh *et al.* 2011). Its trans-formative role is quite evident from the responses from our subjects. While it has played a vital role in terms of its enabling and facilitating functions, a larger number of its impacts are in terms of its transformation role. Our respondents have recorded progressively their agreement over the four periods of data collection on various impact statements.

A good percentage (66 percent) of respondents feel that they are better informed about the world because of the Internet. Computers are also seen as contributing significantly to family social life in terms of establishing contacts with friends and relatives (55 percent) and also the use of social networking sites (21 percent), which though small, is a recent phenomenon and likely to grow. Certainly there is agreement that those that are not knowledgeable about computers are falling behind (70 percent). Computers are seen as replacing newspapers as an information source (40 percent in 2008) – a sign of digital living. A large number (61 percent) agreed that it would be difficult to imagine life now without a computer and a larger number (72 percent) feel that the computer has become part of the daily routine. Time savings (55 percent) are also reported because of the computer as well as being more productive (48 percent). However, very few (15 percent in 2008) feel that the computer has replaced the telephone which is still the most important tool for voice communication. In this context, it would be interesting to see what role smartphones would play especially because smartphones do have computer-like capabilities.

In sum, the transformation is occurring in terms of technological dependence and initiatives, and the indispensable nature of computers to conduct family activities and especially in the areas of communication, information, home management, and social networking.

Conclusion

We began by identifying eight major activity centers: information, communication, shopping, home management, education/learning, job/work/employment, entertainment/hobbies and social. We selected five major activities for analysis: reading newspapers (information), paper records (home management), watching programs on TV (entertainment), substituting for landline phones (voice communication), and sharing photos (social). We also noted that 98 percent of the households use computers for emailing (written communication) and 75 percent for home shopping.

There are clear changes in some household physical devices as a result of the home computer and most importantly the Internet. In some instances it may just be that the next replacement will be that of the home computer as smartphones like the iPhone and androids become more affordable to a wider number of people. In any case, at the moment, we are observing the significant reduction in physical newspaper ownership and what might be generally thought of as the physical photo album as more people opt for viewing photos online or in rotating digital frames. On the other hand, what probably 10 years ago might have been considered, i.e., the elimination of the landline phone with the replacement of the computer as phone, has not evolved as originally thought. In place of that changeover, the landline phone is being replaced by the mobile phone. Instead of a family phone, the phone becomes individual. Thus far, the TV is not in danger of being replaced; rather, it is more likely that the TV will be further integrated into the Internet. Indeed, in this survey, 22 percent of the respondents indicated that their TV is connected to the Internet. As a consequence, it will be interesting to see if the computer replaces TV or the TV becomes more like a computer. Finally, despite corporate efforts and incentives, the paperless home is still very much in the future. The majority of households still rely on the paper versions of bills, claims, insurance documents, etc. In other words, taken as a whole, the developments seem to suggest that "digitizing physical objects" in the home seems to be an on-going project perhaps pointing to an evolving "convergence culture."

Acknowledgments

This material is based upon work funded by the U.S. National Science Foundation under Grant No. 0121232. Any opinions, findings and conclusions reflected in the material are those of the authors and do not necessarily reflect the views of the National Science Foundation.

Note

1 The survey was conducted using a national RDD sample. Any adult 18 years and over who was knowledgeable about the household's use of computers in the home was eligible to be interviewed. A total of 1030 interviews were completed with respondents with a landline phone; 170 interviews with respondents who have only a mobile phone and no landline in the home. AAPOR response rates for the mobile phone sample: response rate 1 = .217; response rate 2 = .223; response rate 3 = .235; response rate 4 = .241. AAPOR response rates for the landline sample: response rate 1 = .216; response rate = .229; response rate = .290; response rate = .307. The survey was conducted by telephone by Abt SRBI (New York) during the period April 15, 2010 to May 24, 2010. The interview took approximately 18–20 minutes.

Further reading

Harper, R. (ed.) (2011) *The Connected Home: The Future of Domestic Life*, London: Springer Verlag,
Haddon, L. (ed.) (2011) *The Contemporary Internet*, London: Peter Lang.
Annamma, J., Sherry Jr., J.F., Venkatesh, A. and Deschenes, J. (2009) "Perceiving Images and Telling Tales: A Visual and Verbal Analysis of the Meaning of the Internet," *Journal of Consumer Psychology*, 19(3): 556–66.

References

Benjamin, W. ([1936] 1972) "The Work of Art in the Age of Mechanical Reproduction," in *Illuminations*, London: Fontana.
Fischer, C. (1994) *America Calling: The History of the Telephone to 1940*, Berkeley, CA: University of California Press.
Fiske, J. (1987) *The Television Culture*, London: Methuen Company.
Flink, J.J. (1970) *America Adopts the Automobile*, Cambridge, MA: The MIT Press.
Hilmes, M. and Laviglio, J. (eds) (2002) *Essays in the Cultural History of Radio in America*, London: Routledge.
Hoffman, D.L. and Novak, T.P. (1996) "Marketing in Hypermedia Environment Computer-Mediated Environments: Conceptual Foundations," *Journal of Marketing*, 60: 50–68.
Hoffman, D.L., Novak, T.P. and Venkatesh, A. (2004) "Has the Internet Become Indispensable?: Empirical Findings and Model Development," *Communications of the ACM*, July: 37–44.
Ito, M., Horst, H., Bittani, M., boyd, d., Herr-Stephenson, B., Lange, P.G., Pearce, C.J. and Robinson, L. (2009) *Living and Learning with New Media: Summary of Findings from the Digital Youth Project*, Cambridge, MA: The MIT Press.

Jaye, B.K. and Johnson, T.J. (2003) "From Here to Obscurity: Media Substitution Theory and Traditional Media in an Online World," *Journal of the American Society for American Science and Technology*, 54(3): 260–73.

Jenkins, H. (2006) *Convergence Culture: Where Old and New Ideas Collide*, New York: New York University Press.

Joy, A., Sherry Jr., J.F., Venkatesh, A. and Deschenes, J. (2009) "Perceiving Images and Telling Tales: A Visual and Verbal Analysis of the Meaning of the Internet," *Journal of Consumer Psychology*, 19: 556–66.

Kozinets, R.V., de Valck, K., Wojnicki, A. and Wilner, S. (2010) "Networked Narratives: Understanding Word-of-mouth Marketing in Online Communities," *Journal of Marketing*, 74: 71–89.

Paterson, C. and Domingo, D. (2008) *Making Online News: The Ethnography of New Media Production*, New York: Peter Lang.

Ribeiro, G.L. (1998) "Cybercultural Politics: Political Activism at a Distance in a Transnational World," in S.E. Alvarez, E. Dagnino, and A. Escobar (eds), *Cultures of Politics, Politics of Cultures: Revisioning Latin American Social Movements*, Boulder, CO: Westview Press, pp. 325–52.

RoAne, S. (2008) *Face to Face: How to Reclaim the Personal Touch in a Digital World*, New York: Simon & Schuster.

Rogers, E. (1986) *Communication Technology: The New Media and Society*, New York: The Free Press.

Shankar, V., Venkatesh, A., Hofacker, C. and Naik, P. (2010) "Mobile Marketing in the Retailing Environment: Current Insights and Future Research Avenues," *Journal of Interactive Marketing*, 24(2): 111–20.

Shih, E. and Venkatesh, A. (2004) "Beyond Adoption: Development and Application of a Use-Diffusion Model," *Journal of Marketing*, 68(1): 59–72.

Stanley, P.H. (1978) *The Celluloid Empire: A History of the American Movie Industry*, London: Hastings House.

Vaidyanathan, S. (2011) *Googlization of Everything (and Why We Should Worry)*, Berkeley, CA: University of California Press.

Venkatesh, A. (1996) "Computers and Other Interactive Technologies for the Home," *Communications of the ACM*, 39(12): 47–55.

——(2008) "Digital Home Technologies and Transformation of the Household," *Information Systems Frontiers*, 10(4): 391–5.

Venkatesh, A. and Behairy, N. (2012) "Young American Consumers and New Technologies: Everyday Life in the Digitally Networked World," in M. Molesworth and J. Denegri-Knott (eds), *Digital Virtual Consumption*, Abingdon: Routledge, pp. 29–45.

Venkatesh, A., Dunkle, D. and Wortman, A. (2011) "Home Computer Uses and Impacts on Family Life: Children and Feminization of Computing," in R. Harper (ed.), *At Home with Smart Technologies*, New York: Springer.

Venkatesh, A., Kruse, E. and Shih, E. (2003) "The Networked Home: An Analysis of Current Developments and Future Trends," *Cognition, Technology and Work*, 5(1): 23–32.

Vitalari, N., Gronhaug, K. and Venkatesh, A. (1985) "Computing in the Home: Shifts in the Time Allocation Patterns of Household," *Communications of the ACM*, 28(5): 512–22.

3

THE DIGITAL CONSUMER

Donna L. Hoffman, Thomas P. Novak and Randy Stein

Keywords

motivations, social media, social networks, well-being

Introduction

The time for predicting whether social media applications will become indispensable to people in their everyday lives is over, because that time has arrived. In the United States, Facebook usage now surpasses Google, accounting for 25 percent of all pages views and 10 percent of all internet activity (Dougherty 2010). One quarter of total online time is spent on social media, with social media usage increasing 82 percent between December 2008 and December 2009 (Nielsen Wire 2010). Facebook is not the only social media application enjoying a phenomenal surge in usage. Thirty-five hours of video are uploaded to www.youtube.com every minute (Schmidt 2010). As of May 2011, yelp.com receives 50 million unique daily visitors (Kincaid 2011). And as early as 2006, one in three South Koreans was a member of the Korean social networking site cyworld.com (BBC News 2006).

As social media continues to evolve and become even more ubiquitous, and as user-generated content replaces marketer-generated content, researchers are beginning to examine how social media is likely to shape consumer behavior. For example, who is influencing whom in social media? How do online reviews, and information about friends' buying behavior, influence consumers' attitudes and purchase behavior? How do people decide what content to create (e.g., what goes in a Facebook profile, and how do users decide what to Tweet about?) What content is most likely to go viral? More generally, why do people use social media at all and become customers of social media applications?

Of course, the ubiquity and scope of social media usage make such investigations daunting. Research on specific topics in how social media impacts consumer behavior has begun to proliferate in the past several years, but organizing and drawing conclusions from this work present significant challenges. Since social media applications themselves are just coming out of a nascent stage, theoretical frameworks guiding broad research questions are still scarce. That is, while many specific topics have been covered, drawing generalizations can be difficult.

On this note, Novak (2008) synthesized research on social media to identify 22 distinct motivations why people use social media, noting that the lack of an organizing framework hampered conceptual progress. From this broad range of goals, Hoffman and Novak (forthcoming) developed a social media version of the 4Ps marketing mix model to account for the goals users have when using social media. Specifically, they identified four higher-order goals they argued account for the lion's share of motivations people have in using social media applications: connect, create, consume, and control. People might use social media simply to *connect* with other users. They might also use an application to *create* content, for example, by posting updates on Facebook or tweeting brief reviews with Twitter. Alternatively, people might *consume* content that other users have created. Finally, users might also choose to exercise *control* over how they use social media, such as by adjusting privacy settings or by modifying the visual appearance of an application. These "4Cs" are not necessarily mutually exclusive as the same behavior could fulfill one or more of the goals; for example, playing Farmville could fulfill the need to connect for one user, and the need to control for another. Similarly, people may approach social media use with more than one goal at the same time, for example with the goals of creating content in order to connect with others. Together, the ability to fulfill these four goals online likely explains why people spend so much time on social media applications.

Since the 4Cs framework helps understand why people use social media, it also indicates the implications social media use should have for consumption behavior. A review of the literature on social media use according to the 4Cs therefore provides a useful organizing framework, as well as a mechanism to identify important areas for future research. Our review that follows is organized by the 4Cs higher-order social media goals. The research we discuss is organized by the primary goal that consumers in a given study were most directly trying to fulfill, or by the type of goal that was most directly examined. For each goal, we define how it relates to social media use, describe research relevant to the goal, and conclude with ideas for future research relating to how consumers might be seeking to fulfill these goals through their social media usage behaviors.

Connect

We define social media as the set of

> web-based and mobile tools and applications that allow people to create (consume) content that can be consumed (created) by others and which enables and facilitates connections.

Thus, social media are not so much about specific technologies (i.e. Facebook today, Viewdle tomorrow), but rather what the technologies let consumers *do*. Arguably, more than any other reason, people use social media to connect with others. Indeed, the ability to connect with large numbers of other users across time and space is largely responsible for much of the success of social media. However, interactions via social media are quite different than offline interactions: conversations are replaced with tweets, wall posts, video uploads, status updates, and "likes." Users are no longer limited to information gleaned from their friends in real-time, real-life interactions; instead, they can display their musical interests, photos of what they did last weekend and relationship status with just a few keystrokes. Social media therefore changes the way people connect with each other, both in the type of interactions that take place and in the quantity and quality of information that is available.

These changes naturally lead to several questions concerning the changing landscape of people's social lives. When seeking a connection with others online, what information do consumers get from others, and how do they use it? Also, does connection with others online lead to positive effects on well-being?

As far as seeking connections with others online, social media is unique in that first impressions can be formed by looking at someone's profile and content created, rather than from a face-to-face meeting. Despite this difference, liking stems from cues of sociability in both modes of meeting: liking of people in real-life meetings is predicted by non-verbal expressivity, while liking from examining a Facebook profile is predicted by the expressivity of the profile (e.g. number of photos posted and how much contact the person has with others; Weisbuch *et al.* 2009). However, impressions will be shaped by the method utilized to find information. People who actively choose which information to use on Facebook to form an impression of another user like the user less than those passively given a set amount of information on the same user (Waggoner *et al.* 2009). Notably, Waggoner *et al.* also found increased amounts of information increased confidence in judgments in passive perceivers (those who are given information to look at), but not active perceivers (those who decide what information to look at, and how much of it to look at). Ironically, this suggests that actively trying to find someone to form a bond with over a social network might be a more difficult task than it initially seems due to the overabundance of information available.

The amount of information available on social media sites is also changing the way we acquire information about our real-life friends. Before social networking websites, impressions of friends were limited by information obtained through face-to-face (i.e. direct) interactions. However, social media enables computer-mediated interactions, so what people post on their Facebook profiles need not be limited to what they choose to share during in-person interactions. Indeed, members of social networks are unaware of disagreements with friends, even on topics they say they discuss, instead applying stereotypes and projecting their own views on their friends (Goel *et al.* 2010). Presumably, as more and more information about friends becomes available online, differences between friends will become more salient. Research has yet to address how noticing this chasm cascades back into real-life interactions, but it is clear that users of social media now have access to information that directly contradicts their natural tendency to assume that their friends' beliefs and attitudes are similar to their own.

Since online interaction has the potential to at least partially replace offline interaction, research examining the impact of social media use on well-being has begun to emerge in recent years. Research has uncovered several relevant moderators and caveat-laden relationships between social media use and well-being. For example, though direct communication between pairs on Facebook (e.g., trading wall posts) increases feelings of bonding and decreases felt loneliness, it is paradoxically those who consume the most content that feel least bonded and most lonely (Burke *et al.* 2010). Also, Facebook usage is correlated with feelings of *both* connection and disconnection, because feelings of disconnection motivate increased use of Facebook, which ultimately leads to feelings of connection (Sheldon *et al.* 2011). However, given the myriad of people using social media and reasons why they use it, there is unlikely to be a clear-cut, unidimensional and unidirectional effect of social media on well-being.

Recently, Hoffman and Novak (2011a) evaluated the relationship between social media goal pursuit and the experience of feeling connected. Results showed that social goals and connect goals lead to different levels of relatedness, but the relationship between goal pursuit and relatedness is moderated by online social identity and motivational orientations. Further research is necessary to connect these feelings of connection to life outcomes. Indeed, users themselves may over-estimate the effect of social media usage on their well-being. Research done after the university shootings at Virginia Tech and Northern Illinois University found that students who turned to Internet-related activities for support after the shootings *thought* those activities were beneficial, but there was no actual effect on well-being, as measured by depressive and PTSD symptoms (Vicary and Fraley 2010). Of course, not all sources of stress that might lead people to seek support online are as extreme as those school shootings, but it is clear that care must be taken when judging the accuracy of users' predictions about their own well-being.

While most research on connection online focuses on the use of social media to become more connected, it is of course possible to prefer an online version of an activity to *avoid* social interactions with others. For example, some users prefer online gambling to casino gambling, viewing the online version as a way to experience the joy of gambling with the added bonus of anonymity, preferring not to have to interact with the other gamblers (Cotte and LaTour 2010). While that study did not involve social media, *per se*, the implication is clear: users may turn to social media to participate in stigmatized behavior, or simply to have a more low-intensity form of social interaction. The effects on well-being of using social media in this way still need to be addressed.

While less researched, it is worth noting that social media is not only a way for users to connect with each other, but also offers businesses these opportunities as well. Online sellers can increase their economic value by connecting with other sellers on social networks, because it makes the seller's marketplace more accessible, essentially creating an "online shopping mall" (Stephen and Toubia 2010). Presumably, seamless integration into customers' social networks would also provide greater feelings of trust between customers and sellers, though further research is necessary to address this question.

Is the connection that people experience online a "real" connection? Considerable research has established that behavior in online virtual environments parallels real-world behavior in many important ways, indicating that the connections people establish online are as real as the ones they establish in the physical world. Slater *et al.* (2006) replicated Milgram's (1963) obedience study and found that participants administering virtual electric shocks to virtual subjects behaved in similar ways as did participants in Milgram's original study. Yee *et al.* (2007) found that single and mixed gender dyad norms for interpersonal distance in avatar-based online social environments paralleled norms in the real world. Similarly, social cues involving the size of successive requests for cooperation made in online environments (i.e. large followed by moderate, vs. small followed by moderate) produced identical outcomes in both virtual and physical world settings (Eastwick and Gardner 2008).

It is clear from research on how people are connecting online that the wealth of information and connection opportunities available is a double-edged sword. The relationship between social media usage and actual feelings of connection is complex (Burke *et al.* 2010; Sheldon *et al.* 2011). Perhaps this is because, with increased information and connection opportunities, expectations may inflate and therefore be more difficult to meet (cf. Goel *et al.* 2010; Vicary and Fraley, 2010; Waggoner *et al.* 2009). The amount of information available on social networks could also de-motivate effective connection-seeking behavior (see Iyengar and Lepper 2000). Future research should address what strategies users could or should use to cut down on this information overload.

Thus, it is clear that social media presents users with a wide array of opportunities to connect with others. However, important questions for the future revolve around how people deal with the massive amount of information available, how feelings of connection are actually derived from interactions online, and online connections improve psychological well-being, if they do so at all.

Consume

Undoubtedly one of the competitive advantages of social media is the amount of user-generated content. People now have access to a huge amount of information created by others, with moment-to-moment access to others users' current moods, thoughts, reviews, and often their purchasing behaviors. However, how does consuming user-generated content online influence users' behaviors, both online and offline?

Notably, some social media websites, like yelp.com are set up for the explicit purpose of shaping users' behaviors with their user-generated content. Users can look online for reviews of businesses and products when they need help with a purchasing decision. However, consuming content online, even when users are not explicitly looking for information to help with a decision, is likely to impact behavior, both online and offline. For example, updates posted through social media applications, such as Facebook, Cyworld, and Twitter, often contain references to what products they are using. Even if users are consuming online content just to pass the time, consuming content from friends online may influence subsequent attitudes and behavior.

Guided by the distinction that users can be influenced by consuming content online intentionally or not, two broad research areas emerge. First, when users explicitly consume content online to shape their decisions, what determines whether online word of mouth will shape user opinions, and in what direction? Second, more indirectly how does the everyday consumption of content online (e.g., aside from an explicit, directed search for reviews) shape users' opinions and behaviors? However, a more fundamental question needs to be addressed first. If we are to discuss how consumers influence each other through the content they create online, how do we know who is most influential? Users will obviously tend to consume and be influenced by content created by those who are most influential, yet what is meant by "influential" is not clear.

Recent research has addressed – with some degree of disagreement – which users are responsible for the most effective change via word of mouth. Using computer simulations, Watts and Dodds (2007) found that, contrary to the long-standing idea that a minority of exceptional individuals are responsible for the diffusion of information in social networks, diffusion is actually due to a larger mass of easily influenced individuals. However, Goldenberg *et al.* (2009) note that there are two types of highly influential people – innovators and followers – who impact information diffusion, albeit in different ways. Innovators adopt new products and trends earlier in the diffusion process and affect speed of adoption, while followers have a greater impact on market size. Similarly, arguing for the need to segment influential users from non-influential users, research has shown that only one-fifth of a user's friends on a social network site impact the user's general behavior on the site (Trusov *et al.* 2010). This suggests that users will exercise a fair amount of selectivity in choosing whose reviews to read.

What then determines whether online word of mouth will actually shape user opinions? While most word of mouth is positive, negative word of mouth is actually most effective (Chen *et al.* 2011). However, the relationship between word of mouth and consumer behavior also varies by product type and who is consuming the online content. Online reviews are more influential for products consumers are unfamiliar with, and for relatively experienced online users (Zhu and Zhang 2010). Consumers also have the ability to look at multiple reviews from the same user. When doing this, consumers might find some that reviewers like the same things as them, while other reviewers dislike the same things as them. Consumers are more likely to follow the opinions of the former, due to the ambiguity of reasons for negative reviews (Gershoff *et al.* 2007).The particular goal that users have when examining reviews also impacts how they process reviews. Users explicitly trying to make a decision are impressed with breadth of information on a topic, while consumers simply trying to learn are more impressed with deep knowledge of the focal topic (Weiss *et al.* 2008).

Of course, not all consumers will read reviews so closely that the details of the review become relevant for their choices. Thus, it is important to look at how content containing thin slices of opinions on products in turn shape viewers' opinions, albeit in ways that are less direct than full reviews do. Indeed, social media sites such as last.fm, and the "like" feature on Facebook, provide a simpler bit of information than a full review, just noting whether a product or business is popular, and who in particular is using it.

Intriguingly, online popularity is self-propagating. Studies of online music markets (Salganik *et al.* 2006; Salganik and Watts 2008) have shown that quality takes a back seat to perceived popularity, at least initially. Although the highest quality songs tended to do well over time, if other songs were perceived as popular, they became and remained popular, regardless of quality. Even when users do not have an explicit goal to find a product to consume, though, they still might be influenced – positively or negatively – by simply seeing what other users are purchasing. This effect also appears to occur when consumers simply observe online content trends, such as brand search trends or YouTube viewing statistics. In a series of studies examining the impact of brand volume trends on brand attitudes, Hoffman and Novak (2011b) found that when consumers simply viewed positive (negative) volume trends about a brand, they were more likely to have positive (negative) attitudes toward the brand, even after controlling for valence effects. They also found that the effects were more pronounced when consumers believed the trends were generated from others more similar to them. Relatedly, those who are moderately connected to others tend to copy the purchases of those in their social networks; those who are on the low end of connection do not copy others' purchases, and those on the high end actively avoid making purchases that mimic people in their networks (Iyengar *et al.* 2009).

Simple popularity information delivered this way is unique to social media, begging the question of whether online interactions impact consumption in ways that other ways of learning about products cannot. Indeed, word of mouth from social networking sites leads to longer carryover effects on consumer behavior than traditional marketing efforts, such as promotional events and media appearances (Trusov *et al.* 2009). Compared to another source of information about others' consumption behavior – simple observational learning – while negative word of mouth is more influential than positive, the reverse is true for observational learning (Chen *et al.* 2011).

Additional research is needed to address whether consumers construct word-of-mouth communications, such as reviews, differently online than they would offline. For example, an examination of offline word of mouth has shown that people tend to use abstract language when an experience matches expectations, and readers likewise infer a positive experience from abstract language (Shellekens *et al.* 2010). Given the emergence of word-of-mouth websites like yelp.com, care needs to be taken before assuming that these results will apply to online reviews as well.

Thus, several lines of research suggest that the online consumption marketplace has several unique features not shared by the offline marketplace. Online content consumption inundates users with information on products and how other users are using them. The research conducted thus far suggests that additional work should continue to examine what moderates user-to-user influence, as well as how content created and delivered on social media differs from its offline counterparts.

Create

One of the major innovations of online social media is the shift of the job of content creation from marketers to consumers. Consumers post personal status updates, send tweets, post reviews for local businesses and products they are using, and "check-in" online when they reach a notable destination offline. This ability to create content leads to two questions: First, how can we predict who is most likely to create content?, and, second, how do consumers decide what content to create?

Given the high volume of people using social media, and the effort involved in creating content, it follows that not every user has an active hand in creation. On Twitter, for example, half of all tweets are generated by a mere 20,000 users, and most content is actually generated by media outlets (Wu *et al.* 2011). Personality attributes predict who is creating what content: for example, trait narcissism predicts creating content that is self-promoting (Buffaradi and Campbell 2008). Additionally, those high in need of uniqueness are less likely to generate positive reviews for, or recommend, products that signal a lack of uniqueness (Cheema and Kaikati 2010). Future research will undoubtedly uncover additional relationships between chronic dispositions and social media usage behaviors.

On message boards, the distinction between those who create content and those who only consume it separates users into two groups: posters and lurkers. In addition to differing with respect to whether they create content, posters and lurkers react differently to created content. Posters are affected primarily by negative opinions and adjust their opinions downward, while lurkers (which, as the Wu *et al.* (2011) research suggests, account for the majority of users) are less impacted by negative opinions (Schlosser 2005).

As far as content creation is concerned, one robust finding seems to be that social media users tend to create content based on information that creates positive affect. That is, content that leads to positive affect tends to go "viral." For example, eliciting positive affect makes tweets more likely to spread (Bakshy *et al.* 2011). However, Bakshy *et al.* note that, despite this relationship, predicting *a priori* which tweets will go viral is difficult to predict. Perhaps suggestive on this point, Berger and Milkman (2011) showed that awe-inspiring content is especially likely to go viral, with users tending to send articles that inspire the awe. Thus, discriminating among types of positive affect might be one way to gain power in *a priori* predictions of which content will spread.

Of course, everyone on a social network is a creator of content to the extent that users must decide what content to put in their profiles. How do users decide what goes in their profiles? Do they represent themselves accurately? Though it seems intuitive that users might exaggerate ideal personality attributes on their profiles, Back *et al.* (2010) found that Facebook profiles are, in fact, accurate. Observers' ratings of users' personalities based on their Facebook profiles, correlated with those users' actual, rather than ideal, personalities.

Research is just beginning to reveal which people are more likely to create content, and what they create. One fruitful area for future exploration might be an examination of what goals people tend to have when creating content. For example, what might prompt a user to post a status update on Facebook about a coffee shop he just visited? Important here might be tying the reason in to the other goals one has for using social media. For example, a consumer might want to vent about a negative experience (influencing other users' consume goals), but also might be posting the status update to indirectly invite friends to join him (exercising a connect goal). The goal users have in mind when creating content will surely impact the extent to which the content is likely to spread, so examining content creation in this way should provide a fuller picture of how people consume content as well.

Control

Usage of social media provides people with not only the chance to create content, but also the opportunity to choose which content they consume. In the process of doing so, users can personalize and customize their privacy and usage settings, essentially creating a user-maintained checks and balances system giving them control over the extent to which their own content is private and others' content is delivered to them. Since these settings are the gatekeeper from the application to the user, it is naturally important to examine what factors shape how users determine what these settings should be. However, research addressing this has been scant relative to the other social media goal types, perhaps since adjusting control settings, while important, is not necessarily seen as part of a user's everyday social media use. This would be an incorrect perspective, since the extent to which a consumer seeks out and implements control over a social media application directly impacts the manner in which one creates and consumes content, and connects with others. Control thus underlies the other "Cs."

Consumers will likely exercise weaker control over content on websites to which they feel a more intimate connection. For example, research on online social capital has shown that social capital is generated when people exhibit volunteerism, reciprocity, and social trust (Mathwick *et al.* 2008). Presumably, this means that consumers will be more likely to share their content when other consumers – and social media application owners, like Facebook – exhibit those three characteristics. There are other steps that website owners can take to encourage content sharing, as well. Eliciting advice from users increases intimacy, while, conversely, eliciting expectations decreases intimacy (Liu and Gal 2011). However, additional research is necessary to understand how social media usage builds online social capital, particularly as that usage becomes more routinized and part of consumers' daily routines (Hoffman 2012). However, research directly addressing willingness to disclose information paints a cautionary picture. Users may actually be more likely to disclose information when cues that disclosure is dangerous are present (John *et al.* 2011). For example, an unprofessional-looking website might actually suppress privacy concerns, increasing disclosure, while also (paradoxically) decreasing felt security. In concert with the research on trust cited above, this research suggests there may be counter-intuitive, and perhaps potentially dangerous ways of "tricking" users into disclosure they ordinarily would not do.

As applications like Foursquare and features like Facebook's check-in become more popular, understanding how users adjust privacy settings will be important for illuminating the extent to which consumers are willing to remove boundaries between their online and offline worlds. Consumers also should be made aware of potential hazards that may make them likely to disclose inappropriately.

Control in social media settings extends not just to control over content, but also to control over interactions with other people, or even control or influence over oneself. Fox and Bailenson (2009) found that individuals who viewed an avatar of themselves exercising in a virtual online environment were more likely to voluntarily exercise in the real world the next day. Similarly, Yee and Bailenson (2007) found that participants who negotiated in online settings with taller, rather than shorter, avatars were more aggressive in subsequent face-to-face negotiations with actual people. Thus, to the degree that choices people make in online environments influence their subsequent offline behavior, people may choose to engage in specific types of online behavior in order to gain this control over themselves or others. For example, participation in virtual worlds may positively influence quality of life for those with physical disabilities (Novak 2012). Marketers can also exert this control by manipulating how people interact with online social environments. Yang and Chattopadhyay (2009) have shown that consumers who are given the opportunity to customize a pre-specified type of online persona (i.e. a conservative, business-line persona), will be more receptive to advertising targeted to that persona.

From the handful of research done on control behaviors thus far, it is clear that control behaviors online represent an important way that users express traits that are important to them. Research has started to uncover how features of the application shape how users balance this self-expression with privacy, but other questions such as what dispositions impact control behavior, and how social influence online impacts control behavior are still largely open. Since control behaviors are the gateway for all other behaviors online, predicting the extent to which users put barriers between their offline and online worlds will become increasingly important as social media applications continue to become pervasive in everyday life.

Conclusion

In this chapter, we used the 4Cs framework to organize current research on the impact of social media usage on consumer behavior and we have identified several promising directions for future research. We hope that consumer behavior researchers can further refine and extend this framework as additional research emerges. From the wide range of research we summarized here, it is clear that many fascinating phenomena of social media usage have been identified. However, the diversity of these findings also underscores the point that these investigations were guided by quite myriad questions, making theoretical generalizations difficult. We suspect and hope that, in the future, theoretical debates (such as the one we cited over which users are most influential online) will become more common. With that in mind, we will briefly discuss the potential of three interrelated research areas of social media usage that could benefit from a theoretical framework.

First is the impact of social media usage on well-being. Research has certainly uncovered that online interactions can be meaningful (Burke *et al.* 2010; Sheldon *et al.*, 2011). However, we have also reviewed how charting the impact of meaningful interactions on well-being can be difficult (e.g., Vicary and Fraley 2010). Moreover, social media presents unprecedented access to information about one's friends in at least two ways that real-life interactions cannot match – information on friends' beliefs (Goel *et al.* 2010) and information on friends' consumption behavior (Iyengar *et al.* 2009; Salganik *et al.* 2006; Salganik and Watts 2008). Ideas about how people deal with this mass of information will be necessary to gauge the impact of social media usage on well-being.

Second is the extent to which online interactions differ from offline interactions, specifically the long-term consequences of decisions made online. That is, as just mentioned, we have good reason to think that social media will change how people make friends and purchasing decisions. However, we do not know anything about the long-term satisfaction of these decisions. Since the inputs to these decisions have changed, new theories may be necessary to address the life cycles of these decisions.

Third is the distinction between the explicit and implicit ways users are influenced by social media. That is, we have identified how users process information when they explicitly look at reviews online (e.g., Shellekens *et al.* 2010). However, we have also reviewed more subtle ways in which social media shapes consumer behavior (Iyengar *et al.* 2009) and interactions between friends (Berger and Milkman 2011). This suggests that future theories of how social media influences users will need to take into account how implicit attitudes and specific types of emotions shape social media usage in ways that might not be accessible to users themselves.

References

Back, M.D., Stopfer, J.M., Vazire, S., Gaddis, S., Schmukle, S.C., Egloff, B. and Gosling, S.D. (2010) "Facebook Profiles Reflect Actual Personality Not Self-Idealization," *Psychological Science*, 21: 372–4.

Bakshy, E., Hofman, J.M., Mason, W.A. and Watts, D.J. (2011) "Everyone's an Influencer: Quantifying Influence on Twitter," paper presented at Fourth International Conference on Web Search and Data Mining.

BBC News (2006) "Koreans Playing the Game of Life," available at: http://news.bbc.co.uk/2/hi/technology/4968314.stm.

Berger, J. and Milkman, K. (2011) "Social Transmission, Emotion, and the Virality of Online Content," Marketing Science Institute, Working Paper, available at: www.msi.org/publications/publication.cfm?pub=1779.

Buffardi, L. E. and Campbell, W.K. (2008) "Narcissism and Social Networking Web Sites," *Personality and Social Psychology Bulletin*, 34: 1303–14.

Burke, M., Marlow, C. and Lento, T. (2010) "Social Network Activity and Social Well-Being," in *Proceedings of ACM CHI 2010: Conference on Human Factors in Computing Systems*, pp. 1909–12.

Cheema, A. and Kaikati, A. (2010) "The Effect of Need for Uniqueness on Word-of-Mouth," *Journal of Marketing Research*, 47(3): 553–63.

Chen, Y., Wang, Q. and Xie, J. (2011) "Online Social Interactions: A Natural Experiment on Word of Mouth Versus Observational Learning," *Journal of Marketing Research*, 48: 238–54.

Cotte, J. and LaTour, K. (2009) "Blackjack in the Kitchen: Understanding Online versus Casino Gambling," *Journal of Consumer Research*, 35(5): 742–58.

Dougherty, H. (2010) "Facebook.com Generates Nearly 1 in 4 Page Views in the US," available at: http://weblogs.hitwise.com/heatherdougherty/2010/11/facebookcom_generates_nearly_1_1.html.

Eastwick, P.W. and Gardner, W.L. (2008) "Is It a Game? Evidence for Social Influence in the Virtual World," *Social Influence*, 4(1): 18–32.

Fox, J. and Bailenson, J. (2009) "Virtual Self-Modeling: The Effects of Vicarious Reinforcement and Identification on Exercise Behaviors," *Media Psychology*, 12: 1–25.

Gershoff, A.D., Mukherjee, A. and Mukhopadhya, A. (2007) "Few Ways to Love, But Many Ways to Hate: Attribute Ambiguity and the Positivity Effect in Agent Evaluation," *Journal of Consumer Research*, 33: 499–505.

Goel, S., Mason, W. and Watts, D.J. (2010) "Real and Perceived Attitude Agreement in Social Networks," *Journal of Personality and Social Psychology*, 99(4): 611–21.

Goldenberg, J., Han, S., Lehmann, D.R. and Hong, J.W. (2009) "The Role of Hubs in the Adoption Process," *Journal of Marketing*, 73, 1–13.

Hoffman, D.L. (2012) "Internet Indispensability, Online Social Capital, and Consumer Well-Being," in D.G. Mick, S. Pettigrew, C. Pechmann and J.L. Ozanne (eds), *Transformative Consumer Research for Personal and Collective Well Being*, New York: Routledge.

Hoffman, D L. and Novak, T.P. (2011a) "Why People Use Social Media: How Online Social Identity and Motivations Influence the Experience of Being Connected," Working Paper, UCR Sloan Center, August.

——(2011b) "Are Brand Attitudes Contagious? Consumer Response to Organic Search Trends," Working Paper, UCR Sloan Center, August.

——(forthcoming) "Social Media Strategy," in V. Shankar and G.S. Carpenter (eds), *Handbook on Marketing Strategy*, Edward Elgar Publishing, Ltd.

Iyengar, R., Han, S. and Gupta, S. (2009) "Do Friends Influence Purchases in a Social Network?" Harvard Working Paper 09–123.

Iyengar, S. S. and Lepper, M. (2000) "When Choice is Demotivating: Can One Desire Too Much of a Good Thing?" *Journal of Personality and Social Psychology*, 79: 995–1006.

John, L., Acquisti, A. and Loewenstein, G. (2011) "Strangers on a Plane: Context-dependent Willingness to Divulge Sensitive Information," *Journal of Consumer Research*, 37: 858–73.

Kincaid, J. (2011) "Yelp Now Drawing 50 Million Users a Month to its 17 Million Reviews," available at: http://techcrunch.com/2011/04/04/yelp-now-drawing-50-million-users-a-month-to-its-17-million-reviews/.

Liu, W. and Gal, D. (2011) "Bringing Us Closer or Driving Us Apart: The Effect of Consumer Input on Propensity to Transact with an Organization," *Journal of Consumer Research*, 38: 242–59.

Mathwick, C., Wiertz, C. and Ruyter, K.D. (2008) "Social Capital Production in a Virtual P3 Community," *Journal of Consumer Research*, 34: 832–49.

Milgram, S. (1963) "Behavioral Study of Obedience," *Journal of Abnormal and Social Psychology*, 67: 371–8.

Nielsen Wire (2010) "What Americans Do Online: Social Media and Games Dominate Activity," available at: http://blog.nielsen.com/nielsenwire/online_mobile/what-americans-do-online-social-media-and-games-dominate-activity/.

Novak, T.P. (2008) "The Social Web," in *Proceedings of Marketing Science Institute Immersion Conference*, Boston, MA, October 14–15.

——(2012) "Quality of Virtual Life (QOVL)," in D.G. Mick, S. Pettigrew, C. Pechmann and J.L. Ozanne (eds), *Transformative Consumer Research for Personal and Collective Well Being*, New York: Routledge.

Salganik, M.J., Dodds, P.S. and Watts, D.J. (2006) "Experimental Study of Inequality and Unpredictability in an Artificial Cultural Market," *Science*, 311: 854–6.

Salganik, M.J. and Watts, D.J. (2008) "Leading the Herd Astray: An Experimental Study of Self-fulfilling Prophecies in an Artificial Cultural Market," *Social Psychology Quarterly*, 71: 338–55.

Schlosser, A. E. (2005) "Posting Versus Lurking: Communicating in a Multiple Audience Context," *Journal of Consumer Research*, 32: 260–5.

Schmidt, E. (2010) "A Conversation with Eric Schmidt," Web 2.0 Summit, November 15,

Palace Hotel, San Francisco, CA. Available at: http://www.youtube.com/watch?v=AKOWK2dR4Dg& p=2737D508F656CCF8.

Sheldon, K.M., Abad , N. and Hinsch, C.A. (2011) "A Two-Process View of Facebook Use and Relatedness Need-Satisfaction: Disconnection Drives Use, and Connection Rewards It," *Journal of Personality and Social Psychology*, 100(4): 766–75.

Shellekens, G.A.C., Verlegh, P.W.J. and Smidts, A. (2010) "Language Abstraction in Word of Mouth," *Journal of Consumer Research*, 37: 207–23.

Slater, M., Antley, A., Davison, A. Swapp, D. Guger, C., Barker, C. *et al.* (2006) "A Virtual Reprise of the Stanley Milgram Obedience Experiments", *PLoS One*, 1: e39.

Stephen, A.T. and Toubia, O. (2010) "Deriving Value from Social Commerce Networks," *Journal of Marketing Research*, 47(2): 215–28.

Trusov, M., Bodapati, A. and Bucklin, R.E. (2010) "Determining Influential Users in Internet Social Networks," *Journal of Marketing Research*, 47(3): 643–58.

Trusov, M., Bucklin, R.E. and Pauwels, K. (2009) "Effects of Word-of-Mouth Versus Traditional Marketing: Findings from an Internet Social Networking Site," *Journal of Marketing*, 73: 90–102.

Vicary, A.M. and Fraley, R.C. (2010) "Student Reactions to the Shootings at Virginia Tech and Northern Illinois University: Does Sharing Grief and Support over the Internet Affect Recovery?" *Personality and Social Psychology Bulletin*, 36: 1555–63.

Waggoner, A.S., Smith, E.L. and Collins, E.C. (2009) "Person Perception by Active Versus Passive Perceivers," *Journal of Experimental Social Psychology*, 45: 1028–31.

Watts, D.J. and Dodds, P.S. (2007) "Influentials, Networks, and Public Opinion Formation," *Journal of Consumer Research*, 34: 441–58.

Weisbuch, M., Ivevic, Z. and Ambady, N. (2009) "On Being Liked on the Web and in the 'Real World': Consistency in First Impressions across Personal Webpages and Spontaneous Behavior," *Journal of Experimental Social Psychology*, 45: 573–6.

Weiss, A.M., Lurie, H.N. and MacInnis, D.J. (2008) "Listening to Strangers: Whose Responses Are Valuable, How Valuable Are They, and Why?" *Journal of Marketing Research*, 45: 425–36.

Wu, S., Hofman, J.M., Mason, W.A. and Watts, D.J. (2011) "Who Says What to Whom on Twitter?" Unpublished manuscript.

Yang, H. and Chattopadhyay, A. (2009) "Marketing to Avatars: The Impact of Metaverse Embodiment on Consumer Self-Concept and Behavior," Working Paper, INSEAD.

Yee, N. and Bailenson, J.N. (2007) "The Proteus Effect: The Effect of Transformed Self-Representation on Behavior," *Human Communication Research*, 33(3): 271–90.

Yee, N., Bailenson, J.N., Urbanek, M., Chang, G., and Merget, D. (2007) "The Unbearable Likeness of Being Digital: The Persistence of Nonverbal Social Norms in Online Virtual Environments," *Journal of CyberPsychology and Behavior*, 10(1): 115–21.

Zhu, F. and Zhang, X. (2010) "Impact of Online Consumer Reviews on Sales: The Moderating Role of Product and Consumer Characteristics," *Journal of Marketing*, 74: 133–48.

4

THE POSTHUMAN CONSUMER

Norah Campbell

Keywords

consumer, laboratorisation, miniaturisation, posthumanism

Introduction: the future of consumption

> Human nature, if it is proper to speak of such a thing, is not fixed: it has changed in the
> past and could change again ... How much nature has to change before our descendants
> cease to be human is a question we are not yet ready to answer. In this respect it
> resembles the question about when, in the course of evolution, our ancestors became
> human – which is also unanswerable at the present stage of our thinking and knowledge.
>
> (Fernández-Armesto 2005, pp. 169–70)

There is something which seems fundamentally *human* about the act of consumption. Presented
with the concept of consumption, most people intuitively think of all the ways in which we
humans assimilate or act on objects. The idea of 'posthuman consumption' stops us in our tracks,
and raises immediate questions; 'If the human is not the one consuming, who is?', 'Is this about
animals consuming, or the dead consuming?', 'Is posthuman consumption something to do with
the use of futuristic technologies?' And of course, 'Why is any of this important to consumer
research?'

In consumer research, we take for granted that our starting point is the human consumer;
investigations into how animals themselves consume (Bettany and Daly 2008), or indeed the
numinous agentic status of the dead consumer (Turley and O'Donohoe 2010) are few and far
between. However, in this chapter I am going to use the term 'posthuman' to describe how late
twentieth- and early twenty-first-century technosciences – in particular computation, artificial
life sciences, biotechnology and nanotechnology – have radically changed and continue to change
the everyday conception of what the human is. More pertinently, they make the fundamentally
'human' aspects of consumption such as learning, decision-making, reason, perception, ethics,
agency, desire and choice, less centred in a discrete human brain and body, and more accurately
as something that arises in new spaces *between* humans and intelligent machines. In other words,
the posthuman can be thought of as a move which seeks to locate being, or aliveness, or

meaning, not in the realm of the exclusively biological or technological but in the not-quite-human-as-we-know-it. Thought of this way, the posthuman calls for changes in humanist epistemology, that is, how we investigate and describe the world, and also in humanist ontology, that is, how we understand what constitutes life and objecthood.

This could help consumer research in three ways. First, it expands its range of temporal reference. While most consumer research deals with present or (recently) past phenomena, little emphasis is placed on considering what consumption will look like in, for example, one hundred, or one thousand years from now. Why is this important? Some artificial intelligent theorists declare that today the (Western) world is undergoing two simultaneous revolutions that will out-scale the agricultural, industrial and information revolutions put together – these are the robotic and the biotechnology revolutions. Imagine if such a vision were even partially true. It would call for changes in theorizing humans and their consumption in ways which would be as profound as those that came with previous revolutions.

Prognoses of what future human will be abound. Hans Moravec (1990) envisages the twenty-first century as the era when human consciousness will be uploaded and run on computer programs, while Marvin Minsky (1988) predicts that within a hundred years humans will have created 'mind children' – sentient computer programs with an evolutionary capability faster (10 billion times faster!) than Darwinian evolution. Many discuss the moment of a technological 'singularity', where humans will reach a point in the future when they create a machine more intelligent than a human being, which in turn will create yet more sophisticated machines (Chalmers 2010). Very interestingly, what unites many accounts of the future is the implicit assumption that the future will herald a *post-consumption* existence, where the messy, materially intensive, wasteful, pleasurable, and human act of consumption will be consigned to an atavistic trait of human history. We as consumer researchers know that the idea of a post-consumption future is most likely a techno-utopian fantasy. But it does mean that it is up to us to provide more nuanced accounts of the future of consumption.

Second, the term 'posthuman consumption' may expand the range of physical reference in consumer research. Presently focussed on the meso-level of the human body and mind, with its attendant human discourses, theories, and sites of investigation, posthuman consumption may expand the focus of consumption. Consider the case of space travel, which is a form of extra-planetary consumption. The sudden proliferation of private enterprise has led to space travel becoming a heavily invested and much-anticipated consumption experience. Consumer researchers are well placed to investigate beyond the hype and novelty of sub-orbital travel, because they have experience in researching what the consumption of place means. Further, posthuman consumption could shift the focus to subcutaneous concerns. Just think of the Virgin Health Bank – a consumer service that allows people to store their child's stem cells. The website states that while there is no practical use for such stem cells at present,

> Many scientists and medical experts believe that there will be breakthroughs in the future reliant on an individual having access to his or her own stored cord blood stem cells ... All we can say with absolute certainty is that the rate of advances in medical science has never been faster and that around the world hundreds of clinical trials are taking place using stem cells to treat conditions.

There are embryonic consumption sites in the contemporary world that leverage as yet unimagined technologies – the future of consumption exists in the present.

Third, the term 'posthuman' is one which has begun to be used in other social sciences and it possesses a complex meaning beyond its obvious futuristic connotations. There is a difference between 'the posthuman' (which is an often ideological account of the future of the human species in annexation with info-bio-technologies) and 'posthumanism', which is a critique of the discourse and epistemologies of humanism. Like other social sciences, consumer research is deeply rooted in humanism, a discourse and ideology predicated on fundamental assumptions about the human – assumptions which are rarely questioned. In order to understand the deeper meaning of posthumanism as anything which disturbs or questions the seemingly transparent logic of humanism, it is of course important to understand what humanism is. Humanism is an ideologically loaded and multifaceted concept. It is taken variously to mean a belief in progress, the technological mastery over nature, the separation of the human and animal kingdom, a therapeutic approach to human behaviour, and a secular approach to scientific inquiry (Ehrenfeld 1981; Soper 1986; Davies 1997). It accords the human a pre-eminent status in the world. Humanism is not just a set of (diverse) beliefs, but an epistemology; that is, a way of investigating the world that is consonant with our human intuition, an intuition which understands life as comprising essentially animate or inanimate, self or other, and human or nonhuman. Sometimes it may seem that such humanist categories are dissolving, but they are in fact extremely enduring. For example, while I may think I am globally interconnected and seamlessly integrated with technology, I only have to think about the horror I feel at the prospect of having a biomedical enhancement surgically implanted to enable some cognitive, affective or behavioural enhancement. This of course shows us the persistence of the inviolability of the body as the seat of identity, a classic humanist assumption. Thus, posthumanism is a way of interrogating the humanist roots of consumer research, as well as highlighting how future consumption underlines as well as undermines our everyday concept of the human.

What is posthumanism?

The posthuman is both a speculative philosophy and a material reality. It is located at the outer edges of fantastical science-fictional visions as well as concrete rationalist science. It is as ancient a concept as it is futuristic. It is exotic and specialised (cellular robotics, telesurgery, amorphous computing), as well as banal and ubiquitous (automobility, computers, eyeglasses). It signals interventions into the (human) body to overcome deficiencies, but also augmentations to the body to develop 'superhuman' capabilities.

Posthumanism is not something that fits into a given disciplinary category; it is empirical science as well as abstract philosophy. It is a term that has been interpreted as oppressive – the posthuman signals the end of humanity as we know it, heralding an apocalyptic era when the human being will be superseded by intelligent machine life. But it also a term that has also been enlisted to describe a new type of ecological ethics where the human is no longer seen as the only and most important life on Earth. Posthuman accounts range in purpose, because anything that collapses, subverts or negates the privileged seat of the human, or human-centred epistemologies can be seen as posthumanist (Halberstam and Livingston 1995; Haraway 1997; Braidotti 2006; Wolfe 2010). Thus the 'post' of posthuman is not automatically a temporal prefix. The term encapsulates both the human *and* the posthuman, reminding us that attempts to overcome humanness are actually age-old human tendencies, with all the complexity and paradox that such attempts involve.

The term posthuman has also been used to describe how diverse types of humans and phenomena over various eras have not fitted into the moulds of humanness as cut by the dominant accounts of the time, exposing that the seemingly resilient and undeconstructible idea of the 'human', or what constitutes 'life' has in fact changed radically over time, These are as diverse as women (Schiebinger 2000), slaves (Douzinas 2006), computer viruses (Parikka 2010), cellular automata (DeLanda 2011), bacteria (Haraway 1995), and swarms (Thacker 2004).

The posthuman has also been used to account for the social world without recourse to how it is important, or how it is perceived, by humans. Posthuman *epistemologies* are therefore research approaches that try not to reproduce humanist distinction and privileging, and range from actor-network theory (Latour 2007), and systems theory (Luhmann 1996), to non-representational theory (Thrift 2007) or strands of Foucauldian thought, where, as Foucault reminds us, that 'life' is a very modern concept of the nineteenth and twentieth centuries, a way of under-standing the universe that replaced the older concept of classification (Foucault 1971). His archaeological approach investigates how the human being is powerfully constituted through social institutions, and argues that 'man is an invention of recent date. And one perhaps nearing its end' (ibid.: 387). Accounts of the world that come from these theories are interesting because they open new ways of knowing the world that are not based on immediately humanly intui-tive accounts. This happens, for example, when brands are not viewed as cultural products, but rather as *living systems* (Giesler and Venkatesh 2005). Just like any other living organism (e.g. a cell), they maintain themselves by distinguishing themselves from their environment, by excluding things from the system that they are not, by communicating with and gaining feedback from their environment, and by replicating themselves (ibid.). In such a posthuman conceptualisation, it is not really relevant to ask whether humans do or do not exist, but rather to ask how systems, by incorporating psychic, social and technological elements, evolve with increasing complexity.

In this chapter, I propose that 'posthuman consumption' indicates a number of increasingly common conditions that are different from human consumption theory and practice. Here, borrowing the structure of Firat and Venkatesh's seminal treatise on postmodern consumption (1995), I tentatively put forward the conditions of posthuman consumption and their main themes. Similar to Firat and Venkatesh, I argue that, rather than poles of past and future, the human and posthuman are ways to describe the weft and warp of forces that are always already present in the human condition. The five conditions I will describe below are: (1) the com-putation of life; (2) the laboratorisation of life; (3) the miniaturisation of life; (4) the complex-ification of life; and (5) the automation of life. The implications of these tendencies to models of human consumption will be discussed.

Conditions of posthuman consumption and their main themes

The computation of life

Conceived in the mid-nineteenth century from weaving technologies, computers became not just tools to make life more efficient, but gave birth to a *logic* of computation – a new way of viewing the universe and its processes. In many different disciplines over the past two decades, the universe has come to be regarded as a giant computer (Wolfram 2002; Margolus 2003; Forbes 2004; Hayles 2005; Jencks and Smith 2005). This is a central and important idea about a posthuman existence. We live in a time when everyone, from philosophers to scientists, are attempting to discover what life itself is, through a better understanding, and appreciation of, the power and seeming omnipresence of computational logic. For her part, Hayles calls this pervasive sentiment the Computational Universe, arguing that it is not simply a claim people make, but a discourse, or way of talking about the world, and, more potently, an ontology which asserts that the 'universe is an immense computer program running on a computational mechanism, underpinning all existence' (2005, p. 3).

It is not surprising that the Computational Universe appears at a time when computers have assumed economic, social and symbolic pre-eminence in the world. Stepping back into previous centuries, we can see how dominant technologies are not just instruments that humans use, but powerful models through which the world is understood, and perhaps sets the limits of thought itself. An interesting predecessor to the Computational Universe of today is perhaps the Clockwork Universe; a prevailing outlook which enframed human understanding during the last four millennia (Maurice and Mayr 1980; Erlich and Dunn 1983). In these centuries, the cosmos was viewed as a giant clock, and it led to a predominately mechanical philosophy of life. For example, people started to formulate their ideas of the universe on the model of the clock and to conceive of the three essential systems within which mankind exists – the cosmos, the state, and the body – as essentially clockwork-like (Maurice and Mayr 1980). Importantly, the Clockwork Universe suppressed the legitimacy of other competing views of reality which were active at different moments, from Romanticism to galvanism, mesmerism and quantum mechanics (see, for example, Miller 1996; Listner *et al.* 2003).

It is important to sketch how computers are not just operational tools, but are philosophical models through which our understanding of the world is shaped. It draws attention to how our tacit models of consumers and consumption behaviour are to a great extent influenced by dominant technologies. How does the computation of life affect our conception of the consumer? There are two ways it does so. First, the most powerful models of the consumer are based on the consumer as computer, or more accurately, computational. The most obvious example of such a tendency was the designation of the consumer as an information processor at a time when computers and their simple processing packages were becoming more widespread (e.g. Hughes 1974). The rise of motivational theories of the consumer – where the consumer was regarded not as a psychological agent, possessing his own free will and reason, but as an automatic subject, whose desires were shaped unconsciously by larger forces – coincided with the growing influence of the science of cybernetics in the 1950s. Within the new discipline of cybernetics, humans were seen to have higher levels of automaticity and feedback than was previously reckoned.

Second, the computation of life has led to the rise of a powerful substance – information. Let us look at this substance called 'information', where it comes from, and what underlying logic it assumes. Information has a history. Although the first appearance of the word 'information' in English was in the fifteenth century (Terranova 2004), it only came to prominence in the social imaginary in the mid-twentieth century – in an era when computers were taking on increasing importance in terms of the tasks they were carrying out (Bateson [1972] 1987, p. 407). At the time, it became important to theorise what exactly it was that computers and other computational devices were holding on punch cards and magnetic cylinders. The question was one of definition – *what did computers do?* They stored electrical impulses and transmitted these from one to another, but what was the nature of this substance? Gleick recalls that at the time, information was a specific and technical term which 'proved as good a word as any, but people had to remember that they were using a specialised value-free term without the usual connotations of facts, learning, wisdom, understanding, enlightenment' (1998, p. 255). It was obvious that this information did not equate with knowledge or wisdom in the conventional sense; instead it was seen as raw data that fed into decisions, models and theories. However, in the second half of the twentieth century, information began to assume a deep and privileged place in the cultural imaginary and in the political economy of the West. In consumer behaviour and research, we can identify a contemporary tendency to 'informationalise' consumer objects and consumer sentiments that had previously been non-informational. For example, the Danish clothing company Jack & Jones brands its jeans as 'intelligent denim', replete with 'vector graphics and pixilation as an expression of your individuality'. The cosmetic giant L'Oréal's Revitalift cream, launched in 2007, comes with 'pro-retinol A nanosomes and Par-Elastyl®' (see Arnould and Tissier-Desbordes 2008).

The laboratorisation of life

The term 'laboratorisation of life' is used here to describe the growing sophistication of the previously simple and straightforward categories of aliveness and deadness, aided in large part by technologies developed since the 1970s. The various dimensions of the biotechnical revolution (stem cell engineering, *in vitro* fertilisation, genomics, virtual surgery, biomaterial engineering, increased reliance on, and sophistication of, pharmaceuticals and prosthetics, and life-support technologies, to mention but a few) do two important things: they make the range of what constitutes 'alive' larger and more complex than before, and they stage the interpenetration of the machinic and the organic to such a degree that is difficult to point to a purely machinic or purely organic entity. These will have wide-ranging implications on consumer behaviour research.

For the sake of brevity, let us take a single example to illuminate how such a development touches on myriad aspects of consumer research. The huge growth in global population, the scarcity of arable land and the environmental intensity of meat production mean it is likely that stem-cell engineering could play a part in creating laboratory-grown chicken, beef, fish and pork. 'In vitro' or cultured meat is estimated to create 96 per cent fewer greenhouse gas emissions, and use 99 per cent less land use (Tuomisto and Teixeira de Mattos 2011). Stem cells of muscle are taken from the animal and grown in a synthetic serum. Such a laboratorisation of life, seemingly unconnected to consumer research, is in fact central. It is often believed that philosophers and scientists are the most influential groups in re-drawing categories of existence, and deciding on what is animate or inanimate, natural or technical. But it is in fact marketers who will in the future play a fundamental role in reconfiguring important categories of what constitutes life in the wake of such changes. Through classical marketing strategies such as positioning and communications, marketers will shape the minds of consumers in deciding the ontological status of cultured meat, and many other numinous products of the new millennium.

In a posthuman age, consumers will be faced increasingly often with paradoxes in their consumption (Kozinets 2008). Such meat appears both identical to and radically different from its predecessor. We may witness post-ethical consumption models whereby former belief systems, grounded in the familiar and well-established dualisms of alive/dead, born/made, or artificial/real are revised. For example, can a consumer still be categorised as a vegetarian if she is only eating a miniscule amount of actual meat (a stem cellular amount)? How will marketing re-enchant food when it is impossible to appeal to a myth of pastoral origin? Meat is of course just one site where the categories of reality engendered by biotechnologies defy simple living/dead and make for sites of new consumer research – others include biomimetic materials, cloned animals, and robots. Debates in consumer research will focus increasingly on this numinous demarcation of the natural versus the artificial. For example, robot companions will pose challenges to our well-established categories of possession and consumption the moment the first consumer marries one.

The complexification of life

Emerging into mainstream science in the 1970s, complexity theory was felt simultaneously in many places, from fluid dynamics to economics, archaeology, linguistics, art and management science (Gleick 1998; Taylor 2003; Capra 2005; Cilliers 2005). Importantly, there is a difference between complex and complicated. As Cilliers (2005, p. 3) explains:

> Some systems have a very large number of components and perform sophisticated tasks, but in a way that can be analysed (in the full sense of the word) accurately. Such a system is complicated. Other systems are constituted by such intricate sets of nonlinear

relationships and feedback loops that only certain aspects of them can be analysed at a time. Moreover, these analyses would always cause distortions. Systems of this kind are complex.

It would be a mistake to suggest that life, or more specifically, consumption behaviours, have become complex. A host of anthropological evidence testifies to the complexity of consumption through time; it is just that modes of analysing and describing such behaviour were not developed until recently. As late as the 1970s, it was taken for granted that in most systems, variables were known, events were causally linked, and they all operated in closed environments. Complexity theory came at a time when the humanist mainstays of science and social science such as measurability and predictability were being challenged. Complex systems have certain properties that have been useful in understanding consumption, such as emergence, bifurcation (more popularly known as the 'tipping point'), and the network effect).

Although it is important to acknowledge that the world of consumption has always been complex, many theorists submit that there has been a *qualitative* shift in the nature of complexity in the past 30 or so years. This is the result of 'new kinds of *technological underlay* that have arisen from a combination of increasingly complex and sophisticated software and new means of registering life' (Thrift 2006, p. 191, emphasis added). Arising from this process are new kinds of objects that are not simple, but involve complex channels of material and non-material flows. To emphasise this qualitative shift: one of the most technologically sophisticated objects of consumer society in 1800 was the Eli Whitney musket, which had 51 components. The Space Shuttle of the 1990s contained ten million (Urry 2005). Urry goes on to sketch this qualitative shift in more striking detail by telling us that,

> Even in 1970 the most valuable products in world trade were still simple products produced by simple processes, such as clothes, paper, yarn, meat, coffee, and so on. But a mere quarter of a century later, only 14% of the most valuable items of world trade are such simple products produced by simple processes.
>
> *(ibid., p. 31)*

Most of the most valuable products today have virtual components (e.g., software and money, Zwick and Dholakia 2006), that would be unrecognisable 25 years ago.

Within the same space of time, fresh complex hybrids completely new to us will appear, posing new challenges to the frameworks of consumer research. Consider, for example, how consumer research will in the future investigate semi-autonomous physical consumer objects. MIT artificial intelligence designers, after creating the world's first AI vacuum cleaner *Roomba*, reported naming their cleaners, and some even took them on vacation. Such relationships will pose new questions for consumer risk, desire, and possession theory that consumer researchers are uniquely placed to investigate.

The miniaturisation of Life

Until the 1980s, the Artificial Intelligence community, like many other scientific communities, was constrained by its conceptualisation of technology as large, expensive, delicate and scarce. Brooks' robotics demanded that technology was cheap, robust, plentiful and 'gnat'-like (Brooks 1989, 1991). His iconic phrase, 'fast, cheap and out-of-control' (Brooks 1989), marked a new paradigm in robotics that eschewed the idea of a central, god-like processor commanding from the top down. Instead, agency was delegated to simple, low-level units that worked autonomously and locally.

The miniaturisation of technology has meant two things for twenty-first-century consumption. First, as distinct from previous eras, technology is no longer locatable within a machine. Technology is dispersed, encouraging a logic of technology not as a *tool* that is separate to the world, but as an *environment* that makes the world. Technology becomes not discrete, but *diffused*. By the depiction of technology as ubiquitous, it no longer is regarded an instrument, an actual 'thing', but rather technology develops a consciousness that envelops the world. Consider, for example, the next generation of digital devices – the Radio Frequency Identification Device, or RFID. Such chips are commonly embedded in objects as diverse as clothing and food products, and can receive and send information about the object's temperature, location, delivery route, and so on, to other devices. Each RFID chip, smaller than a grain of rice, contains a unique 696 Bit electronic code. This is sufficient to generate 80,000 trillion unique identification numbers – probably much more than one for every object on the planet (see Hayles 2009).

Some commentators predict that this technology will give birth to a new revolution in technology, a so-called 'Internet of Things' (Gershenfeld *et al.* 2004), where digitally-enabled objects of all sorts will be able to share and respond to information. While the 1980s celebrated the *processing* of information, as evidenced by the rise of the microprocessor, the 1990s emphasised *networking*, as emblematised by the World Wide Web. The opening decades of the twenty-first century will be the age of *sensing* and *controlling* (Anderson *et al.* 2009). What does a new paradigm of sense and control mean for consumer research? There are possibly many repercussions, so let us take as our example the nature of the consumer object itself. Increasingly, consumer objects have two interpenetrating dimensions. The first is the hard physical dimension of the object, upon which most consumer theory is built. The second is the *data* or the virtual component to the object, that is, diverse information about where the object was bought and when, where it was stored, when it was disposed of, and so on. This informational dimension of the consumer object does not belong to the consumer, but it is a powerful source of information about the consumer. As Sterling so rightly comments, 'My consumption patterns are worth so much that they underwrite my acts of consumption' (in Hayles 2009, p. 54).

Second, the miniaturisation and diffusion of technology encourage the posthuman notion that cognition does not take place exclusively in the brain, but rather is a *product* that emerges between the self and its environment. Because for past humanism, cognition is not locatable inside a single human or a technology, it undermines the human as the seat of consciousness. It stages cognition as a *process*, instead of a predetermined reality, where 'living beings and their environments stand in relation to each other through mutual specification or *codetermination*' (Varela *et al.* 1991, p. 198). This undermines the deeply ingrained imagination we humans in the West have that consciousness is an autonomous immateriality that is housed in the human brain. If consumer researchers subscribe to this processual, co-evolutionary formation of human being, their research will increasingly focus on how technologies and humans create consumption, rather than how humans use technologies in their acts of consumption.

The automation of life

Another long-standing reserve in the arsenal of humanism is the concept of free will. In all our interactions, free will is a basic assumption. The *ius gentium*, for example, refers to the fundamental legal principle that all humans are the same in so far as they are rational human beings in possession of free will (Smith 1997, p. 87). One of the most fundamental implications of twenty-first-century neuroscientific research is its re-evaluation of free will (Gazzaniga and Steven 2005). A tension exists in consumer research between conceptions of the human as a conscious, decision-making agent in control of their environment, and, on the other hand, an unwitting subject of the motivational control of organisations whose sophisticated cognitive manipulations produce the illusion of free will (e.g. Arnould and Thompson 2005; see also Goldman and Papson 1996). Both views are predicated on a binary notion of agency as either free (free will), or determined. Benjamin Libet's conception of 'free won't' (see Libet *et al.* 1999) provides an interesting way of thinking through the binary of free will and determinism in the domain of cognitive science, and perhaps contemporary consumption. Briefly, Libet argues that both free will and determination exist – paradoxically together. Libet's research demonstrated that certain simple voluntarily-induced actions, such as raising one's arm or walking, were initiated by neuronal processes *before* the person was consciously aware they were about to do so. The brain thus prepared for acts before the person was consciously aware of this happening, thus questioning whether the conscious mind is the source of agency. But one important proviso exists. The brain, though initially unaware of the intention to act, becomes aware before the act, thus holding a type of veto power on these acts. In other words, the mind exists in a climate which says yes, but it can also say no.

Consumer researchers realised long before cognitive scientists that consumption acts are often unconscious, automatic, and dependent on the environment. What is new is the extent to which agency is outsourced to systems that are increasingly invisibilised from everyday life, from software systems that decide on whether one gets a mortgage, to 'add a friend' suggestions on Facebook. Consider the case of automobility. Automobile companies predict that in the future, cars will be modelled on a 'drive by wire' philosophy, in effect turning the car into a moving computer. This is already the case with the 2011 Chevy Volt, with its 10 million lines of code – more than Lockheed Martin's F35 Joint Strike Fighter. Many automobile companies are investing in eye tracking software that will monitor driver fatigue, bringing the car to a halt when the driver has been deemed to have reached a certain threshold of tiredness. Devices which track human affect and attempt to intervene will become increasingly sophisticated. The debate will focus on whether this is a positive development that the human will adapt to and change with, or whether it is a tyrannical force that undermines an *a priori* and fundamental humanness.

Conclusion

The posthuman may prove to be one of the most important concepts in social theory of the twenty-first century. I have attempted to show how five nascent conditions – the computation of life, the laboratorisation of life, the miniaturisation of life, the complexification of life, and the automation of life – will have consequences for consumption and for consumer research. Consumer researchers are better positioned than any other group to provide nuanced accounts of the future of consumption. Consumer researchers will engage with embryonic consumption sites, they will use thought experiments and other imaginative methodologies, and their results will be powerful counter-balances to the often too blindly utopian or dystopian accounts of the future.

Further reading

Hayles, N.K. (1999) *How We Became Posthuman: Virtual Bodies in Cybernetics, Literature, and Informatics*, Chicago: University of Chicago Press. [An important critique of the posthuman imagination that formed during the 1950s cybernetic era.]

Wolfe, C. (2010) *What Is Posthumanism?*, Minneapolis: University of Minnesota Press. [An overview of what a 'posthuman' way of thinking, or epistemology, would look like.]

References

Anderson, K., Saffo, P., Siciliano, D.F. and Calo, M.R. (2009) 'Legal Challenges in the Age of Robotics', Stanford University Podcast. Available at: http://blogs.law.stanford.edu/robotics/2010/04/19/legal-challenges-in-an-age-of-robotics/.

Arnould, E.J. and Thompson, C.J. (2005) 'Consumer Culture Theory (CCT): Twenty Years of Research', *Journal of Consumer Research*, 31: 868–82.

Arnould, E. and Tissier-Desbordes, E. (2005) 'Hypermodernity and the New Millennium: Scientific Language as a Tool for Marketing Communications', in A.J. Kimmel (ed.), *Marketing Communication: New Approaches, Technologies and Styles*, Oxford: Oxford University Press, pp. 236–56.

Bateson, G. ([1972] 1987) *Steps to an Ecology of Mind: Collected Essays in Anthropology, Psychiatry, Evolution, and Epistemology*, San Francisco, CA: Chandler.

Bettany, S. and Daly, R. (2008) 'Figuring Companion-Species Consumption: A Multi-Site Ethnography of the Post-Canine Afghan Hound', *Journal of Business Research*. Available at: 10.1016/j.jbusiness.2006.08.010.

Braidotti, R. (2006) 'Posthuman, All Too Human: Towards a New Process Ontology', *Theory, Culture & Society*, 23(7–8): 197–208.

Brooks, R.A. (1989) 'Fast, Cheap, and Out of Control: A Robot Invasion of the Solar System', *Journal of the British Interplanetary Society*, 42: 478–85.

——(1991) 'Intelligence Without Representation', *Artificial Intelligence*, 47: 139–59.

Capra, F. (2005) 'Complexity and Life', *Theory, Culture & Society*, 22(5): 33–44.

Chalmers, D. (2010) 'The Singularity: A Philosophical Analysis', *Journal of Consciousness Studies*, 17: 7–65.

Cilliers, P. (2005) *Complexity and Postmodernism: Understanding Complex Systems*, New York: Routledge.

Davies, T. (1997) *Humanism*, London: Routledge.

DeLanda, M. (2011) *Philosophy and Simulation: The Emergence of Synthetic Reason*, London: Continuum.

Douzinas, C. (2006) 'Who Is the 'Human' of Human Rights?', paper presented at *Forensic Futures: Interrogating the Posthuman Subject*, University of London, Birkbeck College, 16–18 March.

Dunbar, R.I. (1992) 'Neocortex Size as a Constraint on Group Size in Primates', *Journal of Human Evolution*, 22(6): 469–93.

Ehrenfeld, D. (1981) *The Arrogance of Humanism*, Oxford: Oxford University Press.

Erlich, R.D. and Dunn, T P. (eds) (1983) *Clockwork Worlds: Mechanized Environments in Science Fiction*, Westport, CT: Greenwood Press.

Fernández-Armesto, F. (2005) *So You Think You're Human?*, New York: Oxford University Press.

Firat, F. and Venkatesh, A. (1995) 'Liberatory Postmodernism and the Reenchantment of Consumption', *Journal of Consumer Research*, 22: 239–67.

Forbes, N. (2004) *Imitation of Life: How Biology is Inspiring Computation*, Cambridge, MA: MIT Press.

Foucault, M. (1971) *The Order of Things: An Archaeology of the Human Sciences*, New York: Pantheon.

Gazzaniga, M.S. and Steven, M.S. (2005) 'Neuroscience and the Law', *Scientific American Mind*, 3: 43–9.

Gershenfeld, N., Krikorian, R. and Cohen, D. (2004) 'The Internet of Things', *Scientific American*, 291: 76–81.

Giesler, M. and Venkatesh, A. (2005) 'Reframing the Embodied Consumer as Cyborg: A Posthumanist Epistemology of Consumption', *Advances in Consumer Research*, 32: 661–7.

Gleick, J. (1998) *Chaos: The Amazing Science of the Unpredictable*, London: Sphere Books.

Goldman, R. and Papson, S. (1996) *Sign Wars: The Cluttered Landscape of Advertising*, London: Guilford Press.

Halberstam, J. and Livingston, I. (eds) (1995) *Posthuman Bodies*, Bloomington, IN: Indiana University Press, pp. 1–23.

Haraway, D.J. (1995) 'Cyborgs and Symbionts: Living Together in the New World Order', in C. Hables Gray (ed.), *The Cyborg Handbook*, London: Routledge, pp. xi–xx.

——(1997) *Modest_Witness@Second_Millennium.FemaleMan©_Meets_OncoMouse^{TM}: Feminism and Technoscience*, New York: Routledge.

Hayles, N.K. (2005) *My Mother Was a Computer: Digital Subjects and Literary Texts*, Chicago: University of Chicago Press.

——(2009) 'RFID: Human Agency in Information Intensive Environments', *Theory, Culture & Society*, 26 (2–3): 1–24.

Hughes, D. and George, M.L. (1974) *Buyer/Consumer Information Processing*, Durham, NC: University of North Carolina Press.

Jencks, C. and Smith, J.A. (2005) *Qualitative Complexity: Ecology, Cognition and the Re-emergence of Structure in Post-humanist Social Theory*, London: Routledge.

Kozinets, R.V. (2008) 'Technology/Ideology: How Ideological Fields Influence Consumer's Technology Narratives', *Journal of Consumer Research*, 34: 865–81.

Latour, B. (2007) *Reassembling the Social: An Introduction to Actor-Network Theory*, New York: Oxford University Press.

Libet, B., Freeman, A. and Sutherland, K. (eds) (1999) *The Volitional Brain: Towards a Neuroscience of Free Will*, Exeter: Imprint Academic.

Listner, M., Kelly, K., Dovey, J., Giddings, S., and Grant, I. (eds) (2003) *New Media: A Critical Introduction*, London: Routledge.

Luhmann, N. (1996) *Social Systems*, Stanford, CA: Stanford University Press.

Margolus, N. (2003) 'Looking at Nature as a Computer', *International Journal of Theoretical Physics*, 42(2): 309–27.

Maurice, K. and Mayr, O. (1980) *The Clockwork Universe: German Clocks and Automata, 1550–1650*, New York: Neale Watson Academic Publications Ltd.

Mick, D.G. and Fournier, S. (1998) 'Paradoxes of Technology: Consumer Cognizance, Emotions, and Coping Strategies', *Journal of Consumer Research*, 25: 123–43.

Miller, A.I. (1996) 'Visualisation Lost and Regained: The Genesis of the Quantum Theory in the Period 1913–27', in T. Druckery (ed.), *Electronic Culture: Technology and Visual Representation*, New York: Aperture, pp. 86–107.

Minsky, M. (1988) *The Society of the Mind*, New York: Simon & Schuster.

Moravec, H. (1990) *Mind Children: The Future of Robot and Human Intelligence*, Cambridge, MA: Harvard University Press.

Parikka, J. (2010) *Insect Media: An Archaeology of Animals and Technology*, Minneapolis: University of Minnesota Press.

Schiebinger, L. (2000) 'Taxonomy for Human Beings', in G. Kirkup, L. James, K. Woodward and F. Hovenden (eds), *The Gendered Cyborg: A Reader*, London: Routledge, in association with the Open University, pp. 11–37.

Smith, R. (1997) *The Fontana History of the Human Sciences*, London: Collins.

Soper, K. (1986) *Humanism and Anti-Humanism*, London: Routledge.

Taylor, M. (2003) *The Moment of Complexity: Emerging Network Culture*, Chicago: University of Chicago Press.

Terranova, T. (2004) *Network Culture: Politics for the Information Age*, London: Pluto Press.

Thacker, E. (2004) 'Networks, Swarms, Multitudes, Part Two', *CTheory*, available at: http://www.ctheory.net/articles.aspx?id=423.

Thompson, C.J. (2004) 'Marketplace Mythologies and Discourses of Power', *Journal of Consumer Research*, 31: 162–80.

Thrift, N. (2006) 'Donna Haraway's Dreams', *Theory, Culture & Society*, 23(7–8): 189–95.

——(2007) *Non-Representational Theory: Space, Politics, Affect*, London: Routledge.

Tuomisto, H.L. and Teixeira de Mattos, M.J. (2011) 'Environmental Impacts of Cultured Meat Production', *Environmental Science and Technology*, 45(14): 6117–23.

Turley, D. and O'Donohoe, S. (2010) 'Grief Goods: Material Possessions and Meaning Reconstruction in Bereavement', presentation at the European Association for Consumer Research Conference, Royal Holloway College, University of London, July 1–3.

Urry, J. (2005) *Global Complexity*, Cambridge: Polity Press.

Varela, F.J., Thompson, E. and Rosch, E. (1991) *The Embodied Mind: Cognitive Science and Human Experience*, Cambridge, MA: MIT Press.

Wolfe, C. (2010) *What Is Posthumanism?* Minneapolis: University of Minnesota Press.

Wolfram, S. (2002) *A New Kind of Science*, Champaign, IL: Wolfram Media.

Zwick, D. and Dholakia, N. (2006) 'Bringing the Market to Life: Screen Aesthetics and the Epistemic Consumption Object', *Marketing Theory*, 6: 41–62.

PART II

Representing the self and others

5

BLOGS

Zeynep Arsel and Xin Zhao

Keywords

blogs, identity, influence, narratives, representation

It has been almost a decade since Schau and Gilly (2003) described different ways in which personal web pages facilitate conspicious self-presentation. Since then, digital self-presentation has expanded and evolved into a diverse array of outlets, ranging from online social networks (boyd and Ellison 2007) to reverse chronological online diaries (Serfaty 2004) that are now ordinarily referred to as blogs. Blogs are progressively created personal narratives with textual and/or visual content about a variety of topics such as one's everyday life, consumption experiences, political punditry, news, fan culture, and other interests (Reed 2005). A blog presents a world as the blogger sees and understands it, concretizes the blogger's experiences and feelings over time, and provides an extended narrative of identity. Furthermore, bloggers converse with one another through dyadic or more complex forms of interconnectedness (Herring *et al.* 2005) and create networked, communal narratives (Kozinets *et al.* 2010).

In this chapter, we seek to provide an overview of previous studies on blogging and highlight potential areas for future research. At the time of this writing, it is estimated that about 166 million blogs are active across the world, with an average of 947,168 posts per day (BlogPulse 2011). While blogging may have already become an everyday practice for many consumers, current research on it is still underdeveloped, and much more is needed in order to understand this important consumer behavior. In the following sections, we will discuss two central issues about blogs and digital consumers: (1) the production of blogs as a medium for expressing and experimenting with consumer identity through representation and reinterpretation of consumption experiences; and (2) the consumption of blogs as cultural resources and cultural catalysts for social influence. Our focus is on personal blogs through which individuals write about their consumption experiences (Arsel and Zhao 2010; Zhao and Belk 2007), rather than content aggregating and filtering blogs or enhanced columns that provide political viewpoints and debates (Herring *et al.* 2004). We will highlight both emerging issues that characterize the transition from a pre-digital to the digital consumer culture, as well as questions that may bear potential for future research.

Blog as a stage for consumer identity performance

Schau and Gilly (2003) found that maintaining a personal homepage constitutes a communicative project through which consumers perform authenticating acts, explore other selves, fulfill fantasies, engage in self-discovery and conform to social norms. In contrast to the semi-static snapshot telepresence that a personal homepage may provide, blogs are more dynamic documents. Blogs are also more expressive and more permanent than many other forms of consumer-generated content such as online photo albums and discussion boards (Jenkins 2006). While homepages are static digital collages of identity expression (Schau and Gilly 2003), and bulletin boards are fast-paced dynamic outlets for social interaction, blogs are multilayered identity narratives that cross temporal, geographical and physical boundaries.

The narrative power of blogs is rooted in their ability to generate stories through archetypal consumption myths (Woodside *et al.* 2008). These stories are of dramaturgical nature (Goffman 1959; Hookway 2008), and through them authors idealize, mystify, and selectively present their digitalized narratives and maintain a social presence (Arsel and Zhao 2010). Blogs also provide creative identitity management strategies by facilitating consumers to play with the narrative structure through hyperlinking (Bosangit *et al.* 2009; Schau and Gilly 2003), and by enabling them to experiment with intertextuality (Serfaty 2004). In the blogosphere, text is not the only mean of expression: words are often accompanied by other forms of audiovisual material – most frequently depicting an act of consumption – and enriched with links to other blogs on similar subjects and broader cultural references available in the digital universe. Such intertextual and open-ended accumulation of narratives establishes a postmodern act of self-expression (ibid.). In this regard, blogging is a self-expressive aid where consumption takes center stage.

The accumulation of narratives often yields a density of meanings with both of-the-moment immediacy of a particular point of existence (Reed 2005) and with a strong archival quality of a personal trajectory. Blogs can hence be understood as archival extensions of the blogger's sense of self. This diary-like quality (Hookway 2008) provides a subjectively coherent account of a blogger's consumption trajectory that he or she may reflect upon in a later time. Similar to touristic photographs taken to preserve experiences of travel (Belk 2003), the fragmented, ephemeral and constantly changing digital self is relived through rereading the blogs at a later time. As the blog is updated and accumulated over time, the blogger engages in a reflexive relationship with this mirror image, or the *looking-glass self* (Serfaty 2004) and seeks to make sense of it. Blogging also chronologically reconstructs an enjoyable past to which the blogger can always return. One's blog not only communicates to others, but also to a future self; blogging transforms the blogger into a spectator of his own experiences.

As much as a blog is an extension of the blogger's sense of actual self and real-life consumption activities, it could also serve as an avenue for creating imaginary narratives and acting fantasies, a practice that Denegri-Knott and Molesworth (2010) label as *digital virtual consumption*. The blog becomes a stage through which one performs varied cultural scripts. In this context, blogs can be projective tools for individuals to play with an imagined or idealized sense of self that conforms to the dominant consumerist values (Zhao and Belk 2007). It can serve as a virtual lab for identity experimentation as well as for presenting alternative facets of one's identities for others to see.

In storytelling through blogs, consumption experiences often take the spotlight. These stories could range from mundane to extraordinary, and frequently feature brands as supporting actors (Woodside *et al.* 2008). According to Technorati (2011), 42 percent of bloggers write posts regarding brands that they have a strong positive or negative relationship with, and this practice is especially common among women bloggers. In fashion blogging, brands could act as performers that are judged, objects of desire and worship that could serve to anchor an aspiration, or as an equal construction partner that helps bloggers pursue identity goals (Kretz and de Valck 2010). Bloggers also compete with each other based on their cultural capital about brands, such as behind-the-scene stories of designers and product development (Zhao and Belk 2007). Such brand stories are used as important means of status competition among fashion bloggers.

Storytelling in blogs also resonates with varied genres of popular TV shows, novels, and movies; consumption experiences are frequently reinterpreted through the literary lens of pop culture. While storytelling has always been a part of consumer culture, it is its ability to cross four boundaries that makes digitalized storytelling more significant and complex than prior forms of narratives: personal/communal, ordinary/spectacular, private/public and material/symbolic. We will discuss these boundaries below.

Co-construction of the personal

Blogging raises questions regarding authorship in so-called personalized narratives because these are frequently co-constructed between blog creators – at times multiple – and their reacting audience. While there are still many single-authored personal blogs, collaborative blogging, which is also referred to as community blogging (Agarwal and Liu 2008), has become common (Hearst and Dumais 2009; Mutum and Wang 2010). In collaborative blogging, multiple authors may contribute to the same narrative (Reed 2005; Zhao and Belk 2007) and develop a common voice. Rather than individual narratives, blogs could evolve into an important means for small-scale social interactions (Hodkinson 2007). For example, the time delays between different bloggers' writings about a particular event create a sense of dialogue among fellow authors. These interactions not only reinforce social ties among the bloggers (Zhao and Belk 2007) but also create insider languages and a shared subjectivity.

This subjectivity, and its crystallizing narrative, are also subtly co-created with the blog readers. Bloggers often devote considerable attention to the comments left on their blogs and take time to respond to these comments. For many bloggers, reading comments from visitors are a pleasing and rewarding experience (Hodkinson 2007). These comments are taken as inspirations for developing future blog entries or they shape how individuals may seek future experiences so that they can blog about them. The visitors may even request the blogger to write or post particular content (Zhao and Belk 2007). Furthermore, to attract more visitors, the blogger often reinterprets their consumption experiences in a dramatic fashion by carefully framing the story in ways that are more appealing to the assumed audience (Arsel and Zhao 2010; Hookway 2008). Hence, blog visitors often influence how and what consumers write.

Dramatized sharing of ordinary consumption experiences

In real life, we do not enter a public space and start announcing what we ate for lunch, which shampoo we used when we showered in the morning, or which shoes we are coveting. These consumption activities are too mundane or too private to share with strangers and conversations about them are reserved for our close circles. In blogging, the case is the opposite and individuals indiscriminately share-out (Belk 2010) their experiences with strangers. Bloggers, especially young bloggers, create a personalized virtual space that Hodkinson and Lincoln (2008) compare to bedrooms, or what bloggers in Zhao and Belk's (2007) study referred to as a "private closet." In this space, bloggers often downplay their roles as a performer and treat blogging as a spontaneous act to vent about what they have in mind. Blogging is hence taken to be a brain dump (Reed 2005). There is very little restriction on what subject matter a blogger could write about. As Mazur and

Kozarian (2010) indicate, the most common topic in blogs is actually the author's mundane daily activities, such as this: "I am at home, having some fun. I'm eating a banana right now. It's really good. I'm eating it slow though" (quoted in ibid.). Through blogging, a simple, mundane, and perhaps even too trivial act of eating a banana becomes a spectacle. Thus, blogs can not only help us understand the ordinary aspects of the contemporary society (Serfaty 2004) but also raise questions about spectacularization and celebrification of the ordinary.

In an era in which the ordinary becomes celebrated (Turner 2010), a person with little chance of achieving celebrity through traditional means can generate a following and maintain it. This *ordinary celebrity* (Deighton and Kornfeld 2010) gains a voice above others and becomes public and significant (Arsel and Zhao 2010). More than a private and personalized narrative, a blog can become a spectacle performed for the blog's audience. It is a staged display of the blogger's everyday performance, otherwise unseen by most blog readers. The scripted performance behind the transparent veil of the blog is thus subject to both the voyeuristic gaze of blog visitors and the narcissistic gaze of the blogger on himself or herself. It is implicitly understood by both the blogger and the visitor that blogging is a staged and dramaturgical performance (Deighton 1992), for others to consume. The careful management of blogging as backstage and frontstage performance allows the blogger to manipulate others' impressions, freed from many constraints of face-to-face interactions (Goffman 1959). Thus, the blogosphere becomes a liminal space (Turner 1982) that exists between the public and the private.

The liminal space between the private and the public

Whereas some bloggers contend that they blog for themselves and that they are the only audience of their own blogs (Zhao and Belk 2007), they are indeed performing in front of an anonymous audience. For example, in travel blogs, narratives take form as social conversations with an assumed audience that the authors address in a friendly manner (Bosangit *et al.* 2009). This digital performance breaks the intimacy norms of real-life social performance in which the performance is bound with physicality and temporality and framed according to desired level of intimacy. In blogs, targeted and dynamic audience management is impossible, and hence the narrative is sent out to a universal audience without a personalized performance.

Although bloggers have a public audience in mind when writing, a blog also constitutes a realm of solitude in which the blogger can reflectively look into him or herself and experiment with different identities. Gurak and Antonijevic (2008) argue that bloggers can simultaneously experience private and public spheres and cultivate both individual and collective identities. A blog is experienced as a personal showroom for self-display with a "private dressing room" that remains as backstage (Zhao and Belk 2007) and a looking-glass screen that serves as a reflexive instrument (Serfaty 2004). Whereas a bulletin board is considered public, a blog is perceived to be a private narrative where the authors try to keep the audience at arm's length (McCullagh 2008). Bloggers constantly monitor what they write, and often have concerns about co-workers, bosses, parents, and other unintended readers of their blog. In some cases, narratives on experiences are deliberately self-censored so that they cannot be recognized or comprehended by real-life acquaintances. As a precaution, bloggers may also conceal their real identity in order to ease the apparent paradox between desired publicity of blogging and unintended disclosure of the private self to others. In this regard, it is unlike personal web pages where identity is frequently publicized (Schau and Gilly 2003). To avoid offending the potential audience, bloggers also use coded languages that only a closed circle of friends could understand, or replace real names with pseudonyms. As a result of this continuous audience management, bloggers' ability to define and circumscribe their private space in the blogosphere becomes limited.

Dematerialization of the extended self

Blogging also introduces questions regarding materiality of the extended self, or the way we reflect our identities through our possessions as well as our social and symbolic affiliations (Belk 1988). In the blogosphere, individuals can construct digital associations with objects and brands without actual possession of or proximity with them, and in this way they can construct a *digital self* (Schau and Gilly 2003). Self-digitalization may seek a digital likeness, or rather become a quest to impress with a carefully constructed *mise-en-scène* utilizing fictitious and aspirational connections to brands and consumption practices (Kretz 2010). For example, one can identify with a high-end status brand without actually consuming it. Although possessions and actual ownership are important for conspicuous consumption, in the digital era, a blogger thus may also seek status through cyber-consuming status products. Through displaying images of status products and weaving imaginary stories around them, one could extend a sense of self without actually possessing these material goods. For example, Zhao and Belk (2007) found that some young Chinese bloggers, who lack the financial resources needed for luxury consumption, discuss particular products or brands in ways that deliberately give their blog visitors a false impression regarding their ownership of the discussed objects. For many bloggers, these images may provide vicarious consumption experiences and the connection between imagined possessions and self are sometimes felt as real.

Consumers' ability to forge these imaginary, aspirational and staged brand connections through digital representations is in direct contrast with the pre-digital age. Prior research on the extended self often focuses on material possessions in real life. The Internet provides a new means of self-extension through posting images of the ideal self that the blogger aspires to identify with, thus going beyond the blogger's material and geographical constraints. By blogging about aspirational objects, bloggers symbolically take possession of them. Such symbolic possession through visual consumption in the cyberspace can potentially facilitate the extension of self. Expanding these person–object connections to the virtual realm could also enable the researchers to understand what constitutes materiality in the digital age.

Blogs as cultural products and cultural mediators

Americans now read more blogs than newspapers (Pew Research Center 2011). While much has been written about political blogs and civic participation, blog reading has not been conceptualized or studied as a form of consumption itself. Instead, most consumer researchers have focused their investigation on how social influence is arbitrated through blog consumption. We believe that the commodification of information, and its consumption through blogs bear much potential for future research, especially when blogging has changed how opinion leadership and celebrity operate in contemporary society (Arsel and Zhao 2010; Marwick 2010). Mutum and Wang (2010) suggest that one underlying reason for reading blogs is the consumers' need for cognition, but we believe that there is not a singular variable that could alone explain this broad cultural shift, and that exploring why we consume blogs could uncover many aspects of contemporary society.

Not only do we consume blogs, but we also consume through blogs. In 2010, the top 10 most popular blog posts in the world were all consumption-related, such as those discussing new technology products, fashion, green housing, and celebrities (Technorati 2011). This continuous public discourse, or *buzz*, impacts on how word of mouth is co-produced. Word-of-mouth messages permeate into public consumer identity narratives and are further complexified and transformed through the idiosyncratic meaning systems, disclosure strategies, and interpersonal orientation of the bloggers (Kozinets *et al.* 2010). These word-of-mouth messages are frequently labeled as sponsored posts, or *consumer-generated content* (Mutum and Wang 2010). Since blogs are often perceived to be more credible and independent than traditional media outlets (Johnson and Kaye 2004), consumers have an illusion of transparency and authenticity of these messages and cannot differentiate between paid – or compensated for – content and spontaneous endorsement. While some countries like the USA have been proactively adopting legal systems to provide ethical and legal guidelines for product endorsement in blogs (Astrachan 2010), unfortunately, policing and monitoring millions of blogs worldwide would be a futile task.

At the intersection of blogging and digitalization of commodities, we also see a paradigmatic shift in the models that explain how innovations are diffused. As discussed above, blogging has changed how word of mouth spreads in public discourse. However, the possibility of consuming through blogs, for example, in the case of digital media, further complexifies how influence operates. Ramaprasad and Dewan (2009) suggest that "being able to observe others' adoption decisions [online] positively influences subsequent consumption decisions." This, of course, creates an endless feedback loop of buzz influencing sales, and sales generating more buzz (Dewan and Ramaprasad 2009). Thus blogging provides new mechanisms for diffusion and new opportunities for opinion leadership.

Future directions

In this chapter, we have summarized the dynamic landscape of blogging and its impact on consumption. The research on this relatively new phenomenon is still emerging, and a complete picture of the digital consumption cannot easily be depicted at this point, especially with the marketplace changing rapidly with day-to-day innovations. We hence end the chapter with areas of inquiry that we hope that researchers will pursue in the future in order to understand not only digital consumption, but also the society in general.

1   *Understanding consumers thought processes and trajectories*: The chronological and dynamic nature of blog content could enable researchers to conduct inquiries on processes in stark contrast to static forms of data collected through traditional means, such as interviews or surveys. For example, a blogger can document his/her purchase decisions, from the awareness of a need to the disposal stage of consumption. Such complete data could provide an invaluable and non-intrusive way to explore all stages of consumption, as well as documenting long-term processes such as life transitions.

2   *Understanding globalization*: The global flow of people, especially tourists, immigrants and guest workers used to constitute a prominent agent for homogenizing consumption patterns. The spread of consumption-oriented blogs across the globe now adds another dimension to this expansion of global consumer culture. In other words, consumers can now look at the images of other consumers elsewhere in the world for inspiration, emulation, comparison, or envy. Breaking the geographical boundaries, this flow of information accelerates how universal consumerist values, consumer desire and materialism are shaped and spread across the world.

3   *Understanding lifestyle practices*: Blogs can be an excellent data source to understand consumer life-style practices such as parenting, leisure, food, fashion and domestic practices. Lifestyle-oriented blogs provide a gamut of data for researchers of consumer behavior. While the dramaturgical aspect of blog creation could alarm researchers of the authenticity of these narratives, Hookway (2008) suggests that this risk is no different than the participants' social desirability need in face-to-face interviews.

4 *Understanding spatial experiences in the digital era*: A sense of place is fundamental to human existence (Tuan 1977). Similar to the ways blogging has dematerialized the extended self, the rise of computer-mediated environments has also changed how we experience space and place. For example, bloggers often use spatial metaphors such as home or room to describe their blogs and regard visitors as guests to their homes. Future research could explore the different ways in which this sense of place is constructed and experienced in the blogosphere.

5 *Understanding envy and consumer desire*: In the contemporary consumer society, there is a shift from avoiding envy to provoking envy (Matt 2003). Envy constitutes an important motivation for consumption and is frequently experienced by blog readers. Bloggers are often caught in the dilemma between making others envious about their consumption experiences while avoiding jealousy and criticisms of vanity from their blog audience (Zhao and Belk 2007). Blogs provide a new arena to examine this concept, which is underexplored in consumer behavior.

6 *Understanding cyber capitalism*: The celebrification of bloggers has rendered the professional category of blogger as a viable occupation that enables one to gain social, cultural and economic capital. Consequently, popular and professional bloggers attract product placement and targeted word of mouth campaigns that enable marketers to generate more returns. Yet, high profile brand placements may also enable bloggers to further monetize their blog content. Exploring these networked, co-dependent and co-exploitative marketplace relationships could help researchers understand how capitalism works in the virtual age.

Acknowledgments

The project on Blogs is funded by Fonds Québécois de Recherche sur la Société et la Culture.

Further reading

Denegri-Knott, J. and Molesworth, M. (2010) "Concepts and Practices of Digital Virtual Consumption," *Consumption Markets & Culture*, 13(2): 109–32. [A conceptual inquiry on the ways the digital world changes what we experience.]

Goffman, E. (1959) *The Presentation of Self in Everyday Life*, Garden City, NY: Doubleday. [The classic work on self-presentation, pre-digital age.]

Hookway, N. (2008) "'Entering the Blogosphere': Some Strategies for Using Blogs in Social Research," *Qualitative Research*, 8(1): 91–113. [A paper that discusses theoretical, methodological, practical and ethical issues regarding the use of blogs for research.]

Schau, H.J. and Gilly, M.C. (2003) "We Are What We Post? Self-Presentation in Personal Web Space," *Journal of Consumer Research*, 30(3), 385. [A classic article on self-presentation through web pages.]

References

Agarwal, N. and Liu, H. (2008) "Blogosphere: Research Issues, Tools, and Applications," in *ACM SIGKDD Explorations*, New York: ACM.

Arsel, Z. and Zhao, X. (2010) "Personal Blogging, Performance and the Quest for Fame," in D.W. Dahl, G.V. Johar, and S.M.J. van Osselaer (eds), *Advances in Consumer Research*, vol. 38, Duluth, MN: Association for Consumer Research.

Astrachan, J. B. (2010) "Transparency in the New Media," *SSRN eLibrary*, available at: http://ssrn.com/paper=1619506.

Belk, R.W. (1988) "Possessions and the Extended Self," *Journal of Consumer Research*, 15(2): 139–68.

——(2003) *Tourist Photos: Signs of Self*, (video), Salt Lake City, UT: Odyssey Films.

——(2010) "Sharing," *Journal of Consumer Research*, 36(5): 715–34.

BlogPulse (2011) "BlogPulse: Automated Trend Discovery System for Blogs," available at: www.blogpulse.com (accessed 17 July 2011).

Bosangit, C., McCabe, S. and Hibbert, S. (2009) "What Is Told in Travel Blogs? Exploring Travel Blogs for Consumer Narrative Analysis," *Information and Communication Technologies in Tourism*, 2: 61–71.

boyd, d.m. and Ellison, N.B. (2007) "Social Network Sites: Definition, History, and Scholarship," *Journal of Computer-Mediated Communication*, 13(1): 210–30.

Deighton, J. (1992) "The Consumption of Performance," *Journal of Consumer Research*, 19(3): 362–72.

Deighton, J. and Kornfeld, L. (2010) "The Construction of Ordinary Celebrity," in D.W. Dahl, G.V. Johar, and S.M.J. van Osselaer (eds), *Advances in Consumer Research*, vol. 38, Duluth, MN: Association for Consumer Research.

Denegri-Knott, J. and Molesworth, M. (2010) "Concepts and Practices of Digital Virtual Consumption," *Consumption Markets & Culture*, 13(2): 109–32.

Dewan, S. and Ramaprasad, J. (2009) "Chicken and Egg? Interplay between Music Blog Buzz and Album Sales," *PACIS 2009 Proceedings*, paper 87. Available at: http://aisel.aisnet.org/pacis2009/87.

Goffman, E. (1959) *The Presentation of Self in Everyday Life*, Garden City, NY: Doubleday.

Gurak, L.J. and Antonijevic, S. (2008) "The Psychology of Blogging," *American Behavioral Scientist*, 52(1): 60–8.

Hearst, M.A. and Dumais, S.T. (2009) "Blogging Together: An Examination of Group Blogs," in *Proceedings of the 3rd International Conference on Weblogs and Social Media*, AAAI Press.

Herring, S.C., Kouper, I., Paolillo, J.C., Scheidt, L.A., Tyworth, M., Welsch, P., Wright, E. and Yu, N. (2005) "Conversations in the Blogosphere: An Analysis 'From the Bottom Up,'" in *Proceedings of the 38th Annual Hawaii International Conference on System Sciences*, Big Island, HI.

Herring, S.C., Scheidt, L.A., Bonus, S. and Wright, E. (2004) "Bridging the Gap: A Genre Analysis of Weblogs," in *Proceedings of the 37th Hawai'i International Conference on System Sciences (HICSS-37)*, Los Alamitos: IEEE Computer Society Press.

Hodkinson, P. (2007) "Interactive Online Journals and Individualization," *New Media & Society*, 9(4): 625–50.

Hodkinson, P. and Lincoln, S. (2008) "Online Journals as Virtual Bedrooms?," *Young*, 16(1): 27–46.

Hookway, N. (2008) "'Entering the Blogosphere': Some Strategies for Using Blogs in Social Research," *Qualitative Research*, 8(1): 91–113.

Jenkins, H. (2006) *Fans, Bloggers, and Gamers: Exploring Participatory Culture*, New York: New York University Press.

Johnson, T.J. and Kaye, B.K. (2004) "Wag the Blog: How Reliance on Traditional Media and the Internet Influence Credibility Perceptions of Weblogs among Blog Users," *Journalism and Mass Communication Quarterly*, 81(3): 622–42.

Kozinets, R.V., de Valck, K., Wojnicki, A.C. and Wilner, S. (2010) "Networked Narratives: Understanding Word-of-Mouth Marketing in Online Communities," *Journal of Marketing*, 74(2): 71–89.

Kretz, G. (2010) "'Pixelize Me!': A Semiotic Approach of Self-digitalization in Fashion Blogs," in M.C. Campbell, J. Inman, and R. Pieters (eds), *Advances in Consumer Research*, vol. 37, Duluth, MN: Association for Consumer Research.

Kretz, G. and de Valck, K. (2010) "'Pixelize Me!': Digital Storytelling and the Creation of Archetypal Myths through Explicit and Implicit Self-brand Association in Fashion and Luxury Blogs," *Research in Consumer Behavior*, 12: 313–29.

McCullagh, K. (2008) "Blogging: Self Presentation and Privacy," *Information & Communications Technology Law*, 17(1): 3–23.

Marwick, A. (2010) "Status Update: Celebrity, Publicity, and Self-Branding in Web 2.0.," doctoral dissertation, New York University, New York.

Matt, S.J. (2003) *Keeping Up with the Joneses: Envy in American Consumer Society, 1890–1930*, Philadelphia, PA: University of Pennsylvania Press.

Mazur, E. and Kozarian, L. (2010) "Self-Presentation and Interaction in Blogs of Adolescents and Young Emerging Adults," *Journal of Adolescent Research*, 25(1): 124–44.

Mutum, D. and Wang, Q. (2010) "Consumer Generated Advertising in Blogs," in M.S. Eastin, T. Daugherty and N.M. Burns (eds), *Handbook of Research on Digital Media and Advertising*, Hershey, PA: IGI Global.

Pew Research Center (2011) *Internet Gains on Television as Public's Main News Source*, research report, Washington, DC: Pew Research Center.

Ramaprasad, J. and Dewan, S. (2009) "Consumer Choice in an Online Music Community: Bandwagon Effects and Local Network Influence," Working Paper, McGill University.

Reed, A. (2005) "'My Blog Is Me': Texts and Persons in UK Online Journal Culture," *Ethnos*, 70(2): 220–42.

Schau, H.J. and Gilly, M.C. (2003) "We Are What We Post? Self-Presentation in Personal Web Space," *Journal of Consumer Research*, 30(3): 385.

Serfaty, V. (2004) "Online Diaries: Towards a Structural Approach," *Journal of American Studies*, 38(03): 457–71.

Technorati (2011) *Technorati's State of the Blogosphere*, available at: http://technorati.com/state-of-the-blogosphere/ (accessed July 31, 2011).

Tuan, Y.-F. (1977) *Space and Place: The Perspective of Experience*, Minneapolis, MN: University of Minnesota Press.

Turner, G. (2010) *Ordinary People and the Media: The Demotic Turn*, Los Angeles: Sage.

Turner, V.W. (1982) *From Ritual to Theatre: The Human Seriousness of Play*, New York: Performing Arts Journal Publications.

Woodside, A., Sood, S. and Miller, K. (2008) "When Consumers and Brands Talk: Storytelling Theory and Research in Psychology and Marketing," *Psychology and Marketing*, 25(2): 97–145.

Zhao, X. and Belk, R.W. (2007) "Live from Malls: Shopping BLOG (Web Log) and Consumer Desire," in G. Fitzsimons and V. Morwitz (eds), *Advances in Consumer Research*, vol. 34, Valdosta, GA: Association of Consumer Research, pp. 131–7.

6

FASHION BLOGGING

Gachoucha Kretz and Kristine de Valck

Keywords

blogs, brand, digital, fashion, luxury

Introduction

For a long time fashion has had a mixed reputation as a research topic. On the one hand, researchers have often considered fashion too "frivolous" to provide serious ground for scientific analysis (Barnard 2007a; Godart 2009). But, on the other hand, fashion has increasingly grown as a serious business engaging substantial investment and returning considerable profits in ever growing markets.

According to Euromonitor International, however, global consumer expenditures for "fashion" (an aggregation of "clothing and footwear" and "jewellery, silverware, watches and clocks, travel goods") amounted to US$2 trillion, which is more than the US$1.2 trillion spent on the purchase of cars, motorcycles and other vehicles. Besides, fashion plays an essential role in identity construction (Arnold 2001; Davis 1992; Entwistle 2000), including consumer identity (Jackson and Shaw 2006), and contributes to shaping consumer culture (Jackson and Shaw 2006; McCracken 1986; Thompson and Haytko 1997). In a global context where consumers buy more and more fashion goods,[1] a better understanding of how and why consumers make use of fashion products is highly relevant for marketers and consumer researchers.

While fashion *per se* has attracted increased attention from scholars in the realm of cultural studies (Barnard 2007b; Bruzzi and Gibson 2006; Crane 2000; McCracken 1986; Murray 2002; Thompson and Haytko 1997), fashion mediated through social media and specifically through weblogs, has been only partially addressed. With the rise of online communities, and specifically of blogs, branded discussions and word of mouth have dramatically changed (Hoffman and Novak 1996; Kozinets 2006; Kozinets *et al.* 2010). In particular, consumers have gained greater control over brand narratives by sharing and evaluating their consumption experiences through products and brands. Existing research has examined the consequences of new networked narratives within the so-called blogosphere (Kozinets *et al.* 2010) but only very few scholars have studied fashion blogs and blogging. And, yet, a better understanding of fashion blogging and its influence on consumer culture and audiences is important.

Fashion blogs report extensive brand and product experiences including self-fashioning through outfits, information sharing and tips about fashion brands and products (Kretz 2010; Zhao and Belk 2007). Recent studies have shown that consumers trust blogs more than they trust mainstream media as a source of information. In addition, blogs influence their audience: they generate recommendations and purchases: more than 40 percent of the respondents declared they would recommend a brand or a product and that they would purchase it from blogs as an information source.[2] As a consequence, fashion blogs, beyond cultivating consumerism through the cultivation of desire for fashion goods (Zhao and Belk 2007), may well act as a new channel for brand and product promotion. As a consequence, greater understanding of fashion blogging and of blogs' influence regarding consumer culture may suggest new marketing techniques using blogs as recommendation and influence media.

In the present chapter, we report bloggers' motivations to blog and particularly their search for popularity. Existing research on blogging is quite substantial but is scarce on fashion blogging. We review themes that have already been addressed regarding fashion-themed blogs and try and highlight what makes fashion-themed blogs special, compared to other kinds of blogs. Fashion blogs differ from other blogs along two main dimensions: (1) identity hyper-representation; and (2) hyper-connection with the community. Specifically, fashion blogging has introduced new ways of considering identity, representations of beauty and style, and professional and social success. It has also redefined the relationships between brands and consumers and brand advocacy. Finally, we suggest a research agenda for fashion blogging taking into account the growing impact of social network integration.

Fashion blogging motivations

Political and communication studies have already thoroughly analyzed bloggers' motivations to have a news or politics blog. Above all, bloggers have been reported to blog for popularity (da Cunha Recuero 2008). Some bloggers blog for social reasons while others do so for professional reasons (Marlow 2006). In other words, professional bloggers use their blogs to somehow make money while social bloggers seek interactions with their readers to create communal exchanges. Nardi *et al.* (2004) investigated the reasons why people blog and discovered five main reasons: (1) to document their lives, that is, to inform and update readers about their activities; (2) to provide commentary and opinions about topics they are passionate about; (3) to express emotions and make use of the blog as a catharsis; (4) to write and articulate ideas they would not have been able to develop without a blog and to commit to a discipline of regular writing; and (5) to create and maintain interactions within community forums. Schau and Gilly (2003) have already demonstrated that people who have a personal web page manage self-impression and seek "personal growth" and "advocacy" (ibid., p. 391). As a consequence, bloggers may maintain a blog for the sake of identity construction and for communal and commercial reasons. Kozinets *et al.* (2010) added that bloggers write to share with the community branded information through networked word of mouth. In that respect, blogging consists in entertaining both relationships with brands and marketers while engaging in a communal activity.

Style and fashion bloggers blog for identity construction: they often want to construct characters (Kretz 2010), play with identities through "self-fashioning" (Zhao and Belk 2007) and enact individual (Chittenden 2010) and social selves (Palgrem 2010; Pham 2011) in their blogs. Existing findings about blogging suggest that bloggers may also blog for communal and commercial reasons. We collected data through 20 in-depth interviews with fashion bloggers in order to establish style and fashion blog authors' motivations to start a blog (Kretz 2011). We discovered that, indeed, style and fashion bloggers most of the time started to blog for communal reasons and particularly to do the following: overcome the frustration that no one in their close sur-roundings understood their passion for fashion; make friends who share the same passion for fashion and exchange with them; and share tips, recommendations and bargains regarding fashion products. Also, style and fashion bloggers sometimes started a blog for professional motives and specifically to commit to a regular authoring occupation while temporarily unemployed or idle to overcome boredom in their lives, and to display professional competence through authoring performances. What seems to be more specific to fashion-themed blogs is the bloggers' commercial motivations to blog. In particular, style and fashion bloggers said they want to attract brands' attention in order to receive gifts and invitations from brands and monetize their blog through advertisement or sponsored posts (ibid.), and to develop relation-ships and partnerships with them. In fact, brand representatives and advertising agencies do browse the fashion blogosphere to highlight potential brand advocates and promoters. There-fore, style and fashion bloggers often strive to attract their favorite brands' attention in order to receive gifts and money through blog monetization but also to develop relationships and part-nerships with them. Indeed, brands often invite bloggers to special events or visits, to train them in the brand's history, values and craftsmanship. Because brands give carefully selected bloggers access to unique and unseen information, the blog content of those bloggers becomes outstanding and valuable in the eyes of their audience.

Fashion bloggers, however, do not strictly and exclusively blog for themselves, to please an audience of readers or to please potential employers or partner or sponsor brands. We have discovered a blogging psychology that is much more complex, where fashion bloggers usually aim for popularity in their community and, if possible, outside it. In other words, whether they blog to make friends and generate a community of expression about fashion, or to make a living out of their blog, style and fashion bloggers most of the time admit they are caught in the game of popularity and are really happy to see the number of visitors and comments increase on their blog. First, because it satisfies a kind of narcissistic contentment and feeling of usefulness to be read, followed and encouraged to write. Second, because the rise in incoming links to the blog mechanically increases the blog's audience, i.e. popularity online, which in turn increases the probability that new readers and potential employers or partner brands will identify the blog. Generally speaking, bloggers dream of popularity as a reward for their hard blogging work. Popularity is thus quite a general motivation for fashion bloggers.

Fashion bloggers are not always looking for the same kind of popularity. Some may look for a certain visibility within a specific community of readers and for interactions with similar people and peer bloggers, thus displaying prevalent communal popularity motivations. Instead, some others might want to become known to brands and agencies for their skills in the fashion field (photography, design, illustration, styling, content production) and use their blog as a springboard to make a living through advertisement or freelance contracts with fashion brands. They thus show more prevalent professional and commercial popularity motivations. Yet, fashion bloggers do not exclusively seek one kind of popularity, i.e. communal or professional/commercial. They just tend more to one of those options while always keeping in mind that they need to satisfy their readers who are the major providers of the audience for a blog.

The hyper-representation of identity

Arsel and Zhao (Chapter 5 in this volume) discuss blogs as a stage for identity performance. In fashion blogs, identity performance is exacerbated as compared to other kinds of blogs as a way to offer representations of ideal style and beauty.

Personal interpretation of ideal style and beauty

Fashion blogs mainly feature visuals (photographs and sometimes illustrations) and little text (Kretz and De Valck 2010b). Photographs either stage the blogger in carefully selected outfits (Zhao and Belk 2007) and striking carefully studied poses, or everyday models encountered in the street. Most of the time, fashion bloggers make their own photographs, serve as models, visually self-disclose through those pictures, and arrange a *mise-en-scène* mimicking the fashion and luxury ad campaigns they like (Kretz 2010). Alternatively, some popular fashion blogs present pictures of everyday people who have accidentally served as models because the blogger thought their outfit was worth sharing with the community for its originality and creativity. As would style managers in fashion magazines, they suggest inspirations and style models to follow. This kind of picture is also known as "streetstyling." Over time, the number and the quality of the pictures taken and presented in fashion blogs have dramatically improved: bloggers who were their own model have sophisticated their outfits, poses and the setting of the pictures; streetstyle bloggers have hired models and borrowed fashion clothes and accessories and arranged fashion shoots to produce professional quality pictures. Generally speaking, enhancing the pictures' aesthetic appeal through Photoshop has become the usual practice. Fashion blogging has progressively introduced idealized representations of what beauty and style should be through the eyes of everyday fashion consumers. In the same way that journalists have created a fashion discourse and taught the bourgeoisie how to dress through the description of models in fashion shows, fashion bloggers co-produce their personal vision of what beauty and style should be with an audience of readers who react and interact regarding the outfits presented.

Interestingly, though, whereas fashion bloggers imitate fashion designers and stylists' practices in the way they represent identity, on blogs the blogger's personal and amateur touch still remains, even in the ones targeting the most sophistication. This is mainly due to the fact that readers expect authenticity and genuineness from their favorite bloggers. In other words, even if the audience really appreciates inspiring outfits and breathtaking artistic direction from the bloggers, they above all value the bloggers' personal vision and the authenticity of the content produced. For that reason, fashion bloggers who have modeled on their own blog have progressively self-disclosed and abandoned anonymity. When fashion blogs started, model bloggers used to hide their faces, but they now self-stage and exaggerate their features and personality in the pictures they present. Indeed, their readership increases when bloggers self-disclose because people like it better when they can identify, self-compare and update their lives with their favorite blogger.

Personal branding

Along with the decline of anonymity in favor of disclosed identity, bloggers have increasingly committed to personal branding in their blogs. At first, fashion bloggers would choose a name they thought would describe best who they were and their aspiration in blogging. Blog layout and visual identity were quite rough. In a period of five years, fashion blogs have dramatically improved visually and become much more professional. Bloggers manage their blog as a personal brand where the blog's name equals a brand's name; the header banner equals a logo; the signature equals a claim; the blog's visual identity equals a product's packaging; the content promotes a certain personality through a certain tone and plot; and the brands mentioned construct a digital extended self (Kretz and De Valck 2010a). Fashion blogs have now achieved differentiated and recognized identities and associations with their names.

However, similar to commercial brands, awareness is not enough to fully succeed. Bloggers as personal brands have recentl started to adopt audience (popularity) management strategies.

Specifically, they have extended their reach and frequency to recruit more readers and maintain their visibility by linking their blog to social networking websites like Twitter, Facebook, Lookbook, and by appearing in the mass media (in the fashion press, on TV shows) while publishing content at a fast and regular pace. As compared to other kinds of blogs, fashion blogs extensively combine the use of other loci of discussion and interaction with the use of their blog to achieve personal branding objectives. And, as compared to other kinds of blogs, many more fashion bloggers have gained professional and/or social recognition via their blog. Overall, personal branding in fashion is witnessing a new way of contemplating celebrity or professional success: anyone can live a "rags-to-riches" story, provided they know how to self-brand.

Constructing stereotypes through brands

Fashion bloggers present an extension of their sense of self in the real life in their blog. They also use this space as a way to create imagined characters (Kretz 2010) or to project identities in accordance with the surrounding consumerist values and fashion of the times (Zhao and Belk 2007). In particular, they arrange storytelling, including plots featuring brands and products (Kretz and De Valck 2010a), and dramatize their lives by exaggerating elements of their real life and mixing them with fiction to nurture the character they want to construct, to please their audience's need for entertainment and life upgrade. Specifically, consumption narratives contribute to further construct the blogger's identity in the eyes of the audience and to generate empathy and a sense of similarity and connivance because both the author and the readers share the same tastes. This sense of similarity and connivance permits the growing influence and recommendation power between the blogger and their loyal audience. As a consequence, fashion bloggers tend to include a set of recurring brands and products that readers associate with the blogger's identity and personality and that the readers also like. Some brands and products thus contribute to create stereotype blogger identities such as the luxury brand expert, the designer brand addict, or the mass fashion victim. At that point, bloggers are expected not to leave the territory of brand expression that they committed themselves to in the beginning: readers would experience that as a betrayal. For example, if a blogger is used to promoting designers' brands and goes luxury or mass fashion, loyal readers who follow him or her may not appreciate this new editorial line. The fundamentals of the relationship constructed in time between the blogger and the readers represent a specific asset in fashion blogs, which we will discuss later.

Hyper-connection with the community

Most of the present active fashion blogs started as a way to exchange ideas about fashion, brands and purchases and to make connections with people who shared the same passion for fashion and luxury consumption. Communal relationships therefore have underpinned fashion blogging from its very beginning.

Bloggers and readers have built close interactions in time through reading, commenting and answering or linking. Blogs introduced the commenting feature in personal spaces, thus allowing discussion on fashion topics raised by blog posts. Comments in turn have made it possible for people to highlight common interests, similarities, shared tastes and thus to create more or less strong bonds between readers and bloggers but also between readers or between bloggers who read each other. This has triggered linking phenomena where bloggers have mentioned other bloggers they liked in their own blog or where readers linked the posts they liked via their own personal pages (in general social network pages like Facebook or Twitter). Incoming links and visits largely contribute to a blog's popularity and such communal popularity makes up a blog's value. As a consequence, bloggers need to maintain communal relationships to preserve their blog's value. Hyper-connection with the community is both a consequence of the initial motivation to make connections with new people and to share content, but also part of the motivation to remain popular and visible within the crowd of fashion blogs.

What is more specific to fashion blogs in hyper-connecting with the community is: (1) the recommendation power of authors generated by communal links, combined with (2) the management of scarce resources both for the bloggers and the brands.

Recommendation power of authors

Sharing a common interest and taste for specific products and brands creates strong links between bloggers and readers. Specifically, similarity and shared taste create trust relationships between the readers and the blogger: readers feel they can identify with their favorite blogger and trust them as a fashion and style adviser. Time helps create the implicit agreement between the blogger and the readers that the author will follow the same editorial line, that is, remain fresh, not be commercial, and will present brands and products that are expected to fit with the blogger's identity that is constructed and associated with that blogger in the consumers' minds. Such a trust relationship is an asset bloggers construct in the long run, and that guarantees a fashion blogger's influence within a community. Fashion and luxury brands, indeed, actively look for advocates online. For a long time, brands were hesitant to enter the web, as it was feared as a way to let brand discourse control fall into the hands of consumers. Brand managers, however, have found the use of identified advocates to be a reassuring way to take the first steps online to address targeted segments. Specifically, the main advantage offered by bloggers identified by brands as potential advocates is the quality of the relationship entertained with the audience. Since readers like the blogger, trust them, identify with them and share common tastes and interests, relevant brands increase the probability of improving consumers' awareness and chance of purchase in promoting their product through relevant bloggers.

The question then arises of which brand is relevant for which blogger. In traditional marketing, advocacy or celebrity endorsement usually requires a certain "fit" between the promoting brand's values and image and the endorser (Kapferer 2008; McCracken 1989). The fit between a blogger and a brand comes from the commonalities of identity, image and values between the brand and the blogger as the personal brand that brand representatives value. In a social media marketing context, where everyday consumers use word of mouth to discuss brands that brands cannot fully control (Kozinets *et al.* 2010), the "fit" between the brand willing to launch a promotion campaign and the blogger is necessary but not sufficient: readers' adhesion is crucial. Yet, a blog's audience, and particularly loyal readers, usually reject the following features of a blog: commercial content (obvious advertising, sponsored posts) that they think ruin the freshness and trustworthiness of a blog; and identity content (brands promoted that do not belong to the blogger's usual universe, change of fashion style or tone) they feel is not like "their" blogger. Brands thus need to help the blogger keep their perceived identity to nurture the trust link created between them and their audience while entitling the blogger to present the brand the way he or she knows their readers will accept.

That said, what makes content acceptable for bloggers and readers? Readers seek original, genuine and entertaining content. They either care for personal content and stories about the blogger's private life, of for content that teaches them something like how to dress and make up a personal style, or backstage information regarding fashion and luxury brands. That kind of information, however, is scarce and hard to come by. Maintaining a blog's readership therefore requires the ability to obtain and manage scarce resources.

Managing scarce resources

Fashion blog readers follow blogs, first, for entertainment. They particularly like bloggers' report on the VIP parties they were invited to by hip brands, the fashion shows they could attend thanks to their blog or the exclusive encounters they have had, such as meeting Karl Lagerfeld. Backstage information, breaking news and gossip from the fashion world are particularly appreciated. Desire and envy are also drivers for readership: readers like to wonder why and investigate how bloggers are offered valuable gifts like handbags, clothes or shoes. Readers finally like to gain unusual knowledge about brands and products, like the DNA of a luxury brand or the unknown story of the birth of a jewel or a fragrance. A blog's audience, however, do not like to find the same kind of content on the several blogs they read, which means that bloggers attending the same party or the same promotion event should not all report it the same way and at the same time in their blog. This might be rejected as sponsored content. Not every blogger can have access to exclusive information and events relating to fashion and luxury brands, which makes that exclusive blog content all the more desirable. For that reason, bloggers strive to have access to scarce resources on a permanent basis to ensure the success of their blog.

To arrange permanent provision of scarce resources (branded and entertaining content), popular bloggers have become increasingly organized in cliques reserving access to the sources of scarce content. Fashion bloggers gather in subgroups of closely bound peers or cliques. Generally speaking, each member of a clique is connected with a few marketing agencies, brand representatives or designers who provide them with exclusive content and invitations. The blogger then shares access to that content with the other members of the clique, thus excluding outsiders and newcomers. As a consequence, bloggers from the same clique are likely to work with and attract the same brands and the same kind of brands, while new fashion bloggers or bloggers from another subgroup are denied access to those brands. This mostly impacts how brands handle blog marketing: inviting members of different cliques to the same event often leads to total failure as it revives underlying rivalries. It also contributes to pigeonholing bloggers in categories of brands that the blogger has been associated with, according to his or her history of relationships with brands.

Future research on fashion blogging

Fashion blogging and identity are closely linked. Existing research on fashion blogging has already addressed the following issues: social identity construction through fashion-themed blogs (Chittenden 2010; Heffernan 2008; Palmgren 2008; Pham 2011; Zhao and Belk 2007); identity construction on an individual level, particularly through popularity management and personal branding (Kretz 2010, 2011; Kretz and De Valck 2010a); consumerism and spread of consumerist values through identity and/or product display fashion blogs (Zhao and Belk 2007). Femininity construction (Chittenden 2010; Palmgren 2008; Pham 2011), impact of gender (Palmgren 2008), and the reconstruction of genuine cultural and nation-related imagery, for example, "Asianness" (Pham 2011), have all been studied. Further analysis may be carried out on how cultural values are constructed and digitalized, then disseminated on the web. For example, French fashion-themed blogs construct an image of the "French style" and French values as the majority of the readers are not French. How do bloggers construct and disseminate such values and a collective identity? Popular fashion-themed blogs are mostly written by women and may appear a feminist medium: indeed, female bloggers construct femininity by self-disclosing, displaying what they envision as femininity and what the "male gaze" (Palmgren 2008) should expect. However, very little is known about feminist values constructed and diffused through blogs and social media and their impact on consumer culture.

Existing research has pointed to fashion-themed blogs as a way to self-develop and earn a living for everyday authors who know how to construct a popular personal brand. Blogger–brand relationships seem to be crucial to the success of a personal brand in the social media context. Yet, this apparently new brand–blogger relationship has so far not been theorized. If brands and bloggers co-produce value within social networks through popularity and personal branding, what are the processes leading to such value creation? What would be the implications regarding social media marketing? Fashion blogs have increasingly extended their loci of presence to social networks, leading to a web of discussion within a social media context. However, the extension of fashion narratives to other online loci than fashion-themed blogs has not been addressed.

We think bloggers now need to be understood in a wider social media context where visibility and popularity can be increased or at least maintained through extension of "social capital" or "cultural capital" (Bourdieu 1986, 1993, 1996). While social capital and cultural capital have been extensively studied in real-life social networks (Adler and Kwon 2002; Burt 1995, 2000; Lin 1999, 2001), they have not yet been studied in online social networks such as fashion-themed blogs. And yet, style and fashion blogs, because they deal with status, symbolic and cultural products and brands, may provide a unique field for the study of social and cultural capital online. Indeed, greater knowledge of how social and cultural capital interact with online social networks may help us understand phenomena such as the social stratification of social networks where bloggers become more or less popular and successful depending on the resources they can access (i.e., money to finance new projects; genuine content from brands, etc.).

Finally, fashion-themed blogs attract substantial readership and followers. Popular ones are supposed to be highly influential and to drive the purchases of fashion and luxury goods. Yet very little is known regarding the blog audience: What do readers expect from bloggers? Why do they read blogs? Why do they quit blogs? How does influence take place, and why? What can we learn about blog consumers and the consumption of fashion-themed blogs?

Notes

1 Source: Euromonitor International. Global consumer expenditures for the fashion category have increased by 30 percent from 2005 to 2010.
2 Source: Technorati: The State of the Blogosphere 2010. Available at: http://technorati.com/blogging/article/who-bloggers-brands-and-consumers-day/page-3 (accessed July 15, 2011).

Further reading

Barnard, M. (2007) *Fashion Theory: A Reader*, New York: Routledge.
Corrigan, P. (2008) *The Dressed Society*, London: Sage.
Davis, F. (1992) *Fashion, Culture, and Identity*, Chicago: University of Chicago Press.
Godart, F. (2011) *Penser la Mode*, Paris: IFM-Editions du Regard.

References

Adler, P.S. and Kwon, S.W. (2002) "Social Capital: Prospects for a New Concept," *Academy of Management Review*, 27(1): 17–40.
Arnold, R. (2001) *Fashion, Desire and Anxiety: Image and Morality in the 20th Century*, New York: I.B. Tauris & Co.
Barnard, M. (2007a) *Fashion as Communication*, New York: Routledge.
——(2007b) *Fashion Theory: A Reader*, New York: Routledge.
Bourdieu, P (1986) "The Forms of Capital," in J.G. Richardson (ed.), *Handbook of Theory and Research for the Sociology of Education*, New York: Greenwood Press, pp. 241–58.
——(1993) *The Field of Cultural Production*, Cambridge: Polity Press.
——(1996) *The Rules of Art*, Cambridge: Polity Press.

Bruzzi, S. and Gibson, P.C. (2006) *Fashion Cultures: Theories, Explorations and Analysis*, New York: Routledge.

Burt, R.S. (1995) *Structural Holes: The Social Structure of Competition*, Cambridge, MA: Harvard University Press.

——(2000) "The Network Structure of Social Capital," *Research in Organizational Behavior*, 22: 345–423.

Chittenden, T (2010) "Digital Dressing Up: Modelling Female Teen Identity in the Discursive Spaces of the Fashion Blogosphere," *Journal of Youth Studies*, 13(4): 505–20.

Crane, D. (2000) *Fashion and Its Social Agendas: Class, Gender, and Identity in Clothing*, Chicago: University of Chicago Press.

da Cunha Recuero, R. (2008) "Information Flows and Social Capital in Weblogs: A Case Study in the Brazilian Blogosphere," in *Proceedings of the 19th ACM Conference on Hypertext and Media*, Pittsburgh, PA: ACM, pp. 97–106.

Davis, F. (1992) *Fashion, Culture and Identity*, Chicago: University of Chicago Press.

Entwistle, J. (2000) *The Fashioned Body: Fashion, Dress, and Modern Social Theory*, Malden, MA: Polity Press.

Godart, F. (2009) *Status and Style in Creative Industries: The Case of the Fashion System*, New York: Graduate School of Arts and Science, Columbia University.

Heffernan, V. (2008) "Pop Couture: Street-Style Photoblogs Offer a New Way of Presenting Fashion," *New York Times Magazine*, 21 December.

Hoffman, D.L. and Novak, T.P. (1996) "Marketing in Hypermedia Computer-Mediated Environments: Conceptual Foundations," *Journal of Marketing*, 60(July): 50–68.

Jackson, T. and Shaw, D. (2006) *The Fashion Handbook*, New York: Routledge.

Kapferer, J.N. (2008) *The New Strategic Brand Management: Creating and Sustaining Brand Equity Long Term*, London: Kogan Page.

Kozinets, R.V. (2006) "Netnography 2.0," in R.W. Belk (ed.), *Handbook of Qualitative Research Methods in Marketing*, Northampton, MA: Edward Elgar Publishing Inc, pp. 129–55.

Kozinets, R.V., de Valck, K., Wojnicki, A.C. and Wilner, S.J.S. (2010) "Networked Narratives: Understanding Word-of-Mouth Marketing in Online Communities," *Journal of Marketing*, 74(2): 71–89.

Kretz, G. (2010) "'Pixelize Me!': A Semiotic Approach of Self-Digitization in Fashion Blogs," in M.C. Campbell, J. Inman and R. Pieters (eds), *Advances in Consumer Research*, vol. 37, Pittsburgh, PA: Association for Consumer Research.

——(2011) "Popularity Management: How Fashion and Luxury Bloggers Construct and Maintain Their Popularity," report for Marketing Department, HEC PARIS School of Management, Paris.

Kretz, G. and de Valck, K. (2010a) "'Pixelize Me!': Digital Storytelling and the Creation of Archetypal Myths through Explicit and Implicit Self-Brand Association in Fashion and Luxury Blogs," in R.W. Belk (ed.), *Research in Consumer Behavior*, vol. 10, Bingley: Emerald Group Publishing.

——(2010b) *"Pixelize Me!": Digital Storytelling and the Creation of Archetypal Myths through Explicit and Implicit Self-Brand Association in Fashion and Luxury Blogs*, vol. 12, Bingley: Emerald Group Publishing.

Lin, N. (1999) "Social Networks and Status Attainment," *Annual Review of Sociology*, 25: 467–87.

——(2001) "Building a Network Theory of Social Capital," in N. Lin, K. Cook and R.S. Burt (eds), *Social Capital: Theory and Research*, New York: Aldine de Gruyter, pp. 3–29.

McCracken, G. (1986) "Culture and Consumption: A Theoretical Account of the Structure and Movement of the Cultural Meaning of Consumer Goods," *Journal of Consumer Research*, 13(1): 71–84.

——(1989) "Who Is the Celebrity Endorser? Cultural Foundations of the Endorsement Process," *The Journal of Consumer Research*, 16(3): 310–21.

Marlow, C. (2006) "Linking without Thinking: Weblogs, Readership, and Online Social Capital Formation," in *56th International Communication Association Proceedings*, Dresden, Germany.

Murray, J.B. (2002) "The Politics of Consumption: A Re-Inquiry on Thompson and Haytko's (1997) 'Speaking of Fashion'," *Journal of Consumer Research*, 29(3): 427–40.

Nardi, B.A., Schiano, D.J., Gumbrecht, M. and Swartz, L. (2004) "Why We Blog," *Communications of the ACM*, 47(12): 41–6.

Palmgren, A-C. (2008) "Today's Outfit in Swedish Fashion Weblogs: An Ethnographical Study of the Online Body," paper presented at Rethinking Communities, Rethinking Place conference, Copenhagen, Denmark.

——(2010) "Posing My Identity: Today's Outfit, Identity and Gender in Swedish Blogs," *Observatorio Journal*, 4(2): 19–34.

Pham, M-H. T. (2011) "Blog Ambition: Fashion, Feelings, and the Political Economy of the Digital Raced Body," *Camera Obscura*, 26(26): 1–37.

Schau, H.J. and Gilly, M.C. (2003) "We Are What We Post? Self-Presentation in Personal Web Space," *Journal of Consumer Research*, 30: 385–404.

Thompson, C.J. and Haytko, D.L. (1997) "Speaking of Fashion: Consumers' Uses of Fashion Discourses and the Appropriation of Countervailing Cultural Meanings," *Journal of Consumer Research*, 24(1): 15–42.

Zhao, X. and Belk, R.W. (2007) "Live from Shopping Malls: Blogs and Chinese Consumer Desire," in G. Fitzsimons and V. Morwitz (eds), *Advances in Consumer Research*, vol. 34, Valdosta, GA: Association of Consumer Research, pp. 131–7.

7

FROM FREEFORM TO TEMPLATES

The evolution of self-presentation in Cyberia

Hope Jensen Schau and Mary C. Gilly

Keywords

consumer culture theory, consumer identity, digital marketing, online consumer behavior, self-presentation

Introduction

This chapter examines digital self-presentation as it has evolved from the first personal homepages, which were dependent on programming skills and imagination. There were no templates, no norms and no rules in early Cyberia. As templates evolved for creating personal websites, the barriers to participation lowered. We argue that the emergence of elaborate templates and increased scripting encourage less technologically savvy authors to join in digital self-presentation. Further, the software applications that rely most heavily on the corporeal self have enjoyed the largest participation growth. We discuss how digital self-presentation has changed with the development of more user-friendly sites. Also, we take a case study approach and consider three consumers' personal websites as they migrated from early personal websites to more constrained templates.

The digital self we examine here emerged roughly 20 years ago in a blaze of potential glory when the first consumers colonized Cyberia with personal homepages. Assisted by online companies like GeoCities and Earthlink which offered free webspace and publishing tools in exchange for advertising banner displays (Papacharissi 2002), early personal homepages were always "under construction," most often with the conspicuous and popular yellow icon prominently displayed, so that the audience knew the site was a work-in-progress reflecting the owner's latest self-conception (Doring 2002). The first personal websites were highly variable in terms of aesthetics but quite consistent in terms of content. Early studies indicate that these website creators adopted elements from others' home pages when assembling their own site. While it has been called "a medium of nearly unrestricted self-presentation" (ibid., p. 17), these digital self-presentations were unified in their reliance on real-world markers of identity (name, educational achievements, occupation, professional accomplishments, family, and even physical appearance) and on their communicative intent, or their purpose as self-presentation vehicles

(Schau and Gilly 2003). In the early days of personal webspace, authors had to be highly tech-nologically savvy with Internet access and programming skills, or hire someone with that access and those skills. As technology developed, Internet access increased and the social practice of digital self-presentation evolved, easy-to-use templates became available, norms developed and nearly anyone with Internet access could create and share a digital self-presentation within minutes. The introduction of the first Social Networking Site (SNS), Classmates.com in 1995, and the rise of blogging platforms like LiveJournal in the early 2000s lessened the creation of personal webpages (Davies 2010). While the location of online self-presentation was evolving from personal webpages to SNS and blogs, more consumers, and less tech-savvy ones, entered Cyberia with impression management in mind.

This chapter examines the evolution of personal webspace as a form of digital self-presentation from freeform personal homepages to the highly structured templates popular today in blogging (blogger and wordpress) and on SNS (Facebook, Linkedin, Google+ and Twitter). We argue that personal webspace is even more explicitly driven by communicative intent, invites collaboration (which is embedded in the medium itself), and remains anchored in corporeal reality.

The digital frontier: communicative intent and collaborative imperative

Personal webspace is inherently communicative in intent (Doring 2002; Papacharissi 2002; Schau and Gilly 2003). People create and post digital self-presentations to be consumed by known (social networks) and unknown (public) others online. What might be surprising to some is the collaborative nature of the web from its inception.

Cyberspace has been theorized as a shared imagination, or hallucination (Gibson 1984). Rushkoff (1994, p. 84) proclaims: "In Cyberia ... reality is directly dependent on our ability to actively participate in its creation." In fact, as Hafner and Lyon (1996) chronicle the birth of the Internet, computer networking was, and remains today, a collaborative enterprise and mode of communication. Although rumored to have its origins as a vehicle of national defense, Hafner and Lyon demonstrate the first viable computer network, ARPANET, was a government-funded project designed to link research institutions within the computer science discipline. ARPANET, or the Advanced Research Projects Agency's network, was the first usable computer-to-computer interface transmitted along phone lines for the express purpose of communicating, collaborating on research and sharing computing resources. Although eventually operating under the aegis of the US Defense Department, ARPANET was never actually used for military applications *per se*. One of the founding fathers of ARPANET, Joseph Licklider believed from the onset that "Computers had the potential to act as extensions of the whole human being, as tools that could amplify the range of human intelligence and expand the reach of our analytic powers" (Hafner and Lyon 1996, p. 168).

Licklider saw even in the early stages of ARPANET that:

> Hundreds or even thousands more users might gain access to the network without physical proximity to a host computer. Then, the network would no longer be just an experiment for the hardcore computer scientists with mainframe accounts, but open to a whole panoply of more casual users – military officers, government bureaucrats, university administrators, students – who would be brought into the networking community. That would bring the world one step closer to realizing Licklider's vision of the computer as a facilitator of communication and human interaction
>
> *(ibid., p. 171)*

Global telecommunications and mass media expand the popular consumer imagination toward a shared global experience with local manifestations. The techno-social realm available for consumption becomes both the tool for reality engineering and the stimulator of social (re)formation.

Appadurai (1996, p. 4) argues that the advent of globalization through electronic mediation has a significant impact on the imagination:

> Because of the sheer multiplicity of the forms in which they appear (cinema, television, computers, and telephones) and because of the rapid way in which they move through daily life routines, electronic media provide resources for self-imagining as an everyday social project.

Furthermore, "electronic mediation and mass migration mark the world of the present not as technically new forces but as ones that seem to impel (and sometimes compel) the work of the imagination" (ibid., p. 4). In other words, global telecommunications, specifically the Internet, enable and configure shared imaginations. These shared imaginations are collectively and collaboratively derived.

In cyber environments, the construction and maintenance of social reality become a more conspicuous, conscious, and complicated endeavor than in real life (RL). A computer-mediated environment (CME) is "a realm where ... personal identity is defined almost entirely by the words [and symbols] people choose" (Hafner and Lyon 1996, p. 211). Cyber citizens have access to a more expansive array of possible subject positions (organisms– human/animal/machine/hybrid, gender – male/female/neutral/hybrid, etc.) than physical citizens, and are constrained by less fixed social conventions and behavioral standards to govern the interactions (Haraway 1991), therefore more must be socially negotiated.

Cyberia is a space of contestation, of social experiment, of boundary crossing, of inherent ambiguity, perpetual motion, and continuous evolution. It is the habitat of Haraway's cyborg, "a cybernetic organism, a hybrid of machine and organism, a creature of social reality as well as a creature of fiction" (ibid., p. 149). Haraway's cyborgs are resources the imagination uses to make sense of the techno-social realities the collective has created:

> By the late twentieth century, our time, a mythic time, we are all chimeras, theorized and fabricated hybrids of machine and organism; in short, we are cyborgs. The cyborg is our ontology; it gives us our politics. The cyborg is a condensed image of both imagination and material reality, the two joined centres structuring any possibility of historical transformation. In the traditions of 'Western' science and politics – the tradition of racist, male-dominant capitalism; the tradition of progress; the tradition of the appropriation of nature as resource for the productions of culture; the tradition of reproduction of the self from the reflections of the other – the relation between organism and machine has been a border war. The stakes in the border war have been the territories of production, reproduction, and imagination.
>
> *(ibid., p. 150)*

Never is this more apparent than in the new, ever evolving phenomenon of cyberspace, where even the most taken-for-granted identities (self and community) are contested. Much like imagination itself, Cyberia, the set of virtual spaces, is not spatially or temporally bound; people can access it at will, consume it, and interact within it regardless of physical location or geographic time zone. These spaces exist globally, but are locally produced by firms, individuals, or groups in a manner that is inherently culturally influenced. Cyber environments are communicative, social and collaborative.

It is assumed that multiple personas will be interacting in cyberspace, either explicitly or implicitly, in concert.

New technologies impact identity construction, articulation, and expression by expanding the set of socio-cultural tools used in individual and social imagination (Albrow 1996). Stone (1995, p. 168) notes that "[technology] rearranges our thinking apparatus so that different thinking just is." As technology is developed and utilized in everyday life, new ways to imagine and define the self(ves), the body, the individual's relationship to the physical environment, social interaction, and consumption practices emerge. In today's technological climate of computers, global telecommunications, and mass media, new perspectives, signs, symbols, modes of consumer behavior, and rules for social performance are realized. This is exemplified by the seemingly infinite possibilities for self-presentation in cyber environments known as identity hacking (Nguyen and Alexander 1996). New manners of relating to the self(ves), environment, and information are interdependently inspired by, and accomplished through, the technologies that (re)constitute social reality: "electronic media reorganizes social space, breaking down the boundaries between here and there, lived and mediated, personal and public" (Friedberg 1994, p. 179). Carr (2008) suggests the technology and new media have reshaped our collective understanding of the world, business, information and social relations. Fields (2011) refers to "Google brain" as the manner in which people now organize information, specifically the ability to vend out memory to the worldwide web and our collective reliance on these external fact storage systems that are retrievable with any Internet-enabled device at the tap of our thumbs. The technology has rewired our brains from fact storage to smart retrieval systems. No one knows friends' phone numbers anymore because there is no longer the need to memorize them.

Through the proliferation of computer technology, its merger with global telecommunications and the rise of participatory information sharing, a collaboratively created web now exists of digital places, which are not spatially or temporally bound nor unilaterally created. While access has become a commodity (Rifkin 2000), the web itself is a pastiche of multi-authored content that is simultaneously consumed and produced. Within the web's CMEs, social actors work, play, shop, learn, express themselves and develop social networks. Consuming and producing icons, emoticons, images, texts, videos, sound bits, hyperlinks, and entire virtual worlds, social actors express and communicate aspects of their identities to other social actors, institutions, corporations, and also themselves. In these digital spaces, participant-creators demonstrate relationships to material objects and semiotic devices, communicating their identities as an amalgam of meanings inspired by and associated with chosen images, texts and sound bits and relying on the collaborative collective to perpetually renegotiate the meanings. In essence, the Internet was born of collaboration which is embedded in the media and in all enabled interactions.

Cyber pioneers and self-presentation

Cyberspace is a particularly fertile arena to investigate self-presentation (Goffman 1959), because the self as projected into the ether is perceived as a disembodied consciousness without a relevant physical referent, or as Gibson terms it a "consensual hallucination" (1984, p. 51). In other words, digital self-presentation is entirely voluntary and ostensibly unimpeded by real-life physical and economic conditions. It is constructed for audience consumption entirely through digital referents.

Self-presentation in online environments has evolved from the early days of personal homepages in the 1990s when a small percentage (6 percent) of the online population carved out homesteads in the new electronic terrain (Killoran 1999). Personal webspace was the domain of extremely technologically savvy innovators who ventured into the uncharted regions of cyberspace, claiming it as their own. Time and energy to stake a claim online was great. The barriers to entry were imposing. Personal homepages began as freeform self-presentations with authors doing their own programming (literally writing code), using Notepad or FrontPage. People without programming knowledge generally did not have personal homepages, and if they did, they relied on third party programmers to construct and maintain their personal homepages.

Without clear norms, these cyber pioneers were limited by their coding skills and the boundaries of their imaginations (what they could envision). There were no templates, no norms and no rules. Able to create anything and be anyone, most personal homepage authors stayed shockingly close to their corporeal reality (Schau and Gilly 2003). Rooted in the physical realm, these personal cyber incarnations tended toward a professional orientation, or an assemblage of personal information, skill statements and experiences, much like a digital résumé. Both intrapersonal and interpersonal communications were seen to be the key factors in the decision to create a homepage. Links on personal homepages to other sites were intended to signal social association (Papacharissi 2002), and inclusion of brands was common, even if using protected images infringed on copyright laws (Doring 2002).

Due in large part to the state of image technology which was not yet digital in format, photographs and other images were sparse, even though the media was and continues to be highly visually oriented, or ocularcentric (Jenkins 2006). Early personal homepages were text-heavy and text-driven; they were language representations of time and space, or what Bakhtin (1981) terms chronotope. These initial forays into digital self-presentation favored words and readily available stock images and icons over customized pictures and videos, which later emerge as critical content components. Therefore, in addition to computer programming skills, participating in digital self-presentation required a high degree of language acumen.

Despite the chronic presence of the yellow "under construction" icon that site authors used to convey that the site was a work-in-progress, early homepages were relatively static, being modified on average once or twice a month. The programming aspect and access charges (by minute and data size monitored) made it difficult and time-consuming to modify the personal webspace. During updates, the personal website would literally be offline and inaccessible. Modifications were cumbersome and authors often did not achieve their desired outcome in the initial effort, tinkering for hours to perfect even small updates. By today's standards, these self-presentations were static, albeit extremely thoughtful as each modification required time to implement and people would carefully review all modifications prior to posting.

To demonstrate the evolution of personal webspace, we offer three case studies: Dave, Ellie and Jose. Dave is an entertainment promoter and collector of rock-n-roll memorabilia. He set up his initial site in 1997 using FrontPage to tout his professional accomplishments and to showcase his collection. The site consisted of two hyperlinked pages: one containing a small grainy picture of himself alongside an annotated résumé, and the second had 11 descriptions of his most cherished pieces, and one image of a large part of the collection as displayed in his home (none of the individual pieces could be seen in detail). The site took hours to construct and he modified it when significant changes in his résumé or collection occurred. According to Dave's records, he saved each incarnation of his site via the "print screen" function as an MS Word document; he modified the site nine times in the first year. In early 2000, Dave set up an eBay site for a growing part of his collection which he sold and traded. He migrated to MySpace for his personal website, utilizing the customizable music format to augment the text and images he used. In 2001, he hired a professional web designer for his promotions company and included his own professional accomplishments as a subsection of the firm's site. In essence, Dave's two interlocking websites became three separate self-presentations: eBay collector and trader, professional entertainment promoter and personal MySpace site.

Ellie set up her initial site in 1997 on GeoCities. Her site was primarily focused on her journalism and life history. It was a single landing page which one could scroll through. It was text-centric with a single picture of Ellie at the top of the page reminiscent of a byline image in a newspaper or magazine. She claims: "Back in those days I modified my site about once a month ... sometimes a couple of times a week and then nothing for two months ... it was a pain to do and while I modified it the entire site was virtually inaccessible to viewers." Ellie migrated to blogger in 2001 where she created a popular blog commenting on politics and popular culture and detailing her personal musings. The blog was updated daily and sometimes a few times a day via her computer. The blogger site was replete with embedded images and hyperlinks as the blogging template enabled her to add images and texture to her essays.

Unlike Dave and Ellie, Jose's initial site was very complex. Created in 1998, Jose's site contained more than 100 hyperlinks, an animated Harley-Davidson motorcycle where a disembodied hand revved the engine. As a programmer by training and trade, Jose's site was a testament to his skills and garnered a significant cult following. In 2002, Jose created a touch screen version of his website which he maintains today. Jose claims it is "popular with the iPad crowd" as people access and customize the animation at a touch.

In all three cases, the initial freeform personal webspace was challenging and dependent on their varying programming skills. As indicated in the brief descriptions, all three elaborated their self-presentations. As templates emerged, Dave, Ellie and Jose would each take different approaches to using them and leveraging their unique talents.

Templates and scripting

Early reliance on words for digital self-expression led to the explosion of blogging activity we see in the late 1990s through today. Self-presentation online in the late 1990s was dominated by educated tech savvy participants. Later, templates would dissolve barriers to entry such as programming and strong verbal communication.

Templates are skeleton patterns that guide behavior toward a desired and uniform output. In terms of online communication, templates are structures for inputting content that function akin to the popular 1970s and 1980s pastime, MadLibs, where people were given a story with certain words omitted and supplied with a blank line and a cue like "adverb" to know what type of content would best fill the omission to ensure narrative consistency. The MadLib game was designed to produce silly narratives for amusement. The online templates are designed to structure self-presentation into readily digested informational chunks like status updates, educational achievements, and social circles. They free the author from the tyranny of the blank page and designate what type of content should be posted where. Templates also allow for easy sharing, as content is readily portable from one page to the next.

As templates evolved for creating personal websites, the barriers to participation lowered and more authors emerged. Using relatively vague templates like GeoCities and later MySpace, a burgeoning set of authors created and shared their own little part of the web. Interestingly, the trend toward anchoring the digital self on the corporeal self held. Thirty billion pieces of content is shared on Facebook each month and users upload 3,000 images to Flickr (the photo-sharing social media site) every minute (Bullas 2011). This content is cross-posted and tagged and tends to reflect the actual lives of consumers.

Blogger, wordpress for blogging and Facebook, LinkedIn and even the newest Google+ offer highly templated modes of self-presentation including distinct text fields like status updates, picture upload areas, social network assignment options (close friends, colleagues and circles). These prefabricated templates provide explicit norms which even novice users can recognize and utilize. Instead of a blank page facing the would-be self-presenter, the task is chunked into easily constructed and readily digested information units. Paired with mobile technologies, these templates allow for on the fly self-presentation updates that can be achieved in seconds and posted to various social networks for immediate consumption and appropriation.

Yet, the nature of the templated profiles inhibits the user in their self-presentation strategies and constrains communication options differently than the technology constraints of early personal webpages. Marwick (2005, p. 9) suggests that the structure of the profile application encourages the user to frame him/herself as a consumer by asking participants to "define themselves through the entertainment products they consume" such as favorite bands and movies. Liu (2007, p. 1) studied the lists of interests on consumers' social network profiles and found that consumers used these interests to convey "taste statements … that convey prestige, differentiation, authenticity, and theatrical persona."

Further, as boyd and Ellison (2007, p. 2) note, "What makes social network sites unique is not that they allow individuals to meet strangers, but rather that they enable users to articulate and make visible their social networks." The consumer's revealed social network in turn "constitutes a social milieu that contextualizes one's identity" (Liu 2007, p. 3). Thus, the number and type of "friends" appearing on one's social network help to communicate the identity of the consumer.

A more recent venue for self-presentation is Twitter. It launched in 2006 and accounts became mainstream in 2008–9 (Marwick and boyd 2010). Twitter offers the most restricted template for self-presentation: 140 characters. This self-presentation style is inherently referential as links, etc. are often utilized to stand in for more complicated elaborate self-presentation in text or customizable images. Studies of identity presentation in SNS indicate the consumers are attentive to their audience but with Twitter, there is a disconnect between those who tweet and their followers. Marwick and boyd (ibid., p. 9) argue that Twitter "flattens multiple audiences into one – a phenomenon known as 'context collapse'." As a result, it is difficult for consumers to engage in strategies that will allow them to vary the identities they present and engage in impression management. The ongoing "front stage" (Goffman 1959) identity performance of Twitter users creates a tension between revealing and hiding personal information.

Now, especially with mobile technology, self-presentation is less carefully crafted, more constrained by templates and far more dynamic, updating in real time. Researchers speculate that website providers, whether SNS, blog sites or Twitter, influence consumers' self-presentation through the environment they create for their subscribers (Papacharissi 2002; boyd 2004; boyd and Ellison 2007).

Returning to our cases, Dave has fully embraced the templates. He continues to vend out his strictly professional website to a web designer, but Dave utilizes eBay's seller template, Facebook and Twitter on his own. Dave is thankful for the templates, "I like that I can just fill in the blanks and modify from my iPhone … Instead of sweating the programming I focus on my content." For Dave, the digital self-presentation was never about his programming skills; they were merely a means to an end. He updates his Facebook and Twitter many times a day and sometimes simultaneously.

Ellie has also embraced the templates, favoring more customizable ones than Dave. She uses a blogger template that enables her to embed and modify images, sound and video in a single click. Ellie also relishes the freedom from programming, "I love the template. It makes it all so simple. I can set up these elaborate pages with a few keystrokes. I'm a writer … now, I can concentrate on writing." Ellie maintains Facebook pages that link to her blog. She likes Facebook, "I have two [pages] – one for friends and family and one for blog followers." Both support the primary endeavor: the blog. She too updates often and from mobile applications.

Jose has been resistant of the templates. For him, the joy of self-presentation has always been the programming. The templates remove that aspect and subvert his creativity. Jose says, "I have a Facebook, mostly because my wife and family want me to … and it generates traffic to my site." He confesses, "My Facebook page is basic. Why amp it up? It can never do what my site does. I link it to my real site." For him, the digital site is "real" as it authentically reveals his imaginative capacity and his talents. Interestingly, Jose's original personal website has directly fed and even driven his professional aspirations. He is now a sought-after web designer who works with well-known motorcycle shops, celebrity mechanics and reality television restoration garages.

Our cases show that the templates have impacted self-presentation, allowing greater participation through relaxing the programming requirements. More research is needed as to how providers mold, and consumers resist and repurpose sites and self-presentation. Strikingly, our cases also demonstrate that personal webspace remains to some degree personal and reliant on real-world conditions and corporeality. Although Cyberia allows that consumers can be anything, they overwhelmingly opt to present themselves in ways that reference their physical bodies and real world lives.

Conclusion

In this chapter we argue that personal website content may begin as individual interpretations of semiotic signs, but through online posting and iterative and collaborative revisions meanings become culturally determined and socially derived. The individual imagination becomes collective. These virtual spaces reveal the ways their participant-creators imagine objects, brands and symbols to create and express identities (Schau and Gilly 2003) within collaboratively derived social worlds. We show that personal webspace has become increasing template-dependent, relaxing the burden of computer programming that early digital self-presenters faced. Further, we demonstrate that the most popular forums for digital self-presentation are those with explicit links to the corporeal realm.

Further reading

Gilly, Mary C., Celsi, Mary W. and Schau, Hope Jensen (2012) "'It Don't Come Easy': Predictors of Seniors' Internet Adoption and Use," *Journal of Consumer Affairs*, 1: 1–28.

Kozinets, Robert V., Hemetsberger, Andrea and Schau, Hope Jensen (2008) "The Wisdom of Consumer Crowds: Collective Innovation in the Age of Networked Marketing," *Journal of Macromarketing*, 28(4): 339–54.

Schau, Hope Jensen and Mary C. Gilly (2003) "We Are What We Post? The Presentation of Self in Personal Webspace," *Journal of Consumer Research*, 30(4): 385–404.

References

Albrow, Martin (1996) *The Global Age*, Stanford, CA: Stanford University Press.

Appadurai, Arjun (1996) *Modernity at Large: Cultural Dimensions of Globalization*, Minneapolis, MN: University of Minnesota Press.

Bakhtin, M.M. (1981) *The Dialogic Imagination*, trans. C. Emerson and M. Holquist, Austin, TX: University of Texas Press.

boyd, danah michele (2004) "Friendster and Publicly Articulated Social Networking," paper presented at Conference on Human Factors and Computing Systems (CHI), Vienna, ACM, April 24–29.

boyd, danah m. and Ellison, Nicole B. (2007) "Social Network Sites: Definition, History, and Scholarship," *Journal of Computer-Mediated Communication*, 13(1): article 11.

Bullas, Jeff (2011) "20 Stunning Social Media Statistics Plus Infographic," available at: www.jeffbullas.com/2011/09/02/20-stunning-social-media-statistics/ (accessed 15 December 2011).

Carr, Nicholas (2008) *The Big Switch: Rewiring the World, from Edison to Google*, New York: W. W. Norton and Company.

Davies, Laura (2010) "Timeline: A History of Social Networking Sites," available at: http://lauramdavies.wordpress.com/2010/02/11/timeline-a-history-of-social-networking-sites/.

Doring, N. (2002) "Personal Home Pages on the Web: A Review of Research," *Journal of Computer-Mediated Communication*, 7(3).

Fields, R. Douglas (2011) "Genius Across Cultures and the 'Google Brain'," *Scientific American*, August 20. Available at: http://blogs.scientificamerican.com/guest-blog/2011/08/20/genius-across-cultures-and-the-google-brain/.

Friedberg, Anne (1994) *Window Shopping*, Berkeley, CA: The University of California Press.

Gibson, William (1984) *Neuromancer*, New York: Ace Books.

Goffman, Erving (1959) *The Presentation of Self in Everyday Life*, New York: Doubleday.

Hafner, Katie and Lyon, M. (1996) *Where the Wizards Stay Up Late: The Origins of the Internet*, New York: Simon & Schuster.

Haraway, Donna J. (1991) *Simians, Cyborgs and Women: The Reinvention of Nature*, New York: Routledge.

Jenkins, Henry (2006) *Convergence Culture: Where Old and New Media Collide*, New York: New York University Press.

Killoran, John B. (1999) "Moore's Law of Personal Home Pages?" Available at: http://muse.tau.ac.il/maslool/boidem/62estimate.html (accessed November 5, 2003).

Liu, Hugo (2007) "Social Network Profiles as Taste Performances," *Journal of Computer-Mediated Communication*, 13(1): article 13.

Marwick, Alice (2005) "I'm More Than Just a Friendster Profile: Identity, Authenticity, and Power in Social Networking Services," Association for Internet Researchers 6.0, October 5–9.

Marwick, Alice E. and boyd, danah (2010) "I Tweet Honestly, I Tweet Passionately: Twitter Users, Context Collapse, and the Imagined Audience," *New Media Society*, online 7 July, available at: http://nms.sagepub.com/content/early 2010/06/22/1461444810365313.

Nguyen, Dan Thu and Alexander, Jon (1996) "The Coming of Cyberspacetime and the End of the Polity," in Rob Shields (ed.), *Cultures of Internet: Virtual Spaces, Real Histories, Living Bodies*, London: Sage Publications.

Papacharissi, Zizi (2002) "The Presentation of Self in Virtual Life: Characteristics of Personal Home Pages," *Journalism and Mass Communication Quarterly*, 79(3): 643–60.

Rifkin, Jeremy (2000) *The Age of Access*, New York: Putnam.

Rushkoff, Douglas (1994) *Cyberia: Life in the Trenches of Hyperspace*, New York: HarperCollins.

Schau, Hope Jensen and Gilly, Mary C. (2003) "We Are What We Post? The Presentation of Self in Personal Webspace," *Journal of Consumer Research*, 30(4): 385–404.

Stone, Allucquère Rosanne (1995) *The War of Desire and Technology at the Close of the Mechanical Age*, Cambridge, MA: The MIT Press.

PART III

Researching the digital consumer

8

DIGITAL YOUTH, MOBILE PHONES AND TEXT MESSAGING

Assessing the profound impact of a technological afterthought

Anthony Patterson

Keywords

digital youth, Generation C, mobile phones, text messaging, texting, SMS

Inbox

Since real-time conversational interaction with anyone, at any time, from anywhere, until recently, was realisable only in a fictional *Star Trek* universe, it is hardly surprising that a faintly utopian discourse surrounds the use of mobile devices (van den Boomen *et al.* 2009). Understandably, commentators were initially bowled over by the wondrousness of what was once an other-worldly technology, and in their breathless excitement speculated that humankind was entering uncharted territory, that a new virtual reality, a cyberspace of sorts was being colonised (Springer 1996; Danet 2001). The reality, of course, was not nearly so fantastical. While technology such as the mobile phone is undoubtedly a technological marvel, it has quickly become so ubiquitous and ordinary, that it is now a thoroughly mundane experience in everyday life. No one ever leaves the house these days without three things: their keys, wallet and their mobile (Herring 2004). To lose one's phone would amount to a piece of the self being shorn away. Not only could a cherished database of numbers, addresses, notes and messages be lost forever – since an upgrade will inevitably replace the missing phone – the habitual practices of using the device's often esoteric features will also be lost (Berry 2011). It is, in short, an essential lifestyle accessory, especially for young people, a powerful computing device that we need with us at all times, 'to log in', as Gleick (2000, p. 90) notes, 'from the beaches and mountaintops'. So while mobile telephony may be mundane, it still has transformative power. As this chapter will hopefully demonstrate, this device which became the fastest growing consumer device of all time is responsible for consumers displaying many new behaviours, attitudes, and values.

Of all the mobile-embedded features,[1] the most innocuous is the tiny text message. The SMS. The truncated txt. An instantaneously delivered abridged, abbreviated pronounce-ment of the kind most of us social animals regularly receive. The 'OMG, u'll never guess! ... '

The 'where r u?' and the 'cul8r'. Although it played a formative role in a world of abbreviated discourse and other miniature forms of communication, and was the starting gun that gave Twitter and a thousand other instant message platforms their short form factor (Humez *et al.* 2010), these days discussions of digital spaces tend to overlook and under-egg the humble text message. Instead, a fawning discourse devoted to the social media giants, Facebook and Twitter, tends to prevail. Yet, the text message is undoubtedly the unheralded champion of social communication. According to a major study by Lenhart *et al.* (2010) on how teenagers use mobile phones, it might surprise you to learn that by 2009, texting had become the most popular form of communication among teenagers, surpassing email, instant messaging, social networking, and face-to-face communication, and that one-third of them report sending more than 100 texts per day. In total, the expected number of text messages to be sent globally in 2011 is a staggering seven trillion (Martin 2011). One seriously wonders how it was ever possible to arrange a meeting, let someone know your whereabouts, announce your imminent arrival, without the existence of these 'little sugar rushes of contact' (Benson 2000, p. 25), these bursts of textual brevity. Even to the vast majority of non-digital natives, self-proclaimed technophobes and proud luddites, consuming such technology has become entirely second nature.

The practice of text messaging is thus deeply embedded in the fabric of everyday life. Look around you: head-bowed, thumb-poised 'textperts' are everywhere.[2] They have been credited with developing a new shorthand language, vowel-poor, acronym-rich and emoticon-laden that is largely unfathomable to older people. This new language has been praised by linguists for its creativity (Crystal 2008). At the same time, it has been derided by grammar fetishists and punctuation vigilantes predictably incensed by what they perceive to be a gross breach of language convention (Casagrande 2006). Others are infuriated by what has been dubbed 'cell-fishness' whereby mobile phone owners engage in texting while, at the same time, conducting real-time conversations. A survey claims that this behaviour so intensely irritates that many respondents would prefer multi-tasking offenders to pick their nose, rather than to simultaneously talk and text while in their company (Kingston 2011). However one judges the critical reception of text messaging, it is clear, as studies indicate, that along with other instant message formats and computer games, it can be incredibly addictive. In some cases its most ardent fans have even developed repetitive strain injury from over-pressing their keypads, while others have been admitted to addiction clinics to calm their ever-ready-to-text thumbs. The science behind the theory holds that the act of sending and receiving text messages releases dopamine into the brain, which sets up a vicious circle of constant craving that leads to more texting, more craving (Small and Vorgan 2008). It is also clear that texting is proving useful in all kinds of everyday relational situations, whether it be winning over potential partners, conducting illicit affairs, sending lazy birthday greetings,[3] or just keeping in contact with friends. Truly, text messages have beeped and vibrated their way into our cultural conscience. They have reengineered the way people, especially the young, interact, date, socialise and communicate. Like it or not, in this 'mobilized world' (Lindgren *et al.* 2002), it is virtually impossible to venture anywhere – the cinema, the supermarket, the gym, the restaurant – without hearing the beep-beep or ringtone that signals, '1 message received'.

This chapter will discuss how text messaging, alongside a plethora of other digital modes of communication, creates new challenges and opportunities for consumers operating in today's ubiquitously digital realm (Mansvelt 2005). It opens with a brief consideration of the unpredicted, but meteoric rise, of the text message. Drawing primarily on an overview of research which has studied the form, function and meaning of text messaging, the chapter will then reflect on why they have become so pervasive. In doing so, it will analyse the subtleties and significance of sending and receiving text messages as understood by research conducted mainly in the disciplines of sociology, linguistics, consumer behaviour and cultural studies. The discussion will then proceed to delve into some of the potential downsides of texting. It will conclude by exploring the future of texting and suggest a possible strategy that digital consumers might adopt in order to retain more control of their always switched on, always accessible lives. It should be made clear that this chapter neither condemns nor celebrates text messaging, but instead attempts to present a balanced viewpoint between the two extremes.

The history of the truncated txt

Text messaging was developed for digital mobile phones over 20 years ago in 1991. Messages can be up to 160 characters in length, while some people text into several separate messages which allows the total message to be longer. Such a scenario suffices for most users since common mobile contracts come with huge bundles of free text messages. Minor product innovations, predictive text input, the inclusion of dictionaries and the development of an Internet-based SMS capability have since made the technology slightly more palatable. Nonetheless, the act of texting remains awkward, unless you number among the young experts who have inculcated the skill so effectively that some can type 30 words a minute.

It might be intimated from this chapter's consumer slant, and the evident success of text messaging in general, that marketing moguls orchestrated its ascent into the vanguard of culture, but marketing's input was conspicuous by its absence. Texting was not highlighted in market research; nor was it established in conjunction with new product development. The surprising truth is that texting was developed almost entirely by accident. Its anonymous architects, while working on the GSM protocol, noticed spare capacity in the system, so they added the texting facility as an afterthought, in case it might prove useful in the future (Giussani 2001). In the beginning, mobile providers, to be certain, were largely indifferent to the foresight of their engineers. They held little faith in the usefulness of this new technology. Many did not even bother to explain the facility in their instruction booklets (Haig 2005). At the outset they did not even charge consumers for the service, calculating that its main utility lay in delivering modest subscriber information, such as free voicemail notification.[4] If they attributed it with any revenue potential, it was as an extension of paging for busy professionals (Doyle 2001). While the mobile phone providers were pursuing grander ambitions, pouring billions of pounds into WAP technology (deemed a financial failure) and third-generation technologies (which have been more successful), young people quietly and unexpectedly hijacked the text message medium. Today's prolific texters were born after 1990 are are known as Generation C, defined as such because they are, 'connected, communicating, content-centric, computerized, community-oriented, always clicking' (Friedrich *et al.* 2011, p. 1). According to some accounts, they are so adept at texting that 42 per cent of them claim to be able to do it blindfolded (Harris Interactive 2003).

The texture of texting

Research on texting tends to focus on the texting practices of the young people who reside at its epicentre (Hanson 2007; Palfrey and Gasser 2008; Ito 2009; Watkins 2009). This has given scores of academics – myself included – a perfect justification to use the convenient, but frequently criticised, student sample. My own studies encouraged young people to keep qualitative diaries recording all text activity, including both incoming and outgoing messages, as well as the additional thoughts that each text message provoked. My goal was simply to qualitatively explore the, at the time, understudied consumer phenomenon of texting (Patterson *et al.* 2003; Patterson

2005). So what did I discover while sifting through the diaries of my students? Well, contrary to a widespread mythology that today's students are too debt-ridden and exhausted from all the 'McJobbing' they do to actually enjoy themselves, I can confirm that the truth is as it always was. According to the overwhelming weight of data from my study, all the clichés still hold: students sleep into the afternoon; they watch too much TV; rarely attend lectures; get drunk every night; and enjoy healthier sex lives than the rest of us. A key mediator of these intrinsically 'interesting' lives is undoubtedly the very active text message activity that usually begins each and every day with the arrival of a text message pulling them from their slumber. A typical scenario is imagined by Ryan and Jones (2009, p. 28):

> As she gets out of bed her mobile trills: a text has arrived from her college friend Simon. It's about last night's party. Janet stabs at the mobile keypad with one hand, deftly firing off a reply, while her other hand opens up her laptop, logs her on to her various social networking accounts and fires up her e-mail.

Yet despite the matter-of-fact presence of text messaging in their lives and the doggerel that constitutes much of their textual relations, the arrival of a text can be quite an enthralling event in their lives. It is virtually impossible for them not to open it immediately.

You would think that the palpitations and frenzied fumbling in trouser pockets that the unexpected arrival of these messages provokes would be quite enough for any mobile phone user to handle, but for many this is really only the beginning. According to research on texting, the message content often has the potential to provide a satisfaction all of its own. What especially enlivens these digital arrivals is when texters engage in the 'free' exchange of digital items such as pictures, web links, audio and video. Interestingly, it does seem that in this digital space the commercial rarely encroaches, and even if it does, it is easily ignored with a quick press of the delete button. Texting research has also theorised that it gives consumers, what Coyne (2010) labels, a new 'mobility practice'. Rather than being tethered to meeting at a specific time and location, people these days are free to embark with a loose idea of a rendezvous, while remaining completely flexible about when and where. The precise location and time can always be negotiated via text message. This affords people a new flexibility that previously could only be imagined. This heightened mobility has also paved the way for organising flash mobs and the seemingly impromptu swarms of dissenting protestors that can potentially sweep tyrants from power.

Another component of texting that researchers have explained with surprisingly credible sociological contextualisation is what texting can do for one's social standing. While the make and model of the mobile phone can confer considerable credibility onto its owner, as well as offering 'plumage to display', and being 'a perfect fidgeting device', the phone can in social situations promote a person to a stratospheric degree of coolness simply by signalling the delivery of a new, and to any onlooker or listener, mysterious message (Adler 2007, pp. 47–51). The message itself, of course, might just as well be from the recipient's mum. Nonetheless, observing the remote inquisitiveness of those who hear their text messages arrive can make a texter feel socially superior.

In addition to the flush of self-worth that texting can precipitate, another major finding which my research uncovered, was its unique ability to mask the truth, to more easily tell lies, or, at least, to mildly mislead the message receiver. The texting medium lends itself especially to the telling of 'little white lies' principally because texters do not have to undergo the more inquiring inquisition that generally accompanies a face-to-face telling of this same untruth. More often than not, less than forthcoming text messages are fairly harmless, such as: exaggerating the degree of love for a partner, claiming to be ill while in reality being perfectly healthy, or claiming to be unable to attend an event due a prior engagement. Nonetheless, using text messaging for such an end might seem morally reprehensible to some readers, to others perhaps familiar with Oscar Wilde's famous essay entitled *The Decay of Lying*, lying can be infinitely preferable to the finality of truth. 'Lies,' as another brilliant writer put it:

> ramify in all sorts of unexpected directions, complicating things, knotting them up in themselves, thickening the texture of life. Lying makes a dull world more interesting. To lie is to create. Besides, fibs are more fun and liars, I am convinced, live longer.
>
> *(Banville 1993: 191)*

While I'm not certain that texting will actually extend your life expectancy (clearly a longitudinal study is needed, anyone?), texting does seem to suggest that its distance from the sender does, at least, make telling lies easier and absolve some of the associated guilt. Whether or not, as Adorno was convinced, this necessarily means that people in this cellular age will be more inclined towards deceitfulness remains to be seen.

Words-worth

Beyond the manifold pleasures that receiving a text can deliver, researchers report that the actual process of creating a text is an affirmative experience for many texters (Patterson 2005). While there are certainly those who use texting merely as a conduit to communicate personal arrangements or share noteworthy information, as a break from the general tedium of everyday life, many like nothing more than to construct a 'good' text message. Some take great pride in their own linguistic flair, stopping to marvel at their handiwork, perhaps even saving it for future perusal. A 'good' text message it seems should be impulsive, flippant, and off-the-cuff. Ironically, to achieve this effect a texter needs to exercise the pedantic circumspection of an advertising copywriter, ruthlessly scrutinising the tone, style and phraseology of any given message prior to communicating with the intended audience. Writing a text message is not called 'compose' for nothing. Indeed, the English poet laureate, Carol Ann Duffy, believes that the practice of texting is ideal preparation for writing potent poetry. She argues that its power, as a new genre of writing, lies in the fact that it 'allows feelings and ideas to travel big distances in a very condensed form' (Moorhead 2011, p. 39).

This last point empirically illustrates what Mick and Fournier (1998) label as a central paradox of all technological products. On one hand, technological products are often hailed as time-savers, but as their utility becomes apparent, they ultimately steal more and more of our time. The same paradox can be witnessed at the receiver's end. They can spend hours revelling in the analysis of each message received, turning it every which way, exploring all possible motives, meanings and connotations. Each is a written riddle that they have been set to solve. Even after their own text-mortem is complete, they often seek second opinions from their close friends to support or dispute their deeply nuanced reader responses. So meaningful do these messages become that some, as McCarthy and Wright (2004, p. 13) note, 'collect personally significant messages to evoke the moment they were received, to recall, and to reminisce. Some are reluctant to give up their old mobiles for a newer model because the old model holds messages that are dear to them.' Never, as the cliché goes, has so little meant so much.

As an outlet for social interaction, texting offers unparalleled opportunities to solidify and maintain an increasingly global network of relationships with friends and family. Texters too can use text messaging – as is evident from the steady drumbeat of newspapers sporting salacious headlines like *The Joy of Text* and *The Good Txt Guide* – to further romantic aspirations. One, of course, does not want to over-generalise, but there is a considerable weight of evidence in support of the notion that texting is a romance enabler. Large-scale qualitative and quantitative studies that have delved into the utility of text messaging note that for many pursuing new romantic liaisons, acquiring the mobile number of the target of affection is frequently a key determinant of whether a potential relationship will succeed or fail (Harper *et al.* 2005; Crystal 2008). Acquisition of these precious mobile numbers allows an exchange of flirtatious textual relations to ensue, wherein the above-mentioned composure and creation of a text message, and the deeply wrought analysis of messages received, become ever more heightened in the search for deep and meaningful human connectivity. In particular, texting provides a way for tongue-tied adolescents to speak without speaking, spare red-faced blushes, declare intentions, offer invitations, and at the same time, avoid the abjection caused by face-to-face rejection.

It's not all LOL

Texting does have its downsides. One of the most mortifying of which is the embarrassment a text message can cause when it is received in a text-taboo environment like a lecture theatre, cinema or job interview room. An eloquent statement on this subject penned by a student of mine is worth quoting at some length:

> My phone, that's my phone. Shit … I didn't even realise it until the lecture came to an abrupt halt. This new phone. Why did it have to have an unconventional ring tone I'm not familiar with? A lecture theatre filled with 200 people and my phone disrupts this very interesting discussion on … Taylorism. Everyone is shuffling and looking around to see whom the blameworthy culprit is. My face is going red, but feign to be as sinless as the student next to me. I pretend to be concerned and join the crowd in turning my head in every which way, to see who has put a standstill on my concentration and thus harming my education. Suddenly the signs seem to be illuminated, like flashing lights have been fitted around it. 'ALL MOBILE PHONES MUST BE SWITCHED OFF.' My heart beats faster and faster, boom boom, boom boom, boom boom.

The pain of such short-lived embarrassment, however, would be welcomed by a certain tranche of texters, if they could just be given some relief from the bombardment of messages that constantly assault their inbox. Engaging in 'textathons' with all kinds of social reprobates: stalkers, spammers, obsessives and ex-partners is the last thing they want to do, but sometimes there is no escape. Yet a far, far worse fate than receiving too many text messages is, of course, getting too few text messages. It's all very well, having the latest super-duper smartphone of the i-variety, but if you do not have anyone to text or call, well, what is the point? It is akin to being all dressed up with nowhere to go. Life as a 'texter' suffering from empty inbox syndrome can be hard to bear.

Yet these downsides are of little consequence, when compared with some of the more fundamental changes in human behaviour in which texting has been implicated. The most astonishing of which is Palfrey and Gasser's (2008) suggestion that many young people, given the choice, would prefer to send an instant message or text rather than have a face-to-face encounter. Many authors have written on this subject arguing, in essence, that relentless connection has led to a new solitude. Two of the most prominent books that argue this outlook are Small and Vorgan's (2008) *iBrain: Surviving the Technological Alteration of the Modern Mind* and Turkle's (2011) *Alone Together: Why We Expect More from Technology and Less from Each Other*. Both provide a litany of examples illustrating how digital technology is making young people less social. Mobile phones, it is argued, have become 'involvement shields' which people can all too easily hide behind. Coyne (2010, p. 53) also laments the commonplace reality where, 'In a world where most of us are talking to "absent others", the street becomes a potentially lonelier place.' Perhaps though, the degree of loneliness and social exclusion engendered, by mobile phones specifically, is stated in too alarmist a fashion by the authors of these books. It does seem faintly ridiculous to implicate a device whose principal function is to connect people, with the paradoxical disconnection of these same people. Advocates of the digital life would also counter that all change is naturally accompanied by resistance by those who wish to retain the status quo. The on-going readjustment of communication from traditional face-to-face communication towards more mediated forms of communication then may not be as catastrophic as these books predict (Cacioppo and Patrick 2008).

Outbox

Mobile telephony and text messaging have become central to the digital lifestyles of young people. Mobile phones emerged, a generation or two ago, as something 'nice to have', and swiftly became an essential lifestyle accessory that is frequently described as an appendage of the self (Standage 2005). Today, they are recognised as the most ubiquitous consumer devices on Planet Earth. The frequency of their obsolescence with new models typically discontinued after only nine months of production is worrisome, especially since the sensuousness of their exterior conceals innards that contain high levels of lead, arsenic, antimony trioxide, chromium and other carcinogenic substances. Although beyond the scope of this chapter, their unregulated dismantle in shady factories located in remote areas of China and India, at great danger to the workers inside, is an issue that should be given more attention by researchers and government authorities.

The virtues of the mobile phone, and its power to radically transform human behaviour, should not be underrated. For one thing, it provides us with greater control of our busy lives. The effortless mode of communicating it delivers is of enormous utility, even if the message in question amounts to little more than a wife calling her husband from the supermarket to ask what he wants for dinner. Such an act of telemediation, only a short time ago, would have been impossible. Mobile phones are also material props that we use to perform our characters in everyday life. For instance, it is a familiar scene to see many strangers sitting silently on a bus, consumed by the activities offered by the bright-screened phones resting on their laps. In part, these people are partly detached from their immediate environment, not fully present on the bus, but somewhere else. It is this somewhere else that offers intriguing possibilities for future research in terms of investigating the effect this has on sociality. The use of social theory, therefore, could provide a thorough grounding for this field of inquiry. Needless to say, there is also a need for more research on the effect mobile radiation has on our brains. From a purely marketing perspective, another interesting line of investigation would consider what Martin (2011) calls 'the untethered consumer', essentially roaming mobile phone owners who by dint of their device are free from the constraints of traditional marketing, but can still be reached, located, and targeted via their mobile.

On another level, the use of mobiles combines a whole plethora of other digital activities, each of which in their own right is worthy of investigation, whether it is mobile phone cameras, watching movies on tiny screens, shopping while on the move, listening to music, playing games, downloading apps or navigating a city. This chapter focused specifically on the utility of the text message, a technological afterthought that has transformed textual communication. My review of the existing research, to summarise, found that young people, with their remarkably dexterous digits, have mastered a new way to communicate. In doing so, they have been hailed as poets of the digital age. It has been noted that they revel in the construction of these messages, take pleasure in the art of deconstructing them, and, of course, use them to successfully connect with family, friends and love interests.

And yet many charges are commonly invoked against the digitalisation of our lives, of which text messaging is a big part. These include: the blurring of boundaries between work and leisure; the inescapable and perpetual connectivity into which everyone is tethered; that we have become scatterbrains unable to concentrate on anything for very long; that increased connectivity has given rise to a paradoxical alienation; and finally, the frightening prospect, that because the mobile is always on our person, marketers will be able to track our every move and build a staggeringly accurate digital footprint of our consumption activities (Martin 2011). This is not even to detail the specific charges against text messaging: that it has corrupted the English language; that it has afforded 'Generation C' a secret means of communicating beneath the radar of adults (and they are not best pleased); that texting has been partially responsible for young people withdrawing into private digital cocoons; and that these same youngsters find it difficult to communicate with their peers authentically in the real world.

Despite the grumbles, gripes and grievances that have been articulated against the rising digital tide, which I personally think are overwrought; very few of us would ever contemplate relinquishing our gadgets. Our BlackBerries, iPhones, iPads, and Android others, are very much here to stay. In fact, as mobile phone handsets become in effect our digital 'wallet phones', and are directly responsible for the realisation of the seemingly elusive cashless society, they will become even more indispensable. My one piece of advice is simply to remind everyone that these devices do have off buttons that can easily be pressed. I thoroughly recommend trying out this radical, off-the-wall strategy. In fact, I'm about to shut down this computer right now. Consequently, I may not be able to …

Notes

1 The smart phone is the ultimate Swiss Army knife-style gadget incorporating a feature-rich list of integrated technologies, such as a music player, digital camera, video recorder, calculator, web browser, and the ability to instantaneously download thousands of additional useful apps. For instance, if you have an iPhone, it is possible to monitor your blood pressure. In short, the mobile phone is about much more than talking and texting.
2 Ironically, many texters do not look around enough themselves, so absorbed do they become in the act of texting. Texting seems particularly adept at lurching them out of time and context. In fact, a tragic tranche of them have ended their lives by not looking where they are going, falling down open manholes, or causing motorway pileups as a consequence of sending the little blighters.
3 The text message has almost single-handedly decimated both the greeting cards industry and the sending of snail mail. For reasons of cost and convenience many now prefer to send a quick text, rather than trudge to the stationery store to select, purchase and post an expensive card. A further interesting caveat, as Berger (2010) notes, is that the popularity of the cell phone has also led to a decline in people wearing wristwatches primarily because they now use their phones to tell the time.
4 According to Dushinski (2009), text messaging generates $100 billion a year.

Further reading

Hanson, J. (2007) *24/7How Cell Phones and the Internet Change the Way We Live, Work, and Play*, London: Praeger. [Offers an excellent discussion of how technology – mobile phones and text messaging especially – affects our everyday lives.]

Harper, R., Palen, L. and Taylor, A. (2005) *The Inside Text: Social, Cultural and Design Perspectives on the SMS*, Dordrecht: Springer. [As a nuanced discussion on the history and global pervasiveness of text messaging, this edited collection of papers excels.]

Martin, C. (2011) *The Third Screen: Marketing to Your Customers in a World Gone Mobile*, London: Nicholas Brealey Publishing. [This text presents the topics of text messaging and mobile phones for a marketing audience.]

Patterson, A. (2005) 'Processes, Relationships, Settings, Products and Consumers: The Case for Qualitative Diary Research', *Qualitative Market Research: An International Journal*, 8(2): 142–56. [This journal article presents my original research on this topic. It is an interesting read, if only for the richness of the empirical quotations.]

Turkle, S. (2011) *Alone Together: Why We Expect More from Technology and Less from Each Other*, New York: Basic Books. [A highly readable and engaging introduction to the argument that relentless connection through mobile phones and other devices has engendered a new solitude.]

References

Adler, B. (2007) *Boys and Their Toys: Understanding Men by Understanding Their Relationship with Gadgets*, New York: American Management Association.

Banville, J. (1993) *Ghosts*, London: Quality Paperbacks Direct.

Benson, R. (2000) 'The Joy of Text', *The Guardian Weekend* (UK), 3 June: 22–7.

Berger, A.A. (2010) *The Objects of Affection: Semiotics and Consumer Culture*, New York: Palgrave Macmillan.

Berry, D. (2011). *The Philosophy of Software: Code and Meditation in the Digital Age*, London: Palgrave Macmillan.

Cacioppo, J.T. and Patrick, W. (2008) *Loneliness: Human Nature and the Need for Social Connection*, New York: W.W. Norton & Company, Inc.

Casagrande, J. (2006) *Great Big Meanies: A Guide to Language for Fun and Spite*, London: Penguin.

Coyne, R. (2010) *The Tuning of Place: Sociable Spaces and Pervasive Digital Media*, London: The MIT Press.

Crystal, D. (2008) *Txtng: The Gr8 Db8*, Oxford: Oxford University Press.

Danet, B. (2001) *Cyberpl@y: Communicating Online*, Oxford: Berg.

Doyle, S. (2001) 'Software Review: Using Short Message Services as a Marketing Tool', *The Journal of Database Marketing*, 8(3): 273–7.

Dushinski, K. (2009) *The Mobile Marketing Handbook: A Step-by-Step Guide to Creating Dynamic Mobile Marketing Campaigns*, New Jersey: Cyber Age Books.

Friedrich, R., Peterson, M. and Koster, A. (2011) *The Rise of Generation C*, Spring, No. 62, February 22, available at: http://www.strategy-business.com/article/11110?gko=64e54.

Giussani, B. (2001) *Roam: Making Sense of the Wireless Internet*, London: Random House.

Gleick, J. (2000) *Faster: The Acceleration of Just About Everything*, New York: Vintage.

Haig, M. (2005) *Brand Failures: The Truth about the 100 Biggest Branding Mistakes of All Time*, London: Kogan Page.

Hanson, J. (2007) *24/7: How Cell Phones and the Internet Change the Way We Live, Work, and Play*, London: Praeger.

Harper, R., Palen, L., and Taylor, A. (2005) *The Inside Text: Social, Cultural and Design Perspectives on the SMS*, Dordrecht: Springer.

Harris Interactive (2003) *Born to Be Wired: The Role of New Media for a Digital Generation*, Sunnyvale: Teenage Research Unlimited.

Herring, S. (2004) 'Slouching Toward the Ordinary: Current Trends in Computer Mediated Communication', *New Media and Society*, 6(1): 26–36.

Humez, A., Humez, N. and Flynn, R. (2010) *Short Cut: A Guide to Oaths, Ring Tones, Ransom Notes, Famous Last Words, and Other Forms of Minimalist Communication*, New York: Oxford University Press.

Ito, M. (2009) *Hanging Out, Messing Around, and Geeking Out: Kids Living and Learning with New Media*, Cambridge, MA: The MIT Press.

Khan, U., Dhar, R. and Wertenbroch, K. (2005) 'A Behavioral Decision Theory Perspective on Hedonic and Utilitarian Choice', in S. Ratneshwar and D.G. Mick (eds), *Inside Consumption: Consumer Motives, Goals, and Desires*, London: Routledge, pp. 144–65.

Kingston, A. (2011) 'Public Displays of Disaffection', *Macleans*, 19 September, pp. 57–8.

Lenhart, A., Ling, R., Campbell, S., and Purcell, K. (2010) *Teens and Mobile Phones*, Washington, DC: Pew Internet & American Life Project.

Lindgren, M., Jedbratt, J. and Svensson, E. (2002) *Beyond Mobile*, London: Palgrave Macmillan.

McCarthy, J. and Wright, P. (2004) *Technology as Experience*, Cambridge, MA: The MIT Press.

Mansvelt, J. (2005) *Geographies of Consumption*, London: Sage.

Martin, C. (2011) *The Third Screen: Marketing to Your Customers in a World Gone Mobile*, London: Nicholas Brealey.

Mick, D.G. and Fournier, S. (1998) 'Paradoxes of Technology: Consumer Cognizance, Emotions and Coping Strategies', *Journal of Consumer Research*, 25: 123–43.

Miller, S. (2006) *Conversation: A History of a Declining Art*, London: Yale University Press.

Moorhead, J. (2011) 'Shlli Compare Thee 2 an iPad 2?', *The Guardian*, 6 September, p. 39.

Nazareth, L. (2007) *The Leisure Economy: How Changing Demographics, Economics, and Generational Attitudes Will Reshape Our Lives and Our Industries*, London: John Wiley & Sons.

Palfrey, J. and Gasser, U. (2008) *Born Digital: Understanding the First Generation of Digital Natives*, New York: Basic Books.

Patterson, A. (2005) 'Processes, Relationships, Settings, Products and Consumers: The Case for Qualitative Diary Research', *Qualitative Market Research: An International Journal*, 8(2): 142–56.

Patterson, A., Cassidy, K. and Baron, S. (2003) 'Communication and Marketing in a Mobilized World: Diary Research on "Generation Txt"', in D. Turley and S. Brown (eds), *European Advances in Consumer Research*, Dublin: European Association of Consumer Research.

Ryan, D. and Jones, C. (2009) *Understanding Digital Marketing: Marketing Strategies for Engaging the Digital Generation*, London: Kogan Page.

Scott, S. (2009) *Making Sense of Everyday Life*, Cambridge: Polity.

Small, G. and Vorgan, G. (2008) *iBrain: Surviving the Technological Alteration of the Modern Mind*, New York: HarperCollins.

Springer, C. (1996) *Electronic Eros: Bodies and Desire in the Postindustrial Age*, Austin, TX: University of Texas Press.

Standage, T. (2005) *The Future of Technology*, London: Profile Books Ltd.

Tapscott, D. (2009) *Grown Up Digital: How the Net Generation Is Changing Your World*, London: McGraw-Hill.

Turkle, S. (2011) *Alone Together: Why We Expect More from Technology and Less from Each Other*, New York: Basic Books.

van den Boomen, M., Lammes, S., Lehmann, A.S., Raessens, J. and Schäfer, M.T. (2009) *Digital Material: Tracing New Media in Everyday Life and Technology*, Amsterdam: Amsterdam University Press.

Watkins, S.C. (2009) *The Young and the Digital: What the Migration to Social-Network Sites, Games, and Anytime, Anywhere Media Means for Our Future*, Boston: Beacon Press.

9
NETNOGRAPHY AND THE DIGITAL CONSUMER
The quest for cultural insights

Robert V. Kozinets

Keywords

cultural insight, digital consumer, netnography

Who is the digital consumer and what do we need to know about her? Although this exciting new volume is filled with digital dialectics, critical cyborg-oriented conundra, intellectualized information processes, networked New Humans, and postmodern posthumanist post-portraiture, I am going to argue upfront and unabashedly that I see the concept of the "amazing" "new" "digital" consumer as somewhat of a crashing bore.

Posthuman cyborg? Come on. Look up from this book (and I hope you are reading it on a screen), take it to the street, and get real. Do you see that teenager walking down the street with her head completely buried in her mobile phone (maybe she is reading this book too)? That university student cramming for an exam online, texting on Facebook, and simultaneously checking the Patients Like Me online forum for medical information? That grandmom shopping on eBay, paying for it on Paypal, checking her bank balance on her BlackBerry and then Skyping her sister on another continent?

Who are these people, these much-lauded, much-sought, much-studied "consumers" of information and communications technologies? They are the digital consumer, and the digital consumer is, of course, us. That is because digital consumption is nonstop, daily, broadening, local, so constant and invisible it is almost inevitable and indispensable; it is an already inextricable part of our routines and our culture. And so the digital consumer is mundane.

But just because she is mundane does not mean that she is unimportant. In fact, I would like to argue that it is the very mundane and everyday nature of the online-to-offline-to-online consumption of the digital consumer that makes the deep and penetrating understanding of her and her behaviors so vitally important to our understanding of contemporary culture and society. For it is within the crumbs and corners of our daily lives, in the routine conduct we so often take for granted, that lie the deeper clues about our motivations, our values, our social structures, and the meanings that underlie them all.

Like a determined hunter, over the past 15 years I have been tracking the digital consumer. At first, as she first dipped her toes in the rising waters of the information stream we call the Internet, I tried to study the emerging social behaviors that took place largely through textual exchanges in collective online gatherings, newsgroups like the Bitnet and Usenet that followed the development of the World Wide Web in the mid-1990s (see, e.g., Kozinets 1998, 1999; Kozinets and Handelman 1998). After the dotcom boom and bust of the late 1990s, as the Internet and its social uses continue to grow, I followed her communities' use of narratives (Brown *et al.* 2003) and the burgeoning and diversionary ideologies of technology (see Kozinets 2008). Then came the reemergence of the Internet and the burgeoning development of what we now call the social media revolution, with blogs and the way to a democratizing of communications on the Internet and the mass creation of content by a grass-roots army (see Kozinets 2006a, 2006b). Next came the creation of microblogs and social networking sites enabling more and increasingly widespread and sophisticated sharing of personal and other social communications, and the rise of social media marketing that also needed to be investigated, modeled, and understood (see Kozinets *et al.* 2010). In contemporary times, a mere decade and a half from the time that I began this research journey, the small information stream of the Internet has grown into a vast, deep and heavily populated ocean teeming with activity.

In order to understand the world of the digital consumer and the marketplace of digital consumption and social media, I developed a technique called netnography. Netnography combines the participant-observational stance of the traditional anthropological ethnographer with some unique and specially designed procedures that adapt ethnography to the unique contingencies of computer-mediated communications (see Kozinets 1998, 2002, 2010). After a slow initial reception, the technique now is enjoying some adoption in this rapidly expanding sphere of activity and social scientific investigation (Bengry-Howell *et al.* 2011).

There are many articles, conference papers, book chapters, and even a book that offer guidelines about how to conduct netnographic research (see e.g., Kozinets 1998, 2002, 2006a, 2006b, 2010). Instead of reiterating this well-documented advice, this chapter steps back from the procedural elements of netnographic research and wades into their epistemological justification. For netnography is not merely a method for conducting general social scientific research on social media, but it is a particular kind of research, an interrogatory perspective that looks at the cultural worlds of the digital consumer and places a special significance and value on cultural insights. In fact, netnography is a product of the same impetus and movement that led many researchers in the field of marketing and consumer research to define and develop the subfield/ area of "consumer culture theory" or "consumer culture theoretics" (see Arnould and Thompson 2005, 2007).

The goal of this chapter is to begin to develop and explain the necessity and value of applying a cultural lens to an understanding of the social worlds of the digital consumer. In doing so, we will need to examine what is meant by the term "cultural insight" as it applies to the world of the digital consumption. In turn, we are tasked with discussing what types of cultural insights can be gathered from studying the worlds of digital consumption. As the chapter concludes, we will, I hope, begin to see the value for both theory and practice of a culturally inflected perspective on social media and the digital consumers who populate it.

The consumer cultural turn

In their influential article that initially branded consumer culture theory, Arnould and Thompson [2005, p. 869] cite Kozinets' (2001) anthropologically-informed conceptualization of consumer culture as an interconnected system of commercially produced images, texts, and objects the groups use—through the construction of overlapping and even conflicting practices, identities, and meanings—to make collective sense of their environments and to orient their members' experiences and lives. Culture, relatedly, is explained in a haunting metaphor by anthropologist Clifford Geertz (1973) as a type of spider's web of significance and meaning spun by human beings and yet in which we all hang suspended. As Geertz reminds us, although it affects us deeply and individually, meaning, values and culture are very public things. If we understand something of the Other, it is because we share in her or his same culture; we are in some sense both suspended in the strands of the same web. If that Other is completely foreign to us, or acts in a completely inapprehensible way, we stand outside that web, unknowing.

I recall an insightful editorial cartoon in which two women suspiciously pass one another. One woman is cloaked in a full black burqa that covers her entire body, the other in a tiny string bikini but wears big dark sunglasses. The two thought bubbles in the cartoon reveal each woman's impressions of the other. The bikini-clad woman thinks, "Everything covered but her eyes, what a cruel male-dominated culture!" The woman in the burqa correspondingly thinks, "Nothing covered but her eyes, what a cruel male-dominated culture!" Not only is each woman using clothing to interpret the culture of the other, but each woman's interpretation reveals much about her own culture and enculturation, the webs of meaning, value, and significance in which she herself is suspended.

There are parallel processes at work in the worlds of social media. With every phrase used, every acronym, ever intentional misspelling, every reference, avatar, carefully-chosen pseudonym, posting, cross-posting, hyperlink, Tweet, update, photos and video, culture is born, shared, revealed. Our objective as netnographers is to follow and understand the cultural strands of the webs in which these elements of social media meaning are suspended. To understand culture in this way is to understand the deepest shared elements of human groups and their societies. Everything contained in one person's mind—their identity, motivation, emotions, and tightly held personal values—originates in the groupmind and its collective structures of meaning and power. If there is anger, it is because the individual's power in the dyad, the group, or the collective is frustrated. If there is shame, it is because the individual's social standing in the collective is threatened or reduced.

If culture is socially patterned human thought and action, the general term holds within it much more. When we study particular subcultures or general aspects of consumer collectives or even of consumer society, such as we do in the realms of social media, our attention is drawn to a range of distinct cultural elements. We encounter distinct and distinguishing symbol systems, new flourishes and new language. We see rituals, repeated patterns of behavior infused with meaning. We find novel modes of dress, new fashion, and accoutrements of identity. We hear tales of belief, stories of passion, historical narratives, and encounter vast worlds of shared narratives. We see value systems enacted through behaviors like classification and collecting. Social structures emerge with their attendant relations of power, submission and domination, and hierarchies, often within hierarchies.

Cultural insight and ethnography

For the purposes of netnography and understanding the world of the digital consumer, what is a cultural insight? A cultural insight comes from an understanding of some of these above-mentioned cultural elements as they play out in the world of digital consumption. If digital consumers use unique language often drawn from cyberculture, then the netnographer's task is to explore and decode it. If stories and narratives are constructed and shared, it is the netnographer's task to listen, to compare, and to understand them. If power structures and hierarchies are involved, asserted, and reinforced in the searching for and ensuring of consumption knowledge and social status online, it is netnography's job to explore and analyze it. Structures, systems, symbols, values, routines, and meanings are all necessary grist to the netnographic mill.

It is perhaps best *if not only* through a cultural method, a cultural read, an anthropological understanding, that such elements as these can fully be absorbed, understood, and relayed to make sense of the full contextual complexity of the digital consumers' lived world. Netnography is based in ethnography, and ethnography is insight-generation occurring in the friction between observation, participation, thoughts, actions, language, and representations. Ethnography is pattern recognition under conditions of extreme complexity.

Ethnography, thus, is not method. It may be based on methodology, but ethnography cannot be reduced to a mere set of techniques, a checklist of actions, or set of procedures. This simple fact—that it is method-like but not a method—is precisely what is so confusing to novices, vexing to interdisciplinary editors and to those searching for the use of the Holy Grail of clear method descriptions in textbooks about ethnography. Ethnography, it turns out, is more of an approach.

Ethnography can even be said to be a "messy" approach (Marcus 1998), one conducted in complex and convoluted circumstances, full of compromises, contextually constructed out of moment-by-moment decisions and continual and continuous adjustments. Netnography, for better or for worse, follows directly in these messy footsteps. For the mess, like Geertz's webs, is significant, about significance, and of our own making. Culture is not neat and clean. It never was and never will be. Attempts to make it seem so, like Gert Hofstede's much-maligned and yet incredibly popular attempts, are both laughable and tragic reductions to anthropologists. Culture cannot be a dummy variable in a multivariate equation. Culture can only be multivariate itself, the explanation and understanding for why scientists feel compelled to explain culture using Greek symbols and signs (see, e.g., Latour and Woolgar 1979). Culture: alive and thriving and constantly threatening to get out of control. Only a method that itself contains and can accommodate such complexity can ever hope to illuminate even a limited corner of such a phenomenally phenomenological phenomenon.

Ethnographic approaches to understanding

Netnography works in this new world because it is based on the same five elemental principles of cultural understanding of the old one. One of the most fundamental principles of ethnography is its naturalistic approach. Ethnographers go to the field, to where the culture itself manifests and unfolds. The guiding image an imaginary of ethnography is still a scientist on a long and distant voyage of discovery. Translated to the world of social media, the digital consumer interacts with other digital consumers, with organizations and corporations, and with technological interfaces, and this communicative activity creates, manifests and perpetuates culture. To attempt to learn about it by postdoc interviews, focus groups full of reflective similar individuals, or surveys that question consumers about their online behaviors is in some sense to miss and indeed undervalue the lived richness, the phenomenological being-in-cyberspace that is the experience of the digital consumer. That experience requires the researcher to enter and engage with the same social world that the digital consumer experiences, and to engage with it in the same way that the digital consumer experiences it.

The second elemental principle to cultural understanding replicated by netnography is that of the immersive approach. Naturalism means respecting that the phenomenon takes place in its own environment and not necessarily in a location convenient to the researcher. Immersion means being there, but it also means more than this. It means being out there, exposed and vulnerable.

Because of the critical stature of ethnographic immersion during in-person fieldwork, participation is incredibly important to netnography. The immersion of the netnographer in the social media research site requires a membership-like engagement with it and the duty to become in every relevant sense a member of whatever communities she or he is seeking to study. The ultimate test of ethnographic quality for some anthropologists is whether the members of that community have actually accepted the anthropologist into their ranks as a full-blown community member with all rights and privileges accorded to her.

When the researcher completes the transition from outsider to subjectively-knowledgeable insider, the decoding of the culture is assumed to be complete. The next task, that of translating this insider knowledge back into so-called "scientific" "objective" "etic" knowledge (or some might call it "information") is perhaps the most difficult and yet most crucial task of the ethnographic or netnographic researcher. For we can only report time spent in the field, pages of data collected, websites visited, hours of online interviews, numbers of social media members observed, types and quantities of postings and comments. But what we do not know and do not see until it is communicated clearly and unequivocally to us is the depth of insight gathered while the researcher was moving through and within this perhaps-distant social world.

This is related to the next and highly substantial elemental principle of ethnographic and netnographic approaches, the ability to absorb, relate, and represent with considerable verisimilitude the lived subjective reality of culture members as they go about their daily lives in interaction with one another. If ethnography can be considered, as Hobbs (2006, p. 101) suggests, to be "a cocktail of methodologies" which not only share an assumption that "personal engagement with the subject is the key to understanding a particular culture or social setting" but also that "description resides at the core of ethnography and however this description is constructed is the intense meaning of social life from the everyday perspective of group members that is sought," then emotional impact upon the reader and the inspiration of Eureka moments seem to be at its core. They reside in its "intense meaning of social life" representation. This, too, requires not only observational ability but also considerable rhetorical skill. The netnographer, like the ethnographer, must be a skilled architect of social scientific representation, telling stories and painting detailed descriptive portraits that illuminate not only meanings but in a profoundly subjective sense inspire empathy and understanding.

The next elemental principle of ethnography is that it uses multiple methods in order to accomplish its objectives of describing and explaining particular cultures and communities. Although interviews as well as conversational and discourse analysis are among the most common methods added to the central core of participant-observation, a range of other techniques are commonly deployed as needed. Certainly documentary analysis, videography, and photography are very common and often highly useful in bringing the embodied reality of the ethnographic field site to life. The netnographer is also tasked with using these multiple methods in order to illuminate and adequately represent the lived social reality of members of the social media culture and communities. Screenshots and moving screen captures might take the place of still photography and videography; however, the intention to capture some of the dynamism of what is going on in the community remains a common element. Similarly, online interviews, whether conducted via e-mail, chat, in a social networking site's postings and comments, or through Skype or iChat, offer additional windows into the worlds of culture members. Even descriptive statistics and other quantitative representations may have an important role as they sometimes do in anthropological work. Of course, much of the multimethod work of netnography will blur the lines between netnography and ethnography as the exploration of the social field site crosses between embodied, in-person interactions and behaviors and online, technologically-mediated and technoculturally-adapted social media interactions. The cutting edge of netnographic work will be carefully trained and theoretically map the boundaries between in-person and social media communities and communications.

Finally, the last elemental principle of ethnographic work is its adaptability. Ethnography has been adapted to study almost every major culture on the planet. It has been applied to study the vast variety of occupational cultures. It has looked at subcultures, the cultures of age cohorts, and gender cultures. Ethnography has even been adapted to study the cultures of nonhuman primates such as chimpanzees, gorillas, and orangutans, and even intelligent non-primates such as dolphins and wolves. With netnographic work taking place in the ever-expanding universe of social media, these techniques of online anthropology have to deal with a range of different technological and techno-social innovations. So as social media expanded beyond the web forums and crude text-based chat rooms to blogs, wikis, social networking sites, microblogs, and geolocation services and games, the specific nature and practices of netnography have had to adapt and evolve to keep pace. In such a dynamic and relevant site of social expansion, this work of netnographic adaptation is constant, challenging, and exciting.

Netnography can and has been defined as

> [A form of] ethnography conducted on the Internet; a qualitative, interpretive research methodology that adapts the traditional, in-person ethnographic research techniques of anthropology to the study of the online cultures and communities formed through computer-mediated communications ... Netnography adapts common participant-observation ethnographic procedures—such as making cultural entrée, gathering and analyzing data, ensuring trustworthy interpretation, conducting member checks, and conducting ethical research—to these computer-mediated contingencies
>
> *(Kozinets 2006a, p. 135)*

The recommendation of the netnographic approach to social media researchers is therefore based on three arguments: (1) that online social worlds are parallel and in significant ways comparable to off-line social worlds; (2) that online social worlds are significant forums for the enactment of meaningful cultural and human behaviors; and (3) that face-to-face ethnographic techniques should and can be adapted to the unique contingencies of online social worlds. As a result, netnography is said to yield a cultural insight into the world of the digital consumer and the manifold worlds of digital consumption. We can conceptualize and illustrate the unique qualities of netnographic cultural insight, first, by comparing netnography to other methods or approaches used to study social media interactions and texts and, second, by specifying and briefly describing four particular benefits that this cultural insight offers to investigators seeking to understand the lived cultural reality of people as they pursue and continue their social lives online.

The dashboard and the pith helmet

One of the currently favored modes for marketing executives in the world's top corporations to understand digital consumers' online social behaviors and interactions is through what is increasingly becoming known as "the social media dashboard." A typical social media dashboard, such as that offered by SproutSocial looks at a variety of online behaviors and then represents them with a combination of bar and line graphs and pie and other charts. For example, a social scorecard might keep score of how many total "clicks" and also how many new followers, mentions, messages, and postings a particular site has on a daily, weekly, or monthly basis. It might offer demographics of different followers or site members. It might calculate mentions from Twitter or Facebook statistics. Oftentimes marketing dashboards will seek to offer some sort of numerical metric such as "engagement" or "influence" and to provide ongoing calculations regarding its percentage increase or decrease.

In contrast, netnographic analysis offers very little that is quantitative or numeric. A netnographic analysis tends to be far more visually diverse and more narrative. Pie-eating contests are more likely to be featured than pie charts, and cocktail bars more than bar graphs. A netnographic analysis reads more like a deeply structured story, sometimes, in the best cases, with a deep theme and a moral to the tale. Through it all, the words and the lives of real embodied consumers are represented and presented.

The netnographic cultural insight into the worlds of digital consumption is offered by four distinct aptitudes of the approach. First, netnography digs deeply into the lived worlds of significance inherent in the meaningfulness. It penetrates the associations and values behind the symbols that online social media participants share and often take for granted, be they avatars, font colors, emoticons, or videotaped gestures. It identifies the different selves existing behind avatars, pseudonyms, and Facebook profile pages and from them seeks to construct and analyze notions of identity that underlie and impel behavior and that cause and result from the all-penetrating miasma of meaning. Building patterns of significance and representing them theoretically is perhaps the highest order of netnographic analysis and one that cannot be matched for impact or insight by mere aggregations or word counts of posted online texts.

Second, netnography attends not merely to text but to context. Whether flying through a shared videogame world, blogging to a rapt audience, checking into a Foursquare location looking for friends and freebies, tweeting for entrepreneurial purposes, or updating a Facebook status for fun and to stay connected, netnography pays close attention to the form, format, and site of communications. Cultural, communal, technological, and narrative contexts intertwine in the worlds of social media and provide rich fodder for netnographic analysis and representation. In many cases the mere identification of the communities online sharing relevant information about a particular topic is in itself a valuable datum. Similarly, rich description and presentation of these online forums and the behaviors which take place within them are a significant contribution to our knowledge that is unique to the netnographic representation.

Third, netnography tracks culture and its members by representing with as much integrity as possible the actual voice of the digital consumer as she or he interacts with other digital consumers in the worlds of cyberculture. Portraying the naturalistic speech acts of digital consumers as they actually occur avoids essentializing and unnecessarily reducing consumers' online actions and interactions to mere classifications or associations of the so-called 'content' of their texts. Instead, the cultural flux, flow, flavor, and style—the human element of these speech acts (which can also include audio files, artistic works, and audiovisual representations)—is maintained and preserved as part of the uniquely important cultural insight of netnographic work.

Fourth, and finally, netnography not only preserves and analyzes contexts, identities, and meanings, but it also seeks out and works with the stories and narratives of social media. Cultures spark when tales are told and cultures are communicated. Communities are built on these foundations, and identities made in their listening and sharing. Through social media, social stories are constructed. Through social media, identities inflect narratives and fascinating new directions (see Kozinets *et al.* 2010). It is only by carefully attending to these stories that the sensitizing concepts, revelatory incidents, and other hearts and souls of culture's deepest meaning can be gently unpacked and humbly understood.

Transforming insights

Perhaps the underlying importance of these aspects, their common ground, is difficult for many to recognize. That common ground is composed of meaning, meaning contained in the most fundamental particle of human experience: the narrative form, the story. What is the value of understanding the digital consumers stories? Where does it take us? Is it "scientific"? Is it "useful"? From a managerial perspective, what does the understanding of the digital consumers world buy us? Can help us to predict and influence consumers' attitudes and opinions and thus their willingness to open their wallets or purses and thus to buy?

Social sciences of many stripes seek causal relationships between one group of actions and another. Whether it is ticking a box on a survey relating to a person's racist behaviors towards some identified ethnic group, or an economist's interest in aggregate responses to interest rates or money policy, we are constantly looking for rigorously grounded and replicable relationships that can tell us about the workings of our social world. From our observations of daily acts and our aggregations of categories of thought, speech, and action, we devise models of social behavior that in some sense relate particular domains of human existence with one another in specific ways.

In some sense, ethnography and netnography transcend this type of action-to-action causality. By seeking to link up narratives, identities, rituals, myths, stories, interactions, communities, groups, and even technologies, netnography builds a complex network of explanations and observations to map onto and help understand the infinitely-more complex embodied and electronically-mediated social worlds through which many of us now move. For if culture is the ground we walk on, the air we breathe, and the invisible medium through which we all move and interact, then in some sense an understanding of this invisible medium provides the deepest insight of all. And if culture moves through communications, as we know it does, then the technologies that allow us to save and share and spread our communications have also allowed us to create and penetrate new technocultural universes and to permit us to permeate them with ideas and thought forms.

This short chapter sought to explore and think about some of the underlying justifications for a cultural approach to studying the world of the digital consumer. This exploration take place in a milieu in which the social world of the consumer and the consumptive world of the social have already transformed into a world where the physical and the digital are inextricably intertwined. Moreover, as Gossieaux and Moran (2010) argue, the nature of social media is changing organizations from the outside, turning the most responsive and visionary of them into "hyper-social organizations." The consumer originally interacted interpersonally with a myriad of different vendors, each of whom preferred products along with social communications. In the corporate age of mass suffocation, franchising, and the personalized "professional" service, that interpersonal touch was lost. However, social media restores that connection in a new and different way. The consumer once again has access to the producer in order to express his or her delight or deep dissatisfaction.

In this much-noted and oft-overstated empowering evolution, the world of the consumer has changed. Although the underlying reality of the consumer is path dependent in many ways, the way that social reality can manifest in daily life has undergone a profound transformation. As the digital consumer, she interacts with other consumers, with producers, and with the marketplace, the public, the government and even the economy in a totally new and different way. The tribal possibilities of the consumer's world have increased exponentially.

In an ironic twist, technology has allowed much more humanizing of commercial relationships, resulting in a new-and-just-beginning socializing of business, consumers, and consumption itself. Business channels are in the process of transforming into human-to-human-to-human networks, networks of patterned narratives, rituals, and wondrous stories. In every good sense, the organized boxes of organization and society are becoming messier and gloriously messier. In this chapter, I contend that the shift is one that cries out to be understood as a cultural one. These changes are changes of perspective and of stories, of meanings, values, and narratives. They are transformations that we must understand and study, in their origins and their direction, as cultural ones.

References

Arnould, Eric J. and Thompson, Craig J. (2005) "Consumer Culture Theory (CCT): Twenty Years of Research," *Journal of Consumer Research*, 31(March): 868–82.

——(2007) "Consumer Culture Theory (and We Really Mean Theoretics): Dilemmas and Opportunities Posed by an Academic Branding Strategy," in Russell W. Belk and John F. Sherry, Jr. (eds), *Research in Consumer Behavior*, vol. 11, *Consumer Culture Theory*, Oxford: Elsevier, pp. 3–23.

Bengry-Howell, Andrew, Wiles, Rose, Nind, Melanie, and Crow, Graham (2011) "A Review of the Academic Impact of Three Methodological Innovations: Netnography, Child-Led Research and Creative Research Methods,", Working Paper, NCRM Hub University of Southampton.

Brown, Stephen, Kozinets Robert V. and Sherry Jr., John F. (2003) "Teaching Old Brands New Tricks: Retro Branding and the Revival of Brand Meaning," *Journal of Marketing*, 67(3): 19–33.

Geertz, Clifford (1973) *The Interpretation of Cultures*, New York: Basic Books.

Gossieaux, Francois and Moran, Ed. (2010) *The Hyper-Social Organization: Eclipse Your Competition by Leveraging Social Media*, New York: McGraw-Hill.

Hobbs, Dick (2006) "Ethnography," in Victor Jupp (ed.), *The Sage Dictionary of Social Research Methods*, Thousand Oaks, CA: Sage.

Kozinets, Robert V. (1998) "On Netnography: Initial Reflections on Consumer Research Investigations of Cyberculture," in Joseph Alba and Wesley Hutchinson (eds), *Advances in Consumer Research*, vol. 25, Provo, UT: Association for Consumer Research, pp. 366–71.

——(1999) "E-Tribalized Marketing? The Strategic Implications of Virtual Communities of Consumption," *European Management Journal*, 17(3): 252–64.

——(2001) "Utopian Enterprise: Articulating the Meanings of *Star Trek*'s Culture of Consumption," *Journal of Consumer Research*, 28(June): 67–88.

——(2002) "The Field Behind the Screen: Netnography for Marketing Research in Online Communities," *Journal of Marketing Research*, 39(February): 61–72.

——(2005) "Communal Big Bangs and the Ever-Expanding Netnographic Universe," *Thexis*, 3: 38–41.

——(2006a) "Ethnography," in Victor Jupp (ed.), *The Sage Dictionary of Social Research Methods*, Thousand Oaks, CA: Sage.

——(2006b) "Click to Connect: Netnography and Tribal Advertising," *Journal of Advertising Research*, 46 (September): 279–88.

——(2008) "Technology/Ideology: How Ideological Fields Influence Consumers' Technology Narratives." *Journal of Consumer Research*, 34(April): 864–81.

——(2010) *Netnography: Doing Ethnographic Research Online*, London: Sage.

Kozinets, Robert V., de Valck, Kristine, Wojnicki, Andrea and Wilner, Sarah (2010) "Networked Narratives: Understanding Word-of-mouth Marketing in Online Communities," *Journal of Marketing*, 74(March): 71–89.

Kozinets, Robert V. and Handelman, Jay M. (1998) "Ensouling Consumption: A Netnographic Exploration of the Meaning of Boycotting Behavior," in Joseph Alba and Wesley Hutchinson (eds), *Advances in Consumer Research*, vol. 25, Provo, UT: Association for Consumer Research, pp. 475–80.

Latour, Bruno and Woolgar, Steve (1979) *Laboratory Life: The Social Construction of Scientific Facts*, Los Angeles, CA: Sage.

Marcus, George (1998) *Ethnography Through Thick and Thin*, Princeton, NJ: Princeton University Press.

10

THE RISE OF THE CUSTOMER DATABASE

From commercial surveillance to customer production

Jason Pridmore and Detlev Zwick

Keywords

commercial surveillance, consumer production, customer database, Deleuze, Foucault, market practices, marketing, performativity, post-Fordism

Marketing transitions

With the widespread adoption of Fordist regimes of production and Taylorist regimes of management in early twentieth-century America (Gramsci 1971; Hardt and Negri 2000, pp. 219–350), the supply of commodities began to surpass market demand consistently for the first time in history. The advent of mass production required mass consumption and as a consequence, the profession of marketing management was developed. Though marketing management had its roots in agricultural economics and was characterized initially by pragmatic macro-economic concerns about distribution efficiencies and co-operative marketing of agricultural products (Bartels 1988), it obtained an increasingly dominant function within commercial practices as it focused on selling more of a particular product than the competition. The new priorities set by a nascent corporate capitalism that pitches companies directly against each other for scarce consumer resources produced novel needs for knowledge about the market, including knowledge about consumers. Hence, corporate marketing management developed early forms of market research to produce consumer knowledge that would help outsell any rivals. Early market research led to a view of the consumer as a relatively stable, homogeneous, and immobile set of preferences that could be managed and controlled with mass advertising (Beniger 1986). An understanding of the consumer as a psycho-socially complex and mutable collection of needs, wants, and desires did not emerge until the 1940s (Miller and Rose 1997; Rose 1997). But even then, the surveillance of consumers and consumer practices qua market research (or "commercial research" as it was then called, see Elmer 2004), while becoming increasingly sophisticated, was driven by a need of the corporation to control consumers, reduce marketing complexities, and improve production efficiencies (Arvidsson 2004). In other words, the surveillance of consumers was motivated by a company's intention to align consumer preferences for products and brands with what was being produced.

During the 1950s and 1960s, the work undertaken by psychologically-inclined market researchers such as Sidney Levy and management theorist Peter Drucker changed the message coming out of commercial consumer surveillance. They posited that the primary challenge for the firm lies in identifying and responding to consumers' changing needs and wants in the market (see Drucker 1950, 1954; Levy 1959) and that production processes and marketing activities were to be geared toward satisfying consumers' needs and wants rather than controlling them for maximum sales. In other words, these scholars suggested that companies produce what consumers want instead of making consumers want that which the company produces. Similarly, contemporary marketing icon Philip Kotler declared that achieving "customer satisfaction" required the channeling of all efforts of the firm into identifying and meeting customer needs in specific times and spaces. For Kotler, marketing had to take on the character of an "applied behavioral science" (Kotler 1972, p. 46). His promise to the emerging legion of professional marketers was that a concern with production efficiencies should be subordinate to discovering what customers wanted. He assured his students that such acquiescence would ultimately prove to be a superior strategy for securing market share and maximizing profits relative to a production-driven model that assesses opportunities based on a firm's manufacturing efficiencies (see Kotler 1972; Kotler and Levy 1969).

What seems to be little more than a minor adjustment to the dominant view gave birth to a fundamentally new justification for intensified commercial consumer surveillance that dominates contemporary marketing discourse to this day, namely that market research is central to knowing and providing what consumers want. After all, from the vantage point of such early marketing gurus as Levy, Kotler, and Drucker, intense consumer surveillance is akin to providing an important public service because making consumers happy with products they desire, now elevated to something of a social policy, depends on the best possible intelligence about those same consumers (cf. Applbaum 2011). The "applied behavioral science" revolution started a trend in academic and corporate marketing departments toward conceptualizing the consumer as a complex entity whose desire to consume may be boundless (as maintained by the economic branch) but whose motivations to consume (the what and why of consumption) are not well understood and require continuous scrutiny. Sales-through-domination, as Thomas Frank (2000) points out, no longer holds the cachet it once did.

While surveillance of consumers and their consumption practices has been an important task of corporate marketing departments for a long time (Arvidsson 2004), it has increased significantly in the past 20 years. Under conditions of hyper-competition (D'Aveni and Gunther 1994), characterized by excess capacities of progressively more, and more alike, brands and products vying for the same consumer dollar (see also Barber 2007), corporations have sought to collect massive amounts of detailed and accurate information about consumers. The ability to store, retrieve and process this information has become widely recognized as providing a key competitive advantage in contemporary information capitalism (Zwick and Denegri-Knott 2009). The shift to digitized information (as discussed below) is perhaps the most important aspect for under-standing the monitoring and measuring of consumers and their consumption practices as a form of surveillance. Specifically, the customer database has fundamentally changed the speed and degree to which companies are able to collect, sort and process information about consumers and thus erect an increasingly seamless surveillance assemblage (Haggerty and Ericson 2000; Zwick and Dholakia 2004a).

Importantly, as the mundane practices of consumption become important building blocks for the performance of economies, they become subject to both an increased amount of scrutiny and direction. Today, consumption is about more than buying stuff, perhaps about even more than an expression of lifestyles, worldviews and identities. Consumption has become a proxy for proper citizenship, access to desirable socialities, and the possibility of connectedness to modern life and of cosmopolitanism (see Bauman 2001). Furthermore, with the rise of the knowledge economy, and specifically the Internet, the separation between those who 'produce' and those who 'consume' has begun to blur (see e.g. Ritzer and Juergenson 2010). It comes as little surprise, then, that understandings of what constitutes consumption are no longer universally shared (if they ever were) and moreover, that knowing what exactly to monitor about consumers and their consumption practices and more importantly, how to do so, seems to be increasingly difficult to ascertain.

Practices and digitalization

Historically, "assembling" consumers into marketable segments and categories began in earnest in the post-World War II era. It expanded significantly in the years that followed as numerous organizations collected demographic and psychographic data to discover "attitudes, opinions, and interests" of consumers (Arvidsson 2004, p. 464). Differentiated segmentation of markets through these processes gave way to increasingly "smaller and smaller units of analysis" that allowed for increasingly precise targeting of consumers (Holbrook and Hulbert 2002, p. 716). The transition toward smaller segments and clusters of consumers occurred largely in relation to the growth of new information technologies and data processing. Central to this transition was the development of the consumer database.

Large-scale electronic consumer databases were perhaps first employed as part of the development of consumer credit (see e.g., Poon 2007) and large geodemographic information systems (GIS) in the USA in the 1970s. Jonathan Robbin developed a system of consumer segments in the United States according to ZIP codes using the acronym PRIZM, short for Potential Rating Index for ZIP Markets (see Weiss 1988). Richard Webber developed a similar system called ACORN: A Classification Of Residential Neighbourhoods in relation to post codes in the UK at about the same time (see Burrows and Gane 2006). Both Robbin and Webber relied heavily on the nascent fields of information technology and software development to translate the geographic distributions of populations into socio-spatial arrangements, or 'social clusters' "where people tend to congregate among people like themselves" (Weiss 1988, p. 11). It quickly became clear that such GIS-generated population clusters made a very valuable information commodity because location proved to be a "powerful predictor of all manner of consumption practices" (Burrows and Gane 2006, p. 795). Marketers hailed the newly available consumer data as it revealed very clearly the spatial distribution of socio-economic characteristics, tastes, preferences, and lifestyles. Combined with already existing market intelligence, GIS provided an even more solid basis for consumer segmentation as well as selection and de-selection of entire geographic areas for commercial communication, retail development, and product delivery.

In the 1970s and 1980s, adding geographic surveillance to existing forms of lifestyle and socio-demographic surveillance certainly refined and rendered more useful for marketers the notion of consumer clusters and segments. However, real advances in commercial consumer surveillance occurred with the digitalization of information and the rise of data mining. The digital panoptical sort of consumers via algorithmic analysis, cross-referencing of data, and massively populated, electronic consumer profiles allowed for previously unknown and unknowable consumption patterns and behavioral relationships to emerge. As initial data mining techniques improve and begin to include, with the advent of the internet, real-time transactional customer data, descriptions of patterns of behavior and predictions of future behavior become increasingly accurate and meaningful. Real-time collaborative filtering and predictive modeling based on massive amounts of customer information aim at identifying a customer's (or set of customers') propensity to buy certain products, respond to certain marketing campaigns, be at risk of churn and defection, become a credit risk, and so forth.

By constantly (re)producing, storing and analyzing massive amounts of digital data, current forms of commercial surveillance of consumer behavior represent a powerful response to the quickly changing desires, fluid identities, and spatial mobility of contemporary consumers (Featherstone 1991). As databases capture consumer activities ubiquitously and in minute detail, they become electronic repositories of complex consumer lives. While the digital code deconstructs complex, idiosyncratic, and often erratic behavior into individualized and individualizing data points (Poster 1990), the algorithm reconstructs this data into a standardized, rationalized, and comparable structure, making it possible for marketers to identify 'right' and 'wrong' targets for professional marketing intervention. In short, the production of digitized lists of consumers via ubiquitous commercial surveillance serves to reorganize the sensibilities and practices of marketers and the way marketing practice configures and controls spaces of operation, production, and economic value (Leyshon and Thrift 1999; cf. Poon 2007).

The panoptic, the modular, the performative and the productive

Once consumption has been dematerialized and made available as coded, standardized, and manipulable data, there are no more limits to the construction of difference, to classification, and to social sorting (Lyon 2001). The electronic customer list has come to visualize consumption, or rather consumer life phenomena, at the microscopic level, leading to a reorganization of the gaze of marketers and the way marketing practice configures and controls spaces of operation, production, and economic valorization.

Inscribing consumption: the Foucauldian perspective

Over the years, analyses of surveillance and theories about marketing practice have approached commercial and corporate surveillance of consumers in a variety of ways. In one of the earliest pieces to detail consumer surveillance, Oscar Gandy relied on Foucault's use of the panopticon to describe corporate practices. Gandy's text, *The Panoptic Sort*, hinges on mechanisms that act as "a kind of high-tech, cybernetic triage through which individuals and groups of people are being sorted according to their presumed economic or political value" (Gandy 1993, pp. 1–2). Consumer data are gathered and analyzed in ways that serve to dictate corporate offerings to various categories and segmentations of clientele. This panoptic sort draws upon past behavioral data to selectively narrow and limit options presented for future transactions, all of which is based on the identification, classification, and assessments of current and potential consumers. This rationalized marketing sorts out high quality economic targets and discards others in its discriminatory wake, existing, Gandy argues, as an antidemocratic system of control.

These concerns are further expanded upon in a later work in which he indicates part of the issue is that the illusion of choice is maintained against a backdrop of a continually narrowing range of options (Gandy 1996). Gandy shows how the relationship between buyers and sellers has largely become an impersonal transaction controlled by cybernetic intelligence. It uses an increasingly automated collection of personal information to presumably allow for a form of personalized marketing (ibid.). In a later piece co-authored with Anthony Danna, Gandy's perspective is applied to a key element in Customer Relationship Management, viewing data mining as a social sorting process. Danna and Gandy (2002) suggest that the social consequences of data mining practices have consistently been ignored, and that these practices may exclude classes of consumers from full participation in the market place (see also Zwick and Dholakia

2004b). They appeal to corporations to examine the potential cost these discriminatory techniques will have upon certain social groups and suggest that corporations need to consider more than the bottom line when engaging in marketing based on data mining practices.

We can thus argue that marketers consider databases as central agents in the expansion and refinement of demand control strategies based upon the observation of consumer populations. From this vantage, Mark Poster (1995) draws on Foucault to proclaim that customer databases are operating like a market super-Panopticon. Poster approaches databases and profiling machines from a poststructuralist perspective, calling attention to the *discursive effects* of databases in Foucault's sense. Foucault's understanding of discourse and language is of special relevance to Poster's study of customer databases because of the relation Foucault draws between language and the constitution of the subject. Mainly drawing from his genealogical work, Foucault develops a theory of the human being as a subject that is configured, and given cultural significance, in the first instance through language. From this perspective, a new language introduces a new way of constituting cultural objects (such as human beings and customers) and social relationships (such as markets). As Poster argues, computerized databases constitute such a new language altering the way individuals are constituted as subjects and mobilized as identities.

Importantly, a new language changes not only how the consumer subject is constituted but how this subject can be known. From a Foucauldian perspective, the creation of knowledge is the creation of cultural objects and both are functions of linguistic power. In other words, new systems of representation – be it writing, statistics, or digital information flows – articulate newly ordered spaces of knowledge in which the object of representation (e.g. the consumer) becomes observable, measurable, quantifiable, in short, *known*. The customer subject emerges as a known and knowable object upon which the marketer can now act strategically.

Modulating consumption: the Deleuzian perspective

We must keep in mind, however, that the panoptic power of the customer database is not based on the inscription of digital identities, although this process is intrinsic to the recoding of consumer behavior into discrete and virtual "data doubles" (Haggerty and Ericson 2000). Rather, as Elmer (2004, p. 41) observed, thereby extending Poster's focus on the linguistic construction and multiplication of data subjects, the panopticism imposed on consumers by information machines is much more concerned with the collection of personal information to discriminate individuals into previously categorized consumer lifestyle groups or profiles. Hence Elmer puts the spotlight of contemporary market surveillance strategies on the reproductive (or cybernetic) aspect of electronic panopticism. Because data subjects are "always already discriminated and profiled" (ibid.,p. 41), the contemporary mode of data collection and analysis must be understood as a dynamic process where existing surveillance and profiling systems and personal information continuously inform each other with each new interaction between the system and consumers.

This mutability of both the surveillance apparatus and the data subject requires a departure from Foucault's architectural and optical conception of disciplinary power focused on enclosures, molds, and fixed castings (Deleuze 1992). Elmer (2004) proposes instead to draw on Deleuze's (1992) notion of modulation to more successfully conceptualize how control and power operate in and through technological surveillance networks of contemporary information economies. This retheorization of disciplinary forms of control as modular represents more than a semantic move because modulation stresses *simulation, movement, and flexibility* rather than surveillance, enclosure, and documentation. To be sure, simulation relies on surveillance but only as far as documentation, expression, and spatial organization of collective life mapped within the electronic Panopticon provide the foundation for circular, recursive, and self-reproducing strategies of power aimed at forecasting future positions "in an increasingly dispersed and automated infoscape" (Elmer 2004, p. 44).

Elmer's theorization of electronic surveillance and database technologies contrasts fruitfully with the influential Foucauldian analyses associated with the work of Poster (1990) and Gandy (1993, 1996) because it recognizes the need for database marketers to actively solicit consumers for information, hence conceptualizing the building, mining, updating and distributing of the customer database as a systematic modulation of the consumer population (Zwick and Denegri-Knott 2009). Therefore, we can say that in addition to consumer discipline, surveillance technologies perform a complex set of cultural, social and economic functions characteristic of the post-Fordist mode of production, such as the spatial and temporal configuration of markets, the provision of various forms of knowledge, and the flexible connection of consumption and production. It is a departure from Foucault's architectural and optical conception of disciplinary power focused on enclosures, molds and fixed castings (Deleuze 1992). Rather, drawing on Deleuze's notion of modulation better conceptualizes how control and power operate in and through techno-logical surveillance networks of contemporary information economies.

The shift in focus towards modulation and mechanisms of simulation still relies upon panoptic practices, as these provide the foundation for circular, recursive, and self-reproducing strategies of power aimed at forecasting future positions "in an increasingly dispersed and automated infoscape" (Elmer 2004, p. 44, see also Bogard 1996). It draws attention to the reflexive generation and projection onto consumers of market desires through the continuous configuration and reconfiguration of relationships and associations between always changing data points (see Bogard 1996). Recognizing the feedback loop between data collection and analysis and the solicitation of consumers with more inquiries or with 'more of the same' products, this theory of information as modulation better explains how panoptic profiling machines operate to control and homogenize everyday consumption behavior in advanced capitalist societies.

The emphasis on modulation and its co-existence with panoptic framings of surveillance maintain a particular focus on structures of power, ones in which corporate informational power far outmeasures those afforded to consumers themselves. Clearly, as Juliet Schor (2007, p. 28) points out, it is striking that the growing power of corporations in terms of consumer information "has been accompanied by the dominance of an ideology that posits the reverse – that the consumer is king and the corporation is at his or her mercy." However, though corporations are clearly not at the mercy of consumers, they are reliant upon their continued collaboration in the development of current and new market offerings and strategies. Consumers often happily participate in the personal information economy and the surveillance practices that underpin it. They are keen to reap the rewards and benefits found in the "fun" of capitalism (see Thrift 2005). Consumer surveillance therefore must maintain this enticement and continue the reflexive practices described in the mechanisms of modulation and simulation, but this engagement with consumers suggests a surveillance that is performative and highly contingent.

Performing consumption: the contingency perspective

Though the panoptic and the modular framing of consumer surveillance have largely dominated the discourse of marketing practices as forms of surveillance, an additional view sees marketing as having a role in performing and formatting the phenomena it purports to describe (see Callon 1998; Cochoy 1998). This more contingent view of marketing practice and its accompanying conceptions of segments, life-styles, life-stages, desires, and so on are seen as producing consumers as tangible entities that can be understood and engaged (see Araujo 2007). Rather than focusing analysis on marketing, consumption or production practices, this perspective attends to all activities that constitute markets (see Kjellberg and Helgesson 2006). The focus demonstrates how contemporary practices of marketing are less of an enclosure but as part of processes that configure markets: arranging and ordering marketing practices in particular ways. It is inclusive of all actors within the apparatus of marketing, from the marketers themselves to the techniques and technologies that serve to translate particular conceptions of consumption into practice.

With this as a starting point, consumption is more fluid and is interconnected with the systems and practices in which it is constituted. For instance, 'simple' choices made by consumers are embedded in systems of market devices which are deployed by marketers to shape and guide consumptions. These market devices, from measurements to architecture to pricing to analysts, and so on, encompass the "material and discursive assemblages that intervene in the construction [and performance] of markets" (Muniesa *et al.* 2007, p. 2). When marketers develop segmentations as a market device, they do so not as something that "unveils segments already there" (Kjellberg and Helgesson 2007, p. 144). Rather this is an ontological process – an attempt to *produce* segments.

Performance-oriented understanding of markets and 'market making' are about particular enactments of the social that serve to produce both consumption and production through sets of material and discursive practices (see Law and Urry 2004). This demonstrates how the notion of "consumers" is fully susceptible to change, and how the process of assembling and reassembling consumers is continual and indicative of a dynamic and iterative form of surveillance. As corporations attempt to meet the needs of consumers that they "know" and define, they co-construct consumers through the ascription of needs, desires, socio-economic status and more. While this determines corporate offerings and marketing strategies, a performative perspective captures the flexibility of "soft capitalism" to respond to and engage with consumers in ways unanticipated by marketers (see Thrift 2005). It allows for a continual adjustment and evolution of market practices and consumption in ways that are best described as forms of collaborative surveillance (see Pridmore forthcoming).

Manufacturing consumption: the flexible production perspective

A radicalization of the performative model of database marketing requires a shift in focus from the analysis from the technology's panoptic operations to their productive function within post-Fordist regimes of flexible production (Zwick and Denegri-Knott 2009). Drawing on recent re-theorizations of Marx and typically placed under the headings of information capitalism, post-industrial capitalism, and post-Fordism, conceptualizations of the database as a technology of production foregrounds the expanded *economic significance* and *strategic possibilities* of market panopticism in the age of information. Instead of a homogenization of consumption, this approach suggests that the economic strength of panoptic surveillance rests on its ability to detect, valorize, and monetize *consumer heterogeneity*. In particular the database's capacity to spot creative, non-conforming, and unexpected forms of consumer life has not been lost to marketing executives who understand very well that future market opportunities often evolve out of the social and cultural innovations generated in uncontrolled and undisciplined spaces of consumer culture. Indeed, given the need of a growth-dependent, contemporary capitalism to reproduce at an ever-increasing pace new consumer needs, too much consumer homogeneity would constitute a serious challenge for contemporary strategies of accumulation.

Analyses of customer databases from a Deleuzian *and* a Foucauldian perspective are united in their failure to notice that with progressing automation of data collection, analysis, and organization, surveillance-based simulation no longer represents merely a means to discipline or control consumption but *to manufacture consumers*. While this is evident in performative models that serve to configure consumption, it is limited in the critical concerns of market power. Manufacturing consumers, in other words, demonstrates the modular simulation of the consumer population as a site for direct economic value creation while the ambition to control consumers, still important to modern marketers, is increasingly giving way to the possibility of manufacturing customers as valuable information commodities themselves in need of marketing.

Theorizing profiling technologies such as the customer database in terms of production requires a reevaluation of whence these technologies derive their unique power. In particular, while the dominant focus in the current literature on surveillance and simulation technologies has been on spatial politics of consumption "that attempts to locate and map the circulation of information, data, power and control" (Elmer 2004, p. 46), a "production of customers" perspective proposes that the importance of the database for the exploitation of markets and the creation of economic value is derived less from its panoptic capacity than from its ability to produce modular (flexible and reflexive) consumer simulations in little or, better even, *real time*. The recent gains in speed and flexibility of production processes, premised on the unfolding of increasingly powerful data-mining techniques, are hence central for an understanding of how the customer database leads to a reversal of Fordist organizations of production and consumption.

It is important to recall that databases are made up of symbols in data fields. They embody a specific mode of representing the world, what Bolter (2001) calls "numeric inscription." As Poster (1995) puts it, "one does not eat them, handle them, or kick them, at least one hopes not. Databases are configurations of language; the theoretical stance that engages them must take at least this ontological fact into account." Poster, of course, has in mind a post-structuralist analysis when he points to the database as a repository for linguistic power. Yet theories approaching information and communication technologies via an analysis of the digitalization of production also benefit from this insight because it speaks directly to some of the fundamental features of a post-Fordist economic system: the nature of the technological base, the nature of commodities, and time–space compression.

All of these framings of marketing as consumer surveillance are overlapping and interpenetrating (see also Pridmore and Lyon 2011). The panoptic, modular, performative and productive perspectives on consumer surveillance are intended to be illustrative of marketing in practice and demonstrative of the crucial concerns and issues raised by this increasingly pervasive and important form of surveillance. Combined, these perspectives allow us to look at database marketing today as an activity of concrete economic production. But in addition to a strategic analysis of database marketing in post-Fordist capitalism, we should voice clear concerns regarding the systematic exclusion and forms of cumulative disadvantage (Gandy 2009), issues with respect to exploitation of consumers (Andrejevic 2010) and the lack of corporate transparency (see e.g., Pridmore 2010). The trajectories of research in the area of consumer surveillance suggest that these issues and others are only going to become increasingly pertinent given the importance of digital systems of information in the consumption of that which is 'produced' and the production of those who 'consume.' This is particularly true as the lines between the two continue to become irreversibly blurred, giving rise to the notions of 'prosumption' and 'prosumers.'

Prosumption, as Ritzer (2009) reminds us, is neither historically new nor specific to twenty-first-century information capitalism. Rather, by recognizing that production and consumption are two sides of the same coin, prosumption is intrinsic to all forms of capitalist and non-capitalist economies. Nevertheless, recent social transformations such as the emergence of the internet and, in particular, its user-generated version commonly called Web 2.0, have moved practices of prosumption, the constant blurring of the production–consumption line, to the center of economic value creation. It is, thus, this blurring that is most concerning to many social theorists today, including surveillance researchers. In a context in which the internet has become a pervasive tool, mechanism, and medium, the cybernetic and dynamic blurring of boundaries between consumers and producers serves only to heighten social, ethical, political and economic concerns. It should not be surprising, then, that interest in investigating the rise of Web 2.0 and its effects on database marketing and consumer surveillance has increased in the fields of critical media and marketing studies (e.g. Fuchs 2010; Manzerolle and Smeltzer 2010). This work aims to illustrate how contemporary marketing practice relies increasingly upon consumer surveillance practices to scrutinize even the most mundane consumption practices for informational value – a value that can be re-appropriated for the purposes of contemporary capitalism.

Conclusion

Under a post-Fordist regime of capitalist accumulation the flexible production of information has come to dominate value creation and surplus extraction strategies. The ability of the customer database to capture what Arvidsson (2004, p. 467) calls "the communicative action of life in all its walks" effectively turns increasingly complex and mutable consumer practices into value. In other words, ubiquitous information gathering transforms what has previously been seen as a practical marketing problem in need of more control – the mobile, creative, and unpredictable consumer – into a productive and economically important force. Hence, we need to conceive of customer databases as the factories of the twenty-first century because they seamlessly fuse communication and production into a highly flexible manufacturing system that is perfectly adapted to the rules of post-Fordist regimes of accumulation and control.

But we do not limit the analysis of customer database marketing to its strategic use. Rather, we intend this chapter to be a critical starting point from which to launch further investigations of database marketing as consumer surveillance in practice. In many respects such a research project inevitably takes central aim at modern marketing practice more generally or, perhaps more accurately, its performative and productive character. Performing marketing is a complex undertaking that involves a number of actors and tasks, including, centrally, market research. If we are to understand database-driven marketing practice through/as consumer surveillance, we need to study how marketing actually 'works' as a material commercial and social practice, that is, investigate to what effect marketing operates in various social, cultural, and economic contexts; what kind of devices marketers employ and to what end; what kind of knowledge it concerns and, hence, what kind of power it produces; and, finally, what kind of subjectivities on both sides of the exchange relationship it encourages and configures (see Zwick and Cayla 2011). This chapter may provide a rough blueprint to open up this new intellectual space for scholars interested in drawing new links between digital marketing, the digital consumer, and commercial surveillance practices.

References

Andrejevic, M.B. (2010) "Surveillance and Alienation in the Online Economy," *Surveillance and Society*, 8: 278–87.

Applbaum, K. (2011) "Broadening the Marketing Concept: Service to Humanity, or Privatization of the Public Good?" in D. Zwick and J. Cayla (eds), *Inside Marketing: Practices, Ideologies, Devices*, Oxford: Oxford University Press, pp. 269–98.

Araujo, L. (2007) "Markets, Market-making and Marketing," *Marketing Theory*, 7: 211–26.

Arvidsson, A. (2004) "On the 'Pre-History of the Panoptic Sort': Mobility in Market Research," *Surveillance and Society*, 1: 456–74.

Barber, B.R. (2007) *Consumed: How Markets Corrupt Children, Infantilize Adults, and Swallow Citizens Whole*, New York: W.W. Norton and Co.

Bartels, R. (1988) *The History of Marketing Thought*, Columbus, OH: Publishing Horizons, Inc.

Bauman, Z. (2001) "Consuming Life," *Journal of Consumer Culture*, 1: 9–29.

Beniger, J. R. (1986) *The Control Revolution: Technological and Economic Origins of the Information Society*, Cambridge, MA: Harvard University Press.

Bogard, W. (1996) *The Simulation of Surveillance: Hypercontrol in Telematic Societies*, Cambridge: Cambridge University Press.

Bolter, J. D. (2001) *Writing Space: Computers, Hypertext, and the Remediation of Print*, Mahwah, NJ: Lawrence Erlbaum Associates.

Burrows, R. and Gane, N. (2006) "Geodemographics, Software and Class," *Sociology*, 40: 793–812.

Callon, M. (1998) *The Laws of the Markets*, Oxford: Blackwell.

Cochoy, F. (1998) "Another Discipline for the Market Economy: Marketing as a Performative Knowledge and Know-How for Capitalism," in M. Callon (ed.), *The Laws of the Markets*, Oxford: Blackwell, pp. 194–221.

Danna, A. and Gandy, O.H. (2002) "All That Glitters Is Not Gold: Digging Beneath the Surface of Data Mining," *Journal of Business Ethics*, 40: 373–86.

D'Aveni, R.A. and Gunther, R. (1994) *Hypercompetition: Managing the Dynamics of Strategic Maneuvering*, New York: Maxwell Macmillan.

Deleuze, G. (1992) "Postscript on the Societies of Control," *October*, 59: 3–7.

Drucker, P.F. (1950) *The New Society: The Anatomy of the Industrial Order*, New York: Harper.

——(1954) *The Practice of Management*, New York: Harper.

Elmer, G. (2004) *Profiling Machines: Mapping the Personal Information Economy*, Cambridge, MA: MIT Press.

Featherstone, M. (1991) *Consumer Culture and Postmodernism*, London: Sage.

Frank, T. (2000) *One Market Under God: Extreme Capitalism, Market Populism and the End of Economic Democracy*, New York: Doubleday.

Fuchs, C. (2010) "Web 2.0, Prosumption, and Surveillance," *Surveillance and Society*, 8: 288–309.

Gandy, O.H. (1993) *The Panoptic Sort: A Political Economy of Personal Information*, Boulder, CO: Westview Press.

——(1996) "Coming to Terms with the Panoptic Sort," in D. Lyon and E. Zureik (eds), *Computers, Surveillance, and Privacy*, Minneapolis: University of Minnesota Press, pp. 132–55.

——(2009) *Coming to Terms with Chance: Engaging Rational Discrimination and Cumulative Disadvantage*, Farnham: Ashgate.

Gramsci, A. (1971) *Selections from the Prison Notebooks*, New York: International Publishers.

Haggerty, K.D. and Ericson, R.V. (2000) "The Surveillant Assemblage," *British Journal of Sociology*, 51: 605–22.

Hardt, M. and Negri, A. (2000) *Empire*, Cambridge, MA: Harvard University Press.

Holbrook, M.B. and Hulbert, J.M. (2002) "Elegy on the Death of Marketing," *European Journal of Marketing*, 36: 706–32.

Kjellberg, H. and Helgesson, C. (2006) "Multiple Versions of Markets: Multiplicity and Performativity in Market Practice," *Industrial Marketing Management*, 35: 839–55.

——(2007) "On the Nature of Markets and Their Practices," *Marketing Theory*, 7: 137–62.

Kotler, P. (1972) "A Generic Concept of Marketing," *Journal of Marketing*, 36: 46–54.

Kotler, P. and Levy, S. (1969) "Broadening the Concept of Marketing," *Journal of Marketing*, 33: 10–15.

Law, J. and Urry, J. (2004) "Enacting the Social," *Economy and Society*, 33: 390–410.

Levy, S.J. (1959) "Symbols for Sale," *Harvard Business Review*, July–August: 117–24.

Leyshon, A. and Thrift, N. (1999) "Lists Come Alive: Electronic Systems of Knowledge and the Rise of Credit-scoring in Retail Banking," *Economy and Society*, 28: 434–66.

Lyon, D. (2001) *Surveillance Society: Monitoring Everyday Life*, Buckingham: Open University Press.

Manzerolle, V. and Smeltzer, S. (2010) "Consumer Databases, Neoliberalism, and the Commercial Mediation of Identity: A Medium Theory Analysis," *Surveillance and Society*, 8: 323–37.

Miller, P. and Rose, N. (1997) "Mobilizing the Consumer," *Theory, Culture & Society*, 14: 1–36.

Muniesa, F., Millo, Y. and Callon, M. (2007) "An Introduction to Market Devices," *Sociological Review*, 55: 1–12.

Poon, M. (2007) "Scorecards as Devices for Consumer Credit: The Case of Fair, Isaac and Company Incorporated," in M. Callon, Y. Millo, and F. Muniesa (eds), *Market Devices*, Malden, MA: Blackwell, pp. 284–306.

Poster, M. (1990) *The Mode of Information*, Chicago: The University of Chicago Press.

——(1995) "Databases as Discourse, or Electronic Interpellations," in P. Heelas, S. Lash and P. Morris (eds) *Detraditionalization*, Oxford: Blackwell, pp. 277–93.

Pridmore, J.H. (2010) "Reflexive Marketing: The Cultural Circuit of Loyalty Programs," *Identity in the Information Society*, 3: 565–81.

——(forthcoming) "Collaborative Surveillance: Configuring Contemporary Marketing Practice," in L. Snider and K. Ball (eds), *The Political Economy of Surveillance*, Routledge.

Pridmore, J. and Lyon, D. (2011) "Marketing as Surveillance: Assembling Consumers as Brands," in D. Zwick and J. Cayla (eds), *Inside Marketing: Practices, Ideologies, Devices*, Oxford: Oxford University Press, pp. 115–36.

Ritzer, G. (2009) "Correcting an Historical Error," Keynote Address, Conference on Prosumption, Frankfurt, Germany, March.

Ritzer, G. and Juergenson, N. (2010) "Production, Consumption, Prosumption: The Nature of Capitalism in the Age of the Digital 'Prosumer'," *Journal of Consumer Culture*, 10: 13–36.

Rose, N. (1997) *Inventing Ourselves: Psychology, Power, and Personhood*, Cambridge, MA: Cambridge University Press.

Schor, J.B. (2007) "In Defense of Consumer Critique: Revisiting the Consumption Debates of the Twentieth Century," *The Annals of the American Academy of Political and Social Science*, 611: 16–30.

Thrift, N.J. (2005) *Knowing Capitalism*, London: Sage.

Weiss, M.J. (1988) *The Clustering of America*, New York: Harper and Row.

Zwick, D. and Cayla, J. (eds) (2011) *Inside Marketing: Practices, Ideologies, Devices*, Oxford: Oxford University Press.

Zwick, D. and Denegri-Knott, J. (2009) "Manufacturing Customers: The Database as New Means of Production," *Journal of Consumer Culture*, 9: 221–47.

Zwick, D. and Dholakia, N. (2004a) "Consumer Subjectivity in the Age of Internet: The Radical Concept of Marketing Control through Customer Relationship Management," *Information and Organization*, 14: 211–36.

——(2004b) "Whose Identity Is It Anyway? Consumer Representation in the Age of Database Marketing," *Journal of Macromarketing*, 24: 31–43.

11

RESEARCHING CHILDREN IN A DIGITAL AGE

Theoretical perspectives and observations from the field

Vebjørg Tingstad

Keywords

chat rooms, children, methodology, research

Researching new technologies, such as the Internet and mobile phones, or the new and diverse ways in which traditional media such as television are used together with online and mobile communication devices, calls for a discussion of methodology. The routinization and convergence of new media through increased use and access to a variety of new technologies which themselves 'melt together' raise a series of new questions and require a rethinking of how to represent the audience, in this case, when the audience happens to be children. This chapter draws on empirical studies in a Norwegian context, done from 1999 to 2005.

As this field of study has changed and expanded, this also applies to researchers from a variety of disciplines. As Lievrouw and Livingstone argue:

> [T]he inextricably linked phenomena of information, communication and mediation are no longer the sole province of communication research and a few related specialties; today they are the focus of intense interest and study across the social sciences, arts and humanities.
>
> *(2006, p. 3)*

As these authors analyse the current situation, one consequence is that multidisciplinary approaches are essential in new media studies, posing both theoretical and methodological challenges and bringing hitherto distinct fields into conjunction (and sometimes confrontation) with each other. Communication and media research is at a conceptual and disciplinary crossroads, they argue, and it is therefore time to rethink such phenomena as the role of 'the masses' in technology and society, bearing in mind the distinction between mediation today and mediation in the past. Children who have access to new media are often the early adopters and the most frequent ones in terms of use. Some 94 per cent of Norwegian children in the age range of 9–15 used, for instance, the Internet on their home computer on an average day in 2010. 'To stay current, our research methods must follow,' as Kozinets argues in his book, *Netnography* (2010).

Adopting the perspective of the social studies of childhood (James *et al.* 1998; Qvortrup *et al.* 1994), this chapter discusses methodology in relation to three main issues. First, it refers to a contemporary academic discourse in media research, which is criticized for treating this question in a relatively superficial way. Second, the question of representing children in general is treated, referring to changing constructions of children and childhood in contemporary societies. Finally, the chapter describes and discusses the methodology related to two empirical examples based on ethnographically inspired studies of children's online and SMS activities. The main argument in this chapter is that the dynamics and convergence of new media technologies and changing constructions and perceptions of children and childhood must continually be reflected in the academic discourse of child and childhood research methodology, not so much to provide a 'true picture of reality', but rather to encourage methodological creativity and maintain epistemological standards.

Methodology: a 'stepchild' in media research?

One contemporary argument in media research is that questions of methodology and methods have been treated in quite different ways by disciplines in the social sciences compared to those rooted in the humanities (Fetveit 2000; Höijer 2005). Methodology refers here to a meta-perspective on methods, for example, theoretical discussions of the methods to be used, while 'methods' refers to procedures and how to do research (Höijer 2005). As Höijer argues, both of these levels are equally important.

While methodological issues have assumed a central position in the social sciences, generating an extensive body of literature, the humanities, Fetveit (2000) argues, have a tendency to regard such issues as peripheral, as something which is found implicitly in their research traditions, and, in this respect, as nothing to worry about. In addition, some researchers contend that too much time has been wasted on the quantitative/qualitative debate. Even if this latter debate is often perceived as out-dated today, it continues to be an influential part of contemporary academic discourse. The authors of the book *Researching Audiences*, for instance, refer to what they call 'methodological apartheid', arguing against being methodologically narrow-minded by giving either quantitative or qualitative methods paradigmatic status as the one and only way to obtain new insights. Based on what they say is a true story, they refer to a conference where a researcher, having presented a qualitative project, received the following comment from the discussant: 'So altogether, it was an interesting paper, and I am sure you could easily do a quantitative thing to it if you wanted to publish it' (Schrøder *et al.* 2003: 11). The most obvious problem with such kinds of utterances is the question of academic hegemony or, as Höijer (2005) puts it, 'positivistic fundamentalism'. What the utterance above also illustrates is, first, a superficial way of handling the question of methodology, and, second, the lack of recognition and awareness of the many ways of approaching a research question and the challenges involved in representing people in research. In using a narrow methodological approach based on tradition and hegemonic paradigms, the risk is that questions about methodology and methods are only rarely discussed in the wider research community and therefore left to individual exploration or 'recycling' without thorough or shared reflections.

This claim does not imply that research on such topics as the media and childhood is static or that it suffers from a severe lack of updated knowledge and reflections on methods. On the contrary, many researchers often dedicate relatively extensive amounts of time to inform the reader what kinds of procedures were used (before we come to the 'real' thing, that is, the substantive results). However, a critical review or a meta-perspective on these procedures is often conspicuous by its absence. Research procedures and approaches always express ways of understanding. For instance, researching 'children's culture' is not a neutral activity (Mitchell and Reid-Walsh 2002). A discussion of methods and procedures will therefore never be about techniques alone, but also about how the researcher perceives the phenomenon that is studied, the role and position of the researcher, and how the researcher positions the research object (or subject).

Ontology and epistemology

Some researchers argue that it is not the methods, but rather the ontology and epistemology that are the determinants of good social science (Alvesson and Sköldberg [1994] 2000), i.e., how one understands and interprets the world and how one chooses to obtain knowledge about it. Thus the researcher's position in relation to these issues is crucial to the entire research process, from defining the topic, the research problem and the methods, to the analyses, interpretations and conclusions of the study. How the researcher approaches an interview situation reflects in different ways the researcher's view of knowledge production, including the kind of status those interviewed should be given.

Kvale and Brinkmann (2009) use two different metaphors which describe various concepts of knowledge formation in an interview. The *miner* metaphor sees knowledge as buried metal and the interviewer as a miner who is unearthing the valuable metal. In this perspective, knowledge is waiting in the subjects' interior to be uncovered. The alternative is the *traveller* metaphor, in which the interviewer is understood as a traveller on a journey, using *method* in the original Greek meaning of the word: a route leading to a destination. Knowledge is the narratives that emerge from the journey and that are explored and interpreted by the interviewer. The inter-viewer 'walks along with the local inhabitants, asking questions and encouraging them to tell their own stories of their lived world' (Kvale and Brinkmann 2009, p. 48). Qualitative research has developed a tradition of focusing on the encounter between the researcher and the infor-mant. This includes an emphasis on reflexivity, in which the researcher is seen not only as an observer, but also as part of the social world that is being studied (Hammersley and Atkinson 1987). This requires reflections about issues such as the researcher's age, gender and social and cultural background. A part of this reflexivity is to be aware of and take into account the power relations that are implicit in a research context. In the end, the researcher is the person who decides what and how to interpret the informants and their accounts, and how to present them. This is particularly important when studying children, because they are generally dependent on adults and have fewer possibilities to protect themselves than most adults have. Solberg (1988, 1996) asks for more descriptions of the process through which researchers obtain their results. This should be written on 'the blank pages' in the methodology chapters, she argues.

An essential question then is whether doing child research is essentially different from researching adults. Solberg (1991) warns against the researcher becoming ethnocentric by occupying adult roles, thus having difficulties in establishing the necessary distance to reflect on adult ways of conceptualizing children and childhood. She recommends a certain ignorance of age, encouraging researchers to redirect their attention to the situational context within which children act. Solberg argues in favour of concentrating more on the children's doing, i.e., children's actions, and moving away from their being, i.e., how they 'are'. To do this, it is crucial to employ some of their various 'languages' which are indeed strongly linked to new communication devices.

Power and agency

However, what does it mean when we say that we are listening to children (Clark *et al.* 2005)? What does it imply if we intend to 'visit' child informants in new environments like chat sites and via email or SMS? In child research, as in research with adults, a crucial question is: What are the underlying assumptions of the positions of the informants, both as participants in the research and in society in general? What do we mean when we say that we 'adopt the children's perspective'? How do we represent children in research? How do we maintain a reflexive distance from our private and professional biases and adult-centrism? Regardless of age, it is important to establish a good relationship and enter into an explicit agreement about the research (Solberg 1991). Questions must be relevant, and the researcher must be able to listen and show interest. Independent of methods, what should characterize research with children is the absence of adult evaluation or supervision. Motivation, contract and a common focus are key words for conducting a child interview (Andenæs 1991). Reflections on these issues are crucial from the very moment the researcher plans the project to the final phase. In an approach where the aim is, following Kjørholt (1991) and Gullestad (1991), to emphasize the child's world and regard society and culture from the position of children, the researcher has to take into account the power relations between the researcher and the informant. Woodhead and Faulkner (2000) recommend acknowledging the complexities that lie beneath the simple appeal to listen to the child. It is the researchers, not the children, who generally control the research process, they argue.

In the next sections, two empirical examples are presented, in which I as a researcher established my position in two different ways.

Online and SMS data: two empirical examples

This section discusses how new communication technologies may supplement more traditional methods such as observation and interviews. It deals with some of the characteristics of these technologies, but also reflects on challenges by using the data that have emerged from them. It is important to emphasize that these methods are supplementary to, not intended to replace other, more traditional methods, such as observation and interviews. But as online and mobile devices are becoming increasingly familiar to children, they may offer a valuable methodological opportunity. In fact, empirical material from real-time observation of children's online communication and 'staying in touch' on mobile phones may supply the researcher with data about everyday practices that are difficult, perhaps impossible to obtain in other ways, for example, by interviewing or by conducting a questionnaire. An email or a text message may function as a way of establishing a routine or flow of information, maintaining contact between researcher and informants, and offering an easy, accessible and relaxed way of communication. My main argument for choosing this method is that this kind of material can provide rich and sensitizing sets of data and thus modify my interpretations (cf. Spiggle 1994).

In my research with children, I have used technologies such as online observations, emailing and text messaging as additional resources and tools (Tingstad 2003, 2006, 2007, 2012, in press). The first study was about children's chat on the Internet, while the second focused on the TV reality show, *Pop Idol*. Both projects were inspired by media ethnography, as they focus on children as media users rather than the medium itself (Drotner 1993). This does not imply that I have not used traditional ethnographic methods, strictly speaking, such as long-term field studies conducted within the settings of the participants. However, defining ethnography, not as a method, but rather as a combination of different methods and a theory about the research process (Skeggs 1995, p. 192), means that we can relate it to certain major issues, such as, for instance, the researcher in participation and observation, focusing on experience and practice and treating participants as a microcosm of wider structural processes. I interpret these examples as a research approach which recognizes children as subjects and thus meets my theoretical requirement of positioning children neither as powerless and exploited victims of the new media, nor as empowered superheroes (Cook 2004), but as a mixed group of agents within a particular cultural and social structure in society.

Mixed methods

I have combined these methods with other approaches, such as child interviews, both in groups and individually, as well as interviews with parents and using written texts with children's descriptions of the series to a fictitious person who does not know what *Pop Idol* is. The individual interview with children was structured on the model of a 'life form interview', where the focus is on actions that are anchored in time and space and are repeated as a pattern (Haavind 1987; Andenæs 1991). Thus there is a series of social occasions as the child guides the researcher through the house or flat, recalling what has happened during the day. Children may tell and reflect on what happened at home yesterday. Time and space are the organizing principles of the interview. This method is useful in order to obtain concrete and recently experienced actions. What happened? Who participated? How were the interactions? By comparing and reflecting on how things usually are, the interview encourages nuances, complexities and patterns from daily life to emerge.

Study 1: Chat room communication

How children's play in cyberspace (the world of computers tied together in networks) resembles or differs from what is traditionally perceived as play, is a relatively un-mapped field. This study explored two Norwegian chat rooms and how a small sample of children used them. Empirically, the study is based on 14 hours observation of the chat rooms www.popit.no and www.sol.no, in addition to observations, interviews and email communication with eight children aged 11–14 years over a period of two years (Tingstad 2003). In the following transcript we see that complaints about school, and the joys and expectations of the summer holiday, are shared with chat partners:

SUMMER_GIRL: now we don't need to go to school for 3 months
ZOMBIE: and stupid teachers
ZONEBABE: no 12 months
ZONEBABE: hehhe
SUMMER_GIRL: I have 1 year left in barneskolen[1]
SØTJENTE_15:   you have to worry about ungdomsskolen
SØTJENTE_15:   hate school teachers ungdomsskolen
SØTJENTE_15:   ungdomsskolen is awful!!!!
LARS: why do you think ungdomsskolen is awful?
SØTJENTE_15:   because it is
SØTJENTE_15:   I'm soooo glad that I've just finished ungdomsskolen
ZONEBABE: fantastic to have summer holiday. JIPPPPPIIIIIII !!!
ZONEBABE: GOING TO GET A BOY FRIEND DURING THE SUMMER HOLIDAY
DE 2 KULEGUTTENE: is school a dump everybody hates key 111 for yes, key 1234 for no
ZONEBABE: 1234
JORDAN: 1234
DE 2 KULEGUTTENE: is everybody strange school is a dump

These kinds of online encounters have the character of many comings and goings. People can physically leave the computer and still 'be' in a chat room as long as the site is logged on. Thus, a chat room is transient and continuously changing in terms of participants, content and atmosphere. As a result of these characteristics, chat communication often appears to be chaotic, as if on the verge of a breakdown.

What are the difficulties involved in collecting and interpreting this type of empirical material? What distinguishes it from other types of talk or qualitative data, such as classroom observations or an interview, for example? How can we obtain reliable data from this chaos? My approach was to develop tools to make sure that the methodological principles, described above, were taken into account.

First of all, it is obvious that the material represents something particular, which poses a challenge in terms of both data collection and analysis. Chat is typically multiple communication between many individuals simultaneously (Holm Sørensen 2001). Chat is characterized by chaos and transience, regarding both participation and content. As chat is a more or less continuous activity, it is not an easy matter to determine its starting point or obtain a reasonable under-standing of what, in Goffman's terms (1959), the *definition of the situation* is. The communication exists before the researcher arrives, and it continues after the observation is finished. A chat room might be silent for minutes, maybe hours, in terms of utterances until there is a sudden and huge burst of activity, probably when something entertaining or provoking has happened or when a special person has entered the room. This might be someone somebody has waited for or someone who, for some reason, is popular (or unpopular) in the room. The researcher also faces problems when participants make references to things which happened the day before, for example, when accusing each other of changing nicknames. The problem is that the researcher was not present on that special occasion because it happened yesterday. The researcher has to make use of bits and pieces of talk, without knowing in what contexts the communication has been made. Another question is which excerpts of the communication to choose. Karlsson (1997) suggests focusing on one 'chatter' or one topic. However, Karlsson's study was a linguistic one that focused on the details of language. My focus was on the actual interactions between the participants, of which the continuous changes are an essential part. Thus, it was difficult with my chosen focus, even impossible and undesirable, to single out one topic in the way Karlsson suggests and define it as *the* topic of study. Sveningsson (2001) found that most of the conversations in her material were dyads that went on independently from the other dyads in the chat room, a situation that increases the number of simultaneous conversations that the researcher has to keep track of. She chose to isolate conversations in order to avoid distraction from other ongoing conversations. In my material there were obvious dyads, too, but most often the messages were intertwined and difficult to isolate. Since the main aim was to explore the social aspects, I decided to use *content* as my organizing principle.

A second challenge with this kind of material is that there are usually no clearly defined roles between the participants in the sense that one asks the questions and another gives the answers. Messages are literally spoken in a helter-skelter manner, where they are thrown out into the virtual world. Thus, compared to classroom interactions or interviews, chat is not limited to a dialogue where one paragraph is usually to be understood as an answer to a previous question. On the contrary, the contextual structures that normally help a researcher are absent. In a chat room, several parallel dialogues on various topics may be going on or there may be no obvious dialogues at all, just rows of letters, numbers or signs. As the messages are viewed on the screen in the same order as they are keyed, an answer to a question may emerge a long time (or many messages) after the question was asked. Thus, this kind of communication also differs from more traditional forms of conversation in terms of *turn-taking*, i.e. conversations in which one person talks and another listens, and with some system for determining when one person's turn is over and the next person's turn begins (cf. Tannen 1982). Chat communication challenges the observer who must make sense of a flow of parallel and potential dialogues, of simple utterances and statements, often performed in an apparently secret language, at a fast pace and with no regard to traditional systems of turn-taking.

A third aspect that must be taken into account is the uncertainty concerning the identity of the actors and actresses. Who is actually writing the messages? Even if a participant presents a credible identity, such as *boy 14, interested in football and games*, this self-presentation can be questioned. Most of the participants know that this ambiguity is a part of the chat context, whatever their motivations for entering the room might be. Nicknames may be changed: someone who was *coolboy* yesterday might be *hotbabe* today. Consequently, as Holm Sørensen (2001) also argues, chat enables participants to play, pretend and present themselves using shifting identities, thus questioning traditional images of face-to-face interactions, which are often perceived as more authentic than interactions without physical closeness. Finally, in classroom observations or an interview, the talking partners can observe both verbal and non-verbal communication, and adapt questions and answers on behalf of what happens in the context. In a chat room, facial and bodily gestures are absent and therefore cannot be used to derive information: the participants have to rely solely on the written words and other language forms, which must replace emotional expressions and body language. Chat resembles multiply voiced, loud talk in a dark and crowded room. Observing and analysing this talk are more likely to be compared with ethnographic fieldwork in a foreign culture, where meaning has to emerge from and rely on what the researcher is able to observe and make sense of. I will return to this issue when discussing the second empirical example.

Ethical considerations

After having chosen the chat room to observe, a question was how to establish a research situation which takes into account the ethical principles and avoids influencing the activity in the room. What kind of procedure was the most useful for finding authentic information about the phenomenon in the actual chat rooms? I approach this question by describing my strategy for observation and the level of my own participation. A fundamental question was to choose how to observe. One issue was whether I should enter the chat rooms openly as a researcher, as a participant with a common nickname or pretend to be a young person and thus be a hidden observer. When I tried to introduce myself as a researcher, the communication stopped. When I entered the chat room and acted as a participant, other people 'talked' to me and expected me to answer. I therefore usually chose a position with a hidden identity which means that I entered the room with an ordinary nickname and remained 'silent'. This position might, from an ethical perspective, be questioned, even if this is recommended in the methodological literature (Patton 1990). Paccagnella (1997) recommends hidden observation to avoid the observer influencing the situation. My main arguments for choosing this approach lie in the fact that this was what I evaluated as the best possible way to study the phenomenon without disturbing it. Another argument is that this kind of communication actually goes on in a public space. I was one of the crowd. Chat rooms of this type are open and accessible to anyone. Everybody has a nickname, and pretending is a part of the convention. Therefore, it is likely that many of the participants are aware of the room as a public space. Those who want to chat privately, i.e. by creating a sub-room within the chat room, can withdraw from the public room. This chat habit, which continuously emerges in questions like 'anybody who wants to chat privately?' is supposed to increase the chatters' images of the differences between various levels of publicity. However, even if the chat context is a public space and perceived as such, people have a right to be protected from being compromised. In order to protect participants who write personal details, it was an issue not to include private information, for example, real names, addresses, email addresses or phone numbers.

Study 2: *Pop Idol*

The global television concept *Pop Idol* is a singing contest that has been successfully broadcast in different national versions in a number of countries since its creation in 2001. People can vote for their favourite acts with their mobile phones, ask questions on the Internet, participate in online discussions, etc. Audiences can take part in a television quiz, win a day with the contestants, watch previous episodes on web-TV, make their own video to send in, send *Idol* cards electronically to friends, and buy accessories for their mobile phones. This strategy supplements traditional media such as television, newspapers and magazines with the Internet and mobile phones.

This chapter focuses on two series of the Norwegian *Idol* (2003 and 2005), collected with a range of methodological approaches that are comprised of qualitative data. The interview data stem from focus groups of girls and boys between 11 and 13 years old. They consist of recordings of children's conversations while watching a video clip from the programme, their individual descriptions of the series written to a fictitious person who does not know anything about the *Idol* show and individual interviews with the children in their home environment. Also included in the data are text messages (SMS) and emails. The sample consists of 21 children, who were recruited from the same level at two different schools in an urban environment. Given the goal of establishing smaller groups of well-informed children (Patton 1990), I deliberately recruited those who actively said they wanted to participate in the inquiry. This approach yielded a group composed of 71 per cent girls. This way of obtaining data made it easier for children to initiate spontaneous and close responses to the researcher in the immediate context of their television viewing or purchasing of *Idol* items on the Internet, such as accessories for the mobile phone, CDs, hats and cups. One example of a spontaneous message about purchasing an item is the following email from one girl: 'By the way, I bought a picture of Alejandro today, for my mobile … I paid 20 kroner … but can afford that. Hug from Vicky.' Whenever I received such messages, I would continue the exchange by answering and asking questions. This email gave me an opportunity to talk further about the economic aspects of the television concept in terms of, for instance, the children's interest in using money on *Idol* items and whether it was appropriate or 'cool' among the friends to use money on such things. Another issue which emerged from a text message was the question of gender. The following messages between Ingrid and me raise this question for the first time, and I could refer to this issue in the interview later on.

INGRID: Hi! Today I hope that Jorun wins. But anyway, it will be good if a girl wins Idol.
VEBJØRG: Thanks for the message. Can you plz tell me after the show what you think about the judges? Preferably by email.
INGRID: I'm in the hut, so I don't have the internet, but you'll get a message.
VEBJØRG: Excellent!
[TWO HOURS LATER]
INGRID: Tonight I think Tone was the best one. The judges were too kind.

When I received such messages, I knew that the children had something they wanted to say, or that they just wanted to be responsible informants. In any case, I was able to continue the exchange by answering them and asking questions: a method that requires the researcher to be attentive and available on Friday evenings when the programme was shown. The following email, which discusses the judges' changing 'attitudes' throughout the programme series, illustrates the sort of information given in the immediate context of watching the programme, such as questioning the credibility of the series:

> The judges have changed a lot. Tor in particular! In the beginning he was very strict, but now he does not say so many negative things … The other judges have also changed! But sometimes they become too kind too. The hosts are also a bit different … they are more emotional and talk nonsense. In the very beginning, they were very personal and they often cried when others cried after being evicted from Idol. They don't do this any more.

This kind of online and SMS data also poses some fundamental questions, which I will discuss in the next section.

Representing children

In her discussion of the methods, politics and ethics of representation in online ethnography, Markham (2005) argues that Internet-based technologies change the research scenario, altering interactions and their possible outcomes. As referred to in the discussion of chat communication, one interesting question is whether one can trust the information received by these technologies. Informants in Markham's and my own studies support the suggestion that offline information is not necessarily always more trustworthy than information given online. Some girls in my study say that they often feel more 'themselves' when they 'are' in a chat room compared to when they are in their school playground. In Markham's study, one informant says something similar: 'In cyberspace, one dwells in language, and through language, I exist as myself in language online … it feels more like being me than I sometimes feel offline' (ibid., p. 793). By using new technologies as an additional source to give information, children do not control the research process any more so than by using other methods. However, children have the potential to use their expertise to inform, calibrate and extend research projects with rich and unexpected (and easily accessible) data in the different stages of the research process. Seeing the results of the research process as a co-constructed product, contrasting the first study where the researcher was a hidden observer, may lead to a more open-minded approach to both the research situation and the informants. In this way, informants are given opportunities to introduce new subjects (Sveningsson 2001), as well as to facilitate the collection of rich empirical data, new perspectives and interpretations. Kvale and Brinkmann (2009) argue that issues of verification do not belong to a separate stage of the investigation but should rather be addressed throughout the entire research process. One question is whether it is possible to *generalize* results from a small sample to a larger one. According to these authors, the positivist quest for universal knowledge, as well as the cult of the individually unique, should be replaced by an emphasis on the heterogeneity and contextuality of knowledge, with a shift from generalization to contextualization.

Conclusion

This chapter has raised a number of questions, crucially, how to position children and childhood in the social structure and represent children in research. What stories do we tell? How do we obtain the stories? How do we analyse the context, in which we establish the research site in order to offer our informants optimal conditions to become the experts we want them to be? As illustrated in this chapter, I personally pursued quite different approaches. Being relatively passive in one context whereas co-producing the empirical material together with my informants in the other was simply a consequence of a contextual analysis and a reflection on what probably would be the best way to let the children's voices to be heard. A contextual analysis is here not to be confused with a recipe of any kind. A concluding appeal is that we as researchers, whether the topic is digital media or other topics, must continue to ask and discuss questions about methods and methodology thoroughly and across disciplines, as well as within the different research communities to which we belong.

Note

1 Barneskolen (6–12 years) and Ungdomsskolen (13–15 years) in Norway roughly correspond to primary and secondary school in the UK.

Further reading

Buckingham, D. and Tingstad, V. (eds) (2010) *Childhood and Consumer Culture*, London: Palgrave Macmillan. [Anthology with contributions that offer empirical data and challenging critical perspectives on children's engagement with consumer culture.]

Masten, D.L. (2003) 'Digital Ethnography: The Next Wave in Understanding the Consumer Experience', *Design Management Journal*, 3(2): 75–81. [From a marketing perspective, a reflection about using new technologies for rethinking ethnographic principles, methodologies and analyses.]

Schultz, T. (2000) 'Mass Media and the Concept of Interactivity: An Exploratory Study of Online Forums and Reader Email', *Media, Culture & Society*, 22(2): 205–21. [Calls for preserving mass media as institutions of integration and public discourse combined with a new culture of interaction.]

Skaar, H., Buckingham, D. and Tingstad, V. (2011) 'Marketing on the Internet: A New Educational Challenge', *MERJ: The Media Educational Research Journal*, 1(2): 13–30. [Discusses the implications of new marketing strategies towards children on the Internet.]

Tingstad, V. (2008) 'Barn, dataspill og digital kompetanse. Perspektiver og forskningsutfordringer', in *Nordicom Information* Den kompetenta gamern. En konferens om ny mediekompetens, 2(08): 47–57. [An overview of research about children, computer games and digital competence.]

References

Alvesson, M. and Sköldberg, K. ([1994] 2000) *Reflexive Methodology: New Vistas for Qualitative Research*, London: Sage.

Andenæs, A. (1991) 'Livsformsintervju med 4–5 åringer: Motivasjon, kontrakt og felles fokus', *Barn* 4: 20–9.

Clark, A., Kjørholt, A.T. and Moss, P. (eds) (2005) *Beyond Listening: Children's Perspectives on Early Childhood*, Bristol: The Policy Press.

Cook, D.T. (2004) *The Commodification of Childhood: The Children's Clothing Industry and the Rise of the Child Consumer*, Durham, NC: Duke University Press.

Drotner, K. (1993) 'Media Ethnography: An Other Story?', in U. Carlsson (ed.), *Nordisk Forskning om Kvinnor och Medier*, Göteborg: Nordicom, pp. 25–40.

Fetveit, A. (2000) 'Den trojanske hest: om metodebegrepets marginalisering av humanistisk medieforsking', *Norsk Medietidsskrift*, 2: 5–27.

Goffman, E. (1959) *The Presentation of Self in Everyday Life*, New York: Doubleday.

Gullestad, M. (1991) 'Hva legger jeg i begrepet Barneperspektiv?', *Barn*, 1: 63–5.

Haavind, H. (1987) *Liten og stor: kvinners levekår og livsløp*, Oslo: Universitetsforlaget.

Hammersley, M. and Atkinson, P. (1987) *Feltmetodikk: grunnlaget for feltarbeid og feltforskning*, Oslo: Gyldendal Norsk Forlag.

Höijer, B. (2005) 'Håller metodkvaliteten på att utarmas?', *Nordicom Information*, 27(2): 3–7.

Holm Sørensen, B. (ed.) (2001) *Chat, leg, identitet, socialitet og læring*, Copenhagen: Gads Forlag.

James, A., Jenks, C. and Prout, A. (1998) *Theorizing Childhood*, Cambridge: Polity Press.

Karlsson, A.M. (1997) 'Skrivet ungdomsspråk, finnes det? Om datorchatt och internauter', in U.B. Kotsinas, A. B. Stenström and A.M. Karlsson (eds), *Ungdomsspråk i Norden*, Stockholm: Stockholms Universitet, Institutionen för Nordiska Språk, pp. 147–59.

Kjørholt, A.T. (1991) 'Barneperspektivet: Romantiske frihetslengsler og nostalgisk søken etter en tapt barndom, eller nye erkjennelsedimensjoner?', *Barn*, 1: 66–70.

Kozinets, R.V. (2010) *Netnography: Doing Ethnographic Research Online*, London: Sage.

Kvale, S. and Brinkmann, S. (2009) *Interviews: Learning the Craft of Qualitative Research Interviewing*, London: Sage.

Lievrouw, A. and Livingstone, S. (2006) *The Handbook of New Media*, London: Sage.

Markham, A.N. (2005) 'The Methods, Politics and Ethics of Representation in Online Ethnography', in N.K. Denzin, and Y.S. Lincoln (eds), *The Sage Handbook of Qualitative Research*, London: Sage.

Mitchell, C. and Reid-Walsh, J. (2002) *Researching Children's Popular Culture: The Cultural Spaces of Childhood*, London: Routledge.

Paccagnella, L. (1997) 'Getting the Seats of Your Pants Dirty: Strategies for Ethnographic Research on Virtual Communities', *Journal of Computer-Mediated Communication*, 3(1). Available at: http://www.ascusc.org/jcmc/vol3/issue1/paccagnella.html (accessed 8 August 2003).

Patton, M.Q. (1990) *Qualitative Research and Evaluation Methods*, London: Sage.

Qvortrup, J., Bardy, M., Sgritta, G. and Wintersberger, H. (eds) (1994) *Childhood Matters: Social Theory, Practice and Politics*, Aldershot: Avebury.

Schrøder, K., Murray, C., Drotner, K. and Kline, S. (2003) *Researching Audiences*, London: Arnold.

Skeggs, B. (ed.) (1995) *Feminist Cultural Theory: Process and Production*, Manchester: Manchester University Press.

Solberg, A. (1988) 'Metodekapitlenes blanke sider', in B. Dale, M. Jones, and W. Martinussen (eds), *Metode på tvers: Samfunnsvitenskapelige forskningsstrategier som kombinerer metoder og analysenivåer*, Trondheim: Tapir, pp. 85–112.

——(1991) 'Er det annerledes å intervjue barn enn voksne?', *Barn*, 4: 31–6.

——(1996) 'The Challenge in Child Research: From "Being" to "Doing"', in J. Brannen and M. O'Brien (eds), *Children in Families: Research and Policy*, London: Falmer Press, pp. 53–65.

Spiggle, S. (1994) 'Analysis and Interpretation of Qualitative Data in Consumer Research', *Journal of Consumer Research*, 21(3): 491–503.

Sveningsson, M. (2001) 'Creating a Sense of Community: Experiences from a Swedish Web Chat', doctoral dissertation, Linköping University.

Tannen, D. (1982) 'Ethnic Style in Male-Female Conversation', in J.J. Gumperz (ed.), *Language and Social Identity*, Cambridge: Cambridge University Press, pp. 217–31.

Tingstad, V. (2003) 'Children's Chat on the Net: A Study of Children's Social Encounters in Two Norwegian Chat Rooms', doctoral dissertation, NTNU, Trondheim.

——(2006) *Barndom under lupen: Å vokse opp i en foranderlig mediekultur*, Oslo: Cappelen Akademisk Forlag.

——(2007) '"Now It's Up to You!", Children Consuming Commercial Television', *Society and Business Review*, 2(1): 15–36.

——(2010) 'From Chat in Public to Networked Publics: Children's Online Communication and Changing Technologies', *Digital kompetanse: Nordic Journal of Digital Literacy*, 5(1): 22–37.

——(2012) 'Watching Without Voting: Norwegian Child Audiences Questioning *Idol*'s Ethos', in K. Zwaan and J. de Bruin (eds), *Adapting Idols: Authenticity, Identity and Performance in a Global Television Format* (in press).

Woodhead, M. and Faulkner, D. (2000) 'Subjects, Objects or Participants? Dilemmas of Psychological Research with Children', in P. Christensen, and A. James (eds), *Research with Children: Perspectives and Practices*, London: Falmer Press, pp. 9–35.

12

NEW FORMS OF DIGITAL MARKETING RESEARCH

Elanor Colleoni

Keywords

data mining, sentimental analysis, social media, text mining

Introduction

The development of the information society has been characterized by the proliferation of collaborative highly socialized networks (Arvidsson forthcoming). These collaborative networks have transformed traditional marketing (Cova *et al.* 2007; Kozinets *et al.* 2010). Traditionally, purchasing practices have been conceived of as a private act taking place in isolation. To this end, marketing has studied the consumer's preferences in relation to historical and demographic individual consumption patterns. Nowadays, social and emotional structures in which individuals are embedded are increasingly thought to influence consumers' attitudes and behavior.

The implementation and use of ranking and review systems are perhaps the initial best-known embodiment of the new perspective. Amazon.com is the most illustrative example. It is the world's largest online retailer that has based its success on the trust generated by its customer product reviews.

The diffusion of social media sites has further enhanced this process. More and more people gain knowledge about a brand or a product by searching how it is valued and perceived in their social network. Once people have created their own opinion, they share their views and feelings with others and "the subjective truth turns into a collective truth" (Pekka 2010, p. 46). This, in particular, applies to social media platforms, such as Facebook and Twitter that are specifically designed for sharing emotions, feelings and opinions among the users.

Consequently, it has become increasingly important for marketers to acquire the ability to monitor and predict consumer social and emotional behavior in online communities. This has given rise to the emerging marketing discipline of Social Media Analytics, which uses a new set of data mining techniques in order to capture online social and behavioral dynamics. Data mining is the process of automated discovery of hidden patterns and relationships in large datasets. Algorithms, such as real-time trend detection, link prediction and opinion mining, have been deliberately developed to systematically monitor consumer behavior in online social contexts (Pang and Lee 2008).

Several authors have warned about the insidious perils of commercial exploitation of participatory cultures, which contributes to a selective access to knowledge and experiences (Thrift 2005; Lash 2007; Zwick and Dholakia 2008; Beer 2009). As pointed out by Beer (2009), in order to investigate the potential consequences of new digital marketing practices, there is a need for a better understanding of how these algorithms work and their underlying assumptions.

In this chapter, I touch upon data mining techniques for digital marketing research that "mine" three consumers' attributes in the social web: relational (i.e., collaborative and social filtering systems); conversational (i.e., topic trend and novelty detection); and emotional (i.e., automated sentiment analysis).

The aim of the chapter is to provide a clear description of the evolution of data mining techniques for the marketing analysis of the social web. The chapter is organized as follows: in the first section, I describe the research techniques based on the analysis of the relational links in the social web. In this section, I investigate different interpretations of the concept of influence and the implications for digital marketing research. In the second section, I describe the techniques for automated topic extraction and discourse novelty detection and their implications for marketing predictions. In the third section, I focus on opinion mining through using sentiment analysis, a fairly new method that is gaining increasing attention in marketing research. In the final section I discuss the possible future developments and implications of the social web for marketing research.

Studying the relational networks of the digital consumer

The social web can be conceived of as a set of social relations that connect people together over the web, as opposed to the informational web that links websites (Gerlitz and Helmond 2011). The resulting social network is a graph of relationships and interactions within a group of individuals. "Communication that flows in these decentralized networks is referred as 'viral' because ideas, opinions and influence spread like an epidemic though the network *via* word-of-mouth" (Hansen *et al.* 2011). The concept of "viral marketing" is not new in marketing theories and refers to "the potential of these unstructured social relations like gossip, word of mouth, and lately online sociality to function as a medium of marketing communication" (ibid., p. 2).

With the diffusion of social networks, word-of-mouth communication has acquired even more relevance as a communication and marketing tool. As pointed out by Edelman (2010), "earned media," what consumers are saying about a product or brand, has replaced "owned media," what companies pay to say in advertising, as the most strategically important marketing channel.

However, even if the relevance of these online networks in influencing consumer decisions is now recognized by general marketing theories, it is still not clear how ideas and opinions spread in society, and how to efficiently harness this viral potential for commercial purposes. Different theoretical conceptions of influence lead to radically diverse results.

Influence has long been studied in the fields of marketing and communication (Katz and Lazarsfeldt 1955; Godin 2000; Ahonen and Moore 2005; Leskovec *et al.* 2006). Studying influence patterns can help to better understand why certain trends or innovations are adopted while others are not. The concept of influence refers to the capacity of causing an effect in indirect or intangible ways (Cha *et al.* 2010). Influence theories have traditionally seen society as driven by a minority of individuals, who are particularly "influential" in spreading information, i.e., opinion leaders (Katz and Lazarsfeldt 1955; Rogers 1962; Gladwell 2000).

Early on, Tarde (1903) identified two main processes of human behavior that drive the diffusion of ideas in society: imitation and influence. The concept of imitation refers to the human tendency to create homogeneous groups and to affiliate with individuals who are similar in certain attributes, such as beliefs, education, social status and the like, i.e., homophily (Granovetter 1973). Information flow in homophilous networks is perceived as highly trusted because it is based on similarities; these similarities lead to attitude or behavior change.

Following Tarde's distinction, it is possible to identify two different approaches to the analysis of relational networks in the social web: influencer marketing and recommender systems. The main difference between these approaches relies on the idea of consumer preferences. Influence marketing assumes that consumer preferences change over time and can be easily influenced. Recommender systems assume that consumer choices are stable and based on group similarity and imitation, therefore it is possible to identify similar patterns of behavior among peers based on their relational network.

Influencer marketing targets a minority of users, called *influentials*, assuming that they are able to impact on public opinion. Using a two-step flow of communication model, Katz and Lazarsfeld (1955) first suggested that "by targeting these *influentials* in the network, one may achieve a large-scale chain-reaction of influence driven by word-of-mouth, with very small marketing cost" (Cha *et al.* 2010).

Opinion leaders or *influentials* are connectors or "hubs" that are positioned strategically in a social network, and therefore, "act as intermediates between the mass-media and the majority of the society" (Watts and Dodds 2007, p. 441). This idea has gained renewed interest with Malcolm Gladwell's bestseller, *The Tipping Point* (2000). In his popular book, Gladwell provides a number of examples of the power of word of mouth, such as the spread of fashion trends and the precipitous drop in the New York City crime rate after 1990:

> Ahoren (2005) coined the term Alpha user to emphasize that it is now possible to technically isolate the focal point members of any viral campaign thanks to new information technologies, such as mobile phone networks. For example, Yahoo has long been identifying and paying *influencers* to share their opinions in online social network.

However, the influencer marketing approach has been criticized mainly because it underestimates both the interpersonal relationship among ordinary users and the readiness of a society to adopt an innovation (Cha *et al.* 2010, p. 2). In contrast to the idea of opinion leaders, some researchers have argued that the opinion of peers is more relevant in decision-making (Domingos and Richardson 2001; Watts and Dodds 2007).

Watts and Dodds (2007) analyzed the extent to which opinion leaders are important to the formation of public opinion. They found that a long chain of information diffusion is driven "not by *influentials* but by a critical mass of easily influenced individuals" (ibid., p. 441). Watts argued that "when influence or information is propagated *via* word-of-mouth, most of what differentiates successful from unsuccessful diffusion is related to the structural properties of the word-of-mouth network as a whole, not a property of a small number of special individuals" (Watts 2007, p. 202). In this sense, Watts uses the term *accidental influentials*. Domingos and Richardson (2001) introduced the concept of "customer network value" to account for the expected profit from other customers that the customer may influence to buy. Indeed, instead of treating each customer as making a buying decision independently of all other customers, they explicitly assume that "a person's decision to buy a product is often strongly affected by her friends, acquaintances, business partners" (ibid., p. 2). This modern view of influence has led to marketing strategies such as collaborative filtering and social recommender systems (Cha *et al.* 2010).

Collaborative and social filtering

In everyday life, people rely on recommendations from their peers through spoken words, reference letters, news reports, reviews, and so on. Recommender systems assist and augment this natural social process to help people sift through information by applying a filter based on affinity between users and items (i.e., homophily, Huang *et al.* 2008). In so doing, these techniques automate word of mouth by providing a type of mass customization over mass market strategies (Zhang and Krishnamurthy 2004). Suggestions for books on Amazon.com or personal advertising on Facebook are examples of this customized marketing.

Adomavicius and Tuzhilin (2005) classify recommender systems into three main categories: content-based; collaborative; and hybrid approaches. Content-based recommendations are based on similarity between items purchased by the user in the past.

Collaborative filtering recommends items to a user based on information gleaned from all the other users. Collaborative filtering exploits similarities in behavior among users to determine user's choices. The most common approach is nearest-neighbor collaborative filtering or memory-based approach (Herlocker *et al.* 2002), in which a user's rating for an item is predicted as a weighted combination of the most similar users' ratings (i.e., neighbors).

However, other techniques, such as Bayesian Networks, clustering models, or latent semantic analysis are also used. These models assume that the similarity observed is explained by a latent common structure (Melville *et al.* 2009). Hybrid methods combine both content-based and collaborative recommendations.

Research in marketing has mainly focused on personalized promotions, communication, products and services experience. Zhang and Krishnamurthy (2004) have shown how to dynamically customize price promotions in online stores based on consumer behavior. Ansari and Mela (2003) developed a model to personalize the content of email and show that this procedure can attract more customers to the websites. Based on a learning algorithm, Ariely *et al.* (2004) developed a content-based recommendation agent that improves the quality of its recommendations dynamically, based on consumers' buying history. Häubl and Murray (2003) have shown that electronic recommendation agents are able to influence users' opinions and that the effect may persist beyond the initial shopping experience and into subsequent choice settings in which no recommendation agent is available.

Although better than general mass strategies marketing, most of the human-item relations used to generate recommendation in the collaborative filtering approach are not based on "real" social relations and interactions (Huang *et al.* 2008). Only recently, with the diffusion of social media sites has the user's network of friends and people of interest become accessible.

Various works have shown that friend-based recommendations are more trusted than collaborative filtering (Golbeck 2006; Groh and Ehmig 2007; He and Chu 2010; Guy *et al.* 2010). He and Chu (2009) developed a probabilistic model to make personalized recommendations using information in social networks, including user preferences, items' general acceptance, and influence from social friends. They extracted data from a real online social network, and found that friends have a tendency to select the same items and give similar ratings.

According to Walsh (2006), social network sites, including Facebook and MySpace, are driving an increasing volume of traffic to retail sites (i.e., 6 percent of retail traffic in 2006), and are thus becoming a starting point for users interested in e-commerce. Facebook is leading this transformation (Kharif 2010). Facebook was the first to introduce social plugins, generating social recommendations based on personal social networks using traditional referrals.

However, the growing trend in digital marketing concerns the integration of information across different commercial websites, the so-called social commerce (Kim and Srivastava 2007), such as the embodiment of referrals that show Facebook friends' information on external retailers websites, such as Amazon or Levi's, for instance, the use of external referrals for automatic birthday gift suggestions for Facebook friends based on their stated profile preferences.

In a similar fashion, the most promising development is represented by the possibility of incorporating the "like" Facebook function. The embedded "like button" allows the consumer to "like" not only a particular website, but particular products. This information is then shown to the consumer network, both on Facebook and on the website. In the same way, a consumer who is logged into Facebook while visiting, for example, Levi's website, can receive personalized suggestions based on the products "liked" by his friends. As pointed out by Arvidsson (forthcoming), the introduction of social buttons represents a necessary objectification of users' webs of social relations and affective attachments around informational objects, that allows a corporate or a brand to "extract and valorize" the social process for marketing purposes.

Studying the conversational networks of the digital consumer

The spread of social computing services that enable people to easily communicate and effectively share information has dramatically increased the volume of the conversations on brands and products. The amount and richness of these conversations determine large-scale patterns of discussions and allow emerging areas to be revealed (Melville *et al.* 2009).

The possibility of learning the present and future trends from these conversations is of crucial importance for online marketing professionals and opinion tracking companies, as trends record the voice of the public and point to topics that capture the public's attention (Glance *et al.* 2005).

The appropriate approach to understanding actual and emerging topics is to use text mining techniques for automated topic detection (ibid.). "Sifting through vast collections of unstructured or semi-structured data beyond the reach of data mining tools, text mining tracks information sources, links isolated concepts in distant documents, maps relationships between activities, and helps answer questions" (Fan *et al.* 2006: 77). Topic detection refers to the automatic process of discovering new, previously unknown information, by extracting information from a large amount of different unstructured textual resources (Hearst 1999).

This technique is different from a simple tracking system based on keywords or memes. In this case, a topic is defined by the most frequently occurring word. Yahoo offers a free topic-tracking tool that allows a company to track news on itself based on keywords and to be notified when news that matches the keywords become available (Fan *et al.* 2006).

Leskovec *et al.* (2009) have developed an algorithm for monitoring social media to spot emerging memes. An internet meme is a distinct cultural unit that propagates online and can be traced, enabling early discovery of new trends. However, "a challenge with the meme-tracking method is the fact that the vast majority of online memes attracts little attention before fading into obscurity" (Colbaugh and Glass 2011, p. 15). Colbaugh and Glass have created a system that predicts memes that will reach a nontrivial fraction of the population, enabling discovery of *significant topics*. Although the ability to predict which memes will spread is very important for viral marketing campaigns or for crisis communication management, these techniques only track a specific unit of information.

In text mining, the goal is to extract higher-level concepts that describe the conversation regardless of the specific words used and, therefore, to identify "collection of posts expressing cohesive patterns of discussion" (Melville *et al.* 2009, p. 3).

Topic modeling is a concept-linkage algorithm that identifies relationships between sets of documents by identifying their shared concepts. Rather than looking at each word isolated from the others, topic modeling algorithms, such as Latent semantic analysis and Latent Dirichlet

Allocation, map all the documents and the terms within them as a whole into a "concept" space and compare them in this space. These algorithms assume that words that are close in meaning will occur close together in text. For instance, "using a search engine search for *sand*, documents are returned which do not contain the search term *sand* but contains terms like *beach*" (Wilk 2008). Therefore, the model trained on such a corpus has identified a latent relationship, *sand* is semantically close to *beach*. These terms share the concept space and will be classified under the same topic.

The clustering process can be also dynamic, allowing the emergence of novel topics from the real-time stream of discussion. The number of commercial enterprises that base their business model on mining business intelligence from these sources is growing fast (Mishne 2007). Perhaps the best-known company is Nielsen BuzzMetrics. This company retrieves and analyzes information from weblogs and social media using topic, sentiment and social network analysis. Nielsen provides marketers with general information about their customers, such as types of user complaints (Mishne 2007). Rickman and Cosenza (2007) have also examined the potential of using novelty topic detection for the fashion industry in general and street fashion trending in particular.

However, the most promising development of topic modeling regards buzz prediction using time-series models to forecast future topics (Melville *et al.* 2009). Mittermayer (2004) has developed accurate forecasts of intraday stock prices based on information from press releases through the application of text preprocessing techniques.

Gruhl *et al.* (2005) studied the predictive potential of online chatter in book sales by analyzing around half a million sales rank values for 2340 books over a period of four months, and correlating postings in blogs, media, and web pages. They compare bursts of blog posts referring to a given book with spikes in sales according to Amazon, and find that "a sudden increase in blog mentions is a potential predictor of a spike in sales rank" (ibid., p. 5). They found that, even though sales rank motion might be difficult to predict in general, the algorithm can use online postings to successfully predict spikes in sales rank.

Studying the affective networks of the digital consumer

The relevance of consumers' opinions and feelings is well known in business. Marketing and investment strategists have long scanned newspapers, industry publications and the like to investigate how the public and consumers feel about a particular company, brand or product (Ognuva 2010).

The rise of blogs and social networks has fueled the internet of personal opinion: reviews, recommendations and other forms of online expression. The reputation that circulates in these networks has been proved to affect consumer behavior. Using a controlled field experiment, Resnick *et al.* (2006) studied the impact of positive reviews on eBay online retailers. They created two identities for the same seller: a positive high-reputation, established eBay dealer sold matched pairs of lots under his regular identity and under new seller identities. They found that there was a significant difference in buyers' willingness to pay the selling price in favor of the high-reputation profile. Consequently, understanding not only when a brand is being talked about, but also if positively or negatively, has become of crucial importance to brand management and marketing.

Sentiment analysis has been developed in order to process this subjective information effectively (Pang and Lee 2008). Sentiment analysis refers to the process of categorization of unstructured human-authored documents "based on their affective orientation, meaning the emotional attitude of the person expressing the opinion" (Mølgaard and Szewczyk 2010, p. 1). The term sentiment analysis first appeared in 2001 in a paper by Das and Chen aimed at analyzing small investor sentiments from stock message boards. The most common approach to text classification is using a lexicon. This approach requires "the creation of a knowledge base-lexicon of affective words, with additional data characterizing emotional states and relations" (ibid., p. 2). The occurrence of these affective words within texts predicts their polarity or valence (Thelwall *et al.* 2011). The most general sentiment classification allows the polarity classification of a text by distinguishing between positive and negative sentiments. More elaborated classifications include the identification of the strength of a sentiment. In this case, sentiment expressions are classified according to their valence, i.e., how positive or negative the expressed sentiment is, and the arousal, i.e., the level of the emotional excitation (Hansen *et al.* 2011). Several word lists have been labeled with emotional valence, e.g., ANEW, WordNet-Affect, OpinionFinder. However, several issues regarding the employment of automated opinion mining still need to be addressed properly, such as the use of irony and sarcasm, idioms, negation forms, obscene words and slang.

The great potential of sentiment analysis is that it allows subjective perceptions, like the experience of or affective ties that consumers can construct with a brand, to acquire an objective existence as observable reputation trends (Colleoni *et al.* 2011). Therefore, social media marketing experts actively monitor the consumers' discussion across websites for reactions to their products. This allows them to quickly assess public reaction to their communication, and consequently, to adapt marketing campaigns and events. Nowadays, more and more companies, as well as investors and marketers are scanning the Web, extracting brand and product opinion trends by aggregating subjective opinions (Ognuva 2010). Several authors have analyzed online news groups and blogs, automatically collecting people's opinions about target products to obtain the reputations of those products (Morinaga *et al.* 2002; Gamon *et al.* 2005; Ziegler and Skubacz 2006). Jansen *et al.* (2009) first investigated Twitter as a form of electronic word of mouth (eWOM) for sharing consumer opinions concerning brands. The aim of the research was to investigate the possible effect of microblogging via eWOM on brand knowledge and brand relationship. They found evidence that social media are often used to share information about brand experiences: nearly 20 percent contained some expression of brand sentiments. They also found that the brand sentiment is subject to strong variations over time.

Besides reputation management, sentiment analysis has also been used to perform trend prediction in sales or other relevant data. Several studies have shown that consumer opinions in digital media are better predictors of consumer choices than traditional market indicators.

Applying sentiment analysis, Mishne and Glance (2006) have shown that both the volume of discussions and the temporal patterns of sentiments about a movie in weblogs can successfully predict its sales. They also found that posts carrying positive comments posted shortly before the movie release are more powerful in predicting the movie success than the general sentiment around a movie over time.

Gilbert and Karahalios (2010) estimated information about future stock market prices based on the analysis of the emotions expressed in blogs. Based on over 20 million posts made on the site LiveJournal, they found that increases in expressions of anxiety predict downward pressure on the SandP 500 index. Asur and Huberman (2010) have shown that a simple model built from the rate at which tweets are created about particular topics, and the sentiment expressed about a movie extracted from Twitter, can outperform market-based indicators in predicting box-office movie revenue.

Conclusion

The development of the social web and the emergence of collaborative networks have both strengthened the relevance of the creation of relations between companies and consumers and rendered them more vexing. Thanks to information technologies and Web 2.0, consumers are now constantly embedded in social and affective streams of information where companies represent only one of the myriad of voices. In these decentralized networks, consumers' opinion about a brand or a product is built more independently in relation to companies.

But the more the perception of a brand or a product is built within these communication networks, the more concepts like community, social recognition and affective proximity are becoming central to online marketing. This has implied a shift from the traditional conception of marketing as the art of persuading consumers, using conventional communication strategies or more sophisticated customer relationship management practices, to a more compelling idea as the ability to predict consumers' behavior.

The *pluralization* of information sources, the giant volume of consumer-generated-content and the consumer decision-making process increasingly relying on these social and affective networks are all reasons for that shift. As a consequence, new data mining techniques have rapidly been developed for marketing purposes. These new techniques have focused on the prediction of consumers' behavior based on their social, affective and conversational relationships. The evolution of these techniques points now to the creation of an algorithm that can integrate these three aspects of the consumer's social life. A few examples of this tendency are the development of algorithms to predict potential connections among consumers based on common interest in a network (i.e., link prediction) or the integration of discourse and emotion into a personalized marketing campaign to consumers who share opinions and interests (i.e., predicting topics and sentiment simultaneously).

The development of digital marketing research based on large databases seems to point in two main directions: (1) towards the creation of a "radical transparency" (Boyd 2010) in order to build trust relations of information exchange and advice; and (2) towards a fully personalized and "portable" extraction of the "collective knowledge" embedded in personal social networks.

Radical transparency is an expression of an attempt to preserve the basic mechanism underlying people's willingness to share and to follow others' advice: trust. Trust, in the form of formal reputation, enables more fluid and secure (i.e., controlled) exchanges of information and advice among users. It is indeed of vital importance for marketers and social media companies to control the reliability of the data produced. This also includes anti-spam techniques and anti-fraud systems. A well-known example of this pressure is Google's attempt to force users to provide real data while subscribing to Google+. However, this tendency is not related to profiling issues, but to the need of this data-driven industry to establish an objectified measure of reputation and trust to strengthen the opinion-sharing mechanisms, and in so doing, to protect their core business.

The improvement of techniques that enable recommendations based simultaneously on social, affective and relational features of consumer social networks and show the consumer "what your friends or relatives or parents would do in the same situation" in commercial websites is the other dominant interest.

Further reading

Asur, S. and Huberman, B. (2010) "Predicting the Future with Social Media," *IEEE/WIC/ACM International Conference on Web Intelligence and Intelligent Agent*, 1: 492–9.

Dellarocas, C. (2003) "The Digitization of Word of Mouth: Promise and Challenges of Online Feedback Mechanisms," *Management Science*, 49(10): 1407–24.

Domingos, P. and Richardson, M. (2001) "Mining the Network Value of Customers," in *Proceedings of SIGKDD Conference on Knowledge Discovery and Data Mining*, pp. 57–66.

Gerlitz, C. and Helmond, A. (2011) "Hit, Link and Share: Organizing the Social and the Fabric of the Web in a Like Economy," paper presented at the DMI mini-conference, 24–25 January, University of Amsterdam, Amsterdam.

Pang, B. and Lee, L. (2008) "Opinion Mining and Sentiment Analysis," *Foundations and Trends in Information Retrieval*, 2(1): 1–135.

References

Adomavicius, G. and Tuzhilin, A. (2005) "Toward the Next Generation of Recommender Systems: A Survey of the State-of-the-Art and Possible Extensions," *IEEE Transactions on Knowledge and Data Engineering*, 17(6): 734–49.

Ahonen, T. and Moore, A. (2005) *Communities Dominate Brands: Business and Marketing Challenges for the 21st Century*, London: Futuretext.

Ansari, A. and Mela, C.F. (2003) "E-customization," *Journal of Marketing Research*, 40(2): 131–45.

Ariely, D., Lynch, J. and Aparicio IV, M. (2004) "Learning by Collaborative and Individual-Based Recommendation Agents," *Journal of Consumer Psychology*, 14: 81–94.

Arvidsson, A. (forthcoming) "General Sentiment: How Value and Affect Converge in the Information Economy," *Sociological Enquiry*.

Asur, S. and Huberman, B. (2010) "Predicting the Future with Social Media," in *Proceedings of the IEEE/WIC/ACM International Conference on Web Intelligence and Intelligent Agent*, 1: 492–9.

Beer, D. (2009) "Power through the Algorithm? Participatory Web Cultures and the Technological Unconscious," *New Media and Society*, 11(6): 985–1002.

Boyd, D. (2010) *Facebook and "Radical Transparency" (A Rant)*, available at: www.zephoria.org/thoughts/archives/2010/05/14/facebook-and-radical-transparency-a-rant.html.

Cha, M., Haddadi, H., Benevenuto, F. and Gummadi, K.P. (2010) "Measuring User Influence in Twitter: The Million Follower Fallacy," in *Proceedings of the 4th International AAAI Conference on Weblogs and Social Media (ICWSM)*.

Colbaugh, R. and Glass, K. (2011) "Emerging Topic Detection for Business Intelligence via Predictive Analysis of Meme Dynamics," *Artificial Intelligence for Business Agility Spring Symposium (AAAI)*, pp. 15–24.

Colleoni, E., Arvidsson, A., Hansen, L.K. and Marchesini, A. (2011) "Measuring Corporate Reputation in Social Media Using Real-time Sentiment Analysis," paper presented at the Reputation Institute Conference, May 6–7, New Orleans.

Cova, B., Kozinets, R. and Shankar, A. (2007) *Consumer Tribes*, London: Heinemann.

Das, S.R. and Chen, M.Y. (2001) "Yahoo! for Amazon: Extracting Market Sentiment from Stock Message Boards," *Management Science*, 53(9): 1375–88.

Dellarocas, C. (2003) "The Digitization of Word of Mouth: Promise and Challenges of Online Feedback Mechanisms," *Management Science*, 49(10): 1407–24.

Domingos, P. and Richardson, M.(2001) "Mining the Network Value of Customers," in *Proceedings of SIGKDD Conference on Knowledge Discovery and Data Mining*, pp. 57–66.

Edelman, D. (2010) "Branding in the Digital Age," *Harvard Business Review*, December: 62–9.

Fan, W., Wallace, L., Rich, S. and Zhang, Z. (2006) "Tapping into the Power of Text Mining," *Communications of ACM*, 49(9): 77–83.

Gamon, M., Aue, A., Corston-Oliver, S. and Ringger, E. (2005) "Pulse: Mining Customer Opinions from Free Text," in *Proceedings of the 6th International Symposium on Intelligent Data Analysis*, vol. 3646 of Lecture Notes in Computer Science: 121–32.

Gerlitz, C. and Helmond, A. (2011) "Hit, Link and Share: Organizing the Social and the Fabric of the Web in a Like Economy," paper presented at the DMI mini-conference, 24–25 January, University of Amsterdam.

Gilbert, E. and Karahalios, K. (2010) "Widespread Worry and the Stock Market," in *Proceedings of Association for the Advancement of Artificial Intelligence*, pp. 122–9.

Gladwell, M. (2000) *The Tipping Point: How Little Things Can Make a Big Difference*, London: Little Brown.

Glance, N., Hurst, M., Nigam, K., Siegler, M., Stockton, R. and Tomokiyo, T. (2005) "Deriving Marketing Intelligence from Online Discussion," in *Proceedings of the 11th ACM International Conference on Knowledge Discovery and Data Mining*, pp. 419–24.

Godin, S. (2000) *Unleashing the Idea-Virus*, available at: http://sethgodin.typepad.com/seths_blog/files/2000Ideavirus.pdf.

Golbeck, J. (2006) "Generating Predictive Movie Recommendations from Trust in Social Networks," in *Proceedings of the 4th International Conference on Trust Management*, May, Pisa, Italy.

Granovetter, M. (1973) "The Strength of Weak Ties," *American Journal of Sociology*, 78(6): 1360–80.

Groh, G. and Ehmig, C. (2007) "Recommendations in Taste Related Domains: Collaborative Filtering vs. Social Filtering," paper presented at ACM GROUP'07, November 4–7, Sanibel Island, Florida.

Gruhl, D., Guha, R., Kumar, R., Novak, J. and Tomkins, A. (2005) "The Predictive Power of Online Chatter," in *Proceedings of the SIGKDD Conference on Knowledge Discovery and Data Mining*, pp. 78–87.

Guy, I., Zwerdling, N., Ronen, I., Carmel, D. and Uziel, E. (2010) "Social Media Recommendation Based on People and Tags," in *Proceedings of the ACM SIGIR*, pp. 194–201.

Hansen, L.K., Arvidsson, A., Nielsen, F.Å., Colleoni, E. and Etter, M. (2011) "Good News, Bad Friends: Affect and Virality in Twitter," *Communications in Computer and Information Science*, 185: 34–44.

Häubl, G. and Murray, K.B. (2003) "Preference Construction and Persistence in Digital Marketplaces: The Role of Electronic Recommendation Agents," *Journal of Consumer Psychology*, 13: 75–91.

He, J. and Chu, W.W. (2010) "A Social Network Based Recommender System," in N. Memon, J.J. Xu, D.L. Hicks and H. Chen (eds), *Data Mining for Social Network Data*, New York: Springer, pp. 47–74.

Hearst, M. (1999) "Untangling Text Data Mining," in *Proceedings of ACL'99: The 37th Annual Meeting of the Association for Computational Linguistics*, June, University of Maryland, MD, pp. 20–6.

Herlocker, J., Konstan, J. and Riedl, J.T. (2002) "Empirical Analysis of Design Choices in Neighborhood-based Collaborative Filtering Algorithms," *Information Retrieval*, 5: 287–310.

Huang, Y., Contractor, N. and Yao, Y. (2008) "CI-KNOW: Recommendation Based on Social Networks," in *Proceedings of the 9th Annual International Digital Government Research Conference*, Montreal, pp. 375–6.

Jansen, B., Zhang, M., Sobel, K. and Chowdury, A. (2009) "Twitter Power: Tweets as Electronic Word of Mouth," *Journal of the American Society for Information Science and Technology*, 60(11): 2169–88.

Katz, E. and Lazarsfeldt, P. (1955) *Personal Influence: The Part Played by People in the Flow of Mass Communication*, Glencoe, IL: The Free Press.

Keller, E. and Berry, J. (2003) *The Influentials: One American in Ten Tells the Other Nine How to Vote, Where to Eat, and What to Buy*, New York: Free Press.

Kharif, O. (2010) "Facebook Ramps Up Big E-Commerce Drive," *BusinessWeek*, December, available at: www.businessweek.com/technology/content/dec2010/tc20101217_877527.htm.

Kim, Y. and Srivastava, J. (2007) "Impact of Social Influence in E-Commerce Decision Making," paper presented at ICEC'07 Conference, August 19–22, Minneapolis, Minnesota.

Kozinets, R., De Valck, K., Wojnicki, A.C. and Wilner, S. (2010) "Networked Narratives: Understanding Word of Mouth Marketing in Online Communities," *Journal of Marketing*, 74(2): 71–89.

Lash, S. (2007) "Capitalism and Metaphysics," *Theory, Culture & Society*, 24(3): 1–26.

Leskovec, J., Adamic, L. and Huberman, B. (2006) "The Dynamics of Viral Marketing," in *Proceedings of the 7th ACM Conference on Electronic Commerce*, June 11–15, Ann Arbor, MI.

Leskovec, J., Backstrom, L. and Kleinberg, J. (2009) "Memetracking and the Dynamics of the News Cycle," in *Proceedings of 15th ACM International Conference on Knowledge Discovery and Data Mining*, Paris.

Melville, P. and Sindhwani, V. (2010) "Recommender Systems," in C. Sammut and G.I. Webb (eds), *Encyclopedia of Machine Learning*, Berlin: Springer-Verlag.

Melville, P., Sindhwani, V. and Lawrence, R. (2009) "Social Media Analytics: Channeling the Power of the Blogosphere for Marketing Insight," *Workshop on Information in Networks*, September, New York.

Mishne, G. (2007) "Applied Text Analytics for Blogs," PhD dissertation, Informatics Institute, University of Amsterdam.

Mishne, G. and Glance, N. (2006) "Predicting Movie Sales from Blogger Sentiment," *AAAI 2006 Spring Symposium on Computational Approaches to Analysing Weblogs*, March 27–29, Stanford University, CA.

Mittermayer, M. (2004) "Forecasting Intraday Stock Price Trends with Text Mining Techniques," paper presented at the 37th Hawaii International Conference on System Sciences, January 5–8, Big Island, HI.

Mølgaard, L. and Szewczyk, M. (2010) "Sentiment Analysis Using Machine Learning," Department of Informatics and Mathematical Modeling, Technical University of Denmark, unpublished results.

Morinaga, S., Yamanishi, K., Tateishi, K. and Fukushima, T. (2002) "Mining Product Reputations on the Web," in *Proceedings of the 8th ACM SIGKDD International Conference on Knowledge Discovery and Data Mining*, Edmonton, AL, pp. 341–9.

Ognuva, M. (2010) "How Companies Can Use Sentiment Analysis to Improve Their Business," available at: http://mashable.com/2010/04/19/sentiment-analysis/.

Pan, S., Sanjeev, H., Kulkarni, R. and Cuff, P.W. (2011) "Wisdom of the Crowd: Incorporating Social Influence in Recommendation Models," paper presented at IEEE International Workshop on Hot Topics in Peer-to-Peer Computing and Online Social Networking, December 7, Tainan, Taiwan.

Pang, B. and Lee, L. (2008) "Opinion Mining and Sentiment Analysis," *Foundations and Trends in Information Retrieval*, 2(1): 1–35.

Pekka, A. (2010) "Social Media, Reputation Risk and Ambient Publicity Management," *Strategy and Leadership*, 38(6): 43–9.

Resnick, P., Zeckhauser, R., Swanson, R. and Lockwood, K. (2006) "The Value of Reputation on Ebay: A Controlled Experiment," *Experimental Economics*, 9: 79–101.

Rickman, T.A. and Cosenza, R. (2007) "The Changing Digital Dynamics of Multichannel Marketing The Feasibility of the Weblog: Text Mining Approach for Fast Fashion Trending," *Journal of Fashion Marketing and Management*, 11(4): 604–21.

Rogers, E. (1962) *Diffusion of Innovations*, New York: Free Press.

Tarde, G. (1903) *The Laws of Imitation*, New York: H. Holt and Company Press.

Thelwall, M., Buckley, K. and Paltoglou, G. (2011) "Sentiment in Twitter Events," *Journal of American Society for Information Science and Technology*, 62(2): 406–18.

Thrift, N. (2005) *Knowing Capitalism*, London: Sage.

Walsh, M. (2006) "Social Networking Sites Fuel E-Commerce Traffic," December 7, available at: www.mediapost.com/publications/article/52207/social-networking-sites-fuel-e-commerce-traffic.html.

Watts, D. (2007) "Challenging the Influentials Hypothesis," *WOMMA, Measuring Word of Mouth*, 3: 201–11.

Watts, D. and Dodds, P.S. (2007) "Networks, Influence, and Public Opinion Formation," *Journal of Consumer Research*, 34(4): 441–58.

Wesson, D. (2010) "Social Commerce: The Case for Redesigning the Shopping Experience!," available at: http://davidwesson.typepad.com/david_wessons_digital_cul/2010/11/social-commerce-strategythe-case-for-redesigning-the-shopping-experience-.html.

West, P.M., Ariely, D., Bellman, S., Bradlow, E., Huber, J., Johnson, E., Kahn, B., Little, J. and Schkade, D. (1999) "Agents to the Rescue?," *Marketing Letters*, 10(3): 285–300.

Wilk, J. (2008) "Latent Semantic Analysis in Python," available at: http://blog.josephwilk.net/projects/latent-semantic-analysis-in-python.html.

Zhang, J. and Krishnamurthy, L. (2004) "Customizing Promotions in Online Stores," *Marketing Science*, 23(4): 561–78.

Ziegler, C.N. and Skubacz, M. (2006) "Towards Automated Reputation Monitoring on the Web," in *Proceedings of the 2006 IEEE/WIC/ACM International Conference on Web Intelligence*, pp. 1066–70.

Zwick, D. and Dholakia, N. (2008) "Infotransformation of Markets: Introduction to the Special Issue on Marketing and Information Technology," *Journal of Macromarketing*, 28(4): 318–25.

PART IV

Communicating, interacting and sharing

13

HOW NON-WESTERN CONSUMERS NEGOTIATE COMPETING IDEOLOGIES OF SHARING THROUGH THE CONSUMPTION OF DIGITAL TECHNOLOGY

Anton Siebert

Keywords

ideologies, Indonesia, intimacy, sharing, smartphones

Introduction

> The Western conception of the person as a bounded, unique, more or less integrated motivational and cognitive universe; a dynamic center of awareness, emotion, judgment, and action organized into a distinctive whole and set contrastively both against other such wholes and against a social and natural background is, however incorrigible it may seem to us, a rather peculiar idea within the context of the world's cultures. Rather than attempt to place the experience of others within the framework of such a conception, ... we must, if we are to achieve understanding, set that conception aside and view their experiences within the framework of their own idea of what selfhood is.
>
> (Geertz 1974, p. 31)

Although originally conceptualized in anthropology as fundamentally driven, shaped, and constrained by a cultural context's ideological make-up (e.g., Geertz 1973; Mulder 1978), sharing has been reduced in the consumer literature to a singular, i.e., Western, mechanism of resource distribution. In his recent work, Belk (2010) reviews the extensive literature on sharing and gift giving in both Western and non-Western contexts and develops a framework summarizing the key characteristics of and differences among sharing, commodity exchange, and gift exchange. His model is, however, decidedly Western in orientation. Belk (2010) assumes that people act as free individuals who are not determined by the cultural forces in which they are embedded. This concept of the individual resembles what has been described as the Western conception of the person (Geertz 1974) or the "independent self" (Markus and Kitayama 1991), and what also forms the basis for Belk's (1988) "extended self:" an atomized, separate, autonomous, and unique individual. This assumption renders the applicability of the conceptual distinctions to non-Western contexts hardly possible. What is considered sharing, borrowing and lending, gift giving, and commodity exchange and which of these forms of behavior are perceived as obligatory, reciprocal, or morally desirable are socially constructed and depend upon a combination of factors: the ideologies, norms, and values in a given culture (Triandis 1994; Mulder 2000), the social context (Gell 1992), the personal relationships (Fiske 1992), and the objects or information involved (Giesler 2006).

More empirical work in a variety of cultural contexts is necessary to examine the fundamentally dialectic relationship between the individual and the societal level (Berger and Luckmann 1966), and to illuminate how sharing and its related forms of behavior manifest themselves in everyday consumer cultures. Yet it is surprising to find that there is little empirical research addressing the ubiquitous consumer behavior of sharing, using a framework that is informed by social constructionism, as well as poststructuralism. Two recent exceptions are Giesler (2008) and Humphreys and Giesler (2007). The authors demonstrate how a paradigmatic shift from ownership to access and sharing evolves through cooperative and agonistic consumer–producer conflict in the bookselling and music downloading consumption context. In his 2008 study on drama in marketplace evolution, in turn, Giesler illustrates how consumers and producers variously interpret the salient narrative of intellectual property in order to construct legitimacy for their activities in the cultural creative sphere. Although these studies are useful and visionary, they are also limited to Western ideologies and notions of sharing. In sum, there is a paucity of empirical research exploring how norms, values, and ideologies of sharing in and across different cultures shape market structures and individual consumption experiences.

To address this oversight, I examine the influence of competing ideologies of sharing on the love-relationship related identity work of Javanese smartphone consumers in Indonesia. Smartphones are digital devices that enable consumers not only to communicate with each other but also to create, transfer, access, store, and most importantly, share information about the self and its relation to the social world. As such, smartphone consumption stands at the intersection of two countervailing ideologies of sharing: a traditional Javanese ideology of sharing and a contemporary Western one. Next, I will briefly review these competing ideologies and show the tensions that exist between them. Following the neglected but central insight that humans are as much a product of society as society is a product of humans (Berger and Luckmann 1966), I then examine the identity narratives of Javanese smartphone users to demonstrate how the two ideologies are constantly blended and restructured. I conclude by discussing the implications of the study for consumer culture research on sharing and (digital) technology consumption. Data for the present analysis stems from a larger research project exploring the relationship among romantic love, globalization, and the marketplace.

This research seeks to inform our understanding of sharing and technology consumption by bringing non-Western ideologies of sharing to bear on data from the Indonesian dating scene. First, it reveals and critiques a Western bias in the Consumer Culture Theory (CCT) literature (Arnould and Thompson 2005) on sharing and offers a poststructuralist alternative theorization of sharing based on culturally competing ideologies of sharing. It also contributes to our understanding of globalized consumer culture (ibid.) by demonstrating the influence of competing ideologies of sharing on identity construction in transitional (non-Western) economies. And finally, this study makes a contribution to a nascent body of CCT literature on the consumption of (digital) technology. Previous work has either adopted a decidedly micro-theoretical perspective (Venkatesh 2008) or has analyzed the influence of static cultural forces on technology consumption practices as a one-way process (Mick and Fournier 1998; Kozinets 2008). Thereby, these studies omit the influence of technology consumption on larger institutional and marketplace structures such as the emergent glocalized Indonesian dating marketplace.

Ideologies of sharing

Before analyzing consumers' self-narratives of sharing, it is necessary to review the overarching cultural meaning systems in which these narratives are embedded. Cultural anthropologists and cross-cultural psychologists (Belk 2010; Fiske 1992; Forshee 2006; Geertz 1964, 1974; Kerstan and Berninghausen 1991; Magnis-Suseno 1981; Mulder 1994, 1998, 2000; Triandis 1994) have analyzed and distinguished between the contrasting normative understandings that make up the two conflicting ideologies of sharing that are crucial to illuminating consumption practices in my Javanese context: one emphasizing dependent selves with low individuation and moral autonomy but a high sense of obligation to share and live publicly; and another accentuating independent selves with high individuation, moral autonomy and a high sense of privacy and personal ownership. Next, I review these salient orientations, referred to herein as the collectivistic and individualistic ideology of sharing.[1] After that, I show how the tension between them provides the stage for cultural conflict and alternative consumer narratives of sharing, thereby restructuring larger normative understandings of dating in Indonesia.

The collectivistic ideology of sharing

One ideology of sharing prominently encountered in the Javanese cultural context is the traditional or collectivistic ideology of sharing. Collectivistic sharing is deeply rooted in the Javanese worldview, *kejawen* (Geertz 1964; Koentjaraningrat 1985; Mulder 2000), according to which individuals should always see themselves as a part of their family and community. The underlying conception of personhood is characterized by low individuation but a high "sense of gratitude, of obligation, of dependence and origin" (Mulder 1994, 106). Using the metaphor of a basket of eggs (Mulder, pers. comm., 16 May 2007), Javanese individuals are understood as boiled and peeled eggs whose egg whites blend into each other so that only the yolks can be differentiated. Besides determining the individual's identity, place, and aspirations, the group or clan also serves as a watchdog against non-conformist behavior (Mulder 1978, 2000). Trust is not associated with inner qualities of others but rather with them living publicly and visibly (Mulder 1978). In this model, sharing is expected, often directly demanded, and comes with a moral obligation (*utang budi*) to reciprocate (Mulder 1994). Only the inner core (*batin*, or, the yolk) consisting of the most private emotions and thoughts, one is not obliged to share (Magnis-Suseno 1981).

In its application to my digital technology consumption realm, the collectivistic ideology of sharing emphasizes an expectation to share one's belongings such as smartphones with others in need. Not to share one's smartphone would be an unacceptable behavior that would be taken as a sign of selfishness and "not knowing one's place and obligations," it would be shameful for the social environment, and it would be sanctioned by the collective (Magnis-Suseno 1981; Mulder 1990).

In the traditional Javanese ideology of sharing, actions are not judged by an absolutistic dichotomous morality that emphasizes man's will and moral autonomy (Geertz 1964; Magnis-Suseno 1981). Rather, actions that lead to infractions of the social rules are regarded as not intrinsically bad but a matter of missing comprehension and insight (*durung ngerti*) or of plain stupidity (Mulder 1998). Moral judgements focus on the *lair*, that is, the visible behavior and outward appearance, in the context of social relationships (Magnis-Suseno 1981). It is bad when infractions are noted and not tolerated by one's fellows; moral "conscience is consciousness of others" (Mulder 1998, p. 67). The appropriate measure against infractions is therefore public, social surveillance. Open conflicts and disruptions of the social harmony (*rukun*), the highest and sacrosanct principle in the moral system, are to be avoided.

The individualistic ideology of sharing

Another ideology of sharing of increasing importance in contemporary Javanese culture is the Western or individualistic ideology of sharing. It refers to a legacy of European and North American philosophical traditions that emphasize the autonomy of the individual subject (Descartes [1641] 1996; Kant [1785] 2004; Sartre [1943] 2001). Here, the individual is seen as a bounded, unique, and distinctive whole that sets itself contrastively against other such wholes rather than regard others as part of its identity (Geertz 1974). In the egg basket metaphor, individualistic selves would be hard-boiled eggs that hardly shade off into each other. This concept has driven the idea that mutual trust is a matter of people's characters and inner qualities instead of social control and supervision. It follows that people who live according to this ideology develop high individuation but a low sense of obligation and conformity. While individual privacy and freedom from invasion are highly valued, personal possessions are not to be used by others without permission (Triandis 1994). For proponents of this model, sharing is a voluntary act free of reciprocal expectations and forced compliance (Belk 2010). In its application to my context, the individualistic ideology of sharing accentuates the assumption that digital devices such as smartphones are personal belongings that need not to be shared with others. If they were to be shared, explicit permission would have to be given by the owner based on a 'free' decision.

In addition, the user would respect the tacit privacy concerns of the owner and avoid consuming personal information. From the individualistic perspective, good or bad actions are a matter of absolutistic principles in combination with moral autonomy and man's will (Kant [1785] 2004; Magnis-Suseno 1981). Deeply rooted in Christianity, humans have to take moral responsibility for their own behavior (Kerstan and Berninghausen 1991). Individual moral conscience and the feeling of personal guilt instead of shame in social situations are emphasized (Triandis 1994). Appropriate measures against infractions of the social rules thus relate less to the consciousness of others and the effects of behavior but rather more to the moral conscience of the individual as it is guided by universal principles (Magnis-Suseno 1981).

In sum, collectivistic and individualistic ideologies of sharing serve as justifications, frames, and motivations for consumers' smartphone practices in Indonesia. However, the ideologies are not monolithic but often amalgamated in everyday consumption practices in ways that support the individual consumer's life projects and circumstances. The negotiations of the two ideologies through the marketplace are characterized by consumers striving for the 'right' blend. Thus far, this process has not led to the historical institutionalization of a third ideology or synthesis resolving the tension between the two ideologies of sharing. So in addition to ideology, we need to study how consumers assuage the tensions between the two opposing ideals and create working compromises through their everyday regimes and practices of sharing.

Methodology

To investigate how competing ideologies of sharing play themselves out on the practical level, I chose to investigate smartphone consumption in the practice of dating in Indonesia. Since 2006, I have frequently lived, studied, and conducted research in Yogyakarta, Java, Indonesia. In addition to this experiential dimension during my undergraduate, graduate, and doctoral studies, I immersed myself in background research regarding the historical and cultural conditions relevant to the Javanese and the specific domain of interest in this chapter. Equipped with this background knowledge, I conducted semi-structured, in-depth interviews with 20 Javanese (aged 17–36, $M = 24$, 10 male and 10 female) in Yogyakarta in August 2011. The data collection is part of my larger research project on globalization, the marketplace, and romantic love, illuminating market system dynamics beyond the Western hemisphere. The interviews were conducted at my place, the participants' homes or their friends' places. They lasted between 90 minutes to four hours, yielding conversations on general lifestyle issues and also on more specific love-relationship and dating-related consumption stories, all revealing the importance of digital technologies and innovations, particularly smartphones and social media such as Facebook. Follow-up interviews focusing on the role of smartphones and the concept of sharing within love-relationships were conducted online in September 2011.

All participants are Javanese, born in Central Java and living in Yogyakarta. Most of them adhere to a syncretic form of Islam, characteristic of Java (Geertz 1964), but varied in terms of relationship status (single, in a relationship, married, divorced), upbringing (parents varied from working class through upper-middle class), education (from high school to graduate degrees), and occupation (from unoccupied to skilled craftsmen to entrepreneurs). To interpret the consumption stories of Javanese smartphone consumers within their broader narratives of self-identity, I used Thompson's (1997) hermeneutically grounded interpretive framework. Accordingly, I analyzed the data through a series of part-to-whole iterations. In the intratextual movement, each interview was analyzed separately in full. In the second stage, the intertext cycle, I sought deeper under-standing by looking for commonalities and differences across the interviews (Thompson 1997). I will now turn to the analysis of consumers' narratives of sharing. I use a case study format (e.g., Holt 2002; Holt and Thompson 2004) to illustrate how the interrelationship and tension between the two models of sharing play out in the love-relationship related consumption practices of Javanese consumers.

Consumer narratives of sharing

Case 1: Yani and Ira on the importance of control in sharing

Yani and Ira are sisters from a working-class background who have lived in Yogyakarta their entire lives. While Yani is 23 years old, holds an undergraduate degree, and has been in a relationship for two years, Ira is a 21-year-old undergraduate student who currently does not have a boyfriend. Yani describes the relationship among sharing, trust, and jealousy as she experiences it with her boyfriend:

YANI: My boyfriend and I are open and trust each other, so there is nothing that we hide from each other. Regarding our smartphones, we are both open and share. At the beginning I became a little bit angry or jealous when he sent text messages to his female friends, and I often asked who they were, what his relationship with them was and so on. He told me that they were just friends and rarely sent each other messages, maybe only if there was an important issue. Since then, every time he sends or receives text messages from girls, he surely tells me, and if he does not tell me, he does not delete the messages because he knows that I will definitely check his smartphone [laughs]. But for me this is better than if he were to hide something behind my back ... Besides text messages there are pictures; I once found a picture of him together with a female friend, and because I was angry, he deleted the picture and apologized to me [laughs].

In her interview, Yani draws upon many elements of the collectivistic ideology of sharing to describe and legitimize her use of smartphones. With the existence of these digital devices, partners in love-relationships can share what they do, with whom, where, and when – and they often directly ask the beloved for this information. Ira's statements help to understand why this is the case among many Javanese couples:

INTERVIEWER: Why do you want to find out all this information?

IRA: Because when I am in a love-relationship with someone, I feel that I have rights to him, whatever it is … I have the right to know what he does, where he is, and with whom he is together.

INTERVIEWER: Imagine if he said that his smartphone was his private item and that you were not allowed to check it. What would you think and feel?

IRA: If he would not give me the permission to do so, it would mean that he is hiding something from me … and I have to find it out. Because in a love-relationship you are not supposed to have any secrets.

INTERVIEWER: For you to trust someone, you have to know every bit of information?

IRA: I believe that expressed and revealed information shows the honesty of a person.

For Yani and Ira, sharing is crucial in love-relationships in order to enable partners to shade off into each other, build up trust, and reduce jealousy. But it is not enough to verbally share feelings and thoughts. Rather, personal information that is stored in smartphones is supposed to be shared too. As a variation of the expectation to live one's life publicly and visibly (Mulder 1978), sharing this information is taken as a 'real' sign of the honesty and sincerity of the partner. Yani and Ira feel that they have the right to know their partner's life in detail and they believe that enforced mutual sharing and surveillance are salient measures to achieve happiness in a love-relationship. Yani's boyfriend experienced how critical these aspects were to Yani and eventually shared information about his life and social relationships with her through his smartphone. However, he is less enthusiastic about finding out about Yani's social relationships and activities:

YANI: It is different when my boyfriend checks my smartphone; he will not find any weird messages because I rarely send or receive text messages from other boys. If there are any, he does not get jealous – strange, isn't it? He just asks who that is, and when I tell him, he is just a friend, he says okay, that's fine. It makes me angry and sad that he rarely checks my phone; he is lazy and just says that there are only messages from him.

His lack of enthusiasm to check Yani's smartphone is not taken as a sign of trust towards her honesty or of the quality of their relationship, but instead makes her angry and sad. Drawing on elements from the collectivistic ideology of sharing, Yani believes that a person who is in love and cares is supposed to reciprocate the demanded sharing practices and serve as a watchdog against potential non-conformist behavior by keeping the beloved under close surveillance. She thus expects a behavior from her boyfriend that would be disapproved of as being too possessive and overly jealous, since it violates one's privacy and autonomy, according to the individualistic ideal of sharing. Smartphone consumption practices have become a major means through which such expectations of sharing and notions of love are negotiated. Given the variety of normative guidelines and assumptions of exactly what the 'right' degree of sharing and shading off into each other is, it is not surprising that these negotiations are a continuous struggle. Yani's case illustrates that different understandings of the role and meaning of sharing in love-relationships provide normative instability that sets the stage for reflection, conflict, and compromise. Smartphones and the personal information stored in them play a crucial role in this process.

Case 2: Venna and the quest for trust and privacy in sharing

Venna is a 22-year-old undergraduate student from a working-class background. She was born in Yogyakarta and currently does not have a boyfriend. In contrast to Case 1, her interview illustrates a quest for privacy and trust in a love-relationship with someone who demands detailed sharing practices:

INTERVIEWER: Have you ever experienced a situation like that?

VENNA: Yes, when I was still in a relationship with Joko, my neighbor. At the time I was in touch with a male friend of mine in Jakarta through text messages. We were very close friends so that I already regarded him as my brother and he called me 'say' [honey] in the text messages. Apparently Joko had my smartphone and read my text messages. And he thought that I had something going on with this male friend of mine behind his back. On top of it, Joko is a close friend of this male friend of mine too.

INTERVIEWER: What did you think and feel when this happened?

VENNA: At the time I didn't know that Joko had checked my smartphone. Unexpectedly he asked me straightaway about the text messages. He was angry and asked for an explanation. I was confused; how could he know about it? Because I didn't have anything going on with this male friend of mine, I told him in a calm way that it was just a normal friendship ... Obviously he had sent a message to my male friend and asked him to confirm the messages. He got the same answer from him. But in that moment Joko was angry with my male friend.

INTERVIEWER: What were the consequences of the incident?

VENNA: The consequence in the long run was that he didn't trust me any more. Maybe that was one of the reasons for our break-up. His behavior changed after the incident compared to his behavior when we got close.

Venna experienced the interconnectedness between sharing, trust, jealousy and privacy rather differently from Yani and Ira. When her boyfriend enacted what he thought was his right of reciprocal sharing and checked her smartphone, he came across a message from a male friend of hers who called her "honey," a term used both among close friends and partners in love-relationships. Although the incident could be explained and his anger vanished shortly afterwards, he lost trust in Venna. Trust is a very important but elusive category in Indonesia, as Venna explains:

VENNA: When someone trusts someone else or something else, he or she will guard his trust faithfully. But if you ever do something wrong, even if it is only once, just for a moment, something totally unimportant or minor, then this trust will be lost and will never come back. That's why people try to protect their privacy so heavily.

The idea of strictly protecting one's privacy resembles salient elements of the individualistic ideology of sharing. In a social environment that associates privacy with having something to hide and trust with living one's life publicly, however, a rather pragmatic approach seems to be a suitable way to achieve a working peace. Konde, a 17-year-old Javanese, explicates his way of bridging the two competing ideologies of sharing:

KONDE: Normally I delete the chat or text messages that I receive from or send to my close female friends directly afterwards because I am afraid that my girlfriend will read them. I don't like other people to read my messages because I regard them as private. And I also don't like to read other people's text messages because I regard them as private and I don't need to know what is in them.

Although he strongly believes in the importance of privacy and does not need to shade off into his partner's life to build up trust as much as Yani, Ira, and Joko, for example, he reflected upon the ideological instability provided by the countervailing ideologies of sharing and decides to construct a pragmatic, working compromise that allows him to minimize conflict and drama in his love-relationship. Venna, in contrast, chose a more idealistic, confrontative way of negotation:

INTERVIEWER: Are you going to share your mobile phone with your friends and your boyfriend like before?

VENNA: My smartphone is my private item. I never share my smartphone with anyone without this person asking me for permission.

INTERVIEWER: Has the idea that "my phone really is my own possession" emerged?

VENNA: Yes, definitely.

INTERVIEWER: Do you wish that your friends and your boyfriend would respect your privacy more and would not search for private information on your phone? Are you going to respect others' privacy more than you used to?

VENNA: I follow the principle that I don't want to know someone else's privacy before he or she tells me about it. And I think that they, other people, also have to follow this principle as I do. I don't disturb you so you also don't disturb my privacy.

INTERVIEWER: Will people become more individualistic because of such incidents?

VENNA: I think so. But it's a private decision … If they want to share with other people or not is up to them − and no one else has the right to tell them what to do.

INTERVIEWER: If you could work together with a smartphone company, what would you advise them?

VENNA: Maybe I would suggest using fingerprints [laughs], so that only the owner of the smartphone could unlock and use it.

Instead of relying on the consciousness of others, Venna follows her personal principles that have to be respected by others. She regards her smartphone as her own possession that she never shares with anyone without explicit permission (Triandis 1994). Rather than meeting other people's expectations or demands to reciprocate, she assumes herself to be an individual who can make 'free' decisions (Belk 2010). Similar to Konde, she also believes that a happy love-relationship does not need such a high degree of mutual shading off into each other. However, in contrast to his pragmatic approach, she does not want to superficially play by the rules of the collectivistic game of sharing. Her reluctance to share and her emphasis on individualistic notions of self were the basis of many of the conflicts with her boyfriend and eventually led to their break-up. In her case, no comforting blending of the two opposing ideals of sharing could be constructed within their love-relationship.

Interpretive summary

In summary, the cases illustrate some of the ways in which consumers in Indonesia draw on the two competing ideologies of sharing in their love-relationship related identity work. Indonesian consumers attempt to creatively negotiate and blend the two ideologies through their smartphone consumption practices in ways that support their individual (consumer) life projects and create a working compromise in their love-relationships. It is striking that extreme approaches such as Yani's emphasis on control in sharing or Venna's strict quest for privacy and trust in sharing tend to produce difficult conditions for a love-relationship to flourish as they create continuous misunderstanding and conflict. My analysis further suggests that smartphone consumption practices restructure the Javanese ideology of sharing in at least two important ways. First, open confrontations and conflicts are on the rise as an effect of increasing (mis-)communication via smartphones, which further weakens the concept of harmony or *rukun*, once the most important and sacrosanct principle in the Javanese worldview (Magnis-Suseno 1981; Mulder 2000). Second, the separation between the inner self (*batin*) and the outer world (*lair*) becomes increasingly blurred since smartphones make information about the self and its intimate social relations visible to the outer world, which in turn creates expectations to share. With new digital devices entering the marketplace, new consumption practices will emerge and the search for the 'right' blend and the restructuring of the larger normative understandings of sharing will continue.

Implications

These findings have the potential to inform the literature on sharing, (digital) technology consumption, and the manifestation of consumer culture in non-Western contexts in several important ways. First, my empirical findings suggest that previous research on sharing (Belk 2010) suffers from an ethnocentric Western bias and is thus not suited to illuminate the full complexity of sharing within and across different (non-Western) consumer cultures. The understandings of sharing, privacy, trust, and jealousy that the consumers in my study create, move far beyond the Western conceptions of sharing (ibid.). Indonesian consumers are forced to strike compromises between two competing overarching ideologies of sharing. Given the variety of ideological and institutional abstraction regarding these issues, conflict is the norm and failure to compromise often leads to or facilitates the break-up of relationships. The continuous struggle of consumers to achieve working self-narratives of sharing play a formative role in the restructuring of larger normative understandings of mating, friendship, and love (Berger and Luckmann 1966). Even broader, they also contribute to fundamentally reshaping established social structures such as class or religion (Klein 2001). However, questions of exactly what constitutes the 'right' blend and what new structures of power relationships will evolve remain unanswered, making sharing an ongoing tightrope act. Longitudinal research is needed to unpack how this negotiation process influences the emergence of new market systems as well as shifts in normative understandings and the evolution of consumer cultural practices (Giesler 2008; Humphreys 2010; Karababa and Ger 2011).

The findings further contribute to our understanding of (digital) technology consumption. Former research in the consumer behavior literature has acknowledged and drawn upon the larger cultural forces in which technology consumption is embedded, but it has focused on its influence on micro-level practices as a one-way process (Mick and Fournier 1998; Kozinets 2008). I find that smartphones are one of the most important technological devices Javanese consumers use to share information about the self in their love-relationships and make internal emotions and thoughts strategically available to the outside world. I further demonstrate how smartphones in Indonesia foster a blurring of longstanding cultural boundaries between the internal sphere of emotions, thoughts, and intentions and the external sphere of expressions and behavior. As such, I demonstrate the influence of digital consumer technology beyond the micro-level of individual consumer practices. Digital technology can facilitate ideological instability and help set the stage for conflict and compromise in social relationships. Thereby, it influences the continuous human production of societal-level abstractions (Berger and Luckmann 1966).

Finally, my analysis also responds to the call to further explore the influence of globalization and consumption on transitional economies (Arnould and Thompson 2005). Following established concepts of hybridization and glocalization, I demonstrate how identity construction in a non-Western context draws from the marketplace to blend local traditional and global normativities (Karababa and Ger 2011; Kjeldgaard and Askegaard 2006; Kjeldgaard and Ostberg 2007). My findings further support the thesis that globalization promotes reflexive, self-actualizing consumer subjects (Askegaard and Kjeldgaard 2007). More specifically, I show how Indonesian consumers form particular self-ethics and enact their personal understandings of how and what to share within their love-relationships (Karababa and Ger 2011). Utilizing alternative ideologies of sharing, they overcome the 'natural' notion of traditional dominant normativities and instead actively negotiate the 'right' blending. In this process, the active Indonesian consumer subjects articulate their reflexive identities through the marketplace, thereby producing new glocal forms of ideological and institutional abstractions.

Acknowledgments

The author would like to thank Markus Giesler, Søren Askegaard, Ela Veresiu, the reviewer, and the participants of the doctoral workshop at the University of Arkansas for their many helpful comments and suggestions on earlier versions of the manuscript.

Note

1 The terms individualism and collectivism are not used in the classic Hofstedian (Hofstede 1980) sense of reproducing binary oppositions. Rather, they are understood herein as cultural resources that are leveraged to create specifically tailored relational narratives that, in turn, serve multiple competing interests (Giesler 2008; Holt and Thompson 2004).

Further reading

Ayers, M.D. (ed.) (2006) *Cybersounds: Essays on Virtual Music Culture*, New York: Peter Lang Press. [Collection of essays critically examining the constitution of the digital music consumer.]

Belk, R.W. (2010) "Sharing," *Journal of Consumer Research*, 36(5): 715–34. [The article provides an overview of the literature on sharing and gift giving in consumption.]

Giesler, M. (2008) "Conflict and Compromise: Drama in Marketplace Evolution," *Journal of Consumer Research*, 34(6): 739–53. [The article illustrates the role of technology in shifting normativities of social exchange.]

Zhao, X. and Belk, R.W. (2008) "Politicizing Consumer Culture: Advertising's Appropriation of Political Ideology in China's Social Transition," *Journal of Consumer Research*, 35(2): 231–44. [The article explores the rise of consumer culture in a non-Western transitional country.]

References

Arnould, E.J. and Thompson, C.J. (2005) "Consumer Culture Theory (CCT): Twenty Years of Research," *Journal of Consumer Research*, 31(4): 868–82.

Askegaard, S. and Kjeldgaard, D. (2007) "Here, There, and Everywhere: Place Branding and Gastronomical Globalization in a Macromarketing Perspective," *Journal of Macromarketing*, 27(2): 138–47.

Belk, R.W. (1988) "Possessions and the Extended Self," *Journal of Consumer Research*, 15(2): 139–68.

——(2010) "Sharing," *Journal of Consumer Research*, 36(5): 715–34.

Berger, P.L. and Luckmann, T. (1966) *The Social Construction of Reality*, New York: Anchor.

Descartes, R. ([1641] 1996) *Meditations on First Philosophy*, trans. J. Cottingham, New York: Cambridge University Press.

Fiske, A.P. (1992) "The Four Elementary Forms of Sociality: Framework for a Unified Theory of Social Relations," *Psychological Review*, 99(4): 689–723.

Forshee, J. (2006) *Culture and Customs of Indonesia*, Westport, CT: Greenwood Press.

Geertz, C. (1964) *The Religion of Java*, London: The Free Press of Glencoe, Collier Macmillan Limited.
——(1973) *The Interpretation of Cultures*, New York: Basic Books.
——(1974) "'From the Native's Point of View': On the Nature of Anthropological Understanding," *Bulletin of the American Academy of Arts and Sciences*, 28(1): 26–45.
Gell, A. (1992) "Inter-tribal Commodity Barter and Reproductive Gift-Exchange in Old Melanesia," in C. Humphrey and S. Hugh-Jones (eds), *Barter, Exchange and Value: An Anthropological Approach*, Cambridge: Cambridge University Press, pp. 142–91.
Giesler, M. (2006) "Consumer Gift Systems," *Journal of Consumer Research*, 33(2): 283–90.
——(2008) "Conflict and Compromise: Drama in Marketplace Evolution," *Journal of Consumer Research*, 34(6): 739–53.
Hofstede, G.H. (1980) *Culture's Consequences: International Differences in Work-Related Values*, Beverly Hills, CA: Sage.
Holt, D.B. (2002) "Why Do Brands Cause Trouble? A Dialectical Theory of Consumer Culture and Branding," *Journal of Consumer Research*, 29(1): 70–90.
Holt, D.B. and Thompson, C.J. (2004) "Man-of-Action Heroes: The Pursuit of Heroic Masculinity in Everyday Consumption," *Journal of Consumer Research*, 31(2): 425–40.
Humphreys, A. (2010) "Megamarketing: The Creation of Markets as a Social Process," *Journal of Marketing*, 74: 1–19.
Humphreys, A. and Giesler, M. (2007) "Tensions between Access and Ownership in the Media Marketplace," in *Advances in Consumer Research*, vol. 34, Provo, UT: Association for Consumer Research, pp. 696–9.
Kant, I. ([1785] 2004) *Grundlegung zur Metaphysik der Sitten*, ed. J. Timmermann, Göttingen: Vandenoeck & Ruprecht.
Karababa, E. and Ger, G. (2011) "Early Modern Ottoman Coffeehouse Culture and the Formation of the Consumer Subject," *Journal of Consumer Research*, 37(5): 737–60.
Kerstan, B. and Berninghausen, J. (1991) *Emanzipation wohin? Frauen und Selbsthilfe in Java, Indonesien*, Frankfurt am Main: Verlag für Interkulturelle Kommunikation.
Kjeldgaard, D. and Askegaard, S. (2006) "The Glocalization of Youth Culture: The Global Youth Segment as Structures of Common Difference," *Journal of Consumer Research*, 33(2): 231–47.
Kjeldgaard, D. and Ostberg, J. (2007) "Coffee Grounds and the Global Cup: Glocal Consumer Culture in Scandinavia," *Consumption Markets and Culture*, 10: 175–87.
Klein, T. (ed.) (2001) *Partnerwahl und Heiratsmuster: Sozialstrukturelle Voraussetzungen der Liebe*, Opladen: Leske + Budrich.
Koentjaraningrat (1985) *Javanese Culture*, Singapore: Oxford University Press.
Kozinets, R.V. (2008) "Technology/Ideology: How Ideological Fields Influence Consumers' Technological Narratives," *Journal of Consumer Research*, 34(6): 865–81.
Magnis-Suseno, F. (1981) *Javanische Weisheit und Ethik: Studien zu einer östlichen Moral*, Munich: R. Oldenbourg Verlag.
Markus, H.R. and Kitayama, S. (1991) "Culture and the Self: Implications for Cognition, Emotion and Motivation," *Psychological Review*, 98(2): 224–53.
Mick, D.G. and Fournier, S. (1998) "Paradoxes of Technology: Consumer Cognizance, Emotions, and Coping Strategies," *Journal of Consumer Research*, 25(2): 123–43.
Mulder, N. (1978) *Mysticism and Everyday Life in Contemporary Java: Cultural Persistence and Change*, Singapore: Singapore University Press.
——(1990) *Individuum und Gesellschaft in Java: Eine Untersuchung zur kulturellen Dynamik*, Saarbrücken: Breitenbach.
——(1994) *Inside Indonesian Society: An Interpretation of Cultural Change in Java*, Bangkok: Ed. Duang Kamol.
——(1998) *Mysticism in Java: Ideology in Indonesia*, Amsterdam: The Pepin Press.
——(2000) *Indonesian Images: The Culture of the Public World*, Deresan, Yogyakarta: Kanisius Publishing House.
Sartre, J-P. ([1943] 2001) *Being and Nothingness: An Essay in Phenomenological Ontology*, trans. H. Barnes, New York: Citadel Press.
Thompson, C.J. (1997) "Interpreting Consumers: A Hermeneutical Framework for Deriving Marketing Insights from the Texts of Consumers' Consumption Stories," *Journal of Marketing Research*, 34: 438–55.
——(2004) "Marketplace Mythology and Discourses of Power," *Journal of Consumer Research*, 31(1): 162–80.
Triandis, H.C. (1994) *Culture and Social Behaviour*, New York: McGraw-Hill.
Venkatesh, A. (2008) "Digital Home Technologies and Transformation of Households," *Inf Syst Front*, 10: 391–5.

14

VIRTUALLY 'SECRET' LIVES IN 'HIDDEN' COMMUNITIES

Ekant Veer

Keywords

anorexia nervosa, depression, online communities, online identity, stigmatization

Being part of a collective is part of human nature (Turner 1987). Separation from others, although not impossible, is not a state that many choose to endure (Tajfel 1982). Being a part of those with whom one wants to be associated not only aids in feeling part of a larger collective, but allows the individual to more freely express him or herself, knowing others are likely to accept him or her (Abrams and Hogg 1990; Ashforth and Mael 1989; Hogg and McGarty 1990; Hogg *et al.* 1995; Tajfel 1974; Turner and Oakes 1986). What the Internet has offered digital consumers is the ability not only to belong to offline groups and communities, but to exist equally in online communities; almost like living a second life that could either be a reflection and representation of who they are offline (Schau and Gilly 2003) or be completely divergent from who they present themselves to be offline (Veer 2010). In either case, the Internet plays a vital role in allowing users to find communities online to be a part of, or create communities with relative ease. Digital consumers are able to keep these communities secret and frequent them only when they choose to engage with the community.

In this chapter I explore the notions of online communities and secrecy for the digital consumer and present case studies that describe the role that online communities play in self-expression and community identity formation. It is argued here that the Internet does not create the need for secrecy, but rather, the Internet expedites the facilitation of secrecy. That is, if one wants to create or be part of a secretive community, it is possible offline, but the nature of online communities makes the process far easier and therefore, more accessible to a mass audience.

The nature of secrecy

Secrets exist in all aspects of our lives (Bok 1989). Keeping secrets, knowing a secret, holding knowledge, creating an imbalance of power through secrets are all aspects of secrets that are relatively well understood, but are not readily researched (Kelly and Yip 2006). Keeping secrets, or purposefully hiding information from others (Margolis 1974), is most often discussed in the psychotherapy literature rather than from a sociological perspective. As such, most of the theories surrounding secrets and secretive behaviour focus heavily on how it negatively impacts relationships, rather than whether having a second/secret life can be used as a basis for self-expression. Here, I focus more on the latter perspective in an attempt to show how a secretive existence can be beneficial for those who feel they cannot express themselves freely in an offline life.

Some research has been done on the need for consumers to express their multiple selves through a variety of channels (Lee *et al.* 2008). Other research looks closely at how being able to express one's self, without prejudice, can be used as a means of finding attachment and belonging in social groups (Baumeister and Leary 1995); and the consumer behaviour literature is awash with research looking at the importance and impact of self-concept and multiple selves (Mandel 2003; Markus and Nurius 1986; Oyserman and Saltz 1993; Reed 2004; Schouten 1991; Sirgy 1982). However, relatively little research looks at 'secret selves' or the deliberate concealment of a part of one's self from others. One reason for this is, that by its very nature, a 'secret' identity is difficult to discover and study, as it is concealed. This chapter focuses specifically on the use of the Internet as a means of expressing a side of one's self that is often kept secret to offline social networks.

There are often good reasons for not sharing or expressing one's self to offline social networks. Crandall and Eshleman (2003) discuss how in offline social interactions one's desire to express a prejudice could be suppressed if the person wishing to express the prejudice does not feel it fits with the social norms of the current interaction. That is, if a person who is racially biased against a particular race does not feel he/she is surrounded by others who also hold a similar prejudice, he/she may suppress their prejudicial feelings and not overtly express any of their inner feelings. In a similar way, it can be argued that in offline interactions, a person who feels a side of him/her self is not accepted by social norms may suppress their desire to share this aspect of him/her self. This does not mean that this person is not looking for an excuse or avenue to express this sense of self (Veer and Shankar 2011), just that the time and situation are not conducive to allowing an expression of self. This chapter shows that when a sense of self is kept hidden or secret from offline interactions, some digitally savvy consumers go online to find a means of expressing themselves and seek acceptance for a sense of self that is deemed unacceptable by their offline relationships.

Secret online lives

This chapter presents example cases of communities that exist online, although their existence is often kept secret from offline social relationships. In the presented cases, the individuals are willing to present personal information to anonymous strangers, while keeping the same information hidden from those personally close to them, as opposed to the more commonly understood concept of sharing intimate details with close friends, and keeping them secret from strangers (Gross and Acquisti 2005). I briefly introduce each group before discussing the findings and theoretical advancements from the research into these groups. In each case, the data is taken from video loggers (vloggers) who post video logs (vlogs) on YouTube. These vlogs are then open for anyone to watch and comment on. As viewers find vloggers whose vlogs they enjoy, they are able to subscribe to their video feed so that they can watch future vlogs posted by the vlogger. The larger the subscriber base, the more people watch the vlogs. As the number of people who watch the vlogs increases, there is often a higher number of comments from watchers, which can also be used as data for analysis.

Beyond vlogs on YouTube, there exist a number of online communities that have thrived for many years, especially if it is perceived that being open about an identity in the offline world could subject the individual to persecution. For example, Alexander (2002) discusses the importance of online communities for lesbian, gay, bisexual, transgender, questioning and queer (LGBTQQueer) people who choose to express their identity in a forum where they will find social support, rather than separation. Similarly, Shaw (1997) identified the role that online communities played in bringing gay men closer together through their online narratives and how online communities were instrumental in aiding gay men in understanding their gay identity. The cases presented here reflect a similar pattern of expression when offline expression is, in the minds of the vloggers, not possible. What is different in these cases is that each of the vlogs operates in a public sphere where anyone can watch and comment, as opposed to the LGBTQQueer communities where specific access is often necessary. Having permission-based communities allows greater control over members and easier censorship of members, if necessary. This is still possible on YouTube, but not to the same extent. The vloggers are opening their views to those who are part of the community and those who are not, making their expression more open to attack. However, the vloggers still express a sense of security about presenting online, compared with offline.

Pro-ana online

Pro-anorexia nervosa (pro-ana) online communities have been the focus of much of the attention with regards to 'secretive' online activity (Norris *et al.* 2006). Anorexia nervosa is defined by the American Psychiatric Association as being an inability to maintain a healthy body weight combined with a fear of losing control over one's body weight and, subsequently, becoming fat (American Psychiatric Association 2000). A number of researchers have looked at the role that online pro-ana groups can play in causing a triggering effect, encouraging others who do not suffer from anorexia nervosa to engage in anorexia-like behaviours (Bardone and Cass 2006, 2007; Fox *et al.* 2005; Overbeke 2008; Shade 2003). However, relatively few have looked at the way in which online communities, such as pro-ana groups, act as a means of self-expression. Previous research has also shown that the sufferer's desire for control could be a major contributing factor to the exhibitionist behaviour online (Veer 2010). That is, sufferers' need for control is co-symptomatic of a need to be heard and the need to express themselves so overtly, that it can be likened to a form of exhibitionism. Similarly, Dias (2003) shows that pro-ana communities are used as places of trust and solace where sufferers can feel safe to express themselves without fear of recrimination. Although referred to as 'ana-sanctuaries', these sites are also used as a means of promoting the pro-ana lifestyle with 'how to' advice and encouragement from other members to continue with one's fast (ibid.). In general, the role of websites that are unilaterally pro-ana sites has been condemned by many countries. However, this has not stopped the online pro-ana movement from infiltrating other, more generic sites, such as YouTube.

YouTube is still the most popular video-sharing website available with thousands of videos uploaded and hundreds of thousands viewed every day (YouTube 2010). A number of anorexia nervosa sufferers have turned to YouTube as a means of sharing their experiences and stories. Although many share stories of recovery in an attempt to help others overcome their own struggles with anorexia nervosa, there also exist vlogs which actively encourage anorexia nervosa behaviours. These pro-ana vloggers use YouTube as a platform not only to express their views but also to encourage others to choose anorexia nervosa as a valid lifestyle choice.

Depression vlogs

Depression, although one of the most commonly diagnosed mental illnesses (American Psychiatric Association 2000), continues to be the basis of significant social stigma (Schwenk *et al.* 2010).

Depression is a condition that substantially impairs an individual's ability to cope with daily life and can, in the most severe cases, lead to suicide (Seligman 1975). Very few studies actually have looked at the link between depression and online activity. Finkelstein and Laphsin (2007) show that the stigma associated with depression can be reduced through online media, but many studies focus on curing individuals suffering from depression through medication or psychotherapy, rather than how online spaces and places can be used a means of expressing one's self. In this chapter, I present the brief findings of how some digital consumers are able to use the Internet as a means of expressing their identity as a depressed individual, without having to share such personal details with those close to them in their offline social networks.

Self-injury vlogs

The final case discussed in this chapter is that of people who share their experiences and lives as self-injurers or *cutters*. Cutters are described as persons who actively, consciously and deliberately cause themselves physical harm (American Psychiatric Association 2000). Self-injury has been closely linked with borderline personality disorders and suicidal tendencies (Pattison and Kahan 1983). However, other authors suggest that rather than attempting to end one's life, many cutters use their behaviour as a means of eliminating negative sides of themselves, rather than as an attempt to destroy their entire body (Brown *et al.* 2002; Harris 2000). This may help to explain why so many depressives are turning to social media sites to express themselves to anonymous parties, as they feel they need to share their stories in an attempt to purge the negative aspects of their self and attain a feeling of catharsis from such behaviour (Bloom-Feshbach 2001; Mienczakowski *et al.* 1996).

From these three cases the following three themes are presented: sharing; personal validation; and community-driven validation. The interactive nature of these themes is also discussed along with the implications of the studies and the impact they have on understanding digital consumers.

Themes

Sharing

Every vlog, by its nature, shared a part of the creator for the audience to observe and, if so wished, comment upon. Previous research has shown that some vloggers behave in an exhibitionistic fashion, presenting overly personal and sensitive information in order to attract greater support and attention from their watchers (Veer 2010). Similarly, sharing parts of one's self acts as a way to draw closer to those you wish to attract as part of your in-group (Acquisti and Gross 2006; Haight 2001). Belk's (2010) concept of 'Sharing In' helps to understand how one can aid in expanding one's sense of extended self to incorporate others. Thus, by blurring the boundaries of what is 'you' and 'me' by sharing intimate details, the vloggers are able to actively encourage others in as part of their extended self, with the vlog being used as a ritualistic tool to encourage this extension (Belk and Llamas 2011).

In this study it was evident that both sensitive and deeply personal parts of the vlogger's self and identity were presented, but also that some videos were extremely transactional in nature. In these videos, vloggers offered practical hints, tips and strategies to aid watchers who had found their videos. In the case of Fran, she discusses the best make-up to use to cover scars left by self-injury. I have deliberately not revealed the names of the brands discussed by Fran in order not to inadvertently associate these brands with a behaviour that it is likely the brand owners do not support:

> Alright … you have to stay with me because I'm going to go through this at light speed. Also, write down what I say because those bastards at YouTube are sure to delete this pretty soon. If you have light-coloured skin, like mine, then brand … is the way to go. Rub it on lightly from the centre of your scar to the outside. Don't go against the grain as it'll clump and look like a shadow. Just gently like this and you'll be able to cover them up enough that a person glancing won't notice … not, if someone grabs your arm and stares, you're fucked, but this will get most of you through your normal day without hassles. Most important thing, if you're really worried, is coverage. Sleeves are back in, wear them! This is one of my favourite striped tops [holds up long-sleeved blouse] and I got it from [Retail Store] for only $15 – such a bargain, get one!
>
> *(Fran, female, late teens, cutting vlogger, 18 subscribers)*

In this vlog, Fran was able to share a huge amount of detail about how to physically cope with the after-effects associated with cutting, and help others cover the stigma they carry from being cutters. Much of what Fran shared could be described as being highly secretive information that she would not have been able to discuss openly without others who support her. However, through her vlog she was able to feel as though she has given back something to help those who may be struggling to conceal the scars left by their cutting behaviour.

There are also vloggers who share less practical information, but rather express their own thoughts, feelings and personal history to viewers. Again, it should be noted that many of these viewers are anonymous and not part of the vlogger's offline social network, whom the vloggers feel would disapprove of their behaviour. One prominent web logger (blogger) and vlogger on depression introduces herself by saying:

> I was once told not to tell anyone about my depression, that it should be my personal secret. But I believe keeping secrets only adds to the stigma attached to depression.
>
> *(Annie, female, mid-forties, depression vlogger, 382 subscribers)*

Annie expresses a very personal part of herself that others offline have told her to keep a secret. By sharing such information, she is able to overtly delineate to which viewers she is aiming her vlogs, in the same way that groups are able to distinguish in-group members from out-group members by sharing the focus of the group and the core values of the group (Brewer 1979; Struch and Schwartz 1989). The following themes build upon the effects of sharing.

Personal validation

In all three cases the vloggers discuss the need to seek personal validation through their videos. That is, rather than making the videos for anyone else, many overtly share a need to do this for themselves. For example, Jamie, in one of her first videos says:

> OK … so I know not everyone's going to be happy about this, but it's time to stop hiding, yeah. It's time for me to step up and say something that I'm SOOOOO sick of hiding. I want to be who I want to be and I don't care if no one watches this, I need to say it and I need to be able to say it … I hope I can say it here … .
>
> *(Jamie, female, late teens, anorexia nervosa vlogger, 23 subscribers)*

Jamie's need to vlog is driven not from a need to help others, but from a need to express herself. A number of studies have looked at the importance of expression to stimulate a cathartic effect (Bloom-Feshbach 2001; Bushman 2002; Bushman *et al.* 2001; Bushman *et al.* 1999; Feshbagh 1956; Kaplan 1975; Konecni and Doob 1972; Mienczakowski *et al.* 1996; Vieira da Cunha and Orlikowski, 2008). In particular, Kearney (2007) discusses the importance of narrating one's life and pain in a controlled manner as a way to aid understanding of one's life and struggles. The issue here, is that YouTube offers an unmoderated forum for expression, which can be both constructive and destructive (Vieira da Cunha and Orlikowski 2008); as opposed to a therapy session, where a facilitator can lead the individual through a path of constructive expression and catharsis (Bushman *et al.* 1999; Bushman 2002).

Instead of simply looking for an opportunity to share one's experience, some look to share and seek acceptance from their openness and honesty. As vloggers gain more attention from viewers and their community grows, there are more examples of vlogs that express an attachment to the online community and a detachment from their offline social networks. For example, Carol shares her frustration with the dual life she has found herself in:

> No one really understands what I go through, my parents would think I've gone crazy and send me to THAT clinic but it makes me feel so tired sometimes, and suppressed, and alone ... thank you guys so much, I mean it ... it's nice to have someone that I can relate to and talk to ... love you all and thanks for all your supportive messages ... it's such a relief to finally be able to discuss this without people thinking that I'm a freak!
> *(Carol, female, 31, anorexia nervosa vlogger, 57 subscribers)*

Here Carol offers a clear example of a need for belonging and validation (Baumeister and Leary 1995). When a lack of interpersonal belonging exists in real life for these vloggers, they attempt to seek validation and belonging elsewhere. Some vloggers continue to build this need for belonging by further displacing themselves from their real-life friends and families. Without a feeling of being understood by their friends and families and a deep sense of vulnerability, they crave the understanding of those on YouTube. Therefore, as close relationships are formed on YouTube, face-to-face relationships may progressively diminish:

> I have to spend time with my mother today ... not only is she going to complain how I'm not eating but I have to actually have a CONVERSATION with her ... I really don't want to go and want to spend time with you guys ... she is just going to start crying and complaining that she doesn't know how to help me ... I DON'T NEED HELP! ... Anyway ... I promise to let you guys know how it went and will be making a video soooon!
> *(Fran, female, 24, anorexia nervosa vlogger, 22 subscribers)*

Fran's quote not only shows the lack of enthusiasm towards face-to-face interaction but also reveals the closeness of the relationships formed online. Many of the vloggers studied show a desire to spend time with their online viewers rather than with their families. This indicates that YouTube users form online relationships that can be of more value than those formed over many years with their parents or partners as the vlogger finds themselves expressing their 'true' selves to online viewers, resulting in the formation of a stronger connection and therefore high levels of affection and closeness, as shown by Damien:

> It's a weird feeling ... I sit here talking to you guys about how hard my life is with depression ... I tell you after a couple of weeks that I tried to kill myself, but I struggle

to tell my family ... and I definitely don't tell my friends. Is it because it's easier to tell you guys out there because you've all been so supportive? Or is it me and my own fears coming through?

(Damien, male, 33, depression vlogger, 221 subscribers)

The separation from one's offline social relationships and connection with anonymous online interactions is evidence of how Social Identity Theory describes our need to find affirming in-groups and separate ourselves from out-groups that do not represent a self we wish to be associated with (Hogg and McGarty 1990; Hogg *et al.* 1995; Turner 1987, 1991; Turner and Oakes 1986). It is also evident from these online 'secret' posts that affirming in-groups are created and that the vlogger derives significant validation from the community's support.

Community-driven validation

In each case, and for every vlogger followed as part of this study, it was evident that the vlogger was not in isolation, but part of an interactive and evolving in-group that formed around their vlogs. The more that the vloggers posted and interacted with those who commented on their videos, the closer the vlogger and the community of commenters felt. This is particularly evident in Kylie's post regarding her self-injury vlogs:

Well, what can I say? I've received such positive energy from y'all about my videos. It's really cool to see and I'm really happy I can help everyone out there ... it really helps me to open up and I promise I'll share more in my next videos ...

(Kylie, female, mid-teens, cutting vlogger, 12 subscribers)

The interplay between Kylie and her commenters shows the growing relationship between the two parties, but also the increasing need for Kylie to express more to please her community. Her promise to 'share more' to those that value her is also evidence of a need for the vlogger to please her community, which is akin to Belk's (1996) notion of one example of a 'perfect gift'. However, the sharing of self is also a means by which the community draws stronger together through the dissolution of interpersonal boundaries (Belk 2010). This desire to share with the community could also be indicative of the 'mothering' nature that some vloggers take in their videos to support others and encourage them further, as shown in the interactions between Nancy and one of her commenters:

I wish I could do more for you. I wish I knew more and I was a trained psychologist who can sit there with you and talk you through your pain ... But all I can do is to tell you how it feels for me ... and I HOPE that is enough to help you through one more day.

(Nancy, female, mid-forties, depression vlogger, 72 subscribers)

In response to this video, one commenter writes:

I don't know why or how you keep doing it, but you make me feel so loved. Keep it up hun and I hope you know that you're such an inspiration.

(Commenter 132, follower of Nancy for four months)

Nancy returns with a further comment:

Thank you. I wish I could do more. That I could see you all so happy, just like I want to be. Keep strong and I will post more videos ... I promise!

(Nancy, female, mid-forties, depression vlogger, 72 subscribers)

In this case, the vlogger is not only empowering members of the community, but also drawing reciprocal validation from a member. However, there are times where the community unilaterally support the vlogger, especially when he/she is feeling marginalised in other aspects of their life. For example, when the vlogger expresses deep anxiety in their video, there is often a wave of comments of support. This is particularly evident in the pro-ana blogs with the abundance of 'ana buddies' or friends who support one another to maintain a fast. In these situations, it is clear that the vlogger is able to derive confidence and support from her commenters. This is reflected in both the improved mood in subsequent vlogs as well as the increased frequency of vlogs posted soon after receiving supportive messages. As a vlogger receives validation from the community, their desire to share more and receive more from the community also appears to increase.

Conclusion: why secrecy exists online

In each case there exists a level of secrecy that separates the vloggers from the offline world and draws them into the online world. By sharing the secret with the online world, the power shifts from the offline relationships to the online community who now holds the secret knowledge that is unknown to many others (Foucault 1980), even though the secret is available for all to find. This is the paradox of the digital consumer's secret existence online; it is not well hidden, but few ever find them. From the research, the secretive existence of the vloggers and community members can be described as a reinforcing community whereby the vloggers' shared selves aid in validating their sense of self that is marginalised by the offline world, as shown in Figure 14.1.

These 'secret' communities exist because there is someone or some people who look for acceptance and validation. This sense of acceptance and validation is missing from the vloggers' offline inter-relationships and as such, they turn to online communities in search of acceptance, similar to the way we search for offline inter-relationships that validate and accept us (Tajfel 1974, 1982).

Having secrets and living a secret life is not something that was created with the advent of the Internet, nor is it endemic online. However, increasing access to the Internet and the increasing prevalence of the Internet in almost all aspects of our lives have meant that the discussions surrounding online 'secret' communities is gaining greater attention. Future research

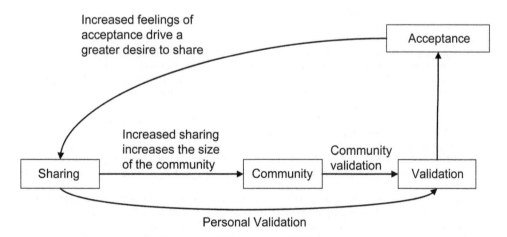

Figure 14.1 Reinforcing nature of secret online communities

should delve further into the world of these online communities, not as a means of judging their users, but in an attempt to understand how the Internet is transforming our inter-connectedness and fostering new means of expression, especially when this is unavailable or not easily attainable in offline settings. Future research should also look at the interaction between one's offline and online self. Much of the research in the area has looked at individuals who are not stigmatised offline and as such, are easily able to express a similar identity online (Schau and Gilly 2003). However, little has looked at how online relationships may be used as a proxy for perceived deficiencies in offline relationships, as shown here.

Further reading

Papacharissi, Z. (2011) *A Networked Self: Identity, Community, and Culture on Social Networking Sites*, New York: Routledge.

Veer, E. (2010) 'Hiding in Plain Sight: "Secret" Anorexia Nervosa Communities on YouTube', *Advances in Consumer Research*, 38. Available at: www.acrwebsite.org/volumes/display.asp?id=15846.

Wellman, B. and Haythornthweait, C. (2002) *The Internet in Everyday Life*, Oxford: Blackwell.

References

Abrams, D. and Hogg, M.A. (1990) 'An Introduction to the Social Identity Approach', in D. Abrams and M.A. Hogg (eds), *Social Identity Theory: Constructive and Critical Advances*, New York: Springer-Verlag, pp. 1–9.

Acquisti, A. and Gross, R. (2006) 'Imagined Communities: Awareness, Information Sharing, and Privacy on the Facebook', *Lecture Notes in Computer Science*, 4258: 36–58.

Alexander, J. (2002) 'Queer Webs: Representations of LGBT People and Communities on the World Wide Web', *International Journal of Sexuality and Gender Studies*, 7(2/3): 77–84.

American Psychiatric Association (2000) *Diagnostic and Statistical Manual of Mental Disorders*, Text Revision, 4th edn, Washington, DC: American Psychiatric Association.

Ashforth, B.E. and Mael, F. (1989) 'Social Identity Theory and the Organization', *Academy of Management Review*, 14(1): 20–39.

Bardone, A.M. and Cass, K.M. (2006) 'Investigating the Impact of Pro-Anorexia Websites: A Pilot Study', *European Eating Disorders Review*, 14(4): 256–62.

——(2007) 'What Does Viewing a Pro-Anorexia Website Do? An Experimental Examination of Website Exposure and Moderating Effects', *International Journal of Eating Disorders*, 40(6): 537–48.

Baumeister, R.F. and Leary, M.R. (1995) 'The Need to Belong: Desire for Interpersonal Attachments as a Fundamental Human Motivation', *Psychological Bulletin*, 117(3): 497–529.

Belk, R.W. (1996) 'The Perfect Gift', in C. Otnes and R. F. Beltramini (eds), *Gift-Giving: A Research Anthology*, Bowling Green, OH: Bowling Green University Popular Press, pp. 59–84.

——(2010) 'Sharing', *Journal of Consumer Research*, 35(5): 715–34.

Belk, R.W. and Llamas, R. (2011) 'Nature and Effects of Sharing in Consumer Behavior', in D. Mick, S. Pettigrew, C. Pechmann and J. Ozanne (eds), *Transformative Consumer Research for Personal and Collective Well Being: Reviews and Frontiers*, New York: Taylor & Francis, pp. 625–46.

Bloom-Feshbach, J. (2001) 'Catharsis as a Constructive Expression of Destructive Affect: Developmental and Clinical Perspectives', in *Constructive and Destructive Behavior: Implications for Family, School, and Society*, Washington, DC: American Psychological Association, pp. 317–25.

Bok, S. (1989) *Secrets: On the Ethics of Concealment and Revelation*, New York: Oxford University Press.

Brewer, M. B. (1979) 'In-Group Bias in the Minimal Intergroup Situation: A Cognitive-Motivational Analysis', *Psychological Bulletin*, 86(2): 307–24.

Brown, M.Z., Comtois, K.A. and Linehan, M.M. (2002) 'Reasons for Suicide Attempts and Nonsuicidal Self-Injury in Women with Borderline Personality Disorder', *Journal of Abnormal Psychology*, 111(1): 198–202.

Bushman, B. J. (2002) 'Does Venting Anger Feed or Extinguish the Flame? Catharsis, Rumination, Distraction, Anger, and Aggressive Responding', *Personality and Social Psychology Bulletin*, 28(6): 724–31.

Bushman, B.J., Baumeister, R.F. and Phillips, C.M. (2001) 'Do People Aggress to Improve Their Mood? Catharsis Beliefs, Affect Regulation Opportunity, and Aggressive Responding', *Journal of Personality and Social Psychology*, 81(1): 17–32.

Bushman, B.J., Baumeister, R.F. and Stack, A.D. (1999) 'Catharsis, Aggression, and Persuasive Influence: Self-Fulfilling or Self-Defeating Prophesies?', *Journal of Personality and Social Psychology*, 76(3): 367–76.

Crandall, C. S. and Eshleman, A. (2003) 'A Justification-Suppression Model of the Expression and Experience of Prejudice', *Psychological Bulletin*, 129(3): 414–46.

Dias, K. (2003) 'The Ana Sanctuary: Women's Pro-Anorexia Narratives in Cyberspace', *Journal of International Women's Studies*, 4(2): 31–45.

Feshbagh, S. (1956) 'The Catharsis Hypothesis and Some Consequences of Interaction with Aggressive and Neutral Play Objects', *Journal of Personality*, 24(4): 449–62.

Finkelstein, J. and Laphsin, O. (2007) 'Reducing Depression Stigma Using a Web-Based Program', *International Journal of Medical Informatics*, 76(10): 726–34.

Foucault, M. (1980) *Power/Knowledge: Selected Interviews and Other Writings, 1972–1977*, New York: Pantheon Books.

Fox, N., Ward, K. and O'Rourke, A. (2005) 'Pro-Anorexia, Weight-Loss Drugs and the Internet: An "Anti-Recovery" Explanatory Model of Anorexia', *Sociology of Health and Illness*, 27(7): 944–71.

Gross, R. and Acquisti, A. (2005) 'Information Revelation and Privacy in Online Social Networks', paper presented at the ACM Workshop on Privacy in the Electronic Society, New York.

Haight, B. (2001) 'Sharing Life Stories: Acts of Intimacy', *Generations*, 25(2): 90–2.

Harris, J. (2000) 'Self-Harm: Cutting the Bad Out of Me', *Qualitative Health Research*, 10(2): 164–73.

Hogg, M.A. and McGarty, C. (1990) 'Self-Categorisation and Social Identity', in D. Abrams and M. A. Hogg (eds), *Social Identification Theory: Constructive and Critical Advances*, New York: Springer-Verlag, pp. 10–27.

Hogg, M.A., Terry, D.J., and White, K.M. (1995) 'A Tale of Two Theories: A Critical Comparison of Identity Theory with Social Identity Theory', *Social Psychology Quarterly*, 58(4): 255–69.

Kaplan, R.M. (1975) 'The Cathartic Value of Self-Expression: Testing, Catharsis, Dissonance, and Interference Exaplanations', *Journal of Social Psychology*, 97(2): 195–207.

Kearney, R. (2007) 'Narrating Pain: The Power of Catharsis', *Paragraph*, 30: 51–66.

Kelly, A.E. and Yip, J.J. (2006) 'Is Keeping a Secret or Being a Secretive Person Linked to Psychological Symptoms?', *Journal of Personality*, 74(5): 1349–70.

Konecni, V.J. and Doob, A.N. (1972) 'Catharsis Through Displacement of Aggression', *Journal of Personality and Social Psychology*, 23(3): 379–87.

Kozinets, R.V. (2002) 'The Field Behind the Screen: Using Netnography for Marketing Research in Online Communities', *Journal of Marketing*, 39(1): 61–72.

Lee, D.-H., Im, S. and Taylor, C.R. (2008) 'Voluntary Self-Disclosure of Information on the Internet: A Multimethod Study of the Motivations and Consequences of Disclosing Information on Blogs', *Psychology and Marketing*, 25(7): 692–710.

Mandel, N. (2003) 'Shifting Selves and Decision Making: The Effects of Self-Construal Priming on Consumer Risk-Taking', *Journal of Consumer Research*, 30(June): 30–40.

Margolis, G. J. (1974) 'The Psychology of Keeping Secrets', *The International Review of Psycho-Analysis*, 1(1): 291–6.

Markus, H. and Nurius, P. (1986) 'Possible Selves', *American Psychologist*, 41(September): 954–68.

Mienczakowski, J., Smith, R. and Sinclair, M. (1996) 'On the Road to Catharsis: A Theoretical Framework for Change', *Qualitative Inquiry*, 2(4): 439–62.

Norris, M. L., Boydell, K.M., Pinhas, L. and Katzman, D.K. (2006) 'Ana and the Internet: A Review of Pro-Anorexia Websites', *International Journal of Eating Disorders*, 39(6): 443–7.

Overbeke, G. (2008) 'Pro-Anorexia Websites: Content, Impact, and Explanations of Popularity', *Mind Matters: The Wesleyan Journal of Psychology*, 3: 49–62.

Oyserman, D. and Saltz, E. (1993) 'Competence, Deliquency, and Attempts to Attain Possible Selves', *Journal of Personality and Social Psychology*, 65(2): 360–74.

Pattison, E.M. and Kahan, J. (1983) 'The Deliberate Self-Harm Syndrome', *American Psychiatric Association*, 140: 867–72.

Reed, A. (2004) 'Activating the Self-Importance of Consumer Selves: Exploring Identity Salience Effects on Judgements', *Journal of Consumer Research*, 31(September): 286–95.

Schau, H.J. and Gilly, M.C. (2003) 'We Are What We Post? Self-Presentation in Personal Web Space', *Journal of Consumer Research*, 30(December): 385–404.

Schouten, J.W. (1991) 'Selves in Transition: Symbolic Consumption in Personal Rites of Passage and Identity Reconstruction', *Journal of Consumer Research*, 17(March): 412–24.

Schwenk, T.L., Davis, L. and Wimsatt, L.A. (2010) 'Depression, Stigma, and Suicidal Ideation in Medical Students', *Journal of the American Medical Association*, 306(4): 343–450.

Seligman, M.E.P. (1975) *Helplessness: On Depression, Development, and Death*, San Francisco, CA: W. H. Freeman.

Shade, L.R. (2003) 'Weborexics: The Ethical Issues Surrounding Pro-Ana Websites', *ACM SIGCAS Computers and Society*, 33(4): 2.

Shaw, D.F. (1997) 'Gay Men and Computer Communication: A Discourse of Sex and Identity in Cyberspace', in S. G. Jones (ed.), *Virtual Culture: Identity and Communication in Cybersociety*, London: Sage Publications, pp. 133–45.

Sirgy, M.J. (1982) 'Self-Concept in Consumer Behaviour: A Critical Review', *Journal of Consumer Research*, 9(December): 287–300.

Struch, N. and Schwartz, S.B. (1989) 'Intergroup Aggression: Its Predictors and Distinctness from In-Group Bias', *Journal of Personality and Social Psychology*, 56(3): 364–73.

Tajfel, H. (1974) 'Social Science and Intergroup Behavior', *Social Science Information*, 13: 265–93.

——(1982) 'Social Psychology of Intergroup Relations', *Annual Review of Psychology*, 33(1): 1–39.

Turner, J.C. (1987) *Rediscovering the Social Group: A Self-Categorisation Theory*, Oxford: Basil Blackwell Ltd.

——(1991) *Social Influence*, Milton Keynes: Open University Press.

Turner, J.C. and Oakes, P.J. (1986) 'The Significance of the Social Identity Concept for Social Psychology with Reference to Individualism, Interactionism and Social Influence', *British Journal of Social Psychology*, 25: 237–52.

Veer, E. (2010) 'Hiding in Plain Sight: "Secret" Anorexia Nervosa Communities on YouTube', *Advances in Consumer Research*, vol. 38. Available at: http://www.acrwebsite.org/volumes/display.asp?id=15846.

Veer, E. and Shankar, A. (2011) 'Forgive Me, Father, for I Did Not Give Full Justification for My Sins: How Religious Consumers Justify the Acquisition of Material Wealth', *Journal of Marketing Management*, 27(5–6): 547–60.

Vieira da Cunha, J. and Orlikowski, W.J. (2008) 'Performing Catharsis: The Use of Online Discussion Forums in Organizational Change', *Information and Organization*, 18(2): 132–56.

YouTube (2010) 'YouTube Fact Sheet', available at: www.youtube.com/t/fact_sheet (accessed 1 December 2010).

15

CROWDSOURCING

Andrea Hemetsberger

Keywords

consumer co-creation, consumer engagement, crowdsourcing, user innovation

A radical transformation

The world is in transformation. It always has been. Yet it is difficult to grasp the potential impact and power of transformative processes while they are emerging. Often these transformative processes involve a rediscovery of long-held social practices and traditions that have been repressed by public institutions, laws and systems. These practices surface again when new opportunities free them from the constraints they have been subject to. They gain momentum when the time is ripe.

The Internet and Web 2.0 technologies have supported radical transformation. They have contributed to a trend of public involvement in problem-solving, idea generation and work that Jeff Howe dubbed "crowdsourcing" in an article in the June 2006 issue of the magazine *Wired*. Crowdsourcing has been widely hailed as an innovative business model and democratic form of co-creation among business partners, including consumers (Surowiecki 2005; Tapscott and Williams 2006; Howe 2008; Tapscott 2008). Yet, the phenomenon as such is not new. As Belk (2010) has observed, sharing expertise, labor, ideas, and more is quite a common practice in people's private domains, and increasingly online. The Internet as a technology and open space has provided a potent infrastructure for sharing on a global basis.

Crowdsourcing was quickly embraced by management research and practice for its obvious advantage of "putting consumers to work" (Zwick *et al.* 2008). Some have expressed moral concerns, seeing it as a typical exploitation strategy with the aim of misusing the brand enthusiasm of consumers for innovation and marketing purposes (Zwick *et al.* 2008; Cova and Dalli 2009; Kozinets *et al.* 2010). Crowdsourcing remains controversial.

Crowdsourcing has become a buzzword with a myriad of connotations. Most of the managerial literature on crowdsourcing, for instance, is mainly of a tactical nature; its strategic implications are still under-theorized (Hemetsberger and Kozinets 2010). This chapter attempts to partly fill this void. I will, first, offer a brief history and a definition of crowdsourcing before I describe its different forms. Several examples will demonstrate the broad range of initiatives subsumed under the umbrella term "crowdsourcing." Subsequent sections will suggest a theoretical approach for organizing crowdsourcing. A critical discussion of the limits and promise of crowdsourcing for the future concludes this chapter.

A brief history of crowdsourcing

Crowdsourcing may be described as a grassroots development. The first Net citizens enthusiastically embraced the exchange opportunities of the Net, and crowdsourcing came naturally as a way of sharing ideas, knowledge, and collaborating on projects. Motivated and gifted coders participated in open-source projects long before the masses were able to do so on the Web, and long before the term crowdsourcing was coined. The first moderated newsgroups were introduced on Usenet in 1984 ("Hobbes' Internet Timeline" at http://www.zakon.org/robert/internet/timeline). From that time on, and even before, tech-savvy engineers, experts, and university staff established regular, remote contact with colleagues and institutions over computer networks to jointly develop the proto-Internet further, share their thoughts and otherwise work together. Already in the 1980s, probably the most radical crowdsource took place when software engineers at MIT and others joined forces to free software from unwanted restrictions, proprietary lock-ins, and software licenses that kept them from contributing to its development (Himanen 2001). The approach was simple. Someone had an idea, started coding, released it openly to the public, and invited contributions from other software engineers (Lakhani and von Hippel 2000). One of the later but most prominent examples is Linux. Linux was programmed from scratch by Linus Torvalds, a Finnish student. He published the source code on the Internet in 1991. Thousands of professional and hobbyist programmers have since contributed to and improved on the Unix-like operating system GNU/Linux. Here, crowdsourcing takes on the quality of sharing the fruits of each and every contributor's labor and synthesizing them into one great piece of work. The outcome seems incredible, even to the contributors themselves.

While the Free and Open-Source Software (FOSS) movement is a striking example, it is also a story of dedicated experts. What is even more astounding is that crowdsourcing also works for companies, who put out calls for ideas for new product designs and new advertising campaigns, for product evaluations and even co-production. It works for anyone who has an idea that inspires a sufficient number of people. The World Wide Web, invented by Tim Berners-Lee at CERN in 1991, is one of its technological foundations and the starting point for the less computer- and software-literate public to get involved in exchanges of all kinds.

The contemporary view

"Crowdsourcing is when a company takes a job which was once performed by employees and outsources it in an open call to a large undefined group of people, generally over the Internet" (http://crowdsourcing.typepad.com). In other words, crowdsourcing is "Wikipedia with everything" (Howe 2008) or the application of the FOSS principle to fields outside of software (http://www.crowdsourcing.org). Whereas today many crowdsourcing projects lack the sophisticated approach visible in FOSS projects, the principle of an open call for contributions is still the common denominator of all forms of crowdsourcing. New technology and best-practice examples originate organically from people who were formerly known as customers/consumers/users, and whose expertise lay idle. Online communities are important building blocks of crowdsourcing as they provide points of access and centers of interest that can be leveraged by organizations.

Crowdsourcing benefits crowdsourcers in many ways. In general, people often face the problem of being biased by previous decision-making and knowledge. Collective intelligence can help mitigate the effects of these biases. It can provide a variety of viewpoints that helps prevent self-serving bias and escalating commitment to prior decisions (Bonabeau 2009). Crowdsourcing also allows access to a wide range of talents. Several intriguing examples have been cited to prove that the crowd is best suited to find solutions to any given problem – from estimating the weight of an ox (Surowiecki 2005) to detecting craters on planets (NASA's Clickworkers project). In other words, crowdsourcing helps to solve problems quickly and at comparatively low cost (Surowiecki 2005).

The view of crowdsourcing outlined above proliferated quickly in business literature as a result of the obvious opportunity it represented for management. Much of the literature that followed concentrated on business uses, which does not do justice to the phenomenon and the vast opportunities provided by the Internet. Other authors have expanded the scope of crowdsourcing. Doan, Ramakrishnan and Halevy (2011), for instance, define a Crowdsourcing System (CS) as a system that enlists a group of humans to help solve a problem defined by the system owners. Users *explicitly* and *implicitly* collaborate to engage in a short-term task or to build a long-lasting artifact (solving problems) that is beneficial to the whole community. Hence, Doan *et al.*'s view on crowdsourcing concentrates on the problem-solving capacity of "crowds."

Doan *et al.* add two important points here. First, crowdsourcing is for the community. Second, many of the contributions on the Internet are *implicit*, that is, not directly aimed at contributing but a side effect of using a system. This means the average Internet user contributes almost daily to a huge pool of resources and assets that are accessible over the Internet. Every picture uploaded to Flickr, every video uploaded to YouTube or Vimeo, every book recommendation written on Amazon, or rating given on a user forum, every little tag, twitter, bug report, or Facebook blog entry contributes to an ever-increasing pool of information and is a thing of value for the global public.

I take this more inclusive point of view and describe crowdsourcing as *an attempt to join forces on the Internet in order to create something of value for humankind*. I adopt Adler, Kwon and Heckscher's (2008) view of the collaborative community as an open, global, interdependent, collegial, and organic form of cooperation based on mutual trust in a generalized exchange of contributions.

Systems and crowds

Crowdsourcing encompasses many notions. It includes systems of open innovation, user innovation (Bogers *et al.* 2010), peer production, co-creation, consumer involvement (Van Doorn *et al.* 2010), collaborative systems, microwork and more. In a wider sense, crowdsourcing denotes all kind of calls for collective work, or task fulfillment. Contributors evaluate (e.g. reviews, votes, tags), share (e.g. items, texts, knowledge), network on social platforms, build artifacts (e.g. software, texts, systems), execute tasks such as looking for extraterrestrials, or create content (Doan *et al.* 2011). Thus it takes on very different forms depending on who is involved, what the purpose is, and how it is organized.

Collective scientific research is probably the most complex collaborative endeavor of what is termed "crowdcreation." Crowdcreation initiatives involve collaborative creation or scientific problem-solving. One specific form of crowdcreation invites gifted individuals to approach scientific problems from different angles. Here the boundaries between science and organizational R&D often are blurred, merging into next-generation innovation projects, called open innovation. FOSS projects probably come closest to this form of crowdsourcing. The full potential of such projects is achieved when users contribute their thoughts, reports, evaluations, or bug reports.

Another form of scientific crowdsourcing invites people to contribute bits and pieces of work, or data that is collected and analyzed by the scientific institution itself. NASA's Clickworkers project, in which space enthusiasts looked for small craters on Mars, is probably the best-known example of this.

Many industries and non-profit, governmental and scientific organizations have established platforms for collaboration. InnoCentive (www.innocentive.com) is probably one of the most prominent examples of such a crowdsourcing platform, where organizations of all kinds can post their "challenges" and contributors can become active workers and problem solvers. The boundaries between organizations and contributors begin to blur on these platforms too. Who is not a consumer, an amateur scientist, a social worker, and who is not involved in business, anyway? Take the example of Threadless.com, which is based on the idea that consumers know best which designs they prefer. First, consumers contribute designs before voting for the ones they like best. Threadless is thus able to gauge consumer demand for new products before making investment decisions. Crowdvoting is a term for public voting or polls that leverage the community's judgment to organize and filter content such as newspaper articles, music and movies (Howe 2008). It is the most popular form of crowdsourcing, and generates the highest levels of participation, as has been demonstrated by popular TV shows, such as *American Idol*.

Another form of collaboration has been described as "crowdfunding." In crowdfunding, collaboration takes on a different role. It demands the collective cooperation, attention and trust of people, who pool their money together, usually via the Internet, in order to support efforts initiated by other people or organizations. Crowdfunding is undertaken for a variety of purposes, from disaster relief to citizen journalism to artisan wine making, to artists seeking support, to political campaigns. *The Age of Stupid* is perhaps the most publicized and successful case to date. This film raised US$1.2 million via crowdfunding, and also used crowdsourcing to distribute it and present it around the world.

"Crowd wisdom" is different in that it premises itself on a democratic principle of problem-solving and decision-making. It is based on the idea that, given a critical mass of people, the most commonly shared solution is the most accurate. The idea was put forward by Surowiecki (2005) even before "crowdsourcing" as a concept was elaborated on.

Up to now descriptions of different CS have provided an overview of different types, but without much theoretical underpinning of the differences among them. Kozinets, Hemetsberger and Schau (2008) offer the first differentiated view of the characteristics of different crowds and their orientation towards contributing. From their observations of numerous online consumer communities, they conclude that some of the communities tend to be focused on reaching generally delimited goals. Kozinets *et al.* (2008) term this type of goal-related focus *telo-specific orientation*. Other communities are innovative as a kind of byproduct of their regular online activities. These online activities often are related to lifestyles, interests, and hobbies, or simply the pursuit of general consumption interests. This type of orientation has a *communo-ludic* character.

In attempting to access these orientations, crowdsourcers should think about the design of their calls, coordination processes, and collaboration. Kozinets *et al.* (2008) only pave the way for thinking about the design of crowdsourcing systems. I approach this open question as a problem of organization, and introduce the concept of "action nets" to describe the way crowdsourcing processes that go beyond the common dyadic view of consumers–producers, or callers and contributors could be organized.

Crowds as action nets

According to Czarniawska, "organizations are but temporary reifications, because organizing never ceases" (1997, p. 780). Studies into crowdsourcing should not ignore that systems of collaboration are in constant flux. They may become institutionalized at some point (cf. Inno-Centive) but within these institutions, organizing continues. Most of today's crowdsourcing attempts are temporary and fluid organizing entities – "action nets" – comprising a multitude of actors, connections, and loci of power. Drawing on the action nets perspective developed by Barbara Czarniawska in 1997, we are able to describe the way "organizing" might work in a complex web of action. According to Czarniawska's theory, *actions* are movements or events to which an intention can be attributed by relating the movement or event to the social order in which it takes place. In a complex web of connections, many different intentions may play a role. Intentions manifest themselves as actions and are fueled by motives and characteristics of actors. In crowdsourcing calls, contributions, or announcing winners may be relevant actions.

Action nets are made up of *actors*. Similar to Actor Network Theory (Latour 2005), humans are but one actor in an action net. Actors construct collaboration, and at the same time are constructed by the collaboration. Actors can be humans, things, machines or institutions. In crowdsourcing, CS and other social platforms, companies, contributors, or technologies might be considered actors (Lanzara and Morner 2005; Hemetsberger and Reinhardt 2009).

Nets draw attention to the central activities of *connecting* and to *knots* in organizing and collaboration. *Connections* can assume a variety of forms: formal contracts, hierarchy, democratic collaboration structures, relationships or friendship. Actions, connected by translations, might produce actors, networks and macro actors. Because connected actions are different, they require *translation*, which happens at connecting points. In CS, translations present themselves in the form of "how to's," cultural norms and rules of conduct, contests, incentive systems, or translating technologies, such as games that signal to actors actions that are appropriate. *Knots* work within this system to hold all of the various parts together. They might be made up of the common goal or mission of a CS, or a platform that hosts a crowdsource.

Observing entire action nets as objects of research unveils a more comprehensive picture of how organizations are formed, stabilized, dissolved and relocated. Action nets are a way of looking at things and not an ontological element of reality (Czarniawska 2004). If we approach different forms of crowdsourcing from the perspective of action nets, we will be able to disentangle the complex ways of how actors and their actions connect, and translate them into the reality and daily routine of potential contributors.

Organizing crowds

From the extant literature, empirical research and the observation of crowds, we may tentatively categorize the way organizing of and in crowds works according to: *activation, participation,* and *collaboration.*

By *activation*, I mean all kinds of little contributions that draw on people's common knowledge and prime interests. This might be professional knowledge, or knowledge gained when pursuing hobbies. Here crowdsourcing is usually quite successful. Most people take part in such crowd-sourcing calls because it does not take too much effort to contribute to something you find fascinating. *Activation* exploits the principle of fractional hiring (Grier 2009) and weak ties (Granovetter 1973) and helps to grow a project dramatically larger than the sum of its parts. Such projects are not bound to a specific actor. Projects range from scientific research to crowd-funding projects, to grassroots collecting and sharing initiatives, to initiatives of governmental and business organizations. Examples of these are Microsoft's Photosynth, NASA's Clickworkers, Mechanical Turk, delicious.com and blogs and support forums. Even Wikipedia might be categorized as a process of activation as most of the contributions are by people who are experts in their field and just need to be activated to donate their knowledge. For them, contributing is not a huge effort. Zheng, Li and Hou (2011) emphasize that tasks should be explicitly specified, not too complex, and require a variety of skills. Kaufmann, Schulze and Veit (2011) corroborate these findings in the context of Mechanical Turk. The main actor in these projects is usually the crowd, a specific technology, as in the case of Microsoft's Photosynth technology, or a good cause as, for instance, with win4causes.com. Actions to be taken in order to establish connections among actors are comprised of: (1) *asking*: explaining why and addressing people's interests; and (2) *responding*: giving back to the community by sharing the outcome. Establishing connections here is quite straightforward. No contracts, no formal structures are required except for a sophisticated platform that collects, coordinates and evaluates contributions. Social relationships among professionals and hobbyists usually already exist, or else can be supported by such crowdsourcing systems so as to provide a social benefit to contributors. The prime motivation for contributing here is genuine interest, social reputation and the feeling of contributing to something of value for the greater collective; it is not primarily the excitement factor or the urge to engage in highly challenging tasks. Still, it is fun to contribute and be part of the crowd and thus the communo-ludic orientation of people is also leveraged.

Participation primarily addresses the communo-ludic but also the telo-specific orientation of creative consumers and takes on the quality of a fun and creative online project. Both the collaborative and the competitive character of a project can be addressed at the same time in order to attract both orientations. This has been described as "communitition" (Hutter *et al.* 2011), or "collaboratition" (Wikipedia.org). A good example of "collaboratition" is the 2009 DARPA experiment in crowdsourcing. DARPA placed 10 balloon markers across the United States and challenged teams to compete to be the first to report the location of all the balloons. Collaboration of effort was required to complete the challenge quickly and competition fueled people's motivation to be first to solve the task. In participative projects, "connections" are often established not just by means of fun hobbyist activities but by addressing social significance and reputation. "Translations" come in various forms but the most prominent examples are designed as idea (IdeaStorm), design (designContest, DesignCrowd, 99designs), or advertising contests (Mypitch, Alternative Genius). Winning is important here but not at all odds.

Actions that provide connection hubs are comprised of (1) *motivating:* the allocation of resources to the consumer community; (2) *asking*: the elicitation of consumer responses and ideas; (3) *measuring*: the evaluation of the outcome of these processes; and (4) *responding*: providing meaningful responses to the creative contributors of the consumer community, and giving back to the community.

Motivating the crowd means providing access to necessary resources, offering interesting tasks and "stuff to play and tinker with." Most of the time, communities of interest are addressed and given an arena for communal play and forms of participation. Motivating involves giving away something of value; the task itself is not motivating enough or rather participants are already intrinsically motivated by what callers are asking for. If they were not, asking for participation would not work at all, because it involves work.

Asking refers to the way companies are able to leverage the creative desire of contributors. Asking is not just about making calls that are appealing; it is primarily about sharing resources and giving clear advice on how to win the contest at hand, or how to earn money or kudos, for instance. In their study on the motives of people for uploading videos to YouTube, Huberman, Romero and Wu (2009) found that such people are primarily seeking the attention of the community.

Measuring is certainly one of the most important steps in participation, because participants' greatest ambition is to be among the best, among the most devoted, among the winners. Therefore, measuring is a very sensitive issue and participants expect to be treated seriously and honestly. They also expect the caller to act as a moderator and take a stance if measuring procedures such as voting, polls, or expert ratings seem opaque to participants.

Hence, *responding* is crucial. It refers to the way companies respond to people's quests and worries. Responding also involves making the value of contributions transparent to every single contributor. Evaluation processes become central "knots" particularly when a winner is to be chosen. Very often, evaluation is a time-consuming task, or as Cisco's chief technology officer described it: "A team of six Cisco people … worked full time on this for three months" (Jouret 2009).

Collaboration specifically addresses the telo-specific orientation; it is goal-oriented and task-focused. Collaboration is more likely to result in long-term involvement. Collaboration is often concerned with concrete outcomes in the form of artifacts, such as software or car design, or complex scientific problems in chemistry, physics, astronomy or the like. Collaboration leverages "sticky" information (von Hippel and von Krogh 2003), i.e. tacit knowledge, from collaborators and callers alike so as to produce highly innovative, and sometimes ground-breaking new solutions. Gigantic databases of knowledge have motivated millions of interested contributors/ users to contribute and increase their knowledge (von Krogh *et al.* 2003; Hemetsberger and Reinhardt 2006). Knowledge not only motivates contributors but also empowers them with a sense of control, mastery, and deep gratification.

Collaboration is fascinating because of its speed and the quality of the results it produces. It is also fascinating for uninformed observers that contributors are willing to contribute so much, and in the case of the many FOSS projects, that people work for "nothing." The fact is, however, that actors here are able to leverage huge gains from contributing. This is sometimes translated into quite lucrative monetary rewards of up to US$250,000 for those who find a solution (see e.g. InnoCentive.com). In the case of FOSS projects, where many collaborators work for free, all have access to a huge pool of free software, which in itself is an enormous economic gain. In addition, the actors involved in programming maintain warm communal relationships, gain social reputation, and improve their career opportunities (Hemetsberger 2002; Lee and Cole 2003; Leimeister *et al.* 2009). Collaboration is characterized by deep involvement and passionate immersion in work freed from corporate strangleholds, and which can develop freely in a re-enchanted form of labor (Hemetsberger 2005). Freedom, voluntary commitment, and democratic decision-making are what drives collaborative forms of crowdsourcing and tie everything together.

Some important steps for successfully establishing connections among actors are: (1) *education*: sharing information, knowledge and know-how; (2) *sharing*: providing appropriate resources and a type of "social contract" governing intellectual-capital sharing; (3) *coordination*: systems and processes to streamline and integrate contributions; (4) *evaluation*: a communally directed, democratic and clear procedure for judging output; and (5) *implementation*: some sort of meaningful conclusion to the process and sharing results or the collective outcome.

Education is often the first step in collaboration. Potential contributors are often attracted by learning opportunities, or by specific communal forms of collaboration. CS platforms educate people. Participants learn about the approach of the project, about the subject matter of the project, about working in a community and about the technology employed.

Sharing is different from exchanging. Whereas both involve providing access to important resources, sharing implies that actors do not claim ownership of any of the resources they share. This is particularly important for FOSS projects. FOSS project results are freely shared on a permanent basis and are safeguarded by specific licensing schemes that keep the source code in the public domain. Yet, even in company-controlled collaboration, companies need to share what otherwise is kept strictly confidential. Collaboration is a serious endeavor and demands high levels of trust and willingness to share not only ideas but also know-how and resources.

The *coordination* of collaborative crowdsources is highly complex and must be tailored to individual project needs. As a general principle, coordination in dispersed crowds requires systems of *coat-tailing* that tie individual work into the collective endeavor (Hemetsberger and Reinhardt 2009).

Evaluation of contributions is not a matter of voting, or expert ratings but rather about getting feedback from the crowd and kudos from well-known experts. Evaluation is meant to increase knowledge, pride and the reputation of collaborators.

The last step, *implementation* and sharing outcomes, is not just a courtesy to the crowd. Collaborators trust in the action net and "re-connect" only when a project has been worth working for in its totality.

To conclude this section, there are some key terms that deserve attention in all three practices of crowdsourcing. These are openness, sharing, alignment of interests, and transparency.

Openness is not just a buzzword for access to all kinds of digital resources. It also means being open to all sorts of unexpected ideas and accepting challenges. It is a prerequisite for a culture of *sharing*, which has nothing to do with some kind of "hippie" attitude but with people wanting other people to share their ideas with them, too. This is only possible when callers are sensitive to the *alignment of interests*. Contributors' interests are passionate work, knowledge, recognition, bonding, and some value from what they have jointly been working for. Crowdsourcers should consider these interests and legitimate their open calls by taking responsibility and making their goals and the values they are sharing *transparent* (Ågerfalk and Fitzgerald 2008). Concern, honesty, collegiality, and making contributions form the basis of trust in collaboration (Adler *et al.* 2008). Callers can build trust by showing the intensity of their own involvement in their crowdsourcing projects (see Gier at: http://dailycrowdsource.com).

The limits

Crowdsourcing and crowds are not good *per se*. Critics have pointed out that crowdsourcing can be exploitative, that it invades people's privacy and attracts people who are looking for a quick gain.

What is not captured in the *explicit* forms of collaboration, participation and activation outlined above are its *implicit* counterparts, in which contributors are mostly unaware of their contribution. Implicit crowdsourcing mechanisms are sophisticated, reaping benefits from the enormous capability of mobile devices and the Internet to collect data from consumers and archive it in huge databases. Consumers are always leaving digital footprints whenever they do a keyword search, upload pictures and messages to Facebook, register for websites, play an online game or when their mobile phone sends their coordinates to a server somewhere. Implicit crowdsourcing demands no activation or motivation procedures, it simply piggybacks on other things people like to do, or have to do (Doan *et al.* 2011). Here, it is part of the responsibility of callers to avoid misuse and, if necessary, even decide *not* to use the data collected so as to protect the privacy of consumers.

Powerful companies that want to reduce overheads and still have top talent work for them are often behind crowdsourcing. It has been argued that contributors, particularly those who never win a contest, or participate for free, are faced with a situation of worker exploitation (Cova and Dalli 2009). When consumers also have to buy what they have been working on, they even pay a price premium for the fruits of their own labor, this is double exploitation (Cova and Dalli 2009; Zwick *et al.* 2008). Creative professionals avoid design contests because such contests simply distract from paid work. Promising models are those that reward all contributors according to the wishes and aspirations that led them, the contributors, to take part in the calls in the first place.

But crowds can also be unkind. Because many calls are competitive in nature, the members of a community can easily move past friendly competition to aggressiveness as they seek to have their work selected over that of their fellow participants. This aggressiveness can take a number of forms, from making disparaging remarks about other participants in open forums (see anonymous at http://dailycrowdsource.com), to cheating by participants by inviting their network of friends to vote for them, or even by cracking and manipulating the voting system. Thus, establishing a code of conduct, including consequences for contributors who ignore it, is mandatory. Great projects do not attempt to crowdsource for everyone. It is a matter of being collegial and honest, enjoying the liberty of the Internet and following democratic principles of collaboration.

The future

The future lies in the progress of technology and society. Recent technological developments include 3D technologies, cloud computing, kinetics, and cyborg science (a combination of biogenetics and technology). We will be confronted with three-dimensional work environments, cloud sourcing, live remote tennis matches (for example) via kinetics, and computer access to human brains. Society will also experience a transformation that will be equally radical and make it possible for people to lead highly flexible and multiple life- and workstyles. Still, our prime motives will remain the same. Our communo-ludic spirit will follow exciting and fun tasks, such as gaming; our telo-specific orientation will fuel much of the complex crowdsourcing work that will be around.

- *The future of work.* People will be able to choose from among a huge variety of working opportunities, from among many different communities and crowds to join, and from among innumerable interesting projects. This will considerably enrich our future workplaces, enabling people to join the workforce even in remote and less developed areas of our planet, and leading to increased speed of productivity. It will be our challenge, however, also to ensure the quality of work and life.
- *The future of gaming.* Even more gamers will implicitly or explicitly contribute to jointly solving problems on our planet. It is the gaming industry's responsibility to develop games that take these problems and translate them into a gaming environment. This will educate people in many ways. In general, it will increase people's ability to define and solve problems collectively.

We should approach this future with what Jane McGonigal (2011) has described as urgent optimism and self-motivation to tackle important problems of society, relying on trustful relationships within the social fabric of the Net. We should engage in blissful productivity, working hard but happily for the right mission that inspires our imagination for a positive future. We should collaborate to come close to being "on the verge of making an epic win" (ibid.).

Conclusion

Much has been written about the massive shift of power from producers to consumers that technology and resulting value-creation practices have made possible. Crowdsourcing has become an established practice and an opportunity to incorporate the voices of consumers and stakeholders of all kinds into everyday decision-making and strategy. It has brought forth democratized forms of collaboration that are well suited to fostering knowledge creation, to developing and evaluating market offers, and to contributing to social and scientific progress. It is in the responsibility of governments and organizations like the World Wide Web Consortium (W3C) to keep the Web an open and accessible place for democratic engagement. For marketers and consumer researchers, the implications are simple yet radical. Instead of mass communication, marketers need to think about how to talk to consumers individually. Instead of developing products and services in-house, they will be co-developed by several stakeholders who have an honest interest in them. Instead of charging for goods and services, marketers might be forced to give them away for free to everyone, or find new business models to compensate for expenses as, for instance, in the case of Free and Open-Source Software, or the music industry. Marketers will also need to think about branding as a co-creative practice considering the increasing number of brands that are created by communities (Schroll *et al.* 2010). Consequently, consumer research must continue to explore sustainable practices of crowdsourcing that adhere to the four principles of collaboration (openness, sharing, alignment of interests, and transparency) and are based on the motives of consumers for engaging in the co-creation process.

Crowdsourcing works. For both open callers and contributors. For everyone, because everyone involved is contributing to society. Crowdsourcing – in the end – will not only be measured by the increased speed of innovation and scientific progress it is helping to drive (Tapscott 2008). It will also be measured by its potential to empower people and enrich work, and by the value it creates for society at large. It will create this value by doing what the first Net citizens did – connect and share.

Further reading

Czarniawska, B. (1997) *Narrating the Organization: Dramas of Institutional Identity*, Chicago: University of Chicago Press. [Classic read on organizing and action nets.]

Grier, D.A. (2009) *Too Soon to Tell: Essays for the End of Computer Revolution*, Hoboken, NJ: John Wiley & Sons, Inc. [For those who want a historical and contemporary view on the relation between machines and human institutions; also visit his blog and biweekly podcasts @ http://dailycrowdsource.com/author/david-alan-grier/.]

Howe, J. (2008) *Crowdsourcing: Why the Power of the Crowd Is Driving the Future of Business*, New York: Crown Publishing Group. [The classic book from the author who coined the expression Crowdsourcing.]

McGonigal, J. (2012) *Reality Is Broken: Why Games Make Us Better and How They Can Change the World*. New York: Penguin. [A plea for the future of gaming – highly interesting; read with caution.]

References

Adler, P.S., Kwon, S.-W. and Heckscher, C. (2008) "Professional Work: The Emergence of Collaborative Community," *Organization Science*, 19(2): 359–76.

Ågerfalk, P.J. and Fitzgerald, B. (2008) "Outsourcing to an Unknown Workforce: Exploring Opensourcing as a Global Sourcing Strategy," *MIS Quarterly*, 32(2): 385–409.

Belk, R. (2010) "Sharing," *Journal of Consumer Research*, 36(February): 715–34.

Bogers, M., Afuah, A. and Bastian, B. (2010) "Users as Innovators: A Review, Critique, and Future Research Directions," *Journal of Management*, 36(4): 857–75.

Bonabeau, E. (2009) "Decisions 2.0: The Power of Collective Intelligence," *MIT Sloan Management Review*, 50(2): 45–52.

Cova, B. and Dalli, D. (2009) "Working Consumers: The Next Step In Marketing Theory?," *Marketing Theory*, 9(3): 315–39.

Czarniawska, B. (1997) *Narrating the Organization: Dramas of Institutional Identity*, Chicago: University of Chicago Press.

——(2004) "On Time, Space, and Action Nets," *Organization*, 11(6): 773–91.

Doan, A., Ramakrishnan, R. and Halevy, A.Y. (2011) "Crowdsourcing Systems on the World-Wide Web," *Communications of the ACM*, 54(4): 86–96.

Granovetter, M.S. (1973) "The Strength of Weak Ties," *American Journal of Sociology*, 78: 1360–80.

Grier, D.A. (2009) *Too Soon to Tell: Essays for the End of Computer Revolution*, Hoboken, NJ: John Wiley & Sons, Inc.

Hemetsberger, A. (2002) "Fostering Cooperation on the Internet: Social Exchange Processes in Innovative Virtual Consumer Communities," in S.M. Broniarczyk and K. Nakamoto (eds), *Advances in Consumer Research*, vol. 29, Duluth, MN: Association for Consumer Research, pp. 354–6.

——(2005) "Creative Cyborgs: How Consumers Use the Internet for Self-realization," in G. Menon and A.R. Rao (eds), *Advances in Consumer Research*, vol. 32, Provo: UT, pp. 653–60.

Hemetsberger A. and Kozinets, R.V. (2010) "Talking to Creative Consumer Crowds in the Age of Networked Marketing," in N. Kornum and H. Mühlbacher (eds), "Virtual Stakeholder Dialogue in Interactive Marketing," special interest group abstract, in *Proceedings of the 39th EMAC Conference*, Copenhagen, CD-ROM.

Hemetsberger, A. and Reinhardt, C. (2006) "Learning and Knowledge-building in Open-Source Communities: A Social-experiential Approach," *Management Learning*, 37(2): 187–214.

——(2009) "Collective Development in Open-Source Communities: An Activity Theoretical Perspective on Successful Online Collaboration," *Organization Studies*, 30(9): 987–1008.

Himanen, P. (2001) *The Hacker Ethic and the Spirit of the Information Age*, London: Vintage Books.

Howe, J. (2008) *Crowdsourcing: Why the Power of the Crowd Is Driving the Future of Business*, New York: Crown Publishing Group.

Huberman, B.A., Romero, D.M. and Wu, F. (2009) "Crowdsourcing, Attention and Productivity," *Journal of Information Science*, 35(6): 758–65.

Hutter, J., Hautz, J., Füller, J., Müller, J. and Matzler, K. (2011) "Communitition: The Tension between Competition and Collaboration in Community-Based Design Contests," *Creativity and Innovation Management*, 20(1): 3–21.

Jouret, G. (2009) "Inside Cisco's Search for the Next Big Idea," *Harvard Business Review*, September: 43–5.

Kaufmann, N., Schulze, T. and Veit, D. (2011) "More Than Fun and Money: Worker Motivation in Crowdsourcing : A Study on Mechanical Turk," in *Proceedings of the Seventeenth American Conference on Information Systems*, Detroit, Michigan, August.

Kozinets, R. V., de Valck, K., Wojnicki, A.J. and Wilner, S. (2010) "Networked Narratives: Understanding Word-of-Mouth Marketing in Online Communities," *Journal of Marketing*, 74(2): 71–89.

Kozinets, R. V., Hemetsberger, A. and Schau, H.J. (2008) "The Wisdom of Consumer Crowds: Collective Innovation in the Age of Networked Marketing," *Journal of Macromarketing*, 28(4): 339–54.

Lakhani, K. R. and von Hippel, E. (2000) "How Open Source Software Works: 'Free' User-To-User Assistance," Working Paper #4117, MIT Sloan School of Management.

Lanzara, G.F. and Morner, M. (2005) "Artifacts Rule! How Organizing Happens in Open Source Software," in B. Czarniawska and T. Hernes (eds), *Actor Network Theory and Organizing*, Copenhagen: Liber and Copenhagen Business School Press, pp. 67–90.

Latour, B. (2005) *Reassembling the Social: An Introduction to Actor-Network-Theory*, Oxford: Oxford University Press.

Lee, G.K. and Cole, R.E. (2003) "The Linux Kernel Development: An Evolutionary Model of Knowledge Creation," *Organization Science*, 14(6): 633–49.

Leimeister, J.M., Huber, M., Bretschneider, U. and Krcmar, H. (2009) "Leveraging Crowdsourcing: Activation-Supporting Components for IT-Based Ideas Competition," *Journal of Management Information Systems*, 26(1): 197–224.

McGonigal, J. (2011) *Reality Is Broken: Why Games Make Us Better and How They Can Change the World*, Harmondsworth: Penguin.

Schroll, R., Hemetsberger, A. and Füller, J. (2010) "Fine Feathers Make Fine Birds: Community Brands and Branded Communities," in D.W. Dahl, G.V. Johar and S.M.J. van Osselaer (eds), *Advances in Consumer Research*, vol. 38, Duluth, MN: Association for Consumer Research, pp. 1–19.

Surowiecki, J. (2005) *The Wisdom of Crowds*, New York: Anchor Books.

Tapscott, D. (2008) *Grown Up Digital: How the Net Generation Is Changing Your World*, New York: McGraw-Hill.

Tapscott, D. and Williams, A.D. (2006) *Wikinomics: How Mass Collaboration Changes Everything*, New York: Penguin Group.

van Doorn, J., Lemon, K.N., Mittal, V., Nass, S., Pick, D., Pirner, P. and Verhoef, P.C. (2010) "Customer Engagement Behavior: Theoretical Foundations and Research Directions," *Journal of Services Research*, 13(3): 253–66.

von Hippel, E. and von Krogh, G. (2003) "Open Source Software and the Private-Collective Innovation Model: Issues for Organization Science," *Organization Science*, 14(2): 209–23.

von Krogh, G., Spaeth, S. and Lakhani, K.R. (2003) "Community, Joining, and Specialization in Open Source Software Innovation: A Case Study," *Research Policy*, 32(7): 1217–42.

Zheng, H., Li, D. and Hou, W. (2011) "Task Design, Motivation, and Participation in Crowdsourcing Contests," *International Journal of Electronic Commerce*, 15(4): 57–88.

Zwick, D., Bonsu, S.K. and Darmody. A. (2008) "Putting Consumers to Work: 'Co-creation' and New Marketing Govern-Mentality," *Journal of Consumer Culture*, 8(2): 163–96.

16

INTERACTIVE ONLINE AUDIENCES

Marie-Agnès Parmentier and Eileen Fischer

Keywords

interactive audiences, objects of attention, online fandom, participatory culture, virtual communities of consumption

Introduction

> I love reading what people have to say; it's almost as interesting as watching the shows. I like to find out if others share my reactions.
>
> (Mike, late twenties, *America's Next Top Model* fan)

For millennia, audiences have been entertained by a broad variety of spectacles in a broad variety of venues. And for millennia, those audiences have interacted to varying degrees and in diverse ways depending in part on norms that have emerged for specific types of spectacles and venues. Today, of course, audience interactions continue to happen as performances occur, in the locale where those performances are taking place; those offline interactions are likely to conform to the norms that have evolved for particular types of venues and objects of audience interest. But increasingly, audience interactions are also taking place online. Consumers are avidly embracing and experimenting with the possibilities afforded by new media and *interactive online audiences* are burgeoning, whether that interaction entails chatting online about what happened on *America's Next Top Model* after a new episode has aired (as reflected in the epigraph), participating in virtual fantasy pools during the *Stanley Cup* playoffs, exchanging tweets about the latest utterances of Lady Gaga, authoring a short story inspired by *Harry Potter* and publishing it on *fanfiction.net* or … the list is truly endless, and expanding every day.

This chapter helps to organize what we know about the phenomenon of interactive online audiences, and to highlight areas for future research on this dynamic phenomenon. It does so by: identifying how interactive online audiences compare with other types of audiences; examining evolving perspectives that inform our understanding of interactive online audiences; highlighting what we know about how online audiences interact, about why they pay attention to certain things more than others, and about what the consequences are of interacting and attending to content. We end our chapter by identifying some issues related to interactive online audiences that are inviting avenues for future research.

Types of audiences

Abercrombie and Longhurst (1998) propose a tripartite model of audiences: the simple audience, the mass audience, and the diffused audience. They argue that these three types of audiences co-exist and "feed-off one another" (ibid., p. 69). In simple audiences, audience members, i.e. spectators, are consuming a live, i.e. local, direct, i.e. unmediated, and public performance, such as a play at the theater or a sports game at a stadium. Mass audiences, in comparison, refer to audience members consuming a mass media performance (e.g., a fashion show or soccer game on television). They are typically less invested in the performance in terms of emotions, knowledge, and attention since greater social and physical distance exists between mass audience members and performers. Mass audiences also experience performances in a less ceremonious way than simple audiences do; whereas performances to simple audiences constitute exceptional events, performances to mass audiences are everyday events consumed in the private sphere. In both cases, however, a clear delineation between performer and audience exists: there are those who perform and those who watch. Diffused audiences, by contrast, break down this delineation. Performances to diffused audiences are no longer events, but "constitutive of everyday life" (ibid., p. 69). As life turns into a constant performance and everyone is both performer and audience member:

> Cultural consumers become cultural producers and vice versa ... This homogenization of producers and consumers is related to the acquisition by the audience of skills of various kinds, the absence of which previously emphasized the distance between per-formers and audience. In the right circumstances, audience members use these skills to become cultural producers in their own right.
>
> *(ibid., p. 75)*

Abercrombie and Longhurst distinguish between crowds and audiences in that the attention of crowds is unfocused whereas that of audiences is engaged with the object of attention; diffused audiences may devolve into crowds with relative ease and rapidity if their attention is not held.

Following Abercrombie and Longhurst's (1998) tripartite model, we argue that interactive online audiences emerge from diffused audiences, as new tools and technologies enable audience members to participate in various production processes, from media content (e.g., *Star Trek*, Kozinets 2007), to product development (e.g., *Jones Soda*, Schau *et al.* 2009), to celebrity (e.g., *America's Next Top Model*, Parmentier and Fischer 2010). Interactive online audiences include (though are not limited to) knowledgeable, enthusiastic, invested, and producerly active consumers. In other words, interactive online audience members are *fans*, who not only consume performances/texts and performers/public figures but also extend and enrich these products and person brands. If the term *fan* once possessed negative connotations, as in obsessed or weird *fanatic* (e.g., Trekkies), fandom today is practically mainstream, as "most people are fans of something" (Gray *et al.* 2007, p. 1), and as new media facilitates fan activities and interactions (Jenkins 2006a).

Interactive audiences do not override prior forms of audiences; rather they imbricate with them. For instance, through mobile technology, simple audience members can communicate and share bits and pieces of a live performance with those connected to their networks (e.g., sharing smartphone pictures of Will and Kate's royal Canadian tour through a social network). Through online platforms, mass audience members can be mobilized and rallied in larger numbers to influence the unfolding of a mass-mediated performance (e.g., organizing protesting efforts to save a television program from being pulled off the air through a Facebook group). And through video-sharing websites, diffused audience members can access worldwide potential audiences and perform for them from their bedroom (e.g., an aspiring teenage singer from small-town Ontario, Justin Bieber, was "discovered" by an American talent agent through YouTube).

Some of the characteristics of interactive online audiences are, however, distinctive, owing to the nature of the Internet. For example, online interactions are typically systematically archived; this constitutes a vast recorded base of ideas, opinions and artifacts that can be shared, annotated, commented upon, and circulated among both audience members and producers. Further, members of interactive online audiences communicate with a potentially vast, unknown, and unknowable "imagined audience": when interacting online, one can never be quite sure of who, if anyone, is the actual reader of an entry, a post, a profile, a tweet (Marwick and boyd 2011). Another distinctive feature of interactive online audiences is the possibility for members to present multiple selves or identities through, for example, multiple accounts; online audience members can also conceal, alter, or enhance their identities (e.g., Labrecque *et al.* 2011; Schau and Gilly 2003). Finally, interactive online audiences are liberated from the restrictions of time and place, and have the opportunity to maintain interactivity for extended periods, while in remote locations or while in transit, via a host of networked technologies.

Perspectives on interactive audiences

In this section, we outline three recent perspectives that have developed to characterize interactive audiences (see also Gray *et al.* 2007). Each view is in some sense a response to traditional notions, inspired by critical theory, of audiences as nothing more than an "unidentifiable mass who passively consumes" (Livingston 2005, p. 24, cited in Marwick and boyd 2011: 129). Habermas, for example, argued that the hierarchical structure of modern mass communication imposed a "don't talk back" format on audiences (Habermas 1962, p. 261). The three perspectives we review below move away from viewing audiences as being dominated by mass culture, and the system that produces it. While these perspectives are not specific to audiences that interact online, each is directly relevant for interactive online audiences.

The first wave of scholars who challenged the passive perspective on audiences included scholars like Henry Jenkins (e.g, *Textual Poachers*, 1992), John Tulloch (Tulloch and Jenkins, *Science Fiction Audiences*, 1995), and Camille Bacon-Smith (*Enterprising Women*, 1992). These scholars explored ideas like de Certeau's interest in the practices of the disempowered (in terms of race, gender, or class), and Fiske's emphasis on fans' resistant readings and the grassroots construction of the popular (Gray *et al.* 2007). Instead of casting audiences as passive and isolated receivers of cultural content, early fan scholars thus focused on the guerrilla-style tactics of audiences constructing meanings as well as their subcultural resistance to the preferred, intended, and dominant interpretation of a cultural product (ibid.). As the foundations of active audience theory crystallized, it became clear that audiences do not blindly consume producers' hegemonic ideologies, but, rather, negotiate the meaning of cultural texts while using interpretive lenses colored by individual experiences to do so (see also Ang 1985; Liebes and Katz 1990; and Radway 1984). Moreover, in this celebratory stance of active audiences, canonical texts such as *Textual Poachers* (1992) acted as platforms to challenge the derogatory status of fandom in the media and among non-fans by recasting it into a positive light while emphasizing its nature as a "collective strategy, a communal effort to form interpretive communities" (Gray *et al.* 2007, p. 2). In other words, rather than conceiving fandom as a pathological condition, scholars working in that tradition repositioned it as a tool of resistance and a space for emancipation. Influential work by Nancy Baym (1999) provides an additional example. Her analysis of the consumption of soap operas by female viewers organized through Usenet – an early Internet platform – emphasized the empowering quality of fandom in allowing for a space where traditional female concerns and values could be honored. Much of the work inspired by this celebratory tradition has focused on active audiences' creative and productive practices, including: fan fiction writing, convention attendance, and mobilization of fans through letter writing-campaigns or fanzine editing (see Gray *et al.* 2007; and also Kozinets 2001). Scholarly work influenced by this perspective typically pays little attention to audience members who are avid fans of something, pay careful attention to it, and talk about it with others, but who do not engage in more publicly observable and labor-intensive fan practices.

A second perspective on fans and their objects of attention emerged during the 1990s, when media markets were fragmenting rapidly into specialized narrowcast offerings, and when the access to the Internet was becoming ever more widespread. These two conditions led the way for the proliferation of *fan cultures* (cf. Jenkins 1992), as fans became more easily connected, but also as they gained recognition from marketing strategists: fans were no longer freaks, they were brand ambassadors. During this period, fan studies furthered its sociological approach as it embraced Pierre Bourdieu's sociology of consumption and segmented taste hierarchies (Bourdieu 1984). Here, rather than envisioning fandom as a space of cultural resistance and a tool for empowerment as did Thornton (1995) who examined questions of gender and tastes in the male-dominant rave subculture), scholars directed attention to how interpretive communities are embedded in wider institutions. They explored how interactive audiences may be accomplices in perpetuating dominant economic, social and cultural logics. Hence, a profound conceptual shift happened with this second stance as active audiences shifted from being conceptualized as "a counterforce to existing social hierarchies and structures" to "agents of maintaining social and cultural systems of classification and thus existing hierarchies" (Gray *et al.* 2007, p. 6).

A third perspective on interactive audiences and their objects of attention is exemplified by contemporary research framed by what Henry Jenkins (2007) has referred to as "participatory culture": networks of consumers embracing the production and circulation of user-generated content through digital platforms (e.g., posting commentaries, sharing fan art, re-editing media performances). This perspective emerged as networked and mobile technologies became integral to contemporary marketing strategy. It builds on the previous two perspectives as it further champions the belief in consumers as active producers, and not mere passive dupes, but also recognizes that digital literacy, skill sets, and access to technology (i.e., social, cultural, economic capital) are necessary to carry on such producerly activities (e.g., Hargittai 2010). Moreover, while the participatory culture perspective allows for the possibility of consumer empowerment, it incorporates a critical reflex by acknowledging potential exploitative consequences such as "arrested emotions" (cf. Bonsu *et al.* 2010), or the commodification of tastes (Jenkins 2009). Interestingly, in this context, the terms "consumers" and "fans" become synonymous, as fandom becomes a hallmark of everyday consumer culture. From a focus on structures of tastes, and meaning embedded in objects of attention, the participatory culture perspective allows for an examination of the ever-expanding range of fan practices and fan communities afforded by networked technologies. This examination matters as scholars argue that understanding contemporary fan cultures and interactive audiences is providing us with the opportunity to "capture fundamental insights into modern life" (Gray *et al.* 2007, p. 9). In doing so, scholars enrich and sometimes challenge previously held views. For instance, work informed by this third perspective has drawn attention to the potential lack of cohesiveness of fan subcultures and to the conflicts and antagonisms within and between fans, communities, faction of fans, and anti-fans (e.g., Chalmers and Acetta 2008; Click 2007; de Valck 2007; Gray 2005; Martin *et al.* 2006; Parmentier 2009a).

Taken together, these perspectives help further our understanding of some of the profound changes that have occurred over the past few decades both in terms of audience interactivity and the ways we understand it. We have moved from seeing mighty broadcasters distributing content unilaterally to undifferentiated, passive audiences, to seeing highly agentic audiences interact as they consume a multiplicity of objects of attention. Our eyes open not only to fans' consumption, in the traditional sense of paying attention, but also to their production of valuable content for themselves, others in the audience, and for those who manage objects of attention.

Current conversations about online audiences

As new perspectives on audiences have become established, and as the sites and types of inter-action have proliferated, certain topics have engaged the interest of those involved in scholarly conversations on interactive online audiences. We review what appear to be the most dominant topics to provide readers some insight into current thinking on each one. Specifically, we review conversations on the topics of "how do online audiences interact?," "why do audiences pay more collective attention to some things than to others?" and "what do audiences derive from their interactions?"

How do online audiences interact?

Not surprisingly, scholars who study interactive online audiences have been intrigued by the range of practices they have observed. Many of the documented practices that have been given different labels depending on the context being studied (e.g., fans of a particular show versus supporters of a political candidate), but can generically be found across a spectrum of online audiences. Some practices are more unique to specific contexts, but warrant attention as well. We review both the relatively generic practices and some which are more localized to certain types of objects of attention.

Schau, Muñiz and Arnould (2009) identified four types of practices that can be observed among devoted fans when they form an interactive audience for virtually any object of attention, be it a brand of soda, an iconic band, or a counter-cultural television program. They used the term social networking practices to refer to actions such as *welcoming* new audience members, *empathizing* with other audience members, and *governing* or attempting to regulate how fellow member audiences interact. Other practices they observed involved trying to create a favorable impression for an object of attention, or for fellow fans of that object. Schau *et al.* (2009) distinguish between *evangelizing*, which entails sharing positive evaluations of the object of fan attention, and *justifying*, which entails articulating rationales for why audience members devote time and effort to the object of attention. A third type of practice Schau *et al.* found common among interactive audience members entails showing one's level of engagement as a fan. *Staking* is a practice through which audience members mark distinctions between fans of different types or levels. *Milestoning* happens when audience members relay tails of seminal events that mark the progression of their fandom. *Badging* refers to creating tangible symbols to mark milestones. Brand use practices formed the fourth category Schau and her colleagues discerned. These included *customizing* practices, in which they include creating fan fiction or fan art, and *commoditizing* practices which are valenced behaviors that can serve either to heighten or diminish the commoditization of the object of attention.

It is useful to note that Schau *et al.* were focused on practices common across (offline and online) interactive audiences whether the objects of attention were brands of conventional consumer packaged goods, consumer durables, or of entertainment. Arguably, some practices that may not occur within interactive audiences across all objects of fan attention are prevalent in certain cases, such as among fans of television programs of various kinds. One practice common among interactive online audiences of television programs is *spoiling* (e.g., Jenkins 2009; Parmentier 2009a) which involves giving away forthcoming plot development that producers have not disclosed. Another practice is *gossiping* which entails sharing information or speculation about actors, about characters played by actors, or about the program itself (e.g., Baym 1999; Parmentier 2009a). A third common practice among fans of television programs is *advocating* which refers to rallying support for certain contestants or characters, and which can include lobbying for the continuation of programs at risk of cancelation (e.g., Jenkins 2009; Parmentier 2009a; Schau and Muñiz 2004; Wilson 2004). A more meta-level practice which can fuel spoiling, gossiping, or advocating is *collective intelligence generation* (Jenkins 2006a; Parmentier 2009a). Collective intelligence refers to "the knowledge of a thinking community" (Lévy (1997), cited in Jenkins (2006a: 27)). The generation of collective intelligence requires audience members not only to search for facts, hints, and clues about intriguing aspects of an object of attention, but also to develop ways to assess the credibility of information brought forward and of the bearers of information themselves. Thus, although democratic in nature, collective intelligence generation nevertheless relies on some adjudication of expertise. As Jenkins (2006b: 134) notes, "Fandom is one of those spaces where people are learning how to live and collaborate within a knowledge community."

Interactive online audiences for entertainment media also often engage in pro-social practices that offer opportunities for interaction that are not tied directly to the object of attention, and can forge closer bonds between particular audience members. One such practice is *gift-giving* (e.g., Giesler 2006; Parmentier 2009a) where members create or share (Belk 2010) something valued by others in the audience; for example, fan art is often provided by one fan to please another member of an online audience. Another practice in this category can be referred to as *playing* by which we mean seeking and providing entertainment for other members of an online audience. For example, fans may develop online games inspired by reality TV show and invite other members of the show's audiences to compete in a digital contest separated from, but thematically related to, the show (Parmentier 2009b).

While this list of practices in which interactive online audiences may engage is not exhaustive, it provides insight into what scholars have thus far discerned in the efforts to understand how online audiences interact. It suggests that some practices may be generic, while others may be specific to a genre or type of object of attention. Moreover, it highlights that both more generic and more context-specific interaction practices can be geared toward engaging with the object of attention, engaging with other members of the audience, and/or with establishing a fan's individual profile within an audience.

Why do online audiences pay attention to some things more than others?

Most objects of attention are complex, in that they are composed of multiple elements. For example, a book has multiple characters, a performer has multiple songs, and a competition-based reality television show has multiple competitors. For any reasonably complex object of interest, audiences will pay more collective attention to some sub-elements or components of that object than others. But why?

One answer to this question lies in the situated tastes and values of particular types of audiences. For example, Jenkins (1995) and Santos (2007) have respectively studied science-oriented versus human-oriented academics who are fans of *Star Trek: The Next Generation*. Interestingly, despite the disparity in both the decade in which the research was conducted and the type of audience examined, both studies report that more attention (and affection) are focused on one character in the series, the android Data, than on other characters appearing with equal frequency in the series. Santos offers an explanation for this phenomenon based on cultural competency, a term she borrows from Bourdieu (1984) and which refers to individuals' socially acquired knowledge of the signification and relative value of a particular kind of element within a particular field of practice. Cultural competencies are rooted in fields of practice, such as the academic field of science versus the academic field of the humanities. She argues that a science- versus humanities-based audience will have different cultural competencies, and see different things as being of value. Each bestows attention on the character of Data, she argues, based on the character's value within their own particular field of practice.

Another perspective on the question of what gets attended to is offered in Jenkins, Ford and Green's (2011) treatise on "spreadability" in which they examine why interactive audiences choose to share (spread) some, but not all, media material. Jenkins acknowledges that the marketing concept of "stickiness" may help to account for why audiences pay more attention to certain websites than to others. Marketers attempt to engineer digital sites to encourage a lingering engagement, but Jenkins argues this engagement is at the individual level and does not stimulate audience interaction. He argues that what triggers audience members to share and discuss element of an object of attention (such as a video of Susan Boyle's audition for *Britain's Got Talent*, which was streamed more than 77 million times on YouTube) is that the material enables them to initiate or advance conversations in both friendship-based and interest-based networks. To illustrate, he argues,

> Some people were passing Boyle's performance along as a gesture of friendship to build interpersonal relationships, as indicated above, while others were using the material to contribute to the community around a key interest. (And, of course, many may have been doing some of both.) As an avowed Christian, Boyle became the focus of online prayer circles. Science blogs discussed how someone with her body could produce such a sound. Karaoke singers debated her technique and reported an incident when she was thrown out of a karaoke bar because she was now viewed as a professional performer. Reality television blogs debated whether her success would have been possible on U.S. television given that *American Idol* excludes people of her age from competing. Fashion blogs critiqued and dissected her make-over for subsequent television appearances. Boyle's video spread, then, as a result of the many conversations the material enabled people to have with each other, whether between or among friends or through communities of common interests.
>
> *(Jenkins* et al. *2011, p. 23)*

Yet another perspective on why some aspects or elements of an object get more attention from audiences can be distilled from the literature on brand narratives (e.g., Brown 2001; Brown *et al.* 2003; Kozinets 2001; Paharia *et al.* 2011; Parmentier 2011). Though studies of brand narratives are many and varied, they converge in underscoring the power of a story or myth (Holt 2004) to engage audience attention. And recent research suggests that some stories have more potential than others to engage audiences, such as a narrative of an "underdog" who triumphs in spite of obstacles (Paharia *et al.* 2011). The rich literature on stories, myths and fairytales underscores that various narrative elements may engage audiences (e.g., Frye 1990). Thus, when one narrative element of an object of attention becomes more compelling – as when a contestant on a reality television show is seen as an underdog relative to other contestants (Parmentier 2009a) – that element may attract more interactive online audience attention than others.

These three explanations of what attracts audience attention are not exhaustive. They serve, however, to draw attention to the multi-faceted drivers of interactions that arise from and give momentum to online audience attention. The field of practice that shapes audience members' values and tastes, audience members' social motivation to contribute to network conversations, and the creative processes that embed specific characters or things in a compelling storyline, are distinct factors that collectively help to explain some of the vast disparity between the attention paid to some, versus other, objects or elements of objects.

So what? Consequences of online audience interactions

Consequences of online audience interaction have been of considerable interest. In our review of perspectives on audience interaction, we noted that an assumption of at least some of the dominant perspectives is that online audience interaction empowers consumers and enables them to become active participants in the co-creation of that which they consume. In particular, it has been argued that consumers participating in interactive audience produce and derive "value" beyond that which producers of materials generate. Specifically, it has been argued that as a result of their interactions with other audience members who share interests in the same objects of attention, people may: acquire cultural capital; discover or develop symbolic resources that can be shared with other people; derive social support from other audience members; increase the social standing of that audience in the wider society; overcome challenges that audience members face in consuming the attention object; create new consumption opportunities; and improve the attention object via customization or augmentation (Schau *et al.* 2009).

These value-producing benefits of online audience interaction might in and of themselves seem like a bonanza for those who market particular objects of attention. Beyond these benefits, marketers are also able to engage in "thought tracing" and "activity tracing" (Deighton and Kornfeld 2009, p. 6) via surveillance of online audience interactions, enabling them to better understand people's interests, motivations and perceptions. As audiences interact online, marketers also can find opportunities to participate in and benefit from the exchanges that occur between audiences members, for example, by recruiting audience members to engage in online word-of-mouth communications about their offerings (Kozinets *et al.* 2010). And online audience interactions afford marketers unprecedented opportunities to contribute to contemporary culture, as audience members put into circulation the words and images marketers create, such as Dove's campaign for Real Beauty (Deighton 2007).

Counterbalancing this inventory of outcomes that benefit marketers and audience members alike are analyses that show how online interactions may have deleterious consequences. For example, audience members who are already marginalized by virtue of race, class, or gender may be even further disenfranchised when the tastes and preferences of those who are more active members of online audiences are legitimated and valorized (cf. Hargittai 2010). And the economic rent arising from audiences' value producing actively is typically unevenly distributed (Zwick *et al.* 2008). Nor are interactive online audiences always linked to positive outcomes for marketers (see e.g., Jenkins *et al.* 2011). Controlling such audiences is difficult, if not impossible. When displeased, online audiences can circulate their complaints rapidly and effectively, leaving marketers looking hapless at best and sinister at worst.

Areas for future research

To stimulate thought on future research, we single out three potential avenues. We highlight these mostly because we ourselves would be an avid audience for scholarly inquiry on these topics.

What about lurkers?

It is only natural that what we know thus far about the consequences of online audience interaction is relevant to those members who actively participate. But what about "lurkers," i.e. those who are avid fans of something, but not particularly inclined to interact with other audience members, even though they may observe those interactions online? Early work by Kozinets (1999) highlighted that those who love some attention object and interact with others fans are likely quite different than those who have the same affection for the object, but do not interact. Yet we know little about whether and how lurkers derive value, or about how the interactions of other audience members affect them – whether positively or negatively, or both. We also know less than is required about how lurkers may add value, for example, by signifying the level of interest in some strand of audience interaction, or whether their actions may diminish something valued by an interactive audience.

From networks to Netwars?

What happens when the interactions of audiences lead to outcomes that producers regard as threatening? Two recent studies have found evidence that producers sometimes wage "war" on networked audiences: Giesler's (2008) study of the clampdown on music downloaders achieved by content owners, and Koulikov's (2010) study of the conflicts between online fans who created subtitled versions of Japanese anime films, and those holding the North American distribution rights to the films. Yet in other cases, marketers have backed away from efforts to constrain actions by audiences that seem to threaten either their control or their profit margins, or both (see examples in Jenkins *et al.* 2011). We would welcome more studies that shed light on diverse cases of clashes between marketers and interactive online audiences, examining what accounts for variation in both short-term dynamics and long-term consequences.

Interactive online audiences' irresponsibility?

One final topic on which we could find no relevant prior research concerns how individuals or groups who are objects of online audience attention may be negatively affected by interactions of online audiences. Recent examples that spark our interest are the public meltdown of Charlie Sheen and the untimely death of Amy Winehouse. Pundits are raising questions about the role of avid interactive audiences in encouraging and accelerating the downward spirals of these artists (Topping 2011). Scholarly attention to the topic seems warranted.

Indeed, scholarly attention to a much deeper and broader range of topics related to interactive online audiences is required. The phenomenon is a dynamic one, fueled by changing technologies and experimentation on the part of audiences and marketers. And the implications of the phenomenon for contemporary individuals and contemporary culture appear enormous.

Further reading

Baym, N.K. (1999) *Tune In, Log On: Soaps, Fandom, and Online Community*, Thousand Oaks, CA: Sage Publications. [A classic read on online fandom.]

Jenkins, H. (2006) *Convergence Culture: Where Old and New Media Collide*, New York: New York University Press. [A contemporary account of interactions between online audiences and media producers.]

Jenkins, H., Ford, S. and Green, J. (2011) *Spreadable Media: Creating Value and Meaning in a Networked Culture*. New York: New York University Press. [Cutting-edge research on how interaction creates value.]

References

Abercrombie, N. and Longhurst, B. (1998) *Audiences: A Sociological Theory of Performance and Imagination*, London: Sage.

Ang, I. (1985) *Watching Dallas: Soap Opera and the Melodramatic Imagination*, New York: Routledge.

Bacon-Smith, C. (1992) *Enterprising Women: Television Fandom and the Creation of Popular Myth*, Philadelphia, PA: University of Pennsylvania.

Baym, N.K. (1999) *Tune In, Log On: Soaps, Fandom, and Online Community*, Thousand Oaks, CA: Sage Publications.

Belk, R. (2010) "Sharing," *Journal of Consumer Research*, 36(February): 715–34.

Bonsu, S.K., Darmody, A. and Parmentier, M.-A. (2010) "Arrested Emotions in Reality Television," *Consumption, Markets & Culture*, 13(1): 91–107.

Bourdieu, P. (1984) *Distinction: A Social Critique of the Judgment of Taste*, Cambridge, MA: Harvard University Press.

Brown, S. (2001) *Marketing: The Retro Revolution*, London: Sage.

Brown, S., Kozinets, R.V. and Sherry, Jr., J.F. (2003) "Teaching Old Brands New Tricks: Retro Branding and the Revival of Brand Meaning," *Journal of Marketing*, 67(July): 19–33.

Chalmers, T.D. and Accetta, R. (2008) "Rejecting the Hard-Core: An Examination of Peripheral Members of Consumption-Oriented Communities," presentation given at the Consumer Culture Theory Conference, Boston, MA.

Click, M. (2007) "Untidy: Fan Response to the Soiling of Martha Stewart's Spotless Image," in J. Gray, C. Sandvoss, and C.L. Harrington (eds), *Fandom: Identities and Communities in a Mediated World*, New York: New York University Press, pp. 305–15.

de Certeau, M. (1984) *The Practice of Everyday Life*, Berkeley, CA: University of California Press.

Deighton, J. (2007) *Dove: Evolution of a Brand*, Boston, MA: Harvard Business School Press.

Deighton, J. and Kornfeld, L. (2009) "Interactivity's Unanticipated Consequences for Marketers and Marketing," *Journal of Interactive Marketing*, 23: 4–10.

de Valck, K. (2007) "The War of the eTribes: Online Conflicts and Communal Consumption," in B. Cova, R. V. Kozinets, and A. Shankar (eds), *Consumer Tribes*, Burlington, MA: Butterworth-Heinemann, pp. 260–73.

Fiske, J. (1989) *Understanding Popular Culture*, Boston: Unwin Hyman.

——(1987) *Television Culture*, New York: Routledge.

Frye, N. (1990) *Myth and Metaphor: Selected Essays, 1974–1988*, ed. R.D. Denham, Charlottesville, VA: University Press of Virginia.

Giesler, M.(2006) "Consumer Gift Systems," *Journal of Consumer Research*, 33(September): 283–90.

——(2008) "Conflict and Compromise: Drama in Marketplace Evolution," *Journal of Consumer Research*, 34(April): 739–53.

Gray, J. (2005) "Antifandom and the Moral Text," *The American Behavioral Scientist*, 48(7): 840–58.

Gray, J., Sandvoss, C. and Harrington, C.L. (2007) *Fandom: Identities and Communities in a Mediated World*, New York: New York University Press.

Habermas, J. (1962) *Strukturwandel der Öffentlichkeit: Untersuchungen zu eine Kategorie der bürgerlichen Gesellschaft*, Frankfurt/M: Suhrkamp.

Hargittai, E. (2010) "Digital Na(t)ives Variation in Internet Skills and Uses among Members of the 'Net Generation,'" *Sociological Inquiry*, 80(1): 92–113.

Holt, D. (2004) *How Brands Become Icons: The Principles of Cultural Branding*, Boston, MA: Harvard Business Press.

Jenkins, H. (1992) *Textual Poachers: Television Fans and Participatory Culture*, New York: Routledge.

——(1995) ""How Many Starfleet Officers Does It Take to Change a Lightbulb?": *Star Trek* at MIT," in J. Tulloch and H. Jenkins (eds), *Science Fiction Audiences: Watching Doctor Who and Star Trek*, London: Routledge, pp. 213–36.

——(2006a) *Convergence Culture: Where Old and New Media Collide*, New York: New York University Press.

——(2006b) *Fans, Bloggers, and Gamers: Exploring Participatory Culture*, New York: New York University Press.

——(2007) "Afterword: The Future of Fandom," in J. Gray, C. Sandvoss, and C.L. Harrington (eds), *Fandom: Identities and Communities in a Mediated World*, New York: New York University Press, pp. 357–64.

——(2009) "Buying into *American Idol*," in S. Murray and L. Ouellette (eds), *Reality TV: Remaking Television Culture*, 2nd edn, New York: New York University Press, pp. 343–62.

Jenkins, H., Ford, S. and Green, J. (2011) *Spreadable Media: Creating Value and Meaning in a Networked Culture*, New York: New York University Press.

Koulikov, M. (2010) "Fighting the Fan Sub War: Conflicts between Media Rights Holders and Unauthorized Creator/Distributor Networks," *Transformative Works and Cultures*, no. 5. doi:10.3983/twc.2010.0115.

Kozinets, R.V. (1999) "E-Tribalized Marketing?: The Strategic Implications of Virtual Communities of Consumption," *European Management Journal*, 17(3): 252–64.

——(2001) "Utopian Enterprise: Articulating the Meanings of *Star Trek*'s Culture of Consumption," *Journal of Consumer Research*, 28(1): 67–88.

——(2007) "Inno-tribes: *Star Trek* as Wikimedia," in B. Cova, R.V. Kozinets, and A. Shankar (eds), *Consumer Tribes*, Burlington, MA: Butterworth-Heinemann, pp. 194–209.

Kozinets, R.V., de Valck, K., Wojnicki, A. and Wilner, S.J.S. (2010) "Networked Narratives: Understanding Word-of-Mouth Marketing in Online Communities," *Journal of Marketing*, 74: 71–89.

Labrecque, L. I., Markos, E. and Milne, G.R. (2011) "Online Personal Branding: Processes, Challenges, and Implications," *Journal of Interactive Marketing*, 25: 37–50.

Lévy, P. (1997) *Collective Intelligence: Mankind's Emerging World in Cyberspace*, Cambridge, MA: Perseus Books.

Liebes, T. and Katz, E. (1990) *The Export of Meaning: Cross-Cultural Readings of Dallas*, New York: Oxford University Press.

Martin, D.M., Schouten, J.W. and McAlexander, J.H. (2006) "Claiming the Throttle: Multiple Femininities in a Hyper-Masculine Subculture," *Consumption, Markets and Culture*, 9(3): 171–205.

Marwick, A.E. and boyd, d. (2011) "I Tweet Honestly, I Tweet Passionately: Twitter Users, Context Collapse, and the Imagined Audience," *New Media & Society*, 13(1): 114–33.

Paharia, N., Keinan, A. Avery, J. and Schor, J. (2011) "The Underdog Effect: The Marketing of Disadvantage through Brand Biography," *Journal of Consumer Research*, 37(5): 775–90.

Parmentier, M.-A. (2009a) "Consuming and Producing Human Brands: A Study of Online Fans of Reality TV," dissertation thesis, York University, Canada.

——(2009b) "Consumer Entrepreneurs: A Netnographic Study of Facebook's Next Top Model," in A.L. McGill and S. Shavitt (eds), *Advances in Consumer Research*, vol. 36, Duluth, MN: Association for Consumer Research, pp. 906–7.

——(2011) "When David Met Victoria: Forging a Strong Family Brand," *Family Business Review*, 23(3): 217–32.

Parmentier, M.-A. and Fischer, E. (2010) "The Role of Brand Communities in the Construction of Celebrity," in D.W. Dahl, G.V. Johar, and S. M.J. van Osselaer (eds), *Advances in Consumer Research*, vol. 38, Duluth, MN: Association for Consumer Research (online).

Radway, J.A. (1984) *Reading the Romance: Women, Patriarchy, and Popular Literature*, Chapel Hill, NC: The University of North Carolina Press.

Santos, J. (2007) "Data on Data: Viewer Responses to *Star Trek: The Next Generation*,"*Particip@tions*, 4(1), available at: www.participations.org/Volume%204/Issue%201/4_01_santos.htm#_edn12 (accessed July 27, 2011).

Schau, H.J. and Gilly, M.C. (2003) "We Are What We Post? The Presentation of Self in Personal Webspace," *Journal of Consumer Research*, 30(4): 385–404.

Schau, H.J. and Muñiz Jr., A. (2004) "If You Can't Find It, Create It: An Analysis of Consumers' Engagement with *Xena: Warrior Princess* and the Creation of Consumer Generated Subtext," in B. Khan and M.F. Luce (eds), *Advances in Consumer Research*, vol. 31, Duluth, MN: Association for Consumer Research, pp. 554–7.

Schau, H.J., Muñiz Jr., A. and Arnould, E.J. (2009) "How Brand Community Practices Create Value," *Journal of Marketing*, 73(September): 30–51.

Thornton, S. (1995) *Club Cultures*, Cambridge: Polity.

Topping, A. (2011) "Amy Winehouse: The Last Days of the Good-Time Girl Who Did Not Want Fame," available at: www.guardian.co.uk/music/2011/jul/27/amy-winehouse-last-days-camden (accessed July 27, 2011).

Tulloch, J. and Jenkins, H. (1995) *Science Fiction Audiences: Watching Dr. Who and Star Trek*, London: Routledge.

Wilson, P. (2004) "Jamming *Big Brother*: Webcasting, Audience Intervention, and Narrative Activism," in S. Murray and L. Ouellette (eds), *Reality TV: Remaking Television Culture*, New York: New York University Press, pp. 323–43.

Zwick, D., Bonsu, S.K. and Darmody, A. (2008) "Putting Consumers to Work: 'Co-Creation' and New Marketing Govern-mentality," *Journal of Consumer Culture*, 8(2): 163–96.

17

DATING ON THE INTERNET

Helene M. Lawson and Kira Leck

Keywords

age, gender, identity, information and communication technologies, interracial, intimacy, LGBT, online dating, self-esteem, trust

New and different media change society. Marshall McLuhan said of television, "The medium is the message" in that media impose an inherent structure which is itself a form of message apart from the inner message, which is what we normally think of as the message, that the medium transmits (McLuhan 1964). The same view can be taken of dating using digital media. The digital medium is an extension of our communication faculties. The Internet and its digital helpers such as photo editors, animated graphics and sound, have made a new dating venue offering new opportunities and restrictions. The Internet has fostered dating for several diverse groups including heterosexuals, homosexuals and those seeking recreational sex. We will examine these three dating moieties and the characteristics of Internet dating that are common to all Internet daters and how the digital age has affected them.

There is an important discovery, the global insignificance of income and education, which condenses a great deal of the statistics about Internet dating. Jessica Sautter (Sautter *et al.* 2006, 2010) examined attitudes towards Internet dating among single American Internet users and found that, apart from being single, simply being on the Internet frequently for whatever reason was the common characteristic of Internet daters. While being on the Internet regularly was controlled primarily by socioeconomic factors affecting Internet access and digital literacy, these same socioeconomic factors had no effect on the choice of whether or not to engage in Internet dating. In her study, Internet users tended to be younger, richer, more educated, not disabled, live in a suburb or city and more likely to be white. Sautter thus identified a "digital divide" separating Internet users from non-users but found all singles on the digital side of the divide equally likely candidates for online dating. A Dutch study (Valkenburg and Peter 2007) found no effect of income and a slight negative effect of increased education on the likelihood of one being an Internet dater. However, the Dutch study recruited its sample using the Internet, thus bypassing any digital divide.

Why daters use the Internet

Daters use the Internet because they can reach a larger pool of potential partners than they could otherwise (Lawson and Leck 2006). The Internet provides them with companionship, emotional support (ibid.), and freedom from commitment and role expectations (McKenna *et al.* 2002; Whitty and Carr 2003, 2006; Lawson and Leck 2006). These are among the immediate reasons for choosing to go online to meet a new other for a conversation and possibly more. Singles ads in print media serve much the same purposes, but the process is slower.

Beyond expediency there are reasons inherent in the digital medium itself. The Internet gives one more control over one's self-presentation. Users can selectively edit which aspects of themselves they will allow prospective dates to see. This option is useful to individuals who possess characteristics that they believe might make them less desirable to others. For example, participants in online newsgroups often omitted details like being overweight and having children. The ability to regulate the rate of flow of information is also valued by online daters (McCown *et al.* 2001; Van Acker 2001; Hardey 2002; Ben-Ze'ev 2004). Because facial expressions are revealing and require skill to control, people who are shy, anxious, and deficient in social skills may prefer to avoid face-to-face contact. Shy and anxious members of Internet newsgroups in McKenna *et al.*'s (2002) sample reported that computer-mediated communication allowed them to express more of their true selves than they felt comfortable sharing in face-to-face communications. The online world offers an enormous selection of people one would never have encountered before.

Heterosexual marriage-seekers

By far the most academically scrutinized group of Internet daters is heterosexual marriage-seekers. Studies centered on the use of online dating services to find long-term heterosexual partners currently constitute most of the literature. These services include not only sites such as eHarmony™ that are specifically oriented toward marriage and suggest possible mates to their clients but sites like Yahoo Personals that are broader in scope and appeal to non-marital date seekers as well. What heterosexual daters seek in a partner as seen in these studies does not appear to be significantly different from that expected for non-Internet daters. Singles ads generally contain information indicating the level of social skill, the financial condition (in the case of males), the level of education and the hobbies of the advertiser. Few significant patterns have been reported based on these characteristics. As expected, males tend to represent themselves as good providers and females tend to represent themselves as young and beautiful. These habits are consistent with the "evolutionary perspective" (Badahdah and Tiemann 2005; Alterovitz and Mendelsohn 2009; Dunn *et al.* 2010) that posits that people unconsciously choose partners for their optimum reproductive benefit. Race, body type and age exert effects on Internet pairing that we will discuss. There appears to be little difference between those who seek marriage and those who just want a casual date although casual dating is not well studied.

Homosexual daters

Although the Internet dating population appears to be predominantly heterosexual and conventional, the Internet is also a valuable resource for daters with alternative sexualities. At the present time the majority of LGBT (lesbian, gay, bisexual and transgender) date recruitment appears to be done online. One of the largest and most complete studies devoted to the demography of Internet dating preferences is the HCMST (how couples meet and stay together) database at Stanford University (Rosenfeld and Thomas 2010). This longitudinal survey studied the effects of the Internet on heterosexual and LGBT relationships. Among the conclusions of this survey was that persons with Internet access were about 30 percent more likely to have a partner than those without Internet access. In the case of same-sex couples still in existence in 2009 who had met in the period between 1994 and 1998, both heterosexual and same-sex couples had about a near-equal 3.4 percent chance of having met online. However, same-sex couples having met in the period from 2007 to 2009 had a 61 percent chance of having met online while heterosexual couples had a 21.5 percent chance, essentially the average of the total population, of having met online. This probably represents the effect of propinquity because 74 percent of couples who met online were total strangers when they met. The mean distance of residence for married heterosexual couples was 50 miles from where they were raised. That for men partnered with men was 150 miles and for women partnered with women was 100 miles. This suggests that the Internet is useful in brokering the typically long-distance meetings of non-heterosexuals.

Lever *et al.* (2008) surveyed Internet users on their sexual preferences and experiences using Internet personals sites. While the actual fractions of LGBT persons in the population is not certain, the fraction of the Internet personals site users sampled was 73.7 percent male. Of all the site users, 10.9 percent were LGBTs. However, only 0.7 percent listed themselves as lesbians. This suggests a large gender bias in the use of Internet personals sites as opposed to the totality of the Internet studied by Rosenfeld and Thomas. Respondents were asked to comment on their impressions including whether they were seeking "discreet" affairs. Those who responded in the affirmative were largely bisexuals (44 percent of men and 22 percent of women). Circumvention of scrutiny and overcoming the geographic restriction of rural communities were among the reasons respondents gave for using the Internet. There are few if any reliable data on frequency of homosexual behavior in the population and most of this is on Internet sites. Reported values range from 1–15 percent for the fraction of the population who are LGBT. Janus and Janus (1993) found 9 percent of men and 5 percent of women report frequent or ongoing homosexual experiences. For definitions of homosexual orientation not based on a person's recent activity, these figures might represent lower bounds.

Daters seeking recreational sex

Not all Internet matchmaking is intended to form permanent partnerships where couples live together as a man and a wife would. Some relationships seem intended for play and evanescence. While there are less data on alternative sexual styles, BDSM has been studied to a limited extent. In order to avoid conflating BDSM with LGBT, we have concentrated our attention on heterosexual BDSM. This phenomenon is largely Internet-based. In BDSM, as in swinging, the Internet has taken over the function of specialty magazines and other venues for personal advertisements. Swinging has a long history of non-Internet recruitment methods (Bartell 1971) but has been little studied as part of Internet dating. Wysocki and Thalken (2007) conducted one of the few surveys to explore this largely uncharted world of Internet dating by using BDSM as a surrogate for all forms of novelty recreational sex. They focused on one site, www.alt.com, which was primarily associated with BDSM, making a textual study of personal advertisements. The study contributes two useful insights. One is the extension of the taxonomy of relationship pairing to meet the needs of this clientele. Most dating sites have the four choices: men looking for women, women looking for men, men looking for men and women looking for women. Wysocki and Thalken (2007) observed six basic pairing categories leading to the possibility of 45 pairing choices based on: men, women, couple, gay couple, lesbian couple and group. The second insight is into the demography of the site's users. The average age is 39, slightly less than the average age of participants in the HCMST study of conventional relationships but the same as in Sautter's study of Internet daters. The percentage of participants with college degrees was 41.3 percent, slightly higher than that seen in the HCMST study of couples and higher than the 37 percent seen for Internet daters in Sautter's study of single daters – although there is some difficulty in matching the different measures used in the different studies. In Wysocki and Thalken's (2007) study, 2.7 percent of site users listed themselves as having doctoral degrees, but race and income were not reported.

Discussion

Tabulating the diversity of Internet daters' motivations establishes that there are different communities. Some of these intersect such as those based on race, religion and sexual orientation. Others, as those based on sexual recreational specialties, do not share the same sites and do not intersect. Yet, in spite of this lack of intersection, the demography of the ages, educations and apparent incomes of all Internet daters seem homogeneous within the broad confidence space of the cross-tabulation of the differently conditioned studies available. Further research is needed in order to identify the key differentiating factors between the groups and contrast their use.

The Internet dating experience

Self-presentation

The first step in entering the world of online dating is posting one's picture and profile on a dating-related site. Because digital media are capable of being rapidly and easily overwritten; the digital age can be characterized as one of ephemeral realities. Protocols, software, storage media, and websites swiftly become obsolete and information in its original form becomes inaccessible and lost. As a result, the online world lives ever in the present, and history must be continually reconstructed. Thus, for the online dater a new face is always available in the form of a new venue, a new and better picture, or a revised profile. There are many tools individuals seeking online partners can use to construct and manage an online persona for others to see.

Self-presentation involves intentional written or verbal communication in the form of "expressions given," paraverbal (tone, emphasis, writing style and the use of popular codes) and nonverbal cues of "expressions given off" (Goffman 1959). The shortage of nonverbal cues may make it easier for online daters to preen their online identity. Furthermore, the perception that some daters have of online interaction as a virtual play may increase the possibility of deceptive self-presentation (Danet 2001; Albright and Conran 2003). Online daters who have as their goal an intimate offline relationship face a dilemma of whether to present an idealized or true self. This pressure tends to create a balance in the self-presentation of online daters (Reis and Shaver 1988; Ellison *et al.* 2006). Daters in Brym and Lenton's (2001) sample believed they were mostly truthful in their online interactions, possibly because they anticipated eventually meeting face-to-face. Similarly, Gibbs, Ellison, and Heino (2006) found that participants whose goal was a long-term relationship tended to be more honest and disclose a greater amount of personal information than users who were more interested in short-term relationships. Toma and Hancock (2010) found that daters whose written goals indicated interest in long-term relationships tended to digitally enhance their photos more than daters looking for short-term relationships. Additionally, more attractive users and users with long-term relationship goals were more likely to post online photos of themselves than were less attractive individuals with short-term relationship goals.

Online daters use a variety of methods to establish credibility. Participants in Ellison *et al.*'s (2006) sample reported that when designing "honest" profiles, they followed some of the same guidelines they used to screen potential partners' profiles. Daters crafted well-written self-descriptions that reflected their education level and seriousness about being in a relationship, and told stories that they believed demonstrated certain personality traits. Most users posted photographs and some reported specifically posting photos in which they were standing due to their belief that people who use leaning poses do so in an attempt to conceal their weight. Similarly, Yurchisin, Watchravesringkan, and McCabe (2005) found that Internet dating service members reported creating profiles that they believed were honest. Other users solicited feedback from friends or family members to verify their self-descriptions, a method which was also reported by Ellison *et al.*'s participants. Brym and Lenton (2001) found that a quarter of their participants admitted to misrepresenting some aspect of their identity, with age, marital status, and appearance being the most common attributes.

Profile examination

The process of dating online often begins with profile examination (Albright and Conran 2003) to determine the superficial suitability of potential partners. This is like checking out a potential date in an office setting except that the available cues are different. In the office, the physical appearance, clothing, body language, tone of voice and manner of a potential date can be examined in detail. These cues are not available online. Rather due to the large numbers of daters, limited time and cognitive capacity, individuals seeking online dates tend to use pre-conceived assumptions based on profile details to exclude undesirables (Ellison *et al.* 2006). Daters have reported seeking profiles that are well-written based on the belief that poorly-written profiles are indicators of lack of education or serious interest in dating (Levine 2000; Ellison *et al.* 2006). Walther and Tidwell's (1995) respondents emphasized the importance of timing of emails (whether users exchanged emails on a tit-for-tat basis or sent multiple emails before receiving a response). Participants in Ellison *et al.*'s sample perceived that the last time users accessed a dating site was a reliable indicator of availability for and seriousness about dating. Daters sought cues to estimate the reliability of their potential dates.

Cues used by online daters include links on homepages or profiles (Kibby 1997), email addresses (Donath 1999), nicknames, and use of emoticons (Albright and Conran 2003). Because online dating is often perceived by a few as being rife with misrepresentation (Brym and Lenton 2001), it is not surprising that users employ multiple methods to gauge the veracity of personas presented online (Berger 1979: Ramirez *et al.* 2002; Tidwell and Walther 2002; Ellison *et al.* 2006). Walther and Parks (2002) discussed the use of "warranting," a method that involves seeking out information that is difficult to misrepresent or control. Some of their respondents reporting reading postings made in newsgroups, blogs, or other online bulletin boards to obtain information about potential dates' identity, values, attitudes, and opinions.

Initial mediated communications

Once a pair have met on the Internet, there follows a period of Internet-mediated communication during which the pair decide their suitability as discussed by Albright and Conran (2003) among others. Conversing in chat rooms or on bulletin boards, or privately through email or messenger services constitutes this stage. When users begin to communicate privately, they may share highly intimate details about their personal lives. In this phase, self-disclosure increases and online daters perceive greater levels of intimacy; they may begin to exchange personal photos and talk on the phone (Couch and Liamputtong 2008), which can result in "falling in love." This may be followed by a "meeting of minds" where partners perceive each other as "soul mates" whose relationship transcends physicality due to their attraction being based primarily on written conversations. If partners then decide to take their relationship to the next level, they may use emails or phone calls to arrange meetings offline (Hardey 2008).

Meeting in person

If Internet daters find each other compatible, they move on to the next step of relationship building: face-to-face meeting. This final stage requires established trust. Basic interpersonal trust may be contractual trust based on social contracts as in family relationships or trust based on time in relations (Govier 1992). Thus the amount of time spent together online is paramount since no social contracts exist at this point. From a psychological standpoint, meeting in person may turn out to confirm that final stage in relationship forming described by Sprecher (2009), that of the "real relationship" in which partners develop mutuality. After having acquired information gathered in previous stages (Levinger 1974), they become attracted to each other and engage in further self-disclosure, invest in each other, and acquire a new identity as a couple. Most users do not begin to perceive themselves as being coupled until they have met face-to-face.

Current phenomenology in Internet dating

Interracial differences and interracial dating

Differences in dating patterns between races and interracial dating are current topics of interest in Internet dating studies. While respondents in both Lawson and Leck's (2006) and Sautter *et al.*'s (2010) samples tended to be white, the conspectus of research papers suggests that the general characteristics of Internet daters' preferences for race and body type do not appear significantly different from those expected for non-Internet daters, except that some minorities have displayed distinct preferences that would not be immediately anticipated. However, the Internet does appear to make interracial dating less difficult. At the present time, the general rule is that those seeking dates on the Internet prefer to date members of their own race but will date whites and some other races. The desired female body tends to be heavier for blacks than that preferred by white and other races.

An example of the general pattern for racial preference given by Sweeny and Borden (2009) found that while some singles are willing to date a person of any race, most are more likely to prefer to date someone of their same race. This research was done using the Internet as a sampling tool and correlating answers to yes-or-no questions with multinomial logistic regression. Based on this type of survey, Yancey (2009) upheld that African-Americans were less willing to interracially date on the Internet than other races. He also found that African-Americans were particularly less willing to date whites. Females were somewhat less willing than males to interracially date and significantly less likely to date Asians. However, a somewhat less xenophobic impression was obtained when responses were more simply grouped and presented as percentages. In this way Wilson *et al.* (2007) examined specifically black American willingness to date interracially through Match.com. Seventy-five percent of males and 56 percent of females were willing to date whites, while 91 percent of males and 75 percent of females were wiling to interracially date. The order of racial preference for black American males, apart from black American, was Hispanic, the most preferred, followed by white, Asian and Native American. For black American females the preference order was the same except that they appeared to prefer Native Americans to Asians. Feliciano (Feliciano *et al.* 2009) found whites somewhat less willing to date interracially. Only 43 percent of white males and 27 percent of females were willing to date interracially. For both white men and women expressing a racial preference, Latinos were the least likely to be excluded for both genders.

Age effects in dating

Studies of Internet daters indicate that they tend to be middle-aged. The average age of users in Rosenfeld and Thomas' (2010) and Sautter *et al.*'s (2010) samples was 39. Participants in Lawson and Leck's (2006) sample were slightly younger at 33. The most active online daters in Valkenburg and Peter's (2007) survey of Dutch Internet users ranged from ages 30–50. Similarly, Stephure, Boon, MacKinnon, and Deveau (2009) found that people may become more involved with online dating as they age, possibly as a result of becoming dissatisfied with traditional dating. The variability in age of Internet daters is surprising. Alterovitz and Mendelsohn (2009) explored ages of Internet daters through the advertisements they posted and found a significant number of participants over the age of 75. Furthermore, they found that 25 percent of these were still employed.

Age preference is a factor in choosing a partner that is itself a function of the age of the chooser. Dunn *et al.*'s (2010) study of online daters' age preferences across 14 cultures examined age preferences for cohorts ranging in age from 20 to 50. For people in most of the cultures studied, the minimum age preference of men for women remained in the twenties until past age 45. The maximum age preferred by men varied more but was about five years greater than the man's age up to 40, at which point the maximum preferred tended to be less than the age of the man.

For women, the minimum preferred age of men was close to the age of the woman up to 35. At that point the minimum age was usually less than that of the female. The maximum age preferred by women tended to be 5 years greater than that of the woman herself but increased with her age and became about 10 years greater than her own age. One notable exception was Kenya, where women seek much older men. Very little difference was seen in the preferences by Moslems versus those by Christians. These findings are consistent with an earlier study limited to Yahoo Personals (Alterovitz and Mendelsohn 2009) that revealed a similar pattern in singles over the age of 50. Men's preferred ages for women demonstrated an ever-widening gap between the age of the man and what he sought in a partner. On the other hand, women over 60 tended to seek younger men.

The importance of physical appearance

Couch and Liamputtong (2008) found that users often "filter" potential dates based on geographical proximity and physical appearance. Like ethnicity, preference for certain physical characteristics is an option that is often specifically engineered into dating service search engines, and preferences tend to mirror those of offline daters. In an examination of user preferences on HOTorNOT.com, Lee, Loewenstein, Ariely, Hong, and Young (2008) found that people tend to seek others who are similarly attractive, though highly attractive people seek more attractive dating partners. In a separate field study, the authors also found that highly attractive users tended to use attractiveness as a primary factor in choosing dates.

Glasser, Robnett, and Feliciano's (2009) sample of 4500 users of Yahoo Personals revealed that ethnicity and gender influence body type preferences for dates. Overall, males and whites were significantly more likely to express strong preferences than women and non-whites, though the likelihood of expressing any preference diminished with increasing education and amount of overweight. The exception was "athletic" women, who were highly likely to express a preference. With the exception of "large" men, white men tended to prefer "thin" women. African-American men showed a decided preference for the "thick" body type in women. Asian men preferred an "average" body type to the extent of shunning other types. When compared to whites, Hispanic/Latino men equally chose "average" and "voluptuous" for prospective partners.

Finally, both Feliciano (Feliciano *et al.* 2009) and Badahdah and Tiemann (2005) found that women are more likely to express height preferences than men. Several investigators (Badahdah and Tiemann 2005; Alterovitz and Mendelsohn 2009; Feliciano *et al.* 2009) have observed that the nature of women's preferences for height and income may exclude more possible mates than men's preferences for physical appearance.

Discussion

Preference and exclusion are the common denominators of these phenomena. In offline dating, preferences do not always have to be voiced or honestly expressed to others. Online date selection is based on sorting through databases with a search code. In order for the computer to construct the search code, preferences must be made explicit. Thus, online dating data directly reveal true preferences. Yet, in order to be encoded, programmers had to anticipate users' preferences. This limits the choices to what a programmer would expect. Perhaps this is why there are few surprises; online dating preferences are much like common expectations of offline ones. Statements that American black men are drawn to heavier women, Hispanic men like large breasts and older women prefer younger men might have been taken as unfair prejudice were there not now these data. Future scholars will be able to track the interplay of expectation and preference.

What the Internet has done to dating

In the early days of online dating, media commentators and theorists alike envisioned technological developments as driving fundamental change in the nature of close relationships (Zuboff 1984; Donath 1999; Van Acker 2001; Hardey 2002; McKenna *et al.* 2002). This does not appear to have happened. Rather, online dating practices strongly resemble those of conventional dating (Link and McCartney 2003; Hikel 2007; Couch and Liamputtong 2008; Rosenfeld and Thomas 2010). Instead, the Internet has become a powerful and convenient tool to study dating practices. In fact, already most studies of dating are carried out online.

Changes in attitudes and academic interest

It is safe to generalize that, while initially suspicious of online dating, both scholars and the general public have become accepting of this practice over time. While unusual at the beginning of the new millennium, now in the beginning of its second decade, online dating is commonplace.

A sample of the articles in SocINDEX^{TM} illustrates both the growth and change in academic interest in online dating. In the four years from 2002 through 2005, the number of articles grew by nearly 300 percent. In that period, counting the different types of websites, a popular topic initially, vanished in significance. While the fraction of articles devoted to international aspects remained about the same, 19 percent, in that period the new topic of homosexual online dating appeared, accounting for about 9 percent of the articles. In the four years from 2006 through 2009, the number of articles again grew by about 300 percent, meaning that the growth of interest was at least exponential from the date of the earliest article found, 1995 to the end of 2009. In the beginning of scholarly research, the question seemed to be, "What is Internet dating?" From the beginning it was recognized as a world-wide phenomenon. With the passage of time, the question became more one of, "Who does it and how does it work? What are the preferred ways?"

The direction of the Internet dating movement

A fortune cookie once said, "The best predictor of the future is the past." If the past is any predictor of the future effects and direction of digitally mediated social communication, then that future will be hard to predict. At best, we can summarize the direction it has taken and caution against extrapolating.

The use of the Internet as a tool for forming relationships began in the 1990s perhaps with the introduction of Usenet and the Gopher protocol by the University of Minnesota (Wikipedia 2011). The authors witnessed how this searchable text-based Internet communication system spawned a mass of message boards, such as one at the University of Iowa in which one of the authors participated. The University of Iowa board included a section devoted to flirtation. In this section users would address each other provocatively using pseudonyms. In such venues Internet courtship began. Internet relationship forming did not become a serious topic of discussion until the new millennium. By then, the World Wide Web was well established and Internet interpersonal relationships were becoming conspicuously global. In the early days, theorists such as Zuboff (1984) had speculated on the Internet's capacity for reducing face-to-face interaction thinking that it merely created an "uncomfortable isolation." What in fact did happen was the evolution of an obsession with connectedness spawning such new media as Internet cellular phones. In 1997, early fears were melting, and the Internet was being credited with facilitating "the healthy development of romantic relationships" (Cooper and Sportolari 1997). By 2001, articles specifically on Internet dating had appeared, and you could see and hear your prospective partner because of the large-scale introduction of webcams, instant messaging and chat rooms. As the popularity of technology for connectedness increased, Internet romance became an article of commerce. Since 2001, many forms of online dating services have appeared. Some such as eHarmony.com use a computer to predict and find your best mate. Now, in the second decade of the second millennium, social gossip relationships have taken center stage away from Internet romance. Called "social networking," these complicated networks of friends, enemies and potential lovers are a popular topic for popular discussion in 2011.

Meeting someone on the Internet is a different experience than meeting someone by looking across the room. Through the Internet, you can meet people on the other side of the Earth and already there have been postings to the social network, Twitter, from outer space. Yet, most of the rituals of courtship have remained essentially the same despite the new medium. And, the same cultural preferences for age, height and beauty still apply. Online partners are probably still constructed in one's romantic imagining but now with the aid of radio buttons to choose their preferred traits. Online, as in the past, one may advertise for a partner with the specific intent of raising children. Now, with the legalization of gay marriage and changing norms, this child-rearing partner may well be homosexual. This may seem an unusual choice, but the Internet is especially well adapted to conjoining distant and unlikely pairs. Future research will have the opportunity of exploring new venues and phenomena. To the eyes of the authors, sexual partnering seems to be becoming in some cases divorced from romantic commitment and re-attached to commitments of other kinds. Thus the authors observe *hooking up* among students because their commitment to college is held in common and romance must be put off for a later time to accommodate careers. They have seen online sexual relationships formed through common interest groups. People can become partners because they draw Manga well together or collaborate well in writing short stories. Since there has always been a blurred line between friends and lovers, one might predict future technology to exploit in some new way that indistinctness – to reflect in electrons the phrase of this moment, "friends with benefits."

Further reading

Lawson, H. and Leck, K. (2006) "Dynamics of Internet Dating," *Social Science Computer Review*, 24: 189–208. [The basic social psychology of computer-mediated romance.]

Rosenfeld, M.J. and Thomas, R.J. (2010) *How Couples Meet and Stay Together, Waves I and II: Public Version 2.04* [Computer file], Stanford, CA: Stanford University Libraries, 2011-Jan-12. [A massive longitudinal database from which new articles are now emerging.]

Sautter, J.M., Tippett, R.M. and Morgan, S.P. (2010) "The Social Demography of Internet Dating in the United States," *Social Science Quarterly*, 91(2): 554–75. [An excellent review of internet dating demographics.]

Whitty, M.T., Baker, A.J. and Inman, J.A. (eds) (2007) *Online Matchmaking*. Basingstoke: Palgrave Macmillan. [A recent edited volume on psychological aspects of online dating.]

Wilson, S.B., McIntosh, W.D. and Insana, S.P. (2007) "Dating Across Race: An Examination of African American Internet Personal Advertisements," *Journal of Black Studies*, 37: 964–82. [A good examination of how the Internet affects interracial dating.]

References

Albright, J.A. and Conran, T. (2003) "Desire, Love, and Betrayal: Constructing and Deconstructing Intimacy Online," *Journal of Systemic Therapies*, 22: 42–53.

Alterovitz, S. and Mendelsohn, G.A. (2009) "Partner Preferences across the Life Span: Online Dating by Older Adults," *Psychology & Aging*, 24: 513–17.

Badahdah, A.M. and Tiemann, K.A. (2005) "Mate Selection Criteria among Muslims Living in America," *Evolution and Human Behavior*, 26: 432–40.

Bartell, G. (1971) *Group Sex: An Eyewitness Report on the American Way of Swinging*, New York: The New American Library.

Ben-Ze'ev, A. (2004) *Love Online: Emotions on the Internet*, Cambridge: Cambridge University Press.

Berger, C.R. (1979) "Beyond Initial Interaction: Uncertainty, Understanding and Development of Interpersonal Relationships," in H. Giles and R. St. Clair (eds), *Language and Social Psychology*, Baltimore, MD: University Park Press, pp. 122–44.

Brym, R.J. and Lenton, R.L. (2001) "Love Online: A Report on Digital Dating in Canada," *MSN.ca* [online] available at: www.bestsoftworks.com/docs/loveonline.pdf (accessed 26 March, 2012).

Cooper, A. and Sportolari, L. (1997) "Romance in Cyberspace: Understanding Online Attraction," *Journal of Sex Education and Therapy*, 22: 7–14.

Couch, D. and Liamputtong, P. (2008) "Online Dating and Mating: The Use of the Internet to Meet Sexual Partners," *Qualitative Health Research*, 18: 268–79.

Danet, B. (2001) *Cyberpl@y: Communicating Online*, New York: New York University Press.

Donath, J.S. (1999) "Identity and Deception in the Virtual Community," in M.A. Smith and P. Kollock (eds), *Communities in Cyberspace*, London: Routledge, pp. 29–59.

Dunn, M.J., Brinton, S. and Clark, L. (2010) "Universal Sex Differences in Online Advertisers' Age Preferences: Comparing Data from 14 Cultures and 2 Religious Groups," *Evolution and Human Behavior*, 31: 383–93.

Ellison, N., Heino, R. and Gibbs, J. (2006) "Managing Impressions Online: Self-Presentation Processes in the Online Dating Environment," *Journal of Computer-Mediated Communication*, 11: 415–41.

Feliciano, C., Robnett, B. and Komaie, G. (2009) "Gendered Racial Exclusion among White Internet Daters," *Social Science Research*, 38 (1): 39–54.

Gibbs, J.L., Ellison, N.B. and Heino, R.D. (2006) "Self-Presentation in Online Personals: The Role of Anticipated Future Interaction, Self-Disclosure, and Perceived Success in Internet Dating," *Communication Research*, 33: 152–76.

Glasser, C., Robnett, B. and Feliciano, C. (2009) "Internet Daters' Body Type Preferences: Race-Ethnic and Gender Differences," *Sex Roles: A Journal of Research*, 61: 14–33.

Goffman, E. (1959) *The Presentation of Self in Everyday Life*, New York: Anchor Books.

Govier, T. (1992) "Trust, Distrust and Feminist Theory," *Hypatia*, 7(1): 16–33.

Hardey, M. (2002) "Life Beyond the Screen: Embodiment and Identity Through the Internet," *The Sociological Review*, 50: 570–84.

——(2008) "The Formation of Social Rules for Digital Interactions," *Information, Communication and Society*, 11: 1111–31.

Hikel, S. (2007) "Social Space and Commodification: Dimensions of the Politics of Love," *Dissertation Abstracts A*, 67(12): 4683.

Janus, S.S. and Janus, C.L. (1993). *The Janus Report on Sexual Behavior*, New York: John Wiley and Sons, Ltd.

Kibby, M. (1997) "Babes on the Web: Sex, Identity and the Home Page," *Media International Australia*, 84: 39–45.

Lawson, H. and Leck, K. (2006) "Dynamics of Internet Dating," *Social Science Computer Review*, 24: 189–208.

Lee, L., Loewenstein, G., Ariely, D., Hong, J. and Young, J. (2008) "If I'm Not Hot, Are You Hot Or Not? Physical Attractiveness Evaluations and Dating Preferences as a Function of One's Own Attractiveness," *Psychological Science*, 19: 669–77.

Lever, J., Grov, C., Royce, T. and Gillespie, B.J. (2008) "Searching for Love in All the 'Write' Places: Exploring Internet Personals Use by Sexual Orientation, Gender, and Age," *International Journal of Sexual Health*, 20: 233–46.

Levine, D. (2000) "Virtual Attraction: What Rocks Your Boat?" *CyberPsychology and Behavior*, 3: 565–73.

Levinger, G. (1974) "A Three-Level Approach to Attraction: Toward an Understanding of Pair Relatedness," in T.L. Huston (ed.), *Foundations of Interpersonal Attraction*, New York: Academic Press, pp. 99–120.

Link, T.C. and McCartney, A. (2003) "Romance.com," in *Proceedings of 66th Annual Meeting of the Southern Sociological Society, New Orleans, LA*, 26–30 March, Knoxville, TN: Southern Sociological Society.

McCown, J.A., Fischer, D., Page, R. and Homant, M. (2001) "Internet Relationships: People who Meet People," *CyberPsychology and Behavior*, 4: 593–96.

McKenna, K., Green, A. and Gleason, M. (2002) "Relationship Formation on the Internet: What's the Big Attraction?," *Journal of Social Issues*, 58: 9–31.

McLuhan, M. (1964) *Understanding Media: The Extensions of Man*, 2nd edn, New York: McGraw-Hill.

Ramirez, A., Walther, J.B., Burgoon, J.K. and Sunnafrank, M. (2002) "Information-Seeking Strategies, Uncertainty, and Computer-Mediated Communication: Toward a Conceptual Model," *Human Communication Research*, 28: 213–28.

Reis, H.T. and Shaver, P. (1988) "Intimacy as an Interpersonal Process," in S.W. Duck (ed.), *Handbook of Personal Relationships: Theory, Research and Interventions*, Chichester: Wiley, pp. 376–89.

Rosenfeld, M.J. and Thomas, R.J. (2010) *How Couples Meet and Stay Together, Waves I and II: Public Version 2.04*, available at: http://data.stanford.edu/hcmst (accessed 12 Jan. 2011).

Sautter, J.M., Tippett, R.M. and Morgan, S.P. (2006) "Check Out My Profile: Demographic Characteristics of the Internet Dating Population," in *Proceedings of 69th Annual Meeting of the Southern Sociological Society, New Orleans, LA*, 22–26 March 2006, Knoxville, TN: Southern Sociological Society.

——(2010) "The Social Demography of Internet Dating in the United States," *Social Science Quarterly*, 91 (2): 554–75.

Sprecher, S. (2009) "Relationship Initiation and Formation on the Internet," *Marriage and Family Review*, 45: 761–82.

Stephure, R.J., Boon, S.D., MacKinnon, S.L. and Deveau, V.L. (2009) "Internet Initiated Relationships: Associations Between Age and Involvement in Online Dating," *Journal of Computer-Mediated Communication*, 14: 658–81.

Sweeny, K.A. and Borden, A.L. (2009) "Crossing the Line Online: Racial Preference of Internet Daters," *Marriage and Family Review*, 45(6–8): 740–60.

Tidwell, L.C. and Walther, J.B. (2002) "Computer-Mediated Communication Effects on Disclosure, Impressions, and Interpersonal Evaluations: Getting to Know One Another a Bit at a Time," *Human Communication Research*, 28: 317–48.

Toma, C.L. and Hancock, J.T. (2010) "Looks and Lies: The Role of Physical Attractiveness in Online Dating," *Communication Research*, 37: 335–51.

Valkenburg, P.M. and Peter, J. (2007) "Who Visits Online Dating Sites? Exploring Some Characteristics of Online Daters," *CyberPsychology and Behavior*, 10: 849–52.

Van Acker, E. (2001) "Contradictory Possibilities of Cyberspace for Generating Romance," *Australian Journal of Communication*, 28: 103–16.

Walther, J.B. and Burgoon, J.K. (1992) "Relational Communication in Computer-Mediated Interaction," *Human Communication Research*, 19: 50–88.

Walther, J.B. and Parks, M.R. (2002) "Cues Filtered Out, Cues Filtered In: Computer-Mediated Communication and Relationships," in M.L. Knapp and J.A. Daly (eds), *Handbook of Interpersonal Communication*, 3rd edn, Thousand Oaks, CA: Sage, pp. 529–63.

Walther, J.B. and Tidwell, L.C. (1995) "Nonverbal Cues in Computer-Mediated Communication, and the Effect of Chronemics on Relational Communication," *Journal of Organizational Computing and Electronic Commerce*, 5: 355–78.

Whitty, M.T. and Carr, A.N. (2003) "Cyberspace as Potential Space: Considering the Web as a Playground to Cyber-Flirt," *Human Relations*, 56: 869–91.

——(2006) *Cyberspace Romance: The Psychology of Online Relationships*, London: Palgrave Macmillan.

Whitty, M. and Gavin, J. (2001) "Age = Sex = Location: Uncovering the Social Cues in the Development of Online Relationships," *CyberPsychology and Behavior*, 4: 623–30.

Wikipedia (2011) *History of the Internet*, available at: http://en.wikipedia.org/wiki/History_of_the_Internet (accessed 12 July 2011).

Wilson, S.B., McIntosh, W.D. and Insana, S.P. (2007) "Dating Across Race: An Examination of African American Internet Personal Advertisements," *Journal of Black Studies*, 37: 964–82.

Wysocki, D.K. and Thalken, J. (2007) "Whips and Chains? Content Analysis of Sadomasochism in Internet Personal Advertisements," in M.T. Whitty, A.J. Baker and J.A. Inman (eds), *Online Matchmaking*, Houndsmills: Palgrave Macmillan, pp. 178–96.

Yancey, G. (2009) "Crossracial Differences in the Racial Preferences of Potential Dating Partners: A Test of the Alienation of African Americans and Social Dominance Orientation," *The Sociological Quarterly*, 50(1): 121–43.

Yurchisin, J., Watchravesringkan, K. and McCabe, D.B. (2005) "An Exploration of Identity Re-Creation in the Context of Internet Dating," *Social Behavior and Personality*, 33: 735–50.

Zuboff, S. (1984) *In the Age of the Smart Machine*, New York: Basic Books.

PART V

Seeking information and shopping

18

MEDICINE 2.0 AND BEYOND

From information seeking to knowledge creation in virtual health communities

Handan Vicdan and Nikhilesh Dholakia

Keywords

co-creation, Medicine 2.0, patient empowerment, sharing, social media, virtual health community

Introduction

This chapter examines how social media technologies and virtual health communities are transforming the current healthcare system. Providing examples from virtual health platforms, we explore the new forms of empowerment that are occurring, and articulate changes in consumer online health information seeking and learning. These changes also open up wider possibilities of post-consumer, post-corporate forms of organizing our world with the help of digital technologies.

By enabling transformation of roles and relations among market actors, Web 2.0 technologies – technologies that facilitate user contributions, collaborations, collective intelligence, co-creation, and cloud-based services (O'Reilly 2009) – increase the potential for collaboration among these actors. These technologies emphasize innovative, data-oriented, service-centered collaboration; increased levels of user contribution; organization of content through non-hierarchical methods; and increased aspirations of community building, sharing and interaction (Bleicher 2006). Despite conflicting views (Eysenbach *et al.* 2004; Jadad *et al.* 2006), Web 2.0 applications present the potential to transform the top-down approach in healthcare. The use of social media for information sharing, collaboration and user-generated content has disrupted the conventional superior-physician/inferior-patient dialectic (Tyson 2000), which had previously led to a one-way surveillance and management of patient care by those claiming superior medical knowledge and rationality (Foucault 1975). Social media applications in healthcare enable the origination and continuation of a mindset that increasingly seeks to navigate alternative platforms for sharing and connecting to different market actors and forming communities with them. Patients now conduct real-time clinical research with other healthcare actors, and manage their own and others' care through social media (Jadad 1999; Perfetto and Dholakia 2010). In this emerging participatory culture, sharing becomes much more prevalent in online platforms than offline platforms (Belk 2010). Through collaborative ownership and collective sharing, online community members together add to knowledge generation, slice and splice it up, reorganize and give it away without losing it (Belk 2007). Health-related collaboration can be seen as part of a wider movement of technology-aided collaborative consumption (Botsman and Rogers 2010). Consumer empowerment through involvement in social media-induced co-production processes is usually imbued with the capability to give away, deliver and distribute available resources of knowledge and experience to others (Hemetsberger 2002).

In the following sections, we will discuss how virtual health communities and social media applications in healthcare are transforming the roles and relations among healthcare actors, and articulate the shifts in information seeking in healthcare.

Changing dynamics of the healthcare market through social media and virtual health communities

In healthcare, physicians were considered as dominating and authoritative, and they suppressed patient capacity to make her/his own decisions (Lupton 1995). In fact, medical paternalism was considered the ultimate beneficial feature of healthcare (Lim 2002), since it endorsed the superiority of physician and the inferiority of the patient. This excessive reliance on physicians' expertise generally stems from the patient's belief in the greater ability of the physician to make judgments, leading to a one-way management of patient care by a presumably superior medical knowledge and rationality (Foucault 1975). Consequently, such a dominant paternalistic approach to patient care prevented partnership among healthcare actors.

Our observations of discourses of patients in one of the virtual health communities also suggest that patients actually had no inherent right to the patient-related information that healthcare providers held, a reality that is beginning to change with the participatory medicine movement. Patients in contemporary American settings argue that participatory medicine will bring the following benefits: (1) easier access to the patient's own medical record enables the patient to question and analyze the information in these records to enhance learning about her/his medical conditions; (2) the ability to spot and correct misinformation in their records by patients; and (3) acceleration of the treatment process through shared access and smoother flow of medical records to healthcare providers. Patients in the virtual health community studied also assessed the past physician–patient relationship as a top-down relationship, a one-way governing by the physician. They argued that physician knowledge is generally limited to the literature s/he has read and patients s/he has treated. Hence, physicians are unable to offer real-time, on-demand health and real-world practical knowledge (e.g., how a patch medication is used). Patients believe that physician–patient relationships suffer from a lack of trust and understanding by physicians. In addition, conventional clinical trials include only a small number of patients and the results are published in medical journals, hence limiting the number of people who benefit from such results. There exists disconnect between not only physicians and patients but also among healthcare providers. Strong privacy was being practiced among these actors, with pressures from state institutions that threatened physicians with the loss of medical licenses for breaching patient privacy.

The long-established relationship between the physician – who is the utmost authority and expert gatekeeper in patient care, and the patient – who is obliged to comply with the doctor's orders (Haug and Lavin 1981), is beginning to evolve to a different phase. With the advent of new technologies and the rise of consumerism (patients as the 'consumers' of medical knowledge provided by the expert physician or websites such as WebMD), the top-down relationship between the patient and the physician is being transformed. The patient has become more critical, assertive, demanding and well equipped with information and experience – paving the way for a joint relationship with the physician (Edenius and Åberg-Wennerholm 2005; Quill and Brody 1996). Patients rely less on the physicians as the sole information source. Indeed, patients are becoming resourceful and are seeking self-help through searching for information online and seeking support from online support groups and other patients who have had similar experiences (Ferguson 2000). The physician–patient encounter is now mediated by negotiations among these parties, the terms of which are determined by the partnership of the informed patient and the receptive doctor (McGregor 2006). More accessible information online has reduced mere reliance on the expert physician (Tyson 2000). Collaboration between patients and physicians (McGregor 2006) is also invigorated by communities formed through social media. Technology, then, provides the means for not just self-help but also collective cooperation through online communities and healthcare support groups that provide informational, social and emotional support (Burrows *et al.* 2000; Eysenbach *et al.* 2004; Ferguson and Frydman 2004; Wright and Bell 2003).

Web 2.0 technologies and social media platforms in the healthcare market are therefore beginning to transform ways consumers seek information and manage their health. Contemporary medicine had long served as a disciplining entity to maximize our lifespan and normalize our bodies. State institutions and healthcare providers used "security" and "fear" as discourses of power in this process (Epstein 2006), particularly as a means to protect patient privacy and increase mortality salience among patients. With the use of the Internet for acquisition, analysis, aggregation, dissemination, deployment and sharing of private health data and information, changes are beginning to occur in healthcare as well as in the state-established policies to protect patient privacy (e.g., Health Insurance Portability and Accountability Act of 1996). Adopting a "hide it or lose it" perspective concerning online privacy (Weitzner *et al.* 2008), these policies set strict boundaries on the flow of patient health records to third parties (e.g., insurance companies, employers), increased consumer sensitivity and fear about privacy, and served as a barrier to research and discovery (Brown 2008). Macro institutions' excessive reliance on secrecy and desire to have control over patient health information (Weitzner *et al.* 2008) are now beginning to be challenged by patient-empowered virtual communities, the foundations of which are based on sharing rather than sequestering private health data.

Consequently, what we observe at this juncture is that in healthcare, patients are forming collectivities with other patients, doctors, caregivers, researchers, and pharmaceutical companies; and share their experiences and learn from others' experiences on a global scale (Perfetto and Dholakia 2010). Such global sharing of experiences of patients with specific illnesses and the resulting collective knowledge produced from these experiences (e.g., symptoms, treatments received, progress of the disease and treatments) enhance the sharing and distribution of patient data. Hence, patients become both consumers and producers of health information and experience (Hardey 2001). Many health-related organizations now design the means whereby consumers and other actors gather to engage in joint production.

There is also, however, the dark side of social media applications in healthcare. Some argue that social media applications in healthcare have spawned a new category of "hyperinformed patients" who engage in guerilla science and self-medication, and increase the risk of death for many through becoming a part of online health communities (Haig 2007). In many online medical communities, consumers gain more control over their personal health data and become active in the management of their health, even engaging in conducting clinical trials. Through these virtual platforms, patients "share" their knowledge and experiences, engage in clinical research with other healthcare actors, and embrace the "shared" world that provides new possibilities of organizing lives. We will elaborate on the reliability and accuracy of these social media-facilitated clinical trials by virtual health communities, and discuss how they change the course of the current healthcare system.

Virtual health platforms

There are several virtual health platforms, in which patients are empowered at different levels. For example, Organized Wisdom – though not a virtual health community – connects patients to health experts and helps them find the most reliable resources to manage their health. It aggregates and organizes online wisdom shared across the Web by numerous health experts and advocates. Organized Wisdom thus serves as an expert-driven platform for health, and inspires doctors and other health experts to embrace the power of digital media and channel it towards the patients' well-being. Microsoft Health Vault and Google Health are very similar in nature. Tools provided in these platforms help patients keep track of their own health status, provide individualized and personalized medicine recommendations, and let patients keep their medical records in one place. They put patients in control of their health information. Patients enter their data, generate reports, analyze trends, connect with pharmacies and hospitals, and share this organized health information with their doctors and family members. Although these platforms empower con-sumers to manage their own health and allow for personalization of healthcare, they lack the community aspect in sharing health information. Revolution Health is a platform that integrates the community aspect into sharing of health information online. In this platform, patients also track their medical history and use this information to prepare for a doctor visit. There are different communities and forums that exist in Revolution Health that promote the sharing of health information among patients at the anecdotal level. The site sells advertising and products through Revolution Health store to make profit as a result of providing this service to the patients.

Our major focus in this chapter is on PatientsLikeMe (PLM). PLM, a site similar to Revolution Health, allows for personalization of healthcare, and enables patients to track their and others' health data, establish communities and communicate with other patients. Distinct from other virtual health platforms, PLM entails sharing of health data and connection among diverse healthcare actors, and enables patients to actively engage in medical research, produce medical knowledge, and have a say in the design of tracking tools. Unlike other virtual health platforms, PLM foregoes advertising to preserve the sanctity of community patient experiences, and relies only on word-of-mouth sus-tainability, which provides feelings of security for patients and promotes greater sharing of private health data. The selling of anonymous aggregated patient data to pharmaceutical firms, however – the only revenue-generating mechanism for PLM – serves as a deterrent to some patients. For patients who want material gain out of sharing their private health data, PLM sponsors patients' fundraising or disease awareness activities; yet avoids the perception of material gain as a stimulant for sharing. Our observations of patient discourses in PLM reveal that patients legitimize PLM's selling of de-identified aggregated data to pharmaceuticals because of many perceived benefits: (1) discovery and advancement of new medical knowledge; (2) increased connectedness among healthcare actors; (3) increased disease awareness and acknowledgment of patient license; (4) transparency in distribution of health data; and (5) increased quality of life. In order to establish a culture of sharing, PLM blurs the boundaries of coercion and consent through using non-dominating discourses and advocating inclusive cultural values (e.g., openness, transparency, personalization, quality of life, hope, destigmatization). Through non-dominating discourses, PLM aims to alleviate the fear and loss of ownership of private information associated with the traditional notions of privacy as well as mortality salience that the state and other influentials typically institute in the healthcare market.

Community intervention in conventional medicine

Some of the communal health platforms aim to be "all inclusive." More than mere information seeking and sharing, virtual health platforms such as Revolution Health and PLM enable patients to commune with one another. In PLM, we observe the broad integration of healthcare actors and their multidirectional relations. PLM gathers different healthcare market actors on its platform, and serves as a co-mediated market system for sharing, organization, production, and distribution of private health data. Different healthcare market actors collaborate for research, seek both emotional and knowledge support, and increase their disease literacy and connectedness to each other through sharing in and through PLM. Interdisciplinary teams of researchers, designers, and engineers in PLM create a platform for patients to share and use health data, and enable them to integrate their experiences into their health decision-making and to improve outcomes. Tools are designed to engage patients to record, reason with, and apply data to inform all types of medical decisions. As a non-state institution, PLM mobilizes diverse market actors through non-dominating discourses (Rose 2007), to achieve prosocial outcomes in healthcare and to cultivate the social production of medicine through collaborative medical research and increased sharing of private health data. Physicians are also enabled to use tracking tools and improve healthcare outcomes and increasingly engage in the production of medicine both inside and outside of PLM.

By engaging patients and other healthcare actors in continuous sharing and medical research via its platform, PLM seeks to contribute to the increased disease literacy of patients and healthcare providers with the research results discovered in the community. The results of the clinical research conducted in PLM offer potential for improved learning about diseases and treatments, and prompt further investigation by researchers. As the patient becomes more literate in terms of her/his disease and symptoms through PLM, s/he can better discuss her/his conditions and effectively communicate with her/his physician, which in turn contributes to physician disease literacy. Both parties analyze and integrate the knowledge gained from PLM into their shared decision-making. There is an ongoing process of mutual confirmation between physicians and patients as they share their medical knowledge and experience. Tracking tools equip patients with information, which they further discuss and analyze with their physician. Some patients use the information gleaned from PLM to validate the information received from their physician, whereas others perceive the physician as a source of validation to confirm the information collected from PLM and other Internet sources.

Sharing and knowledge generation in virtual health communities

From anecdotal to structured and centralized sharing

Virtual health communities bring a structural approach to sharing private health information, which is an important factor in patient involvement in the sharing of her/his health data. In PLM, for example, stories, narratives, and anecdotal sharing of experiences are transformed into systematic, structural sharing – supporting research conducted by a community of patients and other healthcare actors brought together in this platform. This stands in sharp contrast from other virtual platforms mentioned earlier, which serve mainly as providers of online health information and platforms for sharing medical information at the anecdotal level. PLM is open to everyone (e.g., patients, patients' family members and friends, physicians, caregivers, researchers, pharmaceutical firms). Patients quantify their personal health information, turn it into hard data, and track each other's disease conditions through sophisticated tracking tools. They keep journals of their own individual experiences, and list symptoms of the disease, treatments received and different lifestyles led. This individual patient information is pooled for research, systematically recorded for analysis and visualized with graphs. Hence, patient experiences and data are pulled together in ways that allow both the individual and the comprehensive view of the disease. Actors in the community interact with each other anecdotally through private messaging and/or public messaging in forums and the website's general community blog. They create profiles and share their experiences in forums and community blogs. Both forum interactions and profile data are used for medical research.

Structured and *centralized* health data offers several benefits. It contributes to the increased disease literacy of patients and physicians, which leads – somewhat paradoxically – to productive *decentralized* decision-making about patient care across these parties. Patients express their desire for structured sharing and the ability to have a centralized record of their disease information through these virtual health platforms. By creating a centralized record of their disease information, patients gain the ability to facilitate the flow of information among healthcare institutions and actively engage in the distribution of health data.

Real-time sharing

Patients connect with other healthcare actors in real time and collaborate for research, and receive support whenever they need (real-time help). This constant and instant sharing and knowledge support among actors motivates patients to keep sharing and participating in the community. With PLM, patients can have access to personal information of other patients, who have similar or different experiences worldwide. They list their symptoms, treatments that worked or did not work for them, their progression of the disease, and alternative lifestyles they lead. Constant and instant emotional and knowledge support, and real-time commitment to patient care from other patients are considered to be more beneficial compared to the delayed – and highly vicarious – information sharing with a physician outside of these virtual platforms.

Formal and informal sharing

Patients adopt ironic, critical, and playful engagement with diverse modes of life and seek friendly and humorous seriousness in sharing and suffering. For example, in PLM, patients remind each other that they are there to do research and accelerate the discovery of cures, not just to have fun, socialize, and seek emotional support by discussing non-disease-related issues. Yet, this ironic engagement also helps patients cope with their diseases and makes the community not merely a care-bear community. Patients discuss the value of emotional support and confirmation of one's health status, which is enabled by the knowledge gained in the community. Patient discourses also reflect the desire to seek friendly seriousness in sharing and healing, especially when sharing gets too formal. At PLM, patients state that their healing process not only involves the healing of the body through treatments and medications but also the healing of mind and spirit. For many, the well-being and well-becoming process entail conflict, challenge and acceptance simultaneously – while they are sharing and forming relations in the community. Consequently, the accommodation of both disease-related (e.g., scientific, cause-related) and non-disease-related (e.g., play, fun, entertaining) aspects of sharing serves as a potential to maintain interest and participation in the community.

Increased connectedness among healthcare actors

One unique characteristic of PLM is that PLM enables increased connectedness among diverse healthcare actors. This desire for connectedness also serves as a potential to challenge the meaning of communing for the actors of this community. Marketing scholars and consumer researchers have conceptualized "community" as a social phenomenon outside of the organization or separate from the organization (Peñaloza and Venkatesh 2006). Communities of consumers engage in activities that have links to brands and organizations (e.g., brand communities, *Star Trek* fans, Burning Man gatherings), yet they are independent of the organization in terms of offering either support or resistance. In this sense, communities are outside of the organization. In the PLM community, we observe a shift in the meaning of community from a social phenomenon outside of the organization (ibid.) to a new type of interorganizational business phenomenon (Hummel and Lechner 2001). The new "organization" created by PLM serves as a community comprised of multiple firms (partnership with research organizations, universities, pharmaceutical firms), healthcare providers (e.g., physicians, caregivers), patients, family members, and PLM founders.

In PLM, sharing of private health data and patient-generated medical knowledge does not stay within PLM. Patients learn from each other's experiences and research links they provide to each other on several topics. Patients connect to other patients through intra (within sub-community), inter (among sub-communities, e.g., ALS, Mood, MS), and outer (outside the community) communal sharing, constant monitoring of one's own and others' disease through tracking tools, and the resulting enhanced disease literacy and awareness. Patients also connect to pharmaceutical companies through clinical research conducted in the community, which serves as a counterbalancing yardstick for traditional clinical trials, and pharmaceutical recruitment of patients from PLM community. Patients also connect to the state through direct reporting of drug side effects to the Food and Drug Administration (FDA), which also serves as a potential for improved regulation of pharmaceutical practices by the state and the resulting improved medications. Patients connect to physicians through the recruitment of patients for physicians' own trials, personalized medicine through tracking tools, and mutual encouragement to become a part of PLM. In all of these connections among healthcare actors, the patient license to generate and validate medical knowledge and organize sharing and distribution of medical knowledge is beginning to be acknowledged. Patients also have increased access to clinical trials, a process previously dominated and controlled by academics and clinicians. The disciplining culture is slowly being interlaid by a democratizing culture.

Patient empowerment through social media: façade or panacea?

Various social media platforms in healthcare enable people to have a say in the management of their care and monitor their own well-being. We observe increasingly that these virtual health platforms enable users to share their health data with other healthcare actors and involve patients in sharing, distribution, and generation of health information at new levels (Eysenbach 2008). The empowered networked patient now acts as a validator of her/his and others' well-being as well as the validator of physician expert knowledge. This empowerment is based on patient real-world experiences. As patients share their timely and real-world experiential knowledge, they offer recommendations to each other based on their own personal experiences rather than enforcing on each other certain ways of coping with diseases. They mentor each other through presenting their own ways of coping with diseases so others observe and learn from it – in effect, transcending the passive role of a mere consumer (Fırat and Dholakia 1998). Most importantly, in PLM, the patient also becomes an active participant in research and medical knowledge production, and in the reorganization of sharing and interaction among healthcare actors both inside and outside of the community. Such a license in mentoring others, co-producing medical knowledge through active and constructive engagement in medical research (e.g., recruitment of other patients for clinical trials, creation of ideas to use in data generation and design), and reorganizing the "sharing" of private health data in this community is also beginning to be recognized by the influential players in the healthcare market.

With the gradual dilution of top-down provisioning in healthcare, multilateral processes of organizing relations among healthcare actors in these virtual health communities also indicate that the community is not just a means to support, celebrate, or critique the organization – it begins to interpenetrate the (commercial and state) organization, and transforms the nexus of connections into a new quasi-organization that is to some extent free from the bureaucratic and market discipline.

Several strategies adopted by patients and other healthcare actors in virtual health communities indicate the possibility of how these communities can enable a seamless flow of health data among diverse market actors, and how and at what level they engage actors in the production and distribution processes of medical knowledge. In PLM, tolerance for alternative sources of medical research and the use of these knowledge sources as a yardstick for further validation of conventional research discoveries become vital, especially for life-changing diseases that necessitate accelerated research process. Hence, enabling diverse healthcare actors to engage in centralized sharing for decentralized decision-making on patient care and conduct clinical research – not just giving and receiving medical information (anecdotal sharing) – through these virtual health communities could substantially increase collaboration among healthcare actors. Going beyond healthcare and towards the general nature of lifeworlds in the Web 2.0 era, what emerges from such processes are possible forms of post-consumer entities of the digital age: people who do not just consume but also create, critique, cooperate, contest, calibrate, consult, commune, and care.

Issues with patient medical knowledge generation through social media

As patients increasingly engage in medical research and the generation of new medical knowledge, an observation specific to PLM, issues concerning the reliability and validity of patient-driven clinical research have become apparent. For example, some drug side effects discovered in the ALS community through a clinical trial were criticized as not scientific enough. Despite the skepticism about the value of user-generated trials, these clinical trials have been recognized by influentials in the market for their timeliness compared to traditional clinical trials (Editorial 2008). Hence, PLM patient-driven research is considered an opportunity to design new experimental patient-centered research methods such that the resulting data will be informative, patient-centered, and inclusive. Both PLM founders and patients emphasize the discovery-oriented nature of this research, and that this research could be used as a means of validation for randomized clinical trials, and draw attention to the hypotheses generated for further testing. The body of medical knowledge generated with patients may complement traditional clinical trials due to their discovery-oriented nature and hypothesis generation orientation (Arnquist 2009; Arnst 2008; Johnson 2008). Such clinical trials may also increase the potential for the faster discovery of diagnosis, prognosis and treatment knowledge, and be more cost effective compared to traditional medical research (Sheridan 2008).

Issues raised by the conventional and mainstream medical community concerning the reliability, validity, and quality of user-generated clinical trials may indicate the desire to maintain "expert" dominance over the medical research process. Their criticism is that such trials lack scientific rigor, can cause detrimental effects on patients' lives and shorten their lifespan, and, most importantly, exploit patients. Nonetheless, patients in PLM, for example, are aware of these problems and argue that similar risks also exist in the current healthcare system. Jayanti and Singh (2010) also call attention to the risks of learning and sharing in online health communities, which could lead to degenerative learning through ill advice from the members of these communities. Patients in PLM, however, advocate validating (scientifically and anecdotally) claims concerning drugs and treatments by other patients, physicians, and researchers through additional resources and research links.

Patients also call attention to the drawbacks of traditional clinical trials, in which clinicians and academics are in full control of who to choose for trials and what information to make accessible, which results in information sequestration – privileging a limited group of the medical elite. In addition, traditional clinical trials are perceived as a distant hope and not a real-world solution for many people. Many contemporary, digitally-aware patients – and their families – emphasize the importance of fast and real-time clinical trials, particularly for life-changing diseases. In contrast to traditional clinical trials controlled by clinicians and academics, the use of social networking is opening up the clinical trials: it is creating democratic access to research, unfettered by the disciplining rules/criteria of top-down medicine. Additionally, the mutual sharing of health information, online and rapid learning, and doing their own research help patients better understand their conditions and increase their quality of life through making adjustment to their lifestyles and treatments.

Conclusion

In the modern market society, organizations were considered as distinct/detached entities from consumers in the market, providing goods/services to satisfy the needs of their target markets (Fırat and Dholakia 2006; Peñaloza and Venkatesh 2006). However, the transformation of social networking (Web 2.0) into a business phenomenon (Tapscott and Williams 2008) challenges conventional forms of business, which treat organizations and consumers as distinct entities. Organizations now serve as systems of real-time processes, whereby performers in the market together discover and design their needs in actual or virtual collectivities (Fırat and Dholakia 1998; Kozinets 2002). Such transformations indicate that organizations do business with the consumer and increasingly partake in the construction of consumer experiences as *co-constructors* (Fırat and Dholakia 2006: 144), not in a sequential and linear (e.g., gathering of information about consumers to discover their needs and then engaging in exchange relationships through provisioning) but in a real-time discovery process.

Virtual health communities also initiate a shift from state intervention to community intervention in organizing sharing, generation, and distribution of private patient data; and from privacy to sharing as a form of organizing roles and relations in the current healthcare system. The processes of organization, sharing, generation of, and access to private health information are also beginning to be controlled by these virtual platforms, revealing the unfolding power of social media in constituting new roles and relations among market actors. Community intervention to organize business relations is intriguing in that the community comes to serve as a new territory for and a means of organizing relations among diverse actors and institutionalizing new allegiances and responsibilizations (Miller and Rose 2008). Modern marketing's response to these transformations should then center on finding new ways to engage consumers of the connected society in the production processes through forming communities with organizations. Furthering the new dominant logic of marketing (Vargo and Lusch 2004), marketing's focus in the Web 2.0 and subsequent era is beginning to shift away from top-down provisioning, and toward acting on behalf of or for consumers (Zwick *et al.* 2008); to collaboration, enabling people to act and empowering them to partake in communities of co-creating life experiences through social media, and ultimately blurring the distinctions between the consumer and the organization. Indeed, digital platforms such as PLM may open pathways to a world wherein people are able to transcend the circumscribed and organizationally-disciplined life roles that we characterize as "consumers."

Further reading

Avorn, J. (2000) 'Post-Modern Drug Evaluation: The Deconstruction of Evidence-Based Regulation," *Pharmacoeconomics*, 18(Supplement 1): 15–20. [Documents shifts in scientific modern medicine, which enforces regulations that govern conventional medical therapy through evidence-based discourse.]

Benkler, Y. (2006) *The Wealth of Networks: How Social Production Transforms Markets and Freedom*, New Haven, CT: Yale University Press. [Alternative institutional forms – other than the State – of organizing the right to access, use and control resources in a networked society.]

Foucault, M. (2003) *Security, Territory, Population: Lectures at the Collège de France, 1977–78*, Basingstoke: Palgrave Macmillan. [The rise of experts and institutions – other than the State – to mediate, organize and modify roles and relations in society.]

Johnson, G.J. and Ambrose, P. (2006) 'Neo-Tribes: The Power and Potential of Online Communities in Health Care," *Communications of the ACM*, 49(1): 107–13. [Benefits of communal information sharing in virtual health communities to satisfy cognitive, affective, conative and spiritual needs of patients.]

Kliff, S. (2009) 'Pharma's Facebook," *Newsweek*, March 10, Available at: www.newsweek.com/id/187882. [Issues related to patient recruitment for clinical trials in medical research and how pharmaceuticals are incorporating social networking (Web 2.0) into clinical research.]

References

Arnquist, S. (2009) "Research Trove: Patients' Online Data," *New York Times*, August 24.

Arnst, C. (2008) "Health 2.0: Patients as Partners," *Business Week*, December 4.

Belk, R.W. (2007) "Why Not Share Rather Than Own?," *The Annals of the American Academy of Political and Social Science*, 611(1): 126–40.

——(2010) "Sharing," *Journal of Consumer Research*, 36(Feb.): 715–34.

Bleicher, P. (2006) "Web 2.0 Revolution: Power to the People," *Applied Clinical Trials*, 34–6.

Botsman, R. and Rogers, R. (2010) *What's Mine Is Yours: The Rise of Collaborative Consumption*, New York: HarperBusiness.

Brown, B. (2008) "Research and the Privacy Rule: The Chill Is On," *Journal of Health Care Compliance*, 35–6.

Burrows, R., Nettleton, S., Pleace, N., Loader, B. and Steven, M. (2000) "Virtual Community Care? Social Policy and the Emergence of Computer Mediated Social Support," *Information, Communication, and Society*, 3(1): 95–121.

Edenius, M. and Åberg-Wennerholm, M. (2005) "Patient Communities, ICT and the Future: An Explorative Study about Patient Communities and their Status in the ICT-Era," paper presented at the Economic Research Institute Conference, Stockholm School of Economics.

Editorial (2008) 'Calling All Patients," *Nature Biotechnology*, 26: 953.

Epstein, C. (2006) "Guilty Bodies, Productive Bodies, Destructive Bodies: Crossing the Biometric Borders," paper presented at the International Studies Association Conference.

Eysenbach, G., Powell, J., Englesakis, M., Rizo, C. and Stern, A. (2004) "Health-Related Virtual Communities and Electronic Support Groups: Systematic Review of the Effects of Online Peer-To-Peer Interactions," *BMJ*, 328: 1166–70.

——(2008) "Medicine 2.0: Social Networking, Collaboration, Participation, Apomediation, and Openness," *Journal of Medical Internet Research*, 10(3): 1–8.

Ferguson, T. (2000) "Online Patient-Helpers and Physicians Working Together: A New Partnership for High Quality Healthcare," *BMJ*, 321: 1129–32.

Ferguson, T. and Frydman, G. (2004) "The First Generation of E-Patients," *BMJ*, 328: 1148–9.

Fırat, A.F. and Dholakia, N. (1998) *Consuming People: From Political Economy to Theaters of Consumption*, London: Routledge.

——(2006) "Theoretical and Philosophical Implications of Postmodern Debates: Some Challenges to Postmodern Marketing," *Marketing Theory*, 6(2): 123–62.

Foucault, M. (1975) *The Birth of the Clinic: An Archeology of Medical Perception*, New York: Vintage Books.

Haig, S. (2007) "When the Patient Is a Googler," *Time*, November 8, available at: www.time.com/time/health/article/0,8599,1681838,00.html.

Hardey, M. (2001) "E-health: The Internet and the Transformation of Patients into Consumers and Producers of Health Knowledge," *Information, Communication and Society*, 4(3): 388–405.

Haug, M.R. and Lavin, B. (1981) "Patient or Practitioner: Who's in Charge?" *Journal of Health and Social Behavior*, 22(3): 212–29.

Hemetsberger, A. (2002) "Fostering Cooperation on the Internet: Social Exchange Processes in Innovative Virtual Consumer Communities," *Advances in Consumer Research*, 29(1): 354–6.

Hummel, J. and Lechner, U. (2001) "Communities: The Role of Technology," in *Proceedings of the 9th European Conference on Information Systems*.

Jadad, A.R., Enkin, M.W., Glouberman, S., Groff, P. and Stern, A. (1999) "Promoting Partnerships: Challenges for the Internet Age," *BMJ*, 319: 761–4.

——(2006) "Are Virtual Communities Good for Our Health?," *BMJ*, 332: 925–6.

Jayanti, R. K. and Singh, J. (2010) "Pragmatic Learning Theory: An Inquiry-Action Framework for Distributed Consumer Learning in Online Communities," *Journal of Consumer Research*, 36(6): 1058–81.

Johnson, C.Y. (2008) "Through Website, Patients Creating Own Drug Studies," *The Boston Globe*, November 16, available at: www.boston.com/news/health/articles/2008/11/16/through_website_patients_creating_own_drug_studies/?page=full.

Kozinets, R.V. (2002) "Can Consumers Escape the Market? Emancipatory Illuminations from Burning Man," *Journal of Consumer Research*, 29(June): 20–38.

Lim, L.S. (2002) "Medical Paternalism Serves the Patient Best," *Singapore Medical Journal*, 43(3): 143–7.

Lupton, D. (1995) "Perspectives on Power, Communication and the Medical Encounter: Implications for Nursing Theory and Practice," *Nursing Inquiry*, 4: 157–63.

McGregor, S. (2006) "Roles, Power, and Subjective Choice," *Patient Education and Counseling*, 60: 5–9.

Miller, P. and Rose, N. (2008) *Governing the Present: Administering Economic, Social and Personal Life*, Cambridge: Polity Press.

O'Reilly, T. (2009) "What Is Web 2.0? Design Patterns and Business Models for the Next Generation of Software," available at: http://oreilly.com/web2/archive/what-is-web-20.html (accessed July 28, 2011).

Peñaloza, L. and Venkatesh, A. (2006) "Further Evolving the New Dominant Logic of Marketing: From Services to the Social Construction of Markets," *Marketing Theory*, 6(3): 299–316.

Perfetto, R. and Dholakia, N. (2010) "Exploring the Cultural Contradictions of Medical Tourism', *Consumption, Markets and Culture*, 13(4): 399–417.

Quill, T.E. and Brody, H. (1996) "Physician Recommendations and Patient Autonomy: Finding a Balance Between Physician Power and Patient Choice," *Annals of Internal Medicine*, 125(9): 763–9.

Rose, N. (2007) *The Politics of Life Itself: Biomedicine, Power, and Subjectivity in the Twenty-First Century*, Princeton, NJ: Princeton University Press.

Sheridan, B. (2008) "Open Wide: The Open-Source Movement Worked Wonders for Software. Can It Do the Same for Diabetes and Other Illnesses?," *Newsweek*, October 16, available at: /www.newsweek.com/id/164231.

Tapscott, D. and Williams, A.D. (2008) *Wikinomics: How Mass Collaboration Changes Everyything*, New York: Portfolio Penguin Group.

Tyson, T.R. (2000) "The Internet: Tomorrow's Portal to Non-Traditional Health Care Services," *Journal of Ambulatory Care Management*, 23(2): 1–6.

Vargo, S.L. and Lusch, R. F. (2004) "Evolving to a New Dominant Logic for Marketing," *Journal of Marketing*, 68(January): 1–17.

Weitzner, D.J., Abelson, H., Berners-Lee, T., Feigenbaum, J., Hendler, J. and Sussman, G.J. (2008) "Information Accountability," *Communications of the ACM*, 51(6): 82–7.

Wright, K.B. and Bell, S.B. (2003) "Health-Related Support Groups on the Internet: Linking Empirical Findings to Social Support and Computer-Mediated Communication Theory," *Journal of Health Psychology*, 8(1): 39–54.

Zwick, D., Bonsu, S. and Darmody, A. (2008) 'Putting Consumers to Work: 'Co-Creation' and New Marketing Govern-Mentality," *Journal of Consumer Culture*, 8(2): 163–96.

19

STOCK TRADING IN THE DIGITAL AGE

Speed, agency, and the entrepreneurial consumer

Detlev Zwick and Jonathan Schroeder

Keywords

digital capitalism, entrepreneurial consumer subject, kinematic investor, neoliberalism, online investing

Over the past ten to fifteen years, individual investing has evolved from a niche activity to a mass phenomenon, largely due to the virtualization of the stock market and the computerization of buying and selling (Zwick 2005; Zwick and Dholakia 2006). In the United States and some European countries the 1997–99 period witnessed a growing interest in stocks and the stock market in general, spawning something like a gold rush mentality, especially among younger investors. Online investing has been hailed as the democratization of Wall Street and as a major factor in the spreading of the "ownership society." The USA has more investors than any other country in the world (Staute 1998) and perhaps somewhat logically, the United States became the first place to crack the fortress of the "Masters of the Universe" (Wolfe 1987) – those Wall Street insiders who seemed to have exclusive knowledge of the financial world, controlled its transactions, and made the rules.

By the late 1990s, armed with a personal computer, an Internet connection, and an online brokerage account from companies such as e-Trade and Ameritrade, individuals began to take matters into their own hands. Thus, by 2000, individual online stock trading had become the ultimate American pastime. As one commentator remarked:

> This [online investing and day trading] is not about money-grubbing; it's a new democratic revolution. Day trading, like the right to own dirty magazines, the privilege of serving in our armed forces, is a fail-safe against the loss of individual freedom – which for Americans is the same thing as collective freedom – and for that matter is the only sure way to keep your soul intact. Now an investor controls his own life so he can make the final call, so no one can delude him into thinking that the buying and selling of stocks is more complicated than a couple of mouse clicks, so

nothing can obstruct his inherent right to unload his losers on the next bigger dope to come along. And what could be more American than that?

(Klam 1999, p. 70)

A crop of new online brokerage firms were quick to pick up on this new *Zeitgeist* of, as the *Wall Street Journal* slogan puts it, "adventures in capitalism." TV ads showed, for example, a 12-year-old kid buying a helicopter and a seemingly unemployed slacker driving away in a Rolls-Royce towing a yacht, purchases made – so it was suggested – with their stock-market winnings. Then, trying to push the progressiveness of online trading, its young and global allure, as well as its transformational power, the message of the ads shifted away from the Casino image towards a more serious, almost political direction. In one TV ad, a goateed Gen-Xer with an unconcerned, satisfied air, calculated to look cutting-edge yet sophisticated, proclaims "we're pioneers" and a professional thirty-something female pronounces with cool determination "we're renegade capitalists." Finally, one ad shows how a classroom of immigrants studying English begins to rave about an Internet broker (Ameritrade). "They've mistaken it for the word America, they think their English teacher wants to talk about online trading and they all love this new country!" (Klam 1999, p. 70).

In addition to online brokerage firms trying to lure investor capital, traditional media like television, magazines and radio were active agents in the institutionalization of a postmodern investment culture at the turn of the millennium. Because of 24/7 financial news channels such as CNBC and CNN, CEOs gained celebrity status and became role models – with public recognition ratings similar to that of politicians and minor Hollywood actors (a phenomenon that rather quickly vanished after the bursting of the dot-com bubble but had a revival of sorts during the stunning market run-up between the Spring of 2003 and the Fall of 2007). At the same time, school children across the country founded investment clubs and became knowledgeable about the financial world. Contests such as the CNBC Student Stock Tournament encouraged middle school students to become stock-pickers and savvy investors.

Of course, such a media frenzy around the stock market was not new *per se*. Already in the early 1980s, David Snow and Robert Parker (1984, p. 153) had observed, "[W]ith the exception of the weather and sports, few if any other domains of activity receive such extensive media coverage" as the financial world. In addition to journalistic accounts, popular culture depictions of the world of high finance drew much attention. For example, Oliver Stone's movie *Wall Street*, released just 44 days after the worst day (October 19, 1987) in the history of the New York Stock Exchange, "portrays the heyday of Wall Street's frantically bullish market in the 1985–86 period" (Denzin 1990, p. 31). With the rising entertainment value of Wall Street, celebratory journalistic representations of successful investment bankers and brokers during the dot-com era became quite similar to the celebrity profiles found in *People* magazine.

Things have changed since these early days of the Internet boom in general and online stock trading in particular. The irrational technophilia of the turn of the millennium gave way to a (seemingly) more mature, honest and earnest investment climate, run (again) by such established Wall Street players as Merrill Lynch, Lehman Brothers, Goldman Sachs and the like. And just three years after the severe market downturn of 2000 the stock market began to take investors onto a new and exciting ride that would see market capitalization almost double in only five years. But this time, it was said, there would be no massive hangover for investors binging on rising valuations because, unlike the bull market during the late 1990s where company valuations were based on little more than imagination and fantasy, the boom cycle of 2003–7 was believed to be based on solid financials of real and productive companies. The financial crisis of 2008–9 then revealed that what many believed to be a solid and sound (indeed, *real*) stock market – a successful antidote to the illusion of the dot-com era – was perhaps even more a figment of the imagination than the so-called era of irrational exuberance (Shiller 2000).

Having tracked online investors now for well over a decade, with extensive interview data spanning from the height of the dot-com bubble and the lows of the 2000 crash to the heights of the real estate bubble and the lows of the recent financial crisis, we find rather unsurprisingly a change in the attitudes toward, motivations for, and approaches to investing generally and online trading in particular. Specifically, the years running up to the bursting of the dot-com bubble saw the emergence of what we call the *kinematic investor,* who was mesmerized by the experience of dynamism, action, and speed of being in the market.

In the years after the dot-com crash, investors came to realize that their actions have consequences and that the market ought to be considered as a place for achieving fiscal self-realization and economic security rather than for having fun. We call this investor type the *entrepreneurial investor.* Of course, the kinematic investor and the entrepreneurial investor have much in common and should not be considered ideal types of individual investors. In particular, a strong narrative of individual agency characterizes both investor types, albeit not in exactly the same sense. For the kinematic investor, a sense of agency comes from the experience of acting directly on the market, while for the entrepreneurial investor agency represents a broader concept of having to adopt – not necessarily voluntarily – a mentality of personal fiscal responsibility vis-à-vis a diminishing dependability of collectively managed forms of financial securitization.

For the purpose of this chapter, we use the distinction between the kinematic and the entrepreneurial investor largely as an analytical tool to emphasize the most salient features of the online investing experience as it evolved over the past ten or so years through the emergence of the Internet. In the next section we will first discuss the kinematic investor, with a focus on the speed of money, and the aesthetics of investing. Then we describe the entrepreneurial investor before we conclude with some thoughts on how the notion of the entrepreneurial investor can be seen as part of a more general emergence of the entrepreneurial consumer. We draw on a longitudinal set of interviews with online investors to illustrate key points.

1998–2001, the kinematic investor

Popular science writer James Gleick argues in *Faster: The Acceleration of Just About Everything* (1999), that Western cultures are governed by speed. The new social algorithm, speed pushes people to function with the cadence and efficiency of machines. Gleick believes that speed has become embedded physically and psychologically into every aspect of social behavior, often overwhelming our mental and physical ability to cope with its effects (see also Virilio 1995). Anxiety, restlessness, and a sense of helplessness characterize the subjectivities of speed-governed societies. Speed, then, represents the ultimate experience of modernity because it embodies the progress of the technological revolution (Virilio 1977).

In the corporate realm, speed has become a central element for success. The abundant use of terms like "time to market," "just in time," "product development cycle acceleration," and "real-time" – to name but a few – highlights the importance of speed in a business context increasingly characterized by electronically networked organizations, globally linked markets and just-in-time production practices. The "acceleration of everything" has also changed consumers' perception of time as a value. In the lives of many Western consumers time is a scarce resource and products and services that permit time-savings – such as pre-cooked foods, online shopping, and managed investment funds – find viable markets. Similarly, it is a widely held belief that one of the Internet's greatest benefits for consumers lies in its acceleration of transactions, mainly by reducing search costs (Hoffman and Novak 1997; Dholakia 1998; Hoque and Lohse 1999; Smith *et al.* 1999). In the case of online stock trading, however, utilitarian benefits such as time savings and convenience are often supplemented – if not supplanted – by experiential benefits of speed and agency.

The speed of money

In the case of online investing, speed is experienced by the investor in two distinct yet related ways, in what can be called the *speed of money* and the *speed of action* (see Figure 19.1). In short, the speed of money refers to the investor's perception of the movement and volatility of the stock market in general and his or her investment portfolio in particular. Investors believe that the stock market accelerates money – especially if the stock market is mediated by the Internet – and by doing so increases the possibility of gains and losses. Speed of action refers to the perception of the investor to quickly "act on" the moving market. As the instantaneous experiential effects of such "acting on" are witnessed, the individual investor gains a sense of agency in the market. With this newly felt sense of agency, of individual mastery of speed and action, the individual investor is in turn able to experience the speed of money as an exhilarating and thrilling event, not least because of the possibility of accidents (i.e., losing money fast).

The relationship between the growth of the Internet and the rise in stock market participation of private investors, while certainly not causal, is significant. As the Internet collides with the world of financial markets, somehow a seductive mélange emerges that captures the imagination of a growing number of individuals. Personal accounts of individual investors suggest that they are drawn to this (for most) new world of investing by the allure of *fast money*, or more precisely the potential to *accelerate money*. The speed of money in the stock market is thus perceived as the antithesis of the inertia of money found in traditional

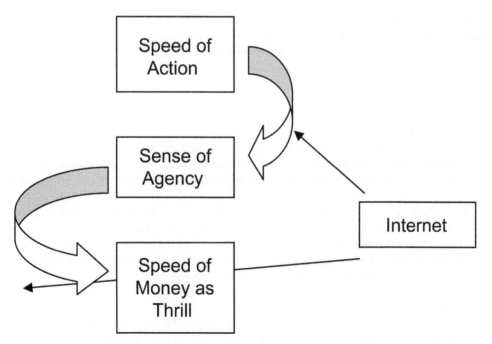

Figure 19.1 Model of the phenomenology of speed in online investing

211

forms of investing. Even mutual funds appear "slow" against the speed of stocks. As some of our informants put it:

> You know, we had $3000 in our savings account and it was just sitting there and the market was going up steadily, it seemed better to take the $3000 and invest it into a decent stock. You could do better that way. You could see some appreciation, right? The numbers where changing every night you checked on your stocks. You wanted to have the Big Mover, right. They have this list of stocks on CNBC, the big movers of the day. And you want to have the Big Mover. Unlike the savings or checking account where nothing happens, you know.
>
> *(Kenny, 42, professor)*

> I don't have any money that is not invested. It would just be lying around and that is wasting it in my eyes.
>
> *(Manfred, 37, IT developer)*

> It started when I was getting some money as a refund from the school. So I had this money just sitting around, so I am, like, what do I do with it? I really didn't think putting it in the bank does any good because like with the other money, it kind of just lies around there, you know, which is fine because you might need it and then it's right there. But if you want to do something with it, you have to invest it. So I was talking to my parents again, and they said, well, why don't you put it in the market?
>
> *(Brad, 21, student)*

So, instead of money just *sitting, hanging,* or *lying around* in a savings account, putting it in the market carries the promise of movement and acceleration – action. Especially during the time of steady and considerable economic growth, to accelerate one's money through the stock market meant for investors to hope for the "jackpot." Thus, the potential to "make it big" and "get the big mover" exerts a strong initial attraction for the individual investor.

At least at this early stage, the financial rationale seems to dominate the investor's disposition toward the market. Early successes reinforce the belief in the market as a moneymaking machine and lead to the build-up of overconfidence in one's own ability to invest (Barber and Odean 1999). But investors realize quickly that money can be lost as well as won and over time, the initial swagger and unfettered exuberance make way for a more nuanced and realistic assessment of the logic of accelerated money. Particularly the market crash of April 2000 brought home to the kinematic investor that stocks are a risky investment choice after all, that speed of money works in both directions. Fast things – cars, trains, airplanes – sometimes crash.

Interestingly, instead of being discouraged or shocked by the market's volatility, some investors actually seemed to be attracted by risk. Once the logic of the market was embraced, it is no longer just the lure of fast gains but the speed of money itself, with the potential to move up *and* down that becomes intriguing for the investor. Markus, for example, sounds like an at-risk casino gambler when describing his experiences in the stock market:

> *So you think more risk is more fun?*
>   Increased excitement. It is this particular edginess. The volatility of these things, 20% is nothing sometimes, that eats you up. Once you've done it and it's all over you think to yourself "never again," and a few weeks later, you get back in. Right now,

I have one from RWE that was already cut in half and currently is in positive territory. I mean, it goes up and down there. You know that is suspense.

(Markus, 25, student)

Similarly, Kenny finds excitement in the fast up and down movements of stock valuations:

Look at Westel here [is playing on the computer again switching quickly between Yahoo! Finance and Quick and Reilly. He now reads off the Westel 1-year chart at Yahoo!]. It was up to $40 right here and I bought it at $12 or $13, maybe. Do you know how much money I made? I never really walked away with that money but I thought I was making a ton of money. I mean it more than doubled, right. Then it went down but here it came back. It was looking good, it was at $30. And there is that drop. Now *that's* a precipitous drop. And then it kept going. Tried to come back. Kept going and now it has come back up to $5. From 3 to 4 to 5, right. 'Cause everybody knows now that this company cannot be trusted. I mean this stock is exciting stuff, right?

(Kenny, 42, professor)

Thus, the sensation of rapidly moving money, its volatility and speed, enters the investors' field of perception through the computer screen (see also Knorr Cetina and Bruegger 2002) and gives rise to a new form of investor subjectivity, what we call the kinematic investor. Unlike other types of investors, the kinematic investor perceives a *dual experience* of speed. First, the rapid up-and-down movement of stock prices is clearly recognized and feared as a threat to personal wealth. Such fast movement causes anxiety and apprehension counteracted by the investors' intensified vigilance and surveillance of the market and their personal portfolios. Second, however, it became possible for the kinematic investor to "envisage speed as a kind of drug, an intensifier, an *excitant moderne*" (Schnapp 1999, p. 3). The movement of invested money now becomes a form of stimulus that is important in and of itself.

The formation of the kinematic investor is closely linked to the emergence of new information and communication technologies such as the Internet and television, which transform our sensitivity to time and distance and create a new "time regime" (Castells 1996, p. 429). As Esther Milne (2000, p. 2) puts it, "[T]he perceptual reconfiguration of time and space is central to an understanding of modernity's preoccupation with speed. Rapid data circulation through digital information systems means that distance appears to shrink and time seems to collapse." David Harvey identified "space–time compression" and the "speed-up in the pace of life" (1989, p. 241) as the fundamental condition of postmodern capitalism. In the interactive age of instantaneous communication, speed is not used solely to make travel more effective.

It is used above all to see, to hear, to perceive, and, thus, to *conceive more intensely* the present world. In the future, speed will be used more and more *to act over distance*, beyond the sphere of influence of the human body and its behavioral biotechnology.

(Virilio 1993, our emphasis)

As far as stock trading is concerned, the future arrived for the masses with the ability to trade online. The Internet and television with its 24/7 financial news cycles have intensified our exposure to the financial realm and the world as a whole. But *exposure* to the speed of money – through mass and interactive media – cannot generate this sense of excitement and suspense that investors express in the face of high volatility. What is needed is the ability, as Virilio puts it, *to act over distance*. In other words, the thrill of high-velocity money does not originate from the objective speed of money itself but the investors' *agency over speed* and it is the Internet that allows investors to act on the market instantaneously. For example, when asked about the difference between using a broker or bank, the telephone, and the internet for investing, one informant replied:

> I think it just became too tedious to always having to walk there and even with the telephone, as I did later. I wanted to have more influence over the whole process but also to be able to better follow market events. The problem with telephone is that you call them up that you want to sell, which is probably OK with long-term investments because you don't want to sell so quickly but with the short-term positions, you just don't know whether it all worked out with your order that day. So you have to inquire about it later and only then they tell you but then sometimes they still don't tell you the exact price they sold it for so you have to wait for the official notification. And with the online brokerage you can follow the process all the way and you see the result immediately. You are much more independent and then the whole thing gets exciting.
>
> *(Oliver, 31, teacher)*

Oliver's comment suggests that *seeing* the market as well as being able to act on it directly changes the experience of investing from a somewhat passive, consumerist activity (when using an intermediary for the execution of trades) to a very dynamic and productive activity (when using the Internet to trade). "Panoptic market vision" is equivalent to being "in or close to the market" and the ability to navigate it. Just like the car driver, who cannot securely steer the vehicle without proper visibility of the road (i.e., the agency of the driver is lost), the individual investor considers vision of the market as perhaps the most critical prerequisite for ensuring a sense of agency as trader. In addition to allowing for total visibility of and telepresence in the market, the Internet also extends agency from the human to the nonhuman (Latour 2005). Technologies such as sell stop orders[1] and limit orders[2] extend the investor's actions and essentially provide him or her with a 24-hour presence in the stock market.

The digital investor

Denegri-Knott and Molesworth (2010) developed a typology of online consumption behavior, what they term *digital virtual consumption*. Whereas their work focused largely on consumption in virtual environments, such as Second Life and World of Warcraft, their insights into how these worlds inhabit user's imaginations are useful for understanding online investors. They consider online environments "liminal – somewhere between the imagination and the material" (ibid., p. 110). We believe that this liminal condition maps onto investing, in which material money is represented by electronic numbers, graphs, and charts (see Zwick and Dholakia 2006). Furthermore, online investing dwells largely in the imaginative world; in particular, our kinematic investors embody this distinction particularly well.

Another important aspect of online investing concerns aesthetics – here considered "non-rational" motives for consumer investment. Aspara (2009) outlined several aesthetic dimensions of investing, arguing that aesthetics plays a large role in individual investor behavior and experience. Specifically, he called attention to what he terms *self-expressive* consumption via the stock market – an aesthetic motivation "that can serve as an additional explanation to many people's stock investment choices, or subjective tastes for particular kind of stocks – beyond the motives related to expected financial returns and mere familiarity" (ibid.:, p. 121). The glut of information available online may contribute to this effect, as consumers learn more about company behavior, they may learn new things, and become sensitive to aesthetic or ethical issues (see e.g., Zwick *et al.* 2007; Hirsto 2011). The ability to engage in self-expressive investment is fundamentally grounded in a perception of agentic movement and engagement. Put differently, kinematic investing – via computer screen and digital networks – opens up new types of motivation and rationality of investing.

Thus, and contrary to media discourse around investing, many consumers report interest in wider activities of companies, and may become sensitized to ethical issues, such as social responsibility, supply chain management, and corporate citizenship via online information sources (Zwick *et al.* 2007). In a recent study of media coverage of investing, Hirsto (2011, p. 72) identified four discourses, each representing a different subject position for the consumer:

> A calculative speculator of the mechanistic discourse; a rationally emotional investor of the psychological discourse; a responsible consumer-investor of the participatory discourse; and a heroic professional of the expert discourse. To some extent, however, these idealized subjects can all be characterized as economistic, that is autonomous, calculative, and motivated by self-interest.

In other words, despite a rapid expansion of consumer participation in investing generally, investment discourse seems to trail behind what investors report about their behavior. Hirsto concludes:

> When consumers are led to think of investing as a technical project of personal wealth management, they may easily fail to recognize the implications of their decisions to broader social and economic practices, and the political and ideological underpinnings of financial practices.
>
> *(ibid., p. 73)*

Importantly, then, the kinematic world of online investing does not over-determine the investor subject. Subject positions such as the (limited) ones promulgated in the media as well as additional positions identified through empirical research by Hirsto and Zwick *et al.*, for example, do not require *necessarily* an online investment environment. However, what the digital investing environment does is to democratize individual investing, thus making experiences of speed and movement of money available to the masses and broadening the range of motivations and dispositions of investors.

The rise of a new investor subject

In sum, the Internet provided individualized and fast access to a stock market that has been rendered fully transparent through its visualization. The Internet thus became the fundamental condition for the experience of speed, both of money and of one's own actions (agency), in addition to expanding the context in which investment occurred (e.g., Zwick *et al.* 2007) It is, hence, too simple to reduce the Internet to a better and more efficient tool for online trading. Rather, the Internet changed entirely the nature and experience of investing, especially during the early years of online trading and therefore is better regarded as an integral part of the production of a new investor subject, the kinematic investor, equipped with a set of perceptions that allow for new kinds of aesthetics, emotions and sensations of investing.

2001–today, the entrepreneurial investor

As the glow of the dot-com era wore off in the aftermath of the 2000 crash, we can see a period of adjustment in the individual online investor's approach – away from the exhilaration of fast money toward a more responsible understanding of investing. That is not to say that investors willingly gave up their newly won independence from banks and professional brokers. Investor agency and the concurrent possibility for excitement and thrill remained important drivers of online trading even after the downturn. Nevertheless, whereas the effect of popular culture and the Internet for the transformation of personal investing into a site for consumerist excitement can hardly be overstated, the traumatic experience of the crash of the dot-com bubble did indeed remind individual investors that investing money takes place in a larger social and economic reality and that one's actions have concrete financial implications – particularly for one's portfolio.

As a result, online investors became more reflexive and earnest about the role of investing in their lives. Investing came to be seen as an opportunity for and even duty to secure a financial future for oneself; an approach to investing suitably for a time when neoliberal social policy in the US and Europe continues to reconstruct society by encouraging individualized forms of security and responsibility, fostering entrepreneurial competitiveness, and relying on the market to provide previously collective goods and services, particularly pension and retirement accounts.

The context in which individual online investors found themselves after the dot-com boom and bust was not new. For a long time, but especially throughout the 1990s, neoliberal social policy had reshaped the social and economic landscape in the US in a way that stresses competitive individualism, entrepreneurial adventurism, and personal responsibility (Harvey 1989; Peck 2010). As a social technology, neoliberalism aspired to create the conditions that encourage and necessitate the production of oneself as new *homo economicus*:[3] a subject that is morally responsible for navigating the social realm using rational choice and cost-benefit calculations grounded on market-based principles to the exclusion of all other ethical values and social interests (Foucault 2008). From this perspective, the stock market emerges as the site *par excellence* for the self-production of the neoliberal subject, a historically specific form of subjectivity, constituted as a free and autonomous "atom" of self-interest (Hamann 2009).

Hence, expanding on the cognitive-phenomenological effect of the technologization of the stock market (speed, agency, thrill), we need to consider recent socio-political transformations, such as the financialization and individualization of risk as well as the general economic insecuritization of the individual, in order to understand more fully the transformation in investor attitudes toward the stock market and stock trading as well as the central role online investing continues to play in the lives of our informants. In particular, we argue that, by being linked in quite direct ways to the production of *oneself* as human capital, online investing represents perhaps more than any other mode of consumption the strategic formation of a new type of individual, "the subject who is an 'entrepreneur of him/herself' who is meant to fit into the frame of society remade as an 'enterprise society'" (Lazzarato 2009, p. 110). The entrepreneurial consumer emerges.

Individualization, insecuritization, financialization

The financialization of risk refers to policies and institutional structures designed to assert "the redistribution of risk and protection, leaving the individual increasingly at the mercy of the market" (ibid., p. 111). As previously collective forms of risk management and financial securitization become individualized and turned over to market mechanism, the individual is left to his/her own devices, compelled to develop the mental hardwiring practical skills required to ensure a secure and prosperous financial future. As one informant put it in an interview conducted almost four years after the first interview [then still enjoying the last months of the dotcom boom times]:

> Yes, absolutely, the recent years have been frustrating for me but also sometimes OK. If you do your research and don't just listen to what the guys from the media say, you

can still find a good stock here and there … and think about it, what options do we, my generation, have in the matter? That pension plan that my father got when he joined the workforce back in the 70s, well, that won't be there for my generation. These days, you have to secure ("absichern") yourself and if you don't, it's your own fault. I wouldn't trust the government, or my employers, to do it for me.

(Oliver, 35, teacher)

Doubt has settled not just on collectively supported long-term financial planning schemes, the financial world itself has become insecure (Beck 1986; Giddens 1990). As traditional and institutional forms of security disappear, risk enters into modern lives from all directions (Bauman 2000). The difference today is that, as the state increasingly withdraws from the collectivization of expenditures for social goods and services (health care, guaranteed retirement income and pensions, education, etc.), individuals learn to accept and live with risk individually, adopting "ways of thinking" adapted to a world where social dependencies vanish and fiscal self-realization is expected. Put differently, the neoliberal subject is exposed to and perceives a riskier world and thus self-fashions an ethics of self-reliance, fiscal agency, and socio-economic independence out of necessity. Kenny, a professor at a state university in New England, expresses this attitude in 2004, more than four years after his first interview with us.

I still do it [trading stocks, investing] all myself. I have come to the conclusion that while I don't know all that much about the stock market, the so-called professionals don't know that much, either. So why rely on someone else? … I invest now with different goals in mind, though, look at the long term and hopefully make some money, real money, that we might need down the road … The state is not doing great, who knows how the university will be doing in twenty years when I want to retire, right? … Playing the market might be my best shot at making sure we are financially OK when I want to retire.

(Kenny, 46, professor)

Indeed, the state Kenny is referring to finds itself in a precarious fiscal position today, after the so-called Great Recession – furloughs have been implemented at his financially strapped university. And as the neoliberal strategy of shifting responsibility onto individuals takes hold in the social body, if things go wrong – as they invariably do in a state-sanctioned finance capitalism, evacuated of democratic accountability and financial consequences for its actors and main beneficiaries – the individual expects to be responsible and left to his or her own devices in dealing with personal fallout. Thus, the neoliberal subject, especially one invested – financially and psychologically – in the stock market, may embrace a perspective that risk and accidents are no longer the exception but the norm, as he is socialized into a world where stark ruptures and serious disruption are as common as they are revocable and (seemingly) repairable, by a government stimulus, for example. In the summer of 2011, eleven years after his first interview, Manfred illustrates this point nicely:

But if you think that maybe now things will normalize a bit and the market will somehow behave more rationally, well, what I mean by that is, somehow more steady, smaller gains or maybe losses of the index over a longer period of time, that kind of thing, I don't count on that to happen. On the contrary, I think these wild swings and bubbles and crashes and all that will get worse. It's not for weak nerves. But in the end, the market always comes back and goes up, so it's really up to you to make the most of these swings. There is a lot of money to be made if you know what you are doing and if you know *when* to do it [laughs]. In fact, I was pretty devastated when the Neuer Markt [best described as the German equivalent of the NSDAQ] crashed in 2000 and I lost a lot of money, back then. But many of my stocks came back and after a couple of years, maybe three or four, I was doing OK again and so, all in all, over the last 10 years I have really come to enjoy the volatility of the stock market because a sharp drop, if you can get out in time, always means a sharp rise in the end and that is where the money is being made now.

By "really enjoying" market volatility, Manfred reveals the power of market socialization, and an important shift in investing behavior and perception. He has aestheticized his experience of online trading. In particular, the market crash in the Spring of 2000 comes up a number of times in our conversation with Manfred. It was a watershed moment for him because the crash was his first experience with a major market shock and massively declining stock valuations. Having survived the market crash and even thrived during the years between the 2000 and 2008 crashes, Manfred has developed an almost deterministic sense of investing, believing that in the end, the stock market will always recover and generate wealth for him. Macro-structural risk and ensuing crises that can move markets in often hysterical fashion, are to be seized as the source of economic opportunity, even if based on the (undeserved) losses of others, and exploited for individual profit.[4] The invasion of Iraq by a US-led NATO coalition force in 2003, for example, drove up stocks of security, weapon and defense contractors, as well as heavy construction companies. As the statement by an American informant illustrates, configuring yourself as a consumer of market opportunity trumps any other consideration:

> It might not always seem fair or the right thing to do when you try to benefit from the misfortune of others but often that is how it works, isn't it? ... I have done really well with defense-related stocks since the invasion of Iraq. It's kinda ironic because I was against the invasion, actually, and still am. But when it comes to making money and making sure my wife and I can retire when we want to, as far as I am concerned, it's OK in my book. I'm taking advantage of an opportunity as an investor. It does not mean that I am a supporter of the war, either.
>
> *(Eric, 46, ad designer)*

The individualization of risk, opportunities, costs, and benefits and the infusion of every aspect of social life with market values also may produce a sense of emancipation from the collective and from a moral duty towards others beyond the letter of the law. The individual is instead exhorted to adopt a mode of self-regulation centered on autonomy, flexibility and instrumentality in professional and institutional life (Binkley 2006). As Bauman (2000, p. 31) summarizes, "'individualization'" consists of transforming human 'identity' from a given into a 'task' and charging the actors with the responsibility for performing that task and for the consequences (also the side-effects) of their performance." Many of the investors we interviewed expressed this sense of "self-made-ness" often related to making things happen in the market. As one informant put it:

> I'll be honest with you, buying and selling stock really excites me, doing the investing myself really excites me, and taking care of our financial future myself really excites me. And it scares me at times but so far, it's been really good. I think it's a control thing with me. I like to be in charge and even when I used a broker, I never liked it. Now, I am completely independent of others and that part feels really good.
>
> *(Eric, 46, ad designer)*

This comment may embody Adam Smith's economic theory, but it neglects his sense of moral sentiments that hold markets and societies together.

According to the new spirit of capitalism (Boltanski and Chiapello 2007) any 'buy-in' to long-term dependencies has the potential to become downright dangerous when individual plans about career, identity, residency, or social relationships must remain nimble, adaptable, and mobile in a world without certainties. Self-directed online investing, rather than state-sanctioned retirement schemes, company pension plans, or "guaranteed" annuities, embodies the new spirit of capitalism by allowing the subject to fashion himself as independent fiscal agent and decisionistic market actor. Echoing the self-confident representations of the Ameritrade advertisements of the late 1990s and in particular the swashbuckling attitude of punk-rock investor Steward, one US-based investor states:

> I take care of my financial needs myself. I don't want to rely on some company or the government when I am older. I don't trust them, so, I'd rather do it myself ... It really is all about people taking responsibility for themselves rather than relying on others to do the work for them. And with the Internet, it's really easy to do.
>
> *(Peter, 28, sales rep.)*

For Peter, Internet investing liberates him from the shackles of investment brokers and government, which smoothly integrates him into the current reality of neoliberalism.

Neoliberalism emphasizes individual liberty and freedom, in particular as expressed through the market, where open and competitive supply responds to consumer desires through the individual liberties of market choice. The freedom of the market becomes the model of freedom *per se* (Brown 2006). From this perspective, neoliberalism is a technique of government, or governmentality (which for Foucault means both governing and a mode of thought) that provides, through specific programs and initiatives, a climate that aims at bringing about the entrepreneurial self (Rose 1992; Dean 1999; Binkley 2006). Hence, the freedom postulated by neoliberalism is not just individual but individual*istic* because "rather than fostering social bonds, the target of neoliberal governmentality is to eliminate precisely those collectivist tendencies, which threaten to stifle self-interested, competitive economic behavior" (Binkley 2009). The stock market, delivered via the computer, tablet or smart phone, fast electronic networks, and near ubiquitous broadband access, became a valid and "natural" site for the performance of the virtues of entrepreneurship and self-realization as the personal ethic for the generation of individual online investors socialized into DIY investing during the heydays of the dot-com era.

Conclusion

The history of online stock trading, at least in its guise as a mass phenomenon, is only about fifteen years old. Yet, a lot has happened in those years with two historical bubbles and respective crashes, and a new generation of investors, lured to the market by the irrational exuberance of the late 1990s and the simultaneous emergence of the Internet, had to adapt to the vagaries of a highly volatile decade. In this chapter we identify two distinct investor types that have been characteristic for the various phases of this brief history of online investing. Representative of investors' attitude during the years running up to the bursting of the dot-com bubble, we call the first investor type the kinematic investor, one who was looking to the stock market as a place for chasing aesthetic experiences of thrill, speed, and agency (see also Zwick 2005). Acting like the super-ego, the dot-com crash forced investors to come to terms with their own foolishness, overconfidence, and limitations and face a reality of tough financial losses and the need for a new definition of the role of investing in their lives. Investors came to realize that their actions have consequences and that the market ought to be considered a place for achieving financial self-realization and economic security rather than for primarily having fun. We called this investor type the entrepreneurial investor.

In the final analysis, we suggest that we can only understand the inner life of investors and the emerging subjectivities when looking at the socio-economic as well as the technological context in which the practice of investing takes place (see also Hirsto 2011). It would therefore be inaccurate to reduce the popular rise of individual online investing to the emergence of the Internet. Rather, the emergence and *especially* the sustained success of individual investing can only be understood when linked to the broader philosophy, discourse, and practical rationality of neoliberalism centered on the maximization of profit and financial security as a form of self-government (cf. Binkley 2009). Neoliberal governmentality, hence, is a political project that focuses on the practical activity of self-producing and self-fashioning oneself as a *homo economicus*. Put differently, the individual must become an entrepreneur of himself, configuring himself as human capital. From this vantage point, the strategy to confer more and more long-term planning tasks, including financial long-term planning, to the logic of the market makes sense for neoliberal subjectivities who, on the one hand, have seen traditional securities and long-standing realities dissolve, and, on the other, have acquired cognitive structures of the "natural" importance of self-reliance and personal responsibility – foundations for entrepreneurial consumption.

Notes

1 The website of the Security Exchange Commission explains that a stop order, also referred to as a stop-loss order, is an order to buy or sell a stock once the price of the stock reaches a specified price, known as the stop price. When the stop price is reached, a stop order becomes a market order. A sell stop order is entered at a stop price below the current market price. Investors generally use a sell stop order to limit a loss or to protect a profit on a stock that they own.

2 A limit order is an order to buy or sell a stock at a specific price or better. A buy limit order can only be executed at the limit price or lower, and a sell limit order can only be executed at the limit price or higher. A limit order is not guaranteed to execute. A limit order can only be filled if the stock's market price reaches the limit price. While limit orders do not guarantee execution, they help ensure that an investor does not pay more than a pre-determined price for a stock.

3 Foucault uses the concept of new *homo oeconomicus* as a form of subjectivation (Milchman and Rosenberg 2009), where individuals are actively fashioning themselves as ethical subjects, and in this case an ethics of autonomy, decisionism, and individualism, the individual as an "entrepreneur of oneself," maximizing himself or herself as "human capital" in competition with all other individuals (see Lazzarato 2009; Klein 2007).

4 As the godfather of American neoliberalism, Milton Friedman, put it (in Klein 2007, p. 47): "Only a crisis—actual or perceived—produces real change. When that crisis occurs, the actions that are taken depend on the ideas that are lying around."

Further reading

Deighton, J. and Kornfeld, L. (2009) "Interactivity's Unanticipated Consequences for Marketers and Marketing," *Journal of Interactive Marketing*, 23: 4–10. [A thoughtful analysis of the Internet's unexpected influences on marketing.]

Knorr Cetina, K.D. (2005) "How Are Global Markets Global? The Architecture of a Flow World," in K.D. Knorr Cetina and A. Preda (eds), *The Sociology of Financial Markets*, New York: Oxford University Press, pp. 103–26). [Looks at global currency exchanges to problematize the notion of "the global" as well as offer a critique to the classic conceptions of markets as networked and embedded.]

Knorr Cetina, K.D. and Preda, A. (2005) *The Sociology of Financial Markets*, New York: Oxford University Press. [Essays provide a sociological perspective of financial markets, asking how do such markets actually work and who is working in them, making the market work? Contributions in this volume trace the actors of financial markets and their operations in a global financial networks.]

MacKenzie, D.A. (2006) *An Engine, Not a Camera: How Financial Models Shape Markets*, Cambridge, MA: MIT Press. [Traces the history of the financial derivatives market to suggest that the development of economic models caused trader behavior to conform to the models, as such performing economics in a way that would then confirm the validity of the models that caused the performance in the first place.]

MacKenzie, D.A., Muniesa, F. and Siu, L. (2007) *Do Economists Make Markets? On the Performativity of Economics*, Princeton, NJ: Princeton University Press. [See above.]

Preda, A. (2009) *Framing Finance: The Boundaries of Markets and Modern Capitalism*, Chicago: University of Chicago Press. [Historical analysis that looks at how the stock market and individual investing have become commonly accepted and largely trusted institutions and practices, thus offering an interesting perspective on the origins of the current economic crisis.]

Zwick, D. and Cayla, J. (eds) (2010) *Inside Marketing*, Oxford: Oxford University Press. [An edited collection that offers a fascinating glimpse at how marketers and marketing work.]

Zwick, D., Denegri-Knott, J. and Schroeder, J.E. (2007) "Stock Trading as Political Activism? The Social Pedagogy of Wall Street," *Journal of Consumer Policy*, 30(3): 177–99. [Argues that digital consumers may learn to appreciate cultural and ethical dimensions of investing.]

References

Aspara, J. (2009) "Aesthetics of Stock Investments," *Consumption, Markets and Culture,* 12: 99–131.

Barber, B.M. and Odean, T. (1999) "The Courage of Misguided Convictions," *Financial Analysts Journal,* 55: 41–55.

Bauman, Z. (2000) *Liquid Modernity*, Cambridge: Polity Press.

Beck, U. (1986) *Risikogesellschaft. Auf dem Weg in eine andere Moderne*, Frankfurt a. M.: Suhrkamp.

Binkley, S. (2006) "The Perilous Freedoms of Consumption: Toward a Theory of the Conduct of Consumer Conduct," *Journal for Cultural Research*, 10: 343–62.

——(2009) "Governing Happiness," conference paper, presented at the Schulich School of Business Consumer Culture Research Series.

Boltanski, L. and Chiapello, E. (2007) *The New Spirit of Capitalism*, London: Verso.

Brown, W. (2006) "American Nightmare: Neoliberalism, Neoconservatism, and De-Democratization," *Political Theory,* 34: 690–714.

Castells, M. (1996) *The Rise of the Network Society*, Malden, MA: Blackwell.

Dean, M. (1999) *Governmentality: Power and Rule in Modern Society*, London: Sage.

Denegri-Knott, J. and Molesworth, M. (2010) "Concepts and Practices of Digital Virtual Consumption," *Consumption, Markets and Culture*, 13: 109–32.

Denzin, N.K. (1990) "Reading 'Wall Street': Postmodern Contradictions in the American Social Structure," in B.S. Turner (ed.), *Theories of Modernity and Postmodernity*, London: Sage.

Dholakia, R.R. (1998) "Introduction: Special Issue on Conducting Business in the New Electronic Environment: Prospects and Problems," *Journal of Business Research*, 41: 175–7.

Foucault, M. (2008) *The Birth of Biopolitics: Lectures at the Collège de France, 1978–79*, New York: Palgrave Macmillan.

Giddens, A. (1990) *The Consequences of Modernity*, Stanford, CA: Stanford University Press.

Gleick, J. (1999) *Faster: The Acceleration of Just About Everything*, New York: Pantheon Books.

Hamann, T.H. (2009) "Neoliberalism, Governmentality, and Ethics," *Foucault Studies*, 6: 37–59.

Harvey, D. (1989) *The Condition of Postmodernity*, Cambridge, MA: Blackwell.

——(2005) *A Brief History of Neoliberalism*, New York: Oxford University Press.

Hirsto, H. (2011) "Everyday Discourses of Stock Market Investing: Searching for Investor Power and Responsibility," *Consumption, Markets and Culture*, 14: 57–77.

Hoffman, D.L. and Novak, T.P. (1997) "A New Marketing Paradigm for Electronic Commerce," *The Information Society*, 13: 43–54.

Hoque, A.Y. and Lohse, G.L. (1999) "An Information Search Cost Perspective for Designing Interfaces for Electronic Commerce," *Journal of Marketing Research*, 36: 387–94.

Klam, M. (1999) "Riding the Mo in the Lime Green Glow," *The New York Times,* July 12.

Klein, N. (2007) *The Shock Doctrine: The Rise of Disaster Capitalism*, New York: Metropolitan Books.

Knorr Cetina, K.D. and Bruegger, U. (2002) "Traders' Engagement with Markets," *Theory, Culture, & Society*, 19: 161–85.

Latour, B. (2005) *Reassembling the Social: An Introduction to Actor-Network-Theory*, New York: Oxford University Press.

Lazzarato, M. (2009) "Neoliberalism in Action: Inequality, Insecurity and the Reconstitution of the Social," *Theory, Culture, & Society*, 26: 109–33.

Milchman, A. and Rosenberg, A. (2009) "The Final Foucault: Government of Others and Government of the Self," in S. Binkley and J. Capetillo (eds), *A Foucault for the 21st Century: Governmentality, Biopolitics and Discipline in the New Millennium*, Newcastle upon Tyne: Cambridge Scholars Publishing.

Milne, E. (2000) "The Ministers of Locomotion: Some Historical Speculations on Velocity Culture," *M/C: A Journal of Media and Culture*, 3, available at: www.api-network.com/mc/0006/ministers.html (accessed March 8, 2001).

Peck, J. (2010) *Constructions of Neoliberal Reason*, Oxford: Oxford University Press.

Rose, N. (1992) "Governing the Enterprising Self," in P. Heelas and P. Morris (eds), *The Values of the Enterprise Culture*, London: Routledge.

Schnapp, J.T. (1999) "Crash (Speed as Engine of Individualation)," *Modernism/Modernity*, 6: 1–49.

Shiller, R.J. (2000) *Irrational Exuberance*, Princeton, NJ: Princeton University Press.

Smith, G.E., Venkatraman, M.P. and Dholakia, R.R. (1999) "Diagnosing the Search Cost Effect: Waiting Time and the Moderating Impact of Prior Category Knowledge," *Journal of Economic Psychology*, 20: 285–314.

Snow, D.A. and Parker, R. (1984) "The Media and the Market," in P.A. Adler, and P. Adler (eds), *The Social Dynamics of Financial Markets*, Greenwich, CT: JAI Press.

Staute, J. (1998) *Borsenfieber: Was Anleger im Aktienrausch wissen sollten*, Frankfurt a. M.: Campus.

Virilio, P. (1977) *Speed and Politics*, New York: Semiotext(e).

——(1993) "The Third Interval: A Critical Transition," in V. Conley (ed.), *Re-thinking Technologies*, Minneapolis: University of Minnesota Press.

——(1995) "Speed and Information: Cyberspace Alarm," *CTheory*, available at: www.ctheory.com/a30-cyberspace_alarm.html.

Wolfe, T. (1987) *The Bonfire of the Vanities*, New York: Farrar Straus Giroux.

Zwick, D. (2005) "Where the Action Is: Internet Stock Trading as Edgework," *Journal of Computer-Mediated Communication*, 10, available at: www.jcmc.indiana.edu/vol11/issue1/zwick.htm.

Zwick, D., Denegri-Knott, J. and Schroeder, J. (2007) "The Social Pedagogy of Wall Street: Stock Trading as Political Activism?" *Journal of Consumer Policy*, 30: 177–99.

Zwick, D. and Dholakia, N. (2006) "Bringing the Market to Life: Screen Aesthetics and the Epistemic Consumption Object," *Marketing Theory*, 6: 41–62.

20

DIGITAL VIRTUAL CONSUMPTION AS TRANSFORMATIVE SPACE

Mike Molesworth and Janice Denegri-Knott

Keywords

desire, digital virtual consumption, eBay, liminoid, practice, transformation, videogames

Introduction

Intuitively, given the tangible presence of consumer goods, we have come to think of consumption as a predominantly material and physical activity that sees us moving around shopping spaces, touching, buying and using goods in physically involved ways. However, we have also come to accept material consumption as a resource for the imagination to the point that much of the magic of goods hinges on pleasurable daydreams about their transformative power (Belk 2001; Belk *et al.* 2003; Campbell 1987; McCracken 1988). In this chapter we consider digital virtual consumption (DVC) as a location that combines aspects of *both* materiality and the imagination allowing for new experiences and with them transformations in consumers and their practices (Denegri-Knott and Molesworth 2012).

We map out possible DVC practices and more specifically focus on the moments of reflection and transformation these may produce in individuals. We do this cognizant of the conceptual pitfalls of perpetuating an erroneous separation between what is physical or material consumption and DVC. So this is not so much about isolating DVC as a distinct terrain then, but rather seeing DVC as a transformative space, about working out the meanings and uses of digital virtual goods, about investing our imaginative prowess in transforming them into objects of desire, and about the accompanying new skills, competencies and knowledge through which we can make sense of ourselves and our place in our social milieus. We present DVC as a potential space to acquire and test out practices and subject positions, not always possible through either the material real or the imagination on its own, but always linked to both.

The chapter is divided into three sections. To begin with, we make a case for why consumption can be understood as being suffused with reflective and transformative potential. From there we explain the conceptual underpinnings of DVC and map out possible relationships between virtual, digital virtual and material consumption. Drawing on research insights we have gained from our decade-long engagement with DVC, we offer a range of examples, namely consumption practices on *eBay* (our central example), popular retail websites and videogames. We conclude by pondering on the angst that the promise of transformation via DVC may bring.

Consumption as transformation

Grant McCracken (2006) has noted that self-reinvention is a major preoccupation of contemporary consumer culture. Self-authorship of the kind McCracken writes about depends on the creation and maintenance of spaces through which change can be sought and a subject who has an unflinching drive to change. Consumers enter consumption experiences in hope that some kind of transformation will ensue, for example, that a desired home will bring idyllic living or that a pair of running shoes will make us more adept runners (McCracken 1988). This drive for transformation has both conceptually and empirically been dealt with through the lens of consumer desire (Belk 2001; Belk *et al.* 2003; Campbell 1987) where research has concluded that any hope of contentment from permanent transformation is always truncated. In part, this is because displaced meanings attached to goods (McCracken 1988) – an imagined future or past – are too ideal to be fully tested, and because desire for desire is too important a fixture to be forsaken (Belk *et al.* 2003; Campbell 1987).

There are, however, more optimistic analyses that see ownership and subsequent use of goods as producing *small* triumphs and transformations (Leadbeater and Miller 2004; Miller 1997; Slater and Miller 2007). Such transformations are namely produced by the kind of reflective activity, which Colin Campbell (2004) has expressed as a form of 'getting to know oneself', by testing, defining and refining our tastes through consumption. For example in the introduction to *The Shopping Experience*, Falk and Campbell (1997, p. 4) note that while shopping:

> The self is mirrored in the potential object of acquisition with questions which are rarely formulated and hardly ever articulated: 'Is that for me?'; 'Am I like that?'; 'Could that be (part of) me?'; 'Could I be like that?'; 'Would I like to be like that?', and so on; an endless series of questions which are acts of self-formation in themselves.

This self-knowing function has now pollinated practice-based research, where it is said to stem from the constant negotiation between various forms of knowing, specific know-hows and skills entangled in using material objects to achieve certain goals and projects (Hand and Shove 2007; Watson and Shove 2008).

Practice theory presents innovation and transformation as a by-product of engaging in a particular practice (Hand and Shove 2007; Warde 2005; Watson and Shove 2008). Warde, for example, notes of practices that 'they are dynamic by virtue of their own internal logic of operation, as people in myriad situations adapt, improvise and experiment' (2005, p. 140) and Watson and Shove (2008, p. 83) describe transformation as something that is 'developed through an iterative process of doing, reflecting and adapting'. In de Certeauan (de Certeau 1984) terms, transformation is manifested within the boundaries of practice itself, where differences in practice are framed by individual projects, for instance, the need to keep in with certain standards of use, or contaminated by other practices as consumers borrow ways of knowing and doing from other domains of experience. Put simply, transformation happens within and through a specific practice.

As consumption itself becomes progressively digitized (Denegri-Knott and Molesworth 2010a), we find the opening of new spaces through which such transformations may be pursued. Websites, videogames, immersive digital virtual worlds, the online stock market and eBay all offer interim platforms – somewhere between the idealism of consumption taking place in consumers' imagination, and material consumption practices – which may expand the scope and opportunity for change. So, for example, where one may not easily become a successful businessperson in the materially real of everyday life, one can exercise entrepreneurial muscle through eBay (Denegri-Knott and Molesworth 2009; Molesworth and Denegri-Knott 2008) or games such as the science fiction trading game EVE online. Consumers may become immersed in digitally created scenarios where exotic goods such as expensive cars and fantastic goods such as magic swords may be bought, experienced and owned (Denegri-Knott and Molesworth 2010a, 2010b; Molesworth and Denegri-Knott 2007, 2008). To make sense of these, we now turn to an explanation of our DVC.

Digital virtual consumption spaces

To understand DVC we draw on Rob Shields's (2000, 2003) theorization of the digital virtual as liminoid space – somewhere between the imagination and the material. As Shields puts it, the ontological stature of the digital virtual as an 'in-between' place allows for experimentation beyond normal consumer subject positions. It is important to note that DVC as a liminoid space implies not only that the material and the virtual are always interwoven, but also that it is impossible to think of DVC without making reference to the changing forms of materiality in social life and to how both the material and ideal contribute to shaping possibilities and constraints of DVC (Denegri-Knott and Molesworth 2012).

Key in this analysis is Shields's insistence that we should not see the imagination as an opposite of the material, but rather that we should recognize that what we imagine (the virtual) is *real*, but *ideal* whereas the material is *real* and *actual*. The *ideal* includes ideas, memories, daydreams, fantasies and intentions that are experienced in the mind, but are not actualized. The *actual*, on the other hand, is what has actually happened in a concrete, physical way.

If the *ideal* and the *actual* are complementary rather than opposites, they may more usefully be compared to what is *ideally possible* and what is *actually possible*. *Possible ideals* are abstractions, or fantasies, for example, a time machine or a dragon. We can know of these things and imagine them, but we cannot physically experience them. Something *actually possible* on the other hand is likely to happen, such as buying a house or a car. The former is abstract, the later probable. Our imagination is constrained only by what is *ideally possible* and this includes all our collected myths, taboos, fictions and fantasies, whereas the material is constrained by what is *actually possible* in everyday experience (see Figure 20.1).

Digital virtual spaces allow for possible ideals to be experienced. A dragon in a videogame is not *only* imagined, yet is not materially real either. Although such things are created from material servers, networks, and digital processors (owned, run, and maintained at a cost and usually for a profit by commercial organization) and audiovisual equipment (bought or leased by consumers), these materialities are not what are experienced in use, rather they are manifest absent (see Law 2004). It follows then, that in DVC an object of consumption lacks material substance so cannot be used in material reality but is also free from the limitations of what is *actually possible* such that the *ideally possible* is made present and can be experienced. For example, a digital virtual car cannot drive its owner to work or the shops but also needs no fossil fuel, finance agreement or warranty plan in order to be experienced; a digital virtual magic sword cannot cut material flesh, but may slay many foes in digital virtual battles.

Although we may be tempted to focus on the fantastical extremes, the practices of DVC also include more mundane aspects of everyday material reality that are otherwise hard to access. As well as the spaceships and magic weapons that can be consumed in videogames and online worlds, DVC allows explorations of nostalgia via the extensive collectables on eBay or the

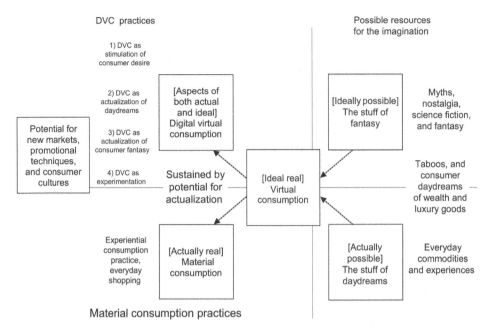

Figure 20.1 Relationships between virtual, material and DVC

experience of shopping for popular car brands via games like Gran Turismo. Consumers may also daydream of and then construct their ideal computer through the 'customize' pages of Dell. DVC therefore includes mechanisms to elaborate and actualize consumers' desires for material commodities and services via their imagination, but also offers the potential to exceed or negate these.

The result is that the range of questions an individual may ask themselves, and the answers about who they are or might be, have the potential for considerable expansion. Indeed, within these spaces an individual may suspend his or her own physical characteristics. They may consume as a different gender, age or even species. For example in World of Warcraft an individual may explore the game world as human, elf, goblin, dwarf, among others and as warrior, druid, priest or warlock.

In these digital virtual spaces the normal rules of materially real quotidian life are suspended, providing a performative matrix for experimenting with different modes of practice. In fact, the potential for individual change is such for Shields (2000, 2003) that it supercharges the potential for transformation present in the liminal, not as a space to manage societal change through the rites of passage that once characterized transitions in life (starting school, starting work, getting married, having children, retiring, etc.) but smaller, individual, liminoid change through personal and often private experimentation. In DVC, the possibility of transformation remains largely wired into commodities and consumer experiences, themselves already liminoid, but also germinates the possibility that the more transgressive practices, which are blocked in the *actually real* because they are too difficult to actualize or because they are taboo, can be enacted in the digital virtual.

DVC practices

DVC practices have two key orientations with accompanying sets of implications and properties. First, under the rubric of *DVC as stimulation of consumer desire* and *DVC as actualization of daydreams*, we discuss DVC practices as ignition, fuelling and actualization of the imagination. We then consider DVC practices as experimentation and transformation.

In the first mode, DVC practices are characterized as a generally harmonious coming together of a desiring consumer and software as epistemic object of consumption which reveals itself progressively through interaction, use and evaluation (Zwick and Dholakia 2006a, 2006b). Like eBay, online worlds, videogames, and interactive websites are always in the process of being defined, acquiring new properties and shedding old ones as closer scrutiny reveals a structure of absence, a chain of always mutating and exploding possibilities. These spaces can never be fully attained because they are always in flux. This makes them, in theory, a perennial source for things to potentially desire.

The material elusiveness and ontological openness of digital virtual spaces demand from its users psychological flexibility and affective investment, which is then returned to the user as emotional stimulation and pleasure by increasingly interesting and exciting possibilities. For example, eBay brings about new wants, as a joint project that is animated by consumers' competences, embodied knowledges and skills to make the technology produce the desired outcomes (Denegri-Knott and Zwick 2012). Users must know what they want, possess the skills to produce and recognize bargains, and have the willingness to compete with others in securing a desired good (Denegri-Knott and Molesworth 2009). Similarly on many other websites, the consumer is invited to always upgrade; always see what is coming next that might fuel desire and lead to actualizing purchases. Amazon allows users the facility to create and manage a 'wish list' of digital virtual items, which may be purchased once finances allow. Yet even when they don't, a user may add to the list those items that arouse their desire, partially actualizing it, changing the status of an item to a possession in waiting. Videogames allow for similar 'wish lists'. Gran Turismo allows players to accumulate a garage full of simulations of increasingly exotic cars. Here the difference is that they may also take them for a spin. Although these cars may one day be purchased 'for real' (and this is no doubt the aim of the growing videogame brand placement business, see Molesworth 2006), something like ownership has already occurred in the game.

These experiences, as we have seen in our research, have potentially transformative properties. DVC practices as experimentation and transformation are possible as a result of the temporary suspension of the quotidian, typical of liminoid spaces (Shields 2000, 2003; Turner 1982, 1988) that allow for the adoption of new subject positions and practices not easily possible in the materially real. This potential for transformation can be explained by invoking Turner's (1982, 1988) metaphor of social dramas to account for individual change with a universal pattern for its management. Social dramas are marked by: a breach (the emergence of a flaw in social norms), crisis (the coming to a head of that flaw that requires action), redressive action (to 'mend' the flaw) and finally reintegration (the return to normal, or coming to terms with the ongoing breach or change). The redressive part of a social drama includes increased reflexivity 'arousing consciousness of ourselves as we see ourselves' (Turner 1982, p. 75) which may activate transformative processes. Through redressive action, there is an attempt to make sense of such experience by looking back at events, to try to 'give the appearance of order to the events leading up to and constituting the experience' (ibid., p. 74).

eBay also provides examples of how DVC may induce individualized social dramas (for example see Denegri-Knott and Molesworth's (2010b) analysis of science fiction writer William Gibson's experience of collecting watches on eBay). In addition, we may see this in the entrepreneurial and 'grand quest' activities undertaken in online worlds such as World of Warcraft. Here a player is removed from the routine practices of everyday life and invited to take part in a world in turmoil and with their own role in it undecided and rich with possibilities for exciting quests and adventures. Alternatively individuals may attempt to explore taboos in videogames such as the Grand Theft Auto series where illegal consumption such as theft, gun crime, prostitution and drug taking are necessary to complete the game. Again the routine and everyday are suspended and players must reflect on the new practices that the game demands.

Transformative practice can be defined as new embodied forms of knowing and doing, including general forms of understanding and a level of commitment to a specific activity, which is perceived as 'new' or constitutes a departure, however slight, from existing practice. Ongoing engagement with eBay or videogames may produce small or temporary transformations at the level of acquiring new skills and competences to perform the role of skilful buyer, seller, thief or hero on a quest. But more significant moments of transformation through reflection derive from the social dramas unfolding in the digital virtual (Shields 2000, 2003). Here, informants reflect on the significance of personal, future aspirations and nostalgic pasts, which promise to fulfil all sorts of otherwise difficult to fulfil possibilities.

DVC as fuel of and actualization of consumer daydreams

Our research on eBay in particular helps illustrate how desire is fuelled, intensified and actualized through DVC. To begin with, eBay awakens a desiring mode through the provision of hope that an elusive item at the right price can be found in its fluctuating landscape of goods. This awakening can be explained by way of a social drama (Turner 1982) where it is eBay's enormous catalogue of goods that induces a crisis based on the possibility that some previously unobtainable possession may now 'suddenly' be available. This produces a drive to mend a flaw or, in Turnerean terminology, a 'breach'. Put differently, latent breaches, which have not been properly addressed, are ignited by the possibility that they may finally be readdressed, from the ongoing wish for an altered state of being associated with a rare and precious item, to the adoption of completely different lifestyles and practices; for example, the recurrent dream of finding financial success by becoming a budding entrepreneur (Siddiqui and Turley 2005, 2007). In order to address a breach, eBay users embark on obsessive and intense episodes of use characterized by careful monitoring of auctions, forms of enhanced *flânerie* where search skills are adopted and deployed to find desired items (Denegri-Knott 2010; Denegri-Knott and Molesworth 2010a, 2010b) or to become more effective sellers.

The harnessing of eBay technology has its moments of enchantment (Denegri-Knott and Zwick 2012). On eBay, the interplay of imagination and possibility, fantasy and reality, is energized by a perceived sense of greater control and autonomy in fuelling desire for goods and in expediting its actualization through material consumption and DVC (Denegri-Knott 2010; Denegri-Knott and Molesworth 2010b). However, this may also produce a contraction in the cycle of desire with the distance between its ignition, consummation and re-ignition, radically shortened (Denegri-Knott 2010). At one level, eBay fuels desire for goods and aids daydreaming activity by giving a more tangible shape to what may have stood as a diffuse daydream and by increasing hope that a desired item may now be had. It also provides an interim, temporary state of ownership, where as an auction's highest bidder, eBay users can indulge in contemplating what life would be like now that a good is almost theirs.

However, the speed of cycles of desire running their course on eBay may be robbing consumers of the pleasures associated with wanting. It is as if continued eBay use threatens desire for desire's sake by giving users a platform for easy actualization through material consumption and DVC. Easy actualization includes easy acquisition only, and not the testing of more substantive promises of transformation that made those items evocative to begin with.

This happens through a process of saturation, where opportunities to learn and gain competence to ignite desire and actualize it, are virtually exhausted, producing complacency and boredom. Additionally, excitement withers away as knowledges are harnessed to acquire goods become settled. This can be explained by seeing the merging of technology and users as involving a redistribution of skills, where eBay absorbs previously embodied skills deployed by users to ignite, fuel and actualize desire. The result is that consumers compensate with creative manoeuvres that assemble new conditions necessary to produce emotional highs, mainly through experimenting with other activities, such as ad hoc collecting and enacting entrepreneurialism (Denegri-Knott and Zwick 2012).

eBay is our substantive case here, but it is not the only digital virtual space that may invite such accelerated cycles of desire. Amazon also presents an apparently limitless list of desirable goods, all just one click away. Long and complex lists of wants can be manufactured in relatively short time. The site invites endless possibilities – the discomfort that drives a desire for actualization – but it also quickly presents the impossibility of ever fulfilling all wishes as well as an over-easy 'one click' solution should finances allow. The problem here then is in desire itself. Sites such as Amazon and eBay may awaken interest in rare, out-of-stock, or nostalgic goods that previously might have taken a lifetime to assemble as a collection, but they also strip away the skilful collecting practices that previously made such projects a worthwhile consumer career. Excessive collecting may be one option – a drive for more and for only the rarest (as we suggested in our analysis of Gibson, see Denegri-Knott and Molesworth 2010b). Yet all too quickly we have all the things we never dreamed were possible, but at the risk that obtaining them has reduced meaning. The extent of the listings for collectables on eBay suggests that similar dramas unfold with many more people. In such circumstances the position of entrepreneur may seem attractive. This re-introduces a need for skill and new knowledge and therefore the potential of a meaningful transformation.

Videogames may solve the problem in a different way. Here material space and financial limitations are removed from the desiring consumer, but new barriers are imposed so that the possibility of 'easy' success is suspended as the scope of what may be achieved is enhanced. If the problem with eBay and Amazon is that they make it both easy to get what you desire *and* make the possibility of every satisfying desire completely all too transparent (you just know you can't ever get all that stuff), this is not the case in the managed environments of games. In *The Sims* we may expand the size of our home with relatively little effort, allowing us to also furnish it with more desirable goods as long as we continue to play the game. We may even create several such homes, each addressing different aspects of who we could be and therefore different reflections. The same is true of racing simulations like Gran Turismo. The game is structured so that as the player progresses with races, more desirable and expensive cars become available to them. As they play, they can actualize the purchase of a new expensive car, then immediately shift their focus to the next one in the range, earning money from winning races to fund an extensive collection of cars. Desire for better cars drives the player to become a better driver. We are now on Gran Turismo 5, and with each version comes the latest cars, from the relatively affordable, to the most exotic.

A final interaction with the market is the possibility that during the process of building a home in The Sims or a garage of exotic cars in Gran Turismo the player may learn more about the material commodities that the games simulate, driving desire for the 'real thing'. Here such games allow both actualization of consumer daydreams with the game and potentially drive desire for expensive commodities (Molesworth and Denegri-Knott 2007). Desirable interior design or cars is understood from playing the game and these desires may eventually be actualized in the material marketplace.

DVC as experimentation and transformative practice

Key elements supporting the reflective and transformative potential of DVC are the awareness of tastes and personal affinities that result from animating a desiring state and the different subject positions that can be adopted and performed. Subject positions may include those that are part of a substantive daydream, for instance, a yearning for a particular lifestyle or an altered sense of self through the accumulation of commodities (cf. Belk *et al.* 2003), or by engaging in new practices, like collecting and selling. Such experiences for Turner can be seen as temporary transgressions or forms of experimentation where the tendency towards order is challenged. These may accelerate processes of transformation initiated through consumption activity. In this scheme then, idealized lifestyles and promises of transformation that are bolted onto commodities are tested through consumption, and this in turn allows, as Campbell (1987) and others have argued elsewhere, a way of reflecting about what one likes and therefore who one is. The associated practices of *flânerie* and crafting of daydreams through eBay may initiate a journey of self-knowing through object knowing. Ultimately though, as cycles of desire run their course, some eBayers find that once a desired object is obtained, associated displaced meanings are not accessible, producing a state of resignation that a given imagined transformation is not possible.

On eBay, the fuelling and actualizing of daydreams themselves become the domain of experimentation or little transformative practices. Consumers learn that they can recycle failed possessions by selling them on eBay, that they can prolong the pleasures of daydreaming by becoming ad hoc collectors, or even at a more parochial level, that certain search words will secure ownership of a desired good. Other small transformations take place at the level of tastes and interests, which often fluctuate and shift, as users gain more expert knowledges about a category of goods and move onto new interests (Denegri-Knott and Molesworth 2010b). More transgressive consumptive practices may also be given into, through a temporary state of almost owning which allows the suspension of moral straitjackets blocking desires in the materially real – users may bid on things they never actually intend to buy (Denegri-Knott 2010).

Browsing and buying on eBay also precipitate more radical transformations than those bound to browsing and shopping practices. As buyers become collectors, buyers, and sellers, individuals mobilize distinct and complex forms of knowing and doing, which in turn produce very distinct practices. In accomplishing specific sales projects, eBayers skilfully mobilize embodied knowledges and embedded knowledge in various objects (Dant 2005), general frameworks of public and private meanings to estimate the value of their own goods against the more precise calibration of economic value they can attain through their scrutiny of eBay's past and current listings (Denegri-Knott and Molesworth 2009). Often, the mobilization of embodied and embedded knowledges extend beyond use and aesthetic values and include complex machinations of demand conditions that help respondents attune the economic value of their goods. Because the selling of once owned possessions is wrapped up in layers of evaluative judgments deriving from personal, affective valuations, as well as commonly held notions of economic, symbolic and use value, the determination of value itself is a thoroughly reflexive enterprise (ibid.).

These role reversals can trigger moments of self-awareness and reflection, necessary for the fourth phase of the social drama, reintegration or schism. In Turner's work, both crisis and redressive actions have liminal characteristics and thus, to cite Turner, furnish a necessary 'distanced replication and critique of events leading to the crisis' (1988, p. 75), needed to 'confront, understand and assign meaning to, and sometime coping with the crisis' (Turner 1982, p. 11). Following Turner, the last phase of social drama requires moments of reflection, for example, by recognizing the irreparable schism that displaced meanings cannot be actualized. Alternatively, this point of self-awareness and reflection can bring forth a new order for the individual.

DVC in videogames provides other and possibly more dramatic routes to these reflective practices through a more direct invitation to take on a new subject position not possible in material reality. For example, the popularity of games like the Grand Theft Auto series suggest that normally law-abiding citizens may gain pleasure from virtual criminal activities. The desirable cars in these games are not saved up for, but simply stolen, and often through violence. Status and progress in the game are also achieved through criminal activity. And other consumption activity that may be considered taboo or very difficult for many to actualize may be a routine part of engagement with the game. For example, gun ownership and use, and the use of prostitutes. Careers within the games which may take hundreds of hours to play, involve knowledge and practices that may be well outside the everyday experiences of most players. But what questions do such activities ask of the player? Do they come to see violence as attractive as the literature of the violent effects of games may suggest? Do they gain sympathy for the impossibility of escaping these apparently deviant lifestyles and therefore for those who find themselves closer to similar material situations? The point is that engagement with such activities forces a reflection on them and perhaps more substantive questions that those asked by shopping in malls.

If Grand Theft Auto represents the transgressive in an otherwise familiar urban environment, other games like World of Warcraft extend DVC into more fantastic realms and with that greater potential to explore and actualize what is otherwise only ideally possible. The World of Warcraft player enters a space where success means engaging with magical goods that are obtained only through heroic quests where they must travel to new lands and do battle with exotic foes. For the jaded consumer who may feel that they already have everything (or know all too well the impossibility of obtaining the desirable), such a game offers new desires and new skills. It also asks more direct questions of the self. Players may be good or evil; they may collaborate with others, or 'go it alone'. They must make and reflect on such roles and decisions.

Conclusion

In this chapter we have argued that DVC may be understood as potentially transformative by recognizing that it opens up a space that combines aspects of both imagined ideals and material actualities. In doing so it invites reflections on the cycles of consumer desire and new transformative practices. It does this through both seemingly mundane marketplace websites and through more exotic videogames and virtual worlds.

We have presented the digital virtual as a wide range of reflective spaces for consumers to look, imagine and consume a range of goods and services including, but also exceeding what is probable through material consumption practices. In some respects the various practices involved may be very similar to those of the reflective *flâneur* shopper (see Falk and Campbell 1997; Featherstone 1990; Molesworth 2007). However, through DVC practices individuals may not only be exposed to a much wider range of stimulus for their imagination – the endless goods presented on online marketplaces, the inaccessible luxury commodities in various brand websites and driving simulation games, and the ideally possible fantasy and science fiction goods in console games, online multi-player games and virtual worlds – but may also come to own and use such things within these virtual spaces. This invites new experiences and with them transformation. Each excursion into a new game or website offers the possibility of some unfolding drama where the status quo of an individual's life is invited into crisis and where they must work to reconcile the tensions in the self they have awoken.

They don't just look and ask 'what might it be like, would it be me?', but may 'try on' being an entrepreneur, someone with wealth, a collector, a trader, an advertiser, a criminal, a hero, a warrior, or many other ways of being. Their possible roles are therefore greatly enhanced as the scripts available to them expand and may be tested within relatively small timescales. The digital virtual individual may be an avid collector one year, a warrior hero the next, and a successful entrepreneur the year after that. The videogame player may be a successful criminal one week, a racing driver the next, etc. With these new practices come new consumers, who through their labours as buyers, seller and consumers maintain the realty of these new consumption spaces.

The many small and individual transformations they undertake therefore invite broader questions about consumption. For example, what might the accelerated ownership of desirable goods, whether material or digital virtual mean for the experience of desire? What might this also tell us about how 'ownership' itself is understood? The 'promiscuous consumer' (Denegri-Knott and Molesworth 2010) who buys commodities with a mind to sell them on via eBay just a short time later (and owns them very much with a view to this) may seem to form much lighter attachments to things while paying more attention to their desires for new goods, for example. The successful player of an online game may on the other hand invest much time and energy in their virtual goods and be less concerned with the pleasures of material shopping. For example, Molesworth (2009) notes the way in which videogame players may contrast their satisfying achievements within digital games with less satisfying aspects of mundane everyday life.

In all, we are yet to fully understand all the ways that consumers may be transformed by the various new practices invited by DVC, but we can see these practices as a further development in Turner's (1982) observations about a society that manages roles, scripts and the necessary transformations between them for individuals through collective, established and easily recognized group rituals, and the individualized and accelerated nature of transformations possible with DVC. We must further ask about strategies consumers adopt to manage all these new knowledges and their accelerated careers. Will this lead to more superficial and transient engagement with practices so that individuals ask 'maybe I'm this, but no worries if I'm not, I can try something else tomorrow', or will we see new angst in individuals who must now try to achieve much more, completing multiple careers and forever feeling that they don't have time to master any of them? Will they ask, 'How can I be all these things?'; 'Where is the time?', or; 'What if I miss something important?'. Whatever the range of answers, we can be sure that more of what constitutes the practices of consumption will take place in front of the screen researching, searching, checking, playing, collecting and selling 'stuff' and the result is also what it means to be a consumer (if indeed such a label retains value) will also be transformed.

Further reading

Belk, R.W., Askegaard, S. and Ger, G. (2003) 'The Fire of Desire: A Multisited Inquiry into Consumer Passion', *Journal of Consumer Research*, 30(3): 326–51. [Comprehensive overview and empirical exploration of consumer desire across three cultural contexts.]

Campbell, C. (1987) *The Romantic Ethic and the Spirit of Modern Consumerism*, New York: Basil Blackwell Ltd. [The definitive text on consumer daydreaming.]

Denegri-Knott, J. and Molesworth, M. (2010) 'Digital Virtual Consumption: Concepts and Practices', *Consumption, Markets and Culture*, 13(2): 109–32. [A conceptual discussion of digital virtual discussion and key consumer practices.]

Shields, R. (2003) *The Virtual*, London: Routledge. [A comprehensive explanation of the digital virtual as a space between the virtual and actually real.]

Turner, V. (1982) *From Ritual to Theatre: The Human Seriousness of Play*, New York: PAJ Publications. [The seminal text on social drama and societal change and individual transformation.]

References

Belk, R. (2001) 'Specialty Magazines and Flights of Fancy: Feeding the Desire to Desire', *European Advances in Consumer Research*, Berlin.

Belk, R.W., Askegaard, S. and Ger, G. (2003) 'The Fire of Desire: A Multisited Inquiry into Consumer Passion', *Journal of Consumer Research*, 30(3): 326–51.

Campbell, C. (1987) *The Romantic Ethic and the Spirit of Modern Consumerism*, New York: Basil Blackwell Ltd.

——(2004) 'I Shop Therefore I Know I Am: The Metaphysical Basis of Modern Consumerism', in H. Brembeck and K.M. Ekström (eds), *Elusive Consumption*, Oxford: Berg Publishers, pp. 27–44.

Dant, T. (2005) *Materiality and Society*, Maidenhead: Open University Press.

de Certeau, M.D. (1984) *The Practice of Everyday Life*, Berkeley, CA: University of California Press.

Denegri-Knott, J. (2010) '"I Want It Now!: eBay and the Acceleration of Consumer Desire', paper presented at European Association for Consumer Research conference, Royal Holloway June 30–July 3.

Denegri-Knott, J. and Molesworth, M. (2009) '"I'll Sell This and I'll Buy Them That": eBay and the Management of Possessions as Stock', *Journal of Consumer Behaviour*, 8(6): 305–15.

——(2010a) 'Digital Virtual Consumption: Concepts and Practices', *Consumption, Markets and Culture*, 13(2): 109–32.

——(2010b) '"Love it. Buy it. Sell it": Consumer Desire and the Social Drama of eBay', *Journal of Consumer Culture*, 56(10): 56–79.

——(2012) 'Introduction', in M. Molesworth and J. Denegri-Knott (eds), *Digital Virtual Consumption*, New York: Routledge,

Denegri-Knott, J. and Zwick, D. (2012) 'Tracking Prosumption on eBay: Desire, Enchantment, and the Challenge of Slow Re-McDonaldization', *American Behavioral Scientist*, 56(4): 1–20.

Falk, P. and Campbell, C. (eds) (1997) *The Shopping Experience*, London: Sage.

Featherstone, M. (1990) *Consumer Culture and Postmodernism*, London: Sage.

Hand, M. and Shove, E. (2007) 'Condensing Practices: Ways of Living with the Freezer', *Journal of Consumer Culture*, 7(1): 79–104.

Law, J. (2004). *After Method: Mess in Social Science Research*, London: Routledge.

Leadbeater, C. and Miller, P. (2004) *The Pro-Am Revolution: How Enthusiasts are Changing our Society and Economy*, London: Demos.

McCracken, G.D. (1988) *Culture and Consumption: New Approaches to the Symbolic Character of Consumer Goods and Activities*, Bloomington, IN: Indiana University Press.

——(2006) *Transformations*, Bloomington, IN: Indiana University Press.

Miller, D. (1997) 'Consumption and its Consequences', in H. Mackay (ed.) *Consumption and Everyday Life*, London: Sage and the Open University, pp. 13–64.

Molesworth, M. (2006) 'Real Brands in Imaginary Worlds: Investigating Players' Experiences of Brand Placement in Digital Games', *Journal of Consumer Behaviour*, 5: 355–66.

——(2007) 'Monsters and the Mall: Videogames and the Scopic Regimes of Shopping, in Situated Play', in *Proceedings of DiGRA 2007 Conference*, Tokyo.

——(2009) 'Adults' Consumption of Videogames as Imaginative Escape From Routine', in A.L. McGill and S. Shavitt (eds), *Advances in Consumer Research*, vol. 36, Duluth, MN: Association for Consumer Research.

Molesworth, M. and Denegri-Knott, J. (2007) 'Digital Play and the Actualization of the Consumer Imagination', *Games and Culture*, 2(2): 114–33.

——(2008) 'The Playfulness of eBay and the Implications for Business as a Game-Maker', *Journal of Macromarketing*, 28(4): 369–80.

Shields, R. (2000) 'Performing Virtualities: Liminality On and Off the "Net",' available at: http://virtualsociety_ sbs_ox.ac.uk/events/pvshields.htm (accessed 4 May 2005).

——(2003) *The Virtual*, London: Routledge.

Siddiqui, S. and Turley, D. (2005) 'Buyer-Seller Role Malleability: A Dip in the eBay', *European Advances in Consumer Research*, 7: 295–6.

——(2007) 'Cries from the Goblin Market: Consumer Narratives in the Marketplace', *European Advances in Consumer Research*, 9: 209–11.

Slater, D. and Miller, D. (2007) 'Moments and Movements in the Study of Consumer Culture: A Discussion between Daniel Miller and Don Slater', *Journal of Consumer Culture*, 7(1): 5–25.

Turner, V. (1982) *From Ritual to Theatre: The Human Seriousness of Play*, New York: PAJ Publications.

——(1988) *The Anthropology of Performance*, New York: PAJ Publications.

Warde, A. (2005) 'Consumption and Theories of Practice', *Journal of Consumer Culture*, 5(2): 131–53.

Watson, M. and Shove, E. (2008) 'Product, Competence, Project and Practice: DIY and the Dynamics of Craft Consumption', *Journal of Consumer Culture*, 8(1): 69–89.

Zwick, D. and Dholakia, N. (2006a) 'Bringing the Market to Life: Screen Aesthetics and the Epistemic Consumption Object', *Marketing Theory*, 6(1): 41–62.

——(2006b) 'The Epistemic Consumption Object and Postsocial Consumption: Expanding Consumer-Object Theory in Consumer Research', *Consumption Markets and Culture*, 9(1): 17–34.

21

CONSUMER DECISION-MAKING IN ONLINE AND OFFLINE ENVIRONMENTS

Elfriede Penz and Margaret K. Hogg

Keywords

e-commerce, emotions, information search, motivation, online shopping, risk, word-of-mouth

Introduction

Digitization has fundamentally changed consumer experiences of shopping. From 2006 to 2011, the share of online shoppers in the EU increased from 27 per cent to 40 per cent of consumers (Eurostat 2011a, 2011b), which reflects the world average pretty well (MarketingCharts 2008). Both companies and consumers have benefitted from the opportunities offered by the Internet. Because of its bidirectional quality, the Internet facilitates communication between companies and consumers as well as between consumers (Godes *et al.* 2005). We can trace a number of changes that have flowed from the growth of the digital age (including in the classical stages of consumer behaviour: search, choice, acquisition/purchase, consumption and use, and disposal) and also developments. First, businesses benefit from consumers communicating with each other online through brand building effects, customer acquisition and retention, product development, and quality assurance (Dellarocas 2003). Other supply-side factors relate to quick information diffusion, expansion in communication channels and reduction in costs of using them and aggregation of interpersonal communication, for example, for market research purposes (Godes *et al.* 2005). Second, consumers have been increasingly empowered by *inter alia* easy access to information and ease of price comparison. The Internet facilitates co-creation of products and services including e-services and in the face of these challenges from an informed consumer, companies have had to move towards innovative collaborations with their customers, incorporating customers' expertise, knowledge and creativity, for instance, in product design and testing (Prandelli *et al.* 2008).

Other developments briefly include different ways of communicating with and reaching consumers, varying channels of distribution, different consumer responses to shopping, and different patterns of consumer purchasing depending on the product category. One such development is belonging to virtual communities, which can become a driver for online shopping (Parsons 2002) and subsequently affects consumers' virtual social identities (Wood and Solomon 2009).

While a comparative approach, which concentrated on the differences between the two modes (offline and online) is preeminent in most past research, this chapter provides, first of all, a survey of the differences between consumer purchasing online and offline, and, second, the context for the new emerging understanding of consumer purchasing strategies. Towards the end of the chapter, we identify changing patterns of consumer behaviour which suggest consumers increasingly are pursuing integrative (rather than different) purchasing strategies between online and offline settings.

Purchase decision making in online versus offline retail contexts

Early research identified some fundamental differences between consumers' online purchase behavior and their traditional or offline shopping (Dennis *et al.* 2002), and established that consumers' motivation to shop online differs from their motivation when shopping in the offline retail environment for identical products (Joines *et al.* 2003; Wolfinbarger and Gilly 2001). Based on their motives, segments of online shoppers are identified. However, consumer segments exist who combine online and offline purchasing, for example, they search for information online (browse websites, use banner ads and search for promotions) but prefer purchasing offline (Kau *et al.* 2003, see Table 21.1).

The technology acceptance model (TAM, Davis 1989) is often used as a theoretical framework with its factors *ease of use*, *usefulness*, and *enjoyment* as drivers for online shopping (Monsuwe *et al.* 2004; Schiffman *et al.* 2003). Overall, motivations to shop online can be grouped into functional (e.g., Bhatnagar and Ghose 2004) versus non-functional (Parsons 2002), and hedonic (i.e., spontaneous, Childers *et al.* 2001, Figure 21.1).

Although prices (functional motivation) are more transparent in online stores and often are more homogeneous, getting the lowest price is not always important. Infomediaries or 'shop-bots' contribute to price savings and well-being on the part of consumers and greater price competition among dealers (Viswanathan *et al.* 2007). Consumers are interested in security of information-transfer and vendor reliability, rather than only in convenience (Bhatnagar and Ghose 2004; Joines *et al.* 2003).

Enjoyment (non-functional motivation) arises partly from the unique features of the Internet and predicts consistently strong attitudes towards interactive shopping. Consumers find it more

Table 21.1 Segments of online shoppers and combined online/offline shoppers

Types	Segments	Author
Online shoppers	Convenience shoppers Variety seekers Balanced buyers Store-oriented shoppers	Rohm and Swaminathan (2004)
	Active shoppers Price sensitives Discerning shoppers Brand loyals Convenience-oriented	Jayawardhena et al.(2007)
Combined online and offline shopping	On-off shoppers Dual shoppers Information surfers	Kau, Tang, and Ghose (2003)

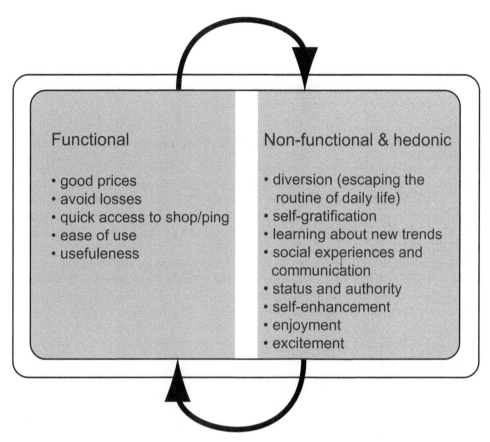

Figure 21.1 Motivations to shop online

enjoyable to shop in interactive environments than shopping in physical environments (Childers *et al.* 2001), and they perceive greater value and higher levels of satisfaction (Scarpi 2006). Eventually, online shoppers' excitement increases the intention to return (Chanaka and Len 2009). On the other hand, consumers are dissatisfied with their offline shopping experience when it comes to service quality, available information and speed of shopping (Burke 2002) and turn to the Internet. Growth of consumer-generated media has allowed consumers to easily compare experiences, which give rise to self-enhancement (Chan and Cui 2011).

Depending on their perceptions about whether a product or service is best bought from one or the other, consumers select a particular shopping mode (offline versus online store, Rajamma *et al.* 2007). Depending whether online purchase is planned or not, consumers engage in directed-purchase visit, search visit to gather information for future purchase (planned purchase) or hedonic browsing visit, and knowledge-building visit (non-planned purchase, Moe and Fader 2001).

Substitutability, that is, the ability of online shopping to compensate for the lack of sensory inputs as compared to traditional 'bricks' shopping (product knowledge, quality, information and its tangible attributes), affects online purchase intentions (Charles *et al.* 2010). If substitutability is perceived as low, despite a positive attitude towards online shopping and past positive online shopping experiences, consumers prefer offline shopping. However, high trust in an online retailer can compensate for low substitutability (Dennis *et al.* 2010).

Trust determines whether a website is perceived as reliable and eventually influences the transaction intention (Gefen 2002; Gefen and Straub 2004; McKnight and Chervany 2001) as well as long-term relationships with the retailer (Kim *et al.* 2009). Important dimensions of trust are ability, integrity and benevolence, which emerge from elements in a website. They impact on the loyalty to a website (Gupta and Kabadayi 2010). In addition, the perceived trustworthiness of Internet merchants influences consumer trust.

The prevalence of information search and reliance on others' opinions

Purchase decision-making is regularly modelled as a process, including *problem recognition, search for information, evaluation and choice of alternatives, purchase of the product or service* and finally *consumption* and *(dis)satisfaction* with the retailer and/or the product (Solomon *et al.* 2010). Considerable research on online shopping focuses on external search (Darley *et al.* 2010; Penz and Kirchler 2006; Peterson and Merino 2003), alternative evaluation and purchase (behavioural intentions) (Darley *et al.* 2010).

Despite similarities, offline and online purchasing differ in the emphasis which shoppers place on different phases of their decision-making (Pan and Zinkhan 2006). Additionally, *purchasing* patterns are not equivalent to online *visit* patterns. Purchasing consists of visiting *and* conversion from browsing to actual buying (Moe and Fader 2001). Besides, online shoppers and online *non*-shoppers are considered to be heterogeneous groups (Swinyard and Smith 2003). In a similar vein, understanding purchase orientations is not necessarily linked to purchase intentions (Jayawardhena *et al.* 2007).

Starting with *problem recognition*, in online decision-making, stimuli can come from different sources, including online marketing communication and traditional communications. Online advertising differs from traditional advertising in that consumers actively search for information by visiting a website. There is wide agreement that website traffic is dependent on offline communication (Jayawardhena *et al.* 2003).

With respect to the *search* for information online (e.g., Peterson and Merino 2003), the Internet empowers consumers by making price, company, product, and competitors' information available in order to improve a decision (e.g., López and Sicilia 2011; van Nierop *et al.* 2011).

In this phase of decision-making, opinions from others influence consumers and their decision-making. These personal conversations, word-of-mouth (WOM), about goods or experiences, mainly take place between people and usually are not commercially influenced (López and Sicilia 2011). Word-of-mouth in the offline setting can be linked to mavenism, i.e., consumers' tendency to offer shopping and marketplace information (Feick and Price 1987), retail opinion sharing, i.e., 'interpersonal communication and influence among friends that is associated with product related and sensate related exchanges that have as their collective focus shopping behavior' (Paridon 2004, p. 88), and susceptibility to interpersonal influence. Susceptibility relates either to shoppers' needs to receive rewards or avoid being punished (i.e., the exertion of *utilitarian* influence), or to shoppers' needs for 'psychological affiliation' (i.e., *value-expressive* influence) (Childers and Rao 1992). The technological advancement of communication through the Internet facilitates the expression of opinions about goods and affects social interaction between consumers and companies (López and Sicilia 2011). With regard to offline and online purchasing, the increased complexity of products combined with the increasing availability of product information favours the eWOM (electronic WOM) channel over the offline WOM channel. eWOM is defined as 'any positive or negative statement made by potential, actual, or former customers about a product or company, which is made available to a multitude of people and institutions via the Internet' (Hennig-Thurau *et al.* 2004: 39). Social interactions involve contexts 'in which one's expected utility for specific choice alternatives is affected by the actions taken by others' (Godes *et al.* 2005, p. 416). Online peer reviews (eWOM) differ in the way communication takes place compared with WOM. Writers of reviews are personally motivated, the writing/reading takes place asynchronously and requires text, and reviews are stored, and not bounded by physical/temporal space (Schlosser 2011). In eWOM, many-to-many communication takes place. Volume of WOM was reported as having a major impact on consumer behaviour; because eWOM can be searched easily, it is assumed to have an even greater influence on decision-making (López and Sicilia 2011).

Consumers utilize eWOM because they are faced with increasingly complex products, vast amounts of information are available and in order to simplify their search for and evaluation of goods they focus on relevant information from eWOM (Godes *et al.* 2005). Taking both forms of WOM into account, it was found that traditional WOM can decrease perceived risk and increase willingness to purchase online (López and Sicilia 2011).

Consumers deal with eWOM in two ways: they actively contribute by writing statements, and they read others' statements (Figure 21.2).

Writing complaints in online forums can help in retrieving balance by expressing positive, negative or mixed emotions (Hennig-Thurau *et al.* 2004; Godes *et al.* 2005). Consumers sometimes express themselves only if they sense that the majority share the same opinion. The same is not true if only a minority supports one's opinion. Because of fear of isolation, consumers who sense they are in the minority do not produce reviews (see spiral of silence, Woong Yun and Park 2011).

Motivation to *write* online reviews

- social interaction utility
- focus-related utility (concern for others, helping the company, receiving social benefits and belonging to a community or exerting power)
- consumption utility (post-purchase stage of problem solving: consumers learn about a product)
- approval utility (communicating how useful a comment has been, includes self-enhancement or financial reward)
- moderator-related utility (receive convenient and problem-solving support)
- homoestase utility (retrieve balance by expression emotions)
- opinion conforms to majority

Motivation to *read* online reviews

- reduce risk
- reduce search time
- establish social position
- reduce dissonance
- belong to virtual community
- learn about market
- learn how to consumer products

Figure 21.2 Motivations to write and to read online reviews

In the *post-purchase phase*, dissatisfaction leads to an unbalanced state according to balance theory (Heider 1967). Writing online reviews can resolve dissatisfaction. In particular, negative WOM plays an important role. Depending on the type of message, negative WOM can have different effects on dissatisfied consumers: attribute-based messages (highlighting the product) trigger a product-evaluative process and result in dissatisfaction aggravation. On the other hand, experience-based messages (highlighting the consumer) trigger a social-comparative process and result in dissatisfaction alleviation. The effect is even stronger when solid reference points or standards do not exist, as with the consumption of new technology. In addition, dissatisfaction alleviation works only when the consumer experience is salient, thus explicitly referred to, in the negative WOM message. Social-comparative rather than product-evaluative processes may predominate in this stage, as dissatisfied consumers find relief in the realization that someone else has had a similar or worse experience (Chan and Cui 2011).

Emotions' role in online decision–making

Emotions represent key components of consumer experiences in both online and offline retail environments (Eroglu *et al.* 2003; Menon and Kahn 2002). While most research focuses on the positive emotions that result from the retail environment, there is some evidence for the influence of negative emotions stimulated by aspects of the retail setting on consumer behaviour. Shopping irritants as identified by d'Astous (2000) fit into the categories of ambience (bad smell, too hot inside the store, music too loud for offline settings; and slow loading of webpages, unpleasant environment, such as an Internet café when browsing for online contexts), and design (unable to locate items, bricks-and-mortar store too small; poor display of products in the online store, bad website design); categories previously identified by Baker (1986). Shopping irritants also stem from social factors, such as crowding or the behaviour of the sales personnel (high-pressure selling) or unfavourable information regarding the product (Mizerski 1982). In the online context, these irritants include negative or ambivalent product reviews and eWOM as well as the appearance of avatars, for example (England and Gray 1998). In addition, overload, i.e., consumers feel 'overwhelmed or ill-prepared during the purchasing process and the sheer volume of purchasing decisions to be made' (Otnes *et al.* 1997, p. 87), which is very likely to happen in an online environment, can cause mixed emotions (i.e., ambivalence). In addition to negative or positive emotions with regard to the retail environment, ambivalence can have severe consequences on consumer behaviour, such as satisfaction with products, repurchase loyalty or conflicts faced by consumers in offline and online retail settings (Otnes *et al.* 1997; Penz and Hogg 2011; Ruth *et al.* 2002). Consumers who experience ambivalence seem to be less loyal, partly because they are also less satisfied. Ambivalent consumers are also less involved in product evaluations (Olsen *et al.* 2005).

A comparative examination of the interplay of a variety of product-relevant, market-relevant and personal factors (Pan and Zinkhan 2006) follows next.

Product–related factors in online purchase decisions

There are differences in purchasing behaviour between the shopping channels with respect to the type of product, indicating that standardized or search goods are usually more suitable for online-shopping (e.g., books, music) when compared with experience goods (e.g., personal care products, clothes, Chiang and Dholakia 2003; Kwak *et al.* 2002; Monsuwe *et al.* 2004; Shim *et al.* 2001); and supporting the argument that the more realizable a product (i.e., products that consumers can imagine without touching, feeling), the more suitable it is for online-shopping (see also Koernig 2003). Usually these are standardized products but that is not the main attribute. When consumers visit an online store to purchase goods, they tend to view only a few categories and review product information a number of times. Time spent per page tends to be short and product information is often not considered in detail (Moe and Fader 2001). Consumers expect durable goods to be described in full; to be offered in conjunction with necessary support services; and the act of purchase needs to be both convenient and quick (Burke 2002).

One area of conflict in both traditional and online shopping is *risk perception* and its consequences. Goods or services involve different levels of perceived risk and of involvement. According to Jarvenpaa, Tractinsky and Saarinen (1999), risk perception is negatively correlated with willingness to buy. Numerous studies emphasize the importance of risk perception with regard to online shopping (Choi and Lee 2003; Mariani and Zappala 2003; Tan 1999). Perceived risk has a negative impact on the evaluation of the experience of online purchasing, which helps to explain barriers to online shopping (Forsythe and Shi 2003). Higher level of Internet experience results in lower perception of risk. Thus, consumers with greater knowledge tend to be less risk-averse (Bhatnagar *et al.* 2000). In order to reduce risk, strategies such as using a reference group appeal, a marketer's reputation or brand image are proposed. In psychology and economics the concept of risk is usually related to choice situations encompassing both potentially positive and negative outcomes. Perceived risk comprises 'subjective expectations of loss' (Stone and Gronhaug 1993: 42) linked to uncertainty and consequences (Conchar *et al.* 2004; Dowling and Staelin 1994; Hansen 1976). *Uncertainty* involves confidence, reliability, dependability, trust likelihood and probability, whereas *consequences* involve trust, danger, relevance and seriousness (Mitchell 1999). Risk perception increases rather than decreases in different phases of the consumer decision-making process (Mitchell and Boustani 1994): prepurchase search and purchase evaluation can be very challenging phases. High involvement products are regarded as more risky than low involvement products (for an overview of perceived risk, see Table 21.2).

Emotions that arise at the beginning of a website visit influence subsequent cognitive processing and shape privacy beliefs. Being afraid could lead to escape behaviour, i.e., leaving the online store; however, relevance of information that is provided on the website and privacy policies can adjust these beliefs (Li *et al.* 2011).

Market-related factors in online purchase decisions

The market and in particular the situation are characterized by a number of environmental variables, many of which have been modelled by earlier researchers (e.g., Donovan *et al.* 1994; Mehrabian and Russell 1974). Consumers are influenced by the rate and amount of information in a store (e.g., its novelty, complexity, density and size, Spies *et al.* 1997), which can stimulate or overwhelm customers; with similar evidence for consumers' experience of websites when shopping online (Fiore *et al.* 2005). Online shopping is affected by a different combination of environmental variables (e.g., complexity including rate of information) compared with offline shopping and can take advantage of these differences by creating a cognitively and aesthetically rich shopping environment in ways not readily imitable in the non-electronic shopping world (Childers *et al.* 2001; Porat and Tractinsky 2008).

Information is mediated by ambient, design and social factors which all affect how customers perceive and experience their physical environment (Baker 1986). Ambient factors are not noticed unless they reach an unpleasant level, e.g., when the lighting is too bright or the music is too loud. Design factors are actively evaluated by shoppers and include aesthetic elements

Table 21.2 Dimensions of risk perception in online purchase decision-making (Dowling and Staelin, 1994, Mitchell, 1999, Kaplan et al., 1974)

Dimension of risk perception	Description	Example
Product performance/ functional risk	Loss incurred when a product does not perform as expected or its function is limited (Ha, 2002) Lack of touching and feeling (Forsythe and Shi, 2003)	Virtual representation of product in online shop
Financial risk	Financial loss Risk of obtaining a poor price (Ha, 2002)	Credit-card fraud Online bought product is cheaper in another shop
Psychological risk	Product consumption harms self-esteem or perception of self	Disclosing personal information on the Internet (Joines et al., 2003, Mariani and Zappalà, 2006)
Social risk	Describes the "relational grouping of individuals who share, and perhaps create, similar risk perceptions" (Scherer and Cho, 2003, p. 261).	Appear up to date (social norms require one to shop online, (e.g. Çelik, 2011).
Physical risk	Possibility of bodily harm (Dholakia and Bagozzi, 2001)	Product contains ingredients which cause allergies or are fake ones

such as architecture, colour and style which can increase a consumer's sense of pleasure when entering a store. Functional elements, such as layout or comfort can also contribute to a shopper's sense of well-being. Social factors include the presence of an audience, fellow customers and/or service personnel who are responsible for generating the atmosphere (which can be positive, e.g., a lively bar, or negative, e.g., busy queues). The attractive appearance and the pleasant behaviour of service personnel, as well as the presence of other customers, can also be reassuring components in a retail environment.

With respect to the online situation, research confirmed the importance of clear user interfaces[1] during all stages of the decision-making process (Palmer 2002; Sinkovics and Penz 2005). In contrast, negative experiences in an online context refer to high effort and frustration (Dennis *et al.* 2002; Chen and Dhillon 2003). When entering an online shop, the first thing a potential customer perceives is the user interface. The interface influences the consumers' emotions in the initial stage of browsing. Consequently, cognitive evaluations and site atmospherics (site informativeness and effectiveness), are influenced by the initially aroused emotions (Mazaheri *et al.* 2011), which in turn affect the evaluation of atmospherics and impact purchase intentions in the long run. The design of the webpage is central to determining the atmosphere experienced by consumers online (McCarthy and Aronson 2000), which can lead to positive emotions, and thus to favourable attitudes towards online shopping and the presented goods, and consequently higher satisfaction with a purchase (Eroglu *et al.* 2003). Table 21.3 illustrates the factors of website design.

Consumers usually visit both online websites and bricks-and-mortar stores to make the best possible decision. Online websites can be of a transactional (i.e., allowing online shopping) or an informational nature (i.e., supports an existing bricks-and-mortar retailer in that it includes information but does not allow transactions). It was found that informational website visitors

Table 21.3 Factors of website design

Factor	Description
Download time	time taken to access and display the website
Navigability	layout of the website, ease of orientation, logical sequence of the site
Site content	amount and variety of information
Interactivity	possibility to adapt the design to personal preferences
Responsiveness	possibility to give or receive feedback as well as the inclusion of frequently asked questions

engage in fewer shopping trips and spend less money (van Nierop *et al.* 2011). These negative effects occur if the online information makes those customers, first, more efficient buyers, who make fewer shopping trips and fewer impulse purchases in the store; and/or, second, it makes them into more critical buyers who use information but buy from competitors or consider the information provided to be insufficient. They show more planned shopping behaviour as a consequence of their access to and use of more information, because information on the website can easily be compared with information from competitive stores.

In contrast to this result, a prior online search leads to higher amounts spent in a retail store (Sands *et al.* 2010), pointing towards a greater search depth facilitated by the Internet. As a consequence, websites should focus on information that has a positive effect, such as references to brand building efforts, the availability and arrival of new services, and any news that makes customers more curious about visiting the store. Online channels should be provided in addition to the traditional store experience (Sands *et al.* 2010; van Nierop *et al.* 2011).

Personal factors in online purchase decisions

Reference groups are 'social groups that are important to a consumer and against which he or she compares himself or herself' (Escalas and Bettman 2003, p. 341). While reference groups play a very important role in traditional brick-and-mortar stores, little is known about social influences on consumers' online shopping. Online shoppers act in a 'lonely crowd' (Burton 2002, p. 793). Consumers might want to use online shopping on purpose to avoid the consumer culture. This provides evidence of the anti-social nature of some of these forms of shopping.

Virtual stores where consumers interact with assistants or avatars and virtual environments developed because of higher levels of immersion, interactivity, and engagement. Navigational aids and orientation cues in general increase users' efficiency and eventually satisfaction (Shukla *et al.* 2011). The interactivity with avatars (i.e., a graphic representation that can be animated by means of computer technology, Holzwarth *et al.* 2006) was found to have positive benefits for online shoppers. Avatars can help in building trust in the store, which ultimately leads to more satisfaction and better evaluations (Solomon and Wood 2009).

Goal orientation and risk disposition are particularly important psychological influences on shopping behaviour. Goals, i.e., 'a concrete cognitive representation of a desired or undesired end state to guide behaviour' (Elliot and Thrash 2002, p. 806), include *mastery, performance-approach* and *performance-avoidance* goals in the shopping environment. *Goal-oriented* consumers prefer purchasing from the Internet because of 'convenience and accessibility; selection; availability of information; and lack of sociality' (Wolfinbarger and Gilly 2001, p. 35). Consumers perceive a product as having a certain value when considering whether to buy it. Thus, *perceived customer value* is 'consumers' perception of the net benefits gained in exchange for the costs incurred in obtaining the desired benefits' (Chen and Dhillon 2003, p. 326). In contrast to bricks-and-mortar shopping, saving costs, time, and effort are perceived as the benefits of online shopping.

Conclusion

Radical technological developments have significantly influenced retailing and consumer behaviour. This chapter reflects the emphasis from the earlier comparative work on online and offline retailing in order to show how an understanding of consumer purchasing online and offline has changed, and to provide the context for the new emerging understanding of consumer purchasing strategies. However, in tracking research into how consumers have responded to digital developments in retailing, we saw that consumers have increasingly tended to adopt overlapping and integrative (rather than necessarily different) purchasing strategies between online and offline settings. It is these consumer forays into integrating the different parts of the retail offering, online and offline, within the phases of the consumer decision-making process, which promises to be the source of many rich research questions in the future as consumers adopt increasingly creative solutions to their purchasing needs, often integrating different aspects of the two modes in seeking solutions to their consumption needs and purchases. Both offline and online retailers have seized the opportunity to exploit the opportunities offered by the digitization of text, images, sound, objects and signals in promoting and distributing their products, and in attracting their customers. Collaboration, co-creation and co-production (e.g., use of eWOM by both retailers and customers in their virtual worlds) will increasingly characterize the consumption landscape represented by the variety of different opportunities offered by all retailers to consumers to tailor their own decision-making strategies from the combination of offline and online aspects of the retail offering. Future academic research will want to examine how far consumers' early learning from their digital experiences impact their future purchasing behaviour online; and within the context of consumer socialization, which theories of learning most effectively account for consumers' varying patterns of behaviour online. A major motivation for consumers to go online is to satisfy their need for information and learn new things. However, the online environment, in contrast to brick-and-mortar retail environment, changes quickly (for example, informational websites become transactional; virtual communities and virtual worlds are combined with e-commerce) and consumers need to adapt to these new aspects. They need to learn how to deal with impersonal information, in the form of eWOM, infomediaries or avatars. Also, websites include a lot of individual cues. In short, information overload requires consumers to carefully select websites and information. In addition, studying consumer socialization processes on online purchase behaviour provides an invaluable opportunity to explore new developments in reverse socialization where younger family members induct older family members into different aspects of the digital online age.

Note

1 User interface is defined as 'the aspects of a computer system or program which can be seen (or heard or otherwise perceived) by the human user, and the commands and mechanisms the user uses to control its operation and input data', n.d., retrieved: September 15, 2011, user interface, from http://dictionary. reference.com/browse/userinterface (ed.) *The Free On-line Dictionary of Computing*. Dictionary.com.

References

Baker, J. (1986) 'The Role of the Environment in Marketing Services: the Consumer Perspective', in J.A. Czepeil, C.A. Congram and J. Shanahan (eds), *The Services Challenge: Integrating for Competitive Advantage*, Chicago: American Marketing Association.

Bhatnagar, A. and Ghose, S. (2004) 'Segmenting Consumers Based on the Benefits and Risks of Internet Shopping', *Journal of Business Research*, 57(12): 1352–60.

Bhatnagar, A., Misra, S. and Rao, R. (2000) 'On Risk, Convenience, and Internet Shopping Behavior', *Association for Computing Machinery: Communications of the ACM*, 43(11): 98–105.

Burke, R.R. (2002) 'Technology and the Customer Interface: What Consumers Want in the Physical and Virtual Store', *Journal of the Academy of Marketing Science*, 30(4): 411–32.

Burton, D. (2002) 'Postmodernism, Social Relations and Remote Shopping', *European Journal of Marketing*, 36(7/8): 792–810.

Çelik, H. (2011) 'Influence of Social Norms, Perceived Playfulness and Online Shopping Anxiety on Customers' Adoption of Online Retail Shopping', *International Journal of Retail and Distribution Management*, 39(6): 390–413.

Chan, H. and Cui, S. (2011) 'The Contrasting Effects of Negative Word of Mouth in the Post-Consumption Stage', *Journal of Consumer Psychology*, 21(3): 324–37.

Chanaka, J. and Len, T.W. (2009) 'An Empirical Investigation into E-Shopping Excitement: Antecedents and Effects', *European Journal of Marketing*, 43(9/10): 1171–87.

Charles, D., Chanaka, J. and Eleni-Konstantina, P. (2010) 'Antecedents of Internet Shopping Intentions and the Moderating Effects of Substitutability', *The International Review of Retail, Distribution and Consumer Research*, 20(4): 411–30.

Chen, S.C. and Dhillon, G.S. (2003) 'Interpreting Dimensions of Consumer Trust in E-Commerce', *Information Technology and Management*, 4(2–3): 303–18.

Chiang, K.P. and Dholakia, R.R. (2003) 'Factors Driving Consumer Intention to Shop Online: An Empirical Investigation', *Journal of Consumer Psychology*, 13(1 and 2): 177–83.

Childers, T.L., Carr, C.L., Peck, J. and Carson, S. (2001) 'Hedonic and Utilitarian Motivations for Online Retail Shopping Behavior', *Journal of Retailing*, 77(4): 511–35.

Childers, T.L. and Rao, A.R. (1992) 'The Influence of Familial and Peer-Based Reference Groups on Consumer Decisions', *Journal of Consumer Research*, 19(2): 198–211.

Choi, J. and Lee, K.-H. (2003) 'Risk Perception and E-Shopping: A Cross-Cultural Study', *Journal of Fashion Marketing and Management*, 7(1): 49–64.

Conchar, M.P., Zinkhan, G.M., Peters, C. and Olavarrieta, S. (2004) 'An Integrated Framework for the Conceptualization of Consumers' Perceived-Risk Processing', *Academy of Marketing Science Journal*, 32(4): 418–36.

Darley, W.K., Blankson, C. and Luethge, D.J. (2010) 'Toward an Integrated Framework for Online Consumer Behavior and Decision Making Process: A Review', *Psychology and Marketing*, 27(2): 94–116.

d'Astous, A. (2000) 'Irritating Aspects of the Shopping Environment', *Journal of Business Research*, 49(2): 149–56.

Davis, F.D. (1989) 'Perceived Usefulness, Perceived Ease of Use, and User Acceptance of Information Technology', *MIS Quarterly*, 13(3): 319–40.

Dellarocas, C. (2003) 'The Digitization of Word of Mouth: Promise and Challenges of Online Feedback Mechanisms', *Management Science*, 49(10): 1407–24.

Dennis, C., Harris, L. and Sandhu, B. (2002) 'From Bricks to Clicks: Understanding the E-Consumer', *Qualitative Market Research*, 5(4): 281–90.

Dennis, C., Jayawardhena, C. and Papamatthaiou, E.-K. (2010) 'Antecedents of Internet Shopping Intentions and the Moderating Effects of Substitutability', *The International Review of Retail, Distribution and Consumer Research*, 20(4): 411–30.

Dholakia, U. and Bagozzi, R.P. (2001) 'Consumer Behavior in Digital Environments', in J. Wind and V. Mahajan (eds), *Digital Marketing: Global Strategies from the World's Leading Experts*, New York: John Wiley and Sons.

Donovan, R.J., Rossiter, J.R., Marcoolyn, G. and Nesdale, A. (1994) 'Store Atmosphere and Purchasing Behavior', *Journal of Retailing*, 70(3): 283–94.

Dowling, G.R. and Staelin, R. (1994) 'A Model of Perceived Risk and Intended Risk-Handling Activity', *Journal of Consumer Research*, 21(1): 119–54.

Elliot, A.J. and Thrash, T.M. (2002) 'Approach-Avoidance Motivation in Personality: Approach and Avoidance Temperaments and Goals', *Journal of Personality and Social Psychology*, 82(5): 804–18.

England, D. and Gray, P. (1998) 'Temporal Aspects of Interaction in Shared Virtual Worlds', *Interacting with Computers*, 11(1): 87–105.

Eroglu, S.A., Machleit, K.A. and Davis, L.M. (2003) 'Empirical Testing of a Model of Online Store Atmospherics and Shopper Responses', *Psychology and Marketing*, 20(2): 139–50.

Escalas, J.E. and Bettman, J.R. (2003) 'You Are What They Eat: The Influence of Reference Groups on Consumers' Connections to Brands', *Journal of Consumer Psychology*, 13(3): 339–48.

Eurostat (2011a) 'Individuals Having Ordered/Bought Goods or Services for Private Use over the Internet in the Last Three Months', available at: ec.europa.eu/eurostat (accessed 5 December 2011).

——(2011b) 'Information Society Statistics at Regional Level', *Statistics Explained*, available at: ec.europa.eu/eurostat.

Feick, L.F. and Price, L.L. (1987) 'The Market Maven: A Diffuser of Marketplace Information', *Journal of Marketing*, 51(1): 83–97.

Fiore, A.M., Jin, H.-J. and Kim, J. (2005) 'For Fun and Profit: Hedonic Value from Image Interactivity and Responses toward an Online Store', *Psychology and Marketing*, 22(8): 669–94.

Forsythe, S.M. and Shi, B. (2003) 'Consumer Patronage and Risk Perceptions in Internet Shopping', *Journal of Business Research*, 56(11): 867–75.

Gefen, D. (2002) 'Reflections on the Dimensions of Trust and Trustworthiness Among Online Consumers', *Database for Advances in Information Systems*, 33(3): 38–53.

Gefen, D. and Straub, D.W. (2004) 'Consumer Trust in B2C E-Commerce and the Importance of Social Presence: Experiments in E-Products and E-Services', *Omega*, 32(6): 407–24.

Godes, D., Mayzlin, D., Chen, Y., Das, S., Dellarocas, C., Pfeiffer, B., Libai, B., Sen, S., Shi, M. and Verlegh, P. (2005) 'The Firm's Management of Social Interactions', *Marketing Letters*, 16(3/4): 415–28.

Gupta, R. and Kabadayi, S. (2010) 'The Relationship Between Trusting Beliefs and Web Site Loyalty: The Moderating Role of Consumer Motives and Flow', *Psychology and Marketing*, 27(2): 166–85.

Ha, H.Y. (2002) 'The Effects of Consumer Risk Perception on Pre-Purchase Information in Online Auctions: Brand, Word-of-Mouth, and Customized Information', *Journal of Computer-Mediated Communication*, 8(1), online.

Hansen, F. (1976) 'Psychological Theories of Consumer Choice', *Journal of Consumer Research*, 3(3): 117–42.

Heider, F. (1967) *The Psychology of Interpersonal Relations*, New York: Wiley.

Hennig-Thurau, T., Gwinner, K.P., Walsh, G. and Gremler, D.D. (2004) 'Electronic Word-of-Mouth Via Consumer-Opinion Platforms: What Motivates Consumers to Articulate Themselves on the Internet?', *Journal of Interactive Marketing*, 18(1): 38–52.

Holzwarth, M., Janiszewski, C. and Neumann, M.M. (2006) 'The Influence of Avatars on Online Consumer Shopping Behavior', *Journal of Marketing*, 70(4): 19–36.

Jarvenpaa, S.L., Tractinsky, N. and Saarinen, L. (1999) 'Consumer Trust in an Internet Store: A Cross-Cultural Validation', *Journal of Computer-Mediated Communication*, 5(2), online.

Jayawardhena, C., Wright, L.T. and Dennis, C. (2007) 'Consumers Online: Intentions, Orientations and Segmentation', *International Journal of Retail and Distribution Management*, 35(6): 515–26.

Jayawardhena, C., Wright, L.T. and Masterson, R. (2003) 'An Investigation of Online Consumer Purchasing', *Qualitative Market Research: An International Journal*, 6(1): 58–65.

Joines, J.L., Scherer, C.W. and Scheufele, D.A. (2003) 'Exploring Motivations For Consumer Web Use and Their Implications for E-Commerce', *The Journal of Consumer Marketing*, 20(2/3): 90–108.

Kaplan, L.B., Szybillo, G.J. and Jacoby, J. (1974) 'Components of Perceived Risk in Product Purchase: A Cross-Validation', *Journal of Applied Psychology*, 59(3): 287–91.

Kau, A.K., Tang, Y.E. and Ghose, S. (2003) 'Typology of Online Shoppers', *The Journal of Consumer Marketing*, 20(2/3): 139–56.

Kim, D.J., Ferrin, D.L. and Rao, H.R. (2009) 'Trust and Satisfaction, Two Stepping Stones for Successful E-Commerce Relationships: A Longitudinal Exploration', *Information Systems Research*, 20(2): 237–57.

Koernig, S.K. (2003) 'E-Scapes: The Electronic Physical Environment and Service Tangibility', *Psychology and Marketing*, 20(2): 151–67.

Kwak, H., Fox, R.J. and Zinkhan, G.M. (2002) 'What Products Can Be Successfully Promoted and Sold Via the Internet?', *Journal of Advertising Research*, January/February: 23–38.

Li, H., Sarathy, R. and Xu, H. (2011) 'The Role of Affect and Cognition on Online Consumers' Decision to Disclose Personal Information to Unfamiliar Online Vendors', *Decision Support Systems*, 51(3): 434–45.

López, M. and Sicilia, M. (2011) 'The Impact of E-WOM: Determinants of Influence', in S. Okazaki (ed.), *Advances in Advertising Research*, New York: Gabler.

McCarthy, R.V. and Aronson, J.E. (2000) 'Activating Consumer Response: A Model For Web Site Design Strategy', *The Journal of Computer Information Systems*, 41(2): 2–8.

McKnight, D.H. and Chervany, N.L. (2001) 'What Trust Means in E-Commerce Customer Relationships: An Interdisciplinary Conceptual Typology', *International Journal of Electronic Commerce*, 6(2): 35–59.

Mariani, M.G. and Zappala, S. (2003) 'Online Shopping: A Web Research on Risk Perception, Trust and Usability', at workshop, Firms and consumers facing e-commerce: Strategies to increase ITs adoption and usage, 2003, Rome, Italy.

——(2006) 'Risk Perception in Online Shopping', in S. Zappalà and C. Gray (eds), *Impact of E-Commerce on Consumers and Small Firms*, Aldershot: Ashgate.

MarketingCharts (2008) '875m Consumers Have Shopped Online: Up 40% in Two Years', available at: www.marketingcharts.com/direct/875mm-consumers-have-shopped-online-up-40-in-two-years-3225/ nielsen-global-ecommerce-most-popular-online-purchases-copyjpg/ (accessed 7 December 2011).

Mazaheri, E., Richard, M.-O. and Laroche, M. (2011) 'Online Consumer Behavior: Comparing Canadian and Chinese Website Visitors', *Journal of Business Research*, 64(9): 958–65.

Mehrabian, A. and Russell, J.A. (1974) *An Approach to Environmental Psychology*, Cambridge, MA: MIT Press.

Menon, S. and Kahn, B. (2002) 'Cross-Category Effects of Induced Arousal and Pleasure on the Internet Shopping Experience', *Journal of Retailing*, 78(1): 31–40.

Mitchell, V.-W. (1999) 'Consumer Perceived Risk: Conceptualisations and Models', *European Journal of Marketing*, 33(1/2): 163–95.

Mitchell, V.-W. and Boustani, P. (1994) 'A Preliminary Investigation into Pre- and Post-Purchase Risk Perception and Reduction', *European Journal of Marketing*, 28(1): 56–71.

Mizerski, R.W. (1982) 'An Attribution Explanation of the Disproportionate Influence of Unfavorable Information', *Journal of Consumer Research*, 9(3): 301–10.

Moe, W.W. and Fader, P.S. (2001) 'Uncovering Patterns in Cybershopping', *California Management Review*, 43(4): 106–17.

Monsuwe, T.P., Dellaert, B.G.C. and de Ruyter, K. (2004) 'What Drives Consumers to Shop Online? A Literature Review', *International Journal of Service Industry Management*, 15(1): 102–21.

Olsen, S.O., Wilcox, J. and Olsson, U. (2005) 'Consequences of Ambivalence on Satisfaction and Loyalty', *Psychology and Marketing*, 22(3): 247–69.

Otnes, C., Lowrey, T.M. and Shrum, L.J.1997) 'Toward an Understanding of Consumer Ambivalence', *Journal of Consumer Research*, 24(1): 80–93.

Palmer, J.W. (2002) 'Web Site Usability, Design, and Performance Metrics', *Information Systems Research*, 13(2): 151–67.

Pan, Y. and Zinkhan, G.M. (2006) 'Determinants of Retail Patronage: A Meta-Analytical Perspective', *Journal of Retailing*, 82(3): 229–43.

Paridon, T.J. (2004) 'Retail Opinion Sharing: Conceptualization and Measurement', *Journal of Retailing and Consumer Services*, 11(2): 87–93.

Parsons, A.G. (2002) 'Non-Functional Motives for Shoppers: Why We Click', *The Journal of Consumer Marketing*, 19(4/5): 380–92.

Penz, E. and Hogg, M.K. (2011) 'The Role of Mixed Emotions in Consumer Behaviour Investigating Ambivalence in Consumers' Experiences of Approach-Avoidance Conflicts in Online and Offline Settings', *European Journal of Marketing*, 45(1–2): 104–32.

Penz, E. and Kirchler, E. (2006) 'Affective States, Purchase Intentions and Perceived Risk in Online Shopping', in S. Zappalà and C. Gray (eds), *Impact of E-Commerce on Consumers and Small Firms*, Aldershot: Ashgate.

Peterson, R.A. and Merino, M.C. (2003) 'Consumer Information Search Behavior and the Internet', *Psychology and Marketing*, 20(2): 99–121.

Porat, T. and Tractinsky, N. (2008) 'Affect as a Mediator between Web-Store Design and Consumers' Attitudes Toward the Store', in C. Peter and R. Beale (eds), *Affect and Emotion in Human–Computer Interaction*, Berlin: Springer.

Prandelli, E., Swahney, M. and Verona, G. (2008) *Collaborating with Customers to Innovate: Conceiving and Marketing Products in the Networking Age*, Cheltenham: Elgar.

Rajamma, R.K., Paswan, A.K. and Ganesh, G. (2007) 'Services Purchased at Brick and Mortar Versus Online Stores, and Shopping Motivation', *The Journal of Services Marketing*, 21(3): 200–12.

Rohm, A.J. and Swaminathan, V. (2004) 'A Typology of Online Shoppers Based on Shopping Motivations', *Journal of Business Research*, 57(7): 748–57.

Ruth, J.A., Brunel, F.F. and Otnes, C.C. (2002) 'Linking Thoughts to Feelings: Investigating Cognitive Appraisals and Consumption Emotions in a Mixed-Emotions Context', *Journal of the Academy of Marketing Science*, 30(1): 44–58.

Sands, S., Ferraro, C. and Luxton, S. (2010) 'Does the Online Channel Pay? A Comparison of Online Versus Offline Information Search on Physical Store Spend', *The International Review of Retail, Distribution and Consumer Research*, 20(4): 397–410.

Scarpi, D. (2006) 'The Fun Side of the Internet', in S. Zappalà and C. Gray C (eds), *Impact of E-Commerce on Consumers and Small Firms*, Aldershot: Ashgate.

Scherer, C.W. and Cho, H. (2003) 'A Social Network Contagion Theory of Risk Perception', *Risk Analysis*, 23(2): 261–7.

Schiffman, L.G., Sherman, E. and Long, M.M. (2003) 'Toward a Better Understanding of the Interplay of Personal Values and the Internet', *Psychology and Marketing*, 20(2): 169–86.

Schlosser, A.E. (2011) 'Can Including Pros and Cons Increase the Helpfulness and Persuasiveness of Online Reviews? The Interactive Effects of Ratings and Arguments', *Journal of Consumer Psychology*, 21(3): 226–39.

Shim, S., Eastlick, M.A., Lotz, S.L. and Warrington, P. (2001) 'An Online Prepurchase Intentions Model: The Role of Intention to Search', *Journal of Retailing*, 77: 397–416.

Shukla, A., Sharma, N.K. and Swami, S. (2011) 'Web Site Classification on Information and Entertainment Profiles', *Journal of Advances in Management Research*, 8(1): 148–57.

Sinkovics, R. and Penz, E. (2005) 'Empowerment of SME Websites: Development of a Web-Empowerment Scale and Preliminary Evidence', *Journal of International Entrepreneurship*, 3(4): 303–15.

Solomon, M.R., Bamossy, G., Askegaard, S. and Hogg, M.K. (2010) *Consumer Behaviour: A European Perspective*, Harlow: Financial Times Prentice Hall.

Solomon, M.R. and Wood, N.T. (2009) 'Introduction: Virtual Social Identity: Welcome to the Metaverse', in N.T. Wood and M.R. Solomon (eds), *Virtual Social Identity and Consumer Behavior*, New York: M.E. Sharpe.

Spies, K., Hesse, F. and Loesch, K. (1997) 'Store Atmosphere, Mood and Purchasing Behavior', *International Journal of Research in Marketing*, 14(1): 1–17.

Stone, R.N. and Gronhaug, K. (1993) 'Perceived Risk: Further Considerations for the Marketing Discipline', *European Journal of Marketing*, 27(3): 39–50.

Swinyard, W.R. and Smith, S.M. (2003) 'Why People (Don't) Shop Online: A Lifestyle Study of the Internet Consumer', *Psychology and Marketing*, 20(7): 567–97.

Tan, S.J. (1999) 'Strategies for Reducing Consumers' Risk Aversion in Internet Shopping', *The Journal of Consumer Marketing*, 16(2): 163–80.

van Nierop, J.E.M., Leeflang, P.S.H., Teerling, M.L. and Huizingh, K.R.E. (2011) 'The Impact of the Introduction and Use of an Informational Website on Offline Customer Buying Behavior', *International Journal of Research in Marketing*, 28(2): 155–65.

Viswanathan, S., Kuruzovich, J., Gosain, S. and Agarwal, R. (2007) 'Online Infomediaries and Price Discrimination: Evidence from the Automotive Retailing Sector', *Journal of Marketing*, 71(3): 89–107.

Wolfinbarger, M. and Gilly, M.C. (2001) 'Shopping Online for Freedom, Control, and Fun', *California Management Review*, 43(2): 34–55.

Wood, N.T. and Solomon, M.R. (eds) (2009) *Virtual Social Identity and Consumer Behavior*, New York: M.E. Sharpe.

Woong Yun, G. and Park, S.-Y. (2011) 'Selective Posting: Willingness to Post a Message Online', *Journal of Computer-Mediated Communication*, 16(2): 201–27.

PART VI

Playing, praying, entertaining and educating

22

VALUE CO-CREATION IN VIRTUAL ENVIRONMENTS

Sammy K. Bonsu

Keywords

co-creation, prosumers, value, virtual environment

In this chapter, I explore the role of value co-creation in the contemporary economy, with an emphasis on its processes and relevance for web environments. Value co-creation posits that a product constitutes no more than a resource for consumers "to work with" and create further value beyond that allowed by the firm, as goods offered on the market are mere "value propositions" that the consumer adapts to fulfill relevant needs (Vargo and Lusch 2004). Thus, the consumer is an "operant resource," to use Vargo and Lusch's term – a necessary part of the machinations of production of value in the market. The firm's primary role in this process is to provide a platform for the consumer to create mutually beneficial value for the firm and the consumer. The value resulting from this joint effort exceeds that which is derived from each party's independent output. Consumers appear to participate willingly in this process whereby they expend their own resources to convert the platform into usable formats. The usable versions of the product are under the direct influence of the consumer. The consumer is thus deemed to have assumed a controlling role in contemporary production processes, suggesting a stronger relevance of the marketing mantra "consumer-is-king" that has guided business practice for decades (Sheth *et al.* 2000).

Some have observed that the active recruitment of consumer inputs into production – which was heretofore the unique province of the firm – indicates consumer freedom from the grips of Fordist capitalism that offered rigid products that consumers accepted as is (Prahalad and Ramaswamy 2000; Tapscott and Williams 2006; Vargo and Lusch 2004). Others, however, have observed that co-creation and its principles support collaborative production only to the extent that it defines a specific enclosure for containing the unmanageable postmodern consumer toward firm profitability (Andrejevic 2008; Arvidsson 2007, 2008; Bonsu and Darmody 2008). This supposed consumer freedom attributable to the market and technology advances is not without question (Terranova 2000). I contribute to this debate by exploring the ideological implications of value co-creation for contemporary marketing participants, focusing on the concept and processes of value co-creation as they relate to virtual environments. Virtual environments as used here include all web applications that support networked interactions among users, e.g., Facebook, YouTube, Flickr, Second Life and World of Warcraft. I begin the discussion with a brief overview of exploitation and its form in the contemporary economy.

Exploitation in the contemporary economy

Contemporary capitalism is necessarily a techno-economic system, an "informational capitalism" (Castells 2000, p. 18) that allows the attendant processes of production, consumption, power, exploitation, and is mediated by networked communication technologies and knowledge (Fuchs 2008). Bell (1973) and Florida (2002), among others, have argued that the resulting knowledge society has funded the demise of socio-economic hierarchies, and so the distinction between capitalist and proletariat is no longer necessary. Several scholars disagree with this viewpoint. For instance, Fuchs (2010, p. 180) notes that:

> Even though some knowledge workers become successful knowledge entrepreneurs and some knowledge workers tend to hold small amounts of share options, class divisions are not vanishing ... For example, Google, Inc., which in 2008 made U.S. $4.23 billion in profits, held capital assets of U.S.$31.77 billion, had a market value of U.S.$106.57 billion, and was ranked number 155 in the Forbes World List of Largest Corporations 2009, is not owned by its workers but by shareholders. Among the major shareholders are top executives such as Eric Schmidt (the chief executive officer), the cofounders Sergey Brin and Larry Page, and L. John Doerr, but not Google's 20,000 workers. In 2009, these top four directors and officers held 93.1 percent of class B stocks and a total of 70.6 percent of the total voting power ... That makes them primarily knowledge capitalists, whereas the 20,000 employees are knowledge workers.

That is, Google's employees constitute Marx's proletariat – "a machine for the production of surplus-value" – while its owners are the knowledge capitalists who constitute "a machine for the transformation of this surplus-value into surplus capital" (Marx 1867, p. 742). The workers are, in a Marxist sense, exploited by the capitalists, a situation that is reproduced across several platforms in contemporary economy. From an audience perspective, for example, Smythe (1981) and Jhally and Livant (1986) exemplify exploitation with how watching/listening to any medium becomes a commodity that is traded on the market for profit. Bonsu *et al.* (2010) point to the arrest and packaging of consumer emotions in reality TV production and consumption for sale. Arvidsson (2007) observes the effective wrestling of economic benefits from knowledge consumers/workers by capitalists through the mobilization of leisure and other activities. Terranova (2000) notes the valorization of free consumer labor by capital through digital platforms.

These observations suggest capital's continued and careful recruitment of unpaid consumer labor, and the continued presence of labor exploitation in a new guise. The information economy presents opportunities for capital to employ heretofore unavailable techniques to extract surplus value from knowledge workers, as in the Google example. Indeed, exploitation of labor by capital remains intact in contemporary society (Fuchs 2010) but it is often couched in the vocabulary of democracy, whereby capitalists and workers are framed as mutual beneficiaries of the relevant production/consumption process (Bonsu and Darmody 2008; Zwick *et al.* 2008). Therefore, the argument that labor exploitation and social hierarchies are no longer significant aspects of contemporary society (Bell 1973; Florida 2002) seems to have overlooked the ideological dimensions of capital and its effects. My aim in this chapter is to explore the continued exploitation of labor in virtual environments through "value co-creation."

Value co-creation

One increasingly important conceptual frame that captures the veiled exploitation in contemporary society is "value co-creation." The concept of "value co-creation" suggests a pivotal role for firm–customer co-operation in defining contemporary market success (Hunt 2000; Prahalad and Ramaswamy 2000, 2004; Sawheney *et al.* 2005). It emphasizes the firm's ability to create mutually beneficial relationships for market participants by rendering consumer resources into innovative products. In the process, the firm's output (brands, products, websites, etc.) serves as a fluid platform for consumers to adapt into whatever use the consumer sees fit (Vargo and Lusch 2004). For proponents of co-creation (e.g., Prahalad and Ramaswamy 2000; Tapscott and Williams 2006), consumers have unique skills and expertise that firms need but lack. As Zwick *et al.* (2008) noted, this situation indicates at least two special challenges for managers: "first, to attract and retain these consumers, and second, to provide a creative and open communications environment where such consumers *qua workers* can effectively apply and enhance their knowledge for the benefit of everyone." The successful practice of co-creation requires careful exchanges of information between parties in a manner that supports the firm's ability to tap the broader social knowledge of the consumer for the firm's socio-economic advantage (Humphreys and Grayson 2008).

Therefore, the market is no longer a mere avenue for exchange but a creative hive where consumers showcase their unique resources and trade these resources for reward – rewards that may include social recognition, bragging rights and respect from peers (Arvidsson 2007, 2008). It would seem then that the firm has lost its exclusive privilege of producing value, sharing this privilege with consumers – even granting more creative authority to consumers – to facilitate co-creation (Prahalad and Ramaswamy 2004; Tapscott and Williams 2006; Vargo and Lusch 2004). In other words, co-creation is a form of consumer empowerment born out of a conscious corporate reconfiguration of the market as a democratized space of collaboration in which firms establish and support protean environments that facilitate consumer creativity (Pine and Gilmore 1999; Prahalad and Ramaswamy 2004; Tapscott and Williams 2006). It connotes the tantalizing notion of the firm relinquishing its authority to the consumer who, as the redefined head of the market, is now free to determine what is produced and its associated production protocols. Consumers produce merrily without ceasing; their activities on corporate-owned production platforms are continually transformed into market value that is shared between firm and consumer, albeit disproportionately.

One is tempted to perceive this seeming changing of the market guard as a noble and altruistic gesture in praise of resourceful consumers. However, the conscious engagement of the consumers seems to be a necessary strategy for the firm to arrest the difficulties associated with an active and demanding consumer whose sophisticated tastes and consumption patterns are increasingly disjointed, heterogeneous, and less amenable to corporate control (Gabriel and Lang 1995; Holt 2002). This is especially so when the task of managing production in unstable markets poses major challenges for firms who seek consistency of returns through strategic design and application of resources (Ritzer 2004). The postmodern consumer who can no longer be contained by the firm through traditional management technologies must be managed in new and innovative ways. Co-creation appears to be one such mode of market control, especially in its ability to render the unmanageable consumer manageable by bringing the consumer into a self-interested partnership with the firm, where consumer resources are carefully redefined and employed to support the firm's goals. This co-creation is enacted vigorously on numerous platforms including TV and the Internet (Bonsu *et al.* 2010; Hearn 2008; Zwick *et al.* 2008).

Co-creating value in Web environments

One ubiquitous element of contemporary society is the Internet and the virtual worlds that it has spawned. Bell (2008, p. 2) defined a virtual world as "synchronous, persistent network of people, represented as avatars, facilitated by networked computers." These environments offer detached forms of interaction that simulate community in synthetic spaces. The intense cooperation between firm and consumer on these virtual platforms leads many to suggest a mutually beneficial relationship (Prahalad and Ramaswamy 2004) that serves both parties well. Consumers are supposedly free to operate in non-traditional ways to develop content (as raw materials or finished products) that serves as the firm's offering on the web while firms profit more by ceding product control to the consumer. Indeed, co-creation practices in these worlds draw on social network obligations as resources for cooperative production while encouraging the use of individual self-fulfillment to mask the social character of labor (Zwick *et al.* 2008). This social formation, anchored in contemporary information culture, is most readily observed in Web 2.0 technologies and applications.

> Web 2.0 is the network as platform, spanning all connected devices; Web 2.0 applications are those that make the most of the intrinsic advantages of that platform: delivering software as a continually-updated service that gets better the more people use it, consuming and remixing data from multiple sources, including individual users, while providing their own data and services in a form that allows remixing by others, creating network effects through an "architecture of participation", and going beyond the page metaphor of Web 1.0 to deliver rich user experiences.
>
> *(O'Reilly 2005)*

This definition of Web 2.0 implies the liberty of the user to define and control content. Such implied consumer control is observed in blogs, social networking, wikis, podcasts and virtual games, among others. The proliferation of Web 2.0 applications has allowed web-users to become willing participants in non-traditional social networks that create content for the Web and relevant firms. Through these applications, the Web diffuses informational materials at minimal cost to support the creation of opportunities for collectivist modes of innovation (Jenkins 2007; Tapscott and Williams 2006). Advances in Web 2.0 have encouraged integration of web applications into networked platforms – one need only to sign into Facebook to access wikis, blogs, games, etc. – for the supposed convenience of users. From a co-creation perspective, the firm provides the relevant platforms on which consumers can develop their innovations for market. It maintains a hands-off approach, all the while ensuring that the consumer behaves in accordance with instruments of control embedded in the production platform (cf. Deleuze 1992).

Several Internet platforms demonstrate co-creation's expropriation of consumer cultural labor for the transformation into economic gain for the firm. Consider Flickr which is a popular web suite and online community created by Ludicorp in 2004. The site hosts images and videos that are uploaded by consumers who wish to share their personal photos with the world. In 2005, the site was purchased by Yahoo for $35 million. Over 51 million registered users and 80 million unique visitors work together to keep Flickr in operation as it relies almost exclusively on the input of its users to maintain the site. According to the Flickr website, in August 2011, the platform hosted over 6 billion images, a number that is growing by the hour. Both registered and non-registered members can access photos at the site, although only registered members can upload images. Obligatory registration and other stipulations provide Flickr with a database by which the firm can manage their users (see Zwick and Denegri-Knott 2009).

To access a wide range of consumer knowledge work, Flickr offers free accounts where users are restricted to 200 active photos; even if more photos are uploaded only the latest 200 are available for free account users. In the contemporary digital era of click-happy consumers – mothers in Western Europe take an average of 81 digital photos of their children every quarter (www. infotrends.com/public/Content/Press/2008/10.06.2008.html); a photographer may take more than 2000 pictures of an event (http://photo.net/wedding-photography-forum/00Wy29) – a limit of 200 images for users is woefully inadequate. Flickr users therefore sign up for paid "pro" accounts that have no limit on the number of photos uploaded. Free Flickr accounts may remain inactive for 90 days, after which time the firm reserves the right to delete the images. Pro accounts are not subject to the 90-day inactive rule but Flickr can choose to delete any account without warning to the user. These are intended to keep the user profile current enough to command high advertising rents for Flickr. Users agree to these and other terms and conditions before they are able to use the platform to upload photos. Flickr is also available on other popular platforms (e.g., iPhone, Windows Phone 7, Google) and consumers use these platforms for the ease of access to their pictures and to enhance their Flickr experience.

It is important to note that users pay Flickr to post images that the users have labored to produce, and without which Flickr would cease to exist. It seems that Flickr recognizes consumer need for uniqueness and self-identity (Tian *et al.* 2001) and supports the "liquid" identity pursuits (Bauman 2000) of the postmodern consumer whose fickle nature supports a chameleon-type self-image that can change on a whim. The consumer seems happy to work and pay for the ability to define himself/herself continually in accordance with the relevant identity of the moment. Through this and similar exercises of production and display, consumers routinely produce and reproduce their senses of self for mass consumption. The user perceives control over identity changes without recognizing the free labor for Flickr and the fact that Flickr can take away this control easily by shutting down the platform. The firm frames this as freedom for the user to express whatever they wish with images, without corporate interference – except where the images conflict with the law. Even so, Flickr relies on the active participation of users to derive its socio-economic value and has every reason to maintain the site for its continued financial viability.

The same can be said of YouTube, which was sold to Google for $1.65 billion two years after its launch. Using a platform similar to Flickr, YouTube invites users to a world where the user defines all content. The user uploads content and can remove this content at will, although very few do. YouTube pays a small fee to consumers through its Partner Program for each view of their video uploads, after the videos have become hits. This payment is so miniscule that one requires hundreds of thousands of views to merit any significant payout. For most YouTube users, the most important motivation for their active participation in YouTube is not financial reward but the feeling of having contributed to something of pop cultural value. Sensationalized examples like Justin Bieber who shot from obscurity to music star remain at the back of many users' minds, encouraging them to continue producing for YouTube without pay. Thus, seeking to become well known – even if only through self-promoting images on Flickr or self-endangering actions captured on video that goes viral by way of YouTube – has become vital for most consumers (Hearn 2008). Consumers seem as eager to offer these resources on the market as firms are ready to harness them for profit.

Through co-creation, the consumer is encultured into a market of players whose hopes and actions are controlled by the firm even as the firm promotes an illusory culture of consumer freedom from the market. The firm gains easy access to consumer resources that were heretofore inaccessible by the firm (Dyer-Witheford 1999), and is then able to mobilize these productive resources on the Web for profitable ends (Prahalad and Ramaswamy 2000; Sawhney *et al.* 2005;

Tapscott and Williams 2006). As firms shift the locus of value creation from its core to the periphery where creative authority is shared with consumers (Arvidsson 2007), the firm's economic success will increasingly rely on consumer input in these artificial spaces. It is in the firm's interest therefore to facilitate co-creation on these web spaces.

Beyond YouTube, Flickr and like platforms are the immensely popular massively multiplayer online games (MMOGs). These virtual environments often have their own cultures, social structures, economies and ecologies and are played simultaneously by millions around the world. The games are available 24/7, creating addicts in its wake. Although marketed as free, MMOGs are not free in any sense of the word (Terranova 2000). In some cases, the basic software that serves as the platform for the game needs to be purchased, but in all cases, players have to pay a regular subscription charge to maintain presence on any of these platforms. Like other Web 2.0 applications, the initial parameters of the games are developed and set by the corporate owner. Following the initial launch, player interactions provide the essence of the game. The corporate owner of the game must manage the voluntary cooperation of the players to maintain control, even though the firm depends on the players to sustain continued patronage (Humphreys and Grayson 2008). In essence, the firm appropriates the collective production of the players of the game toward financial gain (Bonsu and Darmody 2008).

Two of the most popular MMOGs are *World of Warcraft* (WW) and *Second Life* (SL). WW was introduced in 1994 as a slim version of its current iteration that was launched in November 2004. The game is framed as play that invites consumers to descend into the world of myth, magic and adventure. If we accept Huizinga's ([1938] 1950, p. 13) view of play as "an activity connected with no material interest, and no profit can be gained by it," then WW is no play at all. The game had over 11.1 million subscribers as of June 2011. In North America and Europe alone, the game raises $800 million in revenue for Vivendi, the owner of the game.

As the world's most popular MMOG, WW is a phenomenon unto its own rules, with a remarkable proliferation of players, clans, websites, and community forums for creating, consuming, and commenting on WW consumer-created movies based on the game. Players spend an average of 22.7 hours per week in the land of Azeroth (the utopian space where the game takes place), generating more than $800 million in revenue from its European and North American players in 2009 for Vivendi (Hamilton 2010). Clearly, the game is impregnated with significant commercial character having been transformed into a business where the distinct zone of free play no longer exists. Players develop virtually all the items used in the game (apparently with the support of hired programmers). Still, players perceive themselves as being in control of the game and the direction its takes. Focusing on the "ethical surpluses" (Arvidsson 2008) that it creates for them, players are blinded to the corporate imperatives that keep the game on the Web. That they have no real control as Vivendi can take down the platform at any time is not as important to them as is the well-crafted illusion of consumer control designed to serve the financial needs of the firm. It is indeed a "capitalist fairytale" (Rettberg 2008) by reason of its reproduction of capitalist ideologies, corporate goals and management technologies under the guise of play.

Illusory control is even more remarkable in *Second Life* (SL), a burgeoning virtual metropolis simulating the real world and the utopian possibility of a world "imagined and created by its residents" without corporate interference (Second Life 2007). The firm offers absolutely no rules for players, suggesting only that they be guided by good etiquette, national laws and fairness grounded in human rights. All action in SL is determined by protocols invented, developed and interpreted by the "residents" of the game, as players are affectionately called. The corporate owners of SL, Linden Lab – called "the Lindens" – describe SL as a platform that simulates the real world, but also affords the malleability of everything in that world (Rymaszewski *et al.*

2006). The Lindens have used mass media and other communication to position SL as a popular grassroots opposition to the proprietary, highly controlled, and hence confining (in the widest sense of the word) world of traditional forms of capital. They have adopted a hands-off approach to managing the virtual environment, encouraging players to create solutions to problems in the world and to improve the SL status quo.

To support this positioning, the SL "world" functions almost entirely on the input of "residents," who are encouraged to be creative in part through copyright ownership of their inventions in the game. The experience begins with the design and creation of one's avatar through which the resident will live her second life. The development of an avatar from a low-level character to one that is a fully functioning social being within SL requires a great deal of expertise, time, labor, money and other investments. Players make these investments in order to enjoy the game to the fullest. The Lindens' main job is to ensure the presence of the virtual platform on which players can create the necessary tools to facilitate interaction in the world, and to collect revenues for this effort. For the players, however, financial gains from the game are limited, even if possible. Many, therefore, perceive the platform as an avenue to learn about the world in anonymity or as an opportunity to escape the realities of the world momentarily. Players pay subscription charges and can purchase specific items (e.g., virtual real estate) from the Lindens. A currency exchange for converting Linden dollars to real money (and back) is another avenue for the firm to generate revenues (see Boellstorff 2008; Bonsu and Darmody 2008, for a discussion of Second Life).

The foregoing suggests that the Internet and its virtual environments thrive on corporate exploitation of consumer resources as play is impregnated with commercial value and converted to corporate profits. The illusion of control created by the firm encourages consumers to engage in co-creating the relevant virtual worlds. This trend poses a threat to the spirit of free play that is devoid of commercialism. In Web 2.0 environments, the consumer is not liberated from corporate tyranny even if there is a loosening of the noose around the consumer's neck. In this regard, Bonsu and Darmody (2008, p. 356) joined Terranova (2000) in observing that

> The Web has often been constructed as a site of unparalleled democracy and creativity ... [whereby the] ... effective mobilization of customer resources ... requires the imposition of boundaries around customer freedoms. ... [this suggests] a paradox of sorts – the more customers are free to create in co-creation relationships, the more restrictions the firm imposes to extract relevant value. In other words, the ideological recruitment of customer labor under the rhetorical guise of empowerment masks the corporate power grab that facilitates the entrapment of customer labor recruits.

This is especially so when one considers the fact that contemporary virtual products like World of Warcraft, Flickr, YouTube and Second Life constitute digital commodities whose existence depend exclusively on the value that consumers create with it. Like other digital commodities, these virtual worlds are transient in character and fully dependent on the continually variable value determined by the extent of combined creative consumer labor inputs (Terranova 2000). Financial success in these worlds, therefore, rest on the firm's ability to continually extract economic value from unpaid consumer input. Through their co-creative activities in the virtual world, consumers develop a genuine sense of self-fulfillment and opportunities for unrepressed indulgence that would not be available in other places. One can argue then that the consumer gets what he wants and the marketer also get what she wants. Thus, co-creation in Internet environments is indeed a mutually beneficial enterprise, even if the expectations and goals of the parties involved are not the same, and the returns are biased in favor of the firm.

257

Conclusion

In this chapter, I have sought to suggest that while consumers of Web technologies (who are simultaneous producers of content and therefore "prosumers") may consider their activities on the web as leisurely means of escape from the realities of life, firms see these consumers and audiences as profit centers, if their labor is mobilized and organized into knowledge work (Smythe 1981; Dyer-Witheford 2003; Terranova 2004). The seeming consumer freedom from corporate control proffered by co-creation and the Internet is a mere veneer that cloaks capital's exploitation of the consumer. That is, rather than the promise of freedom from Fordist and corporate strictures implied by co-creation and Web 2.0 technologies, co-creation throws the consumer into a web of control whereby the firm puts them to work and takes the bulk of their output (Zwick *et al.* 2008). Co-creation in virtual environments then is about control – control of market resources and the conversion of all relevant resources into corporate financial advantage.

In this respect, Web 2.0 and its related technologies/applications are dynamic platforms (Prahalad and Ramaswamy 2004; Sawhney *et al.* 2005) that recognize the need for capital to adjust to prevailing conditions. In the current era where the consumer is fickle and not amenable to corporate forms of discipline, it appears that the best way to manage the consumer is to create an illusion of consumer control of the market through "platforms for action" – to borrow Lury's (2004) expression – constituted by market-system components that are connected strongly enough to facilitate opportunities for community ties and sustain the communal spirit through various emotional and expressive dimensions.

As informational capitalism grows and more relevant platforms for action are developed for virtual consumers, the Web will approach the traditional methods of labor exploitation whereby Flickr, YouTube, WW and like virtual avenues will come to constitute not only an audience commodity that will be sold to advertisers based on defined measure of watching eyeballs or its equivalent measures (Jhally and Livant 1986; Smythe 1981), but also an effective source of creative outputs that can be utilized for firm advantage. The proposed Web 3.0 platform promises to be a meaningful advance from Web 2.0 that will allow users more control over what is produced. Co-creation will remain a key aspect of Web 3.0 and scholars should perhaps ponder (1) the kind of control it can potentially offer relative to what Web 2.0 proffers; (2) to whose advantage; and (3) the need for ways to ensure some balance of power in the system.

In conclusion, co-creation processes in Web environments constitute a simulacrum of traditional market practice that is carefully woven into the social fabric in a manner that directs consumer expressions in particular and exploitative ways. Even though the opportunity to refashion a platform would seem endless, firm controls embedded in the platform limit consumer freedom to co-create. This form of corporate control which was not dominant in previous eras seems to be the only option open to innovative firms in contemporary economy as the consumer becomes increasingly unpredictable in action, thought and behavior. A distinctive feature of Web 2.0 is the ease with which consumers can professionalize their content and make it ready for market absorption. Increased market fragmentation calls for capital to adapt in order to contain the consumer. Such is the promise of co-creation and web 3.0 working together to grant consumers the ultimate in micro-customization (see Peppers and Rogers 2005). This will further minimize the distance between production and consumption but allow for an even more flexible mode of production that calls for the interdependence of the firm and the consumer. Co-creation can be expected to adapt to these changing conditions in an attempt for capital to maintain control of the consumer, especially in informational capitalism where knowledge – all knowledge including those held by consumers – has become a significant productive force.

References

Andrejevic, M. (2008) "Watching Television Without Pity: The Productivity of Online Fans," *Television and New Media*, 9(1): 24–46.

Arvidsson, A. (2005) "Brands: A Critical Perspective," *Journal of Consumer Culture*, 5(2): 235–58.

——(2006) *Brands: Meaning and Value in Consumer Culture*, London: Routledge.

——(2007) "Creative Class or Administrative Class? On Advertising and the 'Underground'," *Ephemera: Theory and Politics in Organization*, 7(1): 8–23.

——(2008) "The Ethical Economy of Customer Coproduction," *Journal of Macromarketing*, 28(4): 326–38.

Bauman, Z. (2000) *Liquid Modernity*, Cambridge: Polity Press.

Bell, D. (1973) *The Coming of Post-Industrial Society*, Harmondsworth: Penguin.

Bell, M.W. (2008) "Toward a Definition of 'Virtual Worlds'," *Virtual Worlds Research: Past, Present and Future*, 1: 1(July).

Boellstorff, T. (2008) *Coming of Age in Second Life: An Anthropologist Explores the Virtually Human*, Princeton, NJ: Princeton University Press.

Bonsu, S.K., and Darmody, A. (2008) "Co-creating *Second Life*: Market-Consumer Cooperation in Contemporary Economy," *Journal of Macromarketing*, 28 (4): 355–68.

Bonsu, S.K., Darmody, A. and Parmentier, M-A. (2010) "Arrested Emotions in Reality, Television, *Consumption, Markets and Culture*," 13, 1(March): 89–105.

Castells, M. (2000) *The Rise of the Network Society*, Malden, MA: Blackwell.

Castronova, E. (2007) *Exodus to the Virtual World: How Online Fun is Changing Reality*, New York: Palgrave Macmillan.

Deleuze, G. (1992) "Postscript on the Societies of Control," *October*, 59(Winter): 3–7.

Dyer-Witheford, N. (1999) *Cyber-Marx: Cycles and Circuits of Struggle in High-technology Capitalism*, Urbana, IL: University of Illinois Press.

——(2003) "Sim Capital: General Intellect, World Market, Species Being, and the Video Game," *Electronic Book Review*. Available at: www.electronicbookreview.com/thread/technocapitalism/marxinalia (accessed 8 October, 2011).

Firat, F.A. and Dholakia, N. (1998) *Consuming People: From Political Economy to Theatres of Consumption*, London: Routledge.

Florida, R. (2002) *The Rise of the Creative Class*, New York: Basic Books.

Fuchs, C. (2008) *Internet and Society: Social Theory in the Information Age*, New York: Routledge.

——(2010) "Labor in Informational Capitalism and on the Internet," *The Information Society*, 26(3): 179–96.

Gabriel, Y. and Lang, T. (1995) *The Unmanageable Consumer: Contemporary Consumption and Its Fragmentations*, Thousand Oaks, CA: Sage.

Hamilton, I. (2010) "Blizzard's World of Warcraft Revenue Down," Nov. 10, available at: http://ocunwired. ocregister.com/2010/11/08/blizzards-world-of-warcraft-revenue-down/ (accessed October 8, 2011).

Hearn, A. (2008) "Meat, Mask, Burden: Probing the Contours of the Branded Self," *Journal of Consumer Culture*, 8(2): 197–217.

Herz, J.C. (2002) "Harnessing the Hive: How Online Games Drive Networked Innovation," *Release 1.0*, 20(9): 1–22.

Holt, D.B. (2002) "Why Do Brands Cause Trouble? A Dialectical Theory of Consumer Culture and Branding," *Journal of Consumer Research*, 29(1): 70–90.

Huizinga, J. ([1938]1950) *Homo Ludens*, Boston, MA: Beacon Press.

Humphreys, A. and Grayson, K. (2008) "The Intersecting Roles of Consumer and Producer: Contemporary Criticisms and New Analytic Directions," *Sociology Compass*, 2: 1–18.

Humphreys, S. (2008) "Ruling the Virtual World: Governance in Massively Multiplayer Online Games," *European Journal of Cultural Studies*, 11(2): 149–71.

Hunt, S.D. (2000) "*A General Theory of Competition*: Too Eclectic or Not Eclectic Enough? Too Incremental or Not Incremental Enough? Too Neoclassical or Not Neoclassical Enough?," *Journal of Macromarketing*, 20(1): 77–81.

Jenkins, H. (2007) "How Second Life Impacts Our First Life," available at: http://henryjenkins.org/2007/ 03/my_main_question_to_jenkins.html (accessed August 18, 2007).

Jhally, S. and Livant, B. (1986) "Watching as Working: The Valorization of Audience Consciousness," *Journal of Communication*, 36(3): 124–43.

Lowood, H. (2005) "Real-time Performance: Machinima and Game Studies," *International Digital Media Arts Association Journal*, 1(3): 10–18.

Lury, C. (2004) *Brands: The Logos of the Global Economy*, London: Routledge.

Lusch, R.F. and Vargo, S.L. (2006) *The Service-Dominant Logic of Marketing: Dialog, Debate, and Directions*, Armonk, NY: M.E. Sharpe.

Marx, K. (1867) *Capital*, vol. I, London: Penguin.

O'Reilly, T. (2005) "Web 2.0: Compact Definition," available at: http://radar.oreilly.com/archives/2005/10/web_20_compact_definition.html (accessed August 30, 2011).

Peppers, D. and Rogers, M. (2005) *Return on Customer: Creating Maximum Value from Your Scarcest Resource*, New York: Currency/Doubleday.

Pine, B.J. and Gilmore, J.H. (1999) *The Experience Economy: Work Is Theatre and Every Business a Stage*, Boston, MA: Harvard Business School Press.

Prahalad, C.K. and Ramaswamy, V. (2000) "Co-opting Customer Competence," *Harvard Business Review*, 78(January–February): 79–87.

——(2004) *The Future of Competition: Co-Creating Unique Value with Customers*, Boston, MA: Harvard Business School Press.

Rettberg, S. (2008) "Corporate Ideology in *World of Warcraft*," in H.G. Corneliussen and J.W. Rettberg (eds), *Digital Culture, Play and Identity: A World of Warcraft Reader*, Cambridge, MA: MIT Press, pp. 19–38.

Ritzer, G. (2004) *The McDonaldization of Society*, Thousand Oaks, CA: Pine Forge Press.

Rymaszewski, M., Au, W.J., Wallace, M., Winters, C., Ondrejka, C. and Batstone-Cunningham, B. (2006) *Second Life: The Official Guide*, Hoboken, NJ: John Wiley & Sons.

Sawhney, M., Verona, G. and Prandelli, E. (2005) "Collaborating to Create: The Internet as a Platform for Customer Engagement in Product Innovation," *Journal of Interactive Marketing*, 19(4): 4–17.

Second Life (2007) "Second Life Key Metrics," available at: http://s3.amazonaws.com/static-secondlife-com/economy/stats_200710.xls (accessed 5 January 2007).

Sheth, J.N., Sisodia, R.S. and Sharma, A. (2000) "The Antecedents and Consequences of Customer-Centric Marketing," *Journal of the Academy of Marketing Science*, 28(1): 55–66.

Smythe, D.W. (1981) "On the Audience Commodity and its Work," in M.G. Durham, and D.M. Kellner (eds), *Media and Cultural Studies*, Malden, MA: Blackwell, pp. 230–56.

Tapscott, D. and Williams, A.D. (2006) *Wikinomics: How Mass Collaboration Changes Everything*, New York: Portfolio.

Terranova, T. (2000) "Free Labour: Producing Culture for the Digital Economy," *Social Text*, 18(2): 33–57.

——(2004) *Network Culture: Politics for the Information Age*, London: Pluto Press.

Tian, K.T., Bearden, W.O. and Hunter, G.L. (2001) "Consumers' Need for Uniqueness: Scale Development and Validation Uniqueness," *Journal of Consumer Research*, 28(1): 50–66.

Vargo, S.L. and Lusch, R.F. (2004) "Evolving to a New Dominant Logic for Marketing," *Journal of Marketing*, 68(January): 1–17.

Zwick, D., Bonsu, S.K. and Darmody, A. (2008) "Putting Consumers to Work: 'Co-Creation' and New Marketing Govern-Mentality," *Journal of Consumer Culture*, 8: 2.

Zwick, D. and Denegri-Knott, J. (2009) "Manufacturing Customers: The Database as New Means of Production," *Journal of Consumer Culture*, 9(2): 221–47.

23

"I DON'T REALLY KNOW WHERE THE MONEY GOES, DO YOU?"

Online gambling and the naïve screenager

June Cotte

Keywords

digital naïve, online gambling, screenagers, teenage gambling

So, there I was, sitting at the 2011 Consumer Culture Theory conference luncheon. I was eating, but thinking about my agreement to write a chapter for this book. I had gathered data from a group of young online gamblers, but I was flummoxed by what I kept hearing. These young people didn't seem to understand the legal, regulatory, or even the technical aspects of the games into which they were pouring hundreds or thousands of dollars. How could this be? Didn't they care that they didn't know much? And how could I possibly frame these findings of ignorance and apathy online in a way that made any sense to a reader of a book called Digital Consumers? And then I introduced the keynote speaker, Eszter Hargittai, and as I listened to her, my own data began to make a little bit more sense. But before we get to that story, let's discover why online gambling is of interest to an emerging group of scholars.

The rise of online gambling

Analysts expect that by 2012, worldwide proceeds from online gambling will be about $30 billion (*The Economist* 2007). All the games that can be found in a physical casino are now also available online. The digital age of gambling has arrived, with convergence among computer-based, smartphone-based, and even online video-game based gambling (King *et al.* 2009). Even accounting for some recent high profile prosecutions in the United States, there are more than 2,600 online websites in operation around the world (Casino City 2011). Many current researchers argue that online gambling is impossible to criminalize in any one country, and that, because of massive gambling revenue flowing out from one country to another, governments everywhere will be motivated to recoup this "lost" revenue by introducing government-sanctioned (or run) online gambling (Wood and Williams 2007). In North America, this can most clearly be seen in Canadian provinces announcing they will open online gambling for residents, and some American states attempting to do the same (*The New York Times* 2011).

Before this happens, because computer-mediated environments have unique qualities from in-person environments (Hoffman and Novak 1996; Schlosser 2003), there is a need for research steeped in online gambling, rather than research that assumes online gambling is similar to casino spaces (Siemens and Kopp 2011). There are profound risks at stake, as a recent survey found that over 40 percent of a large sample of American online gamblers met the diagnostic criteria for problem gamblers, and online gamblers are three to four times more likely to have a gambling problem than land-based casino gamblers (Wood and Williams 2011). Finally, researchers have shown that online gamblers engage in all forms of gambling more, and spend more money gambling, than casino-only gamblers (ibid.). There is also demonstrated comorbidity between online gambling problems and mood disorders, substance abuse and self-harm (Lloyd *et al.* 2010). Of course, it is hard to determine causality, that is, whether problem gamblers are more drawn to online games in the first place, or whether online gambling inherently creates more problematic gambling behavior. But given the stark differences in problems that are related to online gambling, it is certainly worth investigating these differences. Accordingly, there is a growing stream of research studying differences between the casino and online worlds, including some of my own work (Cotte and Latour 2009).

Online vs. casino gambling

In addition to the research reviewed above, many researchers argue that the risks of online gambling are higher than for casino gambling, based on the objective differences between the two contexts (Griffiths and Barnes 2007; Ladd and Petry 2001; McBride and Derevensky 2009; Petry and Weinstock 2007; Wood and Williams 2011). There are many reasons for this, including the instant access and comfort of playing at home (Cotte and Latour 2009; Wood and Williams 2011). Machines increase speed of play, and the technology is now affordable, anonymous, and readily accessible to any operator who can set up a website (Griffiths 2002). Money wagered is often drawn from an online account, making it less likely players notice when it is running low (Siemens and Kopp 2011), and online gamblers tend to play alone, without friends looking out for them (Cotte and Latour 2009; Smith 2004). In addition, online communication, in general, differs from face-to-face communication (Flaherty *et al.* 1998; McKenna and Bargh 2000), partly because of the lack of social cues such as nonverbal behavior (Sproull and Kiesler 1986). In addition, the anonymity possible during online interactions can have both positive and negative effects on behavior (Moon 2000; Schau and Gilly 2003). Although some research, including my own, has indicated more gambling time and money spent online versus offline, recently, researchers have demonstrated a difference in risk-taking during gambling; in higher risk situations, gamblers were more likely to take a greater risk when the roulette wheel was located in the room with them, rather than seen over a video link (as in some online gambling sites) (Goh *et al.* 2011).

In prior work, my colleague and I discovered that the online gambling experience, at home, is quite unique, and can lead gambling to become a "pernicious, insidiously integrated component of a consumer's life" (Cotte and Latour 2009, p. 755). We concluded that this integration contributed to more money and time spent gambling online than in a casino, partly because of the social isolation from potentially moderating social influences. In support of this, Siemens and Kopp (2011) recently concluded that gamblers use controls in the casino environment (including social influences, enforced waiting times, and the tangibility of the chips) to help them mentally account for their gambling consumption. Most of these controls are not available in the online environment. From an experiment, they concluded that gamblers were more likely to lose track of their spending when using intangible currency (as one does online) and when the pace of play is faster (also a characteristic of online games).

Online gambling and "screenagers"

Griffiths and his colleagues have established quite clearly that children and adolescents, as well as young adults, are the most vulnerable group of gamblers when it comes to online gambling, as they are on the Internet frequently, devote major amounts of time to a screen, are early adopters of digital technologies, and are less concerned about the risks involved with using online technologies (de Freitas and Griffiths 2008; Griffiths 2002; Griffiths and Parke 2010; King *et al.* 2010). Kids like gambling because it is fun, and also because gambling's stimulation can help alleviate painful emotions common in adolescence (Jacobs 1986; King *et al.* 2010). The social nature of the online gambling media, with chats and shared news of big wins more instantly translated, can act as a form of peer approval and pressure (King *et al.* 2010). In addition, both my own research and the work of others have shown that online gambling can become a family activity in the home, normalizing the behavior for children and teens. For example, Griffiths and Wood (2007) reported that 16 percent of teenagers who gamble online are playing along with their parents. Indeed, in a recent survey of over 8,000 British teens (between 12 and 15 years old), 8 percent reported gambling online and almost a third had played the free demonstration games offered by online casino websites. These digital-savvy consumers are, of course, the focus of the current volume.

Back to the lunch

As I've briefly outlined, the focus of the most disturbing online gambling research in the last few years have two loci: the increasing evidence of more potential harm in the online realm (versus land-based casinos), and the younger demographic skew in the online group of gamblers. With those trends in mind, I set out to investigate the younger, digitally-savvy gambler group. Against a backdrop of recent online gambling frauds with extensive media coverage (most relevant to players might be the inside cheating scandals at *Absolute Poker* and *Ultimate Bet* in 2007, but also money laundering charges that shut down *Full Tilt Poker*, *Absolute Poker* and *PokerStars* in 2011), I wondered about young people's trust in gambling sites. For most North Americans, and certainly all US-based consumers, the only options for online gambling currently are unregulated sites located off-shore. How do consumers trust these sites enough to send them large amounts of money? Is their trust based on a belief in regulation or oversight? Or are they simply naïve?

Hargittai's keynote address introduced me to her stream of research, which broadly described, focuses on differences in Internet skills and uses due to age, gender, socioeconomic status, race, and other factors, and the impacts these differences have on such outcomes as social inequality. She warns that assumptions about a young generation of digitally-savvy consumers/citizens are perhaps not warranted, and certainly not backed with empirical evidence. Rather than digital natives, she cautions that there are groups of digital naïves:

> While popular rhetoric would have us believe that young [Internet] users are generally savvy with digital media … considerable variation exists even among fully wired college students … data … do not support the premise that young adults are universally knowledgeable about the Web.
>
> *(Hargittai 2010, pp. 108–9)*

In her talk, Hargittai discussed the ramifications of her findings, using examples of online mistakes that went viral, such as inappropriate postings on social networking sites that led to employment problems and reputational damage to young people seemingly unaware of the ramifications of the online actions. For many of us in the audience, the stock reaction was "What were they thinking?" and/or "Don't they know any better?" Paraphrased, these are similar to my own reactions to my data from young online gamblers. Although what I have discovered is in a very different domain, her research on diverse knowledge and uses of the web by young people echoes throughout my findings concerning young online gamblers (for more of her work, also see Hargittai *et al.* 2010 and Hargittai and Hsieh 2010).

The study

Participants were recruited through posters and flyers across a large Canadian university campus in Ontario. I was deliberately seeking a younger cohort of online gamblers, as prior research has shown that although all ages participate, being younger is a significant predictor of online gambling (Petry and Weinstock 2007; Wood and Williams 2011). The recruitment criteria included prior gambling experiences, however the participant defined gambling. I sought out age of majority participants, but as I will discuss, many of the sample began gambling, primarily online, before they had reached the legal age to do so in a casino (19 years old in Ontario). Nineteen young adults (18–25 years old, 11 males) were interviewed about their online gambling experience. The interviews were conducted in participants' homes or dorm rooms, and ranged from 45 minutes to slightly over two hours. Professionally transcribed verbatim, these interviews yielded 304 pages of single-spaced textual data. (For demographic details on the participants, see Table 23.1.) Each interview began with eliciting stories about the gambler's preferred gambling venues and games, gambling history, favorite/least favorite experiences, and finally worked up to views on regulatory issues in the gambling space, particularly regulation of online gambling.

In presenting my findings, I've chosen to focus on mainly a few informants. These young men are the heaviest and most regular online gamblers in the sample, so their experiences, stories, and attitudes are particularly instructive. All are currently students, either undergrad (Todd, Eric, Andrew) or graduate students (Mike and Adam). Their ages range from 18 (Andrew) to

Table 23.1 Demographic details of young gamblers

Pseudonym	Age	Gender	Gambling Experience (Years)
Matt	18	Male	2 years (began in high school)
Jess	22	Female	4 years (after watching parents gamble for years)
Fran	32	Female	10 years (but grew up playing Bingo with Mom)
Phil	24	Male	7 years (began in high school)
Steph	21	Female	3 years
Victoria	24	Female	3 years
Ryan	25	Male	7 years
Jen	22	Female	3 years
Josh	19	Male	1 year
Sandy	23	Female	2 years
John	23	Male	5 years (began in high school)
Jim	20	Male	1 year
Andrew	18	Male	2 years
Adam	23	Male	5 years
Todd	19	Male	2 years
Eric	22	Male	3 years
Jamie	21	Female	2 years
Sarah	23	Female	10 years (played cards as a teen in China)
Mike	25	Male	4 years (grad student in statistics)

25 (Mike), and thus they are squarely located in the generation often called digital natives or the net generation. They all gamble regularly both in the casino and online. We begin by outlining what participants see as the major differences between these modes of gambling, but for brevity move quickly to the focus of the chapter: their assumptions concerning regulation and risk online.

Differences between online and casino gambling

Regular online gamblers recognize that this gambling mode is potentially more problematic than casino gambling. They themselves identify mainly of the risks researchers have also identified. The most common issues are the ease of betting, the speed of play, and the increased intangibility of online credits, versus casino chips (which themselves as less tangible than cash). All of these issues are recognized as potentially misleading cues into problem/addiction areas, yet participants seem to operate in a realm where these things are important to keep in mind, but not important enough to interrupt play for them. As Todd discusses this, he switched from first person to third person, explaining how intangibility online could be a problem for "people," but not for him:

> That is the most important about the online gambling experience. It makes it so much easier to place a bet. You know – physically not handing over money to someone, afterwards, is so much easier than seeing $15 being taken out of your account, to me. Whether or not that's a good thing, I think it probably isn't a good thing. I think so much more money is made through online gambling because of the fact that people – I don't want to say they don't treat it like real money, but, maybe they don't.
>
> *(Todd, 19, male undergraduate student)*

Eric discusses both the intangibility and the speed together, as he talked about the fact that casino trips are much easier to self-regulate than online gambling:

> At least when you're betting [physically], you have to get up, you have to go out, and you have to do it. Gambling online, I find, can be very, very addicting because it's just game after game after game, you just put your credit card down, you're putting 200 bucks at a time, 300 bucks at a time – and you don't actually see the money going, you're just clicking a couple of buttons and it's really – you can get really hooked on it really quickly. You lose one game and you're just a click away from betting on the next game to try to get your money back. It's very easy to throw money away quickly.
>
> *(Eric, 22, male, undergraduate student)*

In a similar manner, Adam talked about virtual money being much easier to lose. He also brings up a fascinating aspect of online gambling – both the money wagered and the wins/losses can be temporally separated by much longer periods of time. For example, gamblers can deposit $1,000 on an account (and many have balances far in excess of this) and then gamble until it eventually is gone (with wins and losses along the way, of course). The initial deposit is treated as a sunk cost, or past spending, so losing it doesn't seem to hurt as much. However, Adam points out that intangible wins also don't feel as good, especially when the realization of them is temporally removed from the win itself. This should be disturbing to addiction specialists, who know that as the "high" of a win is diminished, the addict will seek out greater risk to recover that initial positive rush, or thrill.

I think it's a little easier to lose online than in person if I'm playing blackjack or something in the casino just because, you know, it's kind of all virtual, the money's almost virtual so it's like "ah, I didn't really have it" because you deposited it all, you know, however long ago … it could be months ago, it feels like it's been gone already so I guess it's a little easier to take on-line but it's definitely still so frustrating. [later, about winning] … when you actually go and cash out in the casino, you get the money right away. You're taking this big stack of chips up. They're counting it all out there in front of you. It's a better feeling than winning online where again it just kind of goes into your virtual account there and you cash out when you want which is whenever and it could be months later when you actually, when you cash out and get the cheque so you don't really tie it back to that one day or that one win.

(Adam, 23, male, graduate student)

Andrew prefers online gambling to a casino experience, in much the same way as many consumers in Cotte and Latour's (2009) research did. Andrew has been gambling online for at least three years before he was able to do so legally, and he simply feels more comfortable gambling at home, and is less embarrassed when losses mount at home, when he is alone. The fact that this may be problematic for increased gambling does not seem to occur to Andrew, but it is a theme I have seen in some of my other research. Without the social monitoring that may intimidate Andrew, and potentially cause him to restrict his gambling, he is free to chase losses, as he demonstrates:

Well, I went to a casino, and I wasn't a big fan just because. It's intimidating, a lot of people are watching you play … [in] the online environment you're behind your monitor, you're in the comfort of your own home, you can think straight, and you don't have to be intimidated by people … I just feel if you lose a lot of money, I'd be personally embarrassed if I lost a lot of money in the casino. But if I lost a lot of money in online poker, I know the next day I'll make some. I track the amount I had not that one day, but for like a month. But if I lost one day in a casino, I'd think I'd take it as a loss.

(Andrew, 18, male undergraduate student)

Trust in online gambling operators and sites

As outlined earlier, online gambling, especially at the time of this data collection, is technically illegal in Ontario. As the sites are located off-shore (in countries where it is allowed), it is unclear what penalties could be levied against individual gamblers, and so most gamblers assume, realistically, that they are not going to be prosecuted for participating. However, knowledge that these sites are located in other countries, and not allowed in Canada, does not seem to worry young male gamblers overtly. Credibility seems to be determined by word-of-mouth, consumer reviews online, advertising spending, and endorsements by pro gamblers, just as it would be for most consumer products.

INTERVIEWER: Do you trust online gambling?
ERIC: Well, it depends on the website. You know, I had trouble getting money from one account, so I don't necessarily trust them very much. Now, if I'm going to do it again, I'm going to go with sites that my friends have said they've got money from and sites you know are credible out there. There's some that are run through, because you can't do it in the States or in Canada, they're run from places down south, so some of them I don't trust. I try

to go with more reliable ones, ones that I know friends have already said they have a good reputation, they already got money from.

(Eric, 22, male, undergraduate student)

Even among gamblers well aware of the potential for consumer fraud there exists a reliance on these factors, especially advertising and endorsements, to establish trust in the site.

> The [online sites] that the pros ... maybe this doesn't make the most sense, but the ones that the pros advocate for, I have more trust for that because it makes it seem more legitimate ... I usually try to find some reviews of it to see if there's a general feeling of trust out there for it. But like I said, I do have less trust for those ones [versus land-based casinos] because you'll hear every once in a while, you'll hear that horror story about when they're scamming people's money or something like that. ... Poker sites that are advertising, if they've advertisements or things like that or if there's a lot of people advocating for it ... if there's a legitimate name attached to a poker site or something like that I have more trust in that one.

INTERVIEWER: Can you give me some examples of ones you trust?
ADAM: Oh yeah, the bigger ones like Poker Stars, or Party Poker, or Full Tilt. They're pretty well known poker sites and they're ... they, I don't know ... they seem better run. There are commercials for them and I've never had any issues with them. I couldn't really find any reviews where people, for lack of a better word, have been screwed by them so. There's a few that I trust.

(Adam, 23, male, graduate student)

Some online gamblers trusted the online casinos more than the payment companies that process the monetary transfers (a step necessary in light of the US government's prosecution of banks and credit card companies who facilitate online gambling). However, as Andrew highlights, the trust here is often misplaced because of a lack of knowledge. Many gamblers assume large public companies, such as the ones that run the Las Vegas casinos, also run these websites (they do not).

> [Re: trusting online gambling sites] Yeah, I do. The only sketchy part is a third party that is used to transfer funds, withdraw and deposit money. You should research that before, because some are scams. But, online poker, if it's a legit company that you researched, yeah, why not? [later, when asked about the owners of the sites:] Oh, I have no clue ... aren't online poker companies owned by casino companies?
> *(Andrew, 18, male, undergraduate student)*

The most knowledgeable of our sample of regular online gamblers was also the oldest participant. Mike is a graduate student in statistics, and a frequent online poker player. Although he spends quite a lot of money and time on these sites, he simultaneously shares the belief that many of them have fraudulent elements not possible in physical casino poker games:

> Sometimes you see these hands that are just unbelievable. I feel like it's almost fixed you know. You never see these hands in casinos. It would be so rare, that you'd be like, Oh my God, I can't believe that happened! ... I've seen this so much online ... Because there is no way this would happen so common ... But the fact that I've seen it so often, you know. I can't be that lucky to see these hands. ... It seems sometimes

a little too good to be true, some of these hands. Never see this in real life. So trust there is questionable definitely when it comes to these sorts of things.

(Mike, 25, male, graduate student)

Knowledge of online gambling legality/regulation

As I mentioned earlier, an aspect of online gambling consumption that fascinates me is the trust needed to send an unknown website hundreds of dollars (or any money, for that matter). As outlined above, trust in these sites is often determined in a very similar way to trust in other sorts of websites (WOM, endorsements, advertising). However, given no regulatory oversight (governments cannot regulate what they have outlawed, after all), the chance that a casino website could simply be set up, take bets, then shut down without paying out anything (a risk that most participants actually acknowledge) would seem to be worthy of consideration. So, why doesn't this stem the fast-growing tide of online gambling among the young? As it turns out, they largely assume someone is actually watching or, perhaps more naïvely, think it is in the business's best interest to regulate itself. Todd takes a fairly libertarian view of personal responsibility, but eventually I discovered that this view is based on the faulty assumption that the government of Canada condones/allows/should monitor this consumption behavior:

> Everything that the person does in their home is their choice … online gambling is, doesn't have to be checked. To a degree, it's not illegal, but I think that … just as with everything that's online – it's so much harder to regulate than anything else, and I think that … Well, when it comes to online gambling, I think it's so hard for so many people to regulate this … A lot of people, whenever they ask me, if I gamble online, they think that, well, isn't that illegal? Well, it's not, *there are specific laws allowing online gambling*, but as far as that goes, there's not much more regulation. You know, you could be giving your money to whatever company that may or may not be swindling you out of it, but I think that that becomes so much more your own risk online, just like with every online business might be. [later] Well … *I think that if the federal government has allowed online gambling to take place, in my opinion, shouldn't it be their responsibility to monitor that it's being done in a sort of accountable and legitimate fashion?*
> *(Todd, 19, male undergraduate student, emphasis added)*

Eric and Adam are very regular participants in offshore online gambling. And they do not seem troubled by the lack of oversight, even when they have personal knowledge of the potential for fraud and misuse. Both assume some monitoring is happening, but neither has any idea who may be doing this monitoring or regulation. A site earns Adam's trust by paying out when he wins, that is his evaluation of credibility. Andrew, one of the youngest in the sample, refers to Wikipedia as his ultimate reference, demonstrating the Internet naïvete that Hargittai identified in her research (e.g. Hargittai *et al.* 2010). (Please note that although I present three informants here, the sentiment that "someone must be watching it" was widespread, albeit erroneous.)

> I don't think [online gambling] is as monitored [as casinos]. I think it might be harder because some of the sites are run not in North America. They're run down south in places that have very low standards, so I think the sites that I have heard are sketchy where friends can't get money back, or I haven't been able to get money back, those obviously aren't monitored very closely because the sites are cheating people out of their money and they're giving incentives for people to gamble – they're giving

$15 on every $100 they deposit or what not, but they're never paying out to people, so they're not monitored as well. [later] Some of the sites – I think there are, I'm not really sure where all the sites are from. I think some sites that are from the States that the government probably monitors them. The ones, the sketchy ones, the ones that are regulated down south, nobody's really monitoring them too closely. But, of course, they have to pay out some money or else people aren't going to go to them, so ... they kind of monitor themselves.

(Eric, 22, male undergraduate student)

The online ones, I have no idea. I don't know who monitors them. I don't know if they're monitored by something. A lot of them are offshore things, so a lot of them, I don't even know what country they are based out of or whatnot, so that's part of the reason I guess why I have less trust in them. So I guess they have to earn my trust whereas with the personal ones [land-based casinos], I feel like they're being monitored well enough that I trust them.

(Adam, 23, male, graduate student)

Who would monitor the owners? A higher power? The government? No, not the government. Would the government? Do you know? [later] I actually am not sure ... I think the government should be monitoring them. Just because they should ... the owner shouldn't be scamming and stuff, and so I think the government should monitor any business ... I don't know about ... I just play the game. I've never actually researched. I'll Wikipedia it tonight, though. [later] I actually think online is monitored more now. Because, recently I heard on the news that the U.S. government or someone, I don't know, some higher power is trying to shut down online poker, and that ... I forgot what site it was ... 'Cuz, the government, I believe, just thinks it's all luck, and a lot of people are losing their money, especially in a bad economy, to gambling ... So I think they're being monitored a lot.

(Andrew, 18, male undergraduate student)

Attitudes towards online gambling regulation

Towards the end of most interviews, the discussion turned towards possible regulation of online gambling. Of course, during most interviews it became clear before this point that a fair bit of faulty information and logic was being relied on by these young people. There was a touching, if slightly frightening, aspect to their trust in online gambling operators and websites that echoes Hargittai's themes of digital naïves. Having grown up with screens and digital media, and being on the more privileged side of the societal Internet access gap (all were attending a major university), many would assume these participants know what they are doing online. But here, in an area where a large amount of their discretionary income is at stake, they frankly do not understand the system under which they are gambling.

There were two main themes concerning regulation. One was a decidedly libertarian take on personal freedom, as evidenced strongly by Eric.

Just like with everything else – smoking, drinking, people have a choice. They can, there's not rules, and the government doesn't step in and say, okay you have to stop drinking, well, they do, kind of, with the police, but, there's really ... People have their own freedom to do what they want, so I think they should have the freedom to, if they want to spend their whole life savings, so be it. That's a dumb decision; that's their own fault, but that's their choice and their money, so, I don't think there need to be regulations there.

(Eric, 22, male undergraduate student)

Another theme was that regulations should not be aimed at the online casinos themselves (who offer a legitimate product to consumers, in participants' views) but aimed at gamblers who have a problem learning to gamble responsibly. Suggestions ranged from reducing the advertisements that are allowed to target online gambling consumers to enforced waiting periods to allow consumers to regulate their spending:

[T]hat's the way the gambling industry makes its most money is by playing off people's excitement – titillating people with the idea of making a maximum amount of money without having to do any work for it. And, you know, that's subsequently the way people get into trouble with gambling. You know, if there were anything I'd like to be regulated, I would say maybe the advertisements to protect the gambler. I think that, if anything, the gambler needs so much protection from themselves.

(Todd, 19, male undergraduate student)

… like a restaurant can't serve you more than this much amount of alcohol … Maybe at least give you like a day to think about how much you lost and to like back off, because … if you lost a lot of money and you're just in that mode and you just want to win it back, win it back, and you'll do just whatever to win it back, but if you have like a day and you're like "Oh, shit, I lost like 500 bucks, I should just calm down, I can't gain it back," it's more likely that I'll lose. So, I think it's just the time they should just give you a limitation on how much you lose and then let you go for the night.

(Andrew, 18, male undergraduate student)

A concluding quote illustrates several troubling aspects of the naïve faith displayed by online gambling participants. Adam is one of the veterans in our sample – he has been online gambling for about five years – and he is a regular participant. His wins and losses are routinely in the thousands column of the mental ledger he keeps. And yet, his knowledge of the consumption infrastructure underlying this behavior is astonishingly thin:

[Re: online gambling companies] I have no idea which is probably the scary thing about it. I have no idea who runs it, who owns it. I don't even know what country they're based out of … There is a lot more advertising … Hopefully, everybody's honest and if it's a regulated industry or a monitored industry, they could still be doing things behind the regulations or tweaking things or … hopefully everybody's honest, I would like to think that they are, but … [trails off]

(Adam, 23, male, graduate student)

Conclusion

As I stated at the beginning of this story, I was initially mystified by what I kept hearing in these interviews. The teenagers and young adults I investigated spent quite a lot of money, quite regularly, on an online consumption activity that they knew very little about. As I worked through this data and the literature on this group of digital consumers, I began to realize that this behavior is of a piece with behaviors such as posting highly inappropriate, seemingly private (at least to my generation) information online without much concern for ramifications. And it is also echoed in the research that shows young people are not very good at distinguishing credible information sources online (Hargittai *et al.* 2010). So although set in a gambling context, this research contributes to the debate about young Internet users: their skills, and their aptitudes.

As the focus of most of my own research is on gambling, however, I'd like to point out some of the challenges derived from my findings. First, the appeal of gambling to less than legal age adolescents, particularly males, is clear: it is a risky behavior with potential for huge highs and the rush that comes with winning. Many researchers, particularly Griffiths, have pointed out the risks of gambling for this age group. Digital advances in gambling have increased access for an incredibly vulnerable group. Although my participants spoke about individual responsibility, social scientists know very well that this group is not well equipped to reduce their own risk-taking behaviors. It is incumbent on regulators and policy-makers to ensure age restrictions are in place, and enforced. This is much easier in jurisdictions that have been allowing regulated online gambling (Ontario will begin in 2012), but the refusal, at the federal level, to allow legal online gambling in the US means that harm reduction strategies cannot be enforced.

There is an additional route to provide some consumer protection for online gamblers though, even in jurisdictions that do not allow it. This would be a marketing approach to consumer education particularly focused on teenagers. Rather than an abolitionist approach (such as teaching abstinence only as sex education), perhaps campaigns could focus on helping teens discern safer websites and more responsible behaviors. As word-of-mouth and endorsements are a major factor for gambling website choice in this cohort, major online teen influencers could perhaps be tapped via social media to investigate and recommend more reputable sites.

Many online young online gamblers, digital consumers of casino offerings, are astonishingly naïve, both about the potentially problematic nature of gambling, as well as about the business and regulatory environment in which it operates. It behooves us to study this group with rigor, to be able to offer policy prescriptions that make sense, and help reduce harm.

Acknowledgments

The author thanks Kenneth Preston for data collection assistance.

Further reading

Cotte, June and Latour, Katherine A. (2009) "Blackjack in the Kitchen: Understanding Online Versus Casino Gambling," *Journal of Consumer Research*, 35(February): 742–58. [A comparison of gambling in casinos vs. online, with an emphasis on the meaning changes that occur as the behavior moves into the home.]
——(2012) "Gambling Myths vs. Reality: Implications for Transformative Public Policy," in David Glen Mick, Simone Pettigrew, Cornelia Pechmann and Julie L. Ozanne (eds), *Transformative Consumer Research for Personal and Collective Well-Being*, New York: Routledge, pp. 485–98. [An overview of lab and field-based gambling research, with implications for policy-makers.]
Hargittai, Eszter (2010) "Digital Na(t)ives? Variation in Internet Skills and Uses Among Members of the 'Net Generation'," *Sociological Inquiry*, 80(1): 92–113. [An excellent discussion of the naïve Net generation and some implications for their behavior.]

References

Casino City (2011) Online Casino City site, available at: http://casinocity.com, (accessed December 2011).
Cotte, June and Latour, Kathryn A. (2009) "Blackjack in the Kitchen: Understanding Online Versus Casino Gambling," *Journal of Consumer Research*, 35(February): 742–58.
de Freitas, S. and Griffiths, Mark D. (2008) "The Convergence of Gaming Practices with Other Media Forms: What Potential for Learning? A Review of the Literature," *Learning, Media and Technology*, 33: 11–20.

The Economist (2007) "Playing a Strong Hand," August 29, p. 59.

Flaherty, Lisa M., Pearce, Kevin J. and Rubin, Rebecca (1998) "Internet and Face-to-Face Communication: Not Functional Alternatives," *Communication Quarterly*, 46(3): 250–68.

Goh, Lynette Y.Q, Phillips, James G. and Blaszczynski, Alex (2011) "Computer-Mediated Communication and Risk-Taking Behavior," *Computers in Human Behavior*, 27: 1794–9.

Griffiths, Mark D. (2002) *Gambling and Gaming Addictions in Adolescence*, Leicester: British Psychological Society/Blackwells.

Griffiths, Mark D. and Barnes, A. (2007) "Internet Gambling: An Online Empirical Study Among Student Gamblers," *International Journal of Mental Health and Addiction*, 6: 194–204.

Griffiths, Mark D. and Parke, Jonathan (2010) "Adolescent Gaming on the Internet: A Review," *International Journal of Adolescent Medicine and Health*, 22: 59–75.

Griffiths, Mark D. and Wood, Robert T. (2007) "Adolescent Internet Gambling: Preliminary Results of a National Survey," *Education and Health*, 25: 23–7.

Hargittai, Eszter (2010) "Digital Na(t)ives? Variation in Internet Skills and Uses Among Members of the 'Net Generation'," *Sociological Inquiry*, 80(1): 92–113.

Hargittai, Eszter, Fullerton, Lindsay. Menchen-Trevino, Ericka, and Thomas, Kristen Yates (2010) "Trust Online: Young Adults' Evaluation of Web Content," *International Journal of Communications*, 4: 468–94.

Hargittai, Eszter and Hsieh, Yu-li Patrick (2010) "From Dabblers to Omnivores: A Typology of Social Network Site Usage," in A. Papacharissi (ed.), *The Networked Self*, London: Routledge, pp. 146–68.

Hoffman, Donna L. and Novak, Thomas P. (1996) "Marketing in Hypermedia Computer-Mediated Environments: Conceptual Foundations," *Journal of Marketing*, 60(July): 50–85.

Jacobs, D.F. (1986) "A General Theory of Addictions: A New Theoretical Model," *Journal of Gambling Behavior*, 2: 15–31.

King, Daniel, Delfabbro, Paul and Griffiths, Mark D. (2002) "The Convergence of Gambling and Digital Media: Implications for Gambling in Young People," *Journal of Gambling Studies*, 26: 175–87.

Ladd, G.T and Petry, N.M. (2002) "Disordered Gambling among University-Based Medical and Dental Patients: A Focus on Internet Gambling," *Psychology of Addictive Behaviors*, 16: 76–9.

Lloyd, Joanne, Doll, Helen, Hawton, Keith, Dutton, William H., Geddes, John R., Goodwin, Guy M. and Rogers, Robert D. (2010) "Internet Gamblers: A Latent Class Analysis of Their Behaviors and Health Experiences," *Journal of Gambling Studies*, 26: 387–99.

McBride, J. and Derevensky, J.L. (2009) "Internet Gambling Behavior in a Sample of Online Gamblers," *International Journal of Mental Health and Addiction*, 7: 149–67.

McKenna, Katelyn Y.A. and Bargh, John A. (2000) "Plan 9 from Cyberspace: The Implications of the Internet for Personality and Social Psychology," *Personality and Social Psychology Review*, 4(1): 57–75.

Moon, Youngme (2000) "Intimate Exchanges: Using Computers to Elicit Self-Disclosure from Consumers," *Journal of Consumer Research*, 26(March): 323–36.

The New York Times (2011) "Starved Budgets Inspire New Look at Web Gambling," August 13.

Petry, N.M. and Weinstock, J. (2007) "Internet Gambling is Common in College Students and Associated with Poor Mental Health," *American Journal on Addictions*, 16: 325–30.

Schau, Hope Jensen and Gilly, Mary C. (2003) "We Are What We Post? Self-Presentation in Personal Web Space," *Journal of Consumer Research*, 30(December): 385–404.

Schlosser, Ann E. (2003) "Computers as Situational Cues: Implications for Consumers' Product Cognitions and Attitudes," *Journal of Consumer Psychology*, 3(1–2): 103–12.

Siemens, Jennifer Christie and Kopp, Steven W. (2011) "The Influence of Online Gambling Environments on Self-Control," *Journal of Public Policy and Marketing*, 30(2): 279–93.

Smith, Alan D. (2004) "Controversial and Emerging Issues Associated with Cybergambling (e-casinos)," *Online Information Review*, 28(6): 435–43.

Sproull, Lee and Kiesler, Sara (1986) "Reducing Social Context Cues: Electronic Organizational Communication," *Management Science*, 32(11): 1492–512.

Wood, Robert T. and Williams, Robert J. (2007) "Problem Gambling on the Internet: Implications for Internet Gambling Policy in North America," *New Media and Society*, 9: 520–42.

——(2011) "A Comparative Profile of the Internet Gambler: Demographic Characteristics, Game-Play Patterns, and Problem Gambling Status," *New Media and Society*, 13(7): 1123–41.

24

VIRAL PROPAGATION OF CONSUMER- OR MARKETER-GENERATED MESSAGES

T. E. Dominic Yeo

Keywords

communication flow, cultural representation, emotion broadcasting, memes, social contagion, word-of-mouth

Viral propagation of consumer- or marketer-generated messages has caused much excitement in recent times not least because of its manifestation in novel and high-profile phenomena such as viral videos, consumer-generated content, and flash mobs. Take the example of Thessa's birthday. Like any other digital native (Tapscott 2009), the German girl had created an event page *Mein 16!* on a social networking site inviting her friends to the birthday party. Much to her horror, more than 1,500 strangers showed up outside her house on the day of the event alongside 100 police officers who were summoned to keep the flash mob under control. It turns out that Thessa had inadvertently listed her party as a public event and the invitation had gone viral. The event received 2,500 responses from random users of the site before Thessa realized her oversight and removed the invitation. But by then, clones of the event page spotting her address and other details had emerged and went on to garner over 15,000 responses.

Given the recent prevalence of similar examples, it is easy to forget that viral propagation – the repeated transmission of a message or idea via peer-to-peer dissemination – has been an age-old phenomenon. Legends, folklores, rumors, and gossips provide longstanding precedents of virally propagated narratives. We can also trace the analog precursors of digital viral media (videos, emails, etc.) to the likes of chain letters and the Samizdat (grassroots literature covertly produced and passed on among known associates to avoid censorship in the Soviet era). The difference is that viral propagation is more visible and extensive in the digital context as the dissemination of messages is much faster, more scalable, and better coordinated. Notably, the mass adoption of media-sharing platforms and social network sites recently has made it easier for marketers and consumers alike to quickly disseminate their messages to an exponentially growing audience via peer-referrals.

Despite more favorable conditions for viral propagation in the digital context, viral propagation remains an elusive phenomenon that we can neither predict nor control. As much as digital channels help to multiply the impact of viral propagation, they also accentuate the potential fallout from poorly executed viral campaigns or unintended viral messages – as Thessa's birthday shows. The unpredictability of viral propagation coupled with its increasing prevalence and impact on public discourse and consumer behaviors warrant a better understanding of its nature and process. To this end, a large corpus of empirical work across several disciplines has proffered many determinants and characteristics of viral propagation. However, the lack of an integrative overview of this vast body of work has left us with a fragmented and limited knowledge of the phenomenon. The goal of this chapter, therefore, is to facilitate further research and theoretical advancement on viral propagation by explicating its conceptual foundations and the factors that shape its manifestation in the digital context.

The chapter comprises two main sections. The first section synthesizes and simplifies a broad range of prior literature to highlight the most pertinent theoretical perspectives of the nature and process of viral propagation. Four perspectives stand out: epidemiological, emotional, communicational, and cultural. The second section reflects on viral propagation in the age of digital technologies and rapidly evolving consumption patterns. It interrogates the impact of technologies at both micro and macro level aspects on the process of viral propagation and the way technology affords the transformation of consumers' individual actions to collectively meaningful outcomes. Areas for further research are explored in the conclusion.

Theories of viral propagation

The phenomenon of viral propagation has attracted considerable multidisciplinary research interests – most notably, sociology of collective behaviors, psychology of rumors, anthropology of cultural diffusion, and consumer research of word-of-mouth behaviors. Questions regarding viral propagation can be broadly summarized in terms of what, who, when, where, why, and how: *what* gets propagated? (types of message that frequently become propagated); *who* is involved in the propagation? (opinion leaders, mavens, early adopters, etc.); *when* does viral propagation arise? (the circumstances leading to the generation and spread of messages); *where* does viral propagation occur? (social networks, online communities, etc.); *why* do individuals propagate messages? (their motives, goals, and desires); and *how* are messages propagated? (the mode of transmission). Prior studies on viral propagation can be loosely organized by their focus on one of the following primary units of analysis: messages, individuals, networks, and contexts. The approach in examining viral propagation in terms of the message that is propagated has been to identify the attributes of messages that induce consumers to pass them on. This is frequently coupled with the approach by which viral propagation is understood in terms of the psychological antecedents and consequences of individuals who pass on messages. Turning to the social networks where messages are propagated, the approach has been to investigate how social relations affect the diffusion of messages. Finally, in terms of the cultural contexts that precipitate viral propagation, the approach is to appreciate consumers' meaning-making activities in relation to the messages being propagated. The respective modes of viral propagation are: social epidemic, emotional sharing, interpersonal communication, and cultural representation (see Table 24.1).

Viral propagation as social epidemic

The social epidemic metaphor is perhaps the most commonly used descriptor for the way messages or ideas spread via peer-to-peer dissemination. Underlying this metaphor is the analogy

Table 24.1 Different theoretical perspectives of viral propagation

	Memetic	*Emotional*	*Communicational*	*Cultural*
Focus on	What	Why	Who	How
Unit of analysis	Viral messages	Individuals	Social networks	Cultural contexts
Determinant	Contagious thoughts	Emotional valence	Relational ties	Social relevance
What is transmitted	Memes	Emotions	Information	Meanings
Mode of transmission	Social epidemic	Emotional sharing	Interpersonal communication	Cultural representation
Key references	Dawkins 1976; Blackmore 1999	Heath et al. 2001; Festinger 1957; Heath 1996; Harber and Cohen 2005	Katz and Lazarsfeld 1955; Rogers 1962	Sperber 1996; de Certeau 1984; Jenkins 1992; Bartlett 1932

between the way ideas and messages diffuse through public consciousness and the way diseases spread during epidemics (Gladwell 2000). This notion is most keenly developed by the proponents of memetics (Dennett 1995; Blackmore 1999). Originally conceived as the cultural equivalent of genes (Dawkins 1976), memes provide a useful catch-all term for all sorts of messages, ideas, behaviors, or cultural elements that are imitated by consumers. Proponents of memetics argue that memes represent contagious thoughts (Lynch 1996) or mind viruses (Dawkins 1993) which promote their own replication by inducing their hosts (the minds of individuals) to propagate them. An example is the St. Jude chain letter (Goodenough and Dawkins 1994) which instigates recipients to pass it on by providing anecdotal accounts of good luck befalling recipients who send copies of the letter to others and bad luck for those who do not. The memetic proposition that viral messages possess certain attributes that promote their propagation is especially helpful in legitimizing the art of designing messages that are more likely to be passed on by consumers.

The research strategy in this area is to identify the specific quality or stickiness of messages (Gladwell 2000) that would spur consumers to pass them on. In an exploratory content analysis of 235 television advertisements and 266 viral advertisements, Porter and Golan (2006) aver that viral advertising relies on provocative content (sex, nudity, and violence) to motivate unpaid peer communication of persuasive messages from identified sponsors. While the small handful of published research that examines the viral attributes of messages clearly draws upon the assumptions of memetics, few studies explicitly associate themselves with the meme concept. Instead, these largely practitioner-oriented studies rely on message strategy models as the theoretical framework in a bid to inform creative strategies in viral advertising. Applying Taylor's (1999) six-segment message strategy wheel, Golan and Zaidner (2008) analyzed the creative strategies of 360 viral advertisements and note the overwhelming use of ego-oriented appeals involving themes such as humor and sexuality. In an analysis of 102 video ads from UK and US which were shown on television and online, Southgate *et al.* (2010) found that the volume of video ad views per week can be correlated to advertising pre-test measures on enjoyment, involvement, and branding. The authors further propose three other creative strategies that contribute to viral viewing: the distinctiveness of the ad, the role of celebrities in spreading the message, and the buzz-worthiness of the content (hilariously funny, edgy, gripping, or sexy).

Apart from a few indirect references, the memetics approach has not caught on with main-stream academic researchers. This is largely because of its highly unrealistic and ambiguous ontological assumptions that cultural ideas can be divided up into discrete and independent entities that are replicated and propagated with a high level of fidelity. The explanatory power of the memetic approach is further curtailed by its fallacious disregard for the role of individuals who pass on messages as active participants in the propagation process. To merely analyze the content of virally propagated messages without considering how they are interpreted by receivers is to mistakenly assume that these messages possess direct and uniform influence on consumers – assumptions which were widely discredited by communication scholars several decades ago (Lazarsfeld *et al.* 1944; Katz and Lazarsfeld 1955). Unlike biological or computer viruses, viral messages are rarely propagated by their human hosts unintentionally. People are also likely to modify or add to the content of a message before passing it on to someone else. Even if we could discount human agency and individual differences, it is spurious to claim that themes and other content characteristics identified through post-hoc analysis of messages that had gone viral constitute message attributes that could predict viral propagation. So while the social epidemics metaphor offers an intuitive description of the spread of messages through consumer-to-consumer propagation, the examination of message attributes alone does not offer a convincing theoretical account of viral propagation. Just as sexual selection and environmental factors determine the propagation of genetic materials, individuals and situations play a determining role in the selection and propagation of viral messages.

Viral propagation as emotional sharing

The emotional sharing perspective of viral propagation refers to the idea that individuals are driven to generate and spread certain messages in response to the emotional valence of an event, situation, or consumption object. The earliest proponent of this notion is Prasad (1935) who proposes that a typical situation that leads to the generation and propagation of rumors: (a) sets up an emotional disturbance; (b) is of an uncommon and unfamiliar type; (c) contains many aspects unknown to the individuals affected; (d) contains several unverifiable factors; and (e) is of group interest. While many scholars have echoed the similar idea that rumors arise and propagate in response to uncertainties or anxieties (Allport and Postman 1945; Rosnow 1991), it was Festinger's (1957) theory of cognitive dissonance that inspired the development of emotional discrepancy theories. The theory of cognitive dissonance posits that people are motivated to change their cognitive beliefs or behaviors in order to reduce the tension caused by holding conflicting ideas simultaneously. It was originally proposed by Festinger (1957) to explain the circulation of rumors after an earthquake. He suggests that people who escaped the earthquake unharmed began to circulate rumors about unforeseeable calamities in order to reduce their unjustified feelings of fear. Expanding on the theory of cognitive dissonance, emotional arousal (or discrepancy) theories propose that emotions arise when information violates expectations. To resolve the event or belief discrepancies, people are prompted to share and talk about their experiences of the situations from which the emotions arise. Harber and Cohen (2005) aver that this intrapsychic need to share emotional experiences with others drives viral propagation of messages.

Several studies have provided empirical support for the emotional driving force of expectation-violations on forwarding behaviors in a range of contexts. Heath (1996) demonstrates that in domains that were emotionally positive, people prefer to pass along news that was exaggeratedly positive and in domains that were emotionally negative, the preference was for exaggeratedly negative news. Similarly, Phelps *et al.* (2004) found that email messages that spark strong emotion – humor, fear, sadness, or inspiration – are most likely to be forwarded. They further observed that emails containing very humorous jokes, touchingly sad stories, or particularly inspirational messages meet the threshold of participants who seldom forward viral emails. In an elaborate study of the role of emotions in successful viral marketing campaigns, Dobele *et al.* (2007) examined consumers' emotional responses and subsequent forwarding behavior on messages containing six emotions: surprise, joy, sadness, anger, fear, and disgust. Surprise was identified as a common emotion across the different viral marketing campaigns; it is suggested that the emotion has to be combined with at least one of the other five emotions in order to generate forwarding behaviors. More recently, Brown *et al.* (2010) contend that comedic violence in advertisements elicits greater emotional involvement with the message and higher pass-along probability.

Besides providing the motivational drive for propagating messages, the emotional sharing perspective also suggests that emotions themselves are propagated (Rimé 2009). This emotional contagion is said to occur when both sender and receivers jointly experience a similar emotion (Howard and Gengler 2001). Pointing to the socializing function of shared emotions, Heath *et al.* (2001) propose that memes are frequently selected and retained because they evoke an emotional reaction that is widely shared across people. They argue that consumers may choose to pass along certain messages that generate emotions not because they enjoy consuming the emotion directly but because the shared emotion enhances their social interactions. For instance, Holt (1995) alludes to the role of shared emotions in consumption practices that involve communing with other consumers and appreciating a consumption experience. In a similar spirit, re-telling stories that tap into certain emotions allows consumers to entertain or sustain the listener's attention and enhance their mutual relationships (Guerin and Miyazaki 2006).

Viral propagation as interpersonal communication

The communication flow metaphor for viral propagation references much of consumer research on diffusion of ideas and messages where the phenomenon is treated as a special case of inter-personal communication transfer of information in a given social system. Viral propagation is regarded as runaway word-of-mouth referrals. The conceptual foundation for this perspective is Katz and Lazarsfeld's (1955) seminal work on the role of personal influence in mediating the direct effects of mass media messages on consumers. According to their two-step flow model, information flows from mass media to individuals (opinion leaders) who then pass it on to others along with their own interpretations. The two-step flow model has inspired the field of diffusion research (Rogers 1962; Gatignon and Robertson 1985) which has informed us of the role of social networks and influential individuals on the adoption and spread of ideas and messages.

Diffusion research has helped to deepen our understanding of viral propagation in three areas. The first area pertains to factors that influence individuals to propagate messages. Viral propagation or word-of-mouth behavior constitutes a form of social exchange (Gatignon and Robertson 1986) which is part of consumers' everyday communicational and relational practices (Carl 2006). Many scholars have pointed to the instrumental value of providing information or exchanging resources in the course of peer-to-peer dissemination of messages such as rumors (Rosnow 1991), urban legends (Donavan *et al.* 1999, 2001), and folklore (Brunvand 1981). For example, Allport and Postman (1945) argue that rumors spread because people seek to understand and simplify complicated events. Rumors, therefore, tend to develop when there is an unsa-tisfied demand for news and disappear when the demand drops or supply becomes adequate (Shibutani 1966). Individuals who are more individualistic or altruistic tend to propagate more messages than others (Ho and Dempsey 2010). In particular, consumers with stronger needs for uniqueness tend to avoid propagating positive word-of-mouth of their possesion as it reduces its uniqueness (Cheema and Kaikati 2010).

The second area is related to the characteristics of certain groups of individuals who are influential in viral propagation. These influential individuals are traditionally conceived as opinion leaders and are considered to exert the most influence during the evaluation stage of adoption (Rogers 1962). Scholars have since developed several nuances of these influential individuals. One leading prototype, for example, is market mavens who possess information about many things and frequently initiate discussions with and respond to requests for information from other consumers (Feick and Price 1987). Unlike traditional opinion leaders who are identified according to product categories and domains (Westbrook and Fornell 1979), market mavens' knowledge and expertise – and therefore influence – are not product-specific. The influential role of selected individuals in viral propagation, however, does not necessarily depend on their knowledge or expertise; it can also be derived from their propensity to engage with other consumers (Goldenberg *et al.* 2009). Through psychological profiling of 656 social media consumers, Yeo (2012) avers that relationally-oriented consumers (who are more likely to propagate an interactive service through their engagement with other consumers) possess distinct consumption goals and personality profiles from traditional innovators (who are more active media users and tend to be early adopters). Taking the concept of opinion leadership further, Gladwell (2000) argues that there is not one group of opinion leaders but three sets of individuals that enable viral propagation: those who provide the message (Mavens), those who spread the message (Connectors), and those who persuade others to act on the message (Salesmen). However, Watts and Dodds (2007) downplay the role of opinion leaders in viral propagation, arguing that large cascades of influence are driven not by influentials but by a critical mass of easily influenced individuals.

The third area relates to the impact of social network characteristics on the flow of information. Two concepts from this area of research are particularly useful for our understanding of viral propagation beyond a small group of individuals: strength of ties and tipping point (or threshold). The strength of social ties among individuals refers to the combination of frequency of contact, emotional intensity, intimacy, and reciprocity between individuals (Granovetter 1973). Diffusion researchers have observed that although strong social ties are more likely to be influential in consumers' decision and behaviors, weak ties play an important bridging function in allowing information to travel across distinct subgroups in the social system (Brown and Reingen 1987; Rogers 1995). For the viral propagation of a message to be sustainable, the average number of persons introduced to the message by each person has to exceed 1: the epidemic tipping point. Once the number of people passing on the message reaches a certain critical mass (which is context-dependent), the bandwagon effect sets in and there is an increased tendency for people to spread the message simply because others have already done so (Granovetter 1978).

Viral propagation as cultural representation

The research reviewed so far has suggested that individuals frequently pass on viral messages because they can emotionally connect to them and this is typically related to some amusing or controversial elements that the messages contain. Further, the relations with others in one's social network have a strong bearing on passing on behaviors because they directly influence the perceived importance and credibility of the message. Studies supporting these conjectures, however, typically make two untenable assumptions: (1) individuals' understandings of the viral message are treated as almost identical throughout a group; and (2) the message is assumed to be minimally transformed as it is virally propagated. In so doing, these studies fail to consider how meanings are created, evolved, and spread among consumers as the message propagates. The cultural representation perspective addresses this oversight by conceiving the viral propagation of a message as a series of cultural representations of that message. It entails the examination of how the virally propagated message is cognized and communicated among participants.

The pioneering work of this perspective is Bartlett's (1932) serial reproduction experiments which demonstrate that as items are passed about from one participant to another, participants develop a conventionalized representation of the items propagated. When asked to pass on seemingly meaningless or ambiguous drawings, participants tend to represent the drawings as something more meaningful. The concept of collective sense-making during viral propagation was further developed by Allport and Postman (1945) who found that as rumors were passed on, they tend to become leveled (made more concise), sharpened (uninteresting details left out), and assimilated (modified for coherence and relevance). We can draw a theoretical parallel with de Certeau's (1984) notion of reading as poaching which describes the way readers take away only elements that seems useful or pleasurable to them. Extending the poaching metaphor from reading to writing, Jenkins (1992) suggests that the way fans select only the most useful and pleasurable meanings from original works in their re-presentations of those works constitutes textual poaching.

The cultural representation approach offers a more contextually-sensitive and consumer-centered alternative to the memetic content analysis of viral messages. This emerging line of research distinguishes itself from meme- and information-centered approaches by emphasizing the salience of consumer participation through examinations of creative activity that occurred around these messages and how they were influenced by social and cultural contexts at the time of production (Burgess 2008; Yeo 2011). In this way, a highly significant quality for going viral is based on how the item becomes elaborated within the group it is popular with. This entails examining what individuals find salient, meaningful, and useful about the item that is being virally propagated (i.e., its social relevance and cultural resonance). For example, Burgess (2008) observed that successful viral videos have textual hooks or key signifiers that become part of the available cultural repertoire of vernacular video via being selected a number of times for repetition.

Viral propagation in the digital age

Over the past few decades, we have witnessed the disruptive changes that the rise of the digital age brings to almost every aspect of our everyday lives. Benkler (2006) describes them as a series of changes in technologies, economic organization, and social practices in a networked information environment which result in better democratic participation and greater scope for cooperative, nonmarket production of information and culture. The popularity and widespread growth of consumer-generated contents and peer-distribution channels that rival those of newspapers and broadcasters illustrate the rise of a new media landscape where traditional media institutions wield little direct control. The dynamics of media production, distribution and consumption have changed significantly with the prevalence of digital technologies. For instance, blogging and citizen journalism have changed the way news is gathered, reported and distributed. Similarly, media-sharing, consumer-ratings, and peer-recommendations facilitated by social media play an increasingly important role in not only influencing the box office success of films but the way they are produced. But more significantly, we are witnessing a significant shift from the conventional broadcast model – a primarily top-down process where professionally produced contents are transmitted to mass audiences – to the viral propagation model: an unprecedented increase in non-commercial, peer production and distribution of media contents from the bottom up.

Communication technologies have been regarded as exerting a pervasive influence on a wide range of human behaviors. Benkler suggests that "different patterns of adoption and use can result in very different social relations that emerge around a technology" (2006, p. 12). In reflecting the implications of the communication technologies for viral propagation, this section focuses on the overlapping dimensions of cultural practices and technological affordances from two directions: macro-to-micro and micro-to-macro. The macro-to-micro perspective illustrates the effects of macro-level technological changes on the practices of individual consumers. Convergence is a macro-level technological characteristic generally thought to be associated with media usage patterns. It is used to describe the ability of different platforms to carry similar kinds of services, or the coming together of consumer devices such as the telephone, the television and personal computers because of digitization. Elaborating on these changes, Jenkins (2006) asserts that the convergence of different media systems – production tools, distribution networks, and services – has helped to enable new forms of consumer participation and collaboration, and harness the collective intelligence of participants. The digitalization of communication technologies is said to enable better communication capacities, namely speed, reach, storage capacity, accuracy, selectivity, interactivity, stimuli richness, and complexity (van Dijk 2006). While digitization and improved communication capacities facilitate better coordination of activities among groups of individuals, they also contribute to increasing uncertainty and a multiplicity of choices for consumers. This multiplicity of choices, in turn, prompts consumers to become more motivated in participating in sharing activities, to cooperate with one another, and to take collective action in the pursuit of authenticating experiences (Arnould and Price 2000).

Rafaeli *et al.* (2005) argue that macro-level changes associated with technological innovations necessarily arise from prior processes on micro, individual, group, and community levels. Examining the influences of technology at the micro-level and exploring how they lead to changes at the macro-level are necessary for a better informed understanding of the role of technology in facilitating viral propagation. The micro-to-macro perspective takes us to the availability of digital platforms and services that leverage consumer participation and aggregate, organize, and coordinate their activities to deliver meaningful collective outcomes. The user interface can play an explicit role in encouraging greater consumer participation by signaling the opportunities to engage in actions that could satisfy both individualistic and relational needs. Technologies have not only made communications more efficient—the ubiquity of consumer devices and platforms that afford dialogue has also expanded the boundaries and limitations of connecting with each other (Duck 2007). Because of the ability to embed or recommend content in blogs and social network sites, many consumers inadvertently propagate messages as a result of their participation in these platforms. Boyd *et al.* (2010) argue that the practices of retweeting – copying and rebroadcasting others' messages – on Twitter are conversational practices that contribute to a shared conversational context.

Viral propagation in the digital context also enables consumer-generated content to receive wide attention without having to satisfy traditional media or cultural gatekeepers. The accessibility and prevalence of digital authoring tools, media-sharing platforms, and social networking sites afford the means for consumers to easily create and share their content and messages. Benkler avers that these tools represent "nonmarket, peer-produced alternative sources of filtration and accreditation in place of the market-based alternatives" (2006, p. 8). He explains that in a nonmarket information environment, consumer contributions that are seen as significant would, after initial vetting from local clusters – communities of interest – increasingly make their way to more visible sites where they obtain widespread attention through peer recommendations. The data management capabilities of social network sites further facilitate the rapid propagation of consumer-generated messages along links established among users, thereby allowing the bandwagon effect to kick in much earlier and lowering the threshold epidemic tipping point for viral propagation. In this way, consumer activities at the micro-level become transformed into collective outcomes at the macro-level. Design and technology help to coordinate individual consumer activities in ways that regularly facilitate the emergence of these meaningful collective outcomes.

Conclusion

Much consumer and marketing research hitherto has been concerned with questions about who, what, and why of viral propagation but not how. Many studies have sought to examine what viral messages do to consumers but few have questioned what consumers do to viral messages. This may be related to the disproportionate focus on the propagation of marketer-generated messages. Despite the unprecedented growth in consumer co-creation activities in recent times, there remains a paucity of consumer research into the viral propagation of consumer-generated messages. Too much research attention has also been placed on the drivers of viral propagation without due consideration for its consequence. Given the elusiveness of viral propagation, the success of a viral campaign is frequently indicated by merely getting a message to go viral (Watts and Peretti 2007). There has been little attempt to understand the attitudinal effect of viral propagation on consumers. While the diffusion literature has informed us of the persuasiveness of opinion leaders in influencing an individual's selection and subsequent propagation of viral messages, we remain uncertain about the persuasiveness of the messages that are propagated. Yeo (2011) found that an individual's decision to view a viral video on others' recommendation bypasses more diligent information processing which is typically associated with long-term attitude change. How can we adapt the elaboration likelihood model of persuasion (Petty and Cacioppo 1981), typically used to research mass media messages, on viral messages?

Although viral propagation has been an age-old phenomenon, its manifestation in the digital age represents a fundamental shift in the way ideas, meanings, and information flow. As mentioned, while the social epidemic metaphor of viral propagation provides an intuitive description of the phenomenon, the epidemiological model of person-to-person message dissemination is not realistic. Much of the research on word-of-mouth communication elaborates on the second stage of Katz and Lazarsfeld's (1955) two-step flow model where the top-down flow of communication from mass media is filtered by one-to-one (or one-to-many) communication. Yet, viral propagation in the digital context largely involves the bottom-up and many-to-many flow of communication. There is also the ontological question of what exactly is being transmitted during viral propagation. Even if we unquestioningly accept memes or information as the items that get propagated, we are still left with the untenable assumption that the item is uniformly perceived by consumers or perfectly replicated during viral propagation. By addressing these issues, the meaning-based, cultural representation approach proposed in this chapter offers a potentially fruitful alternative program of viral propagation research.

Further reading

Bartlett, F.C. (1923) *Psychology and Primitive Culture*, Cambridge: Cambridge University Press. [Forerunner of the cultural representation approach to viral propagation.]

Sperber, D. and Wilson, D. (1995) *Relevance: Communication and Cognition*, 2nd edn., Oxford: Blackwell. [Elaborates on the role of relevance in viral propagation.]

Tarde, G. (1969) *Gabriel Tarde on Communication and Social Influence: Selected Papers*, Chicago: University of Chicago Press. [Conceptual precursor of Katz and Lazarsfeld (1955).]

References

Allport, G.W. and Postman, L.J. (1945) "The Basic Psychology of Rumor," *Transactions of the New York Academy of Sciences*, 8: 61–81.

Arnould, E.J. and Price, L.L. (2000) "Authenticating Acts and Authoritative Performances: Questing for Self and Community," in S. Ratneshwar, D.G. Mick, and C. Huffman (eds), *The Why of Consumption: Contemporary Perspectives on Consumer Motives, Goals, and Desires*, London: Routledge, pp. 140–63.

Bartlett, F.C. (1932) *Remembering: A Study in Experimental and Social Psychology*, Cambridge: Cambridge University Press.

Benkler, Y. (2006) *The Wealth of Networks: How Social Production Transforms Markets and Freedom*, New Haven, CT: Yale University Press.

Blackmore, S.J. (1999) *The Meme Machine*, Oxford: Oxford University Press.

Boyd, D.M., Golder, S. and Lotan, G. (2010) "Tweet, Tweet, Retweet: Conversational Aspects of Retweeting on Twitter," in *Proceedings of the 2010 43rd Hawaii International Conference on System Sciences*, pp. 1–10.

Brown, J.J. and Reingen, P.H. (1987) "Social Ties and Word-of-mouth Referral Behavior," *Journal of Consumer Research*, 14(3): 350–62.

Brown, M.R., Bhadury, R.K. and Pope, N.K.L. (2010) "The Impact of Comedic Violence on Viral Advertising Effectiveness," *Journal of Advertising*, 39(1): 49–66.

Brunvand, J.H. (1981) *The Vanishing Hitchhiker: American Urban Legends and Their Meanings*, New York: Norton.

Burgess, J. (2008) "'All Your Chocolate Rain Are Belong To Us?' Viral Video, YouTube and the Dynamics of Participatory Culture," in G. Lovink and S. Niederer (eds), *Video Vortex Reader: Responses to YouTube*, Amsterdam: Institute of Network Cultures, pp. 101–9.

Carl, W.J. (2006) "What's All the Buzz About? Everyday Communication and the Relational Basis of Word-of-Mouth and Buzz Marketing Practices," *Management Communication Quarterly*, 19(4): 601–34.

Cheema, A. and Kaikati, A.M. (2010) "The Effect of Need for Uniqueness on Word of Mouth," *Journal of Marketing Research*, 47(3): 553–63.

Dawkins, R. (1976) *The Selfish Gene*, Oxford: Oxford University Press.

——(1993) "Viruses of the Mind," in B. Dahlbom (ed.), *Dennett and His Critics: Demystifying Mind*, Oxford: Blackwell, pp. 13–27.

de Certeau, M. (1984) *The Practice of Everyday Life*, Berkeley, CA: University of California Press.

Dennett, D.C. (1995) *Darwin's Dangerous Idea: Evolution and the Meanings of Life*, New York: Simon & Schuster.

Dobele, A. *et al.* (2007) "Why Pass on Viral Messages? Because They Connect Emotionally," *Business Horizons*, 50(4): 291–304.

Donavan, D.T., Mowen, J.C. and Chakraborty, G. (1999) "Urban Legends: The Word-Of-Mouth Communication of Morality Through Negative Story Content," *Marketing Letters*, 10(1): 23–35.

——(2001) "Urban Legends: Diffusion Processes and the Exchange of Resources," *Journal of Consumer Marketing*, 18(6): 521–33.

Duck, S. (2007) *Human Relationships*, London: Sage.

Feick, L.F. and Price, L.L. (1987) "The Market Maven: A Diffuser of Marketplace Information," *The Journal of Marketing*, 51(1): 83–97.

Festinger, L. (1957) *A Theory of Cognitive Dissonance*, Chicago: Row, Peterson, and Company.

Gatignon, H. and Robertson, T.S. (1985) "A Propositional Inventory for New Diffusion Research," *Journal of Consumer Research*, 11(4): 849–67.

——(1986) "An Exchange Theory Model of Interpersonal Communication," in R.J. Lutz (ed.), *Advances in Consumer Research*, Provo, UT: Association for Consumer Research, pp. 534–8.

Gladwell, M. (2000) *The Tipping Point: How Little Things Can Make a Big Difference*, New York: Little, Brown, and Company.

Golan, G.J. and Zaidner, L. (2008) "Creative Strategies in Viral Advertising: An Application of Taylor's Six-Segment Message Strategy Wheel," *Journal of Computer-Mediated Communication*, 13(4): 959–72.

Goldenberg, J. *et al.* (2009) "The Role of Hubs in the Adoption Process," *Journal of Marketing*, 73(2): 1–13.

Goodenough, O.R. and Dawkins, R. (1994) "The "St Jude" Mind Virus," *Nature*, 371(6492): 23–4.

Granovetter, M.S. (1973) "The Strength of Weak Ties," *American Journal of Sociology*, 78(6): 1360–80.

——(1978) "Threshold Models of Collective Behavior," *American Journal of Sociology*, 83(6): 1420–43.

Guerin, B. and Miyazaki, Y. (2006) "Analyzing Rumors, Gossip, and Urban Legends Through Their Conversational Properties," *The Psychological Record*, 56(1): 23–33.

Harber, K.D. and Cohen, D.J. (2005) "The Emotional Broadcaster Theory of Social Sharing," *Journal of Language and Social Psychology*, 24(4): 382–400.

Heath, C. (1996) "Do People Prefer to Pass Along Good or Bad News? Valence and Relevance of News as Predictors of Transmission Propensity," *Organizational Behavior and Human Decision Processes*, 68(2): 79–94.

Heath, C., Bell, C. and Sternberg, E. (2001) "Emotional Selection in Memes: The Case of Urban Legends," *Journal of Personality and Social Psychology*, 81(6): 1028–41.

Ho, J.Y.C. and Dempsey, M. (2010) "Viral Marketing: Motivations to Forward Online Content," *Journal of Business Research*, 63(9–10): 1000–6.

Holt, D.B. (1995) "How Consumers Consume: A Typology of Consumption Practices," *Journal of Consumer Research*, 22(1): 1–16.

Howard, D.J. and Gengler, C. (2001) "Emotional Contagion Effects on Product Attitudes," *Journal of Consumer Research*, 28(2): 189–201.

Jenkins, H. (1992) *Textual Poachers: Television Fans and Participatory Culture*, New York: Routledge.

——(2006) *Convergence Culture: Where Old and New Media Collide*, New York: New York University Press.

Katz, E. and Lazarsfeld, P.F. (1955) *Personal Influence: The Part Played by People in the Flow of Mass Communications*, New York: Free Press.

Lazarsfeld, P.F., Berelson, B. and Gaudet, H. (1944) *The People's Choice: How the Voter Makes up His Mind in a Presidential Campaign*, New York: Duell, Sloan and Pearce.

Lynch, A. (1996) *Thought Contagion: How Belief Spreads Through Society*, New York: Basic Books.

Petty, R.E. and Cacioppo, J.T. (1981) *Attitudes and Persuasion: Classic and Contemporary Approaches*, Dubuque, IA: William Brown.

Phelps, J.E. *et al.* (2004) "Viral Marketing or Electronic Word-Of-Mouth Advertising: Examining Consumer Responses and Motivations to Pass along Email," *Journal of Advertising Research*, 44(4): 333–48.

Porter, L. and Golan, G.J. (2006) "From Subservient Chickens to Brawny Men: A Comparison of Viral Advertising to Television Advertising," *Journal of Interactive Advertising*, 6(2): 30–8.

Prasad, J. (1935) "The Psychology of Rumour: A Study Relating to the Great Indian Earthquake of 1934," *British Journal of Psychology*, 26(1): 1–15.

Rafaeli, S., Raban, D. and Kalman, Y. (2005) "Social Cognition Online," in Y. Amichai-Hamburger (ed.), *The Social Net: Understanding Human Behavior in Cyberspace*, New York: Oxford University Press, pp. 57–90.

Rimé, B. (2009) "Emotion Elicits the Social Sharing of Emotion: Theory and Empirical Review," *Emotion Review*, 1(1): 60–85.

Rogers, E.M. (1962) *Diffusion of Innovations*, New York: Free Press.

——(1995) *Diffusion of Innovations*, 4th edn, New York: Free Press.

Rosnow, R.L. (1991) "Inside Rumor: A Personal Journey," *American Psychologist*, 46(5): 484–96.

Shibutani, T. (1966) *Improvised News: A Sociological Study of Rumor*, Oxford: Bobbs-Merrill.

Southgate, D., Westoby, N. and Page, G. (2010) "Creative Determinants of Viral Video Viewing," *International Journal of Advertising*, 29(3): 349–68.

Sperber, D. (1996) *Explaining Culture: A Naturalistic Approach*, Oxford: Blackwell.

Tapscott, D. (2009) *Grown Up Digital: How the Net Generation Is Changing Your World*, New York: McGraw-Hill.

Taylor, R.E. (1999) "A Six-Segment Message Strategy Wheel," *Journal of Advertising Research*, 39(6): 7–17.

van Dijk, J. (2006) *The Network Society: Social Aspects of New Media*, London: Sage.

Watts, D.J. and Dodds, P.S. (2007) "Influentials, Networks, and Public Opinion Formation," *Journal of Consumer Research*, 34(4): 441–58.

Watts, D.J. and Peretti, J. (2007) "Viral Marketing for the Real World," *Harvard Business Review*, available at: http://research.microsoft.com/apps/pubs/default.aspx?id=164570.

Westbrook, R.A. and Fornell, C. (1979) "Patterns of Information Source Usage among Durable Goods Buyers," *Journal of Marketing Research*, 16(3): 303–12.

Yeo, T.E.D. (2011) "Conversations Sell: How Dialogical Judgments and Goals Underpin the Success of Viral Videos," in D.W. Dahl, G.V. Johar, and S.M.J. van Osselaer (eds), *Advances in Consumer Research*, vol. 38, Duluth, MN: Association for Consumer Research.

——(2012) "Social-Media Early Adopters Don't Count: How to Seed Participation in Interactive Campaigns by Psychological Profiling of Digital Consumers," *Journal of Advertising Research*, 52(3): 297–308.

25

DIGITAL FANDOM

Mediation, remediation, and demediation of fan practices

Clinton D. Lanier, Jr. and Aubrey R. Fowler III

Keywords

Fan fiction, Fan wikis, Machinima, User-Generated content, Fandom, Fans

It has been argued that fans make explicit what everyone else does implicitly (Booth 2010). That is, fans interpret the world around them, communicate these meanings with others, and produce their own meanings based on those parts of the world that they like most (Fiske 1989). While all of us do this to various degrees, fans do so consciously, openly, and overtly (Sandvoss 2005). Also, fans actively appropriate the objects of culture in this process and rework them to further their interests in what has been referred to as a form of participatory culture (Jenkins 2006a). Fans do not merely consume culture; they creatively (re)produce culture, thus contributing directly to societal discourse. While some fan scholars have emphasized fan practices as a form of rebellion (e.g., Lewis 1992; Jenson 1992; Jenkins 1992b), others point out that this is a deeply affective process, even for anti-fans (Grossberg 1992; Johnson 2007; Sandvoss 2005). For most, being a fan is ultimately a form of hedonic experience (Hirschman and Holbrook 1982). Even though many fans devote a considerable amount of time, effort, and energy into their respective fandoms, it is usually a labor of love (Smith *et al.* 2007).

Nowhere is the rebellious, affective, and creative nature of fans more prevalent than in the digital realm. Fan activities and practices have exploded with the digital revolution (Negroponte 1995). Digital technology, including the Internet, has vastly increased the tools and spaces for fan creation, as well as the amount of information available to fans and its means of its distribution. In addition, fans tend to be early adopters of technology and have been quick to transition to and utilize digital media (Coppa 2006). For example, fans created Usenet newsgroups, set up BBS and Listserv forums, and established archives of fan-based creations almost as quickly as those tools appeared. Fans now utilize blogs, wikis, and social networking sites to engage in various forms of fan practices, including music/movie creation, online video gaming, and fantasy football (Jenkins 2006b; Kozinets 2007; Pearson 2010).

One thing that makes digital fandom difficult to study is that digital technology functions simultaneously as a tool (e.g., Microsoft Word), an object (e.g., Fan Fiction), and a medium (e.g., www.fanfiction.net) (Stein 2006). Fans produce, distribute, consume, and interact all within the same digital space. In addition, while this technology provides increasing access to fandom, in a sense making it more mainstream and real, it has also made it more virtual. Not only have the objects of fandoms been digitized, but the fans themselves have become virtual beings in this digital landscape (Denegri-Knott and Molesworth 2010). This shift, while seemingly innocuous, has led to deeper changes in the ontological and epistemological conditions of fandom. As fandom has become more mediated, fan practices and the broader socio-cultural structures in which they operate have become more remediated (i.e., the distinctions between practices break down), which in turn has caused them to become and more demediated (i.e., these transformed practices become the new real). As ardent *Star Trek* fans, the authors are still amazed at Gene Roddenberry's foresight that replication of every aspect of life, including ourselves, would change the very nature of existence. Perhaps we are not quite at that stage, but recent advances in the digital realm and their creative utilization by fans suggest that it is important to examine and understand the current state of affairs of digital fandom and its broader implications.

Defining fandom

Before we examine digital fandom, it is important to step back and address the general nature of fans and fandom (i.e., fan practices regarding particular cultural objects) in order to provide the context for this newer manifestation. "Fan" encompasses a broad category of individuals that includes sports, music, media, and celebrity fans, to name a few (Harris 1998; Jenkins 1992b; Sandvoss 2005). Fans display an intense interest, affection, and attachment for the object of their fandom and are distinguished from non-fans through their respect, admiration, desire, and commitment (Fiske 1989; Jenson 1992; Lewis 1992). (In keeping with the fan lexicon, we will broadly refer to these objects as texts, since they are conceived as primarily carriers of meaning.) Fans, though, are not a homogeneous group, but encompass various types of individuals who differ in their forms of participation and levels of engagement (Hills 2002; Jenkins 2006b; Sandvoss 2005). Also, while we usually think of fans in terms of specific cultural phenomena, researchers argue that being a fan is a much deeper process that underlies the way in which we create meaning, attach value, and make sense of our lived experience (Jenson 1992).

In spite of the broader applicability of fandom, "first-wave" fan scholars (Grey *et al.* 2007) argue that fandom is directed primarily towards the objects of popular culture (e.g., rock music, movies, and sports) (Fiske 1989; Lewis 1992; Storey 2001) – as opposed to the objects of high culture (e.g., classical music, fine art, and performing arts) (Arnold 1932) – and represents a unique form of consumption (Jenkins 1992b). Popular culture, though, does not exist on its own accord, but comes into being through the interactions of consumers with the products of mass culture (i.e., offerings that are mass produced for mass consumption) (Storey 2001). This process involves not merely the selection and rejection of specific mass mediated offerings, but also the productive and meaningful use of these offerings as creative resources (Fiske 1989; Jenkins 1992a). While many of these early scholars associate fans with audiences (Lewis 1992; Abercrombie and Longhurst 1998; Harris 1998), others have criticized this approach because it privileges the text and denies the active nature of fandom, which actually elevates the mass media text to the status of popular culture (Fiske 1989; Jenkins 1992b; Radway 1988).

Hence, fandom must be understood not simply as passive consumption, but also as active production (Fiske 1992). It is important to note that production is not necessarily the creation of an artifact, but encompasses the creation of value and meaning. Ultimately, fans are producers of cultural meanings (Jenkins 1992b). These meanings often go beyond the objects of mass culture as they are reworked and refashioned by fans to articulate concerns and interests that usually go unvoiced in the original text and the dominant media (Fiske 1989). For these first-wave scholars, the relationship between fans and the original text is primarily one of resistance (Bacon-Smith 1992; Jenkins 1992a). Fans typically choose certain texts from mass culture because there is some degree of affinity and compatibility between the meanings of the texts and fans' lived experience (Jenkins 1992b). At the same time, there is usually a certain degree of frustration and antagonism with these popular texts because as cultural commodities, there are other forces (e.g., economic, social, and cultural) that directly affect their meanings, driving them towards the meanings of dominant culture and leaving out subordinate and alternative voices (Fiske 1992; Jenkins 1992b; Jenson 1992). As a result, fans often move beyond the original text and produce their own texts that not only poach from the original, but nomadically draw upon other cultural commodities to construct deeper and relevant meanings for the fan communities (Hills 2002).

The productive nature of fans, though, is not enough to define fandom because this type of behavior is also prevalent among other groups (Grossberg 1992; Storey 2001). For first-wave fandom research, what makes fandom distinct is the socio-cultural nature of this production and its relationship to other forms of cultural creations. Jenkins (1992b) proposes a more specific conceptualization of fandom based on four dimensions. First, fandom is based on a distinctive mode of reception. In particular, fans refuse to maintain and openly resist a separation or critical distance between themselves and the products of popular culture. This directly challenges dominant culture, which needs to maintain the division of text and reader in order for the status quo to possess and defend their economic or cultural capital (Fiske 1989; Jenson 1992). Second, fandom constitutes a particular interpretive community (Jenkins 1992a). While all consumers actively engage in semiotic production (i.e., the production of meaning) (Grossberg 1992), fans also engage in enunciative production (i.e., the social communication and interpretation of meaning) (Fiske 1992). That is, fans share and debate their co-created meanings with others who possess a similar interest in the particular cultural text (Bacon-Smith 1992; Kozinets 2001). Third, fandom constitutes a particular art world (Jenkins 1992b). Although fandom can be viewed in terms of its relation to the production, distribution, and consumption of the commodities of popular culture, it also constitutes a creative world of its own that moves beyond simply consuming pre-existing texts and engages in the production, distribution, and consumption of its own texts (Fiske 1992). Fourth, fandom constitutes an alternative social community (Jenkins 1992b). Having been denied access to official economic and cultural capital, fandom establishes a community that is not based on the traditional markers of status and success, but on what fans directly and openly contribute to the community (Kozinets 2001).

In spite of the detailed explanation of fandom by these early scholars, others argue that this narrow focus on resistance, community, and textual production does not account for many individuals who also consider themselves to be fans, but who do not fit this model (Hills 2002; Scodari 2003; Gray et al. 2007). For instance, models of resistance fail to explain adequately the affective pleasure that fans find in a particular text (Sandvoss 2005). Additionally, if the ultimate goal of fandom is to subvert the status quo, it would make more sense for fans to attack more mainstream texts rather than the esoteric ones that seem to attract their attention. As such, "second-wave" fandom scholars argue that the resistance model not only fails to explain a large majority of mainstream fans, many of whom consume cultural texts individually and produce no fannish creations, but it also fails to hold up under empirical scrutiny of the so-called "elite" fans (Jancovich 2002; Sandvoss 2005; Scodari 2003). Instead, these scholars argue that fan practices are embedded in the economic, social, and cultural structures of society and tend to reproduce, rather than resist, these hierarchical structures, even within fandoms (Hills 2002).

The fact that producers of popular cultural texts still vehemently oppose certain fan practices and attempt to tame these unruly consumers is at least partial evidence that fandom is not one seamlessly integrated into the socio-cultural order (Lothian 2009; Tushnet 2007; Walliss 2010). Whereas first-wave scholars may have been overly functional (Grey *et al.* 2007), second-wave scholars seem to be overly structural. Jenkins (2006a, p. 136) attempts to strike a balance between these two waves of fan research by suggesting that it is wrong to perceive of fans "as either totally autonomous from or totally vulnerable to the culture industries … The interactive audience is more than a marketing concept and less than a semiotic democracy." All fans, even the more mainstream ones, actively negotiate the relationship with their chosen cultural texts and its producers through the constant interpretation, co-creation, and maintenance of those texts (Fiske 1989; Hills 2002; Russo 2009).

This deeper philosophical and meta-theoretical debate among fan scholars has opened the door for "third-wave" fandom research, which now focuses on a broader range of fans and cultural texts, including political, academic, and high culture fandoms (Gray *et al.* 2007). From a micro-level perspective, research has examined the intra-personal pleasures and motivations of fans (Lanier and Schau 2007), as well as issues of identity and personal performance (Sandvoss 2005; Tatum 2009). From a macro-level perspective, research has examined how fans' readings, tastes, and practices are constitutive of the social, cultural, and economic structures in which they are practiced (Harrington and Bielby 2005; Muñiz and Schau 2005; Soukup 2006). While some scholars argue that fandom can shed important light on the economics of modernity (Grey *et al.* 2007), a new wave of scholarship, driven especially by the examination of digital manifestations of fandom, suggests a different economic model is beginning to emerge that moves beyond designations of production and consumption and incorporates ideas from the gift economy and theories of the commons (Booth 2010; Lothian 2009; Pearson 2010).

Digital fandom

Since the advent of modern fandom, fannish activities and practices have expanded greatly and have become, to a certain extent, part of mainstream culture (Coppa 2006; Grey *et al.* 2007; Jenkins 1992b). Nowhere is this more prevalent than in the digital world (Negroponte 1995). The digitization of many products has affected practically all types of fandoms, from sports (e.g., fantasy football), to music (e.g., MP3s and remixes), to media (e.g., fan videos). While some analog fan practices have transferred to the digital realm relatively unchanged (e.g., traditional fan fiction), other fan practices are clearly the result of this new digital medium (e.g., machinima) (Jones 2006). In this section, we examine how some digital fan practices, specifically in the realm of media fandom, have fundamentally altered or extended the ways in which fandom operates. As we have mentioned, what makes this task difficult, yet also revealing, is that digital technology functions in multiple ways (e.g., tool, object, and medium) (Booth 2010; Stein 2006). Unlike in the analog realm where these functions are typically separate, the digital realm not only blurs the distinctions within its own nature, but also those practices that utilize this new technology.

What then is digital fandom? Basically, it is the use of digital technology to engage in fannish activities and practices with respect to specific cultural texts. It is important to note that digital fandom does not constitute a distinct type of fandom such as sports, music, or media fandoms, but instead refers to fannish behavior as mediated through digital technology. While we agree with Booth (2010) that digital technology does not specifically determine fan practices, we argue that it has allowed fan practices to change in ways that are fundamentally different than those within the analog realm. Despite the hype over the digital revolution and the temptation to view these changes positively (Negroponte 1995), both fans and scholars view this technology somewhat ambivalently by arguing that digital fandom is both empowering and disempowering, personal and impersonal, and inclusive and exclusive (e.g., Busse and Hellekson 2006; Jenkins

2006b; Pearson 2010). For example, whereas the Internet has opened up fandoms to a much broader group of people and has allowed for the wider dissemination of fannish texts, it has also distanced fans from each other by allowing them to interact anonymously and has even led to the subversion of fan texts by non-fans and members of other fandoms (Booth 2010; Hadas 2009; Russo 2009). Others have argued from a decidedly negative perspective that digital technology has led to the commodification of fandom itself by various media producers and the exploitation of fan labor purely for economic gain (Lothian 2009; Pearson 2010; Shefrin 2004).

Digital fandom is thus a complex phenomenon encompassing a variety of practices, cooperative and competitive interests, and socio-cultural meanings (Booth 2010). In addition, digital fandom encompasses both offline and online behavior, thus making clear distinctions between practices, participants, and perceptions difficult. As a result of this complexity, digital fandom, like fandom in general, resists a comprehensive definition and is often understood in terms of the perspectives of particular fan cultures (Grey *et al.* 2007; Hills 2002). Two specific perspectives of digital fandom are presented next that capture the traditional fandom dichotomy.

Producer-driven digital fandom

The expansion of multifunctional digital media has led to a form of convergence culture in which media content flows across multiple platforms and where consumers are encouraged to seek out and make connections among the various types of information across these platforms (Jenkins 2006a). One impact of convergence culture on fandom is that media producers are now engaging in transmedia storytelling in which narratives unfold across multiple media platforms. Because of the ease of producing more information than any one fan can assimilate, digital fandom is more often a collective, though somewhat impersonal, process in which fans come together to create a richer experience (Busse and Hellekson 2006). For example, fans of *The Matrix* have to cull information across three movies, an animated series, comics, and video games in order to make sense of the broader text (Booth 2010). While many fans enjoy this added depth and interactivity with their favorite texts, some scholars worry that the utilization of digital technology increases the control of producers over consumers by assimilating fans even deeper into the product and shifting interpretive power to producers (Pearson 2010).

One way that fans have responded to the narrative complexity of these transmediated texts is to develop fan-based wikis (i.e., online databases that allow for the communal creation and editing of virtually infinite content that is hyperlinked as separate web pages) (Booth 2010; Kozinets 2007; Mittell 2009). According to Booth (2010, p. 89), in order to construct these wikis, "fans extract narrative elements from an extant media object, create a separate wiki-page for each one, and then rewrite that narrative in a different form by linking wiki-pages via hyperlinks." Examples of popular fan-based wikis include Lostpedia (*Lost* TV show), Harrypotter.wikia (*Harry Potter*), and Wookieepedia (*Star Wars*). On a basic level, fan-based wikis serve as a form of collective intelligence embodied in a complex archive that provides fans access to factual, cross-referenced data (Busse and Hellekson 2006; Jenkins 2006a). On a more complex level, these wikis move beyond mere repositories of information and challenge our deeper understanding of narrative, authorship, and readership. Whereas most fan-based narratives (e.g., fan fiction), especially analog versions, follow traditional narrative forms (Jenkins 1992b; Kaplan 2006;Pugh 2005), wikis separate the elements of narrative, thus dissolving the "chrono-logic" of the media text and detaching the story from its discourse (Booth 2010). Fans collectively rewrite the media text by deconstructing all of its forms into their constituent parts and then hyperlinking these parts to each other in an infinite array of spatial connections (Booth 2010; Mittell 2009). This allows them to explore narrative possibilities through rereading and reconstructing the story as a multi-authored fan discourse.

Although wikis provide for a fan-centric reading and writing of the media text, the broader social and cultural implications of this practice remain unclear. While most traditional forms of fandom rely on the inter-textual connections among divergent texts, thus causing fandoms to expand outward beyond the producer-driven text (Jenkins 1992b), practices such as fan-based wikis rely on intra-textual connections among transmediated texts that cause the fandom to contract inwards (Booth 2010). These forms of fandoms are not necessarily about creating something "new," but about re-producing something that already exists. While fans can re-produce these texts via wikis in almost infinite ways, they are still relatively confined to the producer-based transmediated stories. Whereas first-wave theorists may view this new digital manifestation of fandom negatively (i.e., reasserting the power of producers), second- and third-wave scholars may view this positively (i.e., active negotiation between producers and consumers). It is important to note that fan-based wikis are not limited to the official canon surrounding the media text or the interpretive authority of the official producers, but also include spaces for unauthorized and non-canonical content (e.g., spoilers, vids, and speculative fan fiction) (Kozinets 2007; Mittell 2009). The degree to which this content is being utilized in the constructions of new texts and the expansion of fandoms, though, is still unclear.

In addition to transmedia storytelling, media producers are also attempting to harness the creative and interpretive power of fans by eliciting user-generated content (i.e., fan-produced texts utilizing aspects of the official media texts) for promotional purposes (Jenkins 2006a; Russo 2009; Pearson 2010). Most forms of user-generated content exist in a quasi-legal limbo between transformative works and copyright infringement (Jenkins 1992b; Lothian 2009; Walliss 2010) and have received a mixed reception from media producers – some tolerate it up to a point while others vigorously attempt to curtail it (Shefrin 2004). Knowing that there is no way for them to fully control these activities, producers have utilized various digital technologies to appropriate these forms of fannish texts and to benefit from these creations (Russo 2009). For example, in 2007, the producers of the new *Battlestar Galactica* (BSG) television series (Sci-Fi 2004–9) invited fans to be part of the BSG experience by making a short tribute film using digital clips provided by the producers. The films, particularly those that followed the rules of the contest, were judged for content and quality and the winner was aired on TV (Pearson 2010; Russo 2009). Although many fans participated in the contest with the hope of having their fan activities legitimized by the media producers, some saw this as a means of capitalizing on free fan labor while reigning in fan creativity that was at odds with the brand (Lothian 2009).

Going even further, some fan-savvy producers are even engaging fans in the creative process of the original media texts through the much more direct and efficient communicative opportunities present in the digital world (Shefrin 2004). Not only are producers now commenting directly about fan interpretations on fan websites, there is some speculation that certain producers may even be taking cues for future episodes of a television program from various fan forums and discussion groups (Jenkins 2006a). More recently, various directors and producers have gone directly to fans, especially to "super" fans like Harry Knowles at Aint-It-Cool-News. com, not just to promote their projects, but to enlist their assistance in getting those projects off the ground (Shefrin 2004). For example, producer and director Peter Jackson directly addressed various fan concerns about his adaptation of the *Lord of the Rings* trilogy. Since then, other directors like Sylvester Stallone, Joss Whedon, and John Favreau have directly solicited input from fans as well. Such behavior on the producer side of the equation seems to suggest that for transmedia storytelling to truly be successful, it must enlist, engage, and entangle fans within the storytelling process itself, thus creating a more positive, constructive relationship between producers and consumers (Booth 2010; Jenkins 2004; Shefrin 2004).

Consumer-driven digital fandoms

Despite the social and cultural embeddedness of fans and fandoms emphasized in second- and third-wave research, fannish interpretive and creative practices have always been somewhat beyond the control of media producers (Fiske 1992). One media fan practice that has received considerable attention in the academic literature is the writing of fan fiction (e.g., original, though unauthorized, stories written by fans that utilize elements of an official media text) (Busse and Hellekson 2006; Jenkins 1992b; Pugh 2005). Fan fiction usually extends or even contradicts the official media text, thus offering fans a space to explore issues that are personally relevant (Jenkins 1992b). Being one of the older forms of fannish practices, fan fiction made the transition to digital media quite early and has a prominent presence on the Internet. While many aspects of online fan fiction mirror those in the analog world, there are some digital practices that seem to be fundamentally different in nature. One of these is the posting of fan fiction to blogs.

While blogs can be used for a variety of purposes (see Chapter 5 by Arsel and Zhao in this volume), some fans utilize them specifically as an outlet for their fan fiction (Booth 2010; Cooper 2007; Stein 2006). Fan authors usually post one chapter (or less) at a time on their blog, and other fans provide comments and feedback on the story. This general process is not new to fan fiction, and actually represents the way that many fan fiction stories have been written from the very beginning of the practice (Busse and Hellekson 2006). What is new in this digital realm is that the story and the criticism are no longer spatially or temporally separate, but are fully integrated in the blog (Booth 2010). While this may appear as a technicality, it subtly alters the ontological and epistemological nature of this particular fannish practice and experience.

There are two aspects of this form of digital fandom that make it a distinct fannish practice. First, both the post and the comments make up a single text on the blog. Readers' comments do not appear on a separate page (as they do on most fan fiction websites), but become part of the text as the reader switches to writer. In addition, this text is not stable, but is constantly in flux as new comments alter the text. Thus, blog fan fiction is a dynamic text that is not composed by a single author, but is the result of everyone who writes on the blog. The resulting fan fiction, given the nature of the blog, becomes a multi-layered and multi-authored text that is forever open (Booth 2010; Cooper 2007; Stein 2006). Second, the original author can also post comments on the blog. The author can either make comments about the post, thus turning the author into a reader, or s/he can comment about the comments, thus putting the author on the same plane as the reader (Booth 2010). As a result of these two conditions, and the additional fact that all participants are typically anonymous, the distinction between writer and reader becomes increasingly problematic in this digital space (Cooper 2007). Although the literature on fandom often talks about consumer-as-producer (Bruns 2008), it still presents these designations as separate states and activities. The mediated nature of digital fandom challenges these notions and their ontological distinctiveness and suggests that these activities become increasingly blurred in some digital fannish practices (Hills 2002).

A related practice of digital fandom is the development of online character profiles by fans on social networking sites (SNS), though this is sometimes done on blogs (Booth 2010; Jenkins 2006b; Stein 2006). For example, fans can create a character profile of Captain Kirk, Harry Potter, or even Darth Vader, and then interact with others on SNS as this particular character. While fan fiction allows fans to identify *with* certain characters and have these characters address issues that are important to the fans, character profiles on SNS allow fans to identify *as* the character and to roleplay these issues directly (Booth 2010). What makes this process even more dramatic is that the distinction between the fictional and the real, as well as the virtual and the actual, begin to break down (Stein 2006). As real people become virtual on social networking sites, fictional characters become actual as they interact with others within the same mediated context. The result is an "interreal" character persona, which exists neither wholly online, nor entirely in the real world (Booth 2010). As more and more people digitize themselves (usually their ideal selves) into existence on the Internet through the creation of virtual identities, these identities begin to take on a life of their own apart from those who created them (Suden 2003). In addition, through the creation of character profiles, fans are able to combine their own virtual identities with the virtual identities of media characters, thus allowing them to be two personas at once (Booth 2010). Although traditional fandom typically frowns on fannish practices that interject the fan into the media text (Jenkins 1992b), digital fandom not only allows, but even encourages, fans to integrate themselves more fully into the text through these virtual personas. As a result of this form of remediation, these new practices further challenge the separation of fan and media text, thus calling into question the very nature of the text itself.

One last digital fandom practice of note is the creation of fan movies. While fan films have been around since the beginning of media fandom, the digital revolution has opened up vast possibilities for fan filmmaking (Jenkins 2004; Walliss 2010; Young 2008). Digital technology now allows fans to create relatively professional-looking films at a fraction of the costs faced by major studios. In fact, digital editing is much simpler than film editing, and digital software now allows for the incorporation of sophisticated special effects and much cleaner productions (Jenkins 2004). The quality of fan films has grown so high and the ease by which fans can distribute their films through the Internet have caused media producers to shift their concerns from issues of copyright infringement to fears of direct competition (Walliss 2010). What this form of digital fandom reveals is that fannish practices can now rival the production value of commercial media texts (Young 2008). In a somewhat ironic twist, professional filmmakers are beginning to utilize fan filmmaking practices in the production of commercial films (Jenkins 2004).

An interesting offshoot of digital fan filmmaking is machinima (Jones 2006; Newman 2008; Wirman 2009). Machinima, which is the combination of the words machine and cinema, is a form of animated filmmaking that utilizes the core software of video games to produce a 3D movie (Marino 2001). Rather than arising from the desire to make films, machinima resulted from gamers' desires to modify the source code of the games. As Jones (2006, p. 266) writes, "The ability to freely play with the medium presents a challenge to previous notions of how audiences conventionally behave. The authorial shift that occurs between gamers and designers differentiates it from other traditional media." More specifically, whereas other forms of fannish practices leave the original text intact, machinima actually alters the text itself. In marketing terms, this authorial shift is not from consumer to consumer-as-producer as it is in other fannish practices, but from consumer to producer. Digital fandom, in the case of machinima, moves beyond models of co-creation and allows for pure production that utilizes the media text simply as a resource in the creative process (Jones 2006; Young 2008; Walliss 2010). In this sense, the mediation of video games becomes demediated in machinima as a work of art in own right.

Conclusion

The breakdown of distinctions among producer, consumer, and product in the realm of digital fandom has led many fan scholars to suggest that we are witnessing the birth of a new economic model (Booth 2010; Jenkins 2006a; Pearson 2010). While it may be somewhat of a stretch to say that the economics of the future (à la *Star Trek*) will be based on a model of digital fandom, it has been shown that fannish practices can shed light on deeper economic practices (Grey *et al.* 2007). For instance, Pearson (2010) argues that the new digital economy is composed not simply of a market economy, but also of a gift economy (Belk 2010). It is a market economy because it still contains and is largely controlled by commercial interests, but it is also a gift economy that focuses on sharing and communal interests. For example, the Internet can be understood as both a repository of information which is bought and sold and as a means for social interaction which is essentially free (Booth 2010). Digital fandom overtly reveals the link between these two through the communal interaction of a commercial text.

The problem with this view of the new economic model is that it still relies on old definitions of production, consumption, and product, and also the traditional assumption that consumption implies destruction (Booth 2010; Firat and Venkatesh 1995). Digital products are inherently different from analog products in that they are infinitely reproducible, alterable, and sharable. The ontological status of digital products not only challenges our idea of consumption, but also of production in terms of who is actually in control of the creation and distribution of the product. Based on the idea of a nondepletable resource that is shared by a group, the new economy is considered a form of digital commons in which both ownership and access of information and ideas are continually negotiated by the group for communal purposes (Booth 2010; Lothian 2009; Pearson 2010). Digital fandom shows how fan texts not only exist as both commodities and gifts, but also how they transcend both forms as the nature of each is transformed through digital mediation, remediation, and demediation (Booth 2010).

Although some fan scholars fear that this new digital economy gives corporations more power and control over fannish practices (Lothian 2009; Russo 2009; Pearson 2010), others claim that this view is based on the assumptions of traditional market-based economies and does not take into account the ontological and epistemological shifts brought about by the digital economy (Booth 2010; Jenkins 2006a; Jones 2006). This does not mean that this new economy is free of problems. In fact, the intersection of fandom and the digital economy not only forces us to rethink traditional marketing concepts like production, consumption, and product, but also socio-cultural concepts such as community, agency, and identity (Pearson 2010). For example, does the *mediated* nature of fan interactions on the Internet constitute fan communities? While some fans reveal their true identities, many others maintain their anonymity through screen names and icons that create a barrier between their fannish activities and everyday lives. In addition, does the *remediation* of media texts through fan-based wikis constitute a new form of agency or does it limit fans' freedom to freely interpret and move beyond these texts? Although the addition of spoilers and some ancillary content allow for fan speculation, it is not yet clear how the vast amount of information on the web, especially in the form of transmediated storytelling, has affected fans' ability to rise above and reimagine their favorite texts to fit their own particular needs and wants. Lastly, does the *demediation* of factual and fictional personas on social networking sites undermine or enhance people's identities? While the real becomes virtual and the virtual becomes real in the digital economy, it is important to understand what happens to fans as they write themselves out of their worlds and into the media texts.

The effects of the digital economy, especially through mediation, remediation, and demediation, on both the market and gift economies, as well as on the socio-cultural practices of fandoms, are still relatively unknown. Although third-wave fandom research has opened up fan research to these broader issues, it still operates primarily under the assumption that fandom is a manifestation of socio-cultural structures rather than as a force that constitutes them. As a result, a fourth wave of fandom research, especially studies that focuses on digital fandom, is needed to shed light on the broader ontological and epistemological changes to our economic, social, and cultural structures through fan practices. In order to do this, it will need to bridge the gap between empirical and theoretical research and focus on fandom not merely as an interesting descriptive phenomenon, but as a fundamental expression of what it means to be human.

Further reading

Booth, P. (2010) *Digital Fandom*, New York: Peter Lang Publishing. [Provides an extensive overview of digital fandom, suggesting how an exploration of digital fandom will further the understanding of the new media environment.]

Gray, J., Sandvoss, C. and Harrington, C.L. (2007) *Fandom: Identities and Communities in a Mediated World*, New York: New York University Press. [Discusses the nature of fans, fan communities, and various fandoms in relation to contemporary media culture.]

Hellekson, K. and Busse, K. (2006) *Fan Fiction and Fan Communities in the Age of the Internet*, Jefferson, NC: McFarland & Company, Inc. [Addresses multiple dimensions of fan fiction including its history, fan fiction communities, and its future in a digital world.]

Hills, M. (2002) *Fan Cultures*, London: Routledge. [Provides an overview of fans and fan theories, focusing on the contradictions within fandom and concluding with an assessment of how new media may create new types of fandom.]

Jenkins, H. (2006) *Convergence Culture: Where Old and New Media Collide*, New York: New York University Press. [Examines how the convergence of multiple media platforms has transformed contemporary culture and how consumers and producers have addressed these changes.]

References

Abercrombie, N. and Longhurst, B. (1998) *Audiences: A Sociological Theory of Performance and Imagination*, London: Sage.

Arnold, M. (1932) *Culture and Anarchy*, London: Cambridge University Press.

Bacon-Smith, C. (1992) *Enterprising Women: Television Fandom and the Creation of Popular Myth*, Philadelphia, PA: University of Pennsylvania Press.

Belk, R. (2010) "Sharing," *Journal of Consumer Research*, 36(5): 715–34.

Booth, P. (2010) *Digital Fandom: New Media Studies*, New York: Peter Lang.

Bruns, A. (2008) *Blogs, Wikipedia, Second Life, and Beyond*, New York: Peter Lang.

Busse, K. and Hellekson, K. (2006) "Introduction: Work in Progress," in K. Hellekson and K. Busse (eds), *Fan Fiction and Fan Communities in the Age of the Internet*, Jefferson, NC: McFarland, pp. 5–32.

Cooper, D. (2007) "This is Not an Isolated Incident: An Introduction," in D. Cooper (ed.), *Userlands: New Fiction from the Blogging Underground*, New York: Akashic Books.

Coppa, F. (2006) "A Brief History of Media Fandom," in K. Hellekson and K. Busse (eds), *Fan Fiction and Fan Communities in the Age of the Internet*, Jefferson, NC: McFarland, pp. 41–59.

Denegri-Knott, J. and Molesworth, M. (2010) "Concepts and Practices of Digital Virtual Consumption," *Consumption, Markets and Culture*,13(2): 109–32.

Firat, A.F. and Venkatesh, A. (1995) "Liberatory Postmodernism and the Reenchantment of Consumption," *Journal of Consumer Research*, 22(3): 239–67.

Fiske, J. (1989) *Understanding Popular Culture*, Boston: Unwin Hyman.

——(1992) "The Cultural Economy of Fandom," in L.A. Lewis (ed.), *The Adoring Audience: Fan Culture and Popular Media*, New York: Routledge, pp. 30–49.

Grey, J., Sandvoss, C. and Harrington, C.L. (2007) "Introduction: Why Study Fans," in J. Grey, C. Sandvoss, and C. L. Harrington (eds), *Fandom: Identities and Communities in a Mediated World*, New York: New York University Press, pp. 1–16.

Grossberg, L. (1992) "Is There a Fan in the House?: The Affective Sensibility of Fandom," in L. A. Lewis (ed.), *The Adoring Audience: Fan Culture and Popular Media*, New York: Routledge, pp. 50–68.

Hadas, L. (2009) "The Web Planet: How the Changing Internet Divided *Doctor Who* Fan Fiction Writers," *Transformative Works and Cultures*, 3, available at: http://dx.doi.org/10.3983/ twc.2009.0129 (accessed 28 March 2011).

Harrington, C.L. and Bielby, D.D. (2005) "Flow, Home, and Media Pleasures," *Journal of Popular Culture*, 38(5): 834–54.

Harris, C. (1998) "Introduction Theorizing Fandom: Fans, Subcultures and Identity," in C. Harris and A. Alexander (eds), *Theorizing Fandom: Fans, Subcultures and Identity*, Cresskill, NJ: Hampton Press, pp. 3–8.

Hills, M. (2002) *Fan Cultures*, New York: Routledge.

Jancovich, M. (2002) "Cult Fictions: Cult Movies, Subcultural Capital and the Production of Cultural Distinctions," *Cultural Studies*, 16(2): 306–22.

Jenkins, H. (1992a) "'Strangers No More, We Wing': Filking and the Social Construction of the Science Fiction Fan Community," in L.A. Lewis (ed.), *The Adoring Audience: Fan Culture and Popular Media*, New York: Routledge, pp. 208–36.

——(1992b) *Textual Poachers: Television Fans and Participatory Culture*, New York: Routledge.

——(2004) "Quentin Tarantino's *Star Wars*? Digital Cinema, Media Convergence, and Participatory Culture," in D. Thorburn and H. Jenkins (eds), *Rethinking Media Change*, Cambridge, MA: MIT Press, pp. 281–12.

——(2006a) *Convergence Culture: Where Old and New Media Collide*, New York: New York University Press.

——(2006b) *Fans, Bloggers, and Gamers: Exploring Participatory Culture*, New York: New York University Press.

Jenson, J. (1992) "Fandom as Pathology: The Consequences of Characterization," in L. A. Lewis (ed.), *The Adoring Audience: Fan Culture and Popular Media*, New York: Routledge, pp. 9–29.

Johnson, D. (2007) "Fan-Tagonism: Factions, Institutions, and Constitutive Hegemonies of Fandom," in J. Grey, C. Sandvoss, and C. L. Harrington (eds), *Fandom: Identities and Communities in a Mediated World*, New York: New York University Press, pp. 285–300.

Jones, R. (2006) "From Shooting Monsters to Shooting Movies: Machinima and the Transformative Play of Video Game Fan Culture," in K. Hellekson and K. Busse (eds), *Fan Fiction and Fan Communities in the Age of the Internet*, Jefferson, NC: McFarland, pp. 261–80.

Kaplan, D. (2006) "Construction of Fan Fiction Character Through Narrative," in K. Hellekson and K. Busse (eds), *Fan Fiction and Fan Communities in the Age of the Internet*, Jefferson, NC: McFarland, pp. 134–52.

Kozinets, R. (2001) "Utopian Enterprise: Articulating the Meanings of *Star Trek*'s Culture of Consumption," *Journal of Consumer Research*, 28(1): 67–88.

——(2007) "Inno-tribes: *Star Trek* as Wikimedia," in B. Cova and A. Shankar (eds), *Consumer Tribes*, Oxford: Elsevier/Butterworth-Heinemann, pp. 194–211.

Lanier, C.D. Jr. and Schau, H.J. (2007) "Culture and Co-creation: Exploring Consumers' Inspirations and Aspirations for Writing and Posting Online Fan Fiction," in R.W. Belk and J.F. Sherry, Jr. (eds), *Research in Consumer Behavior: Consumer Culture Theory*, vol. 11, Oxford: Elsevier, pp. 321–42.

Lewis, L.A. (1992) "Introduction," in L.A. Lewis (ed.), *The Adoring Audience: Fan Culture and Popular Media*, New York: Routledge, pp. 1–8.

Lothian, A. (2009) "Living in a Den of Thieves: Fan Video and Digital Challenges to Ownership," *Cinema Journal*, 48(4): 130–6.

Marino, P. (2001) *3D Game-Based Filmmaking: The Art of Machinima*, Scottsdale, AZ: Paraglyph.

Mittell, J. (2009) "Sites of Participation: Wiki Fandom and the Case of Lostpedia," *Transformative Works and Culture* 3, available at: http://dx.doi.org/10.3983/twc.2009.0118 (accessed 28 March 2011).

Muñiz, Jr., A.M. and Schau, H.J. (2005) "Religiosity in the Abandoned Apple Newton Brand Community," *Journal of Consumer Research*, 31(4): 737–47.

Negroponte, N. (1995) *Being Digital*, New York: Alfred A. Knopf.

Newman, J. (2008) *Playing with Videogames*, London: Routledge.

Pearson, R. (2010) "Fandom in the Digital Era," *Popular Communication*, 8(1): 84–95.

Pugh, S. (2005) *The Democratic Genre: Fan Fiction in a Literary Context*, Bridgend: Seren.

Radway, J. (1988) "Reception Study: Ethnography and the Problem of Dispersed Audiences and Nomadic Subjects," *Cultural Studies*, 2(3): 359–76.

Russo, J.L. (2009) "User-Penetrated Content: Fan Video in the Age of Convergence," *Cinema Journal*, 48 (4): 125–30.

Sandvoss, C. (2005) *Fans: The Mirror of Consumption*, Cambridge: Polity Press.

Scodari, C. (2003) "Resistance Re-Examined: Gender, Fan Practices, and Science Fiction Television," *Popular Communications*, 1(2): 111–30.

Sheffrin, E. (2004) "*Lord of the Rings, Star Wars*, and Participatory Fandom: Mapping New Congruencies between the Internet and Media Entertainment Culture," *Critical Studies in Media Communication*, 21(3): 261–81.

Smith, S., Fisher, D. and Cole, S.J (2007) "The Lived Meanings of Fanaticism: Understanding the Role of Labels and Categories in Defining the Self in Consumer Culture," *Consumption, Markets and Culture*, 10(2): 77–94.

Soukup, C. (2006) "Hitching a Ride on a Star: Celebrity, Fandom, and Identification on the World Wide Web," *Southern Communication Journal*, 71(4): 319–37.

Stein, L.E. (2006) "'This Dratted Thing:' Fannish Storytelling Through New Media," in K. Hellekson and K. Busse (eds), *Fan Fiction and Fan Communities in the Age of the Internet*, Jefferson, NC: McFarland, pp. 245–60.

Storey, J. (2001) *Cultural Theory and Popular Culture: An Introduction*, London: Pearson.

Suden, J. (2003) *Material Virtualities*, New York: Peter Lang.

Tatum, M.L. (2009) "Identity and Authenticity in the Filk Community," *Transformative Works and Cultures* 3, available at: http://dx.doi.org/10.3983/twc.2009.0139 (accessed 28 March 2011).

Tushnet, R. (2007) "Copyright Law, Fan Practices, and the Rights of the Author," in J. Grey, C. Sandvoss, and C. L. Harrington (eds), *Fandom: Identities and Communities in a Mediated World*, New York: New York University Press, pp. 60–71.

Walliss, J. (2010) "Fan Filmmaking and Copyright in a Global World: 'Warhammer 40,000' Fan Films and the Case of "Damnatus,'" *Transformative Works and Culture* 3, available at: http://dx.doi.org/10.3983/twc.2010.0178, (accessed 28 March 2011).

Wirman, H. (2009) "On Productivity and Game Fandom," *Transformative Works and Cultures*, 3, available at: http://dx.doi.org/10.3983/twc.2009.0145 (accessed 28 March 2011).

Young, C. (2008) *Homemade Hollywood: Fans Behind the Camera*, London: Continuum.

26

ONLINE GAMES

Consuming, experiencing and interacting in virtual worlds

João Pedro dos Santos Fleck, Marlon Dalmoro and
Carlos Alberto Vargas Rossi

Keywords

online games, virtual identities, virtual worlds

Introduction

Digital phenomena have influenced the way people work, shop, study and communicate, among other activities. Furthermore, the way people play video games has been tremendously impacted by the Internet and digital devices. The possibilities of entertainment offered by video games have been considerably enhanced – and changed – in the past couple of decades due to the possibility of sharing these games with other players online.

Our aim in this chapter is to provide an overview of the consumption of online games, taking into consideration the state of the art in theory as well as research on the evolution of video games and online games in contemporary society.

The Internet brought the video game phenomenon to the virtual world and converted the games into one of the main consumption items of the digital age. According to recent research by the Nielsen Company (2010), Americans spend 10.2 percent of their online time playing games. Another recent study demonstrates that online gaming is one of the most likely reasons for compulsive Internet use (Meerkerk *et al.* 2006).

In the online environment, the interaction between the real and the virtual is an important aspect in understanding why these games are so fascinating. The consumption of online games is a continuous process (Malaby 2007), because only through playing will the gamer be able to develop his or her expertise. The creation and acquisition of value are not based on the purchase of the game, but on what is experienced while the game is played. The player of an online game helps to *create* a complex and nuanced virtual world. Their character and their digital virtual activities – their in-game labor – along with that of other players sustain the digital virtual space as meaningful (Denegri-Knott and Molesworth 2010).

In the following sections of this chapter, we analyze the consumption of online games with a focus on the evolution and the social and experiential aspects they involve. The first section is an overview of the transition from offline to online game, followed by the definition of online games and by a section about the study of online games. Afterwards, social aspects of games are presented in two sections: virtual identities and interactions in virtual worlds. Then, an experiential elements section on game consumptions is presented, followed by our closing arguments.

From offline to online: an overview of games evolution

Since we are talking about online games, it is appropriate to consider some data on the evolution of the consoles market. The dawn of the video games era is linked to consoles such as Atari and Odyssey – in the 1970s – and Nintendo 8-bit – in the 1980s (Shankar and Bayus 2003); however, the explosive growth in sales of this equipment is far more recent.

From 1996 to 2007, video games sales grew 700 percent and in 2008, solely in the United States, the games industry made a profit of $21.3 billion (Matthews 2009). The global online game market reached US$19.3 billion in 2010 and it will increase to US$37.9 billion by 2016 (DFC 2011). This includes revenue from PC online games, console online games, and mobile online games.

The growth of the games market is partly a result of the considerable improvement and changes in the quality of consoles and titles. Since the 1980s, games producers have released new gaming systems, at an average five-year interval, satisfying the desire of consumers who are constantly searching for more powerful games (Clements and Ohashi 2005). According to the ESA report (2011) on the gaming industry, some of the top reasons why gamers purchase a computer or video game are: quality of game graphics, an interesting storyline, a sequel to a favorite game, and word of mouth. Analyzing this market from the consumer focus, we find that this is happening because games evoke our most powerful positive emotions, like curiosity, optimism, pride, and the desire to join forces with others to achieve something extraordinary (McGonigal 2011).

To be able to understand what online gaming gives to the player, it is important to consider, first, what computer games and video games meant to an entire generation that grew up with them during the end of the 1970s, the 1980s and the 1990s. Video games nowadays attract all kinds of users, including females and older players, but in its early years, the console (or computer) could even be considered a refugee for male geeks, nerds, and the socially inept. The average game player in the United States is now 37 years old (18 percent are under 18, 53 percent are 18–49, and 29 percent are 50+) and 42 percent are female (ESA 2011). On the other hand, earlier games were a kind of entertainment directed mainly at children, teenagers, and young adults. To these "players of the past," video games meant the door that opened onto a whole wide world of possibilities that had been nonexistent until that moment. Their fantasies could become reality when the console was turned on, and if by any chance they "died," that wasn't a problem, they could just press "restart" and experience everything over and over, as many times as they wanted.

The gaming world has developed a great deal in its four decades of existence and nowadays you can connect with others in a second, and the social aspect enhances the players' enjoyment of the gaming experience. Online games offer opportunities for social interaction, although players cannot talk to each other as well as they could if they were in the same room, and they cannot give each other high fives. Still, online games offer more social stimulation than most PC or console games (Adams 2009). For instance, in big cities, such as São Paulo, New York and Tokyo that have such intense traffic that make it almost impossible for friends to get together, the possibility of turning on a console, putting on a headset and being on the same race track as your friend and talking about your lives while you enjoy the experience of driving a Formula 1 car is incomparable to anything conceivable before online gaming.

Defining online games

First and foremost, online gaming is a technology rather than a genre; a mechanism for connecting players together rather than a particular pattern of gameplay (Adams 2009). Furthermore, we should also make clear that we are writing about online gaming, and this term should not be confused with online gambling.

As online games cover such a vast topic, we will specify what we understand by the term. Based on Adams (2009), we use the term to refer mainly to multiplayer distributed games, in which the players' machines are connected by a network. This is as opposed to multiplayer local games, in which all the players play on one machine and look at the same screen. While online games can, in principle, include solitary games on the Internet, such as Bejeweled, the online aspect of such games is incidental rather than essential to the experience. We could simply classify Bejeweled as a puzzle game. Online games do not need to be distributed over the Internet; we consider games played over a local area network (LAN) to be identical, from a design standpoint, to those played over the Internet.

These kinds of games are usually multiplayer, allowing users to fantasize and to be entertained through interaction in a virtual world (Hsu and Lu 2004). Online games can be played on a range of devices, such as video game consoles (currently Wii, Xbox and PS3), computers and handhelds (PDAs, tablets and mobile phones). The communication form in online games may vary, but the majority depend on text messages and/or voice communication.

Online games also vary in their purchase and play form. Regarding the purchase, they can be divided into the following main forms: (1) free games that are played directly online; (2) online games with a monthly fee; (3) games requiring purchase of software but taking place completely online; and (4) games requiring software purchase, that can be played either offline or online. The play form is also quite varied and the division is not as simple as the purchase form; we can think about it as a continuum that, at one end has single-player online games and games that can be played offline, but that offer the possibility of online multiplayer action and, at the other end, *persistent world* games, such as World of Warcraft and EverQuest that constitute permanent environments in which players can play, retaining the progressive state of their avatar from one session to another (Adams 2009).

Avatars are a computer user's representation of themselves or an alter ego, in the form of a three-dimensional model representing the embodiment of the user (Jordan 1999). Avatars explore, meet other avatars, socialize, participate in individual and group activities, and create and trade virtual property and services with one another. Game designers tend to favor characters, a usage that dates to Dungeons and Dragons in the early 1970s (Castronova 2005). Several games avatars/characters have virtual possessions (also known as virtual goods, resources, or properties). The concept of virtual possessions is present in some games in which you do not have a virtual avatar representation of yourself (some social games, for instance). A virtual possession can be defined as a computer code that, when processed, mimics some characteristics of real world property, including exclusivity, persistence, and transferability.

It is not our intention to write only about a specific genre/type of games, but it is important to name a few examples of major online games:

- *Massively Multiplayer Online First Person Shooter* (MMOFPS): this is an online gaming genre which features a persistent world and a large number of simultaneous players as first-person shooters – in which the player views the scenario from the eyes of the protagonist. These games provide large-scale, sometimes team-based combat.
- *Massively Multiplayer Online Role-Playing Game* (MMORPG): a genre in which players assume the role of a fictional character through which they interact with an immense

number of players through the Internet. In MMORPGs, the scenario (world) in which the game takes place continues to evolve even when the player is away from the game. The majority of MMORPG are *persistent world* games.

- *Massively Multiplayer Online Real-time Strategy* (MMORTS): combine real-time strategy (RTS) (a category of strategy game that is played in real-time; there are no "turns" in a true RTS – players all move at once) within a *persistent world*. Players often assume the role of a general, king, or other type of figurehead leading an army into battle while maintaining the resources needed for such warfare.
- *Social Gaming*: games that run on or integrate with a social network and use that network to enhance gameplay between players. These games tend to focus on socialization instead of objective-based gameplay.

These are only a few examples of games available to online gaming. Other examples that could be cited are racing games, sports games, fantasy sports games, casual games, and music/rhythm games.

Online games studies

There are several explanations for the emergence of studies on video games as well as the increasing interest in the subject by scholars. First, the significant economic value that the gaming business has generated is enormous (Castronova 2005; Lange 2011; Malaby 2007). Second, our leisure time is decreasing considerably and, as a result, is becoming more valuable to us. Another reason is the improvement in both technical and aesthetical aspects of the games. This evolution already is exercising an influence on other media industries (Wolf 2006).

Studies on games are moving from a peripheral area to a central position in the theorization about social life. This movement has been reinforced by several books, journals and a power-fully interdisciplinary interest (Boellstorff 2006; Shaw 2010). Online games studies fit into different fields, such as: psychology and sociology, especially regarding human–computer interaction (HCI); media studies; computer science, with emphasis on hardware and technologies; and also ludology (Aarseth 2001; Eskelinen 2004) – an autonomous discipline dedicated to the study of games and play. In terms of games consumption, games culture has been analyzed via players' profiles and archetypes, how and when they play, as well as the effects of video games on society and users' behavior, with a special focus on negative aspects such as excessive play and addiction.

The dichotomy between virtual and real is a central focus in online gaming research and can extend the anthropological analysis of the experience value in online games. Several societies did not make a distinction between "work" and "play" (Schwartzman 1980). Thus the daily experience of online game consumption is ripe with meaning. This understanding is in line with the arguments of some anthropologists (Malaby 2007; Schwartzman 1980) that play cannot be analysed as form of activity independent from the everyday activities.

Online games can represent both real and imagined worlds that attract players to interact in a cultural, social, and material milieu that is constantly evolving. Online games promote change in different ways, and also affect those who do not play games. Therefore, exciting research topics become available through this interaction. Figure 26.1 highlights different points of analysis in the emerging online games culture:

Several forms of interactive media go beyond the game itself strengthening the interaction between the virtual world consumed in the game and the real world in which we live: social networking, for instance, which is quite important nowadays, is directly integrated with online gaming. These "synthetic worlds" that are created around/within online games are taking cultural forms in their own right.

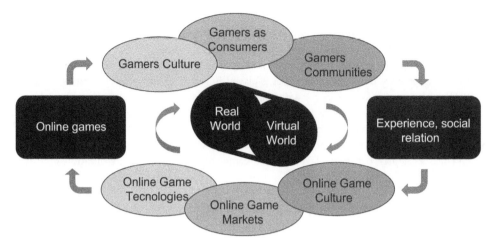

Figure 26.1 Online games research topics

Two principal research topics have emerged: (1) *gamers*, who can be divided into three broad topics: their culture, the consumers, and communities; and (2) *online games*, which can also be divided into three broad topics: technologies, markets, and culture:

- *Gamer culture*: a culture of gaming is emerging, wherein people participate in different types of online games all the time: participating within interactive media, playing on the console, or on the Internet, as shaped by a range of factors from language spoken to quality of Internet connection.
- *Gamers as consumers*: the form of consumption of online games is quite varied. The growing consumption of multiplayer games has become a topic of analysis, mainly due to the social experiences enabled by this kind of play. These games usually require monthly fees, which are quite different from actually acquiring a game and involves a considerable change in the structure of consumption of video games. Another interesting topic of research here is that with the emergence of hardcore gamers, who are seriously involved with their video games, another group of players was created: the casual player who only wants to play a quick and simple game to relax for a while.
- *Gamer communities*: the virtual communities of gamers are one of the main elements that have been created by online games. The interaction and participation in these communities, in some cases, have become more important (and even addictive) than the game. The relationships between participants, the difference between what happens online and offline, the sharing of experiences and sociability are some of the topics that can be studied in these communities.
- *Online game technologies*: this is possibly the most studied topic and continues to be so because technologies are constantly changing and these changes are occurring more rapidly. This topic, among others, relates to innovation and new technologies, competition within the games industry, and changes in the market.
- *Online games markets*: the popularity of video games has resulted in a complex new market that revolves around the gaming culture, such as magazines, special gear, action figures, cards and a huge list of licensed products. Therefore, exploring how this new market is configured and the consumer behavior of gamers, going beyond just the console and the games can be an interesting topic of research.

- *Online game culture*: these games are increasingly affecting interactive media as a whole: television, cell phones, and the Internet among other technologies are used to play. In this sense, cultural meanings provided by online games are shared by consumers of diverse entertainment forms and media.

These lines of research lead to an outline that involves large consumption of experience and social relations and can be extremely valuable for understanding the digital consumer. The consumption of goods in the real world will be increasingly influenced by the virtual world, given the amount of time that is spent in the virtual world by the players.

Virtual worlds and virtual identities

Virtual worlds are simulations. Like a map, they usually start out as reproducing actual worlds, real bodies and situations; but, like simulations, they end up taking on a life of their own (Shields 2003). The virtual is by no means the opposite of the real. On the contrary, it is a fecund and powerful mode of being that expands the process of creation, opens up the future, and injects a core of meaning beneath the plateau of immediate physical presence (Lévy 1998). A virtual world can be defined as an online representation that simulates real-world physics with sufficient fidelity, and in which one or more human participants can control one or more actors in a computer-mediated environment (CME). Based on this definition, several online games take place within virtual worlds – instead of applying this definition strictly to 3D virtual worlds, such as Second Life and Kaneva. Apart from online games, other examples of CMEs are social network websites, such as Facebook and Orkut, 3D virtual worlds, chatrooms, and Multi-User Dungeons (MUDs).

The growth of CMEs allows people to interact, to work, to shop, to learn, to entertain, and to be entertained (Schau and Gilly 2003). CME technologies have lately become a representative form of technological consumption (Siddiqui and Turley 2006). These environments represent new opportunities for self-development, identification and collective affiliation.

Activities in virtual worlds can be representatives of the sense of self. According to Belk (1988), the extended self is achieved by having, doing, and being. In traditional CMEs (e.g. web pages), the identity development is made through "being" and "having" (Schau and Gilly 2003). Conversely, in games, a more interactional environment, the identity development is more dynamic. For instance, as the avatar is the extended self in MMORPGs, this process tends to be more experienced through "doing." But gamers can also use virtual resources to express virtual status through virtual consumption and possessions in CMEs (Wang *et al.* 2009).

Games allow gamers and the gamers' characters to evolve through playing and executing a series of activities. Gamers immersed in a video game have their brain stimulated, which encourages creative solutions and adaptations (ESA 2011). These beneficial ideas and thoughts can then be applied to real-life situations. The results can be surprisingly positive for individuals, communities, and society as a whole. Gamers tend to develop more abilities, expertise and to increase their resources. This progression differentiates the avatars in terms of power and game experience, conferring player status that is available at the click of a button (Mendenhall *et al.* 2010). People search for distinction and recognition, and they are able to achieve this faster in online games than in real life. In the research of Wang *et al.* (2009), some interviewees reported that the time they dedicated in search of an accomplishment would distinguish them from average players.

Belk (1988) developed the notion that material possessions are an integral part of identity construction and self-extension. The representation of the self can also occur in digital media

(Schau and Gilly 2003). Technology is changing forms of consumption; objects of possession and collection are being de-materialized (Siddiqui and Turley 2006) and virtual worlds are described as capable of replicating the sort of buying experience we have in the real world (Hemp 2006). According to Denegri-Knott and Molesworth (2010), for those espousing a cultural or postmodern perspective, digital virtual spaces represent an opportunity for consumers to engage in playful forms of consumption, where the possibilities of "making do" may be magnified.

Therefore, when we think about online games, we have to think also in social and cultural terms. The cyber worlds in which online gamers are involved result in a process of redefinition (Boellstorff 2006). The material world is transformed into a virtual world, with avatars, virtual money, virtual necessities, and so on. Social relations go beyond borders, with a universal network that shares cultural meanings. In this sense, the reason for this mass exodus to virtual worlds is that video games are increasingly fulfilling genuine human needs (McGonigal 2011). It can be argued that every moment spent in a mediated environment entails another moment given up in the real world; each act of consumption in a CME replaces an act of consumption in the real world; each simulated possession replaces a tangible one (Siddiqui and Turley 2006).

Interacting in virtual worlds

Games provide a structured way for people to relax, have fun and learn more about each other in the process (Kim 2000). The sense of gaming as a social practice is even more keenly felt if we look online. As Kerr (2006) analyses, video game play occurs in a wide variety of different contexts and online multiplayer gaming has become an increasingly significant feature of the contemporary medium. Games are a particularly effective way to bond with friends and family, strengthening our real-life and online social networks in ways that no other kinds of social interaction can (McGonigal 2011). The social relationships that are developed in several online games have made the video game become more than just a gaming environment.

The identification with the games' universe stimulates cooperative behavior, which can be seen as an outcome of the sense of trust and reciprocity produced among players. Other factors also make gaming attractive: it is a reasonably cheap form of entertainment and it is something considered "safe" for several players. In a study on the consumption of an online game (Fleck *et al.* 2010), several users mentioned that they did not feel at ease going to parties or going out at night in general because they felt that they were potential victims of violence and theft. They mentioned that they could have as much fun as if they went partying simply by staying indoors and playing with their friends online, particularly due to the fact that they were sharing an experience with another person who was as interested in that experience as they were.

The interaction with other players has a substantial impact on the popularity of online games because sequences of interaction are narrative and thus help to construct a play experience (Choi and Kim 2004). The online environment is a place where teamwork, mutual encouragement and fun can be experienced through group interaction. In a game such as World of Warcraft, social interaction is not only desirable, but necessary, because you need to work in teams with different characters who possess different skills in order to complete a challenge or quest (Cole and Griffiths 2007).

This results in spontaneous *communitas* formation. According to Turner (1969), *communitas* emerges when people step out of their structural roles and obligations, and into a sphere that is decidedly "anti-structural." We can consider the games' virtual spaces as an anti-structural space, given their capacity to generate ambiguity in social life – ideal conditions for the emergence of a social dynamic characterized by feelings of equality, linkage, belonging, and group devotion to a transcendent goal (Arnould and Price 1993). Interaction in *communitas* is free from the culturally defined encumbrances such as status, reputation, class, caste, sex, or other structural categories (Turner 1982). This puts the players on an equal footing to develop intense feelings of comradeship and egalitarianism, since players see others as themselves, people who share their values. When consumers assume the fantasy in the virtual world, they may accept social behaviors that are not considered socially acceptable in the material world (Denegri-Knott and Molesworth 2010).

Since the virtual world does not carry the social restrictions lived in the real world, some social behaviors arise more easily, such as actions of sharing. As stated by Belk (2007), in the online environment of the games, it is easy to share intangible goods like information, opinions, images, and ideas, especially when these things are in digital form and we do not lose them by sharing them. The perception that resources are scarce and materialism are factors that inhibit sharing (Belk 2010). However, to share immaterial goods produced in the virtual world does not require a material detachment and bonds players in solidarity. Gamers share also brand involvement (Muñiz and O'Guinn 2001). In this case, members of a video game brand community share a reverence for the brand, especially each kind of game (hardware and software) that is involved in a network of users formed around the product.

Gamers find in the virtual world a community that provides sociability, support, information, belongingness, and social identity (Dholakia *et al.* 2004). These bonds are defined in social, instead of spatial terms, and the integrating element consists of a shared passion or interest (Kozinets 1999). The social aspect enhances the players' enjoyment of the experience mediated by a communication technology, where the game experience can become more "real" than real life (Adams 2009; Hsu and Lu 2004).

The social production occurs because online games are consumed not simply as a machine/operator action, but as a structure that permits the social exchange between players. In this sense, gamers' consumption is the result of a network of interrelated activities provided by the game structure and embedded in social relations between players. Social capital is produced through the interactions with other players in the game world, which may result in a durable network of more or less institutionalized relationships of mutual acquaintance or recognition (Bourdieu 1980). Although players' relationships are usually packed in a virtual environment, the interactions occur similarly to the real world, because people tend to be close and look for others with whom they previously had an online interaction. Virtual friendships can be very enjoyable for gamers and this virtual relationship can become a real-life friendship (Kendal 2002).

There are also possible negative outcomes, since access to social relationships in a virtual environment may result in the total absence of real relationships (Brewer and Gardner 1996). However, excluding cases closely related to addiction, online games can be seen as a new kind of social interaction rather than a critical absence of relations. Technology is changing forms and modes of consumption, replacing tangible possessions by de-materialized forms: virtual money, e-books, online newspaper (Adams 2009). Similarly, terms such as geeks and nerds that were seen as a negative stereotype are becoming more commonly accepted and even used with pride within such communities. Social interactions in online games now also involve consumers with an adult profile – different from the stereotypical image of an isolated adolescent gamer (ESA 2011; Griffiths *et al.* 2003) – and have allowed a greater recognition in the real world capital of forms generated in the virtual world. In this way, players can appropriate the social capital to strategically play with conventionalized norms and to establish social distinctions (Kates 2002).

Experiential elements in the consumption of online games

The consumption of games is motivated by several experiential elements, such as feelings of challenge, achievement, escapism and the experience of flow. Such elements can also be found in other activities, however, the online game is one of the few that brings a sense of connectedness, engagement and possibilities that are hard to find in our daily lives (Lowood 2008). Denegri-Knott and Molesworth (2010) say that there may be a continuum of imaginative labor from daydreams to fantasy with varying degrees of potential of achievement through virtual consumption forms. Games can be seen as a way for players to access their daydreams in a fantasy world without many requirements.

Games are considered complex interactive structures that facilitate play experiences (Eskelinen 2004) and some games, such as the ones with a persistent world, allow players to decide for themselves what they want to do. They seek out challenges if they desire, resulting in active and expressive experiences rather than reactive (Adams 2009). According to Gee (2000), players are active problem solvers who see mistakes as opportunities for learning and who are constantly searching for newer, better solutions to obstacles and challenges. The greater the capacities of a particular game to maintain a balance between challenges and skills, the longer will be the player's interest in maintaining the experiential consumption (Holbrook *et al.* 1984).

Games allow the creation of fantasies that other entertainment offerings, such as movies and books, do not allow in the same manner. When individuals talk about a film or a book they recall what the characters did in the third person – "they did this" – but when they talk about game experiences they use the first person and possessive pronoun – "I'm going ... "; "my sword" (Molesworth 2008).

The virtual experiences provided by video games can be considered an escape valve for real-life limitations, granting access to fantasy scenarios where players can become heroes, gangsters, sports players and a myriad of other characters. For example, a frustrated desire to be a rock star can be minimized playing a game such as Guitar Hero and characters may even have extraordinary abilities that are incongruent with human biology such as the ability to fly (Mendenhall *et al.* 2010), among others. The escapism provided by the games may lead users to immersion during play. These exceptional moments in which a person loses track of time and self-consciousness can be characterized as flow experiences: a state of concentration or complete absorption with the activity at hand that occurs when a situation demands total participation from the individual, and loss of contact with ordinary reality (Csikszentmihalyi 1990).

Flow transcends mundane experience (Celsi *et al.* 1993). This type of experience is one of the reasons that lead people to play video games, since one of the game's objectives is to create entertainment through intrinsic motivation. One fundamental aspect of flow in games has been linked with learning experienced, since during a game the player may experience an increase of skill for no determined amount of time (Chen 2007; Gee 2000). The balance between challenges and skills provided by the game also contributes to achieving a flow state. If the task is too easy or too difficult, flow cannot occur (Csikszentmihalyi 1990). Online games may magnify the intensity of the flow experience provided by offline video games since the player tends to be more involved during their playing time.

However, it may be argued that online game characteristics create an analogous situation between the individual flow experience and the collective social interaction. Flow is related to an autonomous experience and occurs mostly in environments and situations that are of one's own choosing (ibid.). On the other hand, online games are characterized by interaction between players, resulting in a collective experience. A dichotomy between individual and collective experiences can result in an outcome of shared experiences. In this sense, the self-confidence that emerges from flow experiences gives the participant the confidence to engage in social relationships, thus giving rise to the notion that flow may be an antecedent to *communitas* (McGinnis *et al.* 2008). While flow is transcendent at the individual level of experience, common knowledge of the flow experience creates a bond between members (Celsi *et al.* 1993) and may result in a shared experience that resembles shared flow (Turner 1969).

Conclusion

Video games nowadays have loyal users who strongly defend their hobby (and their favorite brands and games). They are also a major industry, both in economic and technological terms. This form of entertainment – that was initially developed with the objective of entertaining one single player or a group of players, as long as they were together – evolved to become a tool of social interaction creating strong bonds among users, which may be even stronger than the ones created with physical proximity.

Interaction is a tendency of current video games that makes the game a social experience and not an individual one. Allied to that, through the formation of communities, the interaction with other users creates a connection of continually growing strength. Once the game becomes a social experience, this experience is transposed beyond the playing moment. Due to the involvement in the online game communities, the user encounters commonalities with other users who are interested in sharing feelings towards the game. The socialization through the communities creates the opportunity to perform activities online and offline, exchange information, recommend, and disseminate knowledge. Online games have demonstrated that thousands of players can be involved and conected to the game, in different places, but sharing a unique experience at the same time.

But the consumption of digital games still has barriers. For instance, in less developed countries a player cannot follow the technological evolution at the same level as a player in Europe or in North America. This is not only a matter of cost, but also a matter of availability, since games and consoles have a release time lag in different countries. Similar problems as well as connection speed and reliability also have a direct impact on the player's decision to play online or not – the higher the number of virtual possibilities and venues for a player to connect, the higher will be his or her interaction, identification, and level of participation, which will, eventually, increase game consumption as a result.

Our aim in this chapter was to explore different features of the consumption of online games, including the social relations and the experiential aspects provided by the games. We can only suppose that while the digital age continues to alter so many aspects of our daily lives, it will also continue to change the way we play online and how we access the world of online games. It is precisely in this access to online worlds that there exist some of the most interesting questions regarding consumption, since there is still much to be learned about how our real-world desires can actually be satisfied by the virtual worlds created by online games and their players.

Further reading

Bogost, I. (2007) *Persuasive Games: The Expressive Power of Video Games*, Cambridge, MA: MIT Press.
Caillois, R. and Barash, M. (2001) *Man, Play, and Games*, Champaign, IL: University of Illinois Press.
Castronova, E. (2005) *Synthetic Worlds: The Business and Culture of Online Games*, Chicago: University of Chicago Press.
Jenkins, R. (2006) *Fans, Bloggers, and Gamers: Exploring Participatory Culture*, New York: New York University Press.
Newman, J. (2008) *Playing with Videogames*, New York: Routledge.

References

Aarseth, E. (2001) "Computer Game Studies, Year One," *Game Studies*, 1(1): 1–1.

Adams, E. (2009) *Fundamentals of Game Design*, Berkeley, CA: New Riders.

Arnould, E. and Price, L. (1993) "River Magic: Extraordinary Experience and the Extended Service Encounter," *Journal of Consumer Research*, 20(1): 24–45.

Belk, R. (1988) "Possessions and the Extended Self," *Journal of Consumer Research*, 15(2): 139–68.

——(2007) "Why Not Share Rather Than Own?," *The ANNALS of the American Academy of Political and Social Science*, 611(May): 126–40.

——(2010) "Sharing," *Journal of Consumer Research*, 36(February): 715–34.

Boellstorff, T. (2006) "A Ludicrous Discipline? Ethnography and Game Studies," *Games and Culture*, 1(1): 29–35.

Bourdieu, P. (1980) "Le Capital Social: Notes Provisoires", *Actes de la Recherche en Sciences Sociales*, 31: 2–3.

Brewer, M.B. and Gardner, W. (1996) "Who Is This 'We'? Levels of Collective Identity and Self-Representations," *Journal of Personality and Social Psychology*, 71(1): 83–93.

Castronova, E. (2005) *Synthetic Worlds: The Business and Culture of Online Games*, Chicago: University of Chicago Press.

Celsi, R.L., Rose, R.L. and Leigh, T.W. (1993) "An Exploration of High-Risk Leisure Consumption Through Skydiving," *Journal of Consumer Research*, 20(1): 1–23.

Chen, J. (2007) "Flow in Games (and Everything Else)," *Communications of the ACM*, 50(4): 31–4.

Choi, D. and Kim, J. (2004) "Why People Continue to Play Online Games: In Search of Critical Design Factors to Increase Customer Loyalty to Online Contents," *CyberPsychology & Behavior*, 7(1): 11–24.

Clements, M.T. and Ohashi, H. (2005) "Indirect Network Effects and the Product Cycle: Video Games in the U.S. 1994–2002," *Journal of Industrial Economics*, 53(4): 515–42.

Cole, H. and Griffiths, M.D. (2007) "Social Interactions in Massively Multiplayer Online Role-Playing Gamers," *CyberPsychology and Behavior*, 10(4): 575–83.

Csikszentmihalyi, M. (1990) *Flow: The Psychology of Optimal Experience*, New York: Harper and Row.

Denegri-Knott, J. and Molesworth, M. (2010) "Concepts and Practices of Digital Virtual Consumption", *Consumption, Markets, & Culture*, 13(2): 109–32.

DFC (2011) "DFC Intelligence Forecasts Worldwide Video Game Market to Reach $81 Billion by 2016," available at: www.prweb.com/releases/2011/9/prweb8777406.htm (accessed September 28, 2011).

Dholakia, U.M., Bagozzi, R.P. and Pearo, K.L. (2004) "A Social Influence Model of Consumer Participation in Network- and Small-Group-Based Virtual Communities," *International Journal of Research in Marketing*, 21(3): 241–63.

ESA (2011) *2011 Sales, Demographic and Usage Data: Essential Facts about the Computer and Video Game Industry*, Washington, DC: Entertainment Software Association. Available at: http://www.theesa.com/facts/pdfs/ESA_EF_2011.pdf.

Eskelinen, M. (2004) "Toward Computer Game Studies," in P. Harrington and N. Wardrip-Fruin (eds), *First Person: New Media as Story, Performance, and Game*, Cambridge, MA: MIT Press, pp. 36–49.

Fleck, J., Rossi, C.A.V., Segabinazzi, R., Reali, G., Costa, D., and Martins, M. (2010) "Worlds of Warcrafters," in D.W. Dahl, G.V. Johar and S.M.J. van Osselaer (eds), *Advances in Consumer Research*, vol. 38, Duluth, MN: Association for Consumer Research.

Gee, J. (2000) *What Video Games Have to Tell Us about Learning and Literacy*, New York: Palgrave.

Griffiths, M.D., Davies, M.N.O. and Chappel, D. (2003) "Breaking the Stereotype: The Case of Online Gaming," *Cyberpsychology & Behavior*, 6(1): 81–91.

Hemp, P. (2006) "Avatar-Based Marketing," *Harvard Business Review*, 84(6): 48–56.

Holbrook, M.B., Chestnut, R.W., Oliva, T.A. and Greenleaf, E.A. (1984) "Play as a Consumption Experience: The Roles of Emotions, Performance, and Personality in the Enjoyment of Games," *Journal of Consumer Research*, 11(2): 728–39.

Hsu, C.L. and Lu, H.P. (2004) "Why Do People Play On-Line Games? An Extended TAM with Social Influences and Flow Experience," *Information and Management*, 41(7): 853–68.

Jordan, T. (1999) *Cyber Power: The Culture and Politics of Cyberspace and the Internet*, New York: Routledge.

Kates, S.M. (2002) "The Protean Quality of Subcultural Consumption: An Ethnographic Account of Gay Consumers," *Journal of Consumer Research*, 29(December): 383–99.

Kendall, L. (2002) *Hanging out in the Virtual Pub: Masculinities and Relationships Online*, Berkeley, CA: University of California Press.

Kerr, A. (2006) *The Business and Culture of Digital Games*, London: Sage.

Kim, A.J. (2000) *Community Building on the Web*, Berkeley, CA: Peachpit Press.

Kozinets, R.V. (1999) "E-Tribalized Marketing? The Strategic Implications of Virtual Communities of Consumption," *European Management Journal*, 17(3): 252–64.

Lange, P.G. (2011) "Learning Real-Life Lessons from Online Games," *Games and Culture*, 6(1): 17–37.

Lévy, P. (1998) *Becoming Virtual: Reality in the Digital Age*, New York: Plenum Press.

Lowood, H. (2008) "Impotence and Agency: Computer Games as a Post-9/11 Battlefield," in A. Jahn-Sudmann (ed.), *Computer Games as a Sociocultural Phenomenon: Games Without Frontiers, War Without Tears*, New York: Palgrave Macmillan, pp. 78–86.

McGinnis, L.P., Gentry, J.W. and Gao, T. (2008) "The Impact of Flow and Communitas on Enduring Involvement in Extended Service Encounters," *Journal of Service Research*, 11(11): 74–90.

McGonigal, J. (2011) *Reality Is Broken: Why Games Make Us Better and How They Can Change the World*, New York: Penguin Press.

Malaby, T.M. (2007) "Beyond Play: A New Approach to Games," *Games and Culture*, 2(2): 95–113.

Matthews, M. (2009) *NPD: Behind the Numbers*, available at: http://www.gamasutra.com/view/feature/3906/npd_behind_the_numbers_december_.php (accessed June 20, 2011).

Meerkerk, G.J., Van den Eijnden, R. and Garretsen, H.F.L. (2006) "Predicting Compulsive Internet Use: It's All about Sex!" *CyberPsychology & Behavior*, 9(1): 95–103.

Mendenhall, Z., Nepomuceno, M.V. and Saad, G. (2010) "Exploring Video Games from an Evolutionary Psychological Perspective," in I. Lee (ed.), *Encyclopedia of E-Business Development and Management in the Global Economy*, vol. I, Hershey: IGI Global, pp. 734–42.

Molesworth, M. (2008) "Adults' Consumption of Videogames as Imaginative Escape from Routine," in A. McGill and S. Shavitt (eds), *Advances in Consumer Research*, Provo, UT: Association for Consumer Research, pp. 376–83.

Muñiz, A.M.J. and O'Guinn, T.C. (2001) "Brand Community," *Journal of Consumer Research*, 27(March): 412–32.

Nielsen (2010) *What Americans Do Online: Social Media and Games Dominate Activity*, available at: http://blog.nielsen.com/nielsenwire/online_mobile/what-americans-do-online-social-media-and-games-dominate-activity/ (accessed June 20, 2011).

Schau, H. and Gilly, M.C. (2003) "We Are What We Post? Self-Presentation in Personal Web Space", *Journal of Consumer Research*, 30(3): 385–404.

Schwartzman, H.B. (1980) *Play and Culture*, West Point, NY: Leisure.

Shankar, V. and Bayus, B. (2003) "Network Effects and Competition: An Empirical Analysis of the Home Video Game Industry," *Strategic Management Journal*, 24(4): 375–84.

Shaw, A. (2010) "What Is Video Game Culture? Cultural Studies and Game Studies," *Games and Culture*, 5(4): 403–24.

Shields, R. (2003) *The Virtual*, London: Routledge.

Siddiqui, S. and Turley, D. (2006) "Extending the Self in a Virtual World," in C. Pechmann and L. Price (eds), *Advances in Consumer Research*, vol. 33, Duluth, MN: Association for Consumer Research, pp. 647–8.

Turner, V. (1969) *The Ritual Process: Structure and Anti-Structure*, Chicago: Aldine.

——(1982) *From Ritual to Theatre: The Human Seriousness of Play*, New York: Performing Arts Journal Publications.

Wang, J., Zhao, X. and Bamossy, G. (2009) "The Sacred and the Profane in Online Gaming," in N. Wood and M. Solomon (eds), *Virtual Social Identity and Social Behavior*, Armonk, NY: M.E. Sharpe, pp. 109–24.

Wolf, M.J.P. (2006) "Game Studies and Beyond", *Games and Culture*, 1(1): 116–18.

27

THE BRICK TESTAMENT

Religiosity among the adult fans of Lego

Albert M. Muñiz, Jr., Yun Mi Antorini and Hope Jensen Schau

Keywords

brand community, brands, consumer-generated content, self-extension, user-innovation

It is non-controversial to note that brand communities often evoke the magico-religious. Traces of the ethereal have been seen in brand communities centered on Apple Macintosh (Belk and Tumbat 2002; Kahney 2004), Apple Newton (Muñiz and Schau 2005), Saab (Muñiz and O'Guinn 2001), *Star Trek* (Kozinets 2001), *Star Wars* (Brown *et al.* 2003), *Xena: Warrior Princess* (Schau and Muniz 2004), the *X-Files* (Kozinets 1997) and in celebrity fan communities centered on Barry Manilow (O'Guinn 1991), Tom Petty (Schau and Muñiz 2007) and Cliff Richard (Caldwell and Henry 2006).

Looking at the extant exemplars, some patterns begin to emerge. Our knowledge of these phenomena in such contexts is thorough though there still are some obvious gaps. First, as has been noted previously (Schau and Muñiz 2007), many of the magico-religious evoking brands, when initially investigated, were small share, marginal entrants in their respective product categories. The Apple Newton was abandoned and the Apple MacIntosh had less than a 10 percent share of the PC market. Saab was, and is now, low share and imperiled. Still, there are exceptions. Apple has gone on to dominate not one but two electronics categories and is moving toward dominance of a third and yet traces of the magico-religious are still evident there (as the beatification of Steve Jobs in the weeks following his death would attest). *Star Wars* and *Star Trek* have been large market-share brands. From this, we can divine that while marginal, low-share and stigmatized brands can help make a brand capable of producing a community with magico-religious overtones, it is by no means required nor will such a brand absolutely do so. In fact, Muñiz and Schau (2007) detail the presence of magico-religious elements in the community surrounding the mainstream and non-stigmatized rock act, Tom Petty and the Heartbreakers.

The second common theme centers on the categories themselves. Computers and electronics are amply represented, as are cars, science-fantasy dramas and charismatic performers. Some of these brands contain aspects of the magico-religious in their narrative DNA. *Xena: Warrior Princess* was set in an anachronistic fantasy world replete with the supernatural. *Star Wars, Star*

Trek and the *X-Files*, too, routinely evoked ethereal themes. Similarly, the propensity of magico-religious themes to adhere to technology, which figured prominently in these shows, have been amply noted (Davis 1998; Noble 1999). One could argue that the appearance of ethereal themes in such categories was almost pre-ordained.

One category largely unexplored in this realm is toys. The capacity of some toy brands to sustain communities has been suggested before (Kimmel 2010; Park *et al.* 2007; Schau *et al.* 2009). Still, no evidence has been offered of the presence of magico-religious themes in brand communities centered on toys. Thus, such brands are ripe for further investigation, both as hosts for communities and ethereal motifs and themes. In this chapter, we are going to detail the presence of magico-religious themes in the community centered on the LEGO brand. In particular, we are going to show magico-religious themes among the so-called AFOLs (adult fans of LEGO).

LEGO is ostensibly a global toy company that manufacturers children's creative construction toys that are comprised of multi-colored, interlocking building elements. The LEGO System comprises several thousand different elements which are sold as stand-alone elements, or as parts of themed LEGO sets. It is a successful brand that has increasing mainstream awareness and acceptance, including as a hobby for adults (Antorini 2007; Muñiz and Antorini 2011). The high level of involvement with these creative processes probably facilitates the transcendence leading to magico-religious themes found here.

Fieldsite and data

In 1998, LEGO launched the product line: LEGO Mindstorms Robotic Invention System. Sales data for this system revealed quite a surprise: it was mainly adult males and not teenage boys who bought and used the product. Also surprising was the extent to which these consumers, without any encouragement from the firm, re-engineered and wrote new code for the programmable control unit that came with the set. A sizeable, well-organized, non-target market segment was using and innovating the product, frequently quite significantly. These consumers thought of themselves as belonging to a self-organized global brand community exhibiting the cultural and social hallmarks of brand community (Muñiz and O'Guinn 2001). Today, this community comprises over 70,000 members (LEGO Group 2011). During its entire history, user creativity and product innovation have been central activities of the AFOL community. AFOLs innovate all aspects of the LEGO consumption activity. For example, they innovate new LEGO models, new play concepts, and technologically based products, all with the purpose of going "beyond what comes in the box." They also innovate social spaces and means of communication that allow for online as well as offline interaction.

Between 2003 and 2011, we engaged in a multi-site, multi-method research program to examine community development and user innovation in the AFOL community. The multi-site, multi-method program allowed us to study in different contexts and situations. We observed AFOLs at conventions in North America, Denmark and Germany. We also observed AFOLs at smaller and locally arranged gatherings. In addition, we closely followed several LEGO online forums and we collected member profiles uploaded by members of the LEGO User Group Network (Lugnet.com). We conducted 25 depth interviews with members of the community that we met at conventions and events.

Themes and insights

There are several shared practices, thoughts, and feelings that connect AFOLs with the LEGO brand and that can be characterized as magico-religious. These include: an undivided devotion to the LEGO brand; an overwhelming emphasis on notions of purity and cleanliness; and a strongly metaphorical understanding of the period between childhood use of LEGO and adult use and appreciation. We encountered these themes repeatedly in community discussion forum postings, in descriptions offered by AFOLs of LEGO creations and the creative processes underlying them and in interviews with AFOLs.

AFOLs share an undivided devotion to the LEGO brand. Their devotion, however, is centered on the community's understandings of the brand and not necessarily the company's. Thus, not everything branded LEGO is "good." Consequently, although brand community members engage in religious acts and thoughts which concern the brand, these acts and thoughts cannot always be exchanged into brand loyalty. AFOLs frequently describe themselves as purists. They favor work and creative actions that they find pure, and distance themselves from that which they do not deem pure. The way one practices purity in their creative efforts has consequences for the connection between AFOLs and the LEGO brand as well as one's status in the community. AFOLs frequently make use of the term "dark age" to clearly mark the time they were reborn as LEGO consumers. The notion that there is a void before enlightenment (AFOL-hood) is encapsulated in the way AFOLs use the term. Metaphorically, the "dark age" is construed as a break in a chain that is stretched out between childhood, where the AFOL had his or hers first LEGO set, and adulthood where the AFOL takes up LEGO play again and experiences the joy of creativity and imagination. It is fair to say that the "dark age" describes a period in an AFOL's life where he or she loses his or her faith.

In the following, we will offer detailed explanations of these themes and provide illustrative examples. Then, we will divine theoretical insights from the appearance of these themes in a community centered on a toy brand.

Devotion to the LEGO brand

The AFOL community uses only the LEGO brand. As an AFOL declared a decade ago, and which most AFOLs agree with to this day: "It's about LEGO® – The One True Brand of automatic binding bricks." The phrase "automatic binding bricks" goes back to the founding days of the company where it appeared on the very first LEGO boxes in 1949 (it was abandoned by the company in 1953). The use of the descriptor indicates AFOLs' commitment to the original LEGO brand, the One True Brand. They associate this brand with, among other things, unchanging elements and colors, versatile elements, and a certain quality in the way the elements are manufactured and how they perform. These are some of the notions on which AFOLs base their connection with the LEGO brand and with which they defend themselves when challenged, even when it comes to actions undertaken by the company itself. Some AFOLs claim the moral high ground relative to employees of the LEGO Group in their devotion to and understanding of the LEGO brand.

All other brick-based brands (e.g., Mega Block (MB), BestLock, Playgo) are devalued as "clone brands" and are not accepted. As one AFOL explained: "I have many LEGO sets, and many clones, but I keep them by themselves; I would never dream of using even MB bricks in a LEGO MOC [My Own Creation, AFOL term for a self-designed creation]." To AFOLs, LEGO products are in a different league and clone brands are thought of as low in quality, i.e., AFOLs will argue that they are manufactured using "cheap plastic materials," they are inconsistent in colors, they lack stability, and they vary in brick dimensions.

Consider the following, from a posting to a prominent AFOL online discussion forum. Members had been discussing clone brands and the almost visceral intolerance most AFOLs displayed toward them when one AFOL offered a rather matter-of-fact reply:

What makes me ill is seeing reviews of clone brands seep into lugnet.reviews (I think that happened only once, and I screamed quickly), or glorification of clone brands in the main groups, or models glorifying clone brands. That's not what the site is about. It's about LEGO® – The One True Brand of automatic binding bricks. But you knew that. We all know that. :-) I'm sure the LCAD folks don't want to see clone brand poisoning in the CAD stuff either.

Clone bricks pose a real challenge to AFOLs as they often buy large quantities of used LEGO elements. Hence, the purchased collections will often be mixed with clone brand elements which then need to be sorted. AFOLs will easily spot a clone element in a large LEGO layout, so in order to pass for a decent MOC (to other AFOLs), they have to go through the collection and sort clone elements out. The cost of including clone brands in a MOC is devaluation of the MOC, as it becomes impure (see below).

Purity

Purity is a topic which continues to engage AFOLs. Many community discussion forum threads are centered on such questions as: "Are you a purist?," "What do you consider pure?," "How pure are you?," etc. On one much-visited AFOL blog, the authors provide the following (only slightly tongue-in-cheek definition): "Purist: A LEGO creation that does not include any customizations, such as decals, modified parts, or custom accessories from third-party vendors like BrickArms, BrickForge, and Big Ben Bricks. A form of religious fundamentalism." Note, the use of the term "religious fundamentalism" is not arbitrary, nor strictly speaking is it hyperbole, but rather aptly captures the ethos of the pure LEGO movement. Consider the following from a AFOL discussion forum:

> If it's not officially produced by the Lego Company, then I don't use it. I have been known, however, to use some prototype pieces that are available on bricklink (i.e. red wizard hats, black wizard beards, white hair, etc.). I have also been sorely tempted by the BF animals … The part selection that Lego produces are the pallet that we have to work with and we see what we can do with it. Or another metaphor, the parts we have are like the rules in the game. Modifying the parts is like breaking the rules. Any modification feels like cheating to me.

Most AFOLs agree with this understanding of purity. Consequently, this following phrase is often heard among AFOLs: "Cutting/modifying anything is blasphemy in my book. I'm fine with other fans doing it, but you won't catch me doing ANY of those things. I'm not going to tell others how to practice their hobby, but I'm not going to change my ways either."

There are different degrees of purity ranging from the unacceptable (e.g., clone brands and cutting LEGO elements) to the purest of pure, using only elements included in the initial sets marketed by the LEGO Group following its introduction. When the LEGO System was launched (in 1949), red and white elements dominated the sets. As one AFOL noted: "The purest purity probably would be building everything unexceptionally with red and white 2×4 bricks. :-)." The point being made is that a completely pure MOC would consist only of the original colors (red and white) and as a result thereby would be very dull! Consequently, many AFOLs do tolerate some impure behavior, like the use of fan-created stickers or fan-created weapons. However, there are limits to what AFOLs will tolerate (e.g., clone brands and cutting LEGO elements). Impure MOCs will not be tolerated in Best MOC competitions organized by LEGO user groups. Also, one can rest assured that one's work will be criticized if one chooses to upload impure work. So, there is a price to be paid for "stepping out of line."

Interestingly, LEGO branded products are not free from being devalued as impure either. LEGO Jack Stone, LEGO Galidor, LEGO Znap and LEGO Bionicle were alternative building systems which all failed in the market (except LEGO Bionicle) and have been withdrawn. All are examples of product lines that have been called "blasphemy" and "not LEGO" by AFOLs. To many AFOLs, the new LEGO element colors (the grey and brown element colors, among others, were substituted with lighter shades) that were introduced in 2004 are also considered impure. As one AFOL noted, "So, deep down the issue is that LEGO mucked with something we viewed as immutable and permanent. If they can change this, nothing's sacred." The use of the term "sacred" is not uncommon. AFOLs find something sacred in the connection to a cherished part of their childhood.

Cleanliness

Among AFOLs there is the unwritten rule that you don't pick up or touch other AFOLs' MOCs without permission. A MOC is a sacred representation of the creators' creativity. AFOLs explain that MOCs are fragile and will fall apart easily. This is especially true when AFOLs are among non-LEGO people at public conventions. So, to avoid a painful situation, AFOLs often put up fences around their displays to keep people at an arm's length from their MOCs. However, there is also the general issue of greasy fingerprints and dirt which risks contaminating the MOC. AFOLs like their MOCs as well as their LEGO elements clean and fresh looking (i.e., shiny and with a smooth and even surface). Consequently, it is a recurring topic among AFOLs on how to clean and freshen up LEGO elements.

Consider the following, from a forum posting entitled "How do-you-clean your LEGO parts?"

> I'm interested in learning people's techniques, particularly ones that clean a lot of parts at once with little effort. LEGO that's been on display just a short time can be cleaned with compressed air. But for displays that have been sitting out for long periods, the dust tends to stick, so you need to get more aggressive. Then there's the issue of cleaning large quantities of parts that you bought from your neighbor's garage/rummage sale or from eBay. I'm always concerned about how dusty/sticky/whatever those foreign parts could be. How do you dry them after they're cleaned? Water usually stays trapped in the small crevices because of surface tension and takes forever to evaporate. This can also leave soap marks. I've tried the warm soapy water and toothbrush method and the swish-around-in-a-bathtub method, but they're both time-consuming and hard to do with small pieces. It seems to me that using a washing machine or a dishwasher could work, but I've never tried it due to scratches the parts could acquire and potential heat issues.

The list of alternative methods mentioned in the initial posting was more than easily surpassed in the collected methods suggested by responders. Suggested methods ranged in intensity and all required explicit effort.

Cleaning LEGO elements is for some also an act that is part of the transition from one stage to another. For example, one of our informants talked about how he, at the age of 14–15 years, went from being a LEGO set builder to becoming a MOC builder (an implicitly adult designation). During this transition he took apart all his LEGO set models and washed them. His act can be interpreted as a way of cleansing himself of being someone who simply copies what the LEGO Group does to becoming a truly creative LEGO builder who makes original contributions and hence confirms the true meaning and intention of the LEGO System.

The dark age

The dark age is an AFOL term that describes: "That period in a LEGO fan's life when he or she sets aside LEGO in favor of school, dating, motor vehicles, and other non-LEGO pursuits." Typically, the dark age sets in during the teenage years when "wine, women and song" and education become more interesting than building with LEGO. One exits the dark ages when one picks up LEGO play as an adult (thereby becoming an AFOL). Interpreting the dark age from a religious perspective it can be seen as representing rebirth. The gravitas of the stories members tell one another about entering and leaving these unenlightened ages supports this assertion. Through picking up LEGO play as an adult, the AFOL is connected with strong and positive feelings associated with childhood (which is the time AFOLs were given their first LEGO set). The dark age can also be seen as death before life, i.e., a time void of the open-ended and creative play experiences that AFOLs cherish so much.

Consider the following from a AFOL discussion about members' experiences of the dark age. Members were asked to share the length of their dark age, as well as the events that precipitated the beginning and ending of that period.

> My dark ages started when I was about 12 or 13. I couldn't resist the temptation of girls, skateboarding, drugs and/or booze (gasp) and did I mention girls. All of my Lego except for a UCS Tie Intercepter went to my nephew. Many years later the UCS Tie fell off the shelf and shattered into pieces. With no instructions and no knowledge of peeron or Lugnet I gathered the piece, threw them in the box and there it sat for years occasionally pulling it out for a silly bit of drunken building. Years later I was perusing my local TRU and saw the latest Lego line. Exo-Force what a great gateway drug to help kick me out of my dark ages and into the world of AFOL's. It took about 6 months and numerous Exo-Force sets before I found out about my local LUG. I still remember that first meeting feeling a little intimidated by the vast collection at a fellow LUGmates house sorted by piece and color with a large bin of unsorted bley (AFOL slang for the new, disliked blue color (blue + grey = bley) that was introduced as part of the color change in 2004) sitting in a corner unused (crazy castle builder you know who you are) Since then it's become a little ridiculous, Drafting sets buying used lots and discovering the wonders of Bricklink. The clincher was BrickCon last year nothing makes an obsession like ours seem less crazy than a couple hundred others just as crazy about the bricks. So a little less than 3 years out of my dark ages a year and a half of being a LUG member and a little over a year in the flickr Lego community it shows no signs of stopping and I wouldn't have it any other way.

Another AFOL once described it this way

> I'm just coming out of mine now and have had my childhood collection in deep storage in my mum's attic for 20, 25 years. Discovering my stash again recently, I felt like Howard Carter stumbling on Tutankhamun's tomb!

Reasons for magico-religious themes in the AFOL community

There are several reasons why these themes should manifest here. First, LEGO is a portal to AFOLs' childhood. As such, they regard it as sacred. It should not be altered (not too much, at least) or made unpure. The negative reactions of AFOLs to changes in the LEGO color palette mirror the reactions of *Star Wars* fans noted by Brown, Kozinets and Sherry (2003). Brown, Kozinets and Sherry noted the revulsion many *Star Wars* fans felt toward the second trilogy of movies. Many objected to changes made to the notion of The Force with a strong degree of disgust. Something from their childhood had been sullied in Lucas's attempt to update it. The same thing is happening here. LEGO fans appreciate the manner in which LEGO building allows them to express their creativity. They also appreciate the manner in which it connects with their childhoods. LEGO enables AFOLs to reconnect with the childlike wonder and the seemingly limitless creative potential they experienced in their childhood. Changes made to LEGO threaten that special connection.

Second, and closely related, the significance of personal creativity also probably plays a role. Building with LEGO as an adult fan is an intensely creative endeavor, fraught with all the perils, pitfalls and rewards. A Cartesian duality pervades the MOC. Creativity becomes a portal to the soul, the process whereby the creative energy within is made manifest. When we think of how AFOLs understand the MOC, this assertion makes a great deal of sense. AFOLs understand the MOC as a creation from "within." Creativity as a portal to the soul becomes even more meaningful when we look at how some AFOLs perceive their lives. They describe their everyday life as stressful and demanding. They think of their often very specialized work life as satisfying only parts of their need for imaginative and creative expression. Being creative with LEGO allows, as some AFOLs explained, for escaping into "my own little world" where no one is in control (i.e., it's an escape from all the noise, the demands, the mundane everyday life into a better, more fun, unrestricted world). Perhaps this interpretation can explain why some AFOLs have described LEGO play as therapeutic. Certainly, the personal fulfillment AFOLs can feel after a successful act of creation certainly makes for a transcendent experience.

Third, the ethos of the Internet makes it more likely that these themes will emerge. LEGO fans primarily, though not solely, interact online. The Internet certainly made it easier for AFOLs to find one another and to form groups based on the types of LEGO constructions they favor. Consequently, the Internet greatly informs the AFOL experience. This could be another source of the ethereal. Werthheimer sees cyberspace and its promise as an implicitly religious construct, its implicitness being its strength in this increasingly scientific age. She writes: "Great expressions of religion make many uncomfortable today … The spiritual appeal of cyberspace lies in precisely this paradox: it is a repackaging of the old idea of Heaven, but in a secular, technologically sanctioned format" (1999, p. 23).

Similar points have been made by others (Davis 1998; Noble 1999). We agree and assert that it is this property of the medium that facilitates the adherence of ethereal themes to AFOL activities. As has been noted previously (Muñiz and Schau 2005) religious themes and motifs are enduring and quite portable. We assert that this portability is facilitated by a supportive receptacle, one lending itself to themes ethereal.

Discussion

Religiosity is an important aspect of brand communities. It fills a social need that is in many ways missing from modern life (Muñiz and O'Guinn 2001). The Internet allows for homophilious tastes and preferences for commercial offerings to unite people across vast geographic distances to realize a sense of community. The ability to get together through the discussion and use of commercial offerings provides social value that people crave. Thus, this behavior will persist.

Witness the behavior of Apple fans following the death of Steve Jobs. Fans created or contributed to shrines at Apple retail locations and waxed eloquent about the man's (and his brand's) accomplishments in online forums. Clearly, the Apple brand, despite its overwhelming mainstream success, still maintains its capacity for transformative experience. Similarly, consider the death of Michael Jackson and the manner in which his alleged and manifest transgressions were forgiven/ wiped away. Not only were his past misdeeds overlooked, his consumables increased in value and the product offerings surrounding his brand increased exponentially. It was now a necessity to own the boxed set of MJ's own favorite tracks and the digitally remastered *Thriller* video. The doctor who administered the lethal drugs cited in MJ's death was vilified, demonized and ultimately found legally responsible. Michael Jackson, himself formerly the accused and rumored villain, was victimized.

Religiosity provides for transcendent experiences (Muñiz and Schau 2005; Muñiz and Schau 2007). People can both imagine and realize new realities through the use of LEGO, transforming their inert creativity into a tangible masterpiece. The result is an epiphany that echoes that of the most significant religious conversions. Contrary to concerns of critics both classic (Weber [1922] 1978; Freud [1930] 1989; Ellul 1964) and contemporary (Ritzer 1999), AFOLs have a perfectly enchanting consumption (prosumption) experience. Much like the consumers documented by Brown *et al.* (2003), Kozinets (2001), Muñiz and Schau (2005), O'Guinn (1991) and Muñiz and Schau (2007), LEGO offers AFOLs ample opportunity for re-enchantment. The crucial difference this time is that the focal brand is a successful, non-abandoned, mainstream, non-stigmatized, non-technological product that is frequently marketed as a toy. This is a non-insignificant extension.

Further reading

Antorini, Yun Mi, Muñiz, Jr. Albert M. and Askildsen, Tormod (2012) "Collaborating with Customer Communities: Lessons from the Lego Group," *MIT Sloan Management Review*, (March): 73–9.
Chrisman, John, Hanes, Jay and Weisman, Eleanor (2009) "Love of the Brick: A Documentary of Adult Fans of LEGO," film, USA.
von Hippel, Eric (1988) *The Sources of Innovation*, Oxford: Oxford University Press.
——(2005) *Democratizing Innovation*, Cambridge, MA: MIT Press.

References

Antorini, Yun Mi (2007) "Brand Community Innovation: An Intrinsic Case Study of the Adult Fans of LEGO Community," PhD Series 35.2007.
Belk, Russell W. and Gulnur Tumbat (2002) *The Cult of Macintosh*, University of Utah: Odyssey Films.
Brown, Stephen, Kozinets, Robert V. and Sherry, Jr. John F. (2003) "Teaching Old Brands New Tricks: Retro Branding and the Revival of Brand Meaning," *Journal of Marketing*, 67(July): 19–33.
Caldwell, Marylouise and Henry, Paul (2006) "Celebrity Worship Within Affinity Groups: Adopting a Multi-Faceted Perspective," presentation to Association for Consumer Research, Latin America, Monterrey, Mexico.
Coyne, Richard (1999) *Technoromanticism: Digital Narrative, Holism and the Romance of the Real*, Cambridge, MA: The MIT Press.
Davis, Erik (1998) *Techgnosis: Myth, Magic + Mysticism in the Age of Information*, New York: Three Rivers.
Ellul, Jacques (1964) *The Technological Society*, trans. John Wilkinson, New York: Vintage.
Freud, Sigmund ([1930] 1989) *Civilization and Its Discontents*, ed. James Strachey, New York: Norton.
Kahney, Leander (2004) *The Cult of Macintosh*, San Francisco, CA: NO Starch.
Kimmel, Allan J. (2010) *Connecting with Consumers: Marketing for New Marketplace Realities*, New York: Oxford University Press.
Kozinets, Robert V. (1997) "'I Want to Believe':A Netnography of the X-Philes' Subculture of Consumption," in Merrie Brucks and Debbie MacInnis (eds), *Advances in Consumer Research*, vol. 24, Provo, UT: Association for Consumer Research, pp. 470–4.
——(2001) "Utopian Enterprise: Articulating the Meanings of *Star Trek*'s Culture of Consumption," *Journal of Consumer Research*, 28(June): 67–8.

LEGO Group (2011) "Interview with Senior Director Tormod Askildsen," April.

Muñiz, Albert M. Jr. and Antorini, Yun Mi (2011) "Refining and Extending Brand Community: An Evolutionary Perspective," presentation to the annual Association for Consumer Research Conference, St. Louis, Missouri.

Muñiz, Albert M. Jr. and O'Guinn, Thomas C. (2001) "Brand Community," *Journal of Consumer Research*, 27(4): 412–31.

Muniz, Albert M. Jr. and Schau, Hope Jensen (2005) "Religiosity in the Abandoned Apple Newton Brand Community," *Journal of Consumer Research*, March: 737–47.

——(2007) "Vigilante Marketing and Consumer-created Communications," *Journal of Advertising*, 36(3): 187–202.

Noble, David F. (1999) *The Religion of Technology: The Divinity of Man and the Spirit of Invention*, New York: Penguin.

O'Guinn, Thomas C. (1991) "Touching Greatness: The Central Midwest Barry Manilow Fanclub," in Russell W. Belk (ed.) *Highways and Buyways: Naturalistic Research from the Consumer Behavior Odyssey*, Provo, UT: Association for Consumer Research, pp. 102–11.

Park, David J., Deshpande, Sameer, Cova, Bernard and Pace, Stefano (2007) "Seeking Community Through Battle: Understanding the Meaning of Consumption Processes for Warhammer Gamers' Communities Across Borders," in Bernard Cova, Robert V. Kozinets and Avi Shankar (eds), *Consumer Tribes*, Oxford: Elsevier, pp. 212–23.

Ritzer, George (1999) *Enchanting a Disenchanted World: Revolutionizing the Means of Consumption*, Thousand Oaks, CA: Pine Forge.

Schau, Hope Jensen and Muñiz, Jr. Albert M. (2004) "Twenty Years of Consumer Culture Theory: Retrospect and Prospect," presentation to the annual Association for Consumer Research Conference, Portland, Oregon.

Schau, Hope Jensen, Muñiz, Jr. Albert M. and Arnould, Eric J. (2009) "How Brand Community Practices Create Value," *Journal of Marketing*, 73(5): 30–51.

Weber, Max ([1922] 1978) *Economy and Society*, Berkeley, CA: University of California.

Wertheim, Margaret (2000) *Pearly Gates of Cyberspace: A History of Space from Dante to the Internet*, London: Transworld Publishers.

PART VII

Issues of concern in society and culture

28

SURVEILLING CONSUMERS

The social consequences of data processing on Amazon.com

Sachil Singh and David Lyon

Keywords

Amazon.com, customized marketing, surveillance

You open your Internet browser and make your way to http://www.amazon.com. Before you even reach your destination, you are under surveillance. Cookies in your computer, there since your previous visits to the website, identify you to personalize your return to Amazon.com's homepage. "Hello, Peter. We have recommendations for you!" The list of default advertisements is customized to a rubric of your tastes and interests based on your purchase history. One offers photo albums. This reminds you of a conversation with your son the day before. He suggested that you upload your personal photographs to SmugMug for easy online storage. You open a new tab in your Internet browser and make your way to the SmugMug homepage. "Hello, Peter. Click here to donate." How do they know your name? You empathize with the charitable request for donations and get your credit card details ready. But there is no need. Even though you have never before visited this website, it already has a record of these personal details.

This illustrative consumer experience with Amazon.com and one of its partner websites is not mere fiction; neither is it conspiratorial. While the aspects of 'being watched' are not specific to Amazon.com, this e-store's ubiquity in the realm of digital consumption renders it an apt case study. It serves to highlight the relationship between digital consumption and surveillance. The intention of surveillance studies, as we show, is not to assume that technologies, such as those of Amazon.com, are necessarily invasive or even sinister. Neither is it to suggest that the effects of surveillance, as discussed in this chapter, are assumed in all cases where the technological potential of surveillance exists. Rather, the aim of this field of study is to situate a deeper understanding of technology within the realm of the socio-political and economic consequences of 'surveilling' and of 'being surveilled.' Here, then, surveillance refers to a focused and systematic attention to personal details for the purpose of marketing, of producing purchasers, constructing consumers.

Although the effects of the database-driven 'gaze' are reduced when paying with cash at a downtown store, doing so is less convenient for many people than paying with debit, credit or

319

loyalty cards. In cases of embodied transactions, there is neither a record of who buys what nor of the relationship between the buyer and the good that is purchased. However, when paying with plastic at a local store, or online, the electronic mediation of the transaction renders it digital consumption. The relative ease of anonymity which is possible when purchasing with cash is absent once transactions are digitally mediated. In the same way that every *use* of, for example, an e-book generates a *copy* which enforces control for copyright owners, the digital mediation of transactions generates footprints of the respective activities (Lessig 2005, p. 50). This digital mediation not only serves the interests of convenience and security for many consumers. It also seems to create incentives for the influence over, as well as the management and control of, information flows; assiduous attention to consumer habits by those with vested interests; customized marketing, and objectifying consumers to be willing agents of such marketing (Lyon 2002; Andrejevic 2004).

What are the sociological characteristics of these surveillant dimensions that have come to shape digital consumption? Eli Pariser's (2011) popular "filter bubble" analysis provides a useful starting point for a large part of our argument. Pariser argues that social media create "filter bubbles" that, technically, are the creation of matrices of individualized web-user information by codes. More directly, they are the result of companies using algorithms to guess through selection what information users would like to see, based on their past clicking, search behaviour and location. Much so-called self-looping and fragmentation does indeed occur as a consequence of personalization. However, there are further social consequences of digital consumer surveillance. Thus this chapter begins with "customized consumer surveillance and categorical marketing," moves to "the naturalization of surveillance" and then asks "who benefits from Amazon.com?" The intention is that these sections will provide clear overviews of the most recent literature in the field, the relationship between digital consumption and surveillance, and the likely direction of this relationship. This is a social understanding of surveillance rather than one that is technical and software-driven. The first task, however, is to briefly outline key moments in the history of database marketing.

The background: a brief history of surveillance in digital consumption

Surveillance of digital consumption predates by more than a decade the everyday use of the Internet. While electronic surveillance is now comprised of sources, codes and algorithms that are used for the storage, retrieval and processing of data, earlier forms of surveillance had different methods but similar purposes. It is generally acknowledged that a shift in the nature of consumer surveillance – from making consumers want what firms mass produced, to producing what consumers want – occurred after the middle of the last century. This shift was marked by generalized class-based derivations from surveillance of "individuals pursuing *personal* wants in a flourishing *mass* consumption marketplace" to surveillance along the lines of age, class, ethnicity, gender, lifestyle, and race (Cohen 2004, p. 237). While this shift is known in consumer literature, the methods of individual surveillance, especially before 1920, do not receive nearly as much attention.

The exemplar of nineteenth-century entrepreneurialism, the Singer Sewing Machine Company, pioneered mass consumer credit (Godley 2006, p. 295). This was part of its strategy of "aggressive marketing" (Chandler 1977, p. 304). It is from this historical period that Mark Andrejevic (2007, pp. 81–2) identifies the origins of market research. He describes it as an element so significant for the emerging consumer industry that "It is not exaggerating to say that surveillance of the populace became the economic lifeblood of the commercial mass media." Steven Nock (1993, p. 49) argues that by the 1870s, "most household products were available on credit. Thus, the value of various details of consumers' purchases became more significant to marketers as mass consumption expanded and the need for firms to 'monitor and control spending' would grow in sophistication (Evans and Schmalensee 2005, p. 128).

Other forms of consumer surveillance for mass advertising also emerged in this period, particularly as a result of the rise of public communication. The problem, however, was that the reach of the advertisements was unknown as there was no feedback loop to inform advertisers of consumers' reactions. Archibald Crossley answered this call in the 1920s. He used the telephone to conduct individual surveys in order to build a database of audience behaviors and habits. However, with this method, the value of the information gathered is only as reliable as the honesty and consent of the surveilled. Therefore, he expanded the scope of his market research to trails of household garbage. This latter trend away from the active interaction with the surveilled, towards a more passive form, was garnered by Arthur C. Nielsen Sr. He developed a technology that captured, in real time, the behavior of radio listeners and television watchers. Of course, this occurred in affluent households only, which were the ones using such communicative technology. His Audimeter and People Meter, were able to, respectively, measure the popularity of different frequencies at different times of the day, and determine *who* was watching *which* television station. Crossley and Nielsen's contributions built on the ability of technology to shape the direction, not just of society, but of *individual* behavior (Andrejevic 2007, pp. 84–8; Fortier 2001, pp. 4–5).

By the late 1950s, concern had spread in the United States over the ongoing promotion of mass consumption and the belief that this would lead to market saturation, and stagnant economic growth. It is no surprise, therefore, that as methods of surveillance developed, so did the means of consumer market regulation as a form of feedback-based social control (Andrejevic 2007, p. 83). Not only did surveillance render the chances more unlikely of the borrower ever meeting the lender, but it represented growing faith in a system of regulation. This continues today with elaborate but subtle forms of digital surveillance that regulate record-keeping, follow-ups, or legal action of online transactions (Lyon 2007, p. 1). Indeed, as Colin Bennett (2008, p. 11) notes, ironically, in some ways surveillance "is the necessary glue that builds trust throughout a 'society of strangers'."

The emergence of systems of regulation also brought about an individual-centered discourse which as one of us says "entailed the gathering of information on … individuals. Persons were more clearly unique and distinguishable from one another as their individual identities were established but by the same token they became easier to control" (Lyon 2001, p. 28). The methods of control became more sophisticated over the next few decades as consumer surveillance emerged as an established feature of consumerism.

Another means of collecting consumers' personal information was Potential Rating Index for Zip Markets (PRIZM). This computer-based geodemographic system relies on postal or zip code groupings, as a means of consumer surveillance. It was developed in 1974 by Jonathan Robbin. It pays particular attention to the classification of groups according to various lifestyle categories. The computer revolution that defined the late 1970s until the mid-1990s not only contributed to the upgrading of previous methods of consumer surveillance and marketing to make them more sophisticated and widespread, but also facilitated the rapid growth in consumerism. The rise in e-commerce in the mid-1990s added yet another layer of consumer surveillance to those already in place. As American capitalism expanded – particularly through its "golden age" in the mid-late 1990s – so too did consumerism, and the ideological efforts to encourage it (Kofi Annan, cited in Kovel 2007, p. 46).

By 2000, the mutual constitution of capitalism, consumerism and the Internet was providing expanding opportunities for electronic methods of surveillance. Therefore, the ease with which e-shopping can be done, for example, has contributed to almost revolutionary changes in both the ways in which electronic transactions are regulated and in which money is spent. The consumer surveillance potential on the Internet, performed by governments, credit bureaus and e-traders and others, has made the collection of personal information of millions of consumers a potentially very profitable business (Lace 2005, p. 2). That is, despite the ease of shopping online, shoppers, often unknowingly, leave electronic trails as they browse through websites and make credit card purchases (Lyon 2001, p. 43). Similar to Crossely's interest in consumers' garbage, various e-stores and others find financial value in consumers' trails of the websites they visit, the items they peruse and the purchases they make. These trails are created by and stored in cookies and beacons.

Vincent Müller (2009) argues that with such engagement, data collection shifts from an act of simply watching, to a cognitive act of watching *with a purpose* and without the necessary consent of the individual being watched (and thus may be construed as surveillance). As well, Rob Kitchin and Martin Dodge (2011, p. 47) point to the social impact of software that is "addressable, aware, and active." Indeed, the extracted feedback – generated via human or coded means – "becomes the property of private companies that can store, aggregate, sort, and, in many cases, sell the information to others" (Andrejevic 2007, p. 3; see also Pridmore and Zwick 2011). Here lie the social consequences of data processing in the "world wide web of surveillance" (Lyon 2001, p. 101).

Customized consumer surveillance and categorical marketing

Corporations use surveillance on consumers' purchase habits in the hope of predicting their tastes and preferences. Various agencies have different interests in personal information that often originate from digitally-mediated purchases: fraud divisions track consumer activity "for our own protection" every time we pay with plastic; commercial banks track purchases to calculate monthly balances owing; credit unions keep tabs on the consumer's ability to make monthly payments in order to evaluate credit ratings; and telemarketers and e-stores trace tastes and preferences to facilitate customized marketing and profit-seeking.

In light of this chapter's case study of Amazon.com, two important questions must be asked: First, *what kinds of information are generated from one's use of the Amazon.com website?* The account holders' name; address; phone number; credit card details; direct personal association with the purchased item; content of emails to Amazon.com; personal reviews of Amazon.com products; personal descriptions in 'Your Profile' and accompanying photographs; financial information, including Social Security Numbers and drivers' license numbers (Amazon.com 2011a).

Second, *which activities trigger personal data collection on Amazon.com?* Searching for, or purchasing, an item; communicating with Amazon.com by phone or e-mail; completing questionnaires; compiling Wish Lists; and participating in discussion boards (ibid.). The answers to both questions (which, notably, are derived from publicly available information on Amazon.com's website) suggest that browsing and purchasing on Amazon.com, together with customized consumer surveillance that is performed on the website, are mutually constituted. As all acts of digital browsing and consumption are surveilled, they form the lifeblood of consumer surveillance in the electronic world.

Representative of this relationship is Andrejevic's (2007, p. 2) 'digital enclosure' which is "the creation of an interactive realm wherein every action and transaction generates information about itself." One such action is the ability to customize Boolean searches online, which facilitates the filtering through of potentially millions of items. This is a far more individualized, specific and accurate search than having to settle with the limited possibilities on the shelves of a store downtown. At the same time, however, it is also far more invasive. For example, the results of the Boolean search are not necessarily open-ended, but targeted in some form. Jean Baudrillard (1998, p. 27) argues that while consumers certainly do have choices in choosing between products, these choices are not open-ended and often cannot be customized in ways that represent complete freedom of choice.

Another example of invasiveness is to be found in new user registrations on Amazon.com. The customized greeting is followed by "Tell us more about your likes and dislikes by rating products you have an opinion about. The more we know about your interests, the more we can do to improve your recommendations" (Amazon.com 2011b). The release of such information to Amazon.com is the essence of collaborative filtering (Arazy *et al.* 2009, p. 39). This is a process used by the company to make recommendations to consumers based on the similarity of their searches with those made by others users. The surveillance of digital consumers that it enables also highlights the shift from producing and advertising on mass scales to the individualization of both processes in "categorical seduction" (Lyon 2007, p. 185). The information required for this is not only databased, interpreted and categorized for the purposes of one-to-one marketing, but also has ramifications on the "social sorting" of consumers (Lyon 2001, p. 43; 2003).

At some point what we call 'social sorting' shades into what some refer to as 'software sorting.' The claim here is that the sorting is performed by machines as opposed to people (Graham 2005; Müller 2009). Nigel Thrift and Shaun French (cited in Kitchin and Dodge 2011, p. 5) argue that the software needed to make machines 'work' has a "presence as 'local intelligence,'" which is why Kitchin and Dodge (2011, p. 5) believe that technology does indeed possess "characteristics of being alive." Interesting and important though it is to explore such claims, the significant point is that in such software, marketers have even more sophisticated means of classifying consumers in potentially discriminatory ways. The result is that consumer tastes and preferences can be influenced and shaped, and that the outcomes may be even more discriminatory just because softwares operate as it were "on their own" (see Gandy 2009). One does not have to accept the notion that such softwares are alive, act or behave morally to grasp that the capacity of firms to influence how their products are purchased is likely to be enlarged through the use of software to create those crucial classifications. It is a further stage in the historical development of such efforts to extend control to consumers in the marketplace.

Ashlee Humphreys (2006) provides an analysis of Amazon.com's practices of surveillance and marketing in a way which highlights their historical evolution. She proposes that these practices illustrate an extension of Foucauldian self-discipline through the presence of a secularized eye of God. Humphreys' (2006) Foucauldian adaptation suggests a shift from the 'prisoner' to the 'consumer,' from 'mechanisms of discipline' to 'mechanisms of marketing' (and Internet surveillance), from a 'disobeying machine' to a 'desiring machine,' from 'repressed desire' to 'constitutive desire,' and from a subjugated 'human body' to a subjugated 'incorporeal individual.' However, the very nature of the panopticon is to limit interaction between the surveiller and the surveilled. Yet Amazon.com's Wish Lists (and other features) encourage consumer participation in their own surveillance (this is part of 'participatory' and 'peer-to-peer' surveillance). This creates an environment in which there is a *certainty* of one's Wish List being watched, in comparison to the relative *uncertainty* of the inspector's gaze in the panopticon. What is generally unknown to digital consumers (and to other subjects of surveillance), however, is what categories their information generates and into which they are classified (Lyon 2010, p. 329).

Like the panopticon, in which the many are aware of the potential gaze of one, Amazon.com's Wish List makes consumers aware of being surveilled by others. The data that is provided to Amazon.com through this resource presents the company with the opportunity to classify consumers into different categories and formulate "data doubles" (Lyon 2003) or "capta shadows" (Kitchin and Dodge 2011, p. 90). These terms refer to the apparently eternal lifespan of mined data. Oscar Gandy's (1993) *Panoptic Sort* highlights the nature of the classificatory drive behind this. It does so by showing the discriminatory methods of corporations whose rationalized consumer marketing socially sorts based on their perceptions of individuals' economic and political value. The result, as Zygmunt Bauman says, is "flushing the undesirables *away* and keeping the regulars in" (Bauman 2007, p. 4; original emphasis).

Amazon.com combines this kind of sorting with peer-to-peer surveillance. The nature of the Wish List, by its very design, is to enable peer-to-peer surveillance; not in ways that involve snooping, spying or any other form of surveillance that requires discretion, but quite openly and known to the subject. It is so open that if a user does not apply security settings to the Wish List, it is searchable by anyone, provided that the user's email address is known or can be guessed.

But there are other ways to use Michel Foucault's work to illuminate Amazon.com and its ilk. His analysis of the relationship between patient and psychiatrist emphasizes the need to keep a record of every patient's past and present tendencies in order to predict his or her future tendencies. Similarly, the Wish List databases individuals' past and present item selections with the intention of having authority over future tastes and preferences. Arguably, "the ability to sense what customers will want *next*, knowing what they will ask for *before* they actually request it, gains importance" (Franzak *et al.* 2001, p. 634, emphasis added). In this way, the Wish List forms the basis for sorting individuals according to their habits and likes in order to predict the tendencies of many. The Wish List also serves as an illustration of consumers' desires to be watched. Humphreys (2006, p. 304) and Kirstie Ball (2009, p. 643) argue that such desires are the result of an image culture and adds to a fetish value. For example, consumers create Wish Lists with the intention of being seen by other consumers. This arguably plays a significant role in Amazon.com's masking of, or consumers' indifference to, the discreet surveillance that is performed by Amazon.com over Wish Lists. The pleasure derived from being watched, in this case, arguably adds to the implicit tolerance of the Amazon.com gaze in general.

The main success of the Wish List appears to derive from the fact that it capitalizes on the disciplined willingness of consumers to *want* to partake in the consumption that it promotes. This willingness can be likened to Neil Gabler's (2000) *Life the Movie*. He shows the power of the entertainment industry in seducing twentieth-century Americans to live their lives for it – or indeed, *perform* for it. For both the Wish List and Gabler's thesis, the persuasion to make consumers act in certain ways is crucial to the interests of those who encourage the performances. For Amazon.com, this play on desire is of course crucial to consumer surveillance. It only works with willing, even eager, participants, which is a far cry from the intentions of the original panopticon diagram (Rose 1999, pp. 242–5). This qualified disciplinary quality is emphasized by the *amnesiac* qualities of new media technologies which can make users overlook the implications of their intentions (Thrift 2005, p. 21).

Prior to the Wish List, Amazon.com used to customize consumer marketing based on users' *digital* representations of themselves, which were only *assumed* to be representative of reality (Zwick and Dholakia 2004). The malleability and flexibility involved in its more recent form of consumer surveillance offer greater accuracy and completeness for what is known as "captabasing" consumers' personal tastes and preferences. Captabasing refers to the databasing of selectively captured data, in some cases including authorship and tagging data (see Kitchin and Dodge 2011). The reason for this, as Ball (2009, p. 640) argues, is that "the body interior of the surveilled subject is more open to division, classification and scrutiny, because it is seen as a source of truth … which calls for a non-reductive and multi-dimensional approach to the subjective experience of surveillance." The many agencies, known as "digital aggregators," involved in this experience of surveillance connect pieces of various puzzles that consumers leave in different databases, such as names, social security numbers, past residential addresses, credit histories, lifestyle information and various details of friends or associates (Passavant 2005; Lyon 2007, p. 165). While cookies provide accuracy in terms of bridging potential gaps that exist between digital and physical representations of consumption habits, the Wish List provides an incentive for consumers to manage *themselves* and accurately reflect the one form of representation in the other.

The naturalization of surveillance

The use of the word surveillance sometimes misleads by giving the impression that an external force exerts itself on an unwilling subject. But in the case of online shopping, many consumers *choose* to forego the anonymity of paying with cash in a store. They favour the convenience, endless product selections, internationally competitive pricings, and by implication of digital consumption, the surveillance, that accompanies it. The perceived reputability of Amazon.com in the eyes of its e-shoppers is critical to its promotion of the naturalization of surveillance. This is because it provides the basis for the seriousness with which many consumers welcome its methods of collaborative filtering, such as the "recommender system" (Arazy *et al.* 2009, p. 39). The above factors have become such convenient and justifiable incentives for embracing digital consumption, that the immediacy which they are based on makes many consumers overlook the digital means of their consumption (Lash 2002, pp. 2–4; Fisher 2010a, p. 232). That is, focus readily shifts away from both the means of transmitting information and the implicit presence of surveillance. Instead, it shifts towards the act and convenience of transmitting information electronically to make a purchase, as well as the perceived relationship with the e-store, based largely on trust, which improves the advice-taking that stems from recommendations (Arazy *et al.* 2009, pp. 39–40). But why are the roles and effects of surveillance overlooked by many consumers?

The central way in which online stores are able to drastically reduce costs is by almost entirely eliminating market research expenses (Pridmore 2010, pp. 296–7). The consumer information which these stores gather directly, or buy on auction, marks an entire process of consumer marketing, consumer surveillance, advertising and sales. At the center of this process is the productivity of labor in the form of consumer web browsing. Martin Hand (2008, p. 16) reminds us that digital technologies are packaged with "global mobility and marketization not social division and class struggle [as] the watchwords of the new cultural landscape." Perhaps as a result, the surplus labor extraction which data-mining companies derive is not reflected in any reward or remuneration for the online browser (Fortier 2001: pp. 38–9). It only resembles such a form when the online browser purchases an item, as this represents the buying back of the contributed added value (Andrejevic 2007, p. 144). Eran Fisher (2010b, p. 119) notes that this is "not a break but a continuation of the long history of capitalist exploitation, based on increasing levels of surplus value (rather than simply increased levels of productivity)."

One of the premises upon which Amazon.com conducts consumer surveillance is the internal acceptance of surveillance by the targeted web browser. Perhaps this explains why the company is transparent about many forms of surveillance that it performs (Amazon.com 2011a). Another implicit premise is that consumers can be made to enjoy digital consumption, as well as the social consequences that accompany it. These two premises can be understood with closer contextual attention to surveillance. It is important to elaborate on them respectively, as their different aspects overlap and can result in blurred understandings. So why does the digital consumer accept consumer surveillance, and offer little, if any, resistance to it?

First, little is truly understood by consumers about the intricacies and complexities of surveillance practices (Lyon 2007, p. 164; Ball 2009). A lack of such an understanding breeds the belief that when the claim is that police are protecting people from neighborhood crime or terrorism, surveillance is 'good.' 'Bad' surveillance is Orwellian oppression. Also, little attention is paid by consumers to the design of consumer surveillance; typically, consumers 'agree' to "privacy policies" without pausing to read them (Lyon 2001, p. 44).[1] Part of this has to do with the very long, complicated and jargon-laden language used in e-companies' legal policies or terms and conditions. And part of the problem is that 'privacy' seems to refer simply to the notion that one might not wish to disclose certain facts to others for the sake of pride or propriety and does not necessarily touch broader issues of consumer surveillance, particularly those discussed here, of 'social sorting.'

Second, when there are benefits associated with digital consumption, they can readily outweigh any concerns over consumer surveillance. For example, in the case of most credit cards (but particularly with loyalty cards), the more they are used, the more "cash back," air miles and discounts most credit card users are entitled to (Pridmore 2010, p. 295). Of course, the greater usage of such cards creates a more enabling environment for, thus amplifying, consumer surveillance.

Third, digital discourses are largely interpreted as offering a desirable if not literally sublime experience, something that radically transcends previous modes of consumption (Mosco 2004). As early as 1995, *Fortune* magazine offered advice for survival in the chip-driven economy: "Embrace it, for it will transform our lives and the way we work, more profoundly than we can imagine – and nothing is going to stop it" (cited in Cavoukian 1995, p. 6). As a result of such perspectives, digital consumers may favor consumer surveillance technologies for the benefits they confer without considering what they are used for and how they are used beyond the immediate 'customized' needs represented by the transaction.

Following this, fourth, online shoppers are stimulated by interactive technology to what Andrejevic (2007, p. 44) calls "cybernetic participation." It is sometimes simply the desire to partake in the digital experience which overrides any apparent concern with consumer surveillance. Thrift's (2004) development of the "technological unconscious" or Dodge's (2009, p. 18) concern with "automated discrimination" are, respectively, useful explanatory and consequential considerations here. Moreover, Lyon (2001, p. 103) raises concern in arguing that, "[t]he more an individual wishes to participate fully in the consumer society, and especially in electronic commerce, the more she or he will be subject to deeply intrusive surveillance." Such intrusion has consequences. The credit card, of course, seems to make the potential of cybernetic participation materially limitless and infinitely empowering.

Emerging from consumer surveillance, then, are two central issues: consumer exploitation through, and acceptance of, practices of surveillance. While these overlap in the outcome of favor to the firm, they are necessarily rooted in separate issues.

The exploitation of consumers, argue Detlev Zwick *et al.* (2008) (expanded by Cova and Dalli 2009, and Humphreys and Grayson 2008) is in fact "double exploitation." The two elements of this are: the absence of remuneration for consumers' willingness to serve as 'co-creators'; and the imbalance between the offering of 'social cooperation' and the benefits received.[2]

Digital consumers are often oblivious to their own objectification because they are able to provide work which offers financial benefit to Amazon.com in their *leisure* time and from the *comfort* of their homes (2010b, p. 128). They *choose* to incur the costs of their time, health, well-being, and wear and tear to their desktops, laptops, and iPads (Fisher 2010b, p. 128). As Andrejevic (2007, pp. 45–6; original emphasis) correctly points out, "There is a difference between a *deliberative* process whereby goals are collectively defined and a *manipulative* process whereby one group is induced to embrace the goals of another as its own, without deliberation, compromise, or revision." At the core of this lies an institutional legitimation that is based on legal, moral, and cultural forms from which necessary trust is developed, and comes to be assumed by the consumer (Scott 2001; Grayson *et al.* 2008; Cova and Dalli 2009). It is such a legitimating potential which one should keep in mind when considering the ideological arguments that stem from this. François Fortier (2001, pp. 1–2) shows that while some point to the benefits of the digital age, others "vilify cyberspace as the latest mirage of bourgeois mystification, threatening (once again) the working classes with corporate slavery, consumers with mental colonialism, and citizens generally with panoptic totalitarianism."

The acceptance of consumer surveillance arguably lies in the failure to identify the differences in goals of, on the one hand, marketers and e-stores, and on the other hand, consumers themselves. The marketer and e-store are concerned with maximizing profit. The most cost-efficient means to achieve this, it seems, is to offer the consumer the illusion of autonomous choice. Realistically, this illusion is the source of constituting control over consumers. The strategy is that this control, and its implementation, do not necessarily leave the consumer with the feeling of subordination; after all, consumers are not always aware of what personal information is observed, extracted and used. Importantly, this is a kind of control which represents consumers' "*active participation in self-manipulation*" (Andrejevic 2007, p. 255, emphasis added). One of the primary reasons for such power relations is that Amazon.com seeks to achieve the internalization and naturalization of surveillance through "the discipline of marketing" (Humphreys 2006, pp. 297–8).

So how is the naturalization of surveillance achieved through the Wish List's encouragement of consumers' active participation in their own surveillance? One way in which Wish Lists are designed is as shopping tools for users to catalogue the items that they wish to be given as gifts. The front-end of Wish Lists makes the gift-hunting process easier for those wishing to buy gifts, but for the very same reason, also encourages active involvement by users to keep their Wish Lists as frequently updated as possible. The back-end provides Amazon.com with valuable databases of consumer information which can be essentialized to map future tendencies regarding tastes and preferences. Therefore, Wish Lists are not only beneficial to users by giving hints to friends and families regarding what items to potentially buy, but also provide Amazon.com with plots of tastes and preferences which are constantly updated, improved and increasingly accurate (Franzak *et al.* 2001, p. 631). As Frank Franzak *et al.* (ibid., p. 635) note, "The best profiling is continuously updated."

The effect, therefore, is the growing ubiquity of surveillance through encouraging consumers to participate. One key difference between the normalizing agenda in Foucault's psychiatrist–patient relationship and the Amazon.com-customer relationship is that the aim of the former is to correct activity based on the yardstick of a societal norm. In the case of the latter, the aim is to record the consumer tastes and preferences of those who have Wish Lists and then use them as yardsticks to map the typology for a wider audience. The power of individuation which is necessary for the digital consumption that defines this mechanism is only possible through consumer surveillance (Humphreys 2006, p. 302). Quite simply therefore, it is not possible to speak of digital consumption without also speaking of surveillance.

Who benefits from Amazon.com?

Globalization offers consumers increased mobility, interaction and connectedness. These were a few of the factors that facilitated the temporary success of the DotCom boom. However, with the bursting of the DotCom bubble at the turn of the century, and the resulting declarations of bankruptcy by e-corporations, many (such as boo.com, toysmart.com and craftshop.com) turned to selling consumers' personal information as means of saving themselves from insolvency (Foster 2000, p. 140; Fortier 2001, pp. 49–51). These personal forms of information included credit card numbers, addresses, tastes and preferences. Following suit, Amazon.com rewrote portions of its privacy policies to allow it to share consumers' personal information with third parties. This created the possibility for similar redemption should the company also be hit by bankruptcy (Sturges *et al.* 2001, p. 365). Indeed, "Amazon was caught gathering more personal information about customers than the shoppers could possibly have known by reading the site's privacy policy" (Green 2000, p. 14). This is indicative of the financial value that can be garnered from consumer surveillance through the selling of consumers' personal information (Lace 2005, p. 2).

The increased consumer mobility that the Internet has allowed also results in more interaction with people from beyond the boundaries of the local 'village'; interactions with people we have never met before, and possibly will never cross paths with again after a single purchase. Embedded in such interactions are both promises and threats on the relationship between digital consumption and digital technologies (Hand 2008). Connotations of promises include consumer freedom, choice, benefit, pleasure, individuality and empowerment (Gabriel and Lang 2006; Smart 2010, p. 7). This is also suggested by the Amazon.com slogan, " … and you're done" which is indicative of the ease and simplicity presented to digital consumers who use the website.

At the same time, however, the naturalization of surveillance evokes various descriptions of threats: intrusion, invasiveness and exploitation. For example, certain companies, such as Bluekai, collect information about consumers' web activities (such as viewed websites and generated searches) and sell it to other companies for their marketing purposes. Bluekai (2010) advertises this to potential buyers of consumer data as "[a]ccess actionable audience data on more than 200 million users. That's over 80% of the entire US Internet population at your fingertips." This overwhelming percentage offers justification to Susanne Lace's (2005, p. 1) definition of "glass consumers": "others know so much about us, they can almost see through us." However, many digital consumers do not interpret activities such as those of Bluekai as necessarily invasive as much as they are welcomed for empowering digital shopping capabilities.

Perhaps more telling are the efforts by Amazon.com to garner significant control of the Internet in order to increase its 2009 net annual sales of US$24.51 billion (Amazon.com 2010). It is the networked capability of the Internet which is the key element of the horizontal market integration that Amazon.com promotes. For example, between 2001 and 2008, the Amazon Honor System allowed web browsers to make donations (mostly to charities and non-profit organizations) for various causes (such as the American Red Cross' disaster relief initiatives) on many U.S. websites. Once subscribed, an Amazon.com graphic (known as an Amazon Honor System Paybox) was embedded on the partnered website. Intriguingly, even if the web browser had never before visited this partnered website, it contained the same customized greeting that appears when one is logged in on Amazon.com. Unbeknown to most Amazon.com users, the company places cookies on their hard disks when they visit its website. Under the Amazon Honor System, this meant that when the individual browsed a partner website, Amazon.com would search for a cookie on the user's hard disk in order to personalize the experience and retrieve credit card information. Amazon.com (2011c) justifies its intentions to "continue [its] support for charitable giving with new technologies" by allowing customers to make payments "quickly and securely using their existing account information." Despite the goodwill that Amazon.com promotes through these methods, there are concerns regarding its growing dominance over and control of all Internet activity performed by its customers. This is evident in its more recent payment technologies (which are not restricted to charitable incentives) that span across various websites such as eJAMMING and SmugMug.[3]

Finally, the credit card economy benefits from e-stores, since credit card payment is one of the most convenient methods of processing digital consumption. For every digital transaction that is mediated with a credit card, information is relayed, back and forth, via various channels: the acquirer (the bank that handles Amazon.com's transactions based on the user's type of credit card), the respective credit card company's centralized database, the user's bank, and a merchant-processing firm (such as First Data Corporation). Amazon.com generally receives approximately 2 percent less than what consumers acknowledge payment for. This percentage is paid, as commission, to the acquirer. The acquirer pays approximately 1.7 percent (a fee established by the credit card company) of the purchase price to the user's bank.

Clearly, then, there are several significant beneficiaries from the Amazon.com experience. However, if Amazon.com is considered alongside other modes of Internet-based consumption, further responses to the question of benefit would be required. For one thing, the Wish List phenomenon represents a rich dataset through which other marketers may wish to trawl (and even ordinary users without sophisticated software can learn a lot from what is publicly available). Beyond this is the way in which all such online marketing systems, including social media, engage in the classification of consumers according to consumption criteria. It is well known that such social sorting links geodemographics with actual buying habits to create categories of consumers within which to further customize and target advertising (this was noted and popularized early, see e.g. Larsen 1994). Much more recently, Roger Burrows and Nick Gane (2006) have shown that such classification may be analytically connected with studies of social class and thus with more and less access to certain valued resources. And Gandy (2009) argues that in their gender and (especially) racialized dimensions, the "rational discrimination" resulting from consumer classification may produce great benefits for some, but what he calls "cumulative disadvantage" for others.

Conclusion

It is important to note, first of all, that consumer surveillance on Amazon.com or anywhere is no conspiracy. Rather, how user databases are constructed and what happens to them are the result of historical trends towards increasing interest in managing consumption, starting with market research and continuing to present-day offshoots of Customer Relationship Marketing. Amazon.com's Wish List simply follows a well-worn trajectory, albeit with some innovative features. Second, categorical marketing involves collaborative filtering within digital enclosures. We conclude that this produces new forms of consumer self-discipline, especially through Amazon.com's Wish List feature. Third, consumer surveillance becomes naturalized, and (we argued) several overlapping tendencies explain how this occurs with such ease. After all, consuming is generally considered pleasurable and even what might otherwise be construed as self-discipline may be included in that rubric. Lastly, the corporation and those customers whose activities are most synchronized with its practices benefit from the collaborative filtering and social sorting that characterize its model. But at the same time, in a broader context, Amazon.com and its Wish List also contribute unwittingly to the cumulative disadvantage of others who successively slip through the cracks created by a system that rewards winners.

Notes

1 Stephen Marmura (2010, p. 114) reaches the same conclusion regarding surveillance practices in the United States regarding national security. In much the same way, he shows that political leaders are able to design policies of surveillance on the premise of encountering little resistance because patriotism and nationalist sentimentality are still very significant.

2 To Bernard Cova and Daniele Dalli (2009, p. 327), this imbalance is the result of a break in trust that the consumer assumes between him/herself and certain companies.

3 The payment options include: Amazon Simple Pay Donations, Amazon Simple Pay Standard and Amazon Flexible Payments Service.

Further reading

Gandy, O.H. Jr. (2009) *Coming to Terms with Chance: Engaging Rational Discrimination and Cumulative Disadvantage*, London: Ashgate. [An exploration of the gender and (especially) racialized dimensions of consumer classification.]

Kitchin, R. and Dodge, M. (2011) *Code/Space: Software and Everyday Life*, Cambridge, MA: MIT Press. [A critical evaluation of the everyday usage and reliance on codes and algorithms that make up software.]

Pariser, E. (2011) *The Filter Bubble: What the Internet is Hiding from You*, New York: The Penguin Press. [An analysis of the ways in which codes create universes of individualized information (filter bubbles) on the Internet with the intention of shaping our tastes, preferences and the ways in which information and ideas are presented to us.]

References

Amazon.com (2010) "Annual Report 2009," available at: http://phx.corporate-ir.net/phoenix.zhtml?c=97664&p=irol-reportsannual (accessed on 3 November 2010).

——(2011a) "Amazon.com Privacy Notice," available at: www.amazon.com/gp/help/customer/display.html?nodeId=468496 (accessed on 30 May 2011).

——(2011b) "Today's Recommendations for You," available at: www.amazon.com/gp/yourstore?ie=UTF8&ref_=pd_irl_gw_r&new_account=1& (accessed on 30 May 2011).

——(2011c) "Amazon Honor System," available at: www.amazon.com/gp/help/customer/display.html?nodeId=542032 (accessed on 1 June 2011).

Andrejevic, M. (2004) *Reality TV: The Work of Being Watched*, Lanham, MD: Rowman & Littlefield Publishers.

——(2007) *iSpy*, Kansas: University Press of Kansas.

——(2011) "Surveillance and Alienation in the Online Economy," *Surveillance & Society*, 8(3): 278–87.

Arazy, O., Kumar, N. and Shapira, B. (2009) "Improving Social Recommender Systems," *IT Pro*, 38–44.

Ball, K. (2009) "Exposure: Exploring the Subject of Surveillance," *Information, Communication and Society*, 12(5): 639–57.

Baudrillard, J. (1998) *The Consumer Society: Myths and Structures*, London: Sage.

Bauman, Z. (2007) *Consuming Life*, Cambridge: Polity Press.

Bennett, C.J. (2001) "Cookies, Web Bugs, Webcams and Cue Cats: Patterns of Surveillance on the World Wide Web," *Ethics and Information Technology*, 3(3): 197–210.

——(2008) *The Privacy Advocates: Resisting the Spread of Surveillance*, Cambridge, MA: MIT Press.

Bluekai (2010) "The Bluekai Exchange," available at: www.bluekai.com/exchange.php (accessed on 5 December 2010).

Burrows, R. and Gane, N. (2006) "Geodemographics, Software and Class," *Sociology*, 40(5): 793–812.

Cavoukian, A. (1995) *Who Knows: Safeguarding Your Privacy in a Networked World*, Toronto: Random House of Canada.

Chandler, A.D. Jr. (1977) *The Visible Hand: The Managerial Revolution in American Business*, Cambridge, MA: Belknap Press of Harvard University Press.

Cohen, L. (2004) "A Consumers' Republic: The Politics of Mass Consumption in Postwar America," *Journal of Consumer Research*, 31(1): 236–9.

Cova, B. and Dalli, D. (2009) "Working Consumers: The Next Step in Marketing Theory?," *Marketing Theory*, 9(3): 315–39.

Dodge, M. (2009) "Code/Space," *Urbis Research Forum Review*, 1(2): 15–25.

Evans, D.S. and Schmalensee, R. (2005) *Paying with Plastic: The Digital Revolution in Buying and Borrowing*, Cambridge, MA: MIT Press.

Fisher, E. (2010a) "Contemporary Technology Discourse and the Legitimation of Capitalism," *European Journal of Social Theory*, 13(2): 229–52.

——(2010b) *Media and New Capitalism in the Digital Age*, New York: Palgrave Macmillan.

Fortier, F. (2001) *Virtuality Check: Power Relations and Alternative Strategies in the Information Society*, London: Verso.

Foster, E. (2000) "They Are Everywhere You Want Them to Be – and Even Where You Don't Want Them," *Infoworld*, September, 25: 140.

Franceschetti, G. and Grossi, G. (2008) *Homeland Security Technology Challenges: From Sensing and Encrypting to Mining and Modeling*, Cambridge, MA: Artech House.

Franzak, F., Pitta, D. and Fritsche, S. (2001) "Online Relationships and the Consumer's Right to Privacy," *Journal of Consumer Marketing*, 18(7): 631–41.

Gabler, N. (2000) *Life the Movie: How Entertainment Conquered Reality*, New York: Vintage.

Gabriel, Y. and Lang, T. (2006) *The Unmanageable Consumer*, London: Sage.

Gandy, O.H. Jr. (1993) *The Panoptic Sort: A Political Economy of Personal Information*, Boulder: CO: Westview Press.

——(2009) *Coming to Terms with Chance: Engaging Rational Discrimination and Cumulative Disadvantage*, London: Ashgate.

Godley, A. (2006) "Selling the Sewing Machine Around the World: Singer's International Marketing Strategies, 1850–1920," *Enterprise and Society*, 7(2): 266–314.

Graham, S.D.N. (2005) "Software-sorted Geographies," *Progress in Human Geography*, 29(5): 562–80.

Grayson, K., Johnson, D. and Chen, D-F. R. (2008) "Is Firm Trust Essential in a Trusted Environment? How Trust in the Business Context Influences Customers," *Journal of Marketing Research*, 45(2): 241–56.

Green, H. (2000) "1984 in 2000: Getting Too Personal," *Business Week eBiz*, February 7, 14.

Hand, M. (2008) *Making Digital Cultures*, Aldershot: Ashgate.

Heller, S. and Womack, D. (2007) *Becoming a Digital Designer: A Guide to Careers in Web, Video, Broadcast, Game and Animation Design*, Hoboken, NJ: John Wiley & Sons, Inc.

Humphreys, A. (2006) "The Consumer as Foucauldian 'Object of Knowledge'," *Social Science Computer Review*, 24(3): 296–309.

Humphreys, A. and Grayson, K. (2008) "The Intersecting Roles of Consumer and Producer: A Critical Perspective on Co-production, Co-creation and Prosumption," *Sociology Compass*, 2(3): 963–80.

Kitchin, R. and Dodge, M. (2011) *Code/Space: Software and Everyday Life*, Cambridge, MA: MIT Press.

Kovel, J. (2007) *The Enemy of Nature: The End of Capitalism or the End of the World?*, New York: Zed Books.

Lace, S. (ed.) (2005) *The Glass Consumer: Life in a Surveillance Society*, Bristol: Polity Press.

Larsen, E. (1994) *The Naked Consumer*, New York: Penguin.

Lessig, L. (2005) "The People Own Ideas!," *Technology Review*, 108(6): 46–53.

Lyon, D. (2001) *Surveillance Society*, Buckingham: Open University Press.

——(2002) "Surveillance in Cyberspace: The Internet, Personal Data, and Social Control," *Queen's Quarterly*, 109(3): 345–56.

——(2003) "Surveillance as Social Sorting: Computer Codes and Mobile Bodies," in D. Lyon (ed.) *Surveillance as Social Sorting: Privacy, Risk and Digital Discrimination*, London: Routledge.

——(2007) *Surveillance Studies: An Overview*, Cambridge: Polity Press.

——(2010) "Liquid Surveillance: The Contribution of Zygmunt Bauman to Surveillance Studies," *International Political Sociology*, 4(4): 325–38.

MacDougall, R. (2010) "eBay Ethics: Simulating Civility Today, for the 'Digital Democracies' of Tomorrow," *Convergence*, 16(2): 235–44.

Marmura, S. (2010) "Security vs Privacy: Media Messages, State Policies, and American Public Trust in Government," in E. Zureik, S. Harling, L. Lynda, E. Smith, D. Lyon, and Y.E. Chan (eds), *Surveillance, Privacy, and the Globalization of Personal Information: International Comparisons*, Montreal: McGill-Queen's University Press, pp. 110–26.

Mosco, V. (2004) *The Digital Sublime: Myth, Power and Cyberspace*, Cambridge, MA: MIT Press.

Müller, V.C. (2009) "Would You Mind Being Watched by Machines? Privacy Concerns in Data Mining," *Artifical Intelligence and Society*, 23(4): 529–44.

Nock, S.L. (1993) *The Costs of Privacy: Surveillance and Reputation in America*, New York: Walter de Gruyter.

Pariser, E. (2011) *The Filter Bubble: What the Internet is Hiding from You*, New York: The Penguin Press.

Passavant, P.A. (2005) "The Strong Neo-liberal State: Crime, Consumption, Governance," *Theory and Event*, 8(3).

Pridmore, J. (2010) "Loyalty Ambivalence in the United States and Canada: The GDP Survey, the Focus Groups, and the Context of Those Wonderfully Intrusive Loyalty Cards," in E. Zureik, S. Harling, L. Lynda, E. Smith, D. Lyon, and Y.E. Chan (eds), *Surveillance, Privacy, and the Globalisation of Personal Information: International Comparisons*, Montreal: McGill-Queen's University Press, pp. 295–309.

Pridmore, J. and Zwick, D. (2011) "Marketing and the Rise of Commercial Consumer Surveillance," *Surveillance & Society*, 8(3): 269–77.

Rose, N. (1999) *Powers of Freedom: Reframing Political Thought*, Cambridge: Cambridge University Press.

Scott, W.R. (2001) *Institutions and Organizations*, London: Sage.

Smart, B. (2010) *Consumer Society*, London: Sage.

Sturges, P., Teng, V. and Iliffe, U. (2001) "User Privacy in the Digital Library Environment: A Matter of Concern for Information Professionals," *Library Management*, 22(8/9): 364–70.

Thrift, N. (2004) "Remembering the Technological Unconscious by Foregrounding Knowledges of Position," *Environment and Planning D: Society and Space*, 22(1): 175–90.

——(2005) *Knowing Capitalism*, London: Sage.

Zwick, D., Bonsu, S.K. and Darmody, A. (2008) "Putting Consumers to Work: 'Co-Creation' and New Marketing Govern-mentality," *Journal of Consumer Culture*, 8(2): 163–96.

Zwick, D. and Dholakia, N. (2004) "Whose Identity Is It Anyway? Consumer Representation in the Age of Database Marketing," *Journal of Macromarketing*, 24(1): 31–43.

29

ONLINE PRIVACY

Concepts, issues and research avenues for digital consumption

Ian Grant and Kathryn Waite

Keywords

information control, online, privacy, social networks

Introduction

Protecting privacy is a matter of longstanding social and cultural concern (Magi 2011). Privacy is commonly viewed as the individual's 'right to be let alone' (Warren and Brandeis 1890). In the context of consumption, the right to control the collection and subsequent use of personal information has been incorporated into this 'right to be let alone'. For example, in the late 1960s, before the growth of the online medium, concerns emerged regarding the extent to which consumers had true control over the acquisition and use of their personal information (Westin 1967). This concern was reawakened in the 1990s in relation to database construction and direct-mail practice (see Foxman and Kilcoyne 1993; Goodwin 1991; Nowak and Phelps 1992). The ease, speed and completeness by which information on the digital consumer can be gathered, aggregated and shared have again revitalised this area of concern.

The focus of this chapter is on information control. Research into online privacy has divided the concept of information control into two areas: consumer awareness regarding how information is *collected* and consumer control over the subsequent *use* of the information once it has been collected (Sheehan and Hoy 2000). This chapter examines the collection and use of online consumer information in three stages: first, by identifying the methods by which the digital consumer's personal data is collected; second, by examining how that data is used; and third by exploring privacy concern. The chapter concludes with an agenda for research.

Information collection

Digital consumer information can be split into two types: (1) passive collection by organisations and companies as a result of consumer digital use, sometimes without the full knowledge nor full legal consent of original user (such as the recent case of Facebook highlighted by the FTC in the United States) and (2) active inputting by the consumer.

Passive collection

Information that commercial organisations passively collect might include geographical location, information search, browsing patterns, keystroke patterns, and time-related actions. Sometimes the data collected is a side-business (Christiansen 2011), but usually it is intentionally tracked and utilised. This trail of information, also known as a 'digital footprint', is gathered using specific software, which has been given the pejorative term 'spyware' (see Warkentin et al. 2005). Christensen (2011, p. 510) suggests three primary organisational motivations:

- anonymize, aggregate and sell onto third parties and/or to use internally;
- retain personal data within the company but provide the opportunity for advertisers with specific traits for target marketing;
- collect personal data with the intention of selling the information, sometimes including specific profiles, to third parties.

In addition, *location-based services* (LBS) use cellular mobile signals and GPS positioning technology to pinpoint consumers and 'push' information and services based on location information (Xu et al. 2009–10). There has been considerable focus on whether the consumer is aware, and has the right to control the extent to which they are subjected to these forms of 'dataveillance' (Ashworth and Free 2006).

Emerging technologies present increasingly complex means of collecting such data and for some, a daunting environment for privacy concerns. Examples include 'gladvertising', 'a form of advertising that uses cameras and facial recognition to read a consumer's mood, then pushes products relevant to the target's emotional state' (Keats 2011). Perhaps one of the most important technological trends involving passive information collection has been 'facial recognition software', increasingly used for in-store surveillance cameras and online photo software. A recent exhibition at the Tate Modern Gallery in London (2010) highlighted ongoing privacy concerns, reminding us that the United Kingdom is reputed to be the most surveyed country in the world, provoking much discussion surrounding the ethics therein.

Active (consumer) inputting

When conducting an online transaction, active consumer inputs might include information on gender, age or address, and, if a transaction is being undertaken, financial information such as credit card details. Online social networking sites (OSNs) such as Facebook have increased both the scope and quantity of consumer inputted information. The emergence of OSNs has encouraged a more dynamic, open form of communication, ideally suited for immediate gratification between users through shared friendships and forged connections online (Debatin et al. 2009). This is further enhanced by encouraging friends to become connected, exchanging images and video files, 'tagging' others and the communication of online activity via newsfeeds. It has also lead to higher levels of self-disclosure. Debatin et al. argue that the constant updating of this very personal information (which users may not be willing to reveal in other forms of data collection) makes OSNs the ideal targets for commercial activity.

OSNs deeply penetrate their users' everyday lives, and can become taken for granted once they are widely adopted. Hugl (2011, p. 1) cited Facebook figures of 400 million users (now closer to 500 million), 50 per cent of whom log in daily, sharing 25 billion pieces of content each month (including web links, news, blog posts) and 100 million engaging with Facebook on external websites every month. Facebook has now become so much part of everyday life that its taken-for-granted status can sow the seeds for unforeseen consequences and threats to users' and non-users' personal privacy rights. Hugl describes this as the gradual, (and sometimes) voluntary, loss of privacy of the individual.

Information use

The issue of information control extends beyond the method by which data is collected, into how consumer information is used, aggregated, and shared. Technology-based systems not only change the 'quantity, granularity and quality' of what can be collected but also allow data to be explored and analysed in increasingly sophisticated ways (O'Connor 2006, p. 21). In the context of OSNs' use, consumer profiles comprise groupings of personally identifiable information including name, contact information, and demographic data. Data can be gathered from multiple sources (for example, from search engine use, Internet purchase and mobile phone use) and then combined into a composite consumer profile. For example, Achohido (2011, p. 28) reported on recent AT&T research which highlighted how data on webpage visitation is aggregated with more sensitive data disclosed on social networks, such as Facebook and personal health-related sites. This is known as 'co-mingling' of data.

Companies can use a consumer's digital footprint to change content according to usage patterns. An example of this would be 'behavioural advertising'; a practice whereby the selection of advertisements an individual sees is determined by their previous online behaviour. This might mean that, after visiting a website to search for vacation options, a consumer would be repeatedly shown display advertising from a vacation company on any other websites they visited – regardless of whether this was pertinent to the initial search topic. The growth of 'behavioural targeting advertising' is viewed as one indication that the digital consumer has little or no control over their personal data. According to a coalition of privacy-related pressure groups in the US (see Paul 2010, p. 1), this has created a 'gray area in US privacy protection', raising new privacy concerns about how personal data is collected, compiled and distributed.

Companies have been attracted by the prospect of micro-targeted advertising using behavioural tracking systems such as Facebook's Beacon system which provides highly detailed and accurate digital consumer profiles. The vast majority of users are unaware of the scale and complexity of data aggregation that underpin such social networking sites. In the case of Facebook, Debatin et al. (2009, p. 84) suggest that 'for the average user, Facebook-based invasion of privacy and aggregation of data, as well as its potential commercial exploitation by third parties, tend to remain invisible'.

With regard to mobile devices, 'push' tracking technologies can pinpoint the precise location of potential consumers, triggering location-based marketing initiatives. In 2009, the Center for Digital Democracy and the US Digital Public Interest Research Group lodged a formal complaint to the Federal Trade Commission (FTC), listing a range of unacceptable techniques and technologies. They claimed that 'many mobile marketers are eager to exploit what they correctly perceived as a unique opportunity to target consumers by taking advantage of our highly personal relationships with these extremely pervasive devices' (Caverly 2009, p. 1).

Research shows that privacy concerns increase when data is used 'for purposes beyond the initial transaction' (Foxman and Kilcoyne 1993, cited by Ashworth and Free 2006, p. 110). A consumer profile has value and can be shared or sold to third parties (Nowak and Phelps 1992). Moreover, digital data can be transferred efficiently, sometimes across borders, and sometimes without the full knowledge of the parties that were engaged in the initial transaction. Researchers have traditionally argued that concerns about how (their) data is used and disclosed can be lessened if consumers believe they can control when and how their information is disclosed in the future. This is perceived as being less invasive to their privacy and less likely to lead to negative consequences (Bandyopadhyay 2011).

There are several additional examples of how organisations disregard privacy considerations to abuse personal data. Bandyopadhyay (ibid., p. 94), for example, identified a range of negative organisational behaviours that include 'identity theft or fraud (see Acquisti and Gross 2009b), undesirable consumer profiling (Budnitz 1998), the inability to control one's social sphere and being targeted by unwanted advertising messages on the Internet (i.e. spam e-mails)'. Other researchers such as Acquisti and Gross (2009a) have focused on the potential for naïve disclosure without user comprehension of the consequences, demonstrating how information provided about an individual's date of birth and place can be used to accurately predict US social security numbers. The Better Business Bureau back in 2005 estimated that one in eight of identity theft cases were attributed to spyware, online transactions, viruses and phishing. Hence such security-related matters have only served to accentuate privacy concerns relating to control over information use. The global nature of international commerce provides further cause for concern.

Legal protection varies greatly across the globe. In India, there are 'no robust provisions for protecting the privacy rights of Internet users' since the Information Technology (Amendment) Act of 2008 'granted legal sanction to online surveillance, monitoring and identification of data by government agencies' (Bandyopadhyay 2011, p. 93). In the US, legislation has sought only to control highly sensitive data (for example, financial information and the information associated with children) as consumer information has been conceived of as a commodity that develops markets and is in turn controlled by market forces (Zwick and Dholakia 2004). In contrast, in the EU, the 'fundamental right' to privacy is protected and data cannot be transferred to countries that do not ensure an equal level of protection (ibid.). In May 2011, a new privacy directive was issued to UK businesses giving each a year to comply with legislation that requires website visitor consent before passive data collection of browsing activity (*Marketing Week* 2011). What appears to be missing is a clear, unified and international response to the privacy issues.

There is considerable pressure upon commercial organisations to use digital information to ensure competitive advantage. McCreary (2008) argues we face a standoff between society's demands for continued (information) privacy and the excessive exploitation of data by commerce. In common with other sectors, voluntary self-regulation is seen as a course of action to address consumer concerns and prevent more restrictive government regulation being enacted. Kavassalis *et al.* (2003) noted that:

> If mobile marketing is to be an effective and lucrative industry, it has to deliver relevant, requested and interactive content to the customer. End-user privacy must be respected, and therefore permission marketing for opt-in, with clear opt-out instructions, is the efficient way to proceed.

There are several actions available to organisations that wish to legitimise their data collection activity. Industry commentators have proposed the key components codes of best practice. With regards to data collection in a mobile context, Becker and Hanley (2008) argued that four 'tenets of privacy' should guide managerial action; *choice, notice, value* and *trust*. In the US, the FTC determines 'fair information practice' as providing *notice, choice, access and security* (Federal Trade Commission 2000, cited by Milne *et al.* 2006). Two common strategies to meet these requirements are the use of privacy notices and privacy seals.

Privacy notices are designed both to educate consumers and to reassure consumers regarding the control and use of digital data. Marketers can provide such notices explicitly on their website, social networks or by enabling privacy 'text triggers' to explain their policies. Milne and Culnan (2004) noted that privacy notices can help consumers decide whether or not to engage with a named website by providing consumers with information about the organisation's information practices. The use of privacy seals or trust marks have been viewed as an alternative to self-regulated company privacy notices. Such independent schemes encourage companies to behave ethically by providing specific guidelines to ensure minimal standards. Examples include BBBOnline and TRUSTe. A privacy seal certifies that a company website in question facilitates the use of that product or service in compliance with country legislation on privacy and data protection.

While these strategies are widespread, the standard of implementation varies. US government research points out that although virtually all websites post some sort of privacy disclosure statement, less than half meet the Federal Trade Commission (FTC) standards. Similarly, a US FTC report (Federal Trade Commission 2000) found that only 8 per cent of all companies used privacy seals, with companies criticised for a lack of enforcement over infringements to seal guidelines. Furthermore, Rifon *et al.* (2005) found that 'sealed' sites were significantly more invasive than unsealed ones with respect to the amount of personal information required. Krasnova *et al.* (2009) calls for organisations to be more proactive in ensuring users know exactly what is to be done with their personal data, offering simple rule-based notices rather than overwhelming legal jargon.

Moreover, the outcome of this strategy varies, and research into the efficacy of privacy notices and seals has produced mixed results. Some studies have shown trust marks to be effective at reassuring consumers, enhancing trust and encouraging them to give more personal information (Miyazaki and Krisnamurthy 2002; Rifon *et al.* 2005). However, there is evidence suggesting that consumer response varies according to familiarity with the organisation. For example, Milne and Culnan (2004) found that only around 3 per cent of consumers actually read privacy notices and that they do so only if they have little or no prior experience of that organisation. This suggests that any organisational action needs to be considered against a backdrop of continued consumer ignorance, complacency or scepticism regarding privacy-related dangers.

Privacy concern

Studies indicate that consumer privacy concern remains one of the dominant barriers preventing consumers from becoming complete digital converts. For example, a recent mobile industry study highlighted concerns over privacy as one of the main barriers to consumer participation in m-commerce (Mobile Marketing Association 2010). Where there is privacy concern, researchers report a range of precautionary measures that consumers may attempt in order to protect their personal information and preserve their privacy. Bandyopadhyay (2011) identified three key measures: non-disclosure (Nam *et al.* 2006); information falsification (Dinev and Hart 2006); and non-adoption of the technology (ibid.). Information falsification is used to counter security risks when actively inputting information, whereas non-disclosure relates to measures that are taken to prevent passive collection taking place.

Information falsification is pervasive and consumers frequently 'disguise their identity through the use of fictitious or false information' (Lwin and Williams 2003). Culnan and Milne (cited by Lwin *et al.* 2007) found that over 30 per cent of users admitted giving false or fictitious information over the Internet, suggesting that a significant minority are involved in deliberate actions to avoid privacy intrusion. Similarly, Fox *et al.* (2000) reported more than half of their sample falsified or misrepresented data 'at least occasionally', suggesting that this was a 'guerrilla' tactic to protect privacy rights. Tactics include varying, using multiple or using fake passwords to achieve such aims.

In contrast, non-disclosure is less frequently employed with some studies indicating a relatively low level of individual action: Fox *et al.* (2000, p. 3) suggested that 'only ten percent of Internet users modify browser settings to reject cookies and five percent employ anonymising software to conceal their computer identity'. To successfully implement these measures it can be argued that technology proficiency and Internet literacy are needed to exercise any degree of information control. Bandyopadhyay (2011), in a survey of 201 Indian Internet users, showed that low levels of Internet literacy and perceived vulnerability to privacy concerns are linked, and that those who were unfamiliar with the technology were also unaware of privacy risks. Furthermore, those with a higher ability to control their privacy protection exhibited reduced levels of concern and perceptions of vulnerability to risk.

In the context of OSNs' use, Madden's (2010) Pew Internet report found that 71 per cent of younger users actively change their privacy settings to limit what they share with others online and 41 per cent remove their names from photos of them posted by others. Recently there have been changes to popular OSNs such as Facebook and Google to facilitate greater control over information disclosure. Facebook CEO Mark Zuckerberg has frequently argued that enhanced privacy controls can only increase user confidence when personal data is shared between users (see Brandimarte *et al.* 2010). However, critics such as Brandimarte *et al.* argue that there is a danger that this more granular approach to user control may have the opposite effect. Their OSN experiments find that giving greater control simply generates a higher willingness to disclose sensitive information. Thus, researchers argue that greater user-control actually equates to reduced privacy.

Changes in concern

Some critics argue that concerns about information control are falling or that they were initially over-estimated. Caudill and Murphy (2000) remind us that the tracking of consumer online behaviour is not new, although they suggest consumers may have been less concerned when shopping data used to be in aggregate form. Norberg *et al.* (2007, p. 106) noted that when there are 'constant and routine requests for information (e.g., postal codes, phone numbers)', then consumers will supply this information and perceive little privacy risk. Other commentators suggest that concern is falling as consumers see little prospect in regaining control. They argue that we are now at a point where information control is impossible due to the variety and volume of tracking behaviour (McCreary 2008). Finally, there are also indications of a possible cohort effect. For example, Gray and Christiansen (2010) found that adolescents are largely unaware and unconcerned about protecting their privacy online, and unaware of the digital footprint they leave behind. This may change, however, as this cohort matures.

There is considerable evidence that younger digital consumers exhibit a lesser degree of privacy concern. Young and Quan-Haase (2009) reported that almost 100 per cent of undergraduate users of an OSN always use their actual first and last names, nearly two-thirds disclose their sexual orientation and interests, over 80 per cent their e-mail address. Some researchers have identified that, for the young, disclosure in the online environment is perceived differently. Livingstone, for example, who has conducted extensive research among younger digital consumers, suggests that OSNs provide adolescents with 'spaces of privacy, to be themselves in and through their connection with their friends' (2008, p. 406). Hence, she argues, we need to think more about 'complex zones of privacy encouraging a more subtle classification, graded by degrees of intimacy, and intrinsically linked to notions of personal identity'.

It is also argued that consumers are willing to surrender control over their personal data in return for the benefits offered through personalisation of the digital offering (Chellappa and Sin 2005).

Ashworth and Free (2006, p. 110) conceptualise information collection as a form of marketing exchange, whereby 'consumers perceive the information that is collected about themselves to be an input ... in return they expect to receive outcomes such as online services, goods, monetary compensation, or something else of value'. The idea of a Privacy Calculus Theory has been proposed to account for the process by which users weigh up the different choices and benefits when dealing with information disclosure issues (Culnan and Armstrong 1999; Krasnova *et al.* 2009; Krasnova *et al.* 2010). With regards to OSN use, Ibrahim (2008) suggests that personal information on relationships and friendships can be thought of as 'social capital', traded and exchanged for personal gain. Ibrahim calls this 'complicit risk communities' and OSN users have been found to be willing to take higher risks for higher rewards.

It is anticipated that information concern will fall as compensation rises and perceived value increases (Sheehan and Hoy 2000). Relating this to the mobile context, Hanley *et al.* (2006) found that nearly 25 per cent of college students were willing to receive mobile advertising if they received a free gift. Some mobile networks offer cheaper rate plans in exchange for sms or other mobile adverts. Several studies have found that users actively negotiate and manage a degree of tension between their perceived privacy risks and benefits that might accrue from passing on personal information (Ibrahim 2008; Tufekci 2008). It is possible that the benefits of disclosure, be it financial, social or personal, may grow to outweigh the increased vulnerabilities inherent.

Implications for research

Digital privacy concern remains an important and productive topic for research activity. There are, however, several issues regarding research design which limit findings. These include the following:

- *Weaknesses in sampling strategies.* Considerable concern is voiced that research into online privacy concerns remains too focused on the United States, and in particular collegiate contexts (Cho 2010; Hoy and Milne 2010; Wirtz *et al.* 2007).
- *Reliance on cross-sectional or experimental data.* There is little research that has used a longitudinal design; the successful use of panel data by Milne and Culnan (2004) suggests that this approach might be productive.
- *Failure to incorporate different ontological perspectives and draw on different disciplines.* The field is dominated by the positivist research tradition and there is scope for contributions to be made from other perspectives. There is also a need for cross-disciplinary research.

Our review of the literature also indicates several gaps in current understanding which we have outlined below.

Gaps in understanding attitudes, behaviours, identities

Researchers have called for research into the relationships between attitudinal, intentional and behavioural constructs. Areas for research include:

- *Exploring the tension between risk perceptions and usage gratifications,* and relating the outcome to privacy protection behaviours (Cho 2010; Debatin *et al.* 2009).
- *Increasing insight and knowledge of actual online privacy behaviour* (Eastlick and Lotz 2011). In particular, the gap between stated intentions and actual behaviour. For example, while

policy seeks to address consumer privacy concern, it has been observed that in practice 'consumers nonchalantly provide their personal information on a regular basis' (Norberg *et al.* 2007, p. 119).

- *Understanding of the range of behaviour that consumers exhibit* when constructing their online identity and the impact of privacy concern on this 'authorship' (Zwick and Dholakia 2004). This research opportunity aligns with recent developments in 'online personal branding' (Labrecque *et al.* 2011).
- *Testing and developing models of information exchange for the digital context.* Research into relationships between information disclosure and reward remains in its infancy (Li *et al.* 2010).

Gaps in understanding consumer differences

Further research is needed, focusing on different cultural, and indeed subcultural contexts (Gupta *et al.* 2010), where online behaviour is shaped by alternative cultural norms. In addition, there is a need for research that examines the extent to which privacy concern and information control vary both between and among consumers. Areas of research include:

- Gaining insight into any variation in privacy concern between individual-oriented cultures (i.e., North America) and collective-oriented cultures (i.e., China and India) (Dinev and Hart 2006).
- Examining how use of how privacy concern differs between consumers according to age and over a consumer's lifetime of usage (Hoy and Milne 2010). Miyazaki and Fernandez (2001, p. 38) found that 'privacy was actually a greater concern for consumers with longer periods of experience'. This is in direct contrast to suggestions that greater experience leads to fewer privacy concerns.
- Identifying how adolescents' notions of privacy are influenced by changing commercial activities (Grant 2007). This research might include linguistic comprehension of privacy notices (Pollach 2005), awareness and understanding of behavioural advertising practices (Miyazaki 2008), and the influence of peers on compliance with website disclosure agreements (ibid.).
- Investigating the extent to which vulnerable consumers perceive and assess privacy risk. Wirtz *et al.* (2007) suggested that traditional concerns about discrimination may now apply to online contexts; one example cited was the degree to which companies ensure that privacy notices are understood by all sections of society.

Gaps in understanding the effect of policy and regulation

Legal structures and cultural orientations are shown to influence privacy concerns and subsequent online behaviour (Caudill and Murphy 2000). There have been growing calls for greater government action and legislative change. However, public policy remains at a crossroads, informed by contradictory evidence on how best to advise consumers on issues of self-disclosure and privacy protection, and with little international consensus. In a number of domains there are calls for further research to investigate the effectiveness and efficacy of both government and self-regulatory approaches. These include:

- Evaluating the effectiveness of different regulatory approaches. For example, contrasting the EU's preference for intervention with the North American preference for self-regulation (O'Connor 2006). In particular, there are calls for an assessment of differences in government response to adolescent privacy concerns on Facebook and other websites aimed at early adolescence (Gray and Christiansen 2010).

- Assessing the effectiveness of self-regulation (Miyazaki 2008) and consumer education programmes (Norberg *et al.* 2007). Given the polarity in current researchers' positions, it would seem imperative that organisations extensively test their privacy protection procedures and not assume future consumer behaviours will simply replicate the past and mirror shifting attitudes.
- Examining the extent to which approaches to consumer protection policy from other domains might be applied to the online context. For example, Larose and Rifon (2007) suggested that there may be scope to develop legislation concerning privacy labelling similar to food nutrition guidelines.
- Describing and accounting for the privacy-related behaviours of supporting intermediary groups such as privacy consumer organisations (Wirtz *et al.* 2007), commercial intermediaries such as online ad agencies (Ashworth and Free 2006), self-regulating industry bodies such as the Internet Advertising Bureau, and the tactics and strategies of commercial organisations.

Gaps in understanding changes in technologies

Online privacy research initially focused on the Internet and more recently on mobile devices. The increasingly sophisticated digital domain has resulted in calls for continued research. These include:

- Exploring consumer privacy management within the next generation social networks such as Google+. These OSNs provide tools that allow for a more managed approach to personal relationships.
- Identifying how consumers utilise and respond to different tools to author identity such as Twitter (Li *et al.* 2010).
- Examining advances in commercial advertising technologies, data collection and mining which extract consumer information and sell onto third parties sometimes without full consumer knowledge: OSNs such as Facebook have been criticised heavily in the past couple of years for such tactics.
- Investigating new technological applications related to privacy concerns such as the collection of consumer data from RFID tags (Zwick and Dholakia 2004) and possible biometric identification schemes (Wirtz *et al.* 2007). There is scope here to extend and test theories that have previously been applied to the online context.

Gaps in understanding context

Nissenbaum (2010: 3) argued that 'what people care about most is not simply *restricting* the flow of information but ensuring that it flows *appropriately*'. She offers a framework of contextual integrity as way to evaluate whether privacy expectations have been contravened. This framework comprises informational norms that operate within distinct social context. There is a need for research that 'fleshes out' these norms and contexts. Researchers might consider the following:

- Determining how the willingness to disclose information can vary depending on subject matter and emotional consequences. Horne and Horne (1998) found that consumers were much more sensitive about disclosing information concerning medical, financial and family matters in comparison to product and brand-related information.

- Exploring how expectations of privacy might vary according to the nature of the online exchange. For example, Waite *et al.* (2011) highlighted how consumer expectations might vary according to the nature of the task within the context of banking.
- Investigating the degree to which the online world influences the offline world and vice versa. For example, Subrahmanyam and Greenfield (2008) argued that further research is needed into how online privacy issues are now affecting 'real-world', peer-to-peer communications and relationships.
- Developing insight into what constitutes 'appropriate information flows' and in particular examining the degree to which consumers are accepting of the 'co-mingling' of public and private data sources (Achohido 2011).

Conclusion

This chapter has provided an overview of the key areas of privacy concern for the digital consumer. Privacy concerns are present in relation to the techniques used to capture data and its subsequent use. Developments in technology and the range of data that is available within the digital domain have provided companies with the opportunity to build detailed consumer profiles. These developments can undoubtedly benefit the consumer. Customer relationship marketing tools, for example, offer e-tailers the ability to 'proactively tailor products and product purchasing experiences to tastes of individual consumers based upon their personal and preference information' (Chellappa and Sin 2005, p. 181). However, we have also identified a range of data misuses for which there is limited legal protection offered worldwide.

The pervasive nature of digital data collection has resulted in several commentators arguing that information control is impossible (McCreary 2008). Indeed, emerging thinking indicates that rather than considering privacy as a right, we should be viewing it as a socially constructed, context-dependent information norm that each individual subjects to a cost-benefit calculus. Drawing on this background, we have identified several opportunities for further research which we hope will inform investigators in this important and dynamic area.

Further reading

Caoukian, A., Polonetsky, J. and Wolf, C. (2010) 'SmartPrivacy for the Smart Grid: Embedding Privacy into the Design of Electricity Conservation', *Identity in the Information Society*, 3(2): 275–94. [Applies the conceptual model of 'SmartPrivacy' to the context of digital surveillance of energy consumption. Examines the tension between public good (energy conservation) and individual right to privacy.]

Goldfarb, A. and Tucker, C.E. (2011) 'Online Advertising, Behavioural Targeting and Privacy', *Communications of the ACM*, 45(5): 25–7. [Reports on research findings into the effect of the EU Privacy and Electronic communications on consumer response to advertising.]

Manzarolle, V. and Smeltzer, S. (2011) 'Consumer Databases, Neoliberalism and the Commercial Mediation of Identity: A Medium Theory Analysis', *Surveillance and Society*, 8(3). Available at: www.surveillance-and-society.org/ojs/index.php/journal/article/view/mediation. [A theoretical article that suggests that the database should be considered as a distinct communication medium. Argues that surveillance should be accepted as a necessary condition for consumer sovereignty.]

References

Achohido, R. (2011) 'Online Tracking Takes a Scary Turn', *USA Today*, August 4, pp. 27–8.

Acquisti, A. and Gross, R. (2009a) 'Predicting Social Security Numbers from Public Data', *Proceedings of the National Academy of Sciences (PNAS)*, 106(2): 10975–80.

——(2009b) 'Social Insecurity: The Unintended Consequences of Identity Fraud Prevention Policies', paper presented at the *Workshop on the Economics of Information Security*, 24–25 June, University College London, UK.

Ashworth, L. and Free, C. (2006) 'Marketing Dataveillance and Digital Privacy: Using Theories of Justice to Understand Consumers' Online Privacy Concerns', *Journal of Business Ethics*, 67(2): 107–23.

Bandyopadhyay, S. (2011) 'Online Privacy Concerns of Indian Consumers', *The International Business & Economics Research Journal*, 10(2): 93–101.

Becker, M. and Hanley, M. (2008) 'The Mediating Effects of Privacy and Preference Management on Trust and Consumer Participation in a Mobile Marketing Initiative: A Proposed Conceptual Model', in T. Kautonen and H. Karjaluoto (eds), *Trust and New Technologies: Marketing and Management on the Internet and Mobile Media*, Cheltenham: Edward Elgar Publishing, pp. 127–45.

Better Business Bureau (2005) 'New Research Shows that Identity Theft is More Prevalent Offline with Paper Than Online', *Better Business Bureau*. Available at: www.bbb.org/us/article/new-research-shows-that-identity-theft-is-more-prevalent-offline-with-paper-than-online-519 (accessed August 1, 2011).

Brandimarte, L., Acquisti, A. and Loewenstein, G. (2010) 'Privacy Concerns and Information Disclosure: An Illusion of Control Hypothesis', paper presented at *CIST*. Available at: www.heinz.cmu.edu/~acquisti/research.htm (accessed November 5, 2011).

Budnitz, M. (1998) 'Privacy Protection for Consumer Transactions in Electronic Commerce: Why Self Regulation is Inadequate', *South Carolina Law Review*, 49(1): 847–86.

Caudill, E.M. and Murphy, P.E. (2000) 'Consumer Online Privacy: Legal and Ethical Issues', *Journal of Public Policy & Marketing*, 19(1): 7–19.

Caverly, D. (2009) 'Privacy Groups Protect Mobile Advertising Practices', January 13, *WebProNews*. Available at: www.webpronews.com/privacy-groups-protest-mobile-advertising-practices-2009–01 (accessed July 21, 2011).

Chellappa, R. and Sin, R. (2005) 'Personalization Versus Privacy: An Empirical Examination of the Online Consumer's Dilemma', *Information Technology and Management*, 6: 181–202.

Cho, H. (2010) 'Determinants of Behavioural Responses to Online Privacy: The Effects of Concern, Risk Beliefs, Self-Efficacy, and Communication Sources on Self-Protection Strategies', *Journal of Information Privacy & Security*, 6(1): 3–28.

Christiansen, L. (2011) 'Personal Privacy and Internet Marketing: An Impossible Conflict or a Marriage Made in Heaven?' *Business Horizons*, 54: 509–14.

Culnan, M.J. and Armstrong, P. (1999) 'Information Privacy Concerns, Procedural Fairness and Impersonal Trust: An Empirical Investigation', *Organisational Science*, 10(1): 104–15.

Debatin, B., Lovejoy, J.P., Horn, A-K. and Hughes, B.N. (2009) 'Facebook and Online Privacy: Attitudes, Behaviours, and Unintended Consequences', *Journal of Computer-Mediated Communication*, 15(1), 83–108.

De Cew, J.W. (1997) *In Pursuit of Privacy: Law, Ethics and the Rise of Technology*, Ithaca, NY: Cornell University Press.

——(2006) 'Privacy', in *Stanford Encyclopaedia of Philosophy*, Stanford, CA: Metaphysics Research Lab, Center for the Study of Language and Information, Stanford University.

Dinev, T. and Hart, P. (2006) 'Internet Privacy Concerns and Social Awareness as Determinants of Intention to Transact', *International Journal of Electronic Commerce*, 10(2): 7–29.

Eastlick, M.A. and Lotz, S. (2011) 'Cognitive and Institutional Predictors of Initial Trust Toward an Online Retailer', *International Journal of Retail & Distribution Management*, 39(4): 234–55.

Fox, S. (2005) *Spyware*, Washington, DC: Pew Internet & American Life Project, July 6.

Fox, S., Lee, R., Horrigan, J., Lenhart, A., Tom, S. and Carter, C. (2000) 'Trust and Privacy Online: Why Americans Want to Rewrite the Rules', *The Pew Internet & American Life Project*. Available at: http://pewinternet.org/ (accessed July 21, 2011).

Foxman, E.R. and Kilcoyne, P. (1993) 'Information Technology, Marketing Practice, and Consumer Privacy', *Journal of Public Policy & Marketing*, 12(Spring): 106–19.

Goodwin, C. (1991) 'Privacy: Recognition of a Consumer Right', *Journal of Public Policy & Marketing*, 10(1): 149–66.

Grant, I. (2007) 'Online Privacy: An Issue for Children', in K.M. Ekström and B. Tufte (eds), *Children, Media and Consumption: On the Front Edge*, Goteborg: Nordicom Yearbooks, pp. 63–78.

Gray, D.M. and Christiansen, L. (2010) 'A Call to Action: The Privacy Dangers Adolescents Face Through Use of Facebook.Com', *Journal of Information Privacy & Security*, 6(2): 17–33.

Gupta, B., Iyer, L.S. and Weisskirch, R.S. (2010) 'Facilitating Global E-Commerce: A Comparison of Consumers' Willingness to Disclose Personal Information Online in the U.S. and in India', *Journal of Electronic Commerce Research*, 11(1): 41–53.

Hanley, M., Becker, M. and Martinsen, J. (2006) 'Factors Influencing Mobile Advertising Acceptance: Will Incentives Motivate College Students to Accept Mobile Advertising?' *International Journal of Mobile Advertising*, 1: 50–8.

Horne, D.A. and Horne, D.R. (2002) 'Database Marketing: When Does Good Practice Become an Invasion of Privacy?' in K. Evans and L. Scheer (eds) *Marketing Theory & Applications*, Chicago: American Marketing Association, vol. 13, pp. 480–6.

Horne, D.R. and Horne, D.A. (1998) 'Domains of Privacy: Toward an Understanding of Underlying Factors', paper presented at the Direct Marketing Educators' Conference, San Francisco, October 11.

Hoy, M.G. and Milne, G. (2010) 'Gender Differences in Privacy-Related Measures for Young Adult Facebook Users', *Journal of Interactive Advertising*, 10(2): 28–45.

Hugl, U. (2011) 'Reviewing Person's Value of Privacy Online Social Networking', *Internet Research*, 21(4): 384–407.

Ibrahim, Y. (2008) 'The New Risk Communities: Social Networking Sites and Risk', *International Journal of Media & Cultural Politics*, 4(2): 245–53.

JungKook, L. and Lehto, X. (2010) 'E-Personization and Online Privacy Features: The Case with Travel Websites', *Journal of Management and Marketing Research*, 4(March): 1–14.

Kavassalis, P.N., Spyropoulou, D., Drossos, E.G., Mitrokostas, G., Gikas, G. and Hatzistamatiou, A. (2003) 'Mobile Permission Marketing: Framing the Market Inquiry', *International Journal of Electronic Commerce*, 8: 55–79.

Keats, J. (2011) 'Jargonwatch: Gladvertising, Photonic Hyperhighway, Quebecol, Flyjin', *Wired Magazine*, June 28.

Krasnova, H. Günther, O., Spiekermann, S. and Koroleva, K. (2009) 'Privacy Concerns and Identity in Online Social Networks', *Identity in the Information Society*, 2(1): 39–63.

Krasnova, H., Spiekermann, S., Koroleva, K. and Hildebrand, T. (2010) 'Online Social Networks: Why We Disclose', *Journal of Information Technology*, 25(2): 109–25.

Labrecque, L.I. Markos, E. and Milne, G.R. (2011) 'Online Personal Branding: Processes, Challenges, and Implications', *Journal of Interactive Marketing*, 25: 37–50.

Larose R. and Rifon, N.J. (2007) 'Promoting i-Safety: Effects of Privacy Warnings and Privacy Seals on Risk Assessment and Online Privacy Behaviour', *The Journal of Consumer Affairs*, 41(1): 127–40.

Li, H., Sarathy, R. and Xu, H. (2010) 'Understanding Situational Online Information Disclosure as a Privacy Calculus', *Journal of Computer Information Systems*, 51(1): 62–71.

Livingstone, S. (2008) 'Taking Risky Opportunities in Youthful Content Creation: Teenagers' Use of Social Networking Sites for Intimacy, Privacy and Self-Expression', *New Media & Society*, 10(3): 393–411.

Lwin, M.O. and Williams, J.D. (2003) 'A Model Interpreting the Multidimensional Developmental Theory of Privacy and Theory of Planned Behaviour to Examine Fabrication of Information Online', *Marketing Letters*, 14(4): 257–72.

Lwin, M.O., Wirtz, J. and William, J.D. (2007) 'Consumer Online Privacy Concerns and Responses: A Power-Responsibility Equilibrium Perspective', *Journal of Academy of Marketing Science Journal*, 35(4): 572–85.

McCreary, L. (2008) 'What Was Privacy?' *Harvard Business Review*, October: 123–30.

Madden, M (2010) 'Reputation Management and Social Media: How People Monitor Their Identity and Search for Others Online', *Pew Research Centre Internet & American Life Project*, May 26. Available at: www.pewinternet.org/Press-Releases/2010/Reputation-Management.aspx. (accessed August 1, 2011).

Magi, T.J. (2011) 'Fourteen Reasons Why Privacy Matters: A Multi-Disciplinary Review of Scholarly Literature', *The Library Quarterly*, 81(2): 187–209.

Marketing Week (2011) 'Guidelines on Behavioural Advertising Rules Issued', *Marketing Week*, Tuesday 10 May. Available at: www.marketingweek.co.uk/disciplines/digital/guidelines-on-behavioral-advertising-rules-issued/3026200.article (accessed 31 May 2011).

Milne, G.R. and Culnan, M.J. (2004) 'Strategies for Reducing Online Privacy Risks: Why Consumers Read (or Don't Read) Online Privacy Notices', *Journal of Interactive Marketing*, 18(3): 15–29.

Milne, G.R., Culnan, M.J. and Greene, H. (2006) 'A Longitudinal Assessment of Online Privacy Notice Readability', *Journal of Public Policy & Marketing*, 25(2): 238–49.

Miyazaki, A.D. (2008) 'Online Privacy and the Disclosure of Cookie Use: Effects on Consumer Trust and Anticipated Patronage', *Journal of Public Policy & Marketing*, 27(1): 19–33.

Miyazaki, A.D. and Fernandez, A. (2001) 'Consumer Perceptions of Privacy and Security Risks for Online Shopping', *Journal of Consumer Affairs*, 35(Summer): 27–44.

Miyazaki, A.D. and Krisnamurthy, S. (2002) 'Internet Seals of Approval: Effects on Online Privacy Policies and Consumer Perceptions', *The Journal of Consumer Affairs*, 36(1): 28–49.

Mobile Marketing Association (2010) 'Mobile Marketing Association Top Ten Mobile Marketing Trends to Watch in 2011', *MMAGlobal*, Singapore, December. Available at www.mmaglobal.com/news/mobile-marketing-association-outlines-top-ten-trends (accessed August 1, 2011).

Nam, C., Song, C, Lee, E., Park, C.I., Lee, E. and Park, C.I. (2006) 'Consumer's Privacy Concerns and Willingness to Provide Marketing-Related Personal Information Online', in C. Pechmann and L. Price (eds), *Advances in Consumer Research*, vol. 33, Duluth, MN: Association for Consumer Research, pp. 212–17.

Nissenbaum, H.F. (2010) *Privacy in Context: Technology, Policy and the Integrity of Social Life*, Palo Alto, CA: Stanford University Press.

Norberg, P.A., Horne, D.R. and Horne, D.A. (2007) 'The Privacy Paradox: Personal Information Disclosure Intentions Versus Behaviours', *Journal of Consumer Affairs*, 14(1): 100–26.

Nowak, G.J. and Phelps, J. (1992) 'Understanding Privacy Concerns', *Journal of Direct Marketing*, 6(4): 28–39.

O'Connor, P. (2006) 'An International Comparison of Approaches to Online Privacy Protection: Implications for the Hotel Sector', *Journal of Services Research*, 6(7): 20–41.

Paul, R. (2010) 'Privacy Advocates Want Regulation of Behavioral Advertising', available at: http://arstechnica.com/tech-policy/news/2009/09/privacy-advocates-want-regulation-of-behavioral-advertising.ars (accessed July 27, 2011).

Pollach, I. (2005) 'A Typology of Communication Strategies on Online Privacy Policies: Ethics, Power and Informed Consent', *Journal of Business Ethics*, 62(3): 221–35.

Rifon, N.J., LaRose, R and Choi, S. (2005) 'Your Privacy is Sealed: Effects of Web Privacy Seals on Trust and Personal Disclosures', *The Journal of Consumer Affairs*, 39(2): 339–63.

Sheehan, K.B. and Hoy, M.G. (2000) 'Dimensions of Privacy Concerns Among Online Consumers', *Journal of Public Policy & Marketing*, 19(1): 62–73.

Solove, D.J. (2002) 'Conceptualising Privacy', *California Law Review*, 90(4): 1087–155.

Subrahmanyam, K. and Greenfield, P. (2008) 'Online Communication and Adolescent Relationships', *The Future of Children*, 18(1): 119–46.

Tate Modern (2010) *Exposed: Voyeurism, Surveillance & the Camera*, Exhibition, London. Available at: www.tate.org.uk/modern/exhibitions/exposure/default.shtm (accessed 1 November, 2011).

Tufekci, Z. (2008) 'Can You See Me Now? Audience and Disclosure Regulation in Online Social Network Sites', *Bulletin of Science, Technology & Society*, 28(1): 20–36.

Waite, K., Harrison, T. and Hunter, G. (2011) 'Exploring Bank Website Expectations Across Two Task Scenarios', *Journal of Financial Services*, 16(1): 76–85.

Warkentin, M., Luo, X. and Templeton, G.F. (2005) 'A Framework for Spyware Assessment', *Communications of the ACM*, 48(8): 79–84.

Warren, S.D. and Brandeis, L.D. (1890) 'The Right To Privacy', *Harvard Law Review*, 4(4).

Westin, A. (1967) *Privacy and Freedom*, New York: Athenaeum.

Wirtz, J., Lwin, M.O. and Williams, J.D. (2007) 'Causes and Consequences of Consumer Privacy Concern', *International Journal of Service Industry Management*, 18(4): 326–48.

Xu, H., Teo, H., Tan, B.C.Y. and Agarwal, R. (2009–10) 'The Role of Push-Pull Technology in Privacy Calculus: The Case of Location-Based Services', *Journal of Management Information Systems*, 26(3): 135–74.

Young, A.L. and Quan-Haase, A. (2009) 'Information Revelation and Internet Privacy Concerns on Social Network Sites: A Case Study of Facebook', in ACM (ed.) *Proceedings of the 4th International Conference on Communities & Technologies*, 25–27 June, Pennsylvania, ACM.

Zwick, D. and Dholakia, N. (2004) 'Whose Identity Is It Anyway? Consumer Representation in the Age of Database Marketing', *Journal of Macromarketing*, 24(1): 31–43.

30

SELF-DISCLOSURE

Henri Weijo

Keywords

communication, digital self, digitalization, privacy, relationship marketing, self-disclosure

> Obviously, all relationships which people have to one another are based on their knowing something about one another.
>
> (Simmel 1964, p. 307)

We are social beings who make sense of the world through our various relationships. We have family members, friends, acquaintances, teammates, neighbors, colleagues, golfing buddies, girlfriends and boyfriends, loved ones and even enemies, just to name a few. Some of these relationships evolve through a force of their own; we can't choose our parents or siblings, and we can lose touch with our neighbors as they move to a new neighborhood. Culture and social norms will heavily influence the way we manage our relationships: it is a lot more acceptable to lose touch with your college buddies than with your mother. For the most part, however, we have a great deal of control over our relationships and we get to decide which relationships are most worthy of our attention. While we can't choose our siblings, we can choose the person who we want to have children of our own with. We also go through considerable effort to keep some relationships intact even when our life situations change.

The quote by Simmel illustrates how different relationships evolve from casual to more meaningful ones. When we want to let certain people into our lives, we engage in self-disclosure and start sharing information with them that we wouldn't divulge to just anybody, even making ourselves vulnerable (Jourard and Lasakow 1958; Archer 1980; McKenna *et al.* 2002). If other people react to our self-disclosing acts the way we had hoped and engage in reciprocal self-disclosure, the relationship will deepen (Gouldner 1960; Jourard 1964; Cozby 1972). As an example, think of how dating usually works: on the first date a couple might discuss mundane subjects such as where they went to college or their favorite films, but if they get along, soon they might be sharing their personal hopes and dreams or even sexual fantasies.

Self-disclosure happens as acts within communication, as specific utterances within the flow of a conversation. The primary focus of this chapter is to investigate how self-disclosure has been affected by the massive changes the digital revolution has brought to how we communicate with one another. We now communicate via instant messages, social media, emails, video chat, forum platforms and the like. We can now transcend the spatial boundaries that would deny us from interacting whenever and with whomever we wish to. Self-disclosure is a staple and well-studied subject in social sciences, especially within social psychology (see e.g., Cozby 1973; Derlega *et al.* 1993). To do justice to the rich body of literature within the pages of this chapter is a near-impossible task, but I will attempt to provide a passable overview on previous research. As my own background is in more culturally oriented consumer research, a large part of this chapter is dedicated to discussing some of the cultural changes that the digital revolution has brought to self-disclosure. I argue that there is a growing demand for more transparency of the self, which is driven by marketers, techno-cultural evangelists and even consumers. From the marketers' side, this shift for demanding more consumer self-disclosure is due to the rise of so-called *relationship marketing*. I will discuss the implications of these developments and what kind of new directions they offer for researchers. Self-disclosure has some rather obvious over-lapping aspects with consumer privacy issues (Andrejevic 2002; John *et al.* 2010). However, as this volume already contains a dedicated chapter on privacy, discussing privacy issues within this chapter will be limited.

Studying the self and self-disclosure

The concept of the self has been problematic and contested in social sciences, including consumer research (Gecas 1982; Sirgy 1982). This naturally has an effect on self-disclosure literature as well if it is indeed unclear what is this thing called self we are looking to disclose. Broadly speaking, however, we can say the conversation regarding the self has moved from early conceptualizations that saw the self as a bounded, unchanging Cartesian essence to more contemporary accounts where the self is seen as increasingly plural, contextual, embodied, and socially constructed (Holstein and Gubrium 2000; Robinson 2007). Two theoretical contributions by Charles H. Cooley and George H. Mead in particular were paramount in shifting the conversation regarding the self. Cooley (1902) spoke of *a looking-glass self* where the self is shaped by *a generalized other* (other people and instances we interact with) and its constant judgment and validation. Mead's (1934) view of the self is very similar to Cooley's, but Mead further stressed people's reflexive ability in the emergence of the self, which permits a person to see their self's otherness, its objective position in regards to the generalized other(s) across different social contexts and even society at large.

This reflexive ability is also what enables the self to take a plurality of forms, as later contributions have come to argue. For example, we create selves that define what we could or should be in the future and these future selves are subset of the more totalizing self. Self-discrepancy theory suggests that people have an ideal normative *ought self* in addition to the regular self (Higgins 1987). Similarly, the *aspired self* is how a person would like to see herself in the future (Zhao 2005, p. 395). These different selves (or different sides to the self, if you will) have become of par-ticular importance in consumer research and the understanding of consumer goals in consumption (Sirgy 1982). The self becoming seen as plural has created some calamity and boundary issues within the field and has naturally had an impact on understanding self-disclosure as well. Most self-disclosure literature, however, tends to use a rather general definition of the self. Rosenberg's (1979, p. 7) definition of "the totality of the individual's thoughts and feelings having references to himself as an object" is one generally accepted and often-cited definition.

Self-disclosure has been defined as the act of "revealing personal information about oneself to others" (Archer 1980, p. 183) or "the process of making the self known to others" (Jourard and Lasakow 1958, p. 91). Self-disclosure has received considerable attention in social sciences and as noted earlier, is seen as an integral element in the development of interpersonal relationships (Cozby 1973; Derlega *et al.* 1993). While there is some disagreement on the matter, self-disclosure is for the most part seen as a verbal, and explicitly intentional act of telling something about oneself to one or more people (Cozby 1973). As the dating example from earlier suggested, self-disclosure is more likely to occur if disclosure escalates gradually, proceeding from casual exchanges to increasingly intimate ones (Altman and Taylor 1973; Cozby 1973). Once a relationship has reached a deeper level, it needs more disclosure to be maintained. If our significant others stop disclosing of themselves to us, we lose trust and begin to doubt if that person will be as important to us in the future as she has in the past (Berger and Bradac 1982).

Not all disclosed information is equally meaningful. The meaningfulness of the self-disclosing act depends on: (1) the amount of information disclosed; (2) the intimacy of disclosed information; (3) the duration of the disclosing act; (4) the intentionality of disclosure; (5) the accuracy of disclosure; (6) the nature of disclosure (e.g. good vs. bad information); and (7) the relevance of the information to the listener (Altman and Taylor 1973; Cozby 1973; Derlega *et al.* 1993). Logic would thus dictate that we will disclose our most intimate thoughts only to people we have intimate relationships with. Surprisingly, however, this is not always the case. In the right context, people may be willing to disclose very personal information even to complete strangers. For example, during a plane trip, people may disclose quite openly to each other as they figure they will not see that person ever again and thus the risk of embarrassment is limited (Rubin 1975).

Overall, context matters immensely in self-disclosure to the point where one act could be classified as an act of self-disclosure in one context, but not in others. And because of the dynamics of reciprocity, it may be impossible to consider spontaneous acts of disclosure as independent out of the overall conversational dynamic (Joinson and Paine 2006). Another problem for studying self-disclosure is that no communication exchange is ever simply a transfer of information from person A to person B. Self-disclosing acts are often an exercise in impression management and thus being on the receiving end of disclosure entails a lot of interpretation (Qian and Scott 2007). In Goffmanian (Goffman 1959) terms, people judge not only what is being said (what is "given") but also how it is being said (what is "given off"). Our body language, gestures, and even what we *don't* say can reveal more than we originally intended (Zhao 2005). Even our possessions (particularly our clothes) will tell a lot about ourselves to other people and may interfere with the interpretation of the disclosing act (Belk 1988).

Still, while it is important to acknowledge that self-disclosure is moderate by different variables and "noise," self-disclosure as such is commonly understood as solely the willing and often verbal disclosure of the self. This may also explain why self-disclosure has not received as visible a role in consumer research as in other social sciences. What consumers aspire to do through consumption and their identity projects falls more tidily into the realm of self-presentation rather than self-disclosure (Schau and Gilly 2003). Broadly defined, self-presentation is about the proper manipulation of signs and other cultural resources to create a desired impression onto the multiple others that people interact with every day, whereas self-disclosure deals more with communication in more contextual and interpersonal interactions and relationship development (Jourard 1971; Derlega *et al.* 1993). This is not to say that self-disclosure has not been studied at all in consumer research, quite the contrary. Self-disclosure has been a central tenet in some very influential studies, for example, studies regarding the use of communication products through which we self-disclose (Moon 2000), consumers' likelihood of self-disclosure to marketers in consumer–marketer interactions (Goodwin 1996; Andrade *et al.* 2002; White 2004; Lee *et al.* 2008) or how people's expectations to engage in self-disclosure have changed due to changes in consumer culture (Andrejevic 2002; John *et al.* 2010).

Disclosing the digital self

As we established earlier, the self emerges and is defined through social interaction and the digital self is no different in this regard. Zhao (2005) defined four distinct characteristics where the digital self differs from the non-digital self: (1) *inward oriented*; (2) *multiplied*; (3) *retractable*; and (4) *narrative in nature*. I argue that all four are indicative of the two main dimensions in how digital communication and especially digital self-disclosure have been seen to differ from non-digital: *anonymity* and *disembodiment* (Gunkel 2010). Broadly defined, anonymity in communication refers to a state where the person is not identifiable, and the disembodiment of communication refers to communication without the presence or necessity of the human body (Joinson 2001; Qian and Scott 2007). Both anonymity and disembodiment have been traditionally privileged accounts of digital communication, and especially anonymity was once one of the core ideals upon which the Internet was founded (Turkle 1995; Qian and Scott 2007; Streeter 2011).

Of Zhao's four characteristics, the notions of multiplied and retractable relate very closely to anonymity in digital communication. When online interaction first emerged, the ability to communicate with other people without exposing the self was celebrated as a form of emancipation; people were free to present themselves in practically unlimited ways and they had total control over their self-disclosure (Gunkel 2010). This early research was particularly fascinated by findings that seemed to indicate that through computer-mediated communication people were much more likely to disclose personal information to one another than when interacting face-to-face (Joinson 2004). People's surprising willingness to self-disclose digitally may be due to the retractable nature of the digital self: in online interaction we can often make sure our offline identity cannot be linked back to the digital identity and simply "pull out" from the interaction if things get too uncomfortable. Many people are also engaging in communication through a variety of digital channels and arenas, which makes the digital self emerge as (more) multiple in nature. However, not all researchers are enamored by the anonymity of online interaction. Some have linked anonymity to deindividualidation and the loss of self, which has been feared to lead to unruly and antisocial behavior (Qian and Scott 2007).

The remaining two of Zhao's characteristics of the digital self, inward-oriented and narrative in nature, relate closely to the notion of disembodiment. Early research on digital communication and self-disclosure came to see digital communication as an idealized form of communication as we did not have to worry about our body language or gestures getting in the way of what we wanted to communicate (Robinson 2007; Gunkel 2010). As the digital self is not concerned about our embodied self (our height, looks, etc.), it becomes inward-oriented and focuses more on thoughts and feelings in the person's inner world. The digital self, being narrative in nature, refers to people getting to know us exclusively through the gradual fragments and information nuggets we decide to disclose of ourselves in digital channels (lines of text in chatrooms, carefully selected photographs, etc.). However, precisely for these reasons some see digital communication as a flawed form of communication as there is a distinct lack of richness compared to normal face-to-face interaction (Joinson 2001). There is indeed an interesting tradeoff between control over self-disclosing acts and the nonverbal cues we use to judge if our self-disclosure had the effect we intended to. Some have argued that if we accept self-disclosure done through digital communication channels to be flawed, then it follows that the relationships we forge through them cannot be as meaningful as offline relationships. Zhao (2005) quite bluntly referred to our intimate online acquaintances as "intimate strangers" or "anonymous friends" because while reciprocal self-disclosure may have occurred in online interaction, people will ultimately remain strangers because they likely would not recognize each other should they meet in real life. Similarly, Bargh, McKenna and Fitzsimons (2002) referred to the relationships we create online as little more than extended versions of the strangers on a train phenomenon: relative strangers disclosing freely because of a limited potential for social repercussions for improper self-disclosure.

More recent studies seem to go against the somewhat prevailing view of online interaction being a celebration of anonymity or an ongoing act of identity shopping. McKenna *et al.* (2002) found that those who were willing to portray their true self in cyberspace were more likely to have formed close online relationships as true self-disclosure led to an increase in intimacy and trust. The prevailing view of people looking to either create an idealized self or not disclose of oneself at all was severely challenged by Schau and Gilly (2003) who found that people often try to portray a very accurate view of their real self, even their physical appearances. Indeed, the voluntary disclosure of the self through some newer platforms, such as blogs, run counter to what we have come to believe about consumers' willingness to self-disclose and, interestingly, this type of disclosure is often done without any particular expectation of reciprocity (Joinson 2001; Lee *et al.* 2008). It should be noted that consumers often engage in heavy impression manage-ment when disclosing of themselves in the online realm and will self-disclose only when it is voluntary and when they are in control of the process (Lee *et al.* 2008). Still, these new exam-ples of online behavior go against the somewhat prevalent belief that people somehow prefer anonymity and not disclosing of their true bodily self in digital communication.

Some even feel the demarcation between embodied and disembodied communication has become outdated and artificial. Kozinets (2010, p. 15) argues that the supposed "real world" of offline has blended into one world with the online realm and consumers are increasingly willing to portray themselves as they are in all their facets. Some newer studies also serve as a reminder that much of the earlier research on self-ing in cyberspace was conducted during a time when access to digital communication was not as commonplace and democratized as it is today (Robinson 2007). A lot more people are now communicating using digital technologies with much richer communication possibilities. During some of the early studies, digital commu-nication was generally seen as a strictly text-based exchange between anonymous nicknames. The contemporary use of avatars, voice calls and even video chats has obvious ramifications for both opportunities and expectations for being more "as you are" in digital interaction. While we cannot say digital communication has become a completely embodied practice, we can say with some confidence that the digital self has recently taken steps away from disembodiment. But this may be just the beginning. In the next section I will argue that marketers and online service providers have a vested interest in enticing consumers to self-disclose as much of themselves as possible which has clear implications to anonymity in particular.

Relationship marketing and self-disclosure

Self-disclosure as such is not a new phenomenon in consumption as many consumption activities would be quite difficult or even impossible without some amount of self-disclosure from the customer, such as their credit card or address information. However, during the past few decades there has been a noticeable increase in marketers looking to entice consumers to self-disclose at different stages of their consumption experience. This shift is tied to a larger paradigm shift in marketing from product-based transactional marketing into a new paradigm that emphasizes relationship building with customers and (mass) customization of offerings through *relationship marketing* (cf. Duncan and Moriarty 1998; Vargo and Lusch 2004; Lee *et al.* 2008). Deighton (1996) argues that companies who wish to succeed in this new marketing paradigm are ones who successfully gather and leverage customer information, hence the incentive to get consumers to self-disclose. Through these information-driven relationships, marketers strive to acquire knowledge about consumers' preferences to better meet their needs, improve customer service, learn about new product ideas, and target their advertising more accurately (White 2004).

The emergence of relationship marketing started well before the more recent digital revolution with the early use of data received from bar codes, frequent flyer points, visitor counts, and quarterly sales, but without contemporary digital technologies this trend would not be as important as it is today and it has in many ways changed what it means to be a consumer in the contemporary marketplace. Andrejevic (2002) argues that due to the rise of relationship marketing, the role of the consumer has become not only to buy products but also to provide information, to self-disclose at every marketing touch point of the marketing surveillance society. Every act of consumption through digital technologies from mouse clicks to credit card swipes now leaves a trace for companies to analyze. For example, while Amazon has forever redefined the way people buy books via their recommendation system, Amazon makes certain that every search, purchase, or recommendation is attributed to a database entry that carries the customer's name.

In all truthfulness, the concept of relationship marketing may a bit overstated in that it implies marketers and consumers enjoying real and somehow mutual relationships. Indeed, if we have established that relationships are formed and deepened through reciprocal self-disclosure, are companies even capable of disclosing about themselves in a manner that would make reciprocity possible? Moon (2000) dismisses this notion and notes that to achieve proper reciprocity with customers, companies would have to engage in nigh one-to-one interaction with each and every one of them, which would be both costly and time-consuming. Still, while marketers and consumers may never form true relationships in the strictest sense, it does not change the fact that marketers are increasingly interested in getting us to self-disclose. As collecting and storing customer information has become not only possible but also increasingly more affordable, marketers have invested heavily in database technologies (Moon 2000; Zwick and Dholakia 2004). Another interest in getting consumers to engage in self-disclosure in marketer-maintained environments is the increasing interest in different types of consumption communities – particularly of the online variety – and the opportunities they provide companies for learning about their consumers (e.g. Kozinets 1999; McAlexander *et al.* 2002; Muñiz and O'Guinn 2001). Consumers engaging in self-disclosure increases the likelihood of creating lasting communal bonds between consumers and even between consumers and marketers (Goodwin 1996).

Controversies in self-disclosure

While consumers have become used to disclosing among themselves through digital channels, they are still significantly more reluctant to disclose of themselves to marketers (Olivero and Lunt 2004). Marketers have come to understand consumer concerns with the potential risks of betraying consumers' trust in handling their private information and are trying to make their terms of self-disclosure as transparent as possible (Andrade *et al.* 2002; White 2004; Lee *et al.* 2008). Marketers have also turned to third party service providers to gain access to consumers' self-disclosed information through indirect means. Social networks such as Facebook, Orkut and Google+ allow consumers to share and disclose in a variety of ways, but these interactions are saved by the service providers and later sold to marketers as minable consumer data. Different websites, blogs and online services have increasingly started to adopt single sign-on services such as Google ID, Facebook Connect, Open ID, Disqus, and Twitter Sign In, which all promise consumers the ease of signing in to these services securely, but it also assures that all our movements within the online realm will be recorded by these sign-on service providers – and this information is again sold to marketers at a profit.

Though it may not feel like it at times, the reality is that service marketers who run different databases with consumer data and proprietary owners of social media services and platforms have a business interest in shaping consumer (inter)action in a way that benefits them. One way to think of this shift to an era of lesser anonymity is to see it as a capitalist rationalization process of online interaction from its previous idealized and even enchanting anonymous and disembodied form to something that serves the business interests of the service providers and marketers (Andrejevic 2002; Ritzer 1999). Zwick and Dholakia (2004) have expressed worry that consumers' opportunities for online interaction and modes of consumption are increasingly being negotiated and defined without the consumers' say on the matter. Indeed, the proposition for consumers is starting to become quite clear: self-disclose in return for convenience and benefits. With the growing popularity of online networking services, it seems that most consumers are agreeing to this trade. Facebook, led by its CEO Mark Zuckerberg, has been particularly active in pushing for an age of post-anonymity, calling the refusal for transparency a "lack of integrity" (Boyd 2010). *Wired* magazine editor-in-chief Chris Anderson has made similar pleas for embracing "radical transparency" in people's work and online interaction (Anderson 2006).

What is both interesting and problematic about services such as Facebook is that people's personal information is increasingly being exposed through involuntary disclosure, particularly through the actions of their friends and acquaintances. As people have taken up the habit of tagging and commenting on content, they are involuntarily creating breadcrumbs that may help search engines connect to themselves as well as other people, even to those who have closely attempted to protect their privacy at all costs. Contemporary algorithms have become incredibly accurate in connecting one piece of content to another, eventually connecting it to the real person who created it or to whom it refers. So even if marketers show some restraint in enticing consumer self-disclosure, consumers may do a lot of damage to one another or on their own. Google CEO Eric Schmidt recently suggested that in the future young people should be allowed to automatically change their names on their 18th birthday, to get a clean start as they have most likely been willingly and particularly unwillingly been disclosing information about themselves that may come back to haunt them (Jenkins Jr. 2010). So due to the power of search engines and consumers' creation of content, the digital self may be losing its retractable and narrative nature as consumers cannot simply drop what they have disclosed in one channel or context and find another, especially if much of the disclosure is done by other consumers, or even through involuntary self-disclosure.

Andrejevic (2002) lists two reasons why consumers and even academics have been slow to react to the emergence of the marketer-driven push for more consumer self-disclosure. The first reason relates to a simple lack of awareness or naivety of the informational asymmetries and power imbalances in the digital marketplace. Goldman (2006) similarly argues that search engines have for too long been seen in a romanticized way, as selfless enablers of our online whims instead of the media companies with vested business interests that they actually are. The second reason relates to the aforementioned historical discourse of celebratory cyber-romanticism, which has made people believe that the digital market is a consumer paradise where the consumer is in control. As news stories of corporate misbehavior, identity theft and embarrassing or even shocking stories of people overtly exposing themselves through social media have become more frequent, we have started to shed a lot of our naivety and cyber-romanticism that caused us to so freely expose ourselves in the past.

While consumers are becoming more aware of the need to manage the exposure of one's digital self, the differences in both awareness and skill between different demographics are proving to be quite profound. In her keynote at the sixth Consumer Culture Theory Conference held at Northwestern University in 2011, media sociologist Eszter Hargittai argued that this difference in skill between demographics is becoming an increasingly important consumer issue, both academically and socially. Holt (1998) had previously argued that certain consumer groups are often more vulnerable to marketer manipulation than others (e.g., children, the elderly). We had come to previously believe that so-called digital natives (Tapscott 2009) are something of a unified demographic in digital skill. The assumption had been that people born post-analog grow up surrounded by digital technologies and thus learn to use them at ease. Thus we had come to assume that any differences in digital skill would simply vanish over time as in the future everybody would be digital natives. Recent research seems to indicate that this will likely not be the case. Even among digital natives there are clear differences in skill and willingness to engage in online participation (Hargittai and Walejko 2008). We should also not forget that thus far much of the digital native debate has been strictly from a Western point of view, ignoring that young people in developing countries do not enjoy the privilege of ubiquitous online access (Apperley 2007).

Conclusion

Despite people's rising awareness of the perils of too much self-disclosure, the movement for more transparency as championed by Zuckerberg and others is still gaining popularity. Is this "radical transparency" a rehash of what Altman and Taylor (1973) dubbed the "tyranny of openness" where individuals have no freedom for private thoughts and full disclosure is demanded in all social encounters? Perhaps it is not that radical a proposition, but there are similarities. The digital realm already seems to have shifted expectations as to how much one is expected to disclose in different social settings to favor more disclosure (John *et al.* 2010). Kozinets (2008) argues that due to the fast and widespread proliferation of consumer-oriented technologies, the total rejection of technology has become an increasingly difficult identity position for consumers. In similar vein we could ask if absence from online interaction and social media – and by extension the refusal to self-disclose in these settings – are becoming a difficult consumer identity position to assume as well. Consumers are indeed increasingly expected to engage in self-disclosure via social media and similar online services if they want to "stay with the times" or even stay in touch with some of their friends as these friends have already adopted these technologies as their preferred modes of communication.

Further reading

Derlega, V.J., Metts, S., Petronio, S. and Margulis, S.T. (1993) *Self-Disclosure*, Thousand Oaks, CA: Sage. [A very comprehensive review of self-disclosure.]

Joinson, A.N., McKenna, K., Postmes, T. and Ulf-Dietrich, R. (eds) (2006) *The Oxford Handbook of Internet Psychology*, New York: Oxford University Press. [Deserves special mention for its sections on self and self-disclosure.]

Lenier, J. (2010) *You Are Not a Gadget: A Manifesto*, New York: Alfred A. Knopf. [At times severely pessimistic but offers very interesting examples on how deindividualization and anonymity can play out on the Internet.]

References

Anderson, C. (2006) "In Praise of Radical Transparency," available at: www.longtail.com/the_long_tail/2006/11/in_praise_of_ra.html (accessed November 21, 2010).

Andrade, E.B., Kaltcheva, V. and Weitz, B. (2002) "Self-Disclosure on the Web: The Impact of Privacy Policy, Reward, and Company Reputation," *Advances in Consumer Research*, 29: 350–3.

Andrejevic, M. (2002) "The Work of Being Watched: Interactive Media and the Exploitation of Self-Disclosure," *Critical Studies in Media Communication*, 19(2): 230–48.

Altman, I. and Taylor, D.A. (1973) *Social Penetration: The Development of Interpersonal Relationships*, New York: Holt, Rinehart and Winston.

Apperley, T. (2007) "Citizenship and Consumption: Convergence Culture, Transmedia Narratives and the Digital Divide," *ACM International Conference Proceeding Series*, 305.

Archer, J.L. (1980) "Self-disclosure," in D. Wegner and R. Vallacher (eds), *The Self in Social Psychology*, Oxford: Oxford University Press, pp. 183–204.

Bargh, J.A., McKenna, K.Y.A. and Fitzsimons, G.M. (2002) "Can You See the Real Me? Activation and Expression of the True Self on the Internet," *Journal of Social Issues*, 58: 33–48.

Belk, R.W. (1988) "Possession and the Extended Self," *Journal of Consumer Research*, 15(2): 139–68.

Berger, C.R. and Bradac, J.J. (1982) *Language and Social Knowledge: Uncertainty in Interpersonal Relations*, London: Edward Arnold.

Boyd, D. (2010) "Facebook and 'Radical Transparency' (A Rant)," available at: http://www.zephoria.org/thoughts/archives/2010/05/14/facebook-and-radical-transparency-a-rant.html (accessed November 21, 2010).

Cooley, C.H. (1902) *Human Nature and the Social Order*, New Brunswick, NJ: Transaction.

Cozby, P.C. (1972) "Self-Disclosure, Reciprocity and Liking," *Sociometry*, 25(1): 151–60.

——(1973) "Self-Disclosure: A Literature Review," *Psychological Bulletin*, 79(2): 73–91.

Deighton, J. (1996) "The Future of Interactive Marketing," *Harvard Business Review*, 74 (November–December): 4–16.

Derlega, V.J., Metts, S., Petrinio, S. and Margulis, S.T. (1993) *Self-Disclosure*, Newbury Park, CA: Sage.

Duncan, T. and Moriarty, S.E. (1998) "A Communication-Based Marketing Model for Managing Relationships," *Journal of Marketing*, 62(2): 1–13.

Gecas, V. (1982) "The Self-Concept," *Annual Review of Sociology*, 8: 1–33.

Goffman, E. (1959) *The Presentation of Self in Everyday Life*, New York: Doubleday.

Goldman, E. (2006) "Search Engine Bias and the Demise of Search Engine Utopiasm," *Yale Journal of Law and Technology*, 8(Spring): 188–200.

Goodwin, C. (1996) "Community as a Dimension of Service Relationships," *Journal of Consumer Psychology*, 5(4): 387–415.

Gouldner, A.W. (1960) "The Norm of Reciprocity: A Preliminary Statement," *American Sociological Review*, 25(April): 161–78.

Gunkel, D.J. (2010) "The Real Problem: Avatars, Metaphysics and Online Social Interaction," *New Media and Society*, 12(1): 127–41.

Hargittai, E. and Walejko, G. (2008) "The Participation Divide: Content Creation and Sharing in the Digital Age," *Information, Communication and Society*, 11(2): 239–56.

Higgins, E.T. (1987) "Self-Discrepancy: A Theory Relating Self and Affect," *Psychological Review*, 94(3): 319–40.

Holstein, J. and Gubrium, J. (2000) *The Self We Live By: Narrative Identity in a Postmodern World*, New York: Oxford University Press.

Holt, D.B. (1998) "Does Cultural Capital Structure American Consumption?" *Journal of Consumer Research*, 25(June): 1–25.

Jenkins Jr., H.W. (2010) "Google and the Search for the Future," *The Wall Street Journal*, available at: http://online.wsj.com/article/SB10001424052748704901104575423294099527212.html (accessed December 18, 2010).

Jhally, S. and Livant, B. (1986) "Watching as Working: The Valorization of Audience Consciousness," *Journal of Communication*, 36: 124–43.

John, L.K., Acquisti, A. and Loewenstein, G. (2010) "Strangers on a Plane: Context-Dependent Willingness to Divulge Sensitive Information," *Journal of Consumer Research*, 37(5): 858–73.

Joinson, A.N. (2001) "Self-Disclosure in Computer-Mediated Communication: The Role of Self-Awareness and Visual Anonymity," *European Journal of Social Psychology*, 31: 177–92.

——(2004) "Self-Esteem, Interpersonal Risk, and Preferences for E-Mail to Face-to-Face Communication," *Cyberpsychology and Behavior*, 7(4): 479–85.

Joinson, A.N. and Paine, C.B. (2006) "Self-Disclosure, Privacy and the Internet," in A.N. Joinson, K. McKenna, T. Postmes, and R. Ulf-Dietrich (eds), *The Oxford Handbook of Internet Psychology*, New York: Oxford University Press, pp. 235–50.

Jourard, S.M. (1964) *The Transparent Self*, Princeton, NJ: Van Nostrand.

——(1971) *Self-Disclosure: An Experimental Analysis of the Transparent Self*, New York: Wiley-Interscience.

Jourard, S.M. and Lasakow, P. (1958) "Some Factors in Self-Disclosure," *Journal of Abnormal and Social Psychology*, 56(1): 91–8.

Kozinets, R.V. (1999) "E-tribalized Marketing?: The Strategic Implications of Virtual Communities of Consumption," *European Management Journal*, 17(3): 252–64.

——(2008) "Technology/Ideology: How Ideological Fields Influence Consumers' Technology Narratives," *Journal of Consumer Research*, 34(6): 865–81.

——(2010) *Netnography: Doing Ethnographic Research Online*, London: Sage.

Lee, D.H., Im, S. and Taylor, C.R. (2008) "Voluntary Self-Disclosure of Information on the Internet: A Multimethod Study of the Motivations and Consequences of Disclosing Information on Blogs," *Psychology and Marketing*, 25(7): 692–710.

McAlexander, J.H., Schouten, J.W. and Koenig, H.F. (2002) "Building Brand Community," *Journal of Marketing*, 66(1): 38–54.

McKenna, K.Y.A., Green, A.S. and Gleason, E.J. (2002) "Relationship Formation on the Internet: What's the Big Attraction?" *Journal of Social Issues*, 58: 9–31.

Mead, G.H. (1934) *Mind, Self, and Society*, Chicago: University of Chicago Press.

Moon, Y. (2000) "Intimate Exchanges: Using Computers to Elicit Self-Disclosure from Consumers," *Journal of Consumer Research*, 26(4): 323–39.

Muñiz Jr., A.M. and O'Guinn, T.C. (2001) "Brand Community," *Journal of Consumer Research*, 27(4): 412–32.

Olivero, N. and Lunt, P. (2004) "Privacy Versus Willingness to Disclose in E-Commerce Exchanges: The Effect of Risk Awareness on the Relative Role of Trust and Control," *Journal of Economic Psychology*, 25(2): 243–62.

Qian, H. and Scott, C.R. (2007) "Anonymity and Self-Disclosure on Weblogs," *Journal of Computer-Mediated Communication*, 12: 1428–51.

Ritzer, G. (1999) *Enchanting a Disenchanted World*, Thousand Oaks, CA: Pine Forge Press.

Robinson, L. (2007) "The Cyberself: The Self-ing Project Goes Online, Symbolic Interaction in the Digital Age," *New Media and Society*, 9(1): 93–100.

Rosenberg, M. (1979) *Conceiving the Self*, New York: Basic Books

Rubin, Z. (1975) "Disclosing Oneself to a Stranger: Reciprocity and Its Limits," *Journal of Experimental Social Psychology*, 11(3): 233–60.

Schau, H.J. and Gilly, M.C. (2003) "We Are What We Post? Self-Presentation in Personal Web Space," *Journal of Consumer Research*, 30(3): 385–404.

Simmel, G. (1964) "The Secret and the Secret Society," in K. Wolff (ed.), *The Sociology of Georg Simmel*, New York: Free Press.

Sirgy, M.J. (1982) "Self-Concept in Consumer Behavior: A Critical Review," *Journal of Consumer Research*, 9(3): 287–300.

Streeter, T. (2011) *The Net Effect: Romanticism, Capitalism, and the Internet*, New York: New York University Press.

Tapscott, D. (2009) *Grown Up Digital: How the Net Generation is Changing Your World*, New York: McGraw-Hill.

Turkle, S. (1995) *Life on the Screen: Identity in the Age of the Internet*, New York: Simon & Schuster.

Vargo, S.L. and Lusch, R.F. (2004) "Evolving to a New Dominant Logic for Marketing," *Journal of Marketing*, 68(1): 1–17.

White, T.B. (2004) "Consumer Disclosure and Disclosure Avoidance: A Motivational Framework," *Journal of Consumer Psychology*, 14(1–2); 41–51.

Zhao, S. (2005) "The Digital Self: Through the Looking Glass of Telecopresent Others", *Symbolic Interaction*, 28(3): 387–405.

Zwick, D., and Dholakia, N. (2004) "Whose Identity Is It Anyway? Consumer Representation in the Age of Database Marketing," *Journal of Macromarketing*, 24(1): 31–43.

31

CONSUMER ACTIVISM 2.0

Tools for social change

Pia A. Albinsson and B. Yasanthi Perera

Keywords

consumer activism, consumer movements, Internet-mediated communication, online mobilization, social media

> Activists have not only incorporated the Internet into their repertoire, but also ... have changed substantially what counts as activism, what counts as community, collective identity, democratic space and political strategy. And online activists challenge us to think about how cyberspace is meant to be used.
>
> (McCaughey and Ayers 2003, pp. 1–2)

Introduction

Consumer activism is important for the progressive evolution of society. Since the Boston Tea Party of 1773, North American history is replete with accounts of consumers using their collective power to spawn social change (Glickman 2005) including the enactment of consumer protection laws and adoption of socially responsible manufacturing standards. In recent decades, with the increasing global penetration of the Internet and its features that allow users to inexpensively create and disseminate information (DiMaggio *et al.* 2001), consumer activism reached a new height. Internet technology was instrumental in the establishment of China's Falun Gong oppositional movement (Lin 2001), and the online-based myBarackObama.com campaign contributed to the success of President Obama's successful 2008 presidential bid (Carty 2011). More recently, the Internet's role in the 2011 democratic uprisings in the Middle East and the Occupy Wall Street movement attests to its power as a medium for mobilizing global citizens on behalf of various causes.

Scholars in consumer behavior, communication studies, political science, and sociology have studied numerous aspects of collective behavior, social movements, and resistance to political and societal ideologies through various theoretical lenses (e.g., resource mobilization, collective identity, and new social movements). However, there is a research gap due to limited consideration of the new Web 2.0 technologies and consumer-generated media (e.g., Facebook, YouTube, Flickr, Twitter, and blogs) in consumer activism. Established organizations, such as

Amnesty International (AI), now utilize social media and encourage consumers to "promote human rights online" by taking action through email, and displaying Amnesty's banner on personal websites and blogs. In addition to Twitter, AI hosts five official Facebook pages for different activist groups and various country-specific web endeavors. On its 50th birthday, May 28, 2011, AI encouraged consumers to "celebrate 50 years of fighting for justice" by adding the Amnesty candle to users' Facebook and Twitter profiles. The organization also posts images on Flickr, utilizes YouTube, and offers an AI iPhone application to help consumers act quickly on issues they care about. Utilizing current technologies, organizations such as Avaaz.org provide consumers with an easily accessible, online platform from which to participate in various activism efforts ranging from poverty elimination to climate change issues. Meaning "voice" in multiple languages, Avaaz.org empowers consumers to take online action by organizing "citizens of all nations to close the gap between the world we have and the world most people everywhere want" (www.avaaz.org). The issues pursued are selected through polling over 10 million members in 193 countries who, collectively, have taken 58,414,636 activist actions since the organization's founding in 2007. Online engagement has certainly influenced the conduct of activism through connecting consumers to local and global issues, increasing the ease of action, and thus offering consumers the ability to participate in activism efforts to varying degrees.

The aim of this chapter is two-fold. First, we offer an overview of contemporary online consumer activism to better understand how consumers utilize Internet-mediated communications in their activism efforts. Second, we assess whether online activism has altered the nature of activism itself. Although we focus on consumer movements that drive social change through altering existing practices and dialog pertaining to consumption and marketing (Kozinets and Handelman 2004), social movements present the context for these behaviors. Additionally, two implicit premises underpin this chapter. First, while the Internet and Internet-based technologies are important as the facilitating medium for online activism, action on the part of consumers is just as important. As Earl and Kimport (2011, p. 14) write, "It is people's uses of technology – not technology itself-that can change social process." Second, we contend that every consumer is a potential activist because each individual's consumption behaviors are statements of value.

Overview of online activism

Consumers simultaneously occupy numerous roles (sender, recipient, modifier of existing messages) in online consumer activism (Illia 2003) thus causing entities, such as corporations, that historically hold power over media messages some loss of control (Holtz 2002). Currently, online activism either manifests completely online or in hybrid form where online action is coupled with physical place-oriented action as in the case of CarrotMob, a consumer movement with the tagline "vote with your money," that organizes online and persuades consumers to gather at predetermined locations for mass buycotts. Online activism is diverse: the Internet hosts varied groups differing in objectives, structure, scope of activities, and life span, organized by individuals, consumer groups, or coalitions of entities with similar interests, and core philosophies, to achieve specific outcomes ranging from tarnishing corporate reputations, to exposing cultural assumptions, and resisting various facets of the consumption-oriented marketplace culture.

Efforts designed to tarnish corporate reputations and encourage change in both consumption and corporate practices include Untied, a customer disservice site created by an unhappy United Airlines traveler, and numerous anti-corporation websites also referred to as anti-brand communities in the literature, including those targeting Wal-Mart, McDonald's, and Starbucks. Additionally, culture jamming, a popular form of online activism 'reorganizes' media by modifying existing advertising to impart a message about the brand in question that is often contrary to that espoused by the company (Pickerel *et al.* 2002). Adbusters, The Institute of Applied Autonomy, and the Bureau of Inverse Technology are popular manifestations of culture jamming that enact their activism efforts by tapping into consumers' emotions (Pickerel *et al.* 2002; Rumbo 2002; Harold 2004; Wettergren 2009). Other forms of online consumer activism entail hacktivism, e-sit-ins, domain squatting, and cyber graffiti that occur on various websites (e.g., www.2600. com, www.attrition.com).

Irrespective of the form in which the activism entity organizes itself, and how consumer resistance is enacted (e.g., hacktivism versus buycotts versus culture jamming), online efforts utilize a variety of e-tactics (Earl and Kimport 2011). The most common e-tactics entail asking consumers to disseminate activism messages (e.g., information via email, blogs, and viral videos) to their social media networks, or to contact corporations or elected representatives on behalf of a given cause's objective. Other e-tactics involve consumers signing online petitions, or participating in boycotts or buycotts of certain corporations. In terms of organizing such efforts, the online environment offers would-be activists a variety of user-friendly tools. Purely online and hybrid-place activism advocating for social change often provide their supporters with websites that offers e-tactics and e-tools such as event calendars, online activism 'how to' guides, RSS-feeds, downloadable flyers, brochures, and links to cause-related/affiliated organizations. For instance, any consumer can initiate an activism effort by visiting PetitionOnline.org, a website that allows consumers to create and post online petitions within minutes. Since its conception in 1999, PetitionOnline.org has allowed activists to gather in excess of 92 million signatures (PetitionOnline.org). Despite some critics, such as Snopes.com's Barbara Mikkelson, who contend that e-signatures are not as effective as "physical" signatures (2007), numerous success stories exist. For example, Ecpat, a British organization that aims to stop trafficking and abuse of children, could not persuade the Hilton Hotel chain to sign a code of conduct to train staff on stopping potential abuse occurring in the hotels. Ecpat ultimately decided to put up billboards in the CEO's hometown instead of delivering a petition to his office. Avaaz.org, the aforementioned platform for various activism efforts, promoted Ecpat's work, 310,000 consumers signed the petition and Hilton Hotels signed the code of conduct before the billboards were posted (Glennie 2011). It is important to note that a given online consumer movement may utilize many e-tactics in order to achieve their objectives. United Students Against Sweatshops, which uses Facebook, Twitter, RSS-feeds and organizes real-life flashmobs, writes on its website "We seek to use a diversity of tactics, especially nonviolent direct action and civil disobedience, which fundamentally challenge the oppressive power structures that exploit the majority of the world's population" (www.usas.org).

The interface of technology and online activism: evolution, opportunities, and challenges

Early technological advances such as TV, radio, and fax assisted many social movements in spreading their messages to larger audiences. The fax machine facilitated the organization of similar events in different locations by duplicating flyers across disperse geographic areas. The 'emergent electronic advocacy' (e.g., Web pages, email, discussion groups, newsgroups), or the second generation of technological advances (Hick and McNutt 2002), further aided activist groups in their mobilization efforts. This computer-mediated communication (CMC), also called information communication technologies (ICT), refers to communication between computer users who utilize a network to exchange digital messages or information. CMC arises in two forms: asynchronous and synchronous (Carty 2011; Chesters and Welsh 2011). Asynchronous communications (e.g., email, discussion forums, wikis, web diaries and blogs) enable one-to-one or one-to-many communication, whereas synchronous CMC is real-time communication between geographically distant individuals or groups (e.g., text communication in chat rooms, instant messaging). Initial online consumer activism research examined how consumers used message boards, listservs, and discussion forums such as Usenet, Yahoo, and AOL groups. Kozinets and Handelman (2004) researched boycotting as a form of individual resistance, not collective behavior, through the study of various discussion and newsgroups such as Alt.activism, misc.activism.progressive, alt.society.labor-unions and talk.politics.theory. They found that activists perceived a difference between themselves and consumers, referring to the latter as "foolish" and "entranced couch potatoes," as they appeared to operate within the dominant consumption-oriented paradigm. In essence, the activists regarded consumers as opponents while, in some instances, the consumers found activists to be "elitist and overzealous" (ibid.: 701). An individual with long-term involvement in progressing the dialogue on climate initiatives echoed the latter point by noting that environmental conservation was hindered by earlier proponents being "esoteric and holier than thou" with the general population (Perera n.d.). Although further research is needed, we contend that organizations like CarrotMob and Avaaz that present user-friendly information, encourage, and empower consumers to take whatever action they are able represent a shift in approach from opposition to cooperation with activists who coordinate efforts that welcome different levels of consumer participation.

The synchronous nature of current Internet-based social media innovations, coupled with technological advancements in the form of smartphones, tablets, and other mobile devices, has enhanced communication efficiency and reduced the costs of real-time conversations between geographically dispersed individuals. As a result, this current generation of Internet-based innovations, the user-generated content, or Web 2.0, technologies, has differentiated modern online consumer campaigns from their predecessors even further. One Twitter tweet may elicit responses from hundreds of followers, or a smartphone may be used to record an unplanned incident and be uploaded to YouTube where thousands around the world can view it in a matter of minutes.

Social media and Internet access have helped to spread many causes to different parts of the world. The CarrotMob movement, which has organized over 175 buycotting (reverse boycotting) community events, spread from San Francisco to over 70 cities in 20 countries within a four-year period. Through the efforts of the movement's coordinators and local organizers, CarrotMobs have occurred in North and South America, Europe, Asia, Australia, and New Zealand; the movement continues to grow with the first African CarrotMob event taking place in Cape Town, South Africa, during November of 2011 (www.CarrotMob.org). CarrotMob makes it easy for consumers to participate in the effort by revamping their website and collaborating with Facebook to allow consumers to login through this popular social media platform. The Internet and social media are important in CarrotMob's efforts: consumers and CarrotMob organizers communicate, strategize, (e-)mobilize, and organize their physical place-oriented mass buycotts through Twitter, tumblr, Facebook, blogs, YouTube, email and other technologies (see Rheingold 2002, for a review of how technology facilitates smart mobs and flashmobs). It would have been unlikely for CarrotMob to spread their movement to its current global level in the absence of these technologies. Several other movements, including 350.org, Greenpeace, and WiserEarth, utilize social media tools to connect online consumers and spread awareness. For instance, 350.org addresses the climate change issue by linking hundreds of "friends and allies" on their website (e.g., WWF climate witness, the Natural Step, Polar bears International, Klimat Aktion, Greenpeace, Go Loco, Carbono Zero, CarrotMob, etc.). With respect to e-mobilization (Earl and Kimport 2011), research has illustrated the importance of recruiting social media/Web 2.0-savvy individuals to solely help with the viral marketing of events since not all consumers are adept and comfortable in using social media on behalf of a cause or an organization (Albinsson and Perera 2012).

By using the Internet and Web 2.0, existing movements have the potential to mobilize the public to take immediate action in varied locations, in contrast to prior forms of activism where organizers had to plan their mobilization efforts in advance. As such, the speed, spontaneity, and element of surprise present an advantage for current online activism. The spread of messages via social media is so ubiquitous that on occasion, mainstream media (i.e., print media, news channels) may also choose to cover these issues as stories of interest. An example is the case of the Nike "sweatshop email" outlining an exchange of communication between an MIT graduate student, Jonah Peretti and Nike. When Peretti placed an order for a personalized pair of Nike shoes displaying the word "sweatshop," Nike refused to fill the order (Peretti with Micheletti 2004; Carty 2011). This exchange was transmitted through micro-media social networks to millions of people across six continents, and ultimately resulted in hundreds of mass media imprints (Carty 2011). In another example of how online efforts are reported in offline media, news channel reports on online activism efforts and the PBS (Public Broadcasting Service) show *Need to Know* helped CarrotMob to spread their message to TV viewers.

Another distinction between current online activism and prior forms of activism lies in who is involved in message dissemination. In earlier forms of activism, organizers typically disseminated the movement's message; in modern-day online activism, consumers may pass on activism-related information without necessarily having deeper involvement with the cause in question or knowing the original organizers. Consumers now have options: they can simply distribute information about a movement; they can create and distribute media about existing movements; utilizing online tools, they can initiate new movements. Online consumer activists exhibit variations in their degree of engagement with a cause that may be influenced by their level of identification with the cause and its objectives. Intuitively, activism movements also exhibit variations on several dimensions (e.g., hierarchical or flat, dependent on a head office for propagation, or open to consumers spreading their message). While the Internet with its enhanced technologies allows consumers the potential for greater, more involved, participation in activism efforts than before, at a basic level, it is simply the interface for, or context of, interaction between consumer activists, and consumer movements. The outcomes of this interaction are dependent upon the interaction between the movement's characteristics (e.g., structure, availability of participation opportunities) and consumer characteristics (e.g., interest, familiarity and access to the Internet). While some consumers prefer anonymity online, for instance through avatars that exist in virtual worlds such as Second Life or through made-up screen names, others have become amateur journalists who report on the events taking place in their local sphere through venues such as YouTube, or news media sites that encourage consumer participation such as CNN's online iReport. Thus, consumers, expecting a certain degree of ethics, social responsibility, and transparency use available technological and social media tools to hold governments, corporations, other institutions, and fellow citizens responsible for their behaviors.

If we visualize consumer commitment to a cause on a linear continuum, on one end we will find 'minimal interest and low commitment,' which entails an interest or an obligation to be interested in a cause to the point of forwarding messages or signing petitions. For example, hungersite.com makes it easy for consumers to donate food to various charities for distributing to the needy. Consumers click on a button daily and advertisers on the website donate a certain amount (stated in terms of cups of food) towards hunger-alleviating charities. Though their collective action can have a significant impact, this example illustrates very limited involvement on part of the consumer. Another recent phenomenon urges consumers to use their mobile phones and text a code to a certain number to make donations in support of a particular organization or current event (e.g., feedingamerica.org). Popular press articles have dubbed this limited involvement somewhat derogatorily as "slactivism" or "clicktivism." A primary criticism of slactivism/clicktivism is that Internet users participate in many activism efforts without being truly committed to them. However, some researchers have argued that slactivists are in essence "convenience activists" (Albinsson and Perera 2012) who participate in consumer movements to the extent that they are able. These consumers essentially participate through "5-minute activism" (Earl and Kimport 2011) and it is important to note that these individuals contribute in some way towards the cause in question instead of completely ignoring it. While they may participate at a surface level in numerous causes, and not undertake "more committed" action (i.e., participating in physical place-oriented activism, or donating money), these consumers are important in signing petitions and spreading a given cause's message to wider networks. As such, this type of participation can be very important in terms of spreading the movement's message and increasing awareness to other consumers who may take more committed or definitive action.

At the other end of the dimension, we find individuals with 'deep interest and strong commitment.' This strong commitment may stem from either strong personal interest in the cause itself due to their values, or due to strong ties (social capital) with others who participate in, or support, a particular activism effort. Adler and Kwon (2002, p. 23) define social capital as "the goodwill available to individuals or groups … [stemming from] the structure and content of the actor's social relations." While there is debate as to whether Internet technologies erode social capital (e.g., Cole 2000; Wellman *et al.* 2001), research suggests that the Internet sustains community bonds by complementing, not replacing, other channels of interaction (DiMaggio *et al.* 2001, pp. 317–19). Higher committed consumers' behavior may entail recruiting others to support the activism movement, making monetary donations, participating in physical place-oriented gatherings, and contributing to the development of the movement. In terms of the latter, there is a distinction between simply participating in the movement via social media, and contributing to the evolution of the movement (e.g., difference between passing messages and other pre-packaged information, or engage in online discussions, sharing user-generated media and interacting with movement organizers, or setting up local community-based physical place-oriented events). It is important to note that both degree of commitment and opportunity for engagement influence individual consumers' behavior of collective action. While it is intuitive to deduce that more committed individuals are more engaged and will therefore undertake "harder" and more demanding actions (e.g., attending a physical place-oriented protest versus signing online petitions), sometimes committed individuals cannot participate to the extent they would like because of lack of opportunity in their local communities. In such instances, consumer activists tend to participate to greater extent online, either in terms of hours spent on a cause, or engaging online to a different degree (e.g., volunteering for other kinds of movement propagation activities like designing websites, or managing movement-related postings on a specific social media site). While physical co-presence is no longer a requisite for successful activism, we note that online consumer activism is very much community-based. For instance, Hollenbeck and Zinkhan (2006), in an early study of online activism in anti-brand communities, found that the benefits afforded by modern technology (speed, convenience, anonymity, and virtual formation) allowed members of online anti-brand communities to create a collective identity. In turn, Kozinets and Belz (2010), in their study of sustainable consumption-oriented online communities, note that social media are often used to foster community, customize participation, and help consumers focus their awareness and attention on various options for social change.

In terms of challenges, consumer movement organizers constantly need to monitor consumer-generated online media about the movement's message to protect the movement's credibility. This is a potential issue because any consumer can express opinions, tag information, and share it across the Internet; based on their content, the information shared by these consumers could either potentially aid or hinder the development of the said consumer movement. As the personal cost of online activism (in terms of money, time, and access) is relatively low, a given movement may have hundreds of thousands to millions of online supporters. Depending on the nature of the campaign, strong online support may be sufficient to reach the activism goal (e.g., bombarding an organization or political representative with emails and phone calls). However, if the campaign calls for further action that requires more commitment on the part of online supporters (e.g., monetary donations, physical place-oriented action), some, like Hesse (2009), argue that the impressive online support may not translate into significant action. Mary Joyce of DigiActive, an organization that helps activists with the effective use of social media to advance their causes, states,

> Commitment levels are opaque. Maybe a maximum of 5 percent are going to take action, and maybe it's closer to 1 percent ... In most cases of Facebook groups, members do nothing. I haven't yet seen a case where the Facebook group has led to a sustained movement.
>
> *(as quoted in Hesse 2009)*

However, for some consumers, such minimal engagement may lead to more engaged activism later (Kerwin 2010).

Discussion and avenues for future research

Our aim in this chapter was to provide an overview of contemporary online consumer activism to gain a deeper understanding of the way consumers utilize Internet-mediated communications in their activism efforts to assess if and how online activism has altered the nature of activism itself. Consumers realize that through engaging in different movements, they have the power to bring about social, cultural, and political change (Chesters and Welsh 2011). Due to the widespread use of Internet technologies and mobile devices, the world is increasingly transparent and consumers often share events and voice their opinions over the Internet to persuade companies, governments, and other institutions to adopt policies and practices that reflect consumer and societal interests. Thus, movements that effectively utilize online technologies garner many advantages.

First, the use of Internet-based technologies has increased the reaction speed to local, national, and global events on part of activism movement organizers as well as consumers. Depending on the nature of the response, immediate reactions to events may have more power in communicating clear messages as the occurrence is fresh in people's minds, and there may be more emotion and effort involved. For example, despite Occupy Wall Street's organizational issues, consumers in major North American cities responded to the first event in New York City with occupy protests in their cities. These actions en masse communicated consumers' unhappiness with certain facets of business and government.

Second, Internet technologies have made consumer participation more convenient. Now, consumers can choose to participate to various degrees that require different actions and different commitments from them. For instance, consumer A participates in his/her favorite cause by forwarding media message to his/her networks, but Consumer B with more time and perhaps tech-savvy skills may choose to create media messages to disperse, and Consumer C may actually decide to participate in a gathering in support of the same cause in his or her town. Moving activism to the online realm has given consumers and causes more options, more participation, and more choices. However, all of this is dependent upon the organizers of a cause recognizing these opportunities and capitalizing upon them. For example, different consumer/social movements may be in competition for various resources including consumers' attention and propensity to take action. A realization on the part of movements that their causes could be further advanced collaboratively, instead of competing for resources, could be an explanation for why consumer movements with similar messages are increasingly joining forces to achieve successful one-time events or longer-term objectives.

Third, Internet technologies and the wide availability of recording technologies have also made it easy for any consumer with enough gumption and tech skills to share an issue with a company or any social injustice with fellow consumers. As such, Consumer D can upload any disturbing footage of a company's practices (e.g., worker treatment at a plant abroad or an unpleasant service encounter on a plane) to YouTube, link it to other social media sites, and spread their message. Additionally, a consumer can now chose to start an online campaign with easy tools such as PetitionsOnline or Twitition, a specific petition site for Twitter users. We contend that the mingling of online technologies and activism has empowered consumers to participate in varying degrees to extract value from certain brands. Thus, with our contention that perhaps the main difference between traditional forms of activism and present-day online activism is ultimately in the nature of consumer engagement. An important point of our chapter is to initiate a conversation that can lead to thoughtful future research that includes an examination of value co-creation in the online consumer movement context.

As the Internet has heightened the level of transparency and facilitated exchange between corporations, political organizations and consumer movements, value co-creation (Prahalad and Ramaswamy 2004) is integral to the discussion of current online consumer activism. Francis Gouillart (2010), co-author of "The Power of Co-Creation," notes that co-creation already occurs in the political arena most notably with respect to Barack Obama's presidential bid. Obama's 2008 campaign encouraged supporter participation through MyBarackObama.com thereby allowing "any supporter to be a self-directed campaign manager" (Errol Louis, as quoted by Gouillart 2010) in direct contrast to the traditional approach where the political party maintains control and supporters are not provided the option of altering, or adding their voices, to the formal political marketing material. Similarly, at a basic level, the ubiquitous presence of the Internet and commonplace Web 2.0 technologies facilitate consumers' communication with corporations and other consumers. A recent example is the uproar over GAP's decision to change its apparently much loved "Blue Box" logo. Consumers' comments and emails on a variety of sites including Facebook led GAP to first engage in a crowdsourcing exercise (i.e., requesting consumers' ideas on what the new logo should look like), which was quickly scrapped in favor of readopting the Blue Box logo. More and more organizations are utilizing crowdsourcing to build goodwill and brand loyalty by involving consumers in the production process (Howe 2009). At a more advanced level, consumers utilize Web 2.0 technologies to add to existing activist communications, or create their own on behalf of a movement, in essence creating value with the movement organizers.

We contend that consumer activists assist in value co-creation through their dialogue in the marketplace with corporations and organizations, and through their actions (boycotts, buycotts, and other retaliating or rewarding behaviors) that communicate what is, and what is not acceptable to them. We expect that, as consumers continue to address lapses in social responsibility by businesses and other institutional entities, the social responsibility practices and the degree of transparency of these organizations may change in response to consumer expectations. We note that at times, different activist groups may communicate contrary messages on the same issue. An example is consumers' reaction to the passing of Arizona's stringent immigration laws SB-1070 in 2010: numerous groups advocated boycotts of Arizona to communicate disapproval, while others with different views called for buycotts to support Arizona lawmakers (Archibold 2010).

As such, interaction between activists groups with differing views may present an area for future exploration.

In terms of further future research, as suggested above, online activism may present a form of value co-creation where consumers interact with corporations to aid in enacting changes that allow for greater value extractions. Thus, the value co-creation lens may prove to be insightful in examining online consumer activism. Future research could also address some of the debates in the field. The first focuses on whether slactivists add value to consumer movements, or whether their minimal participation dilutes activism efforts. A second debate questions the very value of the online activism with the query of whether online action is as powerful and effective as similar physical place-oriented action. This debate questions whether 100,000 Internet signatures are equivalent to 100,000 signatures physically collected by movement organizers by standing in a public venue. While it appears that the degree of effort required, on part of the organizers, seems to be less for online activism, we contend that what ultimately matters is impact and, in this day and age of widespread use and necessity of technology and social media, online signatures should carry as much weight as signatures collected in physical spaces. However, further research regarding the outcomes of online action is necessary to settle this debate. Moreover, with the advent of hybrid activism, that occurs both online and in physical places, the notion of social capital, which has been examined with respect to online communities, becomes important.

Foth (2003, p. 33) contends that the widespread use of the Internet has changed social interactions "away from local anchors and towards the Internet which has the potential to revive social capital." An area of future research could explore the effect of social capital on consumers' willingness to participate in physical place-oriented activism and other forms of deeper engagement. This research is important because of the debate on whether online consumer activism brings about meaningful change or whether online coordination and information sharing must be accompanied by physical place-oriented action for the consumer action to be meaningful. The social capital lens could also be used to examine further collaborations, temporary and longer term, between online activists with similar overarching goals. We posit that a primary difference is in the nature of the activists themselves. Is participation dependent upon characteristics of the consumer, or the movement, or ease of use of the technology? Additionally, as not all tactics are used by all organizations, one could also explore the different tactics favored by different types of organizations, their degree of success in achieving their goals, and the characteristics of their members. An extreme form of consumer resistance that goes beyond real life and the online efforts previously described is consumer resistance through online gaming and virtual worlds such as in Second Life (Bonsu and Darmody 2008). One cannot be more anonymous than having a virtual avatar that spreads awareness of a given cause online. More research is needed to see how consumers' action through their avatars affects social change.

To conclude, current Internet-based innovations, including Web 2.0 tools and the wherewithal to use these tools, have given consumers a new form of freedom, and voice. As such, they are more apt to start campaigns, expose social injustices, and demand change from the institutions concerned. We contend that activism in the online realm may contribute to creating a more empowered consumer who participates to the degree that he or she is able. While this ease of participation and the ability to start consumer campaigns from one's home computer have added to the social conscience and social awareness of society, they have introduced new conundrums to contemplate. One wonders whether the plethora of petitions and viral videos on behalf of various causes have the desired effects or whether they confuse matters. After all, if there are 259 Facebook pages calling for stringent GMO policies, which one does the consumer join? Perhaps the most important contribution of this chapter is to be a starting point for additional empirical research on the various questions surrounding online consumer activism.

Further reading

Carty, V. (2011) *Wired and Mobilizing: Social Movements, New Technology, and Electoral Politics*, New York: Routledge. [A review of social movement theories and four case studies of activism using new technology.]

Earl, J. and Kimport, K. (2011), *Digitally Enabled Social Change: Activism in the Internet Age*: Cambridge, MA: MIT Press. [Empirical investigations of Web activism and its impact on the organization and participation in activism movements.]

Hick, S.F. and McNutt, J.G. (2002), *Advocacy, Activism, and the Internet: Community Organization and Social Policy*, Chicago: Lyceum Books Inc. [Integrates Internet activism for social change with macro social work theory.]

McCaughey, M. and Ayers, M.D. (2003) *Cyberactivism: Online Activism in Theory and Practice*, New York: Routledge. [A research collection of what Internet has brought to activism, how it re-defined what counts as activism and how it challenged the utilization of cyberspace prior to Web 2.0.]

References

Adler, P.S. and Kwon, S. (2002) "Social Capital: Prospects for a New Concept," *Academy of Management Review*, 27(1): 17–40.

Albinsson, P.A. and Perera, B.Y. (2012) "Consumer Activism through Social Media: Carrots vs. Sticks," in A. Close (ed.), *Online Consumer Behavior: Theory and Research in Social Media, Advertising, and E-Tail*, New York: Routledge, pp. 101–32.

Archibold, R. (2010) "Arizona Enacts Stringent Law on Immigration," *New York Times*, April 23 Available at: www.nytimes.com/2010/04/24/us/politics/24immig.html (accessed November 27, 2011).

Bonsu, S. and Darmody, A. (2008) "Co-creating Second Life: Market Consumer Cooperation In Contemporary Economy," *Journal of Macromarketing*, 28: 355–68.

Carty, V. (2011) *Wired and Mobilizing Social Movements, New Technology, and Electoral Politics*, New York: Routledge.

Chesters, G. and Welsh, I. (2011) *Social Movements: The Key Concepts*, New York: Routledge.

Cole, J. (2000) *Surveying the Digital Future*, Los Angeles: UCLA Center for Telecommunication Policy.

DiMaggio, P., Hargittai, E., Neuman, W.R., and Robinson, J.P. (2001) "Social Implications of the Internet," *Annual Review of Sociology*, 27: 307–36.

Earl, J. and Kimport, K. (2011) *Digitally Enabled Social Change: Activism in the Internet Age*, Cambridge, MA: MIT Press.

Foth, M. (2003) "Connectivity Does Not Ensure Community: On Social Capital, Networks and Communities of Place," presentation at the ITIRA Conference, December 2003, Community Informatics.

Glennie, J. (2011) "The Joys of Online Activism," *The Guardian*, January 18. Available at: www.guardian. co.uk/global-development/poverty-matters/2011/jan/18/online-activism-internet-campaign-mobilise (accessed 21 November 2011).

Glickman, L. (2005) "Boycott Mania: As Business Ethics Fall, Consumer Activism Rises," *Boston Globe*, July 31, available at: www.boston.com/news/globe/editorial_opinion/oped/articles/2005/07/31/boy cott_mania/ (accessed 20 April 2011).

Gouillart, F. (2010) "Dialogue with the Authors of The Power of Co-Creation, Co-creating Campaigns and the Social Contract," available at: http://powerofcocreation.com/authors-blog/co-creating-campaigns-and-social-contract) (accessed September 30, 2010).

Harold, C. (2004) "Pranking Rhetoric: 'Culture Jamming' as Media Activism," *Critical Studies in Media Communication*, 21(3): 189–211.

Hesse, M. (2009) "Facebook's Easy Virtue 'Click through Activism' Broad but Fleeting," *Washington Post*, July 2, available at: www.washingtonpost.com/wp-dyn/content/article/2009/07/01/AR2009070103936.html.

Hollenbeck, C.R. and Zinkhan, G.M. (2006) "Consumer Activism on the Internet: The Role of Anti-brand Communities," *Advances in Consumer Research*, 33: 479–85.

Holtz, S. (2002) *Public Relations of the Net*, 2nd edn, New York: Amacom.

Howe, J. (2009) *Crowdsourcing*, New York: Three Rivers Press.

Illia, L. (2003) "Passage to Cyberactivism: How Dynamics of Activism Change," *Journal of Public Affairs*, 3(4): 326–37.

Kerwin, A.M. (2010) "How to Get the Social-Media Generation Behind Your Cause," *Advertising Age*, June 28, p. 8.

Kozinets, R.V. and Belz, F-M. (2010) "Social Media for Social Change: Sustainability-based Community in a Sustainable World", in D.W. Dahl, G.V. Johar, and S.M.J. van Osselaer (eds), *Advances in Consumer Research*, vol. 38, Duluth, MN: Association for Consumer Research.

Kozinets, R.V. and Handelman, J.M. (2004) "Adversaries of Consumption: Consumer Movements, Activism and Ideology," *Journal of Consumer Research*, 31(December): 691–704.

Lin, N. (2001) *Social Capital: A Theory of Social Structure and Action*, New York: Cambridge University Press.

McCaughey, M. and Ayers, M.D. (2003) *Cyberactivism*, New York: Routledge.

Mikkelson, B. (2007) "Internet Petitions," June 9, available at: www.snopes.com/inboxer/petition/internet.asp.

Perera, B.Y. (n.d.) 'How for-Profit Social Entrepreneurs Balance Social and Economic Missions,' Working Paper, New Mexico State University.

Peretti, J. with Micheletti, M. (2004) "The Nike Sweatshop Email: Political Consumerism, Internet and Culture Jamming," in M. Micheletti, A. Follesdal, and D. Stolle (eds), *Politics, Products and Markets: Exploring Political Consumerism Past and Present*, New Brunswick, NJ: Transaction Publishers, pp. 127–42.

Pickerel, W., Jorgensen, H. and Bennett, L. (2002) "Culture Jams and Meme Warfare: Kalle Lasn, Adbusters, and Media Activism: Tactics in Global Activism for the 21st Century," interview with Kalle Lasn, editor of *Adbusters Magazine*, April 19, 2002.

Prahalad, C.K. and Ramaswamy, V. (2004) *The Future of Competition: Co-Creating Unique Value with Customers*, Boston: Harvard Business School Press.

Rheingold, H. (2002) *Smart Mobs: The Next Social Revolution*, Cambridge, MA: Perseus Books.

Rumbo, J.D. (2002) "Consumer Resistance in a World of Advertising Clutter: The Case of Adbusters," *Psychology and Marketing*, 19(2): 127–48.

Wellman, B., Quan Haase, A., Witte, J. and Hampton K. (2001) "Does the Internet Increase, Decrease, or Supplement Social Capital?: Social Networks, Participation, and Community Commitment," *American Behavioral Scientist*, 45(3): 436–55.

Wettergren, A. (2009) "Fun and Laughter: Culture Jamming and the Emotional Regime of Late Capitalism," *Social Movement Studies*, 8(1): 1–16.

32

JACK OF ALL TRADES, MASTER OF ... SOME?

Multitasking in digital consumers

Sydney Chinchanachokchai and Brittany R. L. Duff

Keywords

concurrent, multitasking, sequential

Introduction

In today's fast-paced life, consumers usually engage in multiple tasks at once in a hope to effectively manage their time or to increase the palatability of boring tasks. For example, although we are sure that reading this book is *not* one of those uninteresting tasks, while reading it you may be listening to music, playing a video or texting with a friend. With increasingly accessible entertainment and information, cutting-edge technologies facilitate a digital life.

Increasingly, a single medium is not the sole focus of attention. Studies of college students have shown that 86 percent of respondents say they utilize media in combination (Alperstein 2005). A survey on media multitasking found that 51 percent of the respondents admitted that they paid attention to one medium more than other(s) and 32.9 percent said that they attend to each media equally at the same time (Pilotta and Schultz 2005). Some 72 percent of smartphone owners say that they use them while consuming other media (Google/IPSOS OTX Media CT 2011).

While multitasking in some form has always existed, media multitasking is a phenomenon that recently has become prevalent, especially among younger generations. Media, which may have once been a sole recipient of attention, is used increasingly in conjunction with other tasks and other media. American children between 8 and 18 years old spend more than six hours per day in media use (Roberts and Foehr 2008). In Europe, media multitasking behaviors such as using TV and the Internet simultaneously have grown 38 percent since 2006 (European Interactive Advertising Association Multi-task Report 2009). The behavior is not only observed in the leisure context, but also in classrooms and the workplace. For example, today's classrooms may implement wireless technology including additional visual and auditory information to facilitate the learning process. Some schools allow students to use laptops in class. At home, students often turn on the television or computer while they are doing homework. Interactive media platforms and a proliferation of media options put the consumer in control of their experience to best fit their needs. They choose to interact with and selectively consume media messages. Rather than messages being attended to directly, they may be in the background or periphery or competing against other messages that are being seen at the same time. However, the process of multitasking and its possible effects, both on the consumer and on the perception of the message, have been little studied in the marketing literature.

In this chapter we will provide an overview of some of the relevant research on multitasking behavior, particularly media multitasking. We review the literature in fields that have explored multitasking processing such as psychology and communication as well as identify the gaps and current issues in the body of research. Finally, we discuss potential future research directions in multitasking.

Definition of multitasking and overview of the related theories

Multitasking behaviors have been widely studied across domains such as cognitive psychology, computer science, etc. The term 'multitasking' is considered novel in many fields but the general idea is relatively similar to studies in cognitive psychology on dual-task performance (Pashler 1994; Logan and Gordon 2001). Most multitasking behaviors deal with attentional processes such as divided attention (simultaneously monitoring more than two different inputs) or attention switching (alternately monitoring at least two inputs, one at a time) (McDowd and Birren 1990).

Based on these modes of processing, there are two main ways to think about multitasking as a process. One way to categorize multitasking behavior is by the time spent on one task before switching to another (Salvucci *et al.* 2009). Based on this concept, there are two major categories: sequential multitasking and concurrent multitasking. *Sequential multitasking* refers to when tasks are performed sequentially including "task switching" to accomplish more than one goal at a time (Delbridge 2000). In sequential multitasking, a longer time might be spent on one task before attention is shifted to the other task (Salvucci *et al.* 2009). For example, when students are doing homework and texting friends at the same time, they must allocate their attention to the homework before switching to their phone. *Concurrent multitasking* refers to when tasks are performed simultaneously with almost no switching time between the tasks.

When people perform more than one task at a time, regardless of whether the tasks are performed simultaneously or sequentially, they are likely to interfere with each other because limited attentional resources are shared among those tasks (Pashler 1994). Once a task receives fewer attentional resources, the performance on that task decreases. The next section provides an overview of the existing literature on different models of multitasking.

Sequential multitasking

There are a number of existing studies on multitasking or dual task performance that defines multitasking as performing one task at a time but periodically switching to another task. Dating back to 1927, task switching was studied as people's ability to alternate between two different tasks (Jersild 1927). Jersild gave individuals either pure task blocks (doing the same task throughout the study) or alternating-task blocks (switching between two tasks during the study). Then, he measured the total time they took to respond to the stimuli. The findings showed that the alternating-task condition recorded a slower response time per item compared to the pure task condition.

Effects have also been looked at in terms of switching modalitly of the sensory information given to attend to. Gopher and Kahneman (1971) asked subjects to listen to different auditory information in each ear. Subjects were required to monitor one ear and recite the presented digits. During that time, they had to ignore the information presented to the other ear. Then, they were given a cue to switch the monitoring ear from time to time. They found that the performance was worse than if the task was performed individually.

Other studies have looked at quality of task performance as an indicator of multitasking costs. Delbridge (2000) gave participants in a multitasking group three tasks: a reference task, a situational judgment test, and a logic puzzle-solving test. The multitasking participants were asked to switch between each task during a limited time. Another group was asked to perform each task sequentially without task switching. As expected, the individuals who switched between the tasks performed worse than those who did not switch among tasks.

In order to explain the processes behind the performance costs associated with multiple task switching, Rubinstein *et al.* (2001) introduced Task Switching Theory. The theory explains that we develop a set of rules for each task we perform as well as giving the instructions about the priority of each task. Switching between the tasks induces "switching time costs" because the sets of rules that were developed need to be changed. This change results in performance decrements.

It should be noted that in the task-switching viewpoint, "multitasking" would refer to switching between tasks, not attending to or performing them at the same moment. This point forms one of the main debates on how an individual processes multiple tasks or information.

Concurrent multitasking

Another stream of research is based on the idea of multiple tasks being performed concurrently, which is what many people think of when they consider multitasking. The existing research claims that simultaneously performing two cognitive tasks usually leads to decrements in the performance of one or both tasks (Pashler 1998). Tasks are likely to interfere with each other in this multitasking situation (Pashler 1994; Monsell 2003) because the available mental resources are shared by different tasks in multitasking environment (Kahneman 1973). Dual task interference is thought to occur when concurrent demands on general attentional resources are too great to be met (Bourke *et al.* 1996). Reisberg (1983) looked at interference in concurrent task performance. In the study, subjects were slower in solving and judging ambiguous figures when they were asked to do a counting task at the same time. It should be noted that this concurrent task manipulation is similar to what is more commonly termed "cognitive load" in consumer literature.

Other examples can be found in the visual perception domain. One study showed that subjects responding to light stimuli failed to detect auditory events (Colavita and Weisberg 1979). When perceptual tasks require difficult concurrent processing, accuracy usually suffers. Duncan (1980) asked subjects to make a forced-choice judgment about which of two targets was presented in a display. Stimuli were either simultaneously displayed or successively displayed, controlling for the number of items. When the display size was large and discrimination became difficult, accuracy was significantly worse when the items were simultaneously presented than when they had been presented sequentially. While it is thought that parallel processing can generally only occur for 'gist' or early stage processing, there is also some evidence that even while doing a demanding visual task, participants can rapidly categorize images such as cars or animals (Li *et al.* 2002).

The effects of multitasking have been studied not only in cognitive psychology, but also tested in the classroom environment. In one study, students were randomly assigned into one of the two conditions. One group was told they could use laptops and were allowed to go on the Internet during the lecture. The other group was asked to keep their laptops closed during the lecture. The findings showed that the open-laptop group performed significantly lower on the memory test than the closed-laptop group due to the proportion of time drawn off the lecture (Hembrooke and Gay 2003). Grace-Martin and Gay (2001) reported similar findings in a learning environment. The longer browsing sessions throughout the course of the semester led to lower overall class performance. However, many and shorter browsing sessions during class time actually resulted in higher grades in class, regardless of the content.

Several cognitive variables have also been studied to determine the effects on multitasking performance. Based on simultaneous processing, Konig et al. (2005) indicated that working memory, fluid intelligence, and attention are predictors of successful multitasking. Among the three factors, working memory was the most critical predictor of performance in a complex multitasking scenario reported in the study.

Overall, much of the previous research on dual task performance shows a decrease in performance of one or both tasks. This is thought to be due to the competition for limited attentional resources. However, whether the studies are classified as sequential or concurrent multitasking, the underlying assumption was that the tasks were equally important to the person performing them and they pay the same amount of attention to both of them. Oftentimes, individuals have goals in their mind which serve to prioritize tasks. What remains in question is how motivation or the awareness of task priority affects the multitasking performance. The next section applies these concepts to the consumer behavior domain including the level of attention allocated to the tasks.

Multitasking in media usage

In media and mediated message processing, the conceptualization of "multitasking" is more similar to what has been seen as *concurrent* multitasking in cognitive psychology. *Media multitasking* is defined as consuming media while engaging in a non-mediated task or simultaneously consuming two media (Pilotta *et al.* 2004). As mentioned earlier, media multitasking is a common activity for people who use smartphones. While a majority (72 percent) may use their smartphones in a more active way – while using other media – they also use them during more passive activities, such as waiting in line (59 percent of respondents) or even, yes, using the bathroom (39 percent) (Google/IPSOS OTX Media CT 2011).

A number of studies use memory performance as a measurement to look at when one task is a focal task and the other is in the background, Furnham and Bradley (1997) studied how background music could affect work being done at the same time. In the background music condition, students performed a test while being exposed to a pop music. Students in another condition only performed the test without any background music. They found lowered recall memory when background music was played. Researchers have also examined more active media multitasking behaviors on the effects of background television for reading memory, cognitive complexity, and non-verbal problem solving (Armstrong and Greenberg 1990; Armstrong *et al.* 1991; Furnham *et al.* 1994). This stream of research has begun to show how a secondary, less important task, interferes with the performance of the focal task. However, the task was treated as a distraction.

In addition to memory measurement, some media researchers have used message comprehension and evaluation. Due to competition for limited resources, an increase in demand from tasks results in overloading capacity and leads to interference with effortful processing of mediated messages. Increased production pacing and content arousal in ads, which increases the demand in the task, may lead to consumers evaluating the claims made in ads less favorably (Yoon *et al.* 1998). High cognitive load in individuals can also interfere with message processing. By limiting the amount of time subjects had to process advertising messages, their ability to generate and use imagery when evaluating the advertised product decreases (Bone and Ellen

1992). Other studies have found negative effects of background television on college students' performance on a high school-level standardized reading comprehension measure (Armstrong and Greenberg 1990). Media multitasking has become more important as we are in the digital era where we are surrounded by advertising messages via electronic devices. Future research needs to focus on the levels of consumers' involvement in the medium and how it affects message processing. As discussed above, some media are considered more involving than others. For example, a radio commercial is considered more passive than an interactive advergaming, where a company uses a video game to advertise the product.

Can multitasking behavior improve with practice?

Although the majority of research shows that multitasking impairs the performance of the tasks, other research suggests that the performance can be improved with practice. Practice reduces the cost elicited from dual task performance, even though it is almost impossible to eliminate it (Garavan 1998). In a study to test whether two visual search tasks could be performed simultaneously without a drop in accuracy, Schneider and Fisk (1982) confirmed that secondary task performance improves with practice. Spelke *et al.* (1976) asked subjects to read short stories while copying auditory-presented words. They found that at first the reading speed and comprehension scores were seriously impaired, but they improved after six weeks of practice. It was hypothesized that performance improved because the tasks become automatic after practicing for a certain amount of time. Once a task is automatic, it should be able to combine with other tasks without deficit (Schneider and Detweiler 1988). This factor may distinguish the performance of consumers in the digital era as new generations grow up surrounded by digital devices such as cell phones, iPods, and computers. Children have more practice with these devices, and will now use them as they are growing and forming attentional strategies and habits. However, while practice might diminish impairment over time, it does not make the performance on the tasks equal to when each task is performed separately with full attention.

Benefits of multitasking

As pointed out earlier, many studies have looked at multitasking as consisting of multiple tasks that have similar levels of challenge and are competing for similar resources. But what happens when both tasks are not equally demanding or elicit different levels of interest from the consumer? Does multitasking always lead to worse performance on the tasks involved? Similar to many previous studies, Corr (2003), found that performance was significantly impaired when subjects did both procedural learning (pointing at predictable/random target movement on a screen) and mental arithmetic compared to when they did only one task (procedural learning). However, they classified the mental arithmetic task as a highly demanding task. In a subsequent study, they changed the secondary task to be a less demanding task (counting of nonsense syllables) and found that, unlike in the first experiment, learning was not impaired.

While capacity limitations point to issues with multiple demanding tasks, if one task is less demanding or even boring, would an additional task help with completion of the initial task? It is possible that in certain conditions doing more than one thing at a time may actually have benefits. Most people shift their attention to something else when they find that the task at hand is no longer interesting to them. Therefore, multitasking may be used to alleviate boredom. The performance decrements resulting from the competition for task-specific resources may be eliminated when a secondary task reduces mind wandering (also called stimulus independent thought or daydreaming) that can result from boredom. Mind wandering competes with the primary task for the control and coordination of working memory resources (Teasdale et al. 1995). Building on this idea, Andrade (2009) found that performing two tasks simultaneously does not always lead to a decrease in memory. Instead, some tasks that consume few cognitive resources might actually help explicit memory because they eliminate mind wandering. In the experiment, participants were asked to use a pencil to shade geometric figures while listening for specific information in a boring mock telephone message or they simply listened to the call alone. Subjects in the two-task group recalled more of the monitored information from the boring message than did those in the single task group. Moreover, the two-task group recalled 29 percent more *unmonitored* information that they heard in the call.

Certain characteristics of information may or may not negatively affect the performance of the primary task depending on the familiarity of the message. Students were asked to do a homework assignment under conditions in which they heard a soap opera, popular music video, or nothing at all. The results showed that the number of correct answers on the homework assignment was adversely affected by the soap opera, but not the music video because the music video was more familiar to the students and, thus, required fewer cognitive resources (Pool et al. 2000).

When a primary task is mundane, and motivation is low, boredom can occur. Matthews and Davies (2001) conveyed a similar idea that boring, vigilance tasks lead to depletion of resources as they progress, which then lower the performance of the tasks. Roche et al. (2007) induced disruption of learning a series of focal tasks by introducing another task to interfere during training and found that dual-task performance facilitated the performance of a subsequent related task instead of disrupting. When the task had low resource demands, minimal attention is needed to adequately perform the task. Therefore, the addition of a task may have raised the level of attention rather than only redirecting resources from one task to another. Nonetheless, the performance of the tasks may have a curvilinear effect depending on the resource demands of the secondary task. Too high or too low a demand may deteriorate the performance.

In terms of memory, divided attention may hinder explicit memory, but have less or no impact on the implicit memory. Shapiro and Krishnan (2001) presented subjects with both an audio message and a visual ad on a screen and asked them to pay attention either to both elements (divided attention) or to only the audio message alone. Following the manipulation, the participants completed a memory test. Explicit memory, as measured by the number of correct identification of brands, was found to be impaired. However, implicit memory – measured by asking participants to choose the brands as if they were to purchase the products – showed no differences.

Although the vast majority of studies in multitasking have looked at task performance or memory performance as outcome variables, it is important to also understand what happens with the content that consumers may be exposed to while multitasking. In terms of argument strength of a message, it was found that for weak argument ads seen while multitasking, there was no difference in the support or counterarguments made by the participants. However, for strong argument ads, participants made a fewer supporting statements when the ads were presented simultaneously with a TV program than when the ads were presented sequentially (Chowdhury et al. 2007).

In some circumstance, a secondary task may also benefit both a consumer's memory and judgment. Subjects either copied geometric shapes while listening to a series of radio commercials (dual task condition) or only listened to the commercials (single task condition). Subjects then took a memory test. It was found that when the target commercial was delivered in a more monotone voice, the dual-task subjects actually had higher recognition memory than the single-task subjects. The opposite is true when the target commercial was delivered in a voice designed to grab attention. The subjects in the dual-task group had lower recognition memory than those in the single-task group (Chinchanachokchai *et al.* 2010). The study hypothesized that a mindless secondary task decreases mind wandering, which can occur when a primary task induces boredom. It should be noted that in these studies primary and secondary tasks were prioritized in the instructions given by the researchers and may resemble situations where there is a hierarchy of tasks but may not reflect the exact process by which an individual chooses what to attend to at any given moment.

In the home there are more media options than ever before and with mobile media it is easier than ever for consumers to have access to entertainment, work and information wherever they are and whatever they are doing. However, if consumers can prioritize the importance of the tasks, their performance on tasks may not be always deteriorated. Future research should examine both intrinsic and extrinsic motivation as it relates to consumer multitasking.

One reason that consumers in the digital world multitask is to prevent boredom, which usually leads to mind wandering. They use phones or other mobile devices to keep them cognitively busy and reduce the chance to think about other unrelated events. Mind wandering, therefore, is considered another cognitive task, which occurs without notice and is difficult to detect. It also hinders performance because it represents a breakdown in one's ability to pay attention to information from the external environment (Smallwood *et al.* 2007). If mind wandering is considered a task, future research should look into how much mind wandering can affect an individual's cognitive resources while they are consuming media, for instance, when the TV show is boring and no longer grabs the consumer's attention.

Individual differences

While much research focused on the overall task performance outcomes of multitasking, it is important also to look at individual differences between people on their ability to multitask. Individual propensity to multitask and differences in processing styles of audience members may be crucial to consider when understanding multitasking effects. For example, previous attention research has found that when given an information search task (goal-driven or top-down processing) on a news webpage that has both news content and ads, people rate the ads more negatively when they were not part of the primary task. These effects occur even without explicit recognition of having been exposed to those ads (Duff and Faber 2011). Importantly, these effects differ by individuals high and low in their ability to control their attentional focus (Duff 2009), with those low in attentional control less able to focus on the search task and therefore less able to focus on the primary task of finding the news information (ignoring the ad).

Interestingly, the same underlying difference of control of attentional focus is found in heavy versus light media multitaskers (Ophir *et al.* 2009). Heavy media multitaskers (HMMs) self-report a higher preference to use multiple media simultaneously, however, despite their preference for multitasking, they were found on a series of tests to actually be worse at focusing on tasks, switching tasks and ignoring irrelevant information. It is possible that these heavier media multitaskers might use breadth of information rather than depth, and that they view information more democratically, trying to pull from multiple places in order to get the most possible information, rather than selectively pre-determining which information may be best.

This broad-focused orientation is similar to what is found in holistic processing. Holistic processing is that which involves an orientation to the context or field as a whole. This is in contrast to analytic processing which involves detachment of the object from its context, a tendency to focus on specific attributes of the object (Nisbett *et al.* 2001). Preliminary evidence shows that holistic processors have worse recognition memory (compared to analytic processors) for commercials when watching them is the only task. In a task mimicking multiple windows open on a computer screen, participants were asked to just monitor video ads or monitor them in addition to one or two additional visual tasks on the screen. Analytic processors show the established effect of a drop in performance on a memory task for the video ads. However, holistic processors show no drop in memory for the ad. Recognition memory is the same whether watching the ads is their only (primary) task, or if there are a total of two or even three tasks that they need to monitor (Duff *et al.* 2011).

Delbridge (2000) tested several individual difference factors and found that subjects thought multitasking was stressful due to perceived uncertainty or urgency. The study also reported that the stress from multitasking can lead to the use of avoidance coping strategies and lower per-formance on the reference task, showing that some people are more susceptible to the process losses caused by multitasking.

In media multitasking, differences in performance due to age are potentially important. For example, when given cable TV and laptops and told that they had freedom to browse any websites or change TV channels as they wished, younger participants switched their attention between the laptop and the TV more frequently than older participants did (Brasel and Gips 2011).

Though multitasking with more challenging or novel tasks often leads to performance decrements, there are a minority of people (2.5 percent) who are "supertaskers" (Watson and Strayer 2010). These supertaskers perform exceptionally well with a single-task and show no performance cost with the addition of a task (driving and an auditory task).

Conclusion

As information goes digital, and accessing it is easier and faster than ever, it is being increasingly consumed while people are engaged in other tasks. With so many consumers incorporating it into their daily lives, it is important to understand what multitasking is, why it might occur and what effects it may be having on memory, performance and comprehension.

While multitasking – particularly multitasking with media – has been shown to be on the rise, much of the previous research has shown that people are not usually good at multitasking due to limited processing capacity. Many studies on multitasking look at the concept in terms of divided attention. However, there is little consensus on the exact process that occurs during typical multitasking situations. In this chapter, a range of relevant literature was reviewed and classified into either sequential multitasking (task switching) or simultaneous (concurrent) multitasking. This distinction is important in our conceptualization of what is occurring during the performance of multiple tasks. Studies often also manipulate which task is primary, trying to control how attention is distributed. It is important for future researchers to identify the role of the instructions that are given to participants in their studies as it may be changing the nature of the multitasking that is occurring and may lead to differing effects.

Despite a large number of papers on the negative outcomes of doing more than one thing at once, there is a growing minority that points out the benefits of multitasking. Additionally, there is some evidence that with some tasks, multitasking behavior may be able to be improved with practice. Going forward, better understanding about when multitasking can potentially be beneficial will be important, as will identifying individual differences in ability and propensity to multitask. Because media multitasking is increasing, especially among youth, the characteristics of media, messages and individuals should be studied. This could aid in creating more effective media, better messages or even help consumers understand when they should engage in multitasking and when it might be better to focus on one thing in particular

Moving forward, research needs to focus on the underlying mechanism of media multi-tasking, especially in various stages of information processing as well as investigate the link between each stage and the overall picture. Moreover, the discovery of the benefits of multi-tasking is only at the beginning stage. Multiple studies that we have reviewed here point out some benefits and the fact that multitasking is thought to be increasingly utilized as a way of 'passing time' or alleviating boredom. This may help attention to bothersome tasks that need to get done but it may also operate in a negative feedback loop, leading to an increasing dislike of boring tasks without additional stimulation. Therefore, research that addresses these issues will help us understand and be aware of when and how multitasking would benefit/impair the performance.

Further reading

Andrade, J. (2009) "What Does Doodling Do?" *Applied Cognitive Psychology*, Published online by Wiley InterScience. [Shows how performing another task may benefit the primary task.]

Ophir, E., Nass, C. and Wagner, A.D. (2009) "Cognitive Control in Media Multitaskers," *Proceedings of the National Academy of Sciences*, 106 (37): 15583–7.

Pashler, H. (1994) "Dual-Task Interference in Simple Tasks: Data and Theory," *Psychological Bulletin*, 116(2): 220–44. [Classic dual-task performance theory in cognitive psychology.]

Shapiro, S. and Krishnan, H.S. (2001) "Memory-based Measures for Assessing Advertising Effects: A Comparison of Explicit and Implicit Memory Effects," *Journal of Advertising*, 30(3): 1–13. [Divided attention in advertising and consumer domain.]

References

Alperstein, N. (2005) "Living in an Age of Distraction: Multitasking and Simultaneous Media Use and the Implications for Advertisers," Working Paper. Available at: SRN: http://ssrn.com/abstract=1473864.

Andrade, J. (2009) "What Does Doodling Do?," *Applied Cognitive Psychology*, Published online by Wiley InterScience.

Armstrong, G.B., Boiarsky, G.A. and Mares, M. (1991) "Background Television and Reading Performance," *Communication Monographs*, 58: 235–53.

Armstrong, G.B. and Greenberg, B.S. (1990) "Background Television as an Inhibitor of Cognitive Processing," *Human Communication Research*, 16(3): 355–86.

Baddeley, A. (1996) "Working Memory," *Quarterly Journal of Experimental Psychology*, 49A: 5–28.

Bone, P.F. and Ellen, P.S. (1992) "The Generation and Consequences of Communication-Evoked Imagery," *Journal of Consumer Research*, 19(1): 93–104.

Bourke, P.A., Duncan, J. and Nimmo-Smith, I. (1996) "A General Factor Involved in Dual task Performance Decrement," *The Quarterly Journal of Experimental Psychology*, 49(3): 525–45.

Brasel, S.A. and Gips, J. (2011) "Media Multitasking Behavior: Concurrent Television and Computer Usage," *Cyberpsychology, Behavior, and Social Networking*, 14(9): 527–34.

Chinchanachokchai, S., Duff, B.R.L. and Wyer, R.S. Jr. (2010) "Who Said Multitasking Is Bad? The Benefits of Doing Two Things at the Same Time," in D.W. Dahl, G.V. Johar, and S.M.J. van Osselaer (eds), *Advances in Consumer Research*, vol. 38, Duluth, MN: Association for Consumer Research.

Chowdhury, R.M.M.I., Finn, A. and Olsen, G.D. (2007) "Investigating the Simultaneous Presentation of Advertising and Television Programming," *Journal of Advertising*, 36(3): 85–96.

Colavita, F.B. and Weisberg, D. (1979) "A Further Investigation of Visual Dominance," *Perception and Psychophysics*, 25(4): 345–7.

Corr, P.J. (2003) "Personality and Dual-Task Processing: Disruption of Procedural Learning by Declarative Processing," *Personality and Individual Differences*, 34: 1245–69.

Delbridge, K.A. (2000) "Individual Differences in Multi-Tasking Ability: Exploring a Nomological Network," unpublished doctoral dissertation, University of Michigan.

Duff, B.R.L. (2009) "The Eye of the Beholder: Affective and Attentional Outcomes of Selective Attention to Advertising," unpublished doctoral dissertation, University of Minnesota.

Duff, B.R.L. and Faber, R. (2011) "Missing the Mark: Advertising Avoidance and Distractor Devaluation," *Journal of Advertising*, 40(2): 51–62.

Duff, B.R.L., Sar, S., Oh, S. and Chinchanachokchai, S. (2011) "Seeing the Big Picture: Multitasking and Memory for Ads," in *Proceedings for the Association for Education in Journalism and Mass Communication*.

Duncan, J. (1980) "The Demonstration of Capacity Limitation," *Cognitive Psychology*, 12: 75–96.

European Interactive Advertising Association (2009) "EIAA Media Multi-Tasking Report 2009," available at: http://www.eiaa.net/research/media-consumption.asp?lang=6.

Furnham, A. and Bradley, A. (1997) "Music While You Work: The Differential Distraction of Background Music on the Cognitive Test Performance of Introverts and Extraverts," *Applied Cognitive Psychology*, 11: 445–55.

Furnham, A., Gunter, B. and Peterson, E. (1994) "Television Distraction and the Performance of Introverts and Extroverts," *Applied Cognitive Psychology*, 8: 705–11.

Garavan, H. (1998) "Serial Attention Within Working Memory," *Memory Cognition*, 26: 263–76.

Google/IPSOS OTX Media CT (2011) "The Mobile Movement: Understanding Smartphone Users," available at: http://www.google.com.think/insights.

Gopher, D. (1982) "A Selective Attention Test as a Predictor of Success in Flight Training," *Human Factors: The Journal of the Human Factors and Ergonomics Society*, 24(2): 173–83.

Gopher, D. and Kahneman, D. (1971) "Individual Differences in Attention and the Prediction of Flight Criteria," *Perceptual and Motor Skills*, 33(3): 1335–42.

Grace-Martin, M. and Gay, G. (2001) "Web Browsing, Mobile Computing and Academic Performance," *Educational Technology and Society*, 4(3): 95–107.

Hembrooke, H. and Gay, G. (2003) "The Laptop and the Lecture: The Effects of Multitasking in Learning Environments," *Journal of Computing in Higher Education*, 15(1).

Jersild, A.T. (1927) "Mental Set and Shift," *Archives of Psychology*, 89.

Kahneman, D. (1973) *Attention and Effort*, Englewood Cliffs, NJ: Prentice-Hall.

Konig, C.J., Buhner, M. and Murling, G. (2005) "Working Memory, Fluid Intelligence, and Attention Are Predictors of Multitasking Performance, but Polychronicity and Extraversion Are Not," *Human Performance*, 18(3): 243–66.

Li, F.F., VanRullen, R., Koch, K. and Perona, P. (2002) "Rapid Natural Scene Categorization in the Near Absence of Attention," *PNAS*, 99(14): 9596–601.

Logan, G.D. and Gordon, R.D. (2001) "Executive Control of Visual Attention in Dual-Task Situations," *Psychological Review*, 108(2): 393–434.

McDowd, J. M. and Birren, J.E. (1990) "Aging and Attentional Processes," in J.E. Birren and K.W. Schaie (eds), *Handbook of the Psychology of Aging*, 3rd edn, San Diego, CA: Academic Press, pp. 222–33.

Matthews, G. and Davies, D.R. (2001) "Individual Differences in Energetic Arousal and Sustained Attention: A Dual-Task Study," *Personality and Individual Differences*, 31: 575–89.

Monsell, S. (2003) "Task Switching," *Trends in Cognitive Sciences*, 7(3): 134–40.

Nisbett, R.E., Choi, I., Peng, K., and Norenzayan, A. (2001) "Culture and Systems of Thought: Holistic Versus Analytic Cognition," *Psychological Review*, 108(2): 291–310.

Ophir, E., Nass, C. and Wagner, A.D. (2009) "Cognitive Control in Media Multitaskers," *Proceedings of the National Academy of Sciences*, 106(37): 15583–7.

Pashler, H. (1994) "Dual-Task Interference in Simple Tasks: Data and Theory," *Psychological Bulletin*, 116(2): 220–44.

——(1998) *The Psychology of Attention*, Cambridge, MA: MIT Press.

Pilotta, J.J. and Schultz, D. (2005) "Simultaneous Media Experience and Synesthesia," *Journal of Advertising Research*, March: 19–26.

Pilotta, J.J., Schultz, D.E., Drenik, G. and Rist, P. (2004) "Simultaneous Media Usage: A Critical Consumer Orientation to Media Planning," *Journal of Consumer Behavior*, 3(3): 285–92.

Pool, M.M., Van der Voort, T.H.A., Beentjes, J.W.J. and Koolstra, C.M. (2000) "Background Television as an Inhibitor of Performance on Easy and Difficult Homework Assignments," *Communication Research*, 27: 293–326.

Reisberg, D. (1983) "General Mental Resources and Perceptual Judgments," *Journal of Experimental Psychology: Human Perception and Performance*, 9(6): 966–79.

Roberts, D.F. and Foehr, U.G. (2008) "Trends in Media Use," *The Future of Children*, 18(1): 11–37.

Roche, R., Commins, S., Agnew, F., Cassidy, S., Corapi, K., Lipson, Z., Rickard, J. and O'Mara, S. (2007) "Concurrent Task Performance Enhances Low-level Visuomotor Learning," *Perception and Psychophysics*, 69(4): 513–22.

Roger, R.D. and Monsell, S. (1995) "Costs of a Predictable Switch Between Simple Cognitive Tasks," *Journal of Experimental Psychology*, 124(2): 207–31.

Rubinstein, J.S., Meyer, D.E. and Evans, J.E. (2001) "Executive Control of Cognitive Processes in Task Switching," *Journal of Experimental Psychology: Human Perception and Performance*, 27(4): 763–97.

Salvucci, D. D., Taatgen, N.A. and Borst, J.P. (2009) "Toward a Unified Theory of the Multitasking Continuum: From Concurrent Performance to Task Switching, Interruption, and Resumption," in *Proceedings of the 27th International Conference of Human Factors in Computing Systems*, Boston, MA, pp. 1819–28.

Schneider, W. and Detweiler, M. (1988) "The Role of Practice in Dual-Task Performance: Toward Workload Modeling in a Connectionist/Control Architecture," *Journal of the Human Factors and Ergonomics Society*, 30(5): 539–66.

Schneider, W. and Fisk, A.D. (1982) "Degree of Consistent Training: Improvements In Search Performance and Automatic Process Development," *Perception and Psychophysics*, 31(2): 160–8.

Shapiro, S. and Krishnan, H.S. (2001) "Memory-based Measures for Assessing Advertising Effects: A Comparison of Explicit and Implicit Memory Effects," *Journal of Advertising*, 30(3): 1–13.

Smallwood, J., Fishman, D.J., and Schooler, J.W. (2007) "Counting the Cost of an Absent Mind: Mind Wandering as an Underrecognized Influence on Educational Performance," *Psychonomic Bulletin and Review*, 14(2): 230–6.

Spelke, E., Hirst, W. and Neisser, U. (1976) "Skills of Divided Attention," *Cognition*, 4: 215–30.

Teasdale, J.D., Dritschel, B.H., Taylor, M.J., Proctor, L., Lloyd, C.A., Nimmo-Smith, I., and Baddeley, A.D. (1995) "Stimulus-Independent Thought Depends on Central Executive Resources," *Memory and Cognition*, 23(5): 551–9.

Watson, J.M., and Strayer, D.L. (2010) "Supertaskers: Profiles in Extraordinary Multitasking Ability," *Psychonomic Bulletin and Review*, 17(4): 479–85.

Weber, R.J., Burt, D.B. and Noll, N.C. (1986) "Attention Switching Between Perception And Memory," *Memory and Cognition*, 14: 238–45.

Yoon, K., Bolls, P. and Lang, A. (1998) "The Effects of Arousal on Liking and Believability of Commercials," *Journal of Marketing Communication*, 4(2): 101–14.

33

GENDER ROLES AND GENDER IDENTIFICATION IN RELATION TO MEDIA AND CONSUMPTION

Birgitte Tufte

Keywords

gender identification, gender roles, tweens

Introduction

This chapter will present the results from a study which has examined Danish tween girls' perception of their gender roles and gender identification in relation to their media use and patterns of consumption. It is part of a comparative study between Hong Kong and Denmark. The person responsible in Hong Kong was Professor Kara Chan, Hong Kong Baptist University, and in Denmark, the author of this chapter, at Copenhagen Business School. The title of the project is "Media Consumption and Gender Identity of Tween Girls: A Cross-Cultural Study."

The project is inspired by – and can be considered as a continuation of the project "Children between Media and Consumption" which was carried out from 2004–6 in Denmark (Tufte 2011) and the comparative project: "Tweens and new media in Denmark and Hong Kong" (Andersen *et al.* 2007).

The aim of the latter was to investigate the media ownership, the use of mobile phones and the Internet among tweens in Denmark and Hong Kong. As it was a qualitative study, the results cannot be generalized but just be taken as a trend. The results show – among other things – that Danish tweens own and use more new media than tweens in Hong Kong, and the most significant difference was the way they used the Internet. In Hong Kong, the Internet was primary used for school work whereas the Danish tweens mainly used the Internet for fun, entertainment and communication with peers.

Professor Kara Chan and I discussed the results and due to the fact that it seemed as if gender difference played a role, we agreed to carry out a study with focus on the gender perspective in relation to tweens and the Internet. We discussed how to do this and found out that an interesting perspective would be to get the tween girls' own perception of the images of girls and women in the media. Inspired by anthropological studies where children are given a tape recorder or a camera to register what they find interesting in relation to a specific subject, we decided that we would try to find research means to buy digital cameras for each of the girls involved, ask them to take photographs of girls and women in the media, including as many media as possible. We would then analyse these photographs and interview the girls on the basis of some of the photos that they had taken. Some of the results from the study have already been published (Chan *et al.* 2011; Chan 2011).

Tweens

One could ask why we chose the age group tweens and what interesting aspects there might be in a project like the one described above seen from a consumer and marketing perspective.

First of all, it is a fact that children and young people are increasingly considered as consumers due to the fact that they have their own money and influence the family's consumption. Furthermore, they are pioneers and innovators regarding new media. As a result, companies and advertisers have recently shown a growing interest in them as a consumer segment, and new and still more sophisticated methods for targeting this segment are being developed.

Until recently focus has been very much on teenagers, but in later years children and young people, the so-called tweens, have become an important target group. The interest in the tween group could be compared with the interest in "teenagers" in the 1950s. The term "teenager" connects to the commodity culture of the post-war period. And, as already said, a parallel to the concept of teenagers at that time can be seen in the concept of tweens today. According to Thomas Cook and Susan B. Kaiser (2004) the term "tween" appeared for the first time in 1987 in an article in the journal *Marketing and Media Decisions* where tweens are described as children aged 9–15. And there is general agreement among researchers that we have a new in-between segment, but not agreement how the age of tweens should be defined. According to Martin Lindstrøm (2003), the term tween covers children between 8–14. I think that this is a definition which is far too wide, as there is a great difference between an 8-year-old and a 14-year-old. Siegel, Coffey and Livingston (2001) believe that it would be relevant to operate with the age group 8–12 years and then further distinguish between younger and older tweens.

If we consider the tween group from a gender perspective it is interesting that according to Mitchell and Reid-Walsh (2005) the word tween is commonly understood as a preadolescent and young adolescent age group exclusively or almost exclusively female, defined as a distinct commodity culture. The findings of Michell and Reid-Walsh have – among other studies – inspired the project which is going to be described now.

Methodology

On the basis of the above discussion we decided to focus on 10–12-year-old tween girls. They were asked during a period of seven days to take 5–10 pictures per day with a digital camera, showing with these pictures how they think that young girls and women are portrayed in the media, by choosing pictures which show different activities that the girls/women do and thinking of what young girls, according to the pictures, apparently are expected to do and work with when they grow up. We had a group of 12 girls so I want to emphasize that this is a qualitative study which may show some tendencies, but which cannot be generalized. The study took place in June 2009 in a school north of Copenhagen, i.e., a school where the children generally belong to a higher middle-class segment.

The girls ended up by taking about 60–70 pictures each. We – two researchers – looked at all the pictures thoroughly, making a preliminary analysis, whereupon the girls were interviewed individually about their respective pictures.

The first time we met the girls we explained to them that we were curious to know which of the many pictures that they were surrounded with in their daily life they liked and disliked.

They were asked to take pictures they liked and pictures they disliked. They were asked to take pictures from magazines, from the TV, from the Internet, etc., of girls and women. We explained to them that the girls from Hong Kong would be asked the same questions and that we in the end hopefully would be able to describe similarities and differences between girls in the two countries.

They each received a digital camera which they were going to use to take the pictures and we told them that they could keep the cameras as a gift when they had taken the number of photographs that they were asked to take, i.e. 5–10 pictures per day during a week, and they were told that afterwards we would look at the pictures and interview them. They all seemed to be rather enthusiastic about the project and seemed to think that it was an interesting task, although several of them had questions like "Can I take the photos of myself on my mobile phone?", "What about the picture of myself that I have on Facebook?" To these questions we had to repeat that it was pictures of girls of women in general, not of themselves that they were supposed to take.

After a couple of weeks we visited the school again. As agreed, we interviewed the girls individually, i.e., one of us interviewed the girl and the other took care of the technical things, which means the tape recorder. The point of this kind of approach is that if you are two researchers interviewing one girl, it might be too overwhelming for her, whereas one as a technician seems better, although the 'technician' of course also observes what is going on between the interviewer and the interviewed. They were interviewed in front of their own computer and they chose themselves which of the pictures that they had taken they wanted talk about.

When interviewing, we had a manual that we were using as a basis for the interview:

- Show me some of the pictures you like best and tell why you like them. And show me some of the pictures that you dislike.
- From the pictures that you have taken, how do you think that girls or women should behave – or not behave?
- Who are making these pictures? And why do they look as they do?
- Are you happy about the way girls and women are portrayed in the media today?
- If you were the owner of a magazine, a TV station or responsible for a website, or if you were a media producer, how would you present girls and women?

Results

It turned out that the girls had photographed a great variety of media, from TV as well as the Internet, newspapers, magazines and outdoor advertisements. When we asked about the outdoor advertisements, they said that they often spent time waiting for buses and trains, and then they had plenty of time to look at the outdoor advertisements at the bus stops or stations.

Celebrities

One of the things which is striking is to see to which extent these young girls are interested in and have a knowledge about pop and TV or film stars like Lady Gaga, Britney Spears, Lina Rafn, Paris Hilton, Victoria Beckham, Mary Kate and Ashley and Hanna Montana as well as singers like Beyoncé and others. They are also generally very keen on TV series like *Desperate Housewives*, *Sex and the City*, *Paradise Hotel*, *Friends* and films like, for instance, *Titanic*, *Twilight* and *High School Musical*. A general interest, referred to by all the girls, is an interest in fashion and cosmetics – and shopping.

The following interview is rather representative of many of the girls, i.e., what they express in their interviews with us. Here we have an extract from an interview with a 13-year-old girl about some of the pictures she has taken:

GIRL: It is Lady Gaga. She is a pop star. She always wears strange clothes, that is funny.
INTERVIEWER: Where did you get it?
GIRL: From *Vi Unge* [a magazine for teenagers]

About another picture:

INTERVIEWER: Who is that?
GIRL: Britney Spears.
INTERVIEWER: Is she still popular?
GIRL: Yes ... (smiles)
INTERVIEWER: And where is this picture from?
GIRL: *Twilight*, the film. It is about some vampires. I think she is such a vampire. She is like a kind of hero (about the girl in the picture).

She furthermore talks about a picture of Lina Rafn, which has been on the front page of *Vi Unge* and a band by the name of "Infernal."

We also discuss a picture of the Danish Crown Princess Mary and the famous tennis player, Caroline Wozniacki. The girl admires Princess Mary because she is beautiful and a good mother and Wozniacki because she is such a good tennis player and because of that very famous.

When we ask later on how she would show women if she were the head of a TV station or a magazine, she says:

GIRL: ... well, I would probably take some more "normal" women.
INTERVIEWER: And what is that?
GIRL: Well, not such perfect girls, just some girls who have something interesting to say ...

Fashion, cosmetics, families and age

During the process of analyzing the material, one of the common perspectives is, as already has been said, that fashion and cosmetics play a very important role, as well as stars. However, against these trends there is also the fact that some of the girls chose to take pictures of the organization "doctors without borders," and there are several pictures of families, nuclear families as well as pictures of mother/child relations and babies. An interesting perspective regarding considerations about women's age is expressed by a girl who has photographed a commercial for Dove products (different beauty products). She says:

> It is such an advertisement for Dove. It was, you know, four women, who were not totally young and not really thin. They were about 35–40 years old. I think it was really good ... because I think that they often choose young, pretty girls, because there are some people who would like to live up to look like them. But precisely in this commercial I thought that it was really good that it wasn't those.

We talk about commercials in general, and the interviewer asks if the girl believes that women are influenced by all the commercials for fashion and cosmetics in the media. "Yes, I actually think that they are," she says.

There seems to be a conflict in these young girls. On the one hand, they want to look like the role models in the media and use different cosmetic tools and buy fashion clothes to obtain a perfect look, but on the other hand they have an idea about helping other people, creating a family of their own, and realizing that they will not always be young and slim.

Influence and self-confidence

Similar to the girl just quoted above, many of the girls say that they think that women are influenced by the images of women in the media. They do not think that they themselves are influenced by the media, but that other people may be influenced. This, however, is a general statement, known from other studies. Most people tend to think that other people may be influenced by commercial messages, but you do not want to admit that you yourself may also be influenced.

The girls seemto be both attracted to the pictures of young slim women in fashion clothes and a lot of make-up and be critical of that kind of image. The following is an interview with a 12-year-old girl:

INTERVIEWER: Do you think that women are a little stupid or what?
GIRL: Yes, in a way.
INTERVIEWER: Because they are so easy to influence? – But who makes such advertisements?
GIRL: I don't know … companies probably … I don't know.

It is a general trend that they are aware that the companies just want to sell various products and that they use young and thin models for that:

INTERVIEWER: Can you – from the pictures you have taken – say something about how girls and women are expected to behave and to be?
GIRL: Well, I think they should be themselves. They should stop doing things, others think they should do. Do what they want to do, and look natural. There are really many who, for example, get their teeth pulled out and some get anorexia and they do really a lot – I think that it is stupid. I think you should be like you are. You shouldn't try to change yourself.
INTERVIEWER: So you would show women as they are?
GIRL: Yes, There are really many who change themselves, because then they look slightly better, because the companies want to sell something.
INTERVIEWER: Who is it then, who changes them?
GIRL: It is those who want to sell the product. You know, it's not always exactly the product that they want to sell, which is used, it surely also is something else, which they just don't exactly want to say what is.
INTERVIEWER: Do you think they are lying?
GIRL: Yes, I think they are.

When they are asked how they would present girls and women in the media, if they had some influence, most of them have some very clear ideas that they should be more "natural," as can be seen from the above quotation. The majority of the girls say that girls and women should not be as thin as the models in the commercials.

Accordingly, there seems to be an ambivalence between the pictures they have chosen when they take pictures themselves of super-slim models and pop stars – and the ideals they apparently also have that women ought to be natural.

Regarding their future, several of them have an idea of which profession they are going to choose when they grow up. It is a broad spectrum of professions like doctors, writers, hair stylists, journalists or vets.

Critical perspectives

These Danish 10–12-year-old girls certainly admire some of the role models they see in the media, but, as will be seen from the above quotations, they are also critical. Here are a few more examples. First, an 11-year-old girl:

INTERVIEWER: Could you say something about how women should or should not be expressed in the pictures that you have chosen to show to us?
GIRL: I do not think they should use that much fur, because then I feel sorry for the animals. And then you should think a little bit about the environment, because you hear a lot about that it doesn't go that well there. There is a lot of pollution, and so on. So I think probably that you shouldn't watch that much TV and use cars and so on.

Many of the girls are, as has already been said, very interested in fashion, cosmetics and shopping, but on the other hand they are aware of the fact that the images you see in the media are not very much in accordance with reality. Many of them are focused on the "natural" look and say that this ought to be shown in the media presentation of young girls and women much more than it is today. It is expressed in the following interview with a 12-year-old girl:

INTERVIEWER: If you were the owner of a TV station, a photographer or owned a magazine, how would you present girls or women?
GIRL: I think I would make it more natural, you know. I would follow the fashion a little bit ... but I would choose some natural women who fit better with what you have in reality, so that people won't feel like "Oh, how ugly I am in relation to them" or "Oh, what disgusting legs I have in relation to them" or something like this. More would think like "Oh, they look like me."

And as an example of a different type of model, the same girl mentions Ally McBeal. She says:

I really like her because she seems to really ... She is really unusual, she is really crazy, you know. So I really like that she is so unusual in the series. I think it is nice that not everybody has to be the same.

She goes on to talk about the program *Top Model* and says:

... and then there was a girl, such an Indian, and she was not at all thin, but she was really pretty and she really could get far in this contest and so on, and I think that this was really good. I think it becomes a little role model-like when you see that some of them are so thin, you know – and then you probably think that you also should be like this or look like this.

Apparently the majority of the girls are critical of the typical models presented in the media, some of them are critical of women wearing fur coats and some are worried about the environment and pollution. A funny comment on pollution and not throwing things in the street is the following, where one of the girls says that she hates election posters and explains the reason why she doesn't like them:

> I don't like election posters, because I feel that they are always … firstly, I mean it may be a good picture, and so on, but I just don't like it that, you know, at a certain time, it falls down and then it lies there and messes up the street.

Conclusion and future perspectives

Although this is a qualitative study and therefore cannot be generalized, I am convinced that the result shows some typical trends. The study presents a group of very young girls who express a conflict in their minds and way of thinking between the media images and their own gender role and identification.

It seems as if they, on one hand, are aware that the media images with which they are presented every day are artificial and not in accordance with everyday life, and they admire them, try to imitate them in their way of dressing and using make-up with a focus on shopping. But, on the other hand, they are critical and conscious of other values. They are going through a phase of life where you try to find out who you are, try to form an identity, searching for models. The body is changing and through self-staging using clothes, hair style, make-up and following certain films, TV series, etc., they are trying to send a signal regarding who they are. Thus, we are dealing with an ambivalence, a paradox. It has even been called a "split personality" in tween girls. According to Siegel *et al.* (2001) "We see the defining characteristics as their 'split personality' which toggles between kid behavior and attitudes and those of a teenager."

I think it is an exaggeration and too pessimistic to talk about "split personalities," as it is probably just a question of time before they find their own identity and no longer can be described as "split personalities." These young girls are in an interim period of their life, they are insecure and searching for role models, and many of these role models they find in the media. It is also a fact that although they are interested in fashion and cosmetics, wanting to be good looking, they are also interested in other things such as the environment, their future, including a profession, and having a family. Another interesting aspect is that they are very conscious about the fact that "selling products" are behind most of the images of young girls and women although they are keen consumers themselves. "Shopping" has found its way into the universe of tweens, especially girls, in Denmark and elsewhere: "Shopping in the United States, is the second largest leisure activity after television viewing" (Mitchell and Reid-Walsh 2005). And probably this is a phenomenon which is going to be a characteristic also in the future, for children as well as men and women. Shopping will no doubt continue to be a large leisure activity in the years to come.

As a qualitative study based on a small sample, the current study does not, as already said, allow for generalization of the findings, but the study definitely establishes the need for further studies based on quantitative data which may give further insight into the role of the media in the social and psychological development of tweens.

Furthermore, I want to emphasize that we still need to make a comparison between the Hong Kong and the Danish results, which we hopefully will be able to do soon in order to find similarities as well as differences and publish these findings.

For the time being, a study is being carried out in the Nordic countries: "Gendering ICT in Everyday Life. A comparative study of practices in family and extra-family contexts in three Scandinavian countries" (Norway, Sweden and Denmark 2009–12; Valle-Jo *et al.* 2009–12).

The study explores the use of media in schools and homes among adults as well as among children. It is based on a survey and qualitative interviews among children, parents and teachers with a special focus on comparison between Norway and Denmark. The primary informants are chosen from 10–12-year-old children, so hopefully we will, when the study is finished by the end of 2012, be able to contribute with new knowledge regarding families' and tweens' use of media, and as will be understood from the title of the project, with a focus on the gender perspective.

References

Andersen, L.P., Tufte, B., Rasmussen, J. and Chan, K. (2007) "Tweens and New Media in Denmark and Hong Kong," *Journal of Consumer Marketing*, 24(6).

Chan, K. (2011) "Tween Girls' Sexuality and a Media Scandal in Hong Kong," in C. Feilitzen, U. Carlsson and C. Bucht (eds), *Nordicom Year Book 2011*, Göteborg: Nordicom.

Chan, K., Tufte, B., Cappello, G. and Williams, R.B. (2011) "Tween Girls' Perception of Gender Roles and Gender Identities: A Qualitative Study," *Young Consumers*, 12(1).

Cook, D.T. and Kaiser, S.B. (2004) *Between and Be Tween: Age Ambiguity and Sexualisation of the Female Consuming Subject*, London: Sage Publications.

Kenway, J. and Bullen, E. (2001/2003) *Consuming Children*, Maidenhead: Open University Press.

Lindstrøm, M. (2003) *Brandchild*, Copenhagen: Forlaget Markedsføring.

Mitchell, C. and Reid Walsh, J. (eds) (2005) *Seven Going on Seventeen: Tween Studies in the Culture of Girlhood*, New York: Peter Lang Publishing Inc.

Siegel, D.L., Coffey, T.J. and Livingston, G. (2001) *The Great Tween Buying Machine: Marketing to Today's Tweens*, Ithaca, NY: Paramount Market Publishing, Inc.

Tufte, B. (2011) "Tweens og medier," in L.P. Pynt (ed.), *Tweens: mellem medier og mærkevarer*, Copenhagen: Samfundslitteratur.

Valle-Jo, H., Tufte, B. and Linderoth, J., *et al.* (2009–12) "Gendering ICT in Everyday Life: A Comparative Study in Family and Extra-Family Contexts in Three Scandinavian Countries," a Nordic Research Project, in process.

34

ONLINE CONSUMER MOVEMENTS

Jay M. Handelman

Keywords

consumer activism, consumer movements, history of consumer movements, online activism

Introduction

To live means to buy, to buy means to have power, to have power means to have responsibility.

(Florence Kelley, First General Secretary, National Consumers League, 1899, www.nclnet.org/about-ncl/history)

The idea of a consumer movement is widely regarded to have been born at the dawn of the twentieth century, embodied by the formation of the National Consumers League (NCL) which was established in 1899 (Glickman 2009). While there is a long history of harnessing the purchasing power of consumers (in the form of boycotts, for example) in an effort to impact a myriad of social causes, the rise of a consumer movement is a different and more recent occurrence. As embodied by the NCL, for the first time, consumers themselves came to be recognized as a distinct group that required its own lobby to protect consumer interests and define consumer responsibilities and behaviors. The NCL emerged as the first organization with a mission squarely focused on the consumer, aiming to protect and teach "an ignorant, overmatched, and largely indifferent public new rules of ethical consumption" (ibid.: 161). As can be seen from the above quote from the organization's first leader, the NCL sought to lead a movement aimed at transforming the consumer into a responsible citizen.

Based on the idea that the consumer, just like the worker in the Marxian narrative, was a victim of a highly complex economic system controlled by powerful business elite, leaders of the newly formed consumer movement sought to transform the consumer from helpless victim to societal savior (Glickman 2009; Murray and Ozanne 1991). To do this, the NCL, as a leading organization in the early days of the consumer movement and self-proclaimed 'expert' in consumer matters, sought to resolve what they saw as consumer vulnerability and ineptitude by *investigating* moral and safe consumption options for consumers, *agitating* consumers to alter their consumption behavior accordingly, and then *lobbying* government to legislate restrictions on the power of business as a means of protecting the consumer. As consumer movements continued to evolve throughout the twentieth century, the "investigate, agitate, legislate" mantra has, until recently, continued to capture the scope of the consumer movement (Glickman 2009).

However, in the digital age of the twenty-first century where the disintermediated nature of the Internet has democratized the voice of the consumer, and where localized meaning and micro-emancipation have emerged as the postmodern mantra (Firat and Venkatesh 1995; Holt 2002), the "investigate, agitate, legislate" mantra with its implied hierarchical, paternalistic, top-down approach may no longer capture all aspects of the consumer movement. As developed in this chapter, online consumer movements in a digital age may best be captured by the mantra *pontificate, moralize, obfuscate*, speaking to changes in how we come to understand and research online consumer movements.

Consumer movements of the twentieth century

> On a Friday afternoon in late January 1938, a standing-room crowd of six hundred, including many of the leading society women of the District of Columbia, attended an unusual fashion show at the Wardman Park Theater. The hour-long pageant entitled "Life without Silk: From Morning to Midnight in Cotton and Rayon," sponsored by the League of Women Shoppers (LWS), aimed, quite literally to make a cause fashionable … [T]he LWS organized the show to popularize the nascent campaign to boycott Japanese silk … To promote the boycott, they believed, was also to raise consciousness about socially responsible and stylish modes of nonsilk fashion.
>
> *(Glickman 2009, p. 219)*

From the revolutionaries who dumped the King's tea into Boston Harbor, to Mahatma Gandhi's swadeshi policy of boycotting British-made goods, to acts of culture jamming that subvert corporate control of mainstream media, consumer activism has had an indelible place in American and world history (Glickman 2009; Kozinets *et al.* 2010). By eliciting the commercial power of ordinary consumers, consumer activists have sought to challenge powerful business and political elite in an effort to achieve real political, social, and ideological change (Glickman 2009; Thompson 2004; Witkowski 2010).

Along these lines, the above excerpt describing the "Life Without Silk" fashion show organized by the League of Women Shoppers (LWS) in 1938 may appear as simply another example of consumer activism – in this case, a boycott aimed to hurt the economic apparatus underlying the rising pre-World War II Japanese war machine. However, more than just a boycott against Japanese products, the fashion show organized by the LWS was more pointedly designed to impact the consumer. Formed in 1920 in the same spirit as the NCL, the mission of the LWS was to help consumers – who were seen as predominately women at that time – to exercise their moral responsibilities as citizens by making the causal link between their purchase decisions and the ethical consequences that extend from their purchase behavior (Glickman 2009). The fashion show organized by the LWS in 1938 represented an attempt to raise consumer consciousness about socially responsible consumption behavior (ibid.).

In general, a social movement is an effort by activists with a particular passion and concern for a given social and political arrangement to mobilize people into the collective effort to change the current social order so as to bring about a more desirable state of the world (Den Hond and de Bakker 2007). American colonialists who organized the nonimportation of British products (the Boston Tea Party of 1764) used the power of consumer activism in a social movement against the corruption of the British rulers of the day; in the 1820s, abolitionists called on consumers to only buy non-slave-made products in a social movement to abolish slavery; the anti-Nike boycott of the 1990s called on consumers to join a movement aimed at limiting the globalization of our economic system (Kozinets and Handelman 2004). In all these examples, the power of the consumer was harnessed in a social movement against a target other than the consumer – corrupt governments, slavery, globalized economic arrangements. Therefore, it stands to reason that in a *consumer* social movement, people are mobilized into a collective effort to change the current social order around consumers and what is to be regarded as appropriate consumer behavior.

The consumer movement arose in the early years of the twentieth century in the context of the Progressive Era in the United States. This was a period of great social activism in general whereby Progressives sought two overarching goals: (1) to purify government by giving a stronger voice to all citizens in the country's governance, as witnessed by the women's suffrage movement as one example; and (2) to improve the overall efficiency in business and government operations through the application of science in researching better means of production and management of organizations (Glickman 2009; Witkowski 2010). With the new economic arrangements that ushered in the twentieth century, Progressives recognized the rising power of the consumer as both a potential source of danger and hope in their quest for a better society. If consumers acted selfishly by making consumption decisions without any regard to the consequences of those decisions, what Progressives considered to be immoral consumption, this would potentially undo the social progress made on other fronts. For example, Progressives saw consumers as having a responsibility to the workers who made the products. Consumption decisions that were made without regard to the worker, such as demanding only the lowest priced products even if they were made by non-unionized workers, would undermine much of the progress that had been made to empower workers through the formation of labor unions. By protecting the consumer from the power of corporations while guiding consumers on what was considered by Progressives as moral consumption, consumers could emerge as a powerful force for good in society (Glickman 2009; Witkowski 2010).

While Progressives recognized the power of the consumer, they also regarded the consumer as overwhelmed and ignorant to the complexities of the new economic order of the world. Consistent with the foundations of the Progressive era, it was through expert guidance based on scientific investigation that consumers were to be protected and led (Glickman 2009). This idea of both protecting and leading the consumer gave rise to what became two general strands of the consumer movement throughout much of the twentieth century.

Protecting the consumer

The Progressive Era witnessed the rise of labor unions which were formed to protect and empower workers to confront the power and vagaries of their capitalist employers. In this vein, the NCL and LWS sought to form "consumers unions" to protect the interests of consumers. This era saw the rise of purchasing associations, cooperatives and aggregate buying clubs as organized attempts to protect and empower consumers from being price gauged by powerful businesses. Also with the intent of protecting the consumer, in 1928 a group of professors, journalists, labor leaders, and engineers formed an organization called Consumer Research. The mandate of Consumer Research was to buy consumer products and then, through scientific, laboratory testing, ensure that the products lived up to their marketing hype. Based on these tests, a report was published that rated the acceptability of various categories of consumer products (Glickman 2009). This report was the forerunner to the magazine *Consumer Reports*.

In carrying out their duty to protect the consumer, these consumer movement organizations embarked on intense government lobbying efforts, working to instill legislation that would limit the power of companies and protect consumer interests. Throughout the twentieth century, this lobby has been quite effective as virtually all areas of corporate activity that may impact consumers now fall under government regulations, including marketing communications (Beard and Abernethy 2007), disclosure practices in consumer credit marketing (Burgess *et al.* 2001), food nutrition and labeling (Beales 2003), pricing practices (Hill *et al.* 1998), product safety and warnings (Boedecker *et al.* 1998), and marketers' use of consumer information (Thomas and Maurer 1997). This list of legislation is enacted by a raft of government agencies (such as the Consumer Product Safety Commission, Federal Trade Commission, etc.) and even a Consumer Bill of Rights (Glickman 2009).

Leading the moral consumer

Not all activists throughout the history of the consumer movement have been content to focus on protecting consumers from corporate and government power. By the mid-1930s, many rival consumer movement organizations, including the LWS as one example, were challenging Consumer Research and its narrow focus on product testing and government lobbying. For LWS members and other consumer movement activists in this vein, their focus has been on the consumer's moral responsibility to the workers who made their products, and more recently, on the environmental impact of consumers' consumption decisions (Glickman 2009). These activists organized boycotts as a means of mobilizing consumers to investigate the impact their purchase decisions have on workers and the environment. The motto of the LWS aptly sums up the focus of this strand of the consumer movement: "Use your buying power for justice" (ibid., p. 206). For these activists, the consumer movement is about leading consumers to enact morality and justice in their consumption decisions.

Investigate, agitate, legislate

The consumer movement of the twentieth century, with its combined interest in protecting and leading the consumer, has employed an "investigate, agitate, and legislate" mantra (Glickman 2009). Both strands of the consumer movement saw as their duty the need to investigate – methodically research by employing scientific and expert investigation – the best possible options for consumers. For the protection arm of the consumer movement, their investigation involves scientific laboratory testing of consumer products to ensure that companies are truthful in their product claims. For the moralists, their organizations (such as the NCL and LWS) enlist highly educated people to research the impact of consumption on workers and the environment and to find alternative moral forms of consumption. The adoption of this moralist approach is consistent with a critical theory, Marxist approach to activism which seeks to engage societal members in a process of critical self-reflection so that they may arrive at an awareness of the interests and ideological imperatives that have come to shape the social structures that constrain human potential and freedom (Murray and Ozanne 1991; Kincheloe and McLaren 1994).

Based on a careful examination of consumer products and alternative forms of consumption, both strands of the consumer movement have then agitated for a desirable outcome. The consumer protection activists would use their product research to agitate companies to employ better production standards and more truthful advertising, while at the same time lobby government to enact legislation to force companies to comply. The moralist version of the consumer movement would aim their agitation efforts at consumers themselves, prodding consumers to embed moral decision-making into their consumption decisions. Finally, the "legislate" part of the consumer movement mantra has been of primary importance to the consumer protection activists.

The two versions of the consumer movement of the twentieth century share some important commonalities. First, rooted in Progressive Era thinking, both groups share a suspicion of corporations and governments, advocating the need for constant watchfulness of and lobbying against these two institutional powers. Second, both groups regard the consumer as the primary locus of power in our contemporary market-based system that is able to counter the power of corporations and government. But, third, both groups regard consumers as unaware of their potential power, how to exercise it, the implications of their consumption decisions, and what alternatives to follow (Kincheloe and McLaren 1994; Murray and Ozanne 1991). As a result, consistent with a critical theory approach to activism, the consumer movement of the twentieth century has largely been a top-down, hierarchical arrangement in which "experts" worked to protect and guide supposedly uninformed and naïve consumers (Glickman 2009; Murray and Ozanne 1991).

With the twenty-first century ushering in the digital age and a disintermediated, democratized form of communication where top-down, hierarchical arrangements of the twentieth century are being toppled, it is interesting to consider how these original consumer movement assumptions might play out in this contemporary context. There is reason to consider that the twentieth-century version of the consumer movement may be going through significant changes in the digital age.

Consumer movement in a digital age

To be sure, many vestiges of the consumer movement of the early twentieth century can still be seen today. On the protection front, Consumers Union which has published *Consumer Reports* since the mid-1930s (when the organization transformed itself from the original Consumer Research) is still highly viable as it continues to provide an expert-based, impartial evaluation of consumer products. The National Consumers League still exists today, offering a range of consumer education and protection services including a "LifeSmarts" program that aims to develop consumer and marketplace skills for teens (www.nclnet.org). Other consumer protection organizations such as the American Automobile Association, the Consumer Federation of America, and Public Citizen, to name a few examples, continue to provide consumers with expert advice while lobbying government to enact consumer-friendly legislation. In many ways, the consumer protection strand of the consumer movement has not changed much over the past century.

However, there is reason to consider the possible impact that today's digital revolution may be having on the moralist strand of the consumer movement. Digital technology has enabled a democratization of communication, challenging some of the basic assumptions underlying the history of the consumer movement. The 'average' consumer is now able to access information from any part of the globe with an ease never before possible. For example, a casual keyword search on YouTube using the words "Child Labor" instantaneously calls up hundreds of amateur videos of children working in abhorrent conditions in various countries around the world. Likewise, the online environment provides this consumer with the ability to find an audience for his/her views previously only accessible to an elite few. For instance, an individual consumer's blog espousing concern that the consumption decisions of consumers in developed countries have implications for children in developing countries can attract an audience never possible before the digital age. This dynamic challenges the top-down structure that has been central to the moralist version of the consumer movement. Let us consider what implications might occur as a result of this flattening – democratization – of the structure of the consumer movement.

The moralist consumer movement in the digital age

There are many aspects of today's moralist strand of the consumer movement that provide a consistent extension of the movement's roots. For example, consider the website *The Story of Stuff Project* (www.storyofstuff.org). This website urges a transformation of consumption practices by linking consumption to the physical origins of the products being consumed. This is done through a series of video clips documenting the links between various consumption domains and the corresponding physical consequences. In each video, producer, host and self-proclaimed activist Annie Leonard presents her expertise based on her travels, experience, and research that enables her to reveal the underlying consequences from our consumption of popular brands. For example, in the video "Why 'Designed for the Dump' Is Toxic for People and the Planet," Ms. Leonard documents her travels to developing countries to reveal the "toxic trip around the world" taken by our electronic gadgets, from the assembly of over 1000 different materials per gadget, through to disposal where even recycled gadgets cause toxic harm. Consistent with the founding principles of the consumer movement, Annie Leonard presents herself as an "expert" who has insights into the physical consequences from our consumption behavior, urging consumers to make the 'right' (moral) consumption decisions. *The Story of Stuff Project* is illustrative of a whole genre of websites that take a page directly from the roots of the moralist strand of the consumer movement.

However, what is fundamentally different is that in the digital age the line between expert activist'and average consumer has become blurred to the point of irrelevance. The founders of the original consumer movement organizations of the early twentieth century brought with them a level of education, experience, and charisma that enabled them to form large organizations of followers (Glickman 2009). These characteristics enabled these individuals to utilize mass communication as a means of broadcasting their message out to the population.

In the digital age, a new set of characteristics prevail. The digital age is best captured by a liberatory postmodern lens which reveals the playful and creative power of the independent consumer who is able to celebrate a do-it-yourself version of activism in which consumers find their own freedom from the hegemony of the marketplace through the construction of localized meaning and personal identity (Firat and Venkatesh 1995). No longer a specialized sphere for organized, credentialed, 'professionals' who make a career of researching the societal impacts of consumption, the disintermediated nature of social media has enabled all consumers with the ability to construct themselves as knowledgeable in and outside the influence of powerful corporate arrangements. This dynamic has implications for the consumer movement.

Pontificate instead of investigate

Schau and Gilly (2003) note how in the digital age, postmodern consumers are able to construct and present an online identity that may not be consistent with their self-presentation strategies in real life. This finding is consistent with the postmodern condition in which consumers, driven by the quest for personal authenticity, engage in self-cultivation, self-understanding and ultimately, self-identity construction (Firat and Venkatesh 1995). As we see in a growing number of studies, a common online-enabled identity that consumers construct for themselves is that of the knowledgeable activist who is able to see the hidden consequences to consumption that other consumers, according to these activist consumers, cannot see. Examples include the "oppositional localists" who rail against the effects that global brands, such as Starbucks, have on locally owned alternatives. These activists are "astute at deconstructing the artiface of Starbucks' design" and therefore know when local retailers sell-out by trying to emulate the corporate giant (Thompson and Arsel 2004, p. 638). There are also politically driven brand community members (such as Community-Supported Agriculture groups) that are comprised of consumers who construct themselves as knowledgeable in how to use their buying power to "create a more socially just form of global capitalism" (Thompson and Coskuner-Balli 2007, p. 149). Similarly, in a study of Prius and Hummer drivers, Luedicke, Thompson and Giesler (2010) describe how consumers of one brand construct the consumers of the other brand by way of an enemy narrative as a means of positioning their own moral superiority over the opposing brand community.

In contrast to the founders of the consumer movement's original organizations who were primarily focused on investigating marketplace consumption as a relatively new cultural phenomenon, these studies highlight a different dimension of activism in which online activists expend great effort to construct and present their identity as simply that – activists. This focus on identity construction and presentation leads the online activist to engage in significant amounts of pontification as a means of portraying their activist credentials, expounding their own views while denigrating the behavior of oppositional consumers as immoral (ibid.). Of course, it may have certainly been the case that the consumer movement leaders of the early twentieth century also concerned themselves with building and legitimating their own identities as movement leaders, just as today's online activists may genuinely be attending to investigating real consumption alternatives. However, the studies referenced above point to diverse sets of online consumer activist groups, from "oppositional localists" who stand against Starbucks, to Community-Supported Agriculture groups, to Prius and Hummer drivers, whose primary focus rests with anchoring their own identity projects with a shared set of moral values. Instead of a lifetime commitment to affecting social change that seemed to dominate the portrayal of the consumer movement activist of the early twentieth century (Glickman 2009), the highlight of the current activist of the digital age appears consistent with the postmodern view of identity construction whereby one's online identity construction as activist may be one of many fragmented identities with which the consumer plays (Firat and Venkatesh 1995; Schau and Gilly 2003). Thus, words (by way of pontification) come to be highlighted over actions (by way of experiencing, researching, investigating) as an important tool for today's activist.

Moralize instead of agitate

The consumer movement leaders of the early twentieth century were portrayed as driven to action in a tireless effort to present consumers with alternative (moral) forms of consumption, shame companies into responsible behavior, and lobby government to enact consumer protection legislation. Whether it was the "Life Without Silk" fashion show presenting consumers with specific consumption alternatives; or Consumer Reports exposing instances when products did not live up to marketing hype; or convincing governments to enact legislation, agitation played a central role in the consumer movement's foundation. While these early consumer movement activists were most certainly driven by a moral conviction – and no doubt, a belief that theirs was a morally superior position – their moralizing was accompanied by actions to invoke tangible change.

The postmodern portrayal of the online activist in the digital age highlights the activist effort at identity construction, thus presenting fewer instances of the kind of agitation that was the hallmark of the early consumer movement. Rather than a primary focus on reworking social structures, today's online consumer activist rhetorically vanquishes a socially constructed moral opponent by drawing upon moralistic mythologies and cultural ideologies in performing their individual identity work (Luedicke *et al.* 2010). In so doing, these consumer activists work to "venerate and validate their own ideological beliefs and values" as well as "provide consumers with another cultural means for interjecting a captivating sense of drama and existential significance into their everyday lives" (ibid., p. 1028). This genre of activist identity construction is rich on moralizing, but relatively weak on social change (Kozinets *et al.* 2010).

Obfuscate instead of legislate

With self-identity construction superseding the enactment of social change, it follows that lobbying government to influence consumer-friendly legislation is most likely not high on the agenda of the consumer movement activist in the digital age. Instead of confronting government, the most likely target of confrontation for today's online activist is other consumers/activists. In order to build their own activist identities, consumers construct other consumers as morally inferior (Luedicke *et al.* 2010). However, also consistent with the postmodern condition of fragmented identity construction, these self-proclaimed activists must obfuscate their own positions to ensure that a consistent image of an activist is portrayed. For example, one activist informant in Kozinets and Handelman's (2004) study talks about his own conflicted stance on consumption. On the one hand, he challenges other consumers to constrain their consumption choices for morally desirable ends while at the same time agonizing over how much he enjoys the act of purchasing certain types of products. Where activists of the early twentieth-century consumer movement lived the role of consumer activist (Glickman 2009), studies that examine activists in the digital age present people who are juggling multiple identity roles. As these activists confront each other and their self-proclaimed stances on moral consumption choices, the consumer movement of the digital age may involve more acts of obfuscation than acts of lobbying to enact social change.

Researching online consumer movements

A reader who may look to social movements as a beacon of meaningful social change may come away from this portrayal of the consumer movement in the digital age with a great deal of discouragement. Instead of 'fighting the good fight' like the early twentieth-century consumer movement activists who were determined to enact real social change, the online consumer movement appears to be about consumers' attempts to re-enchant their own lives through the self-identity construction of activist. However, this online dynamic may present an opportunity to rethink how we come to understand social change and the nature of the consumer movement.

Rethinking social change

As mentioned earlier, it stands to reason that social movements should be about social change (Den Hond and De Bakker 2007). The traditional social movement literature speaks to a Marxist type of social change whereby an elite class of activists exposes for consumers the false consciousness they have unwittingly been living under, emancipating them from dominant social structures and leading them to alternative social arrangements (Kozinets and Handelman 2004; Murray and Ozanne 1991). The position developed in this chapter is that this top-down version of social change may be superseded by another view of social change in the digital age.

A research question that emerges from this analysis is: what might social change look like in the context of an online consumer movement where everyone can construct themselves as an activist? Through the self-identity construction of activist, consumers must present themselves as insightfully aware of the implications consumption decisions have on workers and the environment. This raises the intriguing specter of consumers inadvertently confronting each other and even themselves with the very issues that concerned the early founders of the consumer movement – linking consumption decisions with underlying social and environmental implications. Even though consumers' motivations may be driven by self-identity construction, rather than the desire to enact social change, the end result from an online consumer movement may be a more effective march towards social change. Clues to the path of this social change may be revealed through research focused on the consumer–marketer dynamic that might emerge as a result of a consumer movement in a digital age.

Examining the consumer–marketer dynamic

At the core of the traditional postmodern branding enterprise is the marketer's effort to construct an emotional branding story. In constructing this story, marketers must engage in cultural monitoring to identify the latest trends and sources of doppelgänger brand stories. With this knowledge, marketers are able to develop and test new emotional-branding stories that counter, build on, or in some way play off of, the cultural trends identified (Thompson *et al.* 2006).

In this form of postmodern branding, the consumer must be willing to engage in a postmodern dance of meaning co-construction with marketers as the consumer reworks and even subverts the culture-based stories being offered by marketers (Holt 2002; Stern 1994). The online consumer movement presented in this chapter may represent a potential fracture in this postmodern branding arrangement. As consumers become increasingly focused on constructing their own identities as activists, and thus insightfully aware of the arrangements underlying the sourcing and production of the products behind the brand, the relationship between marketers and consumers might change. As online activist consumers seek brands as cultural ingredients in their identity building œuvres, marketers may have to ensure that their brand stories increasingly account for the workers and the environmental impact underlying the physical product. In the meantime, the activist consumer might increasingly seek out third party confirmation of the production sources of the products they consume rather than relying on the marketer-driven brand as a source of cultural material. In the context of a consumer movement in the digital age whereby consumers construct activist identities as people who are "in-the-know" with respect to the human and environmental implications of the brands they consume, a research question arises: Rather than subverting marketer-intended brand meaning, do activist consumers increasingly sidestep and possibly ignore marketers' intended brand meanings altogether? What cultural ingredient status do marketer-intended brand meanings have within the context of a consumer movement in the digital age?

The original consumer movement activists sought to have consumers link their consumption decisions to the corresponding social, cultural, and environmental implications. Research into contemporary online consumer movements may empirically demonstrate an irony whereby an activism driven by identity construction as opposed to social change, may in fact achieve the social change dreams of the consumer movement founders in ways not attainable in the early twentieth century.

Further reading

Heath, J. and Potter, A. (2004) *The Rebel Sell: Why the Culture Can't Be Jammed*, Toronto: HarperCollins. [These authors would most likely disagree with the concluding premise in this chapter – that today's activism can lead to social change – as their examination of the activist counter-culture concludes that it is only subverted by the marketplace, leading to no social change.]

Rao, H. (2009) *Market Rebels: How Activists Make or Break Radical Innovations*, Princeton, NJ: Princeton University Press. [Hayagreeva Rao has written extensively on early consumer movement activism and in this book, he links the history of this activism to how it has shaped contemporary markets.]

References

Beales III, J.H. (2003) "The Federal Trade Commission's Use of Unfairness Authority: Its Rise, Fall, and Resurrection," *Journal of Public Policy and Marketing*, 22(Fall): 192–200.

Beard, T.R. and Abernethy, A.M. (2007) "Costs and Benefits of the Federal Trade Commission's Do-Not-Call Regulations: A Second Look and Reply to Anderson," *Journal of Public Policy and Marketing*, 26(Spring): 149–51.

Boedecker, K.A., Morgan, F.W. and Saviers, A.B. (1998) "Continuing Duty to Warn: Public Policy and Managerial Views," *Journal of Public Policy and Marketing*, 17(Spring): 127–31.

Burgess, D.O., Shank, T.M. and Borgia, D. (2001) "Consumer Lending and Deposit Abuses," *Journal of Public Policy and Marketing*, 20(Spring): 138–43.

Den Hond, F. and De Bakker, F.G.A. (2007) "Ideologically Motivated Activism: How Activist Groups Influence Corporate Social Change Activities," *Academy of Management Review*, 32(3): 901–24.

Firat, A.F. and Venkatesh, A. (1995) "Liberatory Postmodernism and the Reenchantment of Consumption," *Journal of Consumer Research*, 22(December): 239–67.

Glickman, L.B. (2009) *Buying Power: A History of Consumer Activism in America*, Chicago: University of Chicago Press.

Hill, R.P., Ramp, D.L. and Silver, L. (1998) "The Rent-to-Own Industry and Pricing Disclosure Tactics," *Journal of Public Policy and Marketing*, 17(Spring): 3–10.

Holt, D.B. (2002) "Why Do Brands Cause Trouble? A Dialectical Theory of Consumer Culture and Branding," *Journal of Consumer Research*, 29(June): 70–90.

Kincheloe, J.L. and McLaren, P.L. (1994) "Rethinking Critical theory and Qualitative Research," in N.K. Denzin and Y.S. Lincoln (eds), *Handbook of Qualitative Research*, Thousand Oaks, CA: Sage Publications, pp. 463–77.

Kozinets, R.V. and Handelman, J. M. (2004) "Adversaries of Consumption: Consumer Movements, Activism, and Ideology," *Journal of Consumer Research*, 31(December): 691–704.

Kozinets, R.V., Handelman. J.M. and Lee, M.S.W. (2010) "Guest Editorial: Don't Read This: Or, Who Cares What the Hell Anti-Consumption Is, Anyway?" *Consumption, Markets, and Culture*, 13(September): 225–33.

Luedicke, M.K., Thompson, C.J. and Giesler, M. (2010) "Consumer Identity Work as Moral Protagonism: How Myth and Ideology Animate a Brand-Mediated Moral Conflict," *Journal of Consumer Research*, 36(April): 1016–32.

Murray, J.B. and Ozanne, J.L. (1991) "The Critical Imagination: Emancipatory Interests in Consumer Research," *Journal of Consumer Research*, 18(September): 129–44.

Schau, H.J. and Gilly, M.C. (2003) "We Are What We Post? Self-Presentation in Personal Web Space," *Journal of Consumer Research*, 30(December): 385–404.

Stern, B. (1994) "Authenticity and the Textual Persona: Postmodern Paradoxes in Advertising Narrative," *International Journal of Research in Marketing*, 11: 387–400.

Thomas, R.E. and Maurer, V.G. (1997) "Database Marketing Practice: Protecting Consumer Privacy," *Journal of Public Policy and Marketing*, 16(Spring): 147–55.

Thompson, C.J. (2004) "Marketplace Mythology and Discourses of Power," *Journal of Consumer Research*, 31(June): 162–80.

Thompson, C.J. and Arsel, Z. (2004) "The Starbucks Brandscape and Consumers' (Anticorporate) Experiences of Glocalization," *Journal of Consumer Research*, 31(December): 631–42.

Thompson, C.J. and Coskuner-Balli, G. (2007) "Countervailing Market Responses to Corporate Co-optation and the Ideological Recruitment of Consumption Communities," *Journal of Consumer Research*, 34(August): 135–52.

Thompson, C.J., Rindfleisch, A. and Arsel, Z. (2006) "Emotional Branding and the Doppelgänger Brand Image," *Journal of Marketing*, 70(January): 50–64.

Witkowski, T.H. (2010) "A Brief History of Frugality Discourses in the United States," *Consumption, Markets, and Culture*, 3(September): 235–58.

35

THE DIGITAL CONSUMPTION OF DEATH

Reflections on virtual mourning practices on social networking sites

Ming Lim

Keywords

death, digital consumption, social media, social networking, virtual mourning

> The future holds [the] promise of a virtual cadaver nearly indistinguishable from a real person.
> (Richard Satava)

Introduction

The ways in which human beings consecrate, bury, mourn and dispose of the dead are extraordinarily varied across cultures, places, religions and beliefs. What has remained constant across the centuries, however, is the facticity of death as absolute stasis, unconditional finality and the termination of all that might be associated with pleasure, joy, satisfaction, achievement or even pain. Whatever else death may be, it is widely acknowledged by anthropologists and archaeologists that death marks the end of relationships, commitments, activities, feelings and thoughts that occupied one's time and space while one was alive (Scarre 2006). Mourning the death of loved ones, therefore, means mourning the terminal cessation not just of the person herself or himself, but also, arguably, of everything that they enjoyed and consumed while they were alive. More interestingly, perhaps, is the fact that, once I die, others who once either knew or loved me can no longer relate to me as an object of consumption in any meaningful sense of the word. They may lay flowers on my gravestone or have photographs of me around the house, keep a lock of my hair under their pillows or place the urn with my ashes on the mantelpiece, but the 'I' they knew and engaged with is no more.

Yet, the desire to connect with the dead after their death goes back to Biblical times. As an act of consumption, therefore, mourning the death of loved ones (or of any others) appears to offer little prospect of change, let alone *dynamic* change. Even more preposterous is any idea that death can be enjoyed in any way, shape or form. That foremost champion of happy consumption, Epicurus, observed that death has little relevance to either the living or the dead: 'since for the former it is not, and for the latter, it is no more' (Epicurus 1926, p. 85). Clearly, then, death is scarcely relevant to lived enjoyment. It would seem absurd to speak of death as having the potential to offer material possibilities of consumption. Equally, if not more absurd, would be the idea that one could continue to relate to the dead as co-consumers of objects, possessions and experiences. Or would it?

In the digital age, memorialization of the dead is undergoing a radical change. When the British fashion designer Alexander McQueen died last year, over 80,000 'fans' posted messages of grief to him in a week through Facebook (Miller 2010). The sudden death of the Grammy award-winning but troubled British jazz singer, Amy Winehouse, this year generated similar outpourings of grief on Facebook. Virtual mourning has gone mainstream. Facebook itself has responded positively to numerous requests by friends, relatives and survivors of the Virginia Tech shooting in 2007 to allow the pages of Facebook friends to remain active in perpetuity (Miller 2010, p. 42). Facebook's policy as of the 22nd of December, 2010, states: 'If we are notified that a user is deceased, we may memorialize the user's account. In such cases we restrict profile access to confirmed friends, and allow friends and family to write on the user's Wall in remembrance' (www.facebook.com/policy). The memorialization policy is given a human face by employee Max Kelly through the company's official Facebook blog: 'When someone leaves us, they don't leave our memories or our social network (Kelly 2009). As Miller (2010) notes: 'This is how we collectively mourn (in the digital age). Globally. Together. *Online*' (original italics).

As such mass practices gain momentum, it becomes important for consumer researchers to study the epistemological and ontological issues involved in the digital consumption of death. For instance, how *real* is virtual mourning? Do we witness the kind of moral and social commitment, relationships, shared values, truth-telling, exchanges of objects and knowledge and durability in space/time of mourners and mourning practices that we see in 'meatspace'? To what extent does the dead person continue to be a 'thingly being' in cyberspace (Kim 2001, p. 88) with whom loved ones can relate to in ways which mimic or, perhaps, even surpass non-digital/physical commemoration practices and behaviours? How do the grieving mourn the 'digital-being' of the deceased? What do such practices reveal about their perceived relationships with the one(s) who has died? A guiding rubric to address these questions is the notion of materiality, by which I mean the ways in which individuals and groups enact and perform their relationship to the deceased.

In exploring virtual mourning practices and their implications for death consumption in general, new questions in the field of consumer research emerge. It is hoped that once we gain some understanding of how online mourning practices illuminate notions of 'materiality' and/or 'embodiment' in the context of death and dying, we can begin to delineate what is actually new about this phenomenon and what the differences are between online and pre-digital behaviours in the context of the consumption of death. On this basis, then, we can then proceed to ask how consumers' behaviours of digital death consumption are likely to change in the future.

In the rest of this chapter, I explore key insights into the consumption of death in consumer society today, drawing connections between notions of materiality in physical worlds as well as virtual worlds. I draw upon a number of key disciplines for their insights into these issues: sociology (for theories of the desire to perpetuate the tension between ephemeral pleasures and the finality of death); philosophy and anthropology (for an understanding of how we frame embodiment and imagine 'materiality' through the performance of mourning rituals) and computer science (for conceptualizations of interactions on virtual worlds). It is hoped that these explorations can then be synthesized within consumer research theory and practice to enrich our current understandings of how we engage with death consumption in virtual worlds.

To understand the ways in which Social Network Site (SNS) users relate to the dead user via objects and other corporeal practices associated with virtual mourning, exploratory data collection was undertaken. Here, I present a preliminary dataset comprising profile pages of users who have died (using posts and comments left by the public on Facebook, MyDeathSpace and various blogs). Currently, I have collected five interviews from the relatives and friends of a deceased user and present a small sample of data from one of these individuals in order to demonstrate the nuances of how users frame their experiences of relating to the deceased user. A larger set of SNS data along these lines is planned over the coming months.

Materiality: multidisciplinary perspectives

Anthropological, philosophical and other critical humanist perspectives

At some basic, anthropological level, 'materiality' for most of us simply means 'artifacts' (Miller 2005, p. 4). Artifacts, including photographs, human hair, items of clothing, jewellery, family heirlooms and so on, have endured through the centuries as a way of keep our contact with the dead alive, so to speak. They become part of the way we remember the dead and were, historically, a way of anchoring rituals of grieving. In the words of Linkman (2005, p. 49):

> A portrait of the dead at peace could help alleviate the anguish caused to the bereaved by a painful or tragic end … [w]hile portraits of those who had died a 'good' death could serve as an example and role model for the living.

Physical objects also provided our ancestors with strong reminders of the ever-present reality of death and our mortal selves (Ariès 1994); they provide a symbolic (often religiously-defined) chain of continuity between the living and the dead and a way of recognizing our past in the present. Objects, in other words, help the bereaved find 'an appropriate place for the dead in their emotional lives' (Worden 1991, p. 16).

In modern times, the physical manifestations of death have been dis-placed, literally, from the home or community settings to more impersonal venues like hospitals and nursing homes. It is often noted that death in modern Western and Westernized societies has become deeply secularized, to the point that most people rarely witness a corpse first hand and almost never participate in elaborate mourning rituals of any kind (Giddens 1991; Norbert 1985). At the same time, technology has made it possible to decouple acts of grieving and memorialization from the physical fact of death itself. It has become possible to make the dead the basis of wide networks of communication. This means, in the more encompassing world of consumer culture, that materiality can be attributed to the imagination, to the ephemeral, the non-visible, and on on. Materiality, in this sense, is a *technological intermediary* between the corporeal and the non-corporeal. Let us examine this proposition a little more closely.

Cemetery, crematorium and crypt: objectifying and extending the dead

While speaking of the 'materiality of the dead' probably sounds paradoxical or bizarre, or both, this research is partly inspired by prior consumer research which illuminates how consumers locate agency in, and through, objects (Borgerson 2005) and how consumers imbue objects with 'magical thinking' (Fernandez and Lastovicka 2011). Much of this literature points to the 'tangibilization' of non-material processes and connections which consumers feel in relation to objects they use and love. In doing so, they extend themselves into objects, imbuing them with auratic radiance and power (Belk 1988).

In recent years, consumer culture theorists have sought to define the ways in which the living seek to extend, and even redefine, the identities of the dead (Bonsu and Belk 2003). Rituals play a prominent role in the social construction of roles and status on behalf of the dead, allowing all manner of transactions and negotiations to take place after an individual has departed the world of commerce and carnality (ibid.). When rituals cease to have popular currency, however, individuals have to create practices that facilitate a sense of comfort and closure to help them cope with the fact of death. In times past, communities and groups gathered around the cemetery or crypt to mourn the dead. Such rituals would be sombre and sorrowful, marked by formal elegies, songs, prayer. These rituals are giving way to a greater and greater sense that death is what happens to 'other people' and that a kind of biological immortality is well within our reach.

If this is the case, it becomes possible to conceive of the dead as being co-present with the living. Social networking tools and platforms have taken this possibility to new heights.

Techno–death and social media sites

It is in the field of computer science that some of the biggest intellectual strides have been made in terms of elaborating and unpacking some of the issues around how emerging technologies of design aim to capture philosophically challenging notions of identity and subjectivity (Brubaker and Vertesi 2011). Users of Social Network Sites (SNS) have been shown to return again and again (sometimes years after the death of someone they knew) to post messages for and to them, to invoke happy memories of their time with the deceased and to invite the latter to join in on some special occasion. These posts, according to Brubaker and Vertesi, often signify users' conviction that the dead person is somehow present and *co-present* with them as they recount an experience or recall a memory or set of memories.

Virtual reality and materiality: regenerating embodiment?

Fifty or so years ago, virtual reality technologies (VRT) were regarded as disembodying and, paradoxically, somewhat *unreal* because they created an ontological fracture between the mind and the body. This Cartesian split was dominant in VR discourses. The body would be left at the computer interface while the mind would wander off into the nether regions of cyberspace (Murray and Sixsmith 1999). Today, our sense of what is real and what counts as reality is increasingly merging with technologically mediated forms of interaction.

The complexity of this relationship becomes even more obvious with regard to the term virtual reality. Virtual reality, generally understood as the representation and simultaneous perception of reality and its physical characteristics in a real-time, computer-generated, and interactive environment, refers not only to exact copies of *real* environments (i.e. flight simulators for pilot training), but also to imagined *virtual* worlds (such as the online-game World of Warcraft). In general, it is the three-dimensional and high-resolution representation of reality that is regarded as the most important factor for the creation of virtual realities.

Once dead, the person is free to be an object of fantasy. *Because* of this motility, the dead can take on a new lease of life, socially and imaginatively, if not literally. Hallam, Hockey and Howarth (1999) argue that the enlivening of the dead occurs because the bereaved often form communities of discourse around a dead person in order to transform the reality of death into an individualized and personalized construct which they can celebrate and commemorate in myriad ways. Thus, the authors argue, the physically dead can live on in social terms. Similarly, the physically alive may be socially dead. Death, in other words, has only tenuous links with material disembodiment. The lived sense of individuals goes on beyond the material occurrence of physical death. This insight is now expressed by millions of social network site users, creating new innovations in social mourning and commemoration.

The dead are alive: socializing on social network sites

Currently, social network sites (SNS) represent the biggest user-base for online mourning rituals. Social media sites such as Facebook, Twitter and MyDeathSpace.com feature profiles of users who are no longer alive but who are kept alive through digital means. This kind of technologically-driven 'identity persistence' (Brubaker 2009) allows SNS users to sacralize and commemorate other users on global platforms. Social network sites have thus become a new ritualized arena of grieving and memorialization for millions of the bereaved.

An SNS user called Melissa, for example, regularly posts updates on her life to her deceased friend (the friend died three years ago). Her friend clearly continues to have a presence and influence in her life even as she invokes the social network that keeps the deceased in virtual dialogue with all her and all the friends that leave posts on the site:

> You would have loved the cake I made when we all got together last week. Remember how you used to ask me to bake you cakes when you felt down? Andrea said she didn't like it though – can you believe that? We're planning a reunion in a couple of weeks. You've got to come.

A further post from another friend in the network, Sally, says, 'Yes, do!'.

Postings on profiles and comments left on dead users' pages show that the dead are either assigned, or else presumed to have, active social roles. A typical comment is one which plunges straight into making plans for the future or to make specific requests: 'do you think you'll be coming for my birthday party tomorrow? I hope so, cos you missed the last one' or 'could you bring another towel with you for Bik Yoga class next week? I just haven't time to do laundry at all. ... lol'.

The father of 'Jed', a baseball player who was something of a celebrity to his many fans explained to me that he logs onto Farmville at least four to five hours every day without fail to make sure he keeps his son's garden plot looking fresh and green:

> I feel he's watching me. I'm absolutely sure he knows what I'm doing because if I say his name to the plants, they really do seem to grow better. I know it sounds silly, but that's how I feel. The other day, I told off my neighbour (Jed knew him too) for not tending his garden. Jed wouldn't have liked it. His friends got on his case as well.

This man also invited a long-time ex-girlfriend into Jed's allotment, so that she could take care of it as well. This woman, Maria, said she felt 'privileged' to be asked to do something so important: 'I keep it looking really neat. In fact, I think I do a much better job than his Dad (laughs). I told him so and he agrees.'

This sense of aliveness takes on another dimension in the offline world. Jed's father says,

> Sometimes, after talking to Jed – he's up there somewhere – I go to his room and put on his baseball shirt, swing his bat and I feel he's in the room. I feel like I'm him and I know what he's thinking. I tell him, 'Son, it's me in your shirt' (voice breaks slightly) and I then I have to get back to Facebook and tell his friends he's still here.

Discussion and implications

These findings, although brief and highly exploratory, offer some intriguing glimpses of how SNS users conceive of the deceased within the social network. Posts like these reinforce the materiality of the network *as well as that of the deceased*. In a number of instances, the ontological divide between the dead and the living is simply disregarded, or even celebrated. The dead continue to animate past, present and future. Further, the upbeat, cheerful tone of many posts studied are strong indications that virtual technologies are truly changing conventional views on the rejection or denial of death in Western consumer societies. It is difficult to say, based on these samples of exploratory data, whether or not users have comprehended the finality of death; what we get, instead, is a kind of playful badinage with those who are somehow only *temporarily* unavailable.

Materially, too, social network sites appear to offer users a highly convenient and sometimes innovative way of remembering the dead and of celebrating their quirks, personality traits, likes and dislikes. On Farmville, in particular, a veritable ecology of desire is fully exploited by users in the form of gardens, plots of land, fences, flowers, and so on and so forth. Users clearly enjoyed tending to the gardens and to watching them thrive.

The assumption of co-presence with the dead is striking. Whereas some of these posts might, in other contexts, be regarded as the outpourings of the insane or seriously deluded, they appeared natural and convincing in the context of social networking sites. I personally found this both amusing and amazing.

Ultimately, the digital consumption of death says quite a lot about the nature of consumption itself in consumer society. Humans have invented tools and platforms that draw the dead into existing spheres of networks and desires. Bauman (2001), in a provocative piece on the perceived limits to human desire and consumption in life, has argued that limits to consumption are obsolete in consumer societies. Consumption is propelled by self-sustaining and self-perpetuating logics which have nothing to do with the satisfaction of desires: '(t)he 'need' which sets the members of consumer society in motion is, on the contrary, the need to keep the tension alive and, if anything, stronger with every step' (ibid.: 13).

Driving the argument further, the 'need' in modern societies for the acquisition of possessions gives way, in postmodern capitalist societies, to the 'wish' to fulfil fantasies of an entirely different order to that which has come before. The difference is as much an ethical as a cultural one. Bauman, following Ferguson (1996), notes that desire used to function as a way of linking

> consumption to self-expression and to notions of taste and discrimination. The individual expresses himself or herself through their possessions. But for advanced capitalist society, committed to the continuing expansion of production, this is a very limiting psychological framework which ultimately gives way to a quite different psychic 'economy'. The wish replaces desire as the motivating force of consumption.
>
> *(Ferguson 1996: 205, cited by Bauman 2001)*

Desires have been transformed in postmodern societies from objectified needs to solid desires to a 'psychic economy' that overflows modern needs and wants. Immortality is now a cultural reality even if not yet a biological fact.

How will the digital consumption of death evolve in the future? Virtual reality (VR) and human–computer Interaction (HCI) technologies already make it possible not only to speak to, and commune with, the dead but to live, play and work with them through avatars, so the social nature of their manifestations may well change. The meanings of the 'social' in 'social networks' have expanded to include those who have died and not just those who are alive. As these posts show, we already socialize with the dead. Future research could examine the implications of the communal, participatory nature of virtual grieving. Death, in these contexts, is commonly explored as a way for virtual communities to gather in a communal space in order to partake in collective rituals of mourning. Yet, it is entirely possible that this trend will reverse.

That is, we also need to understand how the collectivism of cyberspace is resulting in a kind of backlash. There is evidence to show that more and more people are wanting to choose a more private way to die and to remain buried, left alone. Frustrated by the difficulties of finding reliable information about long-dead relatives and friends, these individuals are choosing to memorialize themselves after death using virtual tombs instead of being buried under gravestones. A French banker, Jacques Mechalaney, has created I-Tomb or what is possibly the world's first virtual cemetery, where, for $50 a year, families can pre-pay for a loved one's tomb in advance, as well as paying for their own, of course (Tett 2011). I-Tomb allows anyone to create memorials using virtual ornaments, virtual flowers and to post messages of tribute and remembrance. These practices are now becoming commonplace and yet there is little consumer research on how they contribute to current notions of materiality and, indeed, dominant cultural prejudices about death, dying and mourning.

This chapter has, hopefully, made a small contribution to the scant research to date on consumers' behaviours in relation to digital death, especially the way in which they construct, manage, modify or otherwise consume the materiality of the ones they mourn in online environments. Hopefully, too, there is now little doubt that this area offers a new frontier for consumer culture researchers.

References

Ariès, P. (1994) *Western Attitudes towards Death: From the Middle Ages to the Present*, Baltimore, MD: Johns Hopkins University Press.

Bauman, Z. (2001) *Community: Seeking Safety in an Insecure World*, Oxford: Polity.

Belk, R.W. (1988) 'Possessions and the Extended Self', *Journal of Consumer Research*, 15(2): September, 139–68.

——(2010) 'Sharing', *Journal of Consumer Research*, 36(5): 715–34.

Bloggs, N. (1982) *A Short History of Trash*, London: Routledge.

Bonsu, S.K. and Belk, R.W. (2003) 'Do Not Go Cheaply into That Good Night: Death–Ritual Consumption in Asante, Ghana', *Journal of Consumer Research*, 30(1): 41–55.

Borgerson, J. (2005) 'Materiality, Agency and the Constitution of Consuming Subjects: Insights for Consumer Research', *Advances in Consumer Research*, 32: 439–43.

Brubaker, J.R. (2009) 'Authoring the Single-Use Identity: Intertechnical Production of the Non-persistent Subject on Craigslist', paper presented at American Comparative Literature Association 2009 Annual Meeting, *Global Languages, Local Cultures*, Harvard University, Cambridge, MA.

Brubaker, J. and Vertesi, J. (2011) 'Death and the Social Network', paper presented at the CHI 2010 Workshop on HCI on *The End of Life: Understanding Death, Dying, and the Digital*, April 10–15, Atlanta, GA.

Dennett, D. (1980) 'Junk Memes', *Journal of Refuse Studies*, 67: 112–25.

Epicurus, D.G. (1926) 'Letter to Menoeceus', in *Epicurus: The Extant Remains*, trans. C. Bailey, Oxford: The Clarendon Press.

Erickson, T. (1997) 'Social Interaction on the Net: Virtual Community as Participatory Genre', in J.F. Nunamaker, Jr and R.H. Sprague, Jr (eds), *Proceedings of the Thirtieth Hawaii International Conference on Systems Science*, 6, pp. 23–30. IEEE Computer Society Press, Los Alamitos, CA., available at: www. pliant.org/personal/Tom_Erickson/VC_as_Genre.html (accessed April 2011).

Ferguson, H. (1996) *The Lure of Dreams: Sigmund Freud and the Construction of Modernity*, London: Routledge.

Fernandez, K.V. and Lastovicka, J.L. (2011) 'Making Magic: Fetishes in Contemporary Consumption', *Journal of Consumer Research*, 38(2): 278–99.

Giddens, A. (1991) *Modernity and Self-Identity*, Oxford: Polity.

Hallam, E., Hockey, J.L. and Howarth, G. (1999) *Beyond the Body: Death and Social Identity*, London: Routledge.

Kelly, M. (2009) 'Memories of Friends Departed Endure on Facebook', posted 26 October 2009, available at: http://blog.facebook.com/blog.php?post=163091042130 (accessed 23 July 2011).

Kim, Y. (2001) 'Phenomenology of Digital-Being', *Human Studies*, 24: 87–111.

Linkman, A. (2005) 'Taken from Life: A Post-Mortem Portraiture in Britain 1860–1910', *Mortality: Promoting the Interdisciplinary Study of Death and Dying*, 10(7): 49.

Miller, D. (2005) 'Materiality: An Introduction', in D. Miller (ed.), *Materiality*, Durham, NC: Duke University Press, pp. 1–50.

Miller, L. (2010) 'R.I.P. on Facebook', *Newsweek*, 3 January, 155(9).

Murray, C. and Sixsmith, J. (1999) 'The Corporeal Body in Virtual Reality', *Ethos*, 27(3): 315–43.

Norbert, E. (1985) *The Loneliness of Dying*, London: Continuum.

Scarre, G. (2006) 'Can Archaeology Harm the Dead?' in C. Scarre and G. Scarre (eds), *The Ethics of Archaeology: Philosophical Perspectives on Archaeological Practice*, Cambridge: Cambridge University Press, pp. 181–98.

Tett, G. (2011) 'Leaving a Digital Legacy', *Financial Times*, 7 October, available at: www.ft.com/cms/s/2/9535180e-efa6–11e0–941e-00144feab49a.html?ftcamp=rss#axzz1dghnECj2 (accessed 10 October 2011).

Worden, J.W. (1991) *Grief Counselling and Grief Therapy: A Handbook for the Mental Health Professional*, London: Routledge.

36

CONSUMER (DIS)TRUST ONLINE

Peter R. Darke, Ray L. Benedicktus and Michael K. Brady

Keywords

consumer, distrust, trust

The dawn of commerce on the Internet was heralded as a leveling of the playing field for business, as well as an opportunity for consumers to gain access to a broader range of sellers, better information, and lower prices (Watson *et al.* 1998). On the marketing side, traditional channels were said to be expensive and favor larger companies with better distribution networks and larger budgets, whereas the Internet offered new, potentially lower cost alternatives to communicate with target consumers and distribute products. For consumers, the Internet offered a very different environment, with greater access to a variety of information from companies and competitors, as well as other consumers, experts and trend setters. These circumstances were expected to intensify market competition in a number of respects (Economist 1997), with potential benefits for consumers, small business, and the economy more broadly. Consumers seemed especially likely to benefit in terms of lower prices and a greater variety of better quality goods and services.

The current reality is quite different from the information utopia anticipated by many. Virtual retailing is instead dominated by big brands, most of which have a substantial bricks-and-mortar presence offline as well (Benedicktus *et al.* 2010). Moreover, consumers are often willing to pay premium prices when purchasing online from brand name retailers (Ba and Pavlou 2002), despite the fact that identical products are available from smaller, lesser-known online retailers. The question is, why has the reality been so different from what was anticipated, and what does this imply about consumer behavior online? Although there are likely to be many other factors involved, one central explanation is that consumers are often highly suspicious when interacting with marketers on the Internet, which can cause them to seek additional assurances such as the confidence offered by dealing with larger, better-established firms (e.g., Yoon 2002). This assertion is in agreement with Reichheld and Schefter (2000, p. 107), who claimed, "price does not rule the web; trust does."

This chapter examines consumer trust and distrust online, including: (1) common definitions and types of trust/distrust; (2) common factors known to increase online trust; (3) the prevalence and likely origins of the consumer suspicion that seems to dominate online perceptions; and (4) traditional and contemporary consumer theories that are useful in understanding the effects of trust and suspicion on consumer evaluation and choice online. Central issues and potential areas for future research are highlighted throughout.

Defining the territory and some important distinctions

Although there are many definitions of trust and distrust (see Kramer 1999, for a more in-depth discussion), most focus on the expectations and vulnerability of the consumer. For instance, Mayer *et al.* (1995, p. 712) define trust as "the willingness of a party to be vulnerable to the actions of another party based on the expectation that the other will perform a particular action important to the trustor." Vulnerability is central to this definition, which suggests that trust is most relevant when consumers stand to lose something of value. Trust is often viewed as the consumer's willingness to rely on the marketer's reliability and integrity (Morgan and Hunt 1994), and the belief that the trusted marketer will engage in actions that result in positive outcomes and avoid negative outcomes for the consumer. Others suggest two fundamentally distinct dimensions of trust (McKnight *et al.* 1998): (1) the *willingness to rely* refers to the consumer's trusting intention or behavior (Currall and Judge 1995); and (2) a *trusting belief* that is indicative of perceptions that the marketer is competent, honest, and benevolent (Mayer *et al.* 1995). More recently, Bart *et al.* (2005) suggest that online trust includes consumer expectations of the site, the believability of the site's information, and the confidence the site inspires among consumers.

Trust and uncertainty or risk

Trust is at times viewed as synonymous with certainty or risk concerning important outcomes that are controlled by others (Mayer *et al.* 1995). This is consistent with the central role that vulnerability and expectations play in the many definitions of trust mentioned above. While risk and uncertainty are common in traditional purchase contexts, these threats seem even greater online (Bart *et al.* 2005). As economists have noted, there tends to be an asymmetry in information that favors sellers over buyers (Akerlof 1970), meaning that consumers face greater uncertainty in determining product quality or the sellers' true intentions compared to the seller's knowledge of these matters. These risks may be exaggerated online given consumers cannot examine products in advance and have minimal interaction with sellers (Bajari and Hortaçsu 2004).

While certainty and trust are related, Mayer *et al.* (1995, p. 711) initially suggested, "It is unclear whether risk is an antecedent to trust, is trust, or is an outcome of trust." More recently, Darke (2004) showed that distrust and uncertainty have similar causes and are positively corre-lated, but that the effects of uncertainty on judgment were fully mediated by distrust. Other evidence suggests that trust can moderate the negative effects risk has on consumer judgment online (Cheema and Papatla 2010). Interestingly, other evidence suggests decision uncertainty can be either positively or negatively related to trust, depending on the coping mechanisms employed by consumers (Wilson and Darke 2012). Additional research clarifying the relationship(s) between certainty and trust seems warranted given the importance of both constructs in consumer judgment.

Trust versus distrust

The literature also suggests important distinctions between trust and distrust. While it seems intuitive to view these as opposite ends of a continuum – where low trust implies high distrust and vice versa – others view trust and distrust as different dimensions with all possible combinations (see Kramer 1999). This implies that consumers may simultaneously maintain both high trust and high distrust, which is an idea that has been empirically supported (Darke and Ritchie 2007; Darke *et al.* 2008). Such simultaneous perceptions of trust and distrust often relate to different facets of the relationship with the same marketer (Lewicki *et al.* 2006). It seems important to recognize the basic idea that mixed trust and distrust may underlie more global measures of trust. Further research examining how such conflicts impact behavior and the maintenance of consumer–marketer relationships in the long term would be of great interest.

Finally, the consumer literature makes additional distinctions for distrust in the form of suspicion and skepticism, which differ somewhat from the terminology used in the broader trust literature. For instance, suspicion may connote the idea that a marketer has hidden motives (Campbell and Kirmani 2000), which is associated with an open-minded approach to determining the true cause(s) of behavior (Fein 1996). In contrast, skepticism is often used to convey a more general tendency to distrust marketers (Obermiller and Spangenberg 1998). Others have used the word cynicism to capture the general tendency to distrust marketers (Pollay 1986), although this concept is broader in including the idea that marketing can also be insulting and disrespectful. More recently, Darke and Ritchie (2007) suggested skepticism and suspicion are best described in terms of *objective* versus *defensive* distrust. The former corresponds to the more open form of distrust that is driven by accuracy goals, whereas defensive distrust is evoked by threat and typically leads to a negative bias in judgments of marketer trustworthiness. Finally, some consumers also seem to employ defensive forms of trust instead of defensive suspicion (Wilson and Darke 2012). These distinctions are further examined in the theoretical discussion below.

Consumer trust and distrust online

Antecedents and consequences of online trust

Trust is recognized as a key component in consumer–marketer interactions in a variety of contexts, including sales (Doney and Cannon 1997; Morgan and Hunt 1994), service (Halliday 2004), advertising (Darke and Ritchie 2007; Pollay 1986), branding (Delgado-Ballester and Munuera-Alemán 2005), and the Internet (Bart *et al.* 2005; Yoon 2002). Indeed, trust often mediates the effects that marketing tactics have on consumer preferences and online purchase intentions (e.g., Ba and Pavlou 2002; Bart *et al.* 2005; Schlosser *et al.* 2006; Yoon 2002), as well as online loyalty (Shankar *et al.* 2003). These findings speak to the central role of trust in determining basic marketing outcomes online.

A substantial empirical literature has identified a long list of factors that can increase consumer trust online. For instance, online trust is fostered by: brand names and the existence of a physical store (Benedicktus *et al.* 2010), third-party satisfaction ratings (Benedicktus 2010); website investment (Schlosser *et al.* 2006); privacy (Hoffman *et al.* 1999); independent seals of approval (Aiken and Boush 2006); interactivity (Burgoon *et al.* 2000); help from virtual advisors (Urban *et al.* 2000); transparency, openness and honesty (Urban 2005); familiarity with the website, and service and satisfaction guarantees (Yoon 2002). More broadly speaking, Bart *et al.* (2005) suggest online trust can be divided into the effects of: (1) website design; (2) privacy and security guarantees; (3) firm-related cues; and (4) consumer characteristics. Their comprehensive study found that the most reliable predictors of online trust were: privacy (protection of individual information), navigation and presentation (site is engaging, clear, and easy to use, etc.), brand strength (familiar, good quality, etc.), website advice (virtual advisors and other features to guide choice), order fulfillment (order, mail, price and service information), and absence of website errors (e.g., complete/correct information, site was fully operational, etc.). In addition, they found 80 percent of consumers belonged to two large segments that used a comprehensive set of all, or almost all, of these factors in judging trust, suggesting the majority of consumers use multiple trust cues online. Finally, consumer experience levels also predicted online trust, including: general Internet experience, Internet shopping experience, experience with chat groups online, and familiarity with the particular website.

The problem of consumer distrust online

Some observers suggest that online trust has steadily improved (Urban *et al.* 2009), based on the substantial increase in online spending by consumers in the past decade. Consistent with this assertion, at least some sources of online information are highly trusted by consumers, particularly trust in branded websites and the posted opinions of other consumers (69 percent and 72 percent trusted; Nielsen 2009). However, most of the evidence suggests a more pessimistic conclusion. Despite its known importance and the considerable attention paid to maintaining trust in online interactions, the level of consumer trust expressed towards online marketing is quite low. For instance, a recent Nielsen poll (2009) suggested online ads from search engine results, online videos and banners were all highly distrusted by North Americans (63 percent, 77 percent and 76 percent of respondents distrusted, respectively) compared to advertising in more traditional channels (television, radio and magazines ads were all distrusted by less than 40 percent of respondents).

A number of factors may be responsible for the prevalence of distrust on the Internet. First, the high incidence of fraud and other white-collar crimes that occur online may play a role (Benedicktus *et al.* 2010). For instance, there were over 300,000 complaints of crime on the Internet by US consumers in 2010, according to the Internet Crime Complaint Center (ICCC), representing an 18-fold increase since the year 2000 (NW3C 2011). Moreover, the web is now the main channel by which consumer fraud is attempted (NCL 2009). Another explanation may be the potentially covert nature of certain online marketing practices. The Internet allows marketers to quietly track consumers, as well as manipulate the kinds of product and pricing information they receive, and such covert tactics are known to generate distrust (Milne *et al.* 2008; see also Wei *et al.* 2008). A final possibility concerns the exaggerated level of information asymmetry online (Bajari and Hortaçsu 2004). Although the Internet is overflowing with information in many respects, it tends to lack the kind of information consumers would typically use to assess trustworthiness in their everyday lives (Gefen 2000; Reichheld and Schefter 2000). For instance, personal interaction with salespeople is a key determinant of trust (Doney and Cannon 1997) but is much less likely to occur online.

Theoretical perspectives of consumer trust online

Research specifically concerning consumer trust online has mainly employed models based on a combination of past research and/or a mix of theoretical perspectives to isolate likely antecedents and consequences. These models tend to be descriptive and strategically focused rather than explanatory in nature. Relationship marketing is perhaps the main identifiable perspective that has been used to model consumer trust in the marketing literature (Bart *et al.* 2005; Ganesan 1994; Doney and Cannon 1997). This considers trust to be a key mediating variable between marketing strategy and consumer loyalty/retention (Morgan and Hunt 1994). Rather than engaging in a detailed examination of the strategic models that have served as the mainstay of research examining online trust, we instead focus on a number of consumer-oriented theories that can be profitably employed to better understand the causes of online trust and suspicion.

Social learning theory

Learning is considered a central component of online trust (Urban et al. 2009). Its origins are provided by Rotter's (1971) social learning theory, where trust is defined as the extent to which an individual or organization lives up to the expectations it creates, whereas distrust occurs when such expectations are not met. Consumers can learn whether to trust based on direct experiences with a specific marketer (*specific trust/distrust*), or alternatively past experiences with marketers as a group can be used to infer the trustworthiness of an unfamiliar marketer (*generalized trust/distrust*). A prescriptive aspect of the theory is that generalized trust/suspicion should be used to inform judgment primarily when there is a lack of direct experience or knowledge about a particular marketer to judge trustworthiness in the more specific sense (ibid.). As such, generalized perceptions of trust/suspicion should dominate consumer judgment in situations that are novel, ambiguous or unstructured. This is likely to be a common situation online, and therefore consumers are likely to rely heavily on perceptions of generalized trust/distrust in online interactions, especially for initial interactions.

Recent evidence in the consumer literature supports the main contentions of social learning theory, but also suggests qualifications. Consistent with the theory, Darke et al. (2010) showed that the failure of a product to live up to expectations created by a marketer's claims can induce generalized suspicion that carries over to other marketers. In contrast to suspicion, trust was less likely to generalize from marketer to marketer. Other evidence (Darke et al. 2008) suggests generalized distrust can impact consumer judgment even when there is specific evidence the particular marketer is trustworthy, contrary to the rational prescription that specific trust should trump generalized trust/distrust. The latter findings are more consistent with the defensive suspicion model described below.

Dual process theories

Dual process theories are a family of models that examine the information processing involved in judgment across a variety of contexts (Chaiken and Trope 1999). Such models share the common view that consumer judgment can occur both through a less effortful automatic process involving little conscious thought, as well as a more effortful deliberative thought process. The various models differ in the extent to which they directly deal with judgments of trust or its effects on other forms of judgment, but they have great potential to serve as the basis for further investigation of online trust.

Persuasion models

Dual process models of attitude judgment such as the Elaboration Likelihood Model (ELM; Petty and Cacioppo 1986) and the Heuristic-Systematic Model (Chen and Chaiken 1999) suggest that trust/suspicion can play multiple roles in consumer evaluation of products or websites. Trust was originally viewed as a simple heuristic source cue, which allowed consumers to easily determine their level of agreement (e.g., "I should agree with a trustworthy source"). This view was later extended to include the idea that distrust can also increase the amount of deliberative thought consumers engage in when making judgments in order to be more accurate. For instance, the warning that a persuasive source was untrustworthy led consumers to make better distinctions between strong versus weak arguments from that source (Priester and Petty 1995). Deliberative thought ironically even led the distrusted source to be more persuasive than a trusted source in some cases. This was because initial distrust led to better appreciation of the merits of the strong arguments, while the same arguments were less likely to be elaborated when they came from a trusted source. Finally, the heuristic-systematic model suggests trust can also act as heuristic cue that *biases* elaborative thoughts and attitudes (Chaiken and Maheswaran 1994). In their study, consumers had more positive thoughts and attitudes when arguments came from the well-trusted *Consumer Reports* compared to the less distrusted *Kmart flyer*. This was said to occur because the heuristic trust cue helped bolster consumer confidence for important decisions when the available product information was ambiguous. Overall, dual process models of attitude judgment suggest trust and suspicion can: (1) act as a simple heuristic cue under low elaboration; (2) increase objective processing; and (3) serve as a heuristic that biases thoughts and judgment under high elaboration conditions when additional confidence is needed.

The Persuasion Knowledge Model (PKM)

The PKM is essentially a dual process theory specific to consumer judgment, which concerns impressions of the marketing source, the tactics used, and the means by which consumers cope with persuasion attempts (Friestad and Wright 1994). The most unique aspect of the model is its focus on consumer lay theories regarding the tactics employed by marketers. Such persuasion knowledge includes beliefs not only about the types of tactics used, but also whether they are likely to be persuasive, or seem appropriate/acceptable for marketers to use. The main focus of the model is on deliberative processing, but the PKM also recognizes that consumers respond to persuasion attempts on the basis of "tactic recognition" heuristics that relate to simple features of the persuasion attempt. For instance, use of a celebrity endorser may lead to the heuristic inference that the marketer is trying to gain the consumer's trust. We would note that although this is a heuristic process, the model seems to suggest the result is a relatively conscious inference in that consumers come to some sort of realization that the marketer is using the tactic for a specific purpose. Finally, the PKM also tends to assume the consumer's primary goal in using persuasion knowledge is to form a valid option (i.e. an accuracy goal), although there is some recognition that defensive goals can motivate consumer coping behavior. The latter is hypo-thesized to lead to rigid generalizations concerning a lack of marketer trustworthiness and broad dismissal of any persuasion attempts involving certain tactics.

The original formulation of the PKM has a broad scope and does not fully elaborate on the specific role of trust and suspicion. Rather, this link was made primarily by Campbell and Kirmani (2000) in their well-known research concerning distrustful responses to the persuasion tactic of flattery from a sales agent. They found that flattery increased consumer distrust when making salient the ulterior motive that this was simply a sales tactic, through greater deliberative processing. These findings not only support the PKM, but are also consistent with prior research by Fein (1996) suggesting the distrust generated by ulterior motives leads to more accurate attributions via deliberative thought. More recent research shows that such persuasion tactics can in fact operate through a combination of heuristic and deliberative processing, and can cause consumers to become suspicious even when an ulterior sales motive is implausible (Main *et al.* 2007). The main implication was that some tactics have the power to trigger suspicion in a relatively direct, automatic fashion, leading consumers to be overly suspicious of marketers, rather than increasing more objective deliberative processing leading to more normative attributions.

While relatively little research has used the PKM to examine trust online, there is at least some evidence consumers respond negatively to website tactics that suggest an ulterior motive. For instance, websites that recommend more expensive product options as the default setting in their order menus can cause consumers to select less expensive options instead, particularly those consumers high in persuasion knowledge (Brown and Krishna 2004). Future research should examine other online tactics that might induce consumer suspicion by activating persuasion knowledge (e.g., pop-up ads, browser hijacking, unexpected mailing costs or additional processing charges, or lack of product availability after ordering). It would also be particularly interesting to identify online tactics that lead to more automatic suspicions. Finally, although the PKM predicts that consumer responses to persuasion tactics may be either positive or negative, the vast majority of evidence examining the PKM shows consumers tend to respond negatively to tactics (Campbell and Kirmani 2008). Research that identifies online tactics that might evoke more positive responses via persuasion knowledge would therefore be of interest for both theoretical and practical reasons (e.g., opt-out policies, presence of product or price comparisons, links to competitors, or free return shipping).

The Defensive Suspicion Model (DSM)

The DSM is a dual process model that deals specifically with the multiple roles trust and suspicion play in consumer judgment (Darke and Ritchie 2007). It recognizes that judgments of suspicion and trust can involve effortful, deliberative processing (Kramer 1999; Campbell and Kirmani 2000), as well as more automatic processing based on simple heuristics (Friestad and Wright 1994; Main *et al.* 2007). Moreover, while accuracy goals may at times drive judgment and information processing relating to trust (e.g., in the presence of ulterior motives), the primary assertion of the DSM is that suspicion often serves more defensive, self-protective goals. The latter arises when the consumer's self-image or material interests are threatened, and tends to bias judgment in a direction that reduces such threats. In particular, defensive suspicion is said to evoke negative systematic processing for direct marketing threats, but operates through heuristic processing for weaker, less direct threats. Finally, the model predicts that defensive suspicion should induce a negative bias in judgment that is relatively persistent, self-reinforcing, and difficult to remedy (see Kramer 1999).

A number of studies support the basic predictions of this model in both offline and online marketing channels (Benedicktus *et al.* 2010; Darke and Ritchie 2007; Darke *et al.* 2008, 2010). In their initial research, Darke and Ritchie (2007) used advertising deception to evoke defensive suspicion and then had consumers evaluate a second ad from either the same or a second-party advertiser. Consistent with the model's predictions, consumers distrusted the same advertiser and actively counterargued any subsequent claims they made in order to avoid being fooled again (direct threat). What was more interesting was that consumer suspicion also generalized to unrelated second-party firms, leading to more negative product evaluations (indirect threat condition). These carryover effects operated through an automatic process known as *defensive stereotyping* (see Kunda and Sinclair 1999), where the initial deception evoked the broad stereotype that no advertising could be trusted. Evidence for the defensive nature of these effects was provided by the fact that ego-threat was a necessary condition for suspicion to generalize across marketing sources, whereas simply observing other consumers being deceived had no such effects. A number of other studies showed that generalized suspicion produces a persistent negative bias on consumer judgment (Darke *et al.* 2008, 2010). For instance, generalized suspicion had negative effects: (1) on both strong and weak arguments; (2) on both trusted brand name retailers and unbranded retailers; (3) despite the opportunity to directly test the product; and (4) that last more than 24 hours after the initial deception.

While the initial tests of the DSM speak to the robust negative bias induced by defensive suspicion, other research has identified important moderators. For instance, whereas initial research showed that a trusted brand name alone was insufficient to protect marketers from generalized suspicion, the use of multiple trust cues (i.e., brand name *and* online customer satisfaction ratings) proved more effective (Benedicktus *et al.* 2010). Consumers seemed to cross-reference the implications of the two cues had for perceptions of trust in the second firm. Other studies show that independent regulators can help buffer against generalized suspicion (Darke *et al.* 2008). For instance, product information provided from the *Consumer Reports* website eliminated the effects of generalized suspicion, and an endorsement from the *Better Business Bureau* displayed on the marketer's website proved just as effective. Finally, a series of studies examining online sales promotions (Darke 2009) suggest that while generalized suspicion has negative effects on promotional tactics that were strongly associated with manipulation and deceit (e.g., price discounts), the same suspicions actually *increased* the perceived value of tactics viewed as incongruent with deceptive marketing practices (e.g., everyday low price offers).

The high levels of suspicion consumers profess towards online commerce seem likely to comprise some combination of objective and defensive distrust, and the DSM suggests it is important to distinguish between the two. Objective distrust (e.g., relating to the presence of ulterior motives) is not necessarily a bad thing for marketers, in the sense that it tends to lead to a more active and open form of information processing that can actually lead to greater persuasion, provided the marketer can offer consumers appropriate arguments or heuristics that would allow them to make valid judgments. In contrast, defensive suspicion is more problematic. It leads to close-minded, often automatic reactions that require clearer, more consistent and independent verification if consumers are to be persuaded. Yet, even this form of suspicion can be advantageous for marketers who use straightforward, no-nonsense tactics in dealing with consumers. Future research should examine other aspects of the consumer behavior process that may be affected by defensive suspicion (e.g., decision-making, customer loyalty), as well as other causes of defensive suspicion. For instance, there are some indications that the threat associated with post-decisional dissonance can also induce defensive suspicion towards marketers (Wilson and Darke 2012).

The Construal Level Theory (CLT)

CLT is a broad theory that predicts the effects psychological distance has on consumer information processing and judgment (Trope and Liberman 2010). Psychological distance is defined as the degree to which an object is *perceived* to be tangible or immediately present. This framework suggests that spatial distance (physical distance of retailer), temporal distance (timing of interaction), social distance (social connection with retailer), and hypotheticality (physical tangibility of retailer) are interchangeable aspects of psychological distance and impact consumer judgment in similar ways. The main prediction of the model is that objects at greater psychological distance tend to be judged using more abstract mental representations, whereas more proximal targets tend to be judged on the basis of more specific, concrete characteristics.

Benedicktus (2008) extended CLT to include the idea that psychological distance also has implications for consumer trust online. The reasoning was that, given stereotyping is a form of abstract construal, and suspicion is a common aspect of marketer stereotypes, it follows that greater psychological distance should cause consumers to stereotype marketers as untrustworthy. It was further proposed that any factors that decrease the psychological distance of a marketing source should help increase consumer trust. Consistent with this extended CLT model, Benedicktus showed consumers were more likely to make online purchases from retailers who also maintained a physical store (hybrids) over purely virtual sellers (pure etailer with no physical store) because the intangibility of the pure etailer created greater psychological distance and distrust. One particularly interesting finding was that even the presence of a physical store at a distance too great to be of any practical benefit (1500 miles) was sufficient to increase online trust over a pure etailer (dubbed the *mere presence effect*). Other evidence suggested hybrids with physical stores in familiar cities evoked greater online trust than stores in unfamiliar locations at the same physical distance, consistent with idea that familiar locations are more tangible and thereby decrease psychological distance. Finally, images of office buildings (increasing tangibility) or employees (decreasing social distance) posted on the website improved consumer trust in pure etailers. In fact, these simple strategies were so successful that they elevated trust and purchase intentions to a level comparable to hybrid firms that had a local physical store. Overall, the extended CLT framework is potentially useful in explaining the effects that a broad range of marketing variables have on online trust. For instance, other aspects of website design may improve online trust by increasing perceptions of tangibility such as the interactivity of the site, or simulation of a physical shopping environment; or by decreasing social distance using computer agents (e.g., avatars) or other tactics that mimic normal social interaction.

Conclusion

Trust is a critical predictor of positive marketing outcomes both online and offline. Consumers' initial trust in online channels is derived through a combination of factors, including: website characteristics (brand name, interactivity, etc.), feedback from other consumers, useful information provided by the website, as well as guarantees and security. However, trust is fragile and can dissolve, or at least weaken, with even a single instance of deception or manipulation. While existing research has been primarily strategic in focus, the current chapter describes a number of consumer-oriented theories that have proven useful in understanding trust both on and offline. In turn, the online environment offers a particularly relevant context for testing consumer models of trust, given the premium that exists for online trust.

Further reading

Campbell, M. and Kirmani, A. (2008) "I Know What You're Doing and Why You're Doing It: The Use of the Persuasion Knowledge Model in Consumer Research," in C. Haugtvedt, P. Herr, and F. Kardes (eds), *Handbook of Consumer Psychology*, New York: Psychology Press, pp. 549–74. [Review of PKM, including its implications for trust and suspicion.]

Darke, P.R. and Ritchie, R. (2007) "The Defensive Consumer: Advertising Deception, Defensive Processing, and Distrust," *Journal of Marketing Research*, 44(1): 114–27. [Original work concerning the defensive suspicion model.]

Kramer, R. (1999) "Trust and Distrust in Organizations: Emerging Perspectives, Enduring Questions," *Annual Review of Psychology*, 50: 569–98. [Broad theoretical overview of trust.]

Pollay, R. (1986) "The Distorted Mirror: Reflections on the Unintended Consequences of Advertising," *Journal of Marketing*, 50(April): 18–36. [Classic paper concerning consumer distrust and other negative connotations of advertising.]

Urban, G.L., Amyx, C. and Lorenzon, A. (2009) "Online Trust: State of the Art, New Frontiers, and Research Potential," *Journal of Interactive Marketing*, 23: 179–90. [Review of managerial research concerning online trust.]

References

Aiken, K. and Boush, M. (2006) "Trustmarks, Objective-Source Ratings, and Implied Investments in Advertising: Investigating Online Trust and the Context-Specific Nature of Internet Signals," *Journal of the Academy of Marketing Science*, 34(3): 308–23.

Akerlof, G. (1970) "The Market for 'Lemons': Quality Uncertainty and the Market Mechanism," *The Quarterly Journal of Economics*, 84(3): 488–500.

Ba, S. and Pavlou, P. (2002) "Evidence of the Effect of Trust Building Technology in Electronic Markets: Price Premiums and Buyer Behavior," *MIS Quarterly*, 26(3): 243–68.

Bajari, P. and Hortaçsu, A. (2004) "Economic Insights from Internet Auctions," *Journal of Economic Literature*, 17: 457–86.

Bart, Y., Shankar, V., Sultan, F. and Urban, G. (2005) "Are the Drivers and Role of Online Trust the Same for All Websites and Consumers? A Large-Scale Exploratory Empirical Study," *Journal of Marketing*, 69(4): 133–52.

Benedicktus, R. (2008) "Psychological Distance Perceptions and Trust Beliefs for Internet-Only and Hybrid Retailers: Implications for Marketers," doctoral dissertation, The Florida State University.

——(2010) "The Effects of 3rd Party Consensus Information on Service Expectations and Online Trust," *Journal of Business Research*, 64(8): 846–53.

Benedicktus, R., Brady, M., Darke, P.R. and Voorhees, C. (2010) "Conveying Trust to Online Consumers: Reactions to Consensus, Physical Store Presence, Brand Familiarity and Generalized Suspicion," *Journal of Retailing*, 86(4): 310–23.

Brown, C. and Krishna, A. (2004) "The Skeptical Shopper: A Metacognitive Account for the Effects of Default Options on Choice," *Journal of Consumer Research*, 31(3): 529–39.

Burgoon, J., Bonito, J., Bengtsson, B., Ramirez, A. and Dunbar, N. (2000) "Testing the Interactivity Model: Communication Processes, Partner Assessments, and the Quality of Collaborative Work," *Journal of Management and Information Systems*, 16: 33–56.

Campbell, M. and Kirmani, A. (2000) "Consumers' Use of Persuasion Knowledge: The Effects of Accessibility and Cognitive Capacity on Perceptions of an Influence Agent," *Journal of Consumer Research*, 27(1): 69–83.

——(2008) "I Know What You're Doing and Why You're Doing It: The Use of the Persuasion Knowledge Model in Consumer Research," in C. Haugtvedt, P. Herr, and F. Kardes (eds), *Handbook of Consumer Psychology*, New York: Psychology Press, pp. 549–74.

Chaiken, S. and Maheswaran, D. (1994) "Heuristic Processing Can Bias Systematic Processing: Effects of Source Credibility, Argument Ambiguity, and Task Importance on Attitude Judgment," *Journal of Personality and Social Psychology*, 66: 460–73.

Chaiken, S. and Trope, Y. (1999) *Dual-Process Theories in Social and Cognitive Psychology*, New York: Guilford Press.

Cheema, A. and Papatla, P. (2010) "Information for Internet Purchases: Product Category and Internet Experience Effects," *Journal of Business Research*, 63(9/10): 979–85.

Chen, S. and Chaiken, S. (1999) "The Heuristic-Systematic Model in Its Broader Context," in S. Chaiken and Y. Trope (eds), *Dual-Process Theories in Social Psychology*, New York: Guilford Press, pp. 73–96.

Currall, S. and Judge, T. (1995) "Measuring Trust Between Organizational Boundary Role Persons," *Organizational Behavior and Human Decision Processes*, 64: 151–70.

Darke, P.R. (2004) "Consumer Reactions to Marketing Practices: Skepticism, Suspicion, and Payback," *Advances in Consumer Research*, 31: 329–32.

——(2009) "Shedding the Veil of Suspicion: Avoiding the Effects of Defensive Suspicion," in *Proceedings of the Association for Consumer Research*, Pittsburgh, PA.

Darke, P.R., Ashworth, L. and Main, K. (2010) "Great Expectations and Broken Promises: Misleading Advertising, Product Failure, Expectancy Disconfirmation and Consumer Suspicion," *Journal of Academy of Marketing Science*, 38(3): 347–62.

Darke, P.R., Ashworth, L. and Ritchie, R. (2008) "Damage from Corrective Advertising: Causes and Cures," *Journal of Marketing*, 72(November): 81–97.

Darke, P.R. and Ritchie, R. (2007) "The Defensive Consumer: Advertising Deception, Defensive Processing, and Distrust," *Journal of Marketing Research*, 44(1): 114–27.

Delgado-Ballester, E. and Munuera-Alemán, J. (2005) "Does Brand Trust Matter to Brand Equity?" *Journal of Product and Brand Management*, 14(2/3): 187–96.

Doney, P. and Cannon, J. (1997) "An Examination of the Nature of Trust in Buyer-Seller Relationships," *Journal of Marketing*, 61(April): 35–52.

Economist (1997) "Survey of Electronic Commerce, Search of the Perfect Market," May 10, pp. 3–26.

Fein, S. (1996) "Effects of Suspicion on Attributional Thinking and the Correspondence Bias," *Journal of Personality and Social Psychology*, 70: 1164–84.

Friestad, M. and Wright, P. (1994) "The Persuasion Knowledge Model: How People Cope with Persuasion Attempts," *Journal of Consumer Research*, 21(1): 1–31.

Ganesan, S. (1994) "Determinants of Long-Term Orientation in Buyer-Seller Relationships," *Journal of Marketing*, 58(April): 1–19.

Gefen, D. (2000) "E-Commerce: The Role of Familiarity and Trust," *Omega*, 28(5): 725–37.

Halliday, S. (2004), "How 'Placed Trust' Works in a Service Encounter," *Journal of Services Marketing*, 18(1): 45–59.

Hoffman, D., Novak, T. and Peralta, M. (1999) "Building Consumer Trust Online," *Communications of the ACM*, 42(4): 80–5.

Kramer, R. (1999) "Trust and Distrust in Organizations: Emerging Perspectives, Enduring Questions," *Annual Review of Psychology*, 50: 569–98.

Kunda, Z. and Sinclair, L. (1999) "Motivated Reasoning with Stereotypes: Activation, Application, and Inhibition," *Psychological Inquiry*, 10(1): 12–22.

Levitt, T. (1983) "After the Sale Is Over," *Harvard Business Review*, 61(5): 87–93.

Lewicki, R., Tomlinson, E. and Gillespie, N. (2006) "Models of Interpersonal Trust Development: Theoretical Approaches, Empirical Evidence, and Future Directions," *Journal of Management*, 32(6): 991–1022.

McKnight, D., Cummings, L. and Chervany, N. (1998) "Initial Trust Formation in New Organizational Relationships," *Academy of Management Review*, 23(July): 472–90.

Main, K., Dahl, D. and Darke, P.R. (2007) "Automatic and Deliberative Bases of Suspicion: Empirical Evidence of the Sinister Attribution Error," *Journal of Consumer Psychology*, 17(1): 59–69.

Mayer, R., Davis, J. and Schoorman, F. (1995) "An Integrative Model of Organizational Trust," *Academy of Management Review*, 20, 709–34.

Milne, G., Bahl, S. and Rohm, A. (2008) "Towards a Framework for Assessing Covert Marketing Practices," *Journal of Public Policy and Marketing*, 27(1): 57–62.

Morgan, R. and Hunt, S. (1994) "The Commitment-Trust Theory of Relationship Marketing," *Journal of Marketing*, 58(July): 20–8.

NCL (2009) "Top Scams of 2009," available at: www.nclnet.org/images/PDF/2009_top_scams.pdf] (accessed Nov. 28, 2011).

Nielsen (2009) "Trust, Value and Engagement in Advertising," Global Online Consumer Survey, July, 1–11.

NW3C (2011) "IC3 2009 Internet Crime Report," National White Collar Crime Center and the Federal Bureau of Investigation, available at: www.ic3.gov/media/annualreport/2010_IC3Report.pdf] (accessed Nov. 29, 2011).

Obermiller, C. and Spangenberg, E. (1998) "Development of a Scale to Measure Consumer Skepticism Toward Advertising," *Journal of Consumer Psychology*, 7(2): 159–86.

Petty, R. and Cacioppo, J. (1986) "The Elaboration Likelihood Model of Persuasion," in L. Berkovitz (ed.), *Advances in Experimental Social Psychology*, New York: Academic Press, pp. 19, 123–205.

Pollay, R. (1986) "The Distorted Mirror: Reflections on the Unintended Consequences of Advertising," *Journal of Marketing*, 50(April): 18–36.

Priester, J. and Petty, R. (1995) "Source Attribution and Persuasion: Perceived Honesty as a Determinant of Message Scrutiny," *Personality and Social Psychology Bulletin*, 21: 639–56.

Reichheld, F. and Schefter, P. (2000) "E-Loyalty: Your Secret Weapon on the Web," *Harvard Business Review*, 78(4): 105–13.

Rotter, J. (1971) "Generalized Expectancies for Interpersonal Trust," *American Psychologist*, 26: 443–52.

Schlosser, A.E., Barnett White, T. and Lloyd, S. (2006) "Converting Website Visitors into Buyers: How Website Investment Increases Consumer Trusting Beliefs and Online Purchase Intentions," *Journal of Marketing*, 70(April): 133–48.

Shankar, V., Smith, A. and Rangaswamy, A. (2003) "Customer Satisfaction and Loyalty in Online and Offline Environments," *International Journal of Research in Marketing*, 20(2): 153–75.

Trope, Y. and Liberman, N. (2010) "Construal-Level Theory of Psychological Distance," *Psychological Review*, 117(2): 440–63.

Urban, G.L. (2005) "Customer Advocacy: A New Era in Marketing?," *Journal of Public Policy and Marketing*, 24(1): 155–9.

Urban, G.L., Amyx, C. and Lorenzon, A. (2009) "Online Trust: State of the Art, New Frontiers, and Research Potential," *Journal of Interactive Marketing*, 23: 179–90.

Urban, G.L., Sultan, F. and Qualls, W.J. (2000) "Placing Trust at the Center of Your Internet Strategy," *MIT Sloan Management Review*, 42(1): 39–48.

Watson, R., Akselsen, S. and Pitt, L. (1998) "Attractors: Building Mountains in the Flat Landscape of the World Wide Web," *California Management Review*, 40(2): 36–56.

Wei, M., Fischer, E. and Main, K. (2008) "An Examination of the Effects of Activating Persuasion Knowledge on Consumer Response to Brands Engaging in Covert Marketing," *Journal of Public Policy and Marketing*, 27(1): 34–44.

Wilson, A.E. and Darke, P.R. (2012) "The Optimistic Trust Effect: Use of Belief in a Just World to Cope with Decision Generated Threat," *Journal of Consumer Research*, 39(3): 615–628.

Yoon, S. (2002) "The Antecedents and Consequences of Trust in Online Purchase Decisions," *Journal of Interactive Marketing*, 16(2): 47–63.

37

AFTERWORD

Consuming the digital

Tom Boellstorff

Keywords

digital consumerism, dubbing, ethnography

Introduction: "dubbing" the digital consumer

The thirty-six chapters making up this edited collection speak to a staggering range of interests in relation to digital consumerism. Since there is no way I can engage at length with any particular chapter, for this afterword I have set myself the goal of identifying shared problematics, interests, and avenues for inquiry. Of course, I approach this task in light of my own scholarly history. As an anthropologist who has conducted extensive research on questions of sexuality and national belonging in Indonesia (e.g., Boellstorff 2005, 2007), I have a longstanding interest in culture, mass media, and consumerism. For instance, in that work, I developed a notion of "dubbing culture," drawn from a debate where the dubbing of foreign films and television shows into the Indonesian language was briefly banned on the grounds that if Indonesians saw Westerners appearing to "speak Indonesian," they would no longer know where Indonesia ended and the West began (Boellstorff 2003).

I have used this concept of "dubbing culture" to theorize forms of globalization where two systems of meaning lie alongside each other without fusing. The difference between dubbing and translation is that while translation is animated by the impossible hope of a total shift from one language to another, in dubbing the moving lips never match with the new soundtrack, nor is there an expectation this will happen. I have found this concept of transformation not predicated on fusion helpful in my research on virtual worlds, particularly my book *Coming of Age in Second Life* (Boellstorff 2008). In this book and more recent work on ethnographic methods for virtual worlds (Boellstorff *et al.* 2012), I explore the "dubbing" of practices and meanings across the physical/virtual divide. These interests resonate with themes evident in *The Routledge Companion to Digital Consumption*.

New frontiers of consumption and consuming

It should not be surprising that novel forms of consumerism represent a strong common thread linking the contributions to this volume. At stake on these digital frontiers are not just new markets, but new understandings of consumption and the commodity form. How, for instance, are notions of "searching" displacing notions of "shopping," such that to shop online and to search online are, in effect, the same activity? This has implications for how we conceive of "choice," a pivotal term of contemporary capitalism that links consumerism to democracy, self-identity, and knowledge production.

Of special interest is that we now face a situation where consumption not only can be enabled by technology (like the steamship allowing for new forms of distribution), but can take place within a digital technology itself. From posting on Facebook to building something in a virtual world or even commenting on a news blog, we encounter new possibilities for virtual locations of consumption—the "markets" without which the concept of "marketing" is meaningless. The very notion of "social media" thus no longer captures how many of these technologies are not media at all: they do not "mediate" between different places, but are (virtual) locations in their own right. In other cases, consumption can take place through associated digital venues (e.g., a fan site for a video game or television show). All this has fundamental consequences for how we theorize value, given the key role of technology in the emergence of modern capitalism. Ideas of marketing and advertising are similarly transformed in the context of the "viral" dissemination of product messages. The viral metaphor presents a parasitic image of agent-less, uncontrolled propagation that obscures the forms of collaborative activity involved in these ostensibly non-directed activities. How are we to understand socialities that have not just "gone online" but have "gone viral?" How do they differ (or not) from forms of rumor, myth, and informal circulation that preexist but also lie alongside digital forms of informal dissemination?

These new digital possibilities for the location of consumption transform the products or services to be consumed, and thus the distinction between purchase and use. For instance, how does blogging rework the temporalities and consuming implications of "fashion?" How is the experience of gambling altered when it can take place online, such that persons can gamble alone, or teenagers can gamble at home with their families? Another area where we are seeing a qualitative transformation in consumption is the rise of virtual goods. These include commodities that historically (and often still) have physical-world forms, like books, magazines, and songs. However, they can also include items without physical-world analogs, such as clothing for avatars or virtual-world homes.

A key issue is that the "digital" is no longer limited to computing devices found on a desktop. Just as desktop computing overshadowed an earlier phase of mainframe computing (though mainframe computers still exist), so desktop and laptop computers are now becoming but one aspect of a digital ecology that includes mobile devices like smart phones and tablets, and also the embedding of networked computational power into everyday objects. How are notions of the public and domestic being transformed in the context of these technologies? These new layerings of place are intimately linked to layerings of activity and engagement that give new valence to the term "multitasking."

Constituting the digital consumer

Many contributions to this volume show how linked to digital consumerism are emergent technologies of selfhood that destabilize the very notion of the consuming person so central to articulations of contemporary capitalism. Here as elsewhere there is a pressing need to avoid, on one hand, the Scylla of presuming a postmodern human that radically breaks from the predigital human, and on the other, the Charybdis of radical continuity, where digital sociality is presumed to be merely superficially distinct from that which came before. These conceptual agendas center on the question of causality: the interplay between how technology amplifies or reflects aspects of society, and how various social formations are enabled by (or even predicated on) digital technologies. This includes the interplay between new forms of creativity versus templates and defaults that canalize social difference.

These questions reflect how our understanding of what it means to be human will shift as we consider forms of selfhood and sociality where online and offline engagements intertwine. For instance, it is not just that social media shape consumer behavior, but that "social" is taking on new meanings. For more people around the world, in some contexts at least, to be "social" means to be "online." This has already had consequences for intimate spheres of life ranging from dating to the "virtual mourning" of the deceased.

The contributions to this volume underscore how in regard to the social construction of the digital consumer, it will prove crucial to examine differences across online technologies and environments. For instance, social networking sites (like Facebook), online games (like World of Warcraft), and virtual worlds (like Second Life) differ in key ways. We cannot assume that consumerism associated with one of these technologies will translate straightforwardly to the others. Yet it is important to examine similarities as well: an intellectual balkanization would lose sight of how these technologies share histories and current features. Notions of avatar embodiment are largely shared between online games and virtual worlds, and influence notions of "profiles" on social networking sites. A distinction between live "chat" and sending "messages" exists across a range of technologies. We thus find the entire spectrum of sameness and difference, from things shared by everything "digital" to things specific to a particular website or online game, or even to a subculture associated with that website or game. Our research agendas and conceptual frameworks must be similarly broad. This includes taking into account the impact of narrowband technologies like texting, which at present are far more commonly used than technologies like virtual worlds. It also includes taking into account forms of "polymedia" where digital consumers use multiple online technologies (Miller 2011, p. 200), often at the same time or even nested inside each other (such as the use of texting inside a social network or within an online game).

It will remain important to track how uses of digital technologies differ by social categories like ethnicity, nation, age, and gender, but it will also be pivotal to consider as well how these categories are shaped by the digital. For instance, the English-language category of the "tween" is hard to separate from online practices, given its origin and widespread adoption during the rise of the Internet in the late 1980s and early 1990s.

The way digital technologies get taken up in varied cultural contexts will not be apparent at the outset. Given the dominance of the West, the United States, and even California in the design and conception of many of these technologies, the question of how they are transformed in non-Western contexts is an important topic for continuing research. For instance, issues of exchange, sharing, and sociocentric selfhood work differently in cultural contexts that in certain respects anticipated the rise of the kinds of distributed subjectivity made possible by Internet technologies. An issue that can get lost in these kinds of "Western versus non-Western" conversations is that we are also witnessing the emergence of cultural formations that are ontologically predicated on the digital, and thus cannot be reduced to any combination of physical world cultures.

Participation, control, and context

Consumerism has always been a social phenomenon, and many contributors to this volume address how forms of participation shape digital consumerism. For instance, we can think of blogs both as something consumed and as sites for consuming other products. In my own work, I have developed the notion of "creationist capitalism" to highlight how forms of crafting and creativity have become central to digital consumer practice (Boellstorff 2008, pp. 205–11). In other words, it is not just that people use digital technologies to create; it is that the very notion of "creating" has shifted. Consumer participation can include highly individualized labor but also forms of "crowdsourced" activity. Here, novel conceptions of sociality, context, and labor intersect with consequences still not fully understood. Even the notion of "audience" is put into question by these developments, since those at the "receiving" end of content are, through forms of commentary, remixing, fandom, and amateur creation, involved in simultaneous production. Could these developments herald the emergence of new forms of consumer exploitation made paradoxically feasible through "collaboration?"

One area where the role of digital technologies in consumption is of particular interest is in fields like medicine, where a significant gap in knowledge and expertise historically separated provider (doctor) from consumer (patient). The sphere of investing and finance is another example, a clear case where the activity itself (the trading of stocks, for instance) is fundamentally altered by digital technologies. This has consequences for notions of consumer activism that can have interweaving online and offline components, while also reconfiguring notions of value. Indeed, several contributors to this volume compel us to ask how control might in fact now represent a form of consumption. This relates to notions of sharing, but also to notions of secrecy and the contextual revealing of aspects of selfhood. It also recalls the rise of the database as not just repository, but active form of social organization that becomes its own context, such that data mining techniques can be used by marketers to conceptualize consumers in their online, real-time socialities.

Context can become a form of surveillance, as online retailers can track not just purchasing histories, but clicks through webpages and how much time is spent on various portions of a website. This in turn can lead to forms of preferential filtering, so that different consumers see, in effect, a different Amazon or Google based upon their past engagements with the digital technology in question. We may be seeing the normalization of surveillance as the *de facto* experience of online sociality. This has important consequences for notions of privacy. It is clear that persons still value privacy when online, but that the meaning of privacy can become highly contextual and distributed, transforming the very notion of self-disclosure. Who is the "self" that "discloses" online? This has implications for how we conceptualize online consumer movements and other forms of consumer activism, as well as the relationship between trust and privacy.

Methods and theories

The various contributors to this volume both summarize existing research from a wide range of disciplines and, in many cases, report on original research the authors themselves have conducted. That research draws upon a palette of methodological approaches including, for instance, surveys and archival research. This is entirely fitting. No one method is perfect: each permits insights into differing aspects of the social. Indeed, the phrase "mixed methods" has become superfluous, since practically all social research projects nowadays employ eclectic toolkits shaped by the perceived needs of the research.

As an ethnographer I am particularly fascinated to see the growing interest in ethnographic methods for researching digital consumerism. "Ethnography" is not a method but the written product of a set of methods, as the suffix "-graphy" indicates. The core method of any ethnographic approach is participant observation. The particular power of this method is that because it is not predicated on elicitation, it allows the researcher to explore commonalities but also divergences between what people "say they do" and "what they do." This helps us avoid presuming not only that people truthfully answer surveys, but that motivations and beliefs are always present to consciousness in the first place.

As many contributions to this volume demonstrate, ethnographic projects usually include other methods alongside the core method of participant observation, for instance, individual interviews. It bears emphasizing that many ethnographers like myself find group interviews (sometimes known as "focus groups") extremely useful. This is the clearest example to my knowledge of an ethnographic method that we owe to the field of market research (Kratz 2010). As I and my colleagues discuss elsewhere (see Boellstorff *et al.* 2012), focus groups provide several specific advantages for ethnographers. Since no culture is unanimous, they provide a means to explore debate and dissention in what might otherwise appear to be a homogeneous culture. They also are useful for oral history work because participants can help fill in gaps in the knowledge of the other members. It is clear that group interviews can play an important role in charting new cultures of digital consumerism.

Overall, these questions of method are crucial because consumerism is often associated with promotion and hype, and thus slippages between descriptive and proscriptive forms of argument—between claims of what "what is" and "what should be." Careful methodological design allows social researchers (including those involved in market research) to avoid these slippages by grounding claims in a descriptive register, allowing us to better understand cultural phenomena in their real contexts of offline and online emergence.

Conclusion

Overall, the contributors to this volume suggest not just new topics for research, but new theoretical frameworks to guide such research. Cultures always have a history and persons draw upon that history when confronted by novel contexts. That is why, for instance, in the world of computing we speak of "desktops," "folders," and web "pages," or even send a "carbon copy" (cc) of an e-"mail." But while such antiquated metaphors for the objects of study amuse, there is a real danger for researchers when our theoretical resources are similarly dated.

There undoubtedly exist a range of possible negative consequences of digital technology and sociality. However, many of the more dismissive or dystopic interpretations are based on a mismatch between theoretical framework and empirical reality. For instance, many concerns about isolation in regard to the use of digital technologies fail to ask how the very meaning of "isolation" is not eternally unchanging, but is itself a cultural phenomenon reshaped by the rise of digital technologies. Similarly, asking after the "influence" of digital technologies must be accompanied by an awareness of how understandings of "influence" are themselves transformed in contexts where persons routinely "follow" or "like" each other's postings in online media, or where forms of modding, hacking, and remixing destabilize any neat distinction between those who are the influencers and those who are influenced. It is by considering these kinds of complex, emergent dynamics through careful empirical and conceptual work that we will attain a robust understanding of the promises and perils of digital consumerism.

References

Boellstorff, T. (2003) "Dubbing Culture: Indonesian Gay and Lesbi Subjectivities and Ethnography in an Already Globalized World," *American Ethnologist*, 30(2): 225–42.
——(2005) *The Gay Archipelago: Sexuality and Nation in Indonesia*, Princeton, NJ: Princeton University Press.

——(2007) *A Coincidence of Desires: Anthropology, Queer Studies, Indonesia*, Durham, NC: Duke University Press.

——(2008) *Coming of Age in Second Life: An Anthropologist Explores the Virtually Human*, Princeton, NJ: Princeton University Press.

Boellstorff, T., Nardi, B., Pearce, C. and Taylor, T.L. (2012) *Ethnography and Virtual Worlds: A Handbook of Method*, Princeton, NJ: Princeton University Press.

Kratz, C.A. (2010) "In and Out of Focus," *American Ethnologist*, 37(4): 805–26.

Miller, D. (2011) *Tales from Facebook*, Cambridge: Polity Press.

INDEX